# Septuagint: History

## Volume 1

SCRIPTURAL RESEARCH INSTITUTE

Published by Digital Ink Productions, 2024

# Copyright

### Septuagint: History, Volume 1

Second Edition. April 8, 2024

Copyright © 2024 Scriptural Research Institute.

ISBN: 978-1-998288-35-9

The Septuagint was translated into Greek at the Library of Alexandria between 250 and 132 BC.

This English translation was created by the Scriptural Research Institute in 2019 through 2023, primarily from the Vaticanus, Sinaiticus, and Alexandrinus codices, although other codices were also used for reference. Additionally, the Leningrad Codex and Aleppo Codex of the Masoretic text, Peshitta, Targums, and Dead Sea Scrolls were used for comparative analysis.

The image used for the cover is 'The Youth Samson' by Léon Joseph Florentin Bonnat, sketched in 1891.

# Table of Contents

# TABLE OF CONTENTS

# TABLE OF CONTENTS

# TABLE OF CONTENTS

# TABLE OF CONTENTS

# TABLE OF CONTENTS

# TABLE OF CONTENTS

# Table of Contents

# TABLE OF CONTENTS

# TABLE OF CONTENTS

# TABLE OF CONTENTS

# TABLE OF CONTENTS

# Introduction

In the mid 3$^{rd}$ century BC, King Ptolemy II Philadelphus of Egypt ordered a translation of the ancient Israelite scriptures for the Library of Alexandria. This translation later became known as the Septuagint, based on the description of the translation by seventy translators in the Letter of Aristeas. The original version, published circa 250 BC, only included the Torah, or in Greek terms, the Pentateuch. The Torah is the five books traditionally credited to Moses, circa 1500 BC: Cosmic Genesis, Exodus, Leviticus, Numbers, and Deuteronomy. According to Jewish tradition, the original Torah was lost when the Babylonians destroyed the Temple of Solomon, and it was then rewritten by Ezra the Scribe from memory during the Second Temple period, circa 350 BC.

The first edition was followed by the second, around 225 BC which added the books of Joshua, Judges, and Ruth, which was later known as the Octateuch. This version of the Septuagint was later carried south into the Kingdom of Kush by the Israelites fleeing Egypt in 200 BC when Judea was in revolt and the Ptolemys attempted to exterminate the Israelites in Egypt. The Octateuch later became the Torah of the Beta Israel community in Sudan and Ethiopia known as the Orit. By 132 BC, the Septuagint included all the books later adopted by the Byzantine Orthodox church as the Old Testament section of the Christian Bible. Some of these books were rejected by the Hebrew translators during the Hasmonean Dynasty of Judea, and never formed part of the Masoretic text. The Septuagint of 132 BC, included four sections: the Torah, History, Wisdom, and Prophets sections.

It is generally accepted that there were several versions of the various books, written in Judahite, Samaritan, or Aramaic, before the translation of the Septuagint. Fragments of some of the History books have been found among the dead sea scrolls, however, only in the Assyrian script of the Hasmonean and Herodian dynasties, and dated to between 140 BC and 6 AD. By this time, the land of Judea passed from the rule of the Ptolemys in Egypt to the rule of the Seleucids in Syria in 200 BC. The Seleucids attempted to Hellenize the Judeans, and effectively banned traditional Judaism. This Hellenizing activity was partially successful, creating the Sadducee faction of Judaism, however also led to the Maccabean Revolt in 165 BC, which itself created the independent Hasmonean Kingdom of Judea. This kingdom was violently xenophobic and led by a priestly monarchy that combined both the powers of the state and the church.

The Hasmonean dynasty attempted to conquer all of the territory that had previously been part of the Persian Province of Judea, and either evicted or exterminated the people that were living there, depending on their ethnicity. When the Edomites were conquered they were allowed to mass-convert to Judaism as they were considered the descendants of Esau, however, most other ethnic groups were not welcome. When the army of Hasmonean King John Hyrcanus annexed Samaria in 113 BC, he slaughtered the Samaritan priests and more than half the Samaritan population and enslaved the rest. His army also destroyed the Samaritan Temple on Mount Gerizim and burned all copies of their holy books. The Samaritans continued to be slaves under the Hasmoneans until the Roman General Pompey's armies freed them in 69 BC, and restored the independent state of Samaria, along with several other states that fell under Rome's protection from that time forward.

While the Hasmoneans ruled Judea, they converted the national script from the old Canaanite script, today called Paleo-Hebrew, to the Assyrian 'block script,' today called Hebrew. As a result, almost all surviving texts found from the Hasmonean era and later are written in the Assyrian script, and it is unclear how much the Hasmoneans redacted the scriptures when they transcribed them. The scriptures the Hasmoneans left the world were later used as the basis of the Masoretic text, which is used today by Rabbinical Jews, as well as by Catholic and Protestant Christians. The Samaritan Torah is believed to have been restored after General Pompey freed the Samaritans, by redacting a copy of the Hasmonean Torah, which is why there are fewer differences between the Samaritan and Jewish (Masoretic) Torahs than either of them and the Septuagint. A copy of the original Samaritan Torah was translated at the Library of Alexandria as well, referred to as the Samareitikon (Σαμαρειτικον), however, it has not survived to the present. Based on the writings of Origen of Alexandria in the early 3<sup>rd</sup> century, and other early Christians, the Samareitikon was more similar to the Septuagint's Pentateuch than it was to either the Samaritan or Jewish Torahs in use at the time.

The differences between the Masoretic and the Septuagint's version of the books are both minor and startling, as the two sets of scriptures contain the same stories, but different Gods. The God of the books in the Septuagint is generally called Lord the God (Κύριοσ ὁ θεὸσ) or simplified to Lord (Κύριοσ), or God (Θεὸσ). These terms are mirrored in the Masoretic versions with Yehwah your god (יְהוָה אֱלֹהֶיךָ), Yhwh my god (יהוה אלהי), and Yehvah (יְהוָֹה). One explanation for the difference between the texts is the Christian redaction of the 3<sup>rd</sup> century AD, when the name Iaô (Ιαω) was removed from the Septuagint, replaced by Lord (Κύριοσ). Fragments of older Septuagint manuscripts still exist that contain the name Iaô (Ιαω), transliterated from the Aramaic Yhw (𐡉𐡄𐡅), however, none of the fragments of the books of History include the name. The name Yhwh (יהוה) is found in some of the fragments of the books of History found among the Dead Sea Scrolls, however, the earliest date to the Hasmonean dynasty, and therefore date to over 85 years after the Septuagint's version of Joshua was translated.

The Aramaic sections of Masoretic Daniel that were not translated into Hebrew maintain the term adonai ha'elohim (אֲדֹנָי הָאֱלֹהִים), meaning the 'Lord the gods' where the Septuagint has 'Lord the god' (Κύριον τὸν θεὸν), however, the Hebrew sections have Yehwah elohim (יְהוָה אֱלֹהִים) where the Septuagint has 'Lord the god,' suggesting the Greek more accurately reflects the Aramaic source texts than the Hebrew translation. According to tractate Sanhedrin (103b) in the Talmud, King Manasseh was blamed for removing the name, however, as his grandson Josiah 'restored' the Torah circa 625 BC, one would expect that he would have restored the name as well, if it had have been in the Torah to begin with. Furthermore, the early Torah appears to have already been translated into Aramaic during the era of Manasseh's father king Hezekiah, suggesting that he removed the name during his religious reforms. This suggests that the name was added to the Hebrew translation by the first Hasmonean High-Priest/King Simon the Zealot to create a national Judean religion with a god having a name similar to the Roman god Jove.

Nevertheless, not all of the books in the Septuagint appear to have been written about the same god. The Septuagint's versions of the book of Esther, as well as the Vetus Latina's book of Esther, both indicate that Mordecai was a worshipper of Moloch, which explains why the Hebrew translation has no reference to any god in it. The Greek terms in the Septuagint's Joshua are translations of well-known terms related to Canaanite god El, the Canaanite creator-god. El translates in Canaanite, Aramaic, and Hebrew as 'God,' and was the primary god worshiped in ancient Canaan in the era Abraham, Isaac, and Jacob were reported to have passed through the area. El was also the patron god of the Temple of El, built by Jacob near the modern city of Nablus in the Palestinian West Bank, which featured in many of the early Hebrew scriptures before Samaria was conquered by the Assyrian Empire. In the Book of Micah, the Temple of El was referred to as Jacob's Temple of El, which confirms that the Israelites in the 8th century BC considered the Temple of El at Shiloh to be the Temple of El that Jacob built, in Genesis chapter 35.

The books appear to have been redacted by the Hasmonean Dynasty circa 140 BC, when they were translated into Hebrew, in an attempt to forge closer ties with Rome, which was still a distant power across the Mediterranean, outside of Greek domination. As the Maccabean Revolt raged against Greek rule in Judea, between 165 and 140 BC, the Romans were fighting the final, and bloodiest of their wars against the Carthaginians, the ancient Canaanite colony base in modern Tunisia. The Carthaginians were once the great power of the Western Mediterranean, dominating northwest Africa, southern and western Iberia, Sicily, Sardinia, and Corsica.

The Romans had been at almost constant war against Carthage for over a century, beginning with the first Punic war in 264 BC, and in 146 BC finally defeated them, and effectively exterminated the race. Roman records report that they forced the surviving Carthaginian warriors to fight to the death in arenas, while the civilians were sold as slaves to anyone that would buy them. The population of northwest Africa became a slave-race for centuries and was not freed until the rise of Christianity in the 4th century. In 139 BC, seven years after the end of the final Punic war, and the year after the Hasmonean dynasty was established in Judea, the Romans evicted all Jews from the republic because the Jews were attempting to promote the idea that the Roman national god Jupiter (Iovis) was their national god Yahweh Sabaoth (Jupiter Sabazius). This was recorded by Valerius Maximus:

> "Gnaeus Cornelius Hispalus, praetor peregrinus in the year of the consulate of Marcus Popilius Laenas and Lucius Calpurnius, ordered the astrologers by an edict to leave Rome and Italy within ten days, since by a fallacious interpretation of the stars they perturbed fickle and silly minds, thereby making profit out of their lies. The same praetor compelled the Jews, who attempted to infect the Roman custom with the cult of Jupiter Sabazius, to return to their homes."

As there had been Judeans living in Rome before 139 BC, and the Romans had interpreted Lord Sabaoth as the Judean version of Dionysus, it is clear something had changed significantly within Judea when the Hasmoneans seized power. The books of the Maccabees, set during the late Greek Era, Maccabean Revolt, and early Hasmonean Dynasty describe Dionysus being worshiped in the Temple in Jerusalem, before the revolution, confirming that the Judeans also considered Lord Sabaoth to be the Judean version of Dionysus. In the Masoretic version of Joshua, the name Lord Sabaoth was entirely replaced by Yhwh (יהוה), indicating that the Masoretic version of Joshua was created after King/High-Priest Simon the Zealot's failed attempt to convert Rome to his religion.

The 'Hebrew' language of the Hasmonean Dynasty, was a reformed version of Judahite, the southern Canaanite dialect spoken in Judea and Edom, written with a specific form of the Aramaic script that the Judeans called 'Assyrian' in the Talmud. While it was a new language in that the Hasmonean Dynasty appear to have been the first government that attempted to standardize it, it was quite similar to both the surviving forms of Ugaritic Canaanite from the Bronze Age, and Phoenician Canaanite from the Iron Age, meaning other than changing the name and script to something that didn't sound or look too Carthaginian, the language was essentially the same as Bronze Age Canaanite.

While the Hasmoneans may have tried to court Rome and the rebels in Phrygia and Assyria, there is little evidence that anyone other than the Assyrians was interested in allying with them. A series of wars including both Julius Caesar's campaigns, and a Parthian invasion led to the weakening of the Hasmonean dynasty, and in 37 AD, the Roman Senate appointed Herod the Great as King of the Jews. Herod's rule wasn't particularly popular, as he allowed the Romans to establish themselves within Judea, however, he did expand Judea, reintegrating the Greek and Samaritan cities, and annexing Galilee and Edom. When he died, his kingdom was divided between four successors, a situation that ended in 66 AD when the Romans conquered the region. An uprising in 120 AD led to the Jews being exiled from Judea, and the region became a Greco-Roman colony. In the wake of the Jews, the Samaritans rose in numbers, along with the Christians once Christianity was legalized. Between 529 and 555 AD, the Samaritans revolted and were effectively annihilated, by Constantinople the Eastern Roman capital.

The modern Samaritan religion is similar to Judaism, in that they have versions of the Torah and the book of Joshua, however, they do not trace their ancestry to ancient Judah, but rather to ancient Samaria also called the Northern Kingdom of Israel. According to the Samaritans, they were the original Israelites, and the Temple of the Lord was not Solomon's Temple in Jerusalem, but rather a Temple of Mount Gerizim, in Samaria. These other Israelites also contributed to the creation of the Septuagint, as the Book of Tobit, was the story of a Samaritan that had been taken to Nineveh, the capital of the Assyrian Empire after the Kingdom of

Israel was conquered by the Assyrians. This book and several others were not considered important to Simon the Zealot, and not translated into Hebrew.

Outside of Judea, the Septuagint was the dominant form of Israelite scriptures across the Greek-speaking world, which at the beginning of the Christian era extended from the Roman Empire in the west, to the Indo-Greek Kingdom in the east. Judean traders had established small colonies along the trade routes of the Red Sea and the Indian Ocean, reaching as far south as Eritrea, and as far east as southern India, and these Judeans spoke Aramaic and Greek and used the Septuagint. The earliest Christians used the Septuagint exclusively, as far as the Israelite scriptures were concerned, and as a result, it is impossible to even understand the chronology of the world they described unless using the Septuagint. It is unclear why the Septuagint, Masoretic text, and Samaritan Asatir each contain a different chronology of the world. Adding the Book of Jubilees, and various variations of the Torah found within the Dead Sea Scrolls, there are no less than six ancient Israelite chronologies.

The Septuagint's Cosmic Genesis includes an additional millennium of human history that was dropped from the Proto-Masoretic texts in order to align the creation of the world with the beginning of the age of El, when the constellation Taurus became the marker of the northern vernal equinox, in 3760 BC. The Bull El was the dominant God of the Canaanite pantheon until circa 1700 BC, when Attar the Goat (Aries) and Yam the Sea-Monster (Cetus) fought for domination of the world beneath the sky, ultimately both being replaced by the god of thunder Ba'al Hadad, in the Canaanite Ba'al Cycle. Traditional Jewish interpretations of the timeline within the Masoretic text, is further hampered by the so-called 'missing years' of Rabbinical Time, in which hundreds of years of the Persian Empire are skipped over in order to make the timeline fit into the era since 3760 BC, a problem Christian chronologists have never had as Christianity developed after the astrology of Babylonian-era Judaism had been forgotten.

The earliest Christian Bibles all used the Septuagint, however, by the 4th century some Christian scholars were debating whether they should retranslate the Old Testament from the version the Jews were using, and some even suggested using the Samaritan version. Both suggestions were generally dismissed as heretical, as Jesus and the Apostles had quoted from the Septuagint, even though they had access to the Hebrew version then in use. This argument held in the west until the Middle Ages, when Catholic Bibles switched to the Masoretic text. In the east, Orthodox Bibles continued to use the Septuagint, as they do today. To the south, the Ethiopian Tewahedo Church continued to use the Septuagint, and across Asia, the Thomas Christians and Nestorians continued to use the Septuagint. Only in Western Europe were the later Masoretic text adopted, abandoning the more ancient Septuagint, on the assumption that the Jews had copied their texts more faithfully than the Greeks had translated them. This assumption was carried forward into the Protestant Churches that broke off from the Catholic Church, and therefore almost all Protestant Bibles use the Masoretic text for the basis of the Old Testament.

Unfortunately, this means that the earliest Christian writings are generally confusing and ignored by Protestants and Catholics. The earliest Christians of the first and second centuries quoted books that are no longer in the Bible, and as such, their writings are not always understood. Septuagint: History is part of a series of 21st century translations aimed at correcting this problem.

# INTRODUCTION

One of the problems with academic translations of the Septuagint, is the use of unfamiliar names or terms, as the Septuagint was written in Greek, and therefore many names are unrecognizable to modern readers who are used to Hebrew-derived names. This project uses the more commonly understood Hebrew-derived names instead of their Greek translations, such as Canaan instead of Chanaan, and Melchizedek instead of Melchisedec. Common modern names are also used instead of either Greek or Hebrew terms when geographical locations are known, such as the archaeological name Uruk instead of the Greek Orech, or the Hebrew Erech, and the archaeological term Sumer instead of Shinar or Senar. While this could be argued as not being a correct academic procedure, it does fulfill the goal of making the translation easy to read and understand.

# Forward to Joshua

It is generally accepted that there were several versions of Joshua written in Samaritan, Judahite, or Aramaic before the translation of the Septuagint. Fragments of the book of Joshua have been found among the dead sea scrolls, however, only in the Assyrian script of the Herodian Dynasty in Judea, and dated to between 37 BC and 6 AD. The Book of Joshua is itself a continuation of the story found in Numbers and Deuteronomy, themselves both continuations of the story found in Exodus. Specifically, it appears to be a direct continuation of Deuteronomy, which it may have originally been part of, as the closing verses of Deuteronomy and opening verses of Joshua fit together seamlessly.

So Moses the servant of the Lord died in the land of Moab by the word of the Lord. They buried him in Gai near the Temple of Peor, and no one has seen his sepulcher to this day. Moses was a hundred and twenty years old at his death, yet his eyes were not dimmed, nor were his natural powers destroyed. The children of Israel wept for Moses in Araboth of Moab at the Jordan near Jericho for thirty days, and the days of the sad mourning for Moses were completed.

Joshua the son of Nun was filled with the spirit of knowledge, for Moses had laid his hands on him, and the children of Israel listened to him, and they did as the Lord commanded Moses. There did not rise another prophet in Israel like Moses, whom the Lord knew face to face, in all the signs and wonders, which the Lord sent him to work in Egypt against Pharaoh and his servants and all his land, and the great wonders, and the mighty hand which Moses displayed before all Israel.

After the death of Moses, the Lord said to Joshua the son of Nun, the minister of Moses, "Moses my servant is dead. Now then rise, go across the Jordan, you and all these people, into the land which I give them. Every place on which you will step I will give to you, as I told Moses. The wilderness and Anti-Lebanon, as far as the great river, the river Euphrates, and as far as the farthest sea, your coasts will be at the setting of the sun. Not a man will stand against you all the days of your life, and as I was with Moses, so will I also be with you, and I will not fail you, or neglect you. Be strong and act like a man, as you will divide the land among these people, which I swore to give to your fathers. Be strong, therefore, and act like a man, and observe and do as Moses my servant commanded you. You will not turn from them to the right hand or the left, that you may be wise in whatever you may do. The book of this law will not leave out of your mouth, and you will meditate on it day and night, that you may know how to do all the things that are written in it. Then you will prosper, and make your ways prosperous, and then you will be wise. Look! I have commanded you 'Be strong and courageous, do not be cowardly nor fearful, for Lord the god is with you in all places, to wherever you go.'"

Joshua commanded the scribes of the people, "Go into the middle of the camp of the people, and command the people, 'Prepare provisions, for in three days you will go across the Jordan, enter into and take possession of the land, which Lord the god of your fathers gives to you."

Joshua also restates the division of the land of Canaan between the twelve tribes, which is previously covered in Numbers but goes into much more depth, stipulating the exact borders of the tribes. This implies that Joshua may have been one of the sources that the Levites used when they cobbled together Numbers for King Josiah. The fact that Deuteronomy and Joshua fit together so seamlessly, indicates it was likely compiled into its pre-Hasmonean form in the Kingdom of Samaria, where Deuteronomy almost certainly originated. Several factors support the book as pre-Josiah and likely ignored entirely by Josiah's reforms, most especially the references to the sun (Shemesh) and moon (Yarikh) obeying Joshua, or possibly Lord the god, depending on interpretation. After Josiah's reforms, the sun and moon were just the sun and moon, two big lights up in the sky that could not listen to anyone. Before his reforms, they were two of the most powerful gods, Shemesh and Yarikh. Certainly, he would not have allowed the heretical implication that they were hearing and thinking and choosing to obey anyone.

The Septuagint's book of Joshua also has the first reference to Sabaoth (Σαβαωθ) in chapter 6, as Lord Sabaoth (Κυρίω Σαβαωθ). Lord Sabaoth was the Judahite God during the rule of the Greeks, whom the Greeks equated with Dionysus, and the Romans equated with Bacchus. In Aramaic, the language which was spoken in Judea during the Persian and Greek eras, Ådny Sbå (אדני צבא) meant 'lord of desires,' however, when the Hasmonean Dynasty seized control of Judea and made the newly invented 'ancient' Hebrew language official, they changed the meaning of the word to 'military' or 'army,' making the Lord of Desires into the Lord of War.

The Hebrew word transliterated as Sabaoth, which the Greeks and Romans treated as the proper name of the Judean god, is a military term, roughly meaning 'army' or 'military.' As such, the fusion of the Hasmonean god Yahweh with Sabaoth created a militaristic version of Yahweh, a war-god, for a warrior-dynasty. The Hasmoneans may have promoted Yahweh Sabaoth, however, in Joshua, Sabaoth is not called Iaw Sabaoth, but Lord Sabaoth. This cannot be as a result of the Christian redaction of the name Iaô (Ιαω) in the 3rd century, as the Masoretic text only have Yahweh, not Yahweh Sabaoth. Lord Sabaoth is only mentioned once in Joshua, with all other references to Lord the god, the Lord, or God. He was mentioned when the Israelites were preparing to attack Jericho, however, his generalissimo (ἀρχιστράτηγοσ) was introduced clumsily at the end of the previous chapter.

When Joshua was in Jericho, he looked up with his eyes and saw a man standing before him, and there was a drawn sword in his hand, and Joshua approached and said to him, "Are you with us, or on the side of our enemies?"

He answered him, "I have now come, the Generalissimo of the army of the Lord."

Joshua fell on his face to the earth, and said to him, "Lord, what do you command of your servant?"

The Generalissimo of the Lord said to Joshua, "Remove your shoes off your feet, for the place on which you now stand is sacred."

This section of the text does not line up with the text before it, or after it. Joshua's people had not attacked Jericho yet, and the Israelites were not in the city. Moreover, if the city was sacred, God should not have destroyed it. This section of text appears to have either been added to the original text, or to be a relic of another, possibly older version of the Jericho story. However it came to be in the book of Joshua, it is in both the Septuagint's and Masoretic version of Joshua, meaning it must have been in the Aramaic version. This generalissimo of the army of the Lord, appears to be Lord Sabaoth, the 'Lord of War' in Canaanite and Hebrew, mentioned in the next chapter, meaning that he was not God, but a soldier sent by the Lord, or a lord, to Jericho, which was apparently sacred to the lord in question. This reference to a Lord other than God is consistent with the early Israelite religion before the reforms of King Josiah circa 625 BC when there were many Lords worshiped in Judah. These reforms are described in detail in the Septuagint's 4th Kingdoms (Masoretic Kings) chapter 23:

The king commanded Hilkiah the high priest, and the priests of the second order, and them that kept the door, to bring out of the temple of the Lord all the vessels that were made for Ba'al, and for

Asherah, and all the army of Shamayim, and he burnt them outside of Jerusalem in the fields of Kidron, and took the ashes of them to the Temple of El. He burnt the sacred male prostitutes, who the kings of Judah had appointed, and those burnt incense in the Bamahs and in the cities of Judah, and the places around Jerusalem, and those that burnt incense to Ba'al, Shemesh, Yarikh, the Zodiac, and the power of the armies of Shamayim.

He carried out the Asherah from the Temple of the Lord to the brook Kidron, and burnt it at the brook Kidron, and ground it to powder, and threw its powder on the sepulchers of the sons of the people. He pulled down the Palace of Qetesh that were by the Temple of the Lord, where the women wove tents for the Asherah. He brought up all the priests from the cities of Judah and defiled the Bamahs where the priests burnt incense, from Geba even to Beersheba.

He pulled down the house of the gates that were by the door of the gate of Joshua the ruler of the city, on a man's left hand at the gate of the city. The priests of the Bamahs did not go up to the altar of the Lord in Jerusalem, and they only ate leavened bread among their brothers. He defiled Tafeth which is in the valley of the son of Hinnom, constructed for a man to cause his son or his daughter to pass through the fire to Moloch. He burnt the horses which the king of Judah had given to Shemesh in the entrance of the Temple of the Lord, by the treasury of Nathan the king's eunuch, in the suburbs, and he burnt the Chariot of Shemesh with fire.

The altars that were on the roof of the upper room of Ahaz, which the kings of Judah had made, and the altars which Manasseh had made in the two courts of the Temple of the Lord, the king pulled down and forcibly removed from there and threw their dust into the Brook of Kidron. The king defiled the temple that was near Jerusalem, on the right hand of the mount of Mosthath, which Solomon king of Israel built to Astarte the abomination of the Sidonians, and to Chemosh the abomination of Moab, and to Moloch the abomination of the Ammanites. He broke in pieces the steles, and completely destroyed Asherah, and filled their places with the bones of men. Also the high altar in the Temple of El, which had been built by Jeroboam the son of Nebat, who made Israel sin, even that high altar he tore down, and broke in pieces the stones of it, and reduced it to powder, and burnt Asherah.

Josiah turned aside, and saw the tombs that were there in the city, and sent, and took the bones out of the tombs, and burnt them on the altar, and defiled it, following the word of the Lord which the prophet spoke...

The reforms that took place in Judah under Josiah were both extreme and lasting, as the god Yahweh continues to be the God of Judaism today. Nevertheless, he has not always been the god of the Judahites. The Septuagint's 1st Ezra recounts how after killing King Josiah, the Pharaoh Necho II restored the worship of the 'Lord' in Judah, which could only be a reference to the sun god Amen, which Necho II is recorded as worshiping in Egyptian records, along with the North Egyptian version of Amen known as Atum. The Septuagint's book of Baruch, written by the scribe Baruch in Babylon after Nebuchadnezzar II had destroyed Jerusalem a couple of decades later, describes his god as the sun, meaning that sun worship had been restored in Judah after Josiah's death. Throughout the subsequent Persian and Greek rules of Judea, several gods were reportedly worshiped in Jerusalem, including Ahura Mazda, the Zoroastrian God, and Lord Sabaoth, who seems to have been very different from the militaristic interpretation of the Hasmonean Yahweh of Armies. The original reference to Lord Sabaoth, in the bronze age cuneiform Joshua, was probably to a military commander, and not a magic genie, like the Aramaic version appears to have read.

The question of who this military commander was, at Jericho, in 1508 BC according to the Septuagint's chronology is generally ignored by those that assume it was God or a supernatural warrior sent by God, however, it is a matter of record that the army of Thutmose I marched through Canaan in the year 1505 BC, using the standard chronology of Egyptian history, and found no one to fight them. According to the archaeological record, the city of Jericho was destroyed sometime shortly before 1500 BC, and not rebuilt until the Iron Age. It is generally accepted that the Egyptian army destroyed the city, although Thutmose I did not report visiting the city himself, and would have mentioned destroying the city. There is no record of an Egyptian military expedition in 1508 BC, however, Egypt was not the only power at the time interested in Canaan, as between 1540 and 1500 BC the Mitanni Empire was rapidly expanding into northern Canaan. It is possible that the Generalissimo was a Mitanni war-chief.

While many scholars have questioned the age of the Book of Joshua, most of the criticism against it seems misdirected at the Hebrew translation, which must date to sometime between 140 and 37 BC. There are other references in Joshua that point to the authorship of Joshua, or at least parts of it, in the late bronze age. Specifically, the treatment of iron. Prior to the bronze-age collapse, circa 1200 BC, iron was rare in the Middle East and mainly used for jewelry. This treatment of iron as a valuable metal shows up in Joshua at the Battle of Jericho, when Joshua orders:

> All the silver, or gold, or brass, or iron, will be holy to the Lord. It will be carried into the treasury of the Lord.

Later, however, iron is treated as a common metal used in chariots, indicating that the Book of Joshua was added to later during the iron age, likely in the centuries before King Josiah's time, when the Israelites were worshiping many gods. The reference to the sun and the moon standing still in the sky would have meant something different to the pre-Josiah Israelites, as Shemesh and Yarikh were gods, but were obeying Joshua. As the author put it:

> The sun and the moon stood still until God executed vengeance on their enemies, and the sun stood still in the middle of the sky. It did not proceed to set until the end of one day. There was not a day like it either before or after, that god should listen to man...

This places the pre-Hasmonean redaction of Joshua before the time of Josiah, likely when the text was originally translated from cuneiform into Aramaic in the Kingdom of Samaria. The geographical references cover all of Canaan from Egypt to Syria, and so it is not easy to place a geographical origin to the text. It does, however, contradict the books of the Kingdoms, as it has Joshua conquering Jebus (Jerusalem), and not David. This would point to a Samaritan origin, as the Samaritans never accepted the city of Jerusalem as having been the capital of Israel, instead claiming that Shechem, and later the city of Samaria were the capital. If the text was translated into Aramaic in Samaria, this would have been between 930 and 720 BC. Nevertheless, some sections of the text must date back to before the bronze age collapse, to explain the value placed on iron.

The longer ending of Joshua is also found in some copies of the Septuagint and is included in this translation. In it, the Israelites turned away from worshiping Lord the god and started worshiping Astarte, Athtart, and the gods of the nations around them, resulting in God withdrawing his protection, and the Israelites being conquered by the Moabites. These two short verses end the book very differently from the Masoretic version, in which the Israelites are, presumably, still worshiping Lord the god, and live happily ever after. The paring of Astarte and Athtart (Ἀστάρτην καὶ Ασταρωθ) also dates the text to the late bronze age, as, by the early iron age, Astarte and Athtart had merged into the goddess simply called Qetesh, meaning 'holiness.'

The two goddesses mentioned are the wives of El from the bronze age Ugaritic Texts: Aṯrt (⊷⟨⊨⊢⊢), later called Ôštrt (𐤕𐤓𐤕𐤔𐤏) by the Phoenicians and Asherah (אשרה) by the Israelites; and Ôṯtrt-ym (⟨⟨⊢⊨⊢⊢ᵢ𝗛⊣), later called Astarte (Ἀστάρτη) by the Greeks and Ashtoret (עַשְׁתֹּרֶת) by the Israelites. The Phoenician Ôštrt (𐤕𐤓𐤕𐤔𐤏) was descended from Ôṯtrt-ym (⟨⟨⊢⊨⊢⊢ᵢ𝗛⊣), the sea goddess which also gave rise to Aphrodite, while the Israelite Åšrh (אשרה) was descended from Åṯrt (⊷⟨⊨⊢⊢), the goddess of the land. In the early Canaanite mythology, the sea and land appear to have been viewed as the two wives of El, the bull in the sky. During the Egyptian New Kingdoms era, which took place at the same time as the events in the books of Joshua and Judges, the two goddesses merged, along with the Egyptian goddess Hathor, into Qetesh, a goddess that assumed the 'sky goddess' role of Hathor, which seems to have been how the Israelites viewed her until King Josiah's reforms of circa 625 BC. This reference to Astarte and Asherah as seperate and equal goddesses, clearly dates the authorship of Joshua to the early New Kingdom Era, circa 1500 BC.

The general view of both historians and biblical scholars is that the Book of Joshua holds no historical value, and is simply a book written during the life of Josiah, or during the Babylonian captivity, or even later by Ezra during the Second Temple Era, however, this is based on analysis of the Masoretic version of the book, which is quite different from the Septuagint's version. In Rabbinical history, as a century and a half have been redacted, Joshua's life is dated to the early-1300s BC, instead of the late 1500s BC. This era does not align with anything found in the archaeo-logical record, and therefore the book reads like fiction. Likewise, the Masoretic version is about a god named Yahweh, a name not known to archaeology until around 800 BC, meaning that the Book of Joshua, if the Masoretic version were the original, would have to have been written after that time.

The Septuagint's version is quite different in the details, as the god of the book is Lord the god, almost certainly a translation of the term adonai hĕlōhîm found in the Aramaic sections of Daniel, and the title of the god El who the ancient Canaanites were worshiping in the 2nd millennium BC. Joshua's invasion of Canaan circa 1508 BC, 42 years after the Minoan Eruption, would also place the Israelites at Jericho at around the time the walls were torn down.

The ruins of Jericho were identified as the mound at Tell es-Sultan in 1869, and this is still generally accepted as ancient Jericho. The city was a major trading center, and heavily fortified city for thousands of years, until circa 1500 BC when the walls were torn down. The exact date when the walls were torn down is unclear, with estimates ranging from 1700 to 1400 BC, however, 1500 BC is the most widely quoted date. In approximately 1504 BC the Egyptian King Thutmose I led an expedition through Canaan and Syria to the Euphrates River, and it is assumed by many historians that he ripped down the walls of Jericho, however, that is not possible. Thutmose recorded that he found no one to fight him in Canaan, and the local peoples submitted to Egyptian power without conflict. Moreover, later the same year he launched his invasion of Nubia, to the south of Egypt, meaning he simply did not have time to secretly lay siege to Jericho. This pacified Canaan ruled by people who were afraid of the Egyptians is consistent with the account in Joshua, however, the Egyptian 'invasion' is not mentioned in Joshua. Given the history between the Israelites and Egyptians, it is not unlikely it would have been omitted, especially if there was no war, and the Israelites surrendered to the Egyptians without a fight.

After 1500 BC the people in Canaan, whoever they were, began fortifying their cities. Thutmose I's heir, Thutmose II, also sent an expedition into Canaan and Syria, and crossed the Euphrates, however, only reported fighting nomads in the Sinai. There are no records of his successor, Queen Hatshepsut invading Canaan. Her heir Thutmose III did send multiple armies through Canaan demanding tribute, however, these campaigns appear to have been mostly peaceful until around 1450 BC, when he marched his army into northern Canaan to invade Syria and occupied all of Canaan in the process. The cities of Kadesh on the Orontes (in modern Syria), and Byblos in modern Lebanon, are mentioned as being major conquests of his campaigns, which laid the foundation for his later attack on the Mitanni Empire in Syria.

After Thutmose's campaign, the region was formally part of the Egyptian Empire for centuries, however, Egyptian records show they generally left the people alone and did not exert much control over the region beyond demanding regular tribute. The Egyptian records show there were many local chieftains during this era, sometimes fighting each other, or a people called the Habiru, which some believe to be an ancient reference to the Hebrews. This era of nominal Egyptian occupation would be the era of the Judges when the Israelites had no king. Obviously, if they did not have a king, they were a subjugated people.

Supporters of the earlier dating for the tearing down of Jericho's walls, generally assume the Hyksos dynasty ripped them down at some point, and as there are few records from the era, it cannot be proven or disproved. Nevertheless, after the walls were ripped down the site was reoccupied briefly, and a small town was present at the ruins until circa 1500 BC, in the dating when the walls were ripped down between 1700 and 1600 BC. In the dating when the walls were ripped down circa 1500, this village existed until circa 1400 BC. In either event, the village was destroyed by someone. If the earlier dating for the walls being torn down is correct, then the walls were already torn down when Joshua's army arrived, and they simply destroyed a small unfortified settlement in the ruins of the ancient city. In that scenario, the story about the walls falling when the Israelites shouted at them was a later fictional element added at some point. However, in either case, whether the Israelites tore down the walls or not, a city or village was destroyed at Jericho circa 1500 BC, according to the archaeological evidence, supporting both the dating of the Minoan eruption in Exodus, and the invasion of Canaan by the Israelites right before the Egyptians occupied the region.

The Israelite invasion of Canaan circa 1508 BC could have been as one-sided as the Book of Joshua depicts it, as the region was divided among many petty 'kings' that emerged from the collapse of the Hyksos Dynasty circa 1540 BC, when their last fortified city, Sharuhen, fell to the armies of Pharaoh Ahmose I. The siege of Sharuhen took the Egyptian army three years, and it was significantly smaller than the ancient fortified city of Jericho, proving Thutmose I could not have leveled Jericho in a few weeks. Between 1540 BC, when Sharuhen fell, and 1450 BC, when Thutmose III formally annexed Canaan into his empire in prelude to his invasion of the Mitanni Empire, the region was in chaos by all accounts, and any resistance the Israelites would have encountered circa 1508 BC would have been minimal and unorganized. The kings they fought would have been in power for less than 40 years, and likely had little control over their dominions.

The Egyptian records report the region was divided among many tribes when they passed through the region in 1504 BC, which, does support the idea that there were 12 autonomous tribes at the time, along with subjugated Hurrians and Canaanites, as described in the Book of Joshua. Some of the names of the tribes are archaeologically attested, such as Dan and Gad, however, most are not, leading to speculation that they may have been later inventions. However, the Egyptians did not have consistent and universal names for countries. For example, the Egyptians called the Mitanni kingdom: Naharin, Maryannu, and Mitanni. Naharin is believed to have been adopted from the Akkadian word for 'river,' making it a geographical name. In this case, it appears an Egyptian asked a local what the river was called, and applied the word 'river' to the entire land. This would make sense to an Egyptian, as the Nile was the only river in Egypt. The name Maryannu is derived from the name of the Indo-Aryan rulers of the Mitanni Empire, known as 'marya' in Mitanni-Aryan, which translates as 'warrior' in Sanskrit. This was the political name of the land, which would have made sense to someone addressing a Pharaoh, as Egypt was his land. The name Mitanni, or 'me-ta-ni' in ancient Egyptian, appears to be a direct transliteration of the local name, however, was the rarest name they used for the land. Therefore, there is no reason to assume the Israelites were either present in Canaan or absent from Canaan, based on the Egyptian records.

Based on the various references to the Israelites worshiping Ba'al, Asherah, Shamayim, Shemesh, Yarikh, and many other Canaanite gods found in the books of Joshua, Judges, and the books of the Kingdoms, as well as the books of the prophets, it is unlikely the Egyptians would have been able to distinguish them from the Canaanites. Modern archaeologists cannot. Until the era of Josiah, the Israelites appear to have been no different from the

Canaanites they supposedly conquered, and most archaeologists doubt there was an invasion. There was the well-documented pillaging of the Habiru, recorded in hundreds of surviving documents from the 2$^{nd}$ millennium BC, by the Canaanites, Egyptians, Akkadians, and Sumerians. These people started out in Sumer and were described as a group of Aramaean nomads that attacked undefended villages and plundered the countryside. Between 1800 and 1200 BC, they lived outside of the major Empires and pillaged the outskirts of Sumer, Akkadia, Babylonia, Assyria, and Canaan.

They were generally described as being murderers and thieves, however, also worked as mercenaries. Based on the Tikunani Prism from around 1550 BC, the majority were Hurrian at the time, although Semitic names were the second most common. In later centuries Indo-Aryan names appeared among them, likely of Mitanni origin. Many have tried to link the history of the Habiru to the Hebrews, and while the names may be connected, there is no evidence of the Habiru having a common god, tribe, or goal. They operated as 'land pirates' marauding their way across the Middle East. In the Amarna Letters, from circa 1350 BC, the warlord Labaya, the ruler of Shechem, one of Egypt's petty kingdoms, hired Habiru as mercenaries and allowed them to settle in Shechem, meaning that if the Israelites were settled in Shechem by that time, they were not the Habiru. These Habiru settlers did nevertheless contribute to the developing Israelite identity and would have been part of the United Kingdom of Israel and Judah if it existed, and the later Kingdom of Samaria. In the Torah, the Israelites were a subset of Hebrews, as Abraham was a Hebrew, however, only the descendants of Jacob were Israelites.

The Book of Joshua has traditionally been very unpopular, both with Jews and Christians, and only 3 copies have been found to date among the Dead Sea Scrolls, compared to 22 for Genesis, 17 for Exodus, 15 for Leviticus, 13 for Numbers, and 33 for Deuteronomy. Even Judges and Ruth were more popular with 4 copies of each discovered among the Dead Sea Scrolls. This unpopularity is generally attributed to the 'heroic' genocidal warfare described, which is the antithesis of Christianity and modern Judaism. Many Christian denominations issue advisories for members reading Joshua, printed directly in their bibles, to 'not take the history seriously,' 'it did not happen,' and to 'focus on the spiritual message.' However, there is little spiritual in the book, other than the first appearance of Lord Sabaoth, who became Yahweh Sabaoth in the Hasmonean redaction.

# Joshua: Chapter 1

After the death of Moses, the Lord[1] said to Joshua the son of Nun, the minister of Moses, "Moses my servant is dead. Now then rise, go across the Jordan, you and all these people, into the land which I give them. Every place on which you will step I will give to you, as I told Moses. The wilderness and Anti-Lebanon, as far as the great river, the river Euphrates, and as far as the farthest sea, your coasts will be at the setting of the sun. Not a man will stand against you all the days of your life, and as I was with Moses, so will I also be with you, and I will not fail you, or neglect you. Be strong and act like a man, as you will divide the land among these people, which I swore to give to your fathers."

"Be strong, therefore, and act like a man, and observe and do as Moses my servant commanded you. You will not turn from them to the right hand or the left, that you may be wise in whatever you may do. The book of this law will not leave out of your mouth, and you will meditate on it day and night, that you may know how to do all the things that are written in it. Then you will prosper, and make your ways prosperous, and then you will be wise. Look! I have commanded you 'Be strong and courageous, do not be cowardly nor fearful, for Lord the god[2] is with you in all places, to wherever you go.'"

Joshua commanded the scribes of the people, "Go into the middle of the camp of the people, and command the people, 'Prepare provisions, for in three days you will go across the Jordan, enter into and take possession of the land, which Lord the god of your fathers gives to you.'"

To Reuben, and to Gad, and to the half-tribe of Manasseh, Joshua said, "Remember the words that Moses the servant of the Lord commanded you, 'The Lord the god has caused you to peace, and has given you this land. Let your wives and your children and your livestock live in the land which he has given you, but you will cross well-armed before your brothers, every one of you who is strong, and you will fight on their side, until Lord the god has given your brothers peace, like you, and they have inherited the land that Lord the god gives them. Then you will leave, each one to his inheritance that Moses gave you to the east of the Jordan."

They answered Joshua, "We will do all things which you command us, and we will go everywhere you will send us. As we listened to Moses, we will listen to you. Only let Lord the god be with you, as he was with Moses. Whoever will disobey you, and whoever will not listen to your words as you will command him, let him die, but you be strong and courageous."

# Joshua: Chapter 1 Notes

**1** Codex Vaticanus: c̅s̅ (κ̅ϲ̅). Translation: lord

- Aleppo Codex: Yhwh (יהוה)

- Leningrad Codex: Yehvah (יְהֶוָה)

- Targum Jerusalem: Yeyah (?). Translation: Yahw

This verse does not survive in the Dead Sea Scrolls, however, the name does show up in later verses that have survived.

- Dead Sea Scroll 4QJosh[a]: Yhwh (𐤉𐤄𐤅𐤄)

- Dead Sea Scroll 4QJosh[b]: Yhwh (𐤉𐤄𐤅𐤄)

The Septuagint's version of the Joshua was translated before 200 BC, as it was carried south by the Israelite community, who left Egypt for Kush (modern Sudan) during the Judean Rebellion against the Ptolemys in 200 BC. This means it predates the Hasmonean redaction and contains the term Lord (Κύριοσ) instead of Iaô (Ιαω), which, if correctly translated from the Aramaic source texts, would have read ådny (𐤀𐤃𐤍𐤉).

The Greeks are believed to have transliterated Yahw (𐤉𐤄𐤅), the Aramaic version of the name Yehvah/Yehvah, as Iaô (Ιαω) in the Book of Leviticus, published circa 250 BC, as evidenced by the Dead Sea Scroll Septuagint fragment 4QpapLXXLev[b], which dates from Hasmonean era Judea. 4QpapLXXLev[b] could be interpreted as a Hasmonean redaction of the Septuagint, however, Leviticus appears to have been written during the rule of King Josiah, and his God was Yahw, supporting the existence of Yahw in the Book of Leviticus.

The Aramaic sections of Masoretic Daniel that were not translated into Hebrew maintain the term adonai ha'elohim (אֲדֹנָי הָאֱלֹהִים), meaning the 'Lord the gods' where the Septuagint has 'Lord the god' (Κύριον τὸν θεὸν), however, the Hebrew sections have Yahweh elohim (יְהֹוָה אֱלֹהִים) where the Septuagint has 'Lord the god,' suggesting the Greek more accurately reflects the Aramaic source texts than the Hebrew translation.

According to the Talmud, this was to repair the damage King Manasseh had done 600 years earlier when he removed the name Yahweh from the Israelite Texts, however, no evidence has survived from the era of Manasseh or earlier that proves the name was originally in the text, suggesting it was an attempt by the first Hasmonean High-Priest/King Simon the Zealot to create a national Judean religion with a god having a name similar to the Roman god Jove.

In the 3rd century AD, the Christians redacted the Septuagint removing the name Iaô, both in Greek, and in Latin translations which transliterated Ιαω as Iaw, replacing it with 'Lord.' This resolved the debate with the Gnostics about whether Iaw was the devil or not. Before that, the various versions of the early-Christian-era Septuagint books that included the name, either used Ιαω, or the name written in Hebrew or Phoenician (Paleo-Hebrew) scripts. According to Origen of Alexandria in the late 2nd century AD, the Phoenician (most ancient script) was the most accurate. According to Theodoret of Cyprus in the 5th century, the Samaritans, who never switched to the Assyrian block letter 'Hebrew,' pronounced the name as Iabe (Ιαβε) or Iabae (Ιαβαι). Hebrews substitute the word 'hasheim,' meaning 'the name,' in all non-scriptural contexts since the Hasmoneans banned the pronunciation of the names of God. Christians have traditionally translated several ways including Jehovah, Jehova, and Jova. As the original Greek translation of Joshua does not appear to have included the name, the term Lord is used in this translation.

**2** Codex Vaticanus: c̅s̅ o t̅h̅s̅ (ⲕⲥⲟⲑⲥ) . Translation: Lord the god

• Aleppo Codex: Yhwh ålhyk (יהוה אלהיך). Translation: Yhwh your god

• Leningrad Codex: Yehvah eloheicha (יְהוָה אֱלֹהֶיךָ). Translation: Yehwah your god

• Targum Jerusalem: daYeyah elahachon (דַיְיָ אֱלָהְכוֹן). Translation: the Yahw your god

This verse does not survive in the Dead Sea Scrolls, however, a similar term does show up in later verses that have survived.

• Dead Sea Scroll 4QJosh[a]: Yhwh ålhy (יהוה אלהי). Translations: Yhwh my god

The Septuagint's version of the Joshua was translated before 200 BC, as it was carried south by the Israelite community, who left Egypt for Kush (modern Sudan) during the Judean Rebellion against the Ptolemys in 200 BC. This means it predates the Hasmonean redaction and contains the term Lord (Κύριοσ) instead of Iaô (Ιαω), which, if correctly translated from the Aramaic source texts, would have read ådny (אדני). The Greeks are believed to have transliterated Yahw (יהו), the Aramaic version of the name Yehvah/Yehvah, as Iaô (Ιαω) in the Book of Leviticus, published circa 250 BC, as evidenced by the Dead Sea Scroll Septuagint fragment 4QpapLXXLev[b], which dates from Hasmonean era Judea. 4QpapLXXLev[b] could be interpreted as a Hasmonean redaction of the Septuagint, however, Leviticus appears to have been written during the rule of King Josiah, and his God was Yahw, supporting the existence of Yahw in the Book of Leviticus.

The Aramaic sections of Masoretic Daniel that were not translated into Hebrew maintain the term adonai ha'elohim (אֲדֹנָי הָאֱלֹהִים), meaning the 'Lord the gods' where the Septuagint has 'Lord the god' (Κύριον τὸν θεὸν), however, the Hebrew sections have Yahweh elohim (יְהוָה אֱלֹהִים) where the Septuagint has 'Lord the god,' suggesting the Greek more accurately reflects the Aramaic source texts than the Hebrew translation. According to some records from the time, this was to repair the damage King Manasseh had done 600 years earlier when he removed the name Yahweh from the Israelite Texts, however, no evidence has survived from the era of Manasseh or earlier that proves the name was originally in the text, suggesting it was an attempt by the first Hasmonean High-Priest/King Simon the Zealot to create a national Judean religion with a god having a name similar to the Roman god Jove.

# JOSHUA: CHAPTER 1 NOTES

In later copies of the Septuagint, the name was replaced by the name written in Phoenician (𐤉𐤄𐤅𐤄) or Hebrew script (יהוה). The name Iaw is found in fragments of the 3rd century AD Papyrus Oxyrhynchus 1007, however, is represented by a double Yod (״), meaning it was copied from a later Hebrew or Aramaic text from that era. After the sixth century AD, the occasional copy of the Septuagint is found which uses the name, either written as Ιαω or a Greek approximation of יהוה (ΠΙΠΙ), however, all of these can be traced back to the Hexapla, Quinta, Sextus, and/or Septima, which attempted to retranslate and harmonize the Old Testament in the 3rd through 6th centuries AD. There are no early surviving copies of the Septuagint's version of Joshua which have the name Iaw (Ιαω / 𐤉𐤄𐤅) in it like some of the other books of the Septuagint. As Κυριοσ ο θεοσ translates directly as Lord God (or Lord the God), that term is used.

# Joshua: Chapter 2

Joshua the son of Nun, sent two young men from Shittim[1] to spy on the land, ordering, "Go up, and view the land around Jericho."

The two young men went to Jericho, and entered into the house of a prostitute, whose name was Rehob, and lodged there. It was reported to the king of Jericho, "Men of the sons of Israel have come in here to spy the land."

The king of Jericho sent and spoke to Rehob, ordering, "Bring out the men that entered into your house tonight, as they have come to spy on the land."

The woman took the two men and hid them, and replied to the messengers, "The men came into me, but after the gate was shut in the dark, the men left. I don't know where they've gone. Chase after them, and you may catch them."

She had taken them up onto the roof to the house, and hidden them in flax-stalks that were spread on her on the roof. The left and men chased after them along the road to ford on the Jordan, where the gate was shut. After the men pursuing them had left, and before the spies had gone to sleep, she went up to them on the top of the house, and said, "I know that the Lord has given you the land, as the fear of you, has fallen on us. For we have heard that Lord the god dried up the Papyrus Sea[2] before you, when you came out of the land of Egypt, and all that he did to the two kings of the Amorites, who were beyond Jordan, to Sihon and Og, whom you completely destroyed. When we heard it we were amazed in our heart, and there was no longer any spirit in any of us because of you, for Lord the god is the god in the sky above and on the land below. Now swear to me by Lord the god, since I dealt mercifully with you, you will also deal mercifully with the house of my father, and save the house of my father, my mother, and my brothers, and all my house, and all that they have, and you will rescue my mind from Mot.[3]

The men answered her, "Our life for yours even to death."

She confirmed, "When the Lord has delivered the city to you, you will deal mercifully and truly with me."

She let them down out her window, and she said to them, "Go into the hill-country, in case the pursuers find you, and hide there for three days until your pursuers return from looking for you, and afterward you can leave on your way."

The men said to her, "This is our oath. Look, we will enter into a part of the city, and you will set the sign: you will bind this scarlet cord in the window, by which you have let us down, and you will bring into your house with yourself, your father, and your mother, and your brothers, and all the family of your father. It will come to pass that whoever will be outside the door of your house, his guilt will be on him, and we will be free of this, your oath. We will be responsible for all that will be found with you in your house. But if anyone should injure us, or betray these our matters, we will be free of this, your oath."

She said to them, "Let it be as you have said," and she sent them out, and they departed. They came to the hill-country and remained there for three days, and the pursuers searched all the roads and did not find them. The two young men returned and came down out of the mountain, and they went over to Joshua the son of Nun, and told him all things that had happened to them. They said to Joshua, "The Lord has delivered all the land into our power, and all the inhabitants of that land tremble because of us."

# Joshua: Chapter 2 Notes

**1** Codex Vaticanus: Sattin (ϲⲀⲧⲧⲓⲚ)

- Aleppo Codex: Štym (שטים)

- Leningrad Codex: Shittim (שִׁטִּ֖ים)

- Targum Jerusalem: Shitin (שִׁטִין)

The location of the Shittim Valley is generally accepted as Khirbet el-Kafrayn, in Jordan. Other Israelite texts, such as Micah refer to the Lord of Peor in association with the Shittim Valley, however, this name appears to have been an insult directed towards Lord Hammon who was worshiped at Tell el-Hammam in the 800s BC. There is no clear link between Hammon and Peor, implying the worshipers of Peor disappeared around the time the Israelites traveled through the Shittim Valley.

The major ruins in the Shittim Valley, are found at Tell el-Hammam, which was occupied from at least 3600 BC until the beginning of the Late Bronze Age (1550 to 1200 BC) when the site was abandoned for unknown reasons. It was rebuilt in the 900s BC as a Samaritan city. As Tell el-Hammam is in the Shittim Valley, and was destroyed or abandoned when the Israelites moved through the region, using either the traditional Christian dating or the Minoan Eruption and collapse of the Hyksos Dynasty from the Book of Exodus, the Bronze-Age city was likely Peor (Φαγωρ). The exact dating of the abandonment of the bronze-age city is unclear, and there is some evidence of occupation for a few decades after 1550 BC, but the site does appear to have been abandoned by 1500 BC.

**2** Codex Vaticanus: erythran thalassan (ⲉⲣⲩⲑⲣⲁⲚⲐⲀⲗⲀⲤⲤⲀⲚ). Translation: Erythrean (or Red) Sea

- Aleppo Codex: ym swp (ים סוף). Translation: sea of reeds (or papyrus)

- Leningrad Codex: yam-suf (יַם־סוּף). Translation: sea of reeds (or papyrus)

- Targum Jerusalem: yama deSuf (יְמָא דְסוּף). Translation: sea of reeds (or papyrus)

The Greek term is not geographically specific, as it is a translation of the Persian term Erostras, which referred to the entire Persian Gulf, Red Sea, and the Indian Ocean. The Greeks were likely referring to the Gulf of Suez, however, this was known to the ancient Egyptians as the 'Sea of Calm,' which is what the Israelites would have called it if that was where they were. The original Sea of Reeds was almost certainly Lake Bardawil on the north coast of the Sinai Peninsula, a shallow saline lake with a surface area of 147,000 acres (59,500 hectares).

The Greeks transliterated the name as the Sea of Siph (ΘΑΛΑϹϹΗϹ Ϲιφ) in the Codex Vaticanus' translation of Judges, confirming that the name Swf was in the Aramaic text they worked from. Both the Aramaic term swf (סוף) and Phoenician term swf (𐤎𐤅𐤐), both meaning papyrus plants were adopted from the Egyptian term tjufi (𓍿𓃀𓆑𓇥), which referred to papyrus, papyrus plants, and papyrus marshes. The Egyptian term continued to be used into the Classical era as the Coptic words čoouf (ϫⲟⲟⲩϥ), conf (ϭⲟⲛϥ), and comf (ϭⲟⲙϥ), all meaning papyrus. Conversely, the Egyptian name of the Red Sea was the Sea of Heh (𓎛), meaning 'very large sea' from the Middle Kingdom era onward, however, it is believed to have originally been named after the ancient Egyptian frog god Heh (𓁨).

As the Greek translation of Erythrean Sea is anachronistic, the translation of Papyrus Sea is imported from the Masoretic text. Based on the described journey out of Egypt, the original Papyrus Sea would have been Lake Bardawil on the north coast of the Sinai Peninsula, a shallow saline lake with a surface area of 147,000 acres (59,500 hectares).


**3** Codex Vaticanus: Thanatou (ΘΑΝΑΤΟΥ). Translation: Thanatos (or death, corpse)

- Aleppo Codex: Mwt (מות). Translation: Mot (or 'to die' in Aramaic, 'death' in Hebrew)

- Leningrad Codex: Mavet (מָוֶת). Translation: Mot (or 'death' in Hebrew)

Mot (ד— / ‏מ‎) was the Canaanite god of death, which the Greeks interpreted as the local version of Thanatos, the Greek god of death. The Israelites viewed Mot as the angel of Death in the era of the prophets, which resulted in Thanatos becoming the Christian angel of death in the early centuries of the Christian era.

# Joshua: Chapter 3

Joshua rose early in the morning and left Shittim, and they came as far as the Jordan and lodged there before they crossed over. After three days, the scribes went through the camp, and they ordered the people, "When you see the box[1] of the covenant of Lord the god, and our priests and the Levites carrying it, you will leave from your places, and you will follow it, but keep a distance from it. You will stand at least two thousand cubits from it. Do not approach it, that you may know which way you are to go, as you have not gone this way previously."

Joshua said to the people, "Sanctify yourselves against tomorrow, for tomorrow the Lord will do wonders among you." Joshua said to the priests, "Take up the box of the covenant of the Lord, and go before the people."

The priests picked up the box of the covenant of the Lord and went before the people. The Lord said to Joshua, "Today I begin to exalt you before all the Israelites, that they may know that as I was with Moses, so will I also be with you. Now order the priests that carry the box of the covenant, 'As soon as you enter on a part of the water of Jordan, then you will stand in the Jordan.'"

Joshua said to the Israelites, "Come here and listen to the word of Lord the god. By this you will know that the living God is among you, and will completely destroy from before us the Canaanites, Cypriots,[2] Perizzites, Mitanni,[3] Amorites, Girgashites, and Jebusites. Look, the box of the covenant of the Lord crosses the Jordan. Choose among yourselves twelve men of the sons of Israel, one from each tribe. It will come to pass, when the feet of the priests that carry the box of the covenant of the Lord enter into the water of the Jordan, the water of Jordan below will stop, and the water coming down from above will stop."

The people packed up their tents to cross the Jordan, and the priests carried the box of the covenant of the Lord before the people. When the priests that carried the box of the covenant of the Lord entered on Jordan, and the feet of the priests that carried the box of the covenant of the Lord were stepped into the water of the Jordan, (now the Jordan, its whole channel overflowed all its banks as in the days of the wheat harvest.) Then the waters that came down from above stopped, frozen and exceedingly violent, as far off as the region of Kariathiarim, and that which came down to the Dead Sea (the salt sea),[4] until it completely failed, and the people stood opposite Jericho. The priests that carried the box of the covenant of the Lord stood on dry land in the middle of Jordan, and all the Israelites went through on dry land until all the people had completely crossed the Jordan.

# Joshua: Chapter 3 Notes

**1** Codex Vaticanus: cibôton (ΚΙΒѠΤΟΝ). Translation: box (or chest)

• Aleppo Codex: årwn (אָרֹון). Translation: box

• Leningrad Codex: aron (אֲרֹון). Translation: box

• Targum Jerusalem: aron (אֲרֹון). Translation: box

The Greek term cibôton (κιβωτὸν) was based on the Aramaic word tybwtå (מ^עוטא), however, the Hebrew translation uses a different word, also meaning 'box.' The reason for the Hebrew substitution is likely due to the Aramaic word being based on the Egyptian word djebåt (𓋃), meaning 'sarcophagus,' since the classical era, which has resulted in many strange translations. The Egyptian word is accepted as being adopted into Canaanite during the New Kingdom Era, when it was pronounced as debåt (𓋃), indicating that the Egyptian word was likely the original in the text. By the Classical era, when the Hebrew text was translated, the related Coptic Egyptian word taibe (ΤΑΙΒє) had come to mean coffin, meaning the 'box of god' would have become the 'coffin of god' explaining the Hebrew substitution of årwn (אָרֹון).

**2** Codex Vaticanus: Chettaeon (ΧєΤΤΑΙΟΝ)

• Aleppo Codex: Ḥty (חתי). Translation: Cypriots

• Leningrad Codex: Chitti (חִתִּי). Translation: Cypriots

• Targum Jerusalem: Chitta'ei (חִתָּאֵי). Translation: Cypriots

This term has created a great deal of confusion since the misidentification of the ruins of the Neshites as being 'Hittite' in the 1800s. The modern archaeological name 'Hittite,' is not derived from an ancient name for the culture applied by themselves, or anyone else, but rather adopted from the biblical reference to a then-unknown civilization somewhere in the region. There was an ancient culture in the region called the Hattians, however, they were conquered by the Nesites

41

before 1700 BC, and subsequently disappeared from the historic records. The name was applied to culture today referred to as 'Hittites,' before the 'Hittite' language had been translated, and is incorrect. Since 1906, excavations at Boğazköy, the ancient 'Hittite' capital Hattusa have uncovered more than 10,000 'Hittite' texts, including the royal achieve. The actual name of the 'Hittite' language and people was Nešili (𒉈𒅆𒇷), which is now rendered in some academic literate as Nesite or Neshite. As early as the mid-1800s some scholars disputed the identification of the Nesites as the Biblical Hittites, including the Orientalist Max Müller, who was one of many claiming the Biblical Hittites were ancient Greeks or some other Mediterranean people. Later in the Septuagint's translation of the Maccabees, the similar term Chettiim (Χεττιιμ) as a reference to all Greek-speaking lands, and therefore the Biblical Hittites were likely the Minoans or the Achaean Greeks.

In the 1st century AD, the Jewish historian Josephus reported that Cethima was the name of Cyrus in Aramaic, and the Chettim were the descendants of Noah's grandson Chethimus, who had settled on Cyprus. Josephus reported that the name was preserved in the Greek name of the town Cition (Κίτιον). Most historians view it as more likely that the Aramaic name was derived from the city-state of Cition, which was known as Kåtjåy ( 𓏤 𓅓 𓇓 𓍃 ) in Egyptian records from the New Kingdom Era in the late Bronze Age, and Kt (𐤊𐤕) or Kty (𐤊𐤕𐤉) in Phoenician records from the early Iron Age. While this may be the origin of the term, by the era of the Neo-Assyrian era, the term must have also referred to other Greek islands, as both the prophets Isaiah and Ezekiel used the term 'Islands of Kittim.' As the term referred to the entire island of Cyprus in Aramaic, the translations of 'Cyprus' and 'Cypriots' are used here.

**3** Codex Vaticanus: Euaion (ΕΥΑΙΟΝ)

- Aleppo Codex: Ḥwy (חוי)

- Leningrad Codex: Chivvi (חִוִּי)

- Targum Jerusalem: Chiva'ei (חִוָאֵי)

The term is believed to have been derived from the name of the Hurrians, however, is derived separately from the other term Chori (חֹרִי). Chori is accepted as referring to the Hurrians, which the Egyptians called Hårw (𓉔𓄿𓂋𓅱), and the Babylonians called Ḫuurri (𒄷𒌨𒊑). The Hurrians were one of the oldest cultures in the Middle East, however, became largely a slave culture within the Akkadian and Old Babylonian empires. Under the Mitanni empire, they rose to a position of wealth, and formed the noble caste. The Greek transliteration of this term was variations of Chorrhaeous (Χορραιους), which, like the Hebrew term, was used interchangeably in the texts with Eyaeon (Ευαῖον) / Chivvi (חִוִּי), although that term generally applied to the rules and priests.

The ultimate origin of the terms Eyaeon (Ευαῖον) and Chivvi (חִוִּי), both appear to be the cuneiform word Éan (𒂍𒀭), meaning temple or sacred. In the Amarna Letters, which date to the 1330s BC, the term Éan (𒂍𒀭) was the name of a people, who appear to be the Mitanni, or the Mitanni-Aryan priesthood within the Mitanni. A similar correlation between the terms is found in the Septuagint's 1st Paralipomenon and Masoretic Divrei-hay Yamim, where the Greek translation uses Beithani (Βαιθανι), however, the Hebrew uses the term Mitni (מִתְנִי). This term also refers to a group of people, meaning the underlying Edomite text the Greeks translated would have been 'people of the House of Ån' (𐤁𐤕𐤀𐤍), a direct Canaanite translation of É An (𒂍𒀭).

While Mitni was the transliteration used in the Edomite text that formed the basis of the Hebrew translation of Divrei-hayYamim, it was replaced with Chivvi (חִוִּי) in the Judahite texts, which served as the basis of most of the Masoretic texts. This likely originated in a Judahite copy of the text, after the Aramaic translation had been made, where an n (𐤍) was replaced with a w (𐤅). The Aramaic translation would have already been made in the time of King Manasseh, were the term was transliterated as Hyån (ח־∧∧י), itself a transliteration of the early Canaanite Hyån (𐤂𐤉𐤀𐤍).

**4** Codex Vaticanus: thalassan Araba thalassan alos (ѲⲀⲗⲀⲤⲤⲀⲚ ⲀⲢⲀⲂⲀѲⲀⲗⲀⲤⲤⲀⲚⲀⲗⲟⲤ). Translation: Sea of Arabah Sea of Salt

• Aleppo Codex: ym hôrbh ym hmlḥ (יס הערבה יס המלח). Translation: Sea of the Plain sea of salt

• Leningrad Codex: yam ha'aravah yam-hammelach ( יָם הָעֲרָבָה יַס־הַמֶּלַח). Translation: Sea of the Plain sea of salt

• Targum Jerusalem: leyama demeishra leyama demilcha ( לְיַמָּא דְמֵישְׁרָא לְיַמָּא דְמִלְחָא). Translation: the sea of the valley the sea of salt

The Sea of Arabah was an ancient name for the Dead Sea. The scribal notes clarifying that the Sea of Arabah was the salt sea appears to have been included in the Aramaic source text that both the Septuagint and Masoretic versions of Joshua were translated from. The fact that the Aramaic translator needed to clarify which sea the Sea of Arabah was, suggests the Aramaic translation of Joshua was made in the north, likely in Gilead or Aram. This note also means the original Book of Joshua was not written in Aramaic, but translated from another language, and, clearly written earlier, when the term Sea of Arabah was commonly used.

# Joshua: Chapter 4

When the people had completely crossed the Jordan, the Lord said to Joshua, "Take men from the people, one from each tribe, and organize them, and you will take out of the middle of the Jordan twelve existing stones, and having carried them across together with yourselves, place them in your camp, where you will camp for the night."

Joshua called twelve distinguished men among the Israelites, one of each tribe, and said to them, "Advance before me in the presence of the Lord into the middle of Jordan, and each pick up a stone from there, let him carry it on your shoulders, according to the number of the twelve tribes of Israel. These may be for you continually an appointed sign, so when your son asks you in the future, 'What are these stones to us?' Then you may explain to your son, 'The river Jordan was dried up from before the box of the covenant of the Lord when it passed it, and these stones will be as a memorial for you for the Israelites forever."

The Israelites did so, as the Lord commanded Joshua. They picked up twelve stones out of the middle of Jordan, (as the Lord commanded Joshua when the Israelites had completely crossed over,) and carried these stones with them into the camp, and laid them down there. Joshua set also another twelve stones in Jordan itself, in the place that was under the feet of the priests that carried the box of the covenant of the Lord, and there they are to this day. The priests that carried the box of the covenant stood in Jordan until Joshua had finished all that the Lord commanded him to report to the people, and the people rushed and crossed over. When all the people had passed over, that the box of the covenant of the Lord crossed over, and the stones before them. The sons of Reuben, and the sons of Gad, and the half-tribe of Manasseh crossed equipped before the Israelites, as Moses commanded them.

Forty thousand armed for battle went over before the Lord to war, to the city of Jericho. On that day the Lord magnified Joshua before all the people of Israel, and they were afraid of him, like they had been of Moses, as long as he lived.

The Lord said to Joshua, "Order the priests that carry the box of the covenant of the testimony of the Lord, to come up out of Jordan."

Joshua ordered the priests, "Come up out of Jordan."

When the priests who carried the box of the covenant of the Lord had come up out of Jordan and set their feet on the land, the water of the Jordan returned rapidly to its place and went as before over all its banks. The people came out of the Jordan on the tenth day of the first month, and the Israelites camped at the circle[1] in the region eastward from Jericho. Joshua set these twelve stones which he took out of Jordan, in a circle, and said, "When your sons ask you, 'What are these stones? Tell your sons, that Israel came over the Jordan on dry land when Lord the god had dried up the water of Jordan from before them until they had passed over. As Lord the god did to the Papyrus Sea, which Lord the god dried up from before us until we passed over. That all the nations of the earth might know, that the power of the Lord is mighty and that you might worship Lord the god in every work."

# Joshua: Chapter 4 Notes

**1** Codex Vaticanus: Galgaloes (ΓΑΛΓΑΛΟΙϹ)

- Aleppo Codex: glgl (גלגל). Translation: circle

- Leningrad Codex: gilgāl (גִּלְגָּל). Translation: circle

- Targum Jerusalem: gilgala (גִלְגָּלָא). Translation: wheel

Gilgal (גִּלְגָּל) is the Hebrew word for circle. Archaeologists have discovered several ceremonial stone circles in Canaan that were used between 1200 and 1000 BC for gatherings that are assumed to be religious in nature. As these stone circles are found down in the valleys, unlike the altars at the tops of hills where the Canaanites worshiped, and 'circles' (גלגל) are mentioned throughout the old Israelite texts, it is assumed they are early Israelite religious centers from before the First Temple was built.

# Joshua: Chapter 5

When the kings of the Amorites who were beyond Jordan heard, and the kings of Phoenicia[1] by the sea, that Lord the god had dried up the river Jordan from before the Israelites when they passed over, that their hearts failed, and their minds melted, and there was no sense in them in the face of the Israelites.

About this time the Lord said to Joshua, "Make yourself stone knives from sharp stone, and sit down and circumcise the Israelites the second time."

Joshua made sharp knives of stone, and circumcised the Israelites at the place called the 'Hill of Foreskins.' This is how Joshua purified the Israelites, as many as were born in the way, and as many as were uncircumcised of them that came out of Egypt, all these Joshua circumcised. For forty-two years Israel wandered among the abandoned places of desert-dwellers.[2] Therefore most of the fighting men that came out of the land of Egypt were uncircumcised, those who disobeyed the commands of God, concerning who he determined should not see the land, which the Lord swore to give to their fathers, a land flowing with milk and honey. In their place he raised up their sons, who Joshua circumcised, because they were uncircumcised, having been born long the way. When they had been circumcised they rested sitting there in the camp until they were healed.

The lord[3] said to Joshua the son of Nun, "On this day have I removed the reproach of Egypt from you," and he called the name of that place Gilgal.

The Israelites kept the Passover on the fourteenth day of the month in the evening, to the west of Jericho on the opposite side of the Jordan in the plain. They ate the grain of the earth unleavened and new grain. On this day the manna stopped after they had eaten of the grain of the land, and the Israelites no longer had manna. They took the fruits of the land of the Phoenicians in that year. When Joshua was in Jericho, that he looked up with his eyes and saw a man standing before him, and there was a drawn sword in his hand, and Joshua approached and said to him, "Are you with us, or on the side of our enemies?"

He answered him, "I have now come, the Generalissimo of the army of the Lord."[4]

Joshua fell on his face to the earth, and said to him, "Lord, what do you command of your servant?"

The Generalissimo of the Lord said to Joshua, "Remove your shoes off your feet, for the place on which you now stand is sacred."

# Joshua: Chapter 5 Notes

**1** Codex Vaticanus: Phoenicês (ϕοινικнc). Translation: Phoenicia

• Aleppo Codex: Knôny (כנעני). Translation: Canaan

• Leningrad Codex: Kena'ani (כְּנַעֲנִי). Translation: Canaan

• Targum Jerusalem: Chena'ana'ah (כְנַעֲנָאָה). Translation: Canaan

Phoenicia and Canaan were two names of the same land and culture. Phoenicia is believed to be derived from the Egyptian name of the people, which then sped through the Mediterranean. Canaan is believed to be derived from the Akkadian name for the people, which was mainly used in Semitic languages of the Middle East. Both terms are believed to be derived from the name 'purple people,' as the Canaanites were mass exporters of purple dye and fabric throughout most of their civilization.

**2** Codex Vaticanus: tê erêmô tê Madbaritidi (THEPHMⲱTH MAΔBAPITIΔI). Translation: the desert (or abandoned places, empty places) the Madbarites

• Aleppo Codex: mdbr (מדבר). Translation: the desert

• Leningrad Codex: midbar (מִדְבָּר). Translation: the desert

• Targum Jerusalem: madbera (מָדְבְּרָא). Translation: the desert

The Greek translation deviates from the Hebrew and Judeo-Aramaic translations, which simply refer to the desert. The Greek could either be read as the 'desert of the Madbarites,' or the 'abandoned places of the Madbarites.' The term Madbaritidi (Μαδβαριτιδι) is a synthesis of the Aramaic mdbrå (ܐܪܒܕܡ) meaning 'desert' and the Greek -itidi (-ιτιδι), meaning 'people of,' the precursor to the modern English '-ites.' This means the term had to be adopted from a term in the Aramaic text which translates as 'desert dweller.' Based on the context, the Aramaic word was likely mdbråyn (ܢܝܪܒܕܡ), meaning 'desert-dweller.' This means the Aramaic text either read the redundant 'desert of the desert-dwellers,' or 'abandoned places of the desert-dwellers,' which is the interpretation used in this translation. As desert-dwellers are nomadic, is suggested the Israelites had occupied their settlements while they were elsewhere.


**3** Codex Vaticanus: c̄s (κ̄c̄). Translation: lord

• Aleppo Codex: Yhwh (יהוה)

• Leningrad Codex: Yehvah (יְהוָה)

• Targum Jerusalem: Yeyah (יְיָ). Translation: Yahw

• Based on the requirement to re-institute the Egyptian practice of circumcision, in order to remove the 'reproach of Egypt,' this appears to be describing the Israelites rejoining Egyptian civilization, which would make the 'lord' in the text King Thutmose I, before the Hasmoneans carelessly changed him to Yahweh.


**4** Codex Vaticanus: architratêgos dynameôs c̄u (ΑΡΧΙϹΤΡΑΤΗΓΟϹ ΔΥΝΑΜΕШϹ κ̄γ̄). Translation: Generalissimo (or high strategist, supreme commander) of the forces of the Lord

• Aleppo Codex: šr ṣbå yhwh (שׂר צבא יהוה). Translation: minister of the army of Yhwh

• Leningrad Codex: sar-tzeva-Yehvah (שַׂר־צְבָא־יְהוָה). Translation: minister of the army of Yehwah

• Targum Jerusalem: Mal'ach sheliach min kodam Yeyah (מַלְאַךְ שְׁלִיחַ מִן קֳדָם יְיָ). Translation: messenger-agent from before Yahw

While the Greeks gave the 'Generalissimo' an impressive rank, the Masoretic texts simply call him a minister or secretary, and the later Jerusalem Targum labels him as a messenger-agent. Assuming that this was not a reference to a supernatural being, or some extraterrestrial being, it was likely the commander of the Egyptian army who was campaigning in Canaan in the year this story is set according to the

Septuagint's chronology. Jericho was destroyed, its walls pulled down around the time that the Egyptian army passed through the region, and most Egyptologists accept that the Egyptian army destroyed the city, regardless of whatever the Israelites were doing there.

# Joshua: Chapter 6

Now Jericho was closely sealed up and besieged, and none went out of it, and none came in.

The Lord said to Joshua, "Look, I deliver Jericho into your power, and its king in it, and its mighty men. Set the warriors around it. It will be that when you will sound with the trumpet, all the people will shout together. When they have shouted, the walls of the city will fall by themselves, and all the people will enter, each one rushing directly into the city."

Joshua the son of Nun went to the priests, and said to them, "Let seven priests having seven sacred trumpets proceed before the Lord, and let them sound loud, and let the box of the covenant of the Lord follow. Order the people to go round, and circle the city, and let your warriors pass by armed before the Lord. Let the warriors proceed before, and the priests bringing up the rear behind the box of the covenant of the Lord proceed sounding the trumpets."

Joshua commanded the people, saying, don't cry out, nor let anyone hear your voice until he himself declares to you the day to cry out, and then you will cry out. The box of the covenant of God having gone around immediately returned into the camp and lodged there. On the second day Joshua rose in the morning, and the priests picked up the box of the covenant of the Lord. The seven priests bearing the seven trumpets went on before the Lord, and afterward, the warriors went on, and the remainder of the multitude went after the box of the covenant of the Lord, and the priests sounded with the trumpets. All the rest of the multitude circled the city six times from within a short distance and went back again into the camp. They did this for six days.

On the seventh day, they rose early and circled the city on that day seven times. It happened at the seventh circuit the priests blew the trumpets, and Joshua said to the Israelites, "Shout, for the Lord has given you the city. The city will be cursed and, and all things that are in it, to Lord Sabaoth,[1] only save Rehob the prostitute, and all things in her house. But keep yourselves strictly from the cursed things, in case you change your mind and take the cursed things, and you make the camp of the Israelites a cursed thing and destroy us. All the silver, or gold, or brass, or iron, will be holy to the Lord. It will be carried into the treasury of the Lord."

The priests sounded with the trumpets, and when the people heard the trumpets, all the people shouted at once with a loud and strong shout, and all the walls fell around it, and all the people went up into the city. Joshua devoted it to destruction and all things that were in the city, man and woman, young man and old, and calf and donkey, by the edge of the sword.[2]

Joshua said to the two young men who had acted as spies, "Go into the house of the woman, and bring her out here, she and all that she has."

The two young men who had spied out the city entered into the house of the woman, and brought out Rehob the prostitute, and her father, and her mother, and her brothers, and her families, and all that she had, and they took her out to the camp of Israel. The city was burnt with fire with all things that were in it, only the silver, and gold, and brass, and iron, they brought into the treasury of the Lord. Joshua saved Rehob the prostitute, and all the house of her father, and allowed her to live in Israel until this day because she hid the spies which Joshua sent to spy out Jericho. Joshua adjured them on that day before The Lord, saying, "Cursed be the man who will build that city, he will lay the foundation of it in his firstborn, and he will set up the gates of it in his youngest son."

(As did Hozan of the Temple of El. He laid the foundation with Abiram, his firstborn, and set up the gates of it with his youngest surviving son.)

The Lord was with Joshua, and his name was in all the land.

# Joshua: Chapter 6 Notes

**1** Codex Vaticanus: Cyriô Sabaôth (ΚΥΡΙШСΔΒΔШΘ). Translation: Lord Sabaoth (or 'forces' in Hebrew, 'desires' in Aramaic)

- Aleppo Codex: Yhwh (יהוה). Translation: Yhwh

- Leningrad Codex: Yehvah (יְהֺוָה). Translation: Yehwah

- Targum Jerusalem: Yeyah (יְּ). Translation: Yahw

This reference to Lord Sabaoth is clearly earlier than the Hasmonean redaction, which replaced most referenced to the various Lords of Canaan with Yhwh. In this case, the entire term Lord Sabaoth was replaced by Yahweh in the Hasmonean redaction, indicating that they considered Lord Sabaoth to be a proper name, and not a title. According to Greek and Roman records from the era, as well as the books of Maccabees, the Judahites worshiped Lord Sabaoth during the Greek rule of Judea. The Greeks associated Lord Sabaoth with Dionysus, while the Romans associated Lord Sabaoth with Bacchus.

Immediately after the Maccabean Revolt had successfully driven out the Greeks and established the Hasmonean Dynasty, the Judeans sent an emissary to Rome to request an alliance against the Greeks, but Roman records indicate that the result was all Judeans being evicted from Rome because the Judean emissaries claimed that their god 'Jupiter Sabazious' was the Roman god Jupiter. As this was the earliest Roman records of a Judean god with a name like Jupiter's (Latin: Iuppiter or Iovis), it seems the first Hasmonean King/High-Priest Simon the Zealot was responsible for the resurgence of the name Yhwh, which completely replaced Lord Sabaoth before the end of the Hasmonean dynasty.

**2** The walled city of Jericho, which has been identified as Tell es-Sultan since 1869, was destroyed sometime circa 1500 BC, and the site was virtually unoccupied until after 1000 BC. The site has been studied extensively, with various dates given for its destruction ranging from 1700 to 1400 BC. The cause of the collapse of the walls is unknown, however, it is theorized, depending on when the walls fell, that they may have been ripped down by the Egyptians circa 1500 BC, as Thutmose I's army campaigned all the way to the Euphrates, however, according to Thutmose I's records, they found no one to fight in Canaan, implying someone had recently campaigned in the region. He claimed that the Canaanite chieftains had pledged loyalty to Egypt, however, archaeological evidence shows after 1500 BC fortifications began being built throughout Canaan.

# Joshua: Chapter 7

But the Israelites committed a great crime and plundered some of the cursed things. Achan the son of Carmi, the son of Zabdi, the son of Zerah, of the tribe of Judah, took of the cursed things, and the Lord was very angry with the Israelites. Joshua sent men to the government office, which is by the Temple of El, ordering, "Spy out the government office,"[1] and the men went up and spied on Gai.

They returned to Joshua, and reported to him, "Don't send all the people up, but send about two or three thousand men up to capture the city by siege. Don't send up there all the people, as the enemy are few."

About three thousand men when up, and they fled from the men of Gai. The men of Gai killed thirty-six of them, and chased them from the gate, and drove them from the steep hill, and the heart of the people was alarmed and became like water. Joshua tore his garments and fell to the earth on his face before the Lord until evening, both he and the elders of Israel, and they threw dirt on their heads.

Joshua said, "I beg, Lord, has your servant brought these people across the Jordan to deliver them to the Amorites to destroy us? We should have remained and settled ourselves beyond Jordan. What will I say since Israel has turned his back before his enemy? When the Canaanites and all the inhabitants of the land hear it, they will surround us and destroy us from off the land. What will you do for your great name?"

The Lord answered Joshua, "Get up! Why have you fallen on your face? The people have sinned and transgressed the covenant which I made with them. They have stolen cursed things and put them into their store. The Israelites will not be able to stand before their enemies. They will turn their back before their enemies, as they have become a cursed thing! I will no longer be with you unless you remove the cursed thing from yourselves. Rise! Sanctify the people and tell them to sanctify themselves for the morning, so says Lord the god of Israel. The cursed thing is among you. You will not be able to stand before your enemies until you have removed the cursed things from among you. You will all be gathered together by your tribes in the morning, and the tribe which the Lord will indicate, you will bring by families. The family which the Lord will indicate, you will bring by household, and the household which the Lord will indicate, you will bring man by man. The man who will be pointed out will be burnt with fire, and all that he has, because he has transgressed the covenant of the Lord, and has worked wickedness in Israel."

Joshua rose early and brought the people by their tribes, and the tribe of Judah was indicated. It was brought by their families, and the family of the Zerahites was indicated. It was brought man by man, and Achan the son of Zabdi the son of Zerah was indicated. Joshua said to Achan, "Give glory this day to Lord the god of Israel, and make a confession, and tell me what you have done, and don't hide it from me."

Achan answered Joshua, "Indeed I have sinned against Lord the god of Israel. I did this: I saw in the spoil an embroidered mantle, and two hundred shekels[2] of silver, and one golden wedge of fifty shekels, and I wanted them and took them, and look, they are hidden in my tent, and the silver is hidden under them."

Joshua sent messengers, and they ran to the tent in the camp, and these things were hidden in his tent, and the silver under them. They brought them out of the tent and brought them to Joshua and the elders of Israel, and they laid them before the

Lord. Joshua took Achan the son of Zerah and brought him to the valley of Achor, and his sons, and his daughters, and his calves, and his donkeys, and all his sheep, and his tent, and all his property, and all the people were with him. He brought them to Emec Achor. Joshua asked Achan, "Why have you destroyed us? The Lord will destroy you today."

All Israel stoned him with stones. They set up over him a great heap of stones, and the Lord ceased from his fierce anger. Therefore he called the place Emecachor until this day.

# Joshua: Chpater 7 Notes

**1** Codex Vaticanus: Gai (ܓܝ)

- Aleppo Codex: Hôy (הֿעי)

- Leningrad Codex: Ha'ai (הָעַי)

- Targum Jerusalem: ay (עַי). Translation: ruins

The Greek translators transliterated this word two different ways from the Aramaic texts they translated. In Genesis it was transliterated as Aggai (Αγγαι), however, both the geographic location and the Hebrew translation of Hôy (העי) confirm it is the same location. The Hebrew term is often translated as 'ruins' however, the place is inhabited during the era of Joshua, indicating 'ruins' is an incorrect interpretation. The term appears to have originated with the Middle Egyptian word Kha (𓉐𓂝), meaning 'government office,' and several 'Khas' are mentioned as existing in Canaan. This 'government office' was the one Abram had built an altar near when he first entered Canaan.

As Canaan had been under the control of the Egyptians during the Middle Kingdom era, as well as during the Canaanite and Hyksos dynasties of the Second Intermediate Period, the colonial offices appear to have been continuously occupied. In the year the story is set, 1504 BC, the armies of Thutmose I had just marched through Canaan, however, he does not appear to have reclaimed the old 'government office' in Samaria, and based on the Israelites attacking 'Gai' immediately after removing the 'reproach of Egypt,' by re-instituting the Egyptian custom of circumcision, and attacking Jericho with the 'Generalissimo of the forces of the Lord,' it suggests that the Israelites attacked the 'government office' for the Egyptians. By the era of Joshua, this Gai appears to have become a town, and the term is used as a proper name.

**2** Codex Vaticanus: didrachma (ΔΙΔΡΑΧΜΑ). Translation: two-drachmas

- Aleppo Codex: šqlym (שְׁקְלִים). Translation: shekels

- Leningrad Codex: shekalim (שְׁקָלִים). Translation: shekels

- Targum Jerusalem: sal'in (סַלְעִין). Translation: selas

The shekel was a unit of weight used throughout the Middle East for thousands of years, weighing approximately 8.6 grams of silver. The Greek drachma was a coin weighing approximately half a shekel, and therefore under Greek rule of the Middle East, a two-drachma coin was used. As the Greeks clearly translated shekel into didrachma, the term shekel is restored in this translation. The term sela, used as the Targum Jerusalem, was a similarly sized coin and weight from the late classical era.

# Joshua: Chapter 8

The Lord said to Joshua, "Don't be afraid or nervous. Take with you all the warriors, and rise, and go up to Gai. I have given into your hands the king of Gai and his land. You will do to Gai, as you did to Jericho and its king, and you will take for yourself the spoils of its livestock. Set an ambush behind the city."

Joshua and all the warriors rose to go up to Gai, and Joshua chose out thirty thousand mighty men, and he sent them away by night. He ordered them, "You lie in ambush behind the city, near the city, and you will all remain ready. I and all with me will come close to the city, the inhabitants of Gai will come out to meet us like before, and we will flee from before them. When they will come out after us, we will draw them away from the city. They will say, 'These men flee from before us, like before.' You will rise up out of the ambuscade, and go into the city. You will do according to this word. Look, I have commanded you."

Joshua sent them, and they went to lie in ambush, and they lay between the Temple of El[1] and the government office, to the west of Gai.

Joshua rose early in the morning and reviewed the people, and he went up, he and the elders before the people to Gai. All the warriors went up with him, and they went forward and approached the city from the east. The ambuscade was on the west side of the city. When the king of Gai saw it, he rushed and went out to meet them immediately in battle, he and all the people that were with him, and he did not know that there was an ambuscade positioned against him behind the city. Joshua and Israel saw them and retreated from before them, and they chased after the Israelites, and traveled a distance from the city. There was no one left in Gai who did not chase after Israel, and they left the city open when they chased after Israel.

The Lord said to Joshua, "Stretch out your hand with the spear towards the city, for I have delivered it into your hands, and those laying in wait will rise quickly from their place."

Joshua stretched out his hand and his spear towards the city, and the ambuscade rose quickly out of their place, and entered into the city and captured it. They quickly set the city on fire. When the inhabitants of Gai looked around them, then they saw the smoke going up out of the city to the sky, and they were no longer able to flee this way or that way. Joshua and all Israel saw that the ambuscade had taken the city and that the smoke of the city went up to the sky, and they turned and attacked the men of Gai. These came out out of the city to meet them, and they were in the middle of the army, some being on this side, and some on that, and they slaughtered them until there was none left of them who survived and escaped.

They took the king of Gai alive and brought him to Joshua. When the Israelites had finished slaying all that were in Gai, and in the fields, and in the mountain on the descent, from where they pursued them even to the end, then Joshua returned to Gai and struck it with the edge of the sword. They who died on that day, men and women were twelve thousand, all the inhabitants of Gai. Beside the spoils that were in the city, all things which the Israelites took as spoil for themselves according to the command of the Lord, as the Lord commanded Joshua. Joshua burnt the city with fire, he made it an uninhabited heap forever, even to this day.

He hanged the king of Gai on a doubletree, and he remained on the tree until evening. When the sun went down, Joshua gave the order, and they took down his body from the tree and threw it into a trench, and they set over him a heap of stones until this day.

# Joshua: Chapters 8 Notes

**1** Codex Vaticanus: Baethêl (ⲃⲁⲓⲑⲏⲗ)

* Aleppo Codex: byt ål (בית אל). Translation: house (or temple) of El (or god)

* Leningrad Codex: veit-el (בֵּית־אֵל). Translation: house (or temple) of El (or god)

* Targum Jerusalem: beit el (בֵּית אֵל). Translation: house (or temple) of El (or god)

* The term Bethel meant several things in ancient Canaan. The term translates as 'house of god,' which can be translated as either 'Temple of God (or El)' or 'sky/heaven.' Bethel was worshiped as a god by the ancient Canaanites, the brother of El and Dagon according to Sanchuniathon, who referred to him as Baitylos, which is the name used in this translation when the god is denoted. The term can also be translated as 'meteorite' as meteorites were believed to be parts of the god Baitylos that had fallen to the Earth, and shrines were built around them. A Temple of El was built in the region by Jacob in Genesis and appears to have been a major town by the time of Joshua.

# Joshua: Chapter 9

When the kings of the Amorites on the other side of Jordan, who were in the mountain country, and in the plain, and in all the coast of the great sea, and those who were near Anti-Lebanon, and the Cypriots, Canaanites, Perizzite, Mitanni, Amorites, Girgashites, and Jebusites heard, they came in an alliance to make war against Joshua and Israel.

Then Joshua built an altar to Lord the god of Israel on Mount Ebal, as Moses the servant of the Lord commanded the Israelites, as it is written in the law of Moses, an altar of uncarved stones, against which iron had not been lifted. There he offered whole burnt offerings to the Lord and a peace offering. Joshua wrote on the stones a copy of the law of Moses, before the Israelites. All Israel, and their elders, and their judges, and their scribes passed on one side and on the other before the box. The priests and the Levites took up the box of the covenant of the Lord. The foreigners and the natives were there, who were half of them near Mount Gerizim and half near Mount Ebal, as Moses the servant of the Lord commanded at first, to bless the people.

Afterward, Joshua read accordingly all the words of this law, the blessings, and the curses, according to all things written in the law of Moses. There was not a word of all that Moses ordered Joshua, which Joshua read not in the ears of all the assembly of the Israelites, the men, and the women, and the children, and the strangers that joined themselves to Israel.

The inhabitants of Gibeon heard of all that the Lord did to Jericho and Gai. They worked cunningly, and they went and made provisions and prepared themselves, and having taken old sacks on their shoulders, and old and tore and patched bottles of wine, and the upper part of their shoes and their sandals old and clouted on their feet, and their old garments on them, and the bread in their provisions was dry, moldy, and partially eaten.

They came to Joshua at the camp of Israel at the circle, and said to Joshua and Israel, "We have come from a far off land, now then make a covenant with us."

The Israelites replied to the Hurrians,[1] "Suppose you live among us, how should I make a covenant with you?"

They replied to Joshua, "We are your servants."

Joshua asked them, "Where are you from, and where have you come from?"

They answered, "Your servants have come from a very far country in the name of Lord the god, for we have heard his name, and all that he did in Egypt, and all that he did to the kings of the Amorites, who were beyond Jordan, to Sihon king of the Amorites, and Og king of Bashan, who lived in Ashteroth and in Edrei. Our elders and all that inhabit our land when they heard said to us, 'Take with yourselves provision for the journey and go to meet them, and you will say to them, 'We are your servants, and now make a covenant with us.' These are the loaves we took hot for our journey on the day on which we came out to come to you, and now they are dried and have become moldy. These are the skins of wine which we filled when new, and they are torn, and our garments and our shoes are worn out because of the very long journey."

The chiefs took of their provision and asked no counsel of the Lord. Joshua made peace with them, and they made a covenant with them to protect them, and the princes of the congregation swore to them. Three days after they had made the covenant with them, they heard that they were near neighbors and that they lived among them. The Israelites departed and came to their cities, and their cities were Gibeon, and Kefireh,[2] and Beirut,[3] and the cities of Ye'arim,[4] and the Israelites did not fight with them, because all the princes swore to them by Lord the god of Israel, and all the congregation murmured at the princes.

The princes said to all the congregation "We have sworn to them by Lord the god of Israel, and now we will not be able to touch them. We will do this, we will capture them alive, and we will preserve them, so there will be no anger against us, because of the oath which we swore to them. They will live and will be lumberjacks and drawers of water for all the congregation," as the princes swore to them.

Joshua called them together and asked them, "Why have you deceived me, saying, 'We live very far from you, whereas you are fellow-countrymen of those who live among us? Now you are cursed. There will not be any of you that is not a slave, or a lumberjack, or a drawer of water for me and my god."

They answered Joshua, "It was reported to us that Lord the god ordered his servant, Moses, to give you this land, and to destroy us and all that lived on it before you. We were very afraid for our lives because of you, and therefore we did this thing. Now look, we are in your power. Do to us as it is pleasing to you, and as it seems good to you."

They did so to them, and Joshua rescued them on that day out of the hands of the Israelites, and they did not kill them. Joshua made them on that day lumberjacks and drawers of water to the whole congregation, and for the altar of God. Therefore the inhabitants of Gibeon became lumberjacks and drawers of water for the altar of God until this day, even for the place which the Lord should choose. Then Joshua built an altar to Lord the god of Israel on Mount Ebal, as Moses the servant of the Lord commanded the

Israelites, as it was written in the law of Moses, an altar of uncarved stones, on which iron had not been lifted, and he offered there whole burnt offerings to the Lord, and a piece offering. Joshua wrote on the stones a copy of the law of Moses, before the Israelites. All Israel, and their elders, and their judges, and their scribes passed on one side and on the other, before the box, and the priests, the Levites took up the box of the covenant of the Lord. The stranger and the native were there, who were half of those near Mount Ebal, as Moses the servant of the Lord commanded before, to bless the people.

# Joshua: Chapter 9 Notes

**1** Codex Vaticanus: Chorrhaeon (ⲬⲞⲢⲢⲀⲒⲞⲚ). This is a Greek transliteration of Chori (חֹרִי), the term generally believed to refer to the Hurrians.

- Aleppo Codex: Hwy (חוי)

- Leningrad Codex: Chivvi (חִוִּי)

- Targum Jerusalem: Chiva'ah (חִוָאָה)

There were two terms used in the Septuagint and Masoretic text for the Hurrians: Chorrhaeon / Chori (Χορραῖον / חֹרִי) and Euaion / Chivvi (Εὐαῖον / חִוִּי), however, in this case, the names do not match between the Septuagint and Masoretic text, indicating that there were two versions of Joshua in circulation. The terms are both believed to derive from the same culture, however, are not interchangeable.

The name Chorrhaeon / Chori, often transliterated as Horite, referred to the Hurrian people, while the term Euaion / Chivvi, referred to the Mitanni-Aryan nobility or Vedic priests. This difference between the Greek and Hebrew texts cannot be accounted for through a transliteration error, or the assumption that the Greeks decided to use the same term for both people, as Euaion (Εὐαῖον) was already used in the Book of Joshua. Hurrians are documented in southern Canaan at the time, as the Adbi-Heba, the chieftain of Jerusalem, had a Hurrian name in the Amarna Letters, circa 1335 BC.


**2** Codex Vaticanus: Cephira (ⲔⲈⲪⲒⲢⲀ)

- Aleppo Codex: Kpyrh (כפירה)

- Leningrad Codex: Kefirah (כְּפִירָה)

- Targum Jerusalem: Chefirah (כְפִירָה)

This is believed to be Khirbet Kefireh in the West Bank of Palestinian Territories.

**3** Codex Vaticanus: Bêrôth (ʙʜⲣⲱⲑ)

• Aleppo Codex: Bårwt (באָרות)

• Leningrad Codex: Ve'erot (בְּאֵרוֹת)

• Targum Jerusalem: Ve'erot (בְּאֵרוֹת)

The location of this town is disputed. Some sources claim it is Al-Bireh, while others claim it is Biddu, both in the West Bank of Palestinian Territories. The Hebrew name is identical to the Phoenician name of Beirut, Bårt (𐤟𐤟𐤟𐤟), however, the modern Hebrew spelling of Beirut is Byyrwt (ביירות), derived from the Arabic Bayrūt (بيروت).

The term used in the Septuagint is not the Greek name for Beirut, which is Bêrytos (Βηρυτός), however, all sources agree that the terms found in the Masoretic text and Septuagint are variant spellings of Beirut, although the town in question is believed to have been in the West Bank, and not Lebanon.

**4** Codex Vaticanus: Iarin (ιⲁⲣιⲛ)

• Aleppo Codex: Qryt Yôrym (קרית יערים)

• Leningrad Codex: Qiryat Ye'arim (קִרְיַת יְעָרִים)

• Targum Jerusalem: Qiryat Ye'arim (קִרְיַת יְעָרִים)

The location of this town is generally assumed to be at the same location as the modern town of Kiryat Ye'arim in Israel.

# Joshua: Chapter 10

When King Adonibezec[1] of Jerusalem heard that Joshua had taken Gai and had destroyed it. That as he'd done to Jericho and its king, he had also done to Gai and its king, and that the inhabitants of Gibeon had gone over to Joshua and Israel, then they were greatly terrified by them, for the king knew that Gibeon was a great city, one of the mother cities, and all its men were mighty. So King Adoni-bezek of Jerusalem sent messages to King Hoham of Hebron, and King Piram of Jarmuth, and King Japhia of Lachish, and King Debir of Adullam, saying, "Come up here to me, and help me, and let us take Gibeon, because the Gibeonites have gone over to Joshua and to the Israelites."

The five kings of the Jebusites went up, the king of Jerusalem, and the king of Hebron, and the king of Jarmuth, and the king of Lachish, and the king of Adullam, they and all their people, and camped around Gibeon, and besieged it. The inhabitants of Gibeon sent word to Joshua at the camp by the circle, saying, "Do not delay from your servants. Come up quickly to us, and help us and save us. All the kings of the Amorites who live in the hill country are gathered against us."

Joshua went up from the circle, he and all the warriors with him, everyone mighty in strength. The Lord said to Joshua, "Don't fear them, for I have delivered them into your hands. There will not be one of them left."

When Joshua came suddenly on them, he had advanced all night from the circle. The Lord struck them with terror before the Israelites, and the Lord destroyed them in a great slaughter at Gibeon, and they chased them by the road going up to the House of Horon,[2] and they slaughtered them to Azekah and to Makkedah. When they fled from the face of the Israelites at the descent of Temple of Horon, then the Lord threw hailstones on them from the sky to Azekah, and more died by the hailstones, than those who the Israelites killed with the sword in the battle.

Then Joshua spoke to the Lord, in the day in which the Lord delivered the Amorites into the power of Israel when he destroyed them in Gibeon, and they were destroyed from before the Israelites. Joshua said, "Let the sun stand over Gibeon and the moon over the valley of Ayalon."

The sun and the moon stood still until God executed vengeance on their enemies, and the sun stood still in the middle of the sky. It did not proceed to set until the end of one day. There was not a day like it either before or after, that god should listen to man because the Lord fought on the side of Israel. The five kings fled, and hid in a cave in Makkedah.

Joshua was told, "The five kings have been found hidden in the cave in Makkedah." Joshua said, "Roll stones to the mouth of the cave and set men to watch over them. Don't stand still, but chase after your enemies and seize of them, and do not allow them to enter into their cities, for Lord the god has delivered them into our hands."

When Joshua and all Israel stopped slaughtering them, they that escaped took refuge in the fortified cities. All the people returned healthy to Joshua at Makkedah, and none of the Israelites murmured with his tongue. Joshua said, "Open the cave, and bring out these five kings from the cave."

They brought the five kings out of the cave, the king of Jerusalem, and the king of Hebron, and the king of Jarmuth, and the king of Lachish, and the king of Adullamite. When they brought them out to Joshua, he called together all Israel, and the chiefs of the army that went with him, and said to them, "Come forward and set your feet on their necks," and they came and set their feet on their necks.

Joshua said to them, "Do not fear them or be cowardly. Be courageous and strong, as the Lord will do this to all your enemies against who you fight."

Joshua killed them and hanged them on five trees, and they hung on the trees until the evening. Towards the setting of the sun, Joshua commanded, and they took them down from the trees and threw them into the cave which they had fled for refuge, and they rolled stones into the cave, which remain until this day. They took Makkedah on that day and killed the inhabitants with the edge of the sword, and they completely destroyed every living thing that was in it, and there was none left in it that was preserved and had escaped. They did to the king of Makkedah, as they did to the king of Jericho. Joshua and all Israel with him departed out of Makkedah to Libnah and besieged Libnah. The Lord delivered it into the hands of Israel, and they took it and its king and killed the inhabitants with the edge of the sword, and everything breathing in it. Nothing was left in it that survived and escaped, and they did to its king as they did to the king of Jericho. Joshua and all Israel with him departed from Libnah to Lachish, and he camped around it and besieged it.

The Lord delivered Lachish into the hands of Israel, and they took it on the second day, and they put the inhabitants to death with the edge of the sword, and completely destroyed it, as they had done to Libnah. Then Horam the king of Gezer went up to help Lachish, and Joshua slaughtered him and his people with the edge of the sword until there was none left of him that was safe and escaped. Joshua and all Israel with him departed from Lachish to Adullam, and he besieged it and attacked it. The Lord delivered it into the hand of Israel, and he took it on that day, and killed the inhabitants with the edge of the sword, and killed everything breathing in it, as they did to Lachish.

Joshua and all Israel with him departed to Hebron and camped around it. He struck it with the edge of the sword, and all the living creatures that were in it. There was no one left alive. They destroyed it and all things in it, as they did to Adullam. Joshua and all Israel returned to Debir, and they camped around it, and they took it, and its king, and its villages. He struck it with the edge of the sword, and they destroyed it, and everything breathing in it. They did not leave in it anyone alive.

They did to Hebron and her king, as they did to Debir and her king. Joshua struck all the land of the hill country, and Negev and the plain country, and Azzah, and her kings, they did not leave of them one alive. They completely destroyed everything that had the breath of life, as Lord the god of Israel commanded, from Kadesh Barnea[3] to Gaza, all Goshen, as far as Gibeon. Joshua slaughtered, once for all, all their kings, and their land, because Lord the god of Israel fought on the side of Israel.

# Joshua: Chapter 10 Notes

**1** Codex Vaticanus: Adônibezec (ΑΔШΝΙΒΕΖΕΚ)

- Aleppo Codex: ådny Sdq (אדני צדק). Translation: Lord Sydyk (or of Justice)

- Leningrad Codex: Adoni-Tzedek (אֲדֹנִי־צֶדֶק). Translation: Lord Sydyk (or of Justice)

- Targum Jerusalem: Adoni Tzedek (אֲדֹנִי צֶדֶק). Translation: Lord Sydyk (or of Justice)

The Greek translators treated the term as a name, Adônibezec, however, the Hebrew translation treats it as a title 'Lord of Justice.' The two translations also deviate on whether it was bezec (βεζεκ) or tzedek (צֶדֶק), which cannot simply be a transliteration error, as the Greeks knew of the Canaanite god Sydyk, and transliterated his name as Sydyc (Συδυκ). Adônibezec is a transliteration of a Semitic term, meaning essentially the 'My Lord in Strength' in Canaanite and Aramaic. During the Roman era, Sydyk was viewed as the Canaanite version of Jupiter, the supreme God of the Roman Empire. As the Septuagint does not agree with the Masoretic text, the Greek name is used in this translation.


**2** Codex Vaticanus: Ôrônin (ШРШΝΙΝ)

- Aleppo Codex: byt Hwrn (בית חורן). Translation: House (or Temple) of Horon

- Leningrad Codex: veit-Chovron (בֵית־חֹורֹן). Translation: House (or Temple) of Horon

- Targum Jerusalem: veit Choron (בֵית חֹורֹון). Translation: House (or Temple) of Horon

Horon was one of the Canaanite underworld gods. He was one of the sons of Mot (Death), who himself later became the Israelite messenger of death Mot, and early Christian angel of death Thanatos. Hwårn

(𓇯𓃀𓈖𓅱𓈙) was also a god of death in ancient Egypt, and the source of the Greek psychopomp Charon (Χάρων) according to Diodorus Siculus. The town around the Temple of Horon is also listed in the inscriptions at the Temple of Karnak, in Egypt, as 'Batae Houarn' in Egyptian hiero-glyphs, one of the towns that Pharaoh Sheshonq I attacked, circa 925 BC, which was later recorded in the 3ʳᵈ Kingdoms (Masoretic Kings). During the era of the two kingdoms, the twin towns of Upper and Lower Beth-Horon served as border towns. These towns have been identified as the Palestinian villages of Beit Ur al-Fauqa and Beit Ur al-Tahta, in the West Bank.

**3** Codex Vaticanus: Cadês Barnê (ΚΑΔΗCΒΑΡΝΗ)

• Aleppo Codex: qdš brnô (קדש ברנע). Translation: Sacred Barnea

• Leningrad Codex: Kadesh Barnea' (קָדֵשׁ בַּרְנֵעַ). Translation: Sacred Barnea

• Targum Jerusalem: Rekam gei'ah (רְקָם גִּיאָה). Translation: Petra (or stony, rocky) hills

The location of Kadesh Barnea has been debated since the Second Temple Era. The Jewish general and historian Josephus reported that the sacred books salvaged from the Second Temple when it was destroyed by the Romans placed Kadesh Barnea at Petra, in modern Jordan. He also claimed that Mount Sinai was nearby, which is the source of the claim that Mountain of the Altar (Jebel al-Madhbah) was Mount Sinai. The name Kadesh Barnea is undoubtedly named after an ancient deity, as the first word, Kadesh (קָדֵשׁ), means holy or sacred. The name Barnea is presumably the name of the deity in question, and the general Hebrew pronunciation of the name as Varne'a is quite similar to the name Mitannian god Aruna, the equivalent of the Vedic god Varuna.

As Deuteronomy chapter 2 reports that Hurrians were living in Seir before the Edomites killed them and inhabited the region, this would support the name Aruna being the source of Barnea, as the Hurrians were the major population base of the Mitanni Empire. This connection between the Mitannian Indo-Aryan Varuna worshipers at Mount Seir would also explain how Mitra-Varuna (𐎣𐎹𐎠 𐎭𐎱𐎡) entered into Judaism, as his earliest recorded Hebrew name Mṭtrwn (מטטרון) is essentially the same as the Mitannian god of covenants  Miitra-Aruna, and played the same role in the Vedic Texts as Metatron did in Second Temple Era Judaism. Subsequent Hebrew pronunciations of the name from the Medieval Era, Mṭtrwn (מטטרון), Metateron (מְטַטְרוֹן), Metatron (מְטַטְרוֹן), Meitatron (מֵיטַטְרוֹן), Mitatron (מִיטַטְרוֹן), and Mattatron (מַטַּטְרוֹן), as well as the Arabic Mītatrūn (ميططرون), are all influenced by the Greek pronunciation of the name Metà-thrónos (Μετὰ-θρόνος), which means 'next to the throne.'

# Joshua: Chapter 11

When King Jabin of Hazor heard, he sent word to King Jobab of Madon, and to the king of Shimron, and the king of Achshaph, and the kings who were by the Sidon the Great,[1] to the hill country and to Arabah across Chinneroth, and to the plain, and to Phenaeddor, and to the Canaanites on the coast to the east, and to the Amorites on the coast, and the Cypriots, and the Perizzites, and the Jebusites in the mountain, and the Mitanni, and those living at the foot of Mount Hermon in the land of Mizpeh. They went out with their kings, like the sand of the sea in numbers, with horses, and a great many chariots. All the kings assembled in person, and came to the same place, and camped at the waters of Madon to make war with Israel.

The Lord said to Joshua, "Do not be afraid of them, for tomorrow at this time I will make them run from Israel. You will hamstring their horses, and burn their chariots with fire."

Joshua and all the warriors suddenly attacked them at the water of Madon and followed them into the hill country. The Lord delivered them into the power of Israel, and they struck them and chased them to Sidon the Great,[2] and to Maseron,[3] and to the plains of Mizpeh in the east. They destroyed them until there was not one of them left that survived. Joshua did to them, as the Lord commanded him, he mutilated their horses, and burnt their chariots with fire.

Joshua returned after that and took Hazor and her king. Previously Hazor was the chief of these kingdoms. They killed with the sword all that breathed in it and completely destroyed them all, and there was nothing living left in it. They burnt Hazor with fire. Joshua took all the cities of the kingdoms, and their kings, and killed them with the edge of the sword, and completely killed them, as Moses the servant of the Lord commanded.

But Israel did not burn all the walled cities, only Hazor was burnt. The Israelites took all its spoils for themselves, and they killed all the men with the edge of the sword, until they destroyed them, and they left none of them breathing. As the Lord commanded his servant Moses, Moses also commanded Joshua, and this Joshua did, he transgressed no law of all that Moses commanded him. Joshua took all the hill country, and all the land of Negev, and all the land of Goshen, and the plain country, and that towards the west, and the mountain of Israel and the low country by the mountain, from the mountain of Halak, and that which goes up to Seir, and as far as Ba'al Gad,[4] and the plains of Lebanon under Mount Hermon.

He took all their kings and destroyed and killed them. For many days, Joshua waged war with these kings. There was no city which Israel did not capture. They took it all in war. For the Lord had hardened their hearts to go out to war against Israel, so they might be completely destroyed, and mercy should not be granted to them, but that they should be completely destroyed, as the Lord told Moses.

Joshua came at that time, and completely destroyed the Anaks[5] out of the hill country, from Hebron and from Debir, and from Anab, and from all the race of Israel, and from all the mountain of Judah with their cities, and Joshua completely destroyed them. There was not anyone left of the Anaks near the Israelites, there were only some of them in Gaza, and in Gath, and in Ashdod. Joshua took all the land, as the Lord commanded Moses, and Joshua gave it for an inheritance to Israel by division according to their tribes, and the land war ended.

# Joshua: Chapter 11 Notes

**1** Codex Vaticanus: Sidôna tên megalên (ϹΙΔѠΝΑΤΗΝΜΕΓΑΛΗΝ). Translation: Sidon the great

- Aleppo Codex: Spwn bhr (צפון בהר). Translation: Zephon (or north) on mountain

- Leningrad Codex: Tzefovn bahar (צְפוֹן בָּהָר). Translation: Zephon (or north) on mountain

- Targum Jerusalem: Tzepuna betura (צְפוּנָא בְּטוּרָא). Translation: Zephon at mountain

The Greek and Hebrew translations differ at this point. The reference to Sidon as the great city, found in the Greek at this point, and also the Hebrew and Aramaic Targums later in the chapter, would date the original text to earlier than circa 980 BC, when Sidon was the mother city of the Phoenicians. Between 980 and 947 BC, King Hiram of Tyre, led the Tyrians in challenging the dominance of Sidon. The Hebrew translation of Mount Zephon (צפון בהר) instead of Sidon is unlikely to have been a Hasmonean redaction, and is something that was likely retained in the Judahite (or Samaritan) texts that the Hebrew translators worked from. Mount Zephon was the holy mountain of northern Canaan, where the temple of the storm-god Ba'al Hadad was located.

**2** Codex Vaticanus: Sidônos tês megalês (ϹΙΔѠΝΟϹΤΗϹΜΕΓΑΛΗϹ). Translation: Sidon the great

- Aleppo Codex: Ṣydwn rbh (צידון רבה). Translation: great Sidon

- Leningrad Codex: Tzidovn Rabbah (צִידוֹן רַבָּה). Translation: great Sidon

- Targum Jerusalem: Tzidovn rabbeta (צִידוֹן רַבְּתָא). Translation: great Sidon

**3** Codex Vaticanus: Maserôn (ΜΑCΕΡѠΝ)

• Aleppo Codex: mšrpwt mym (מִשְׂרְפוֹת מִיַם). Translation: crematoria waters

• Leningrad Codex: misrefovt mayim (מִשְׂרְפוֹת מַיִם). Translation: crematoria waters

• Targum Jerusalem: chartzei yama (חַרְצֵי יַמָא). Translation: sharps (or sharp things, cutting things, cuts) seas

This is considered an unknown location at the southern border of Sidonian control on the Mediterranean coast. It is most likely a reference to the glass production facilities of Sidon, which were the city's largest export during the Late-Bronze Age. As this trade disappeared in the early Iron Age, it would place the origin of the Book of Joshua before the Bronze Age Collapse.

**4** Codex Vaticanus: Baalgad (ΒΑΑΑΓΑΔ)

• Aleppo Codex: Bôl Gd (בעל גד)

• Leningrad Codex: Ba'al Gad (בַּעַל גָד)

• Targum Jerusalem: shar Gad (שַׂר גָד). Translation: prince (or commander) Gad

Ba'al Gad was an ancient Canaanite god, the god of luck, and the god that Jacob's son Gad was named after, and therefore the entire tribe of Gad.

**5** Codex Vaticanus: Enacim (ΕΝΑΚΙΜ)

• Aleppo Codex: Ônqym (עֲנָקִים). Translation: giant, huge, large, big, neck, necklace, Anaks (an ancient tribe of Canaan)

• Leningrad Codex: Anakim (עֲנָקִים). Translation: giant, huge, large, big, neck, necklace, Anaks (an ancient tribe of Canaan)

• Targum Jerusalem: gibbaraya (גִבָּרַיָא). Translation: strong men (or giants, heroes)

The Anaks were transliterated as Enach (Εναχ) in the Book of Numbers, but translated as Gigantes (Γιγάντων) in the Book of Deuteronomy, implying the Greeks considered the Anaks to be like the Gigantes of ancient Greece, who fought a war against the Olympian gods, and lost. The Anaks were a tribe of people also referred to in the book of Judges. According to the book of Judges, they apparently lived in Hebron. The Egyptian Execration Texts from the Middle Kingdom record a group of Canaanites called the 'Anaq' who are generally considered to be the same people.

# Joshua: Chapter 12

These are the kings of the land, whom the Israelites killed, and inherited their land beyond Jordan from the east, from the valley of Arnon to Mount Hermon, and all the land of Arabah on the east. Sihon king of the Amorites, who lived in Heshbon, ruling from Arnon, which is in the valley, on the slope of the valley, and half of Gilead as far as Jabbok, the borders of the Ammonites. Arabah as far as the sea of Galilee[1] to the east, and as far as the Dead Sea, the salt sea to the east by the way to Asimoth, from Teman under Azzah Phasga. King Og of Bashan, who lived in Ashteroth and in Edrei, was what remained of the Gigantes[2] ruling from Mount Hermon and from Salcah, and over all the land of Bashan to the borders of Gergesi, and Machi, and the half of Gilead of the borders of Sihon king of Heshbon. Moses the servant of the Lord and the Israelites struck them down, and Moses gave them by way of inheritance to Reuben, and Gad, and to the half-tribe of Manasseh.

These are the kings of the Amorites, who Joshua and the Israelites killed beyond Jordan by the sea of Ba'al Gad in the plain of Lebanon, and as far as the mountain of Halak, as men go up to Seir, and Joshua gave it to the tribes of Israel to inherit according to their portion, in the mountain, and in the plain, and in Arabah, and in Azzah, and in the wilderness, and the Negev, the Cypriots, Amorites, Canaanites, Perizzites, Mitanni, and Jebusites.

The king of Jericho, and the king of Gai, which is near the Temple of El, the king of Jerusalem, the king of Hebron, the king of Jarmuth, the king of Lachish, the king of Eglon, the king of Gezer, the king of Debir, the king of Geder, the king of Hormah, the king of Arad, the king of Libnah, the king of Adullam, the king of Elath, the king of Tappuah, the king of Hepher, the king of Aphek of Aroc, the king of Hushim, the king of Shimron, the king of Mambroth, the king of Achshaph, the king of Kadesh, the

king of Zachac, the king of Maredoth, the king of Jecom of
Carmel, the king of Adullam belonging to Phennealdor, the king
of Gei of Galilee, and the king of Tirzah. All these were twenty-
nine kings.

# Joshua: Chapter 12 Notes

**1** Codex Vaticanus: Chenereth (ⲭⲉⲛⲉⲣⲉⲑ)

- Aleppo Codex: Knrwt (כנרות)

- Leningrad Codex: Kinarot (כִּנֲרוֹת)

- Targum Jerusalem: Ginosar (גִּינוֹסָר)

These are all alternate names for the region around the Sea of Galilee, also known as Lake Tiberius.


**2** Codex Vaticanus: gigantôn (ⲅⲓⲅⲁⲛⲧⲱⲛ). Translation: Gigantes

- Aleppo Codex: Rpåym (רפאים). Translation: long-dead (in Canaanite), giants (modern Hebrew), Rephaites (theoretical ancient tribe)

- Leningrad Codex: Refa'im (רְפָאִים). Translation: long-dead (in Canaanite), giants (modern Hebrew), Rephaites

- Targum Jerusalem: gibbaraya (גִּבְּרַיָּא). Translation: strong men (or giants, heroes)

The Rpåm (𐤓𐤐𐤀𐤌) were a semi-deified long-dead people by the 1200s BC, as the Ugaritic Texts include the so-called Rephaim Text. They appear to be an ancient people that had been deified and were believed to live in the underworld. The word's etymology implies they were healers. The fact that they were described as 'ruling from Mount Hermon' implies they were the 'watchers' from the Enochian tradition.

The similarities between the name Enach / Ônq (Εναχ / ענק) and Enôch / Ḥnwk (Ενωχ / חנוך) may have led to the confusion in the translation, resulting in both Ônqym (ענקים) and Rpåym (רפאים) as Gigantes in different places in the books of Numbers, Deuteronomy, and Joshua. As the Books of Enoch had to have been translated also before the Beta Israel community left Egypt during the rebellion of 200 BC, the Books of Enoch must have been translated at the same time, and likely by the same translators.

# Joshua: Chapter 13

When Joshua was old and advanced in years, the Lord said to Joshua, "You are advanced in days, and there is much land left to inherit. This is the land that remains: the borders of the Pelesets,[1] the Geshurites, and the Canaanite, from the wilderness near Egypt, as far as the borders of Ekron on the left of the Canaanites the land is reckoned to the five principalities of the Pelesets, to the inhabitants of Gaza, Ashdod, Ashkelon, Gath, and Ekron, and to the Mitanni from Teman, to all the land of Canaan before Gaza, and the Sidonians as far as Aphek, as far as the borders of the Amorites."

"All the land of Giblites of the Pelesets, and all Lebanon east of the circle, under Mount Hermon as far as the entering in of Hamath, everyone that inhabits the hill country from Lebanon as far as Masereth Memphomaim. All the Sidonians, I will destroy them from before Israel, but you give them by inheritance to Israel, as I ordered you. Now divide this land by lot to the nine tribes, and to the half-tribe of Manasseh. From Jordan to the Mediterranean Sea in the west, you will give it to them. The Mediterranean Sea will be the boundary."

"But to the two tribes and to the half-tribe of Manasseh, to Reuben and to Gad Moses gave an inheritance beyond Jordan, Moses the servant of the Lord gave it to them eastward, from Aroer, which is on the bank of the brook of Arnon, and the city in the middle of the valley, and all Misor from Medeba. All the cities of Sihon king of the Amorites, who reigned from Heshbon to the borders of the Ammonites, and the region of Gilead, and the borders of the Geshurites and the Maachathites, the whole of Mount Hermon, and all the land of Bashan to Acha. All the kingdom of Og in the region of Bashan, who reigned in Ashteroth and in Edrei, he was left of the Raphites, and Moses killed him and destroyed him."

But the Israelites did not destroy the Geshurites and the Maachathites and the Canaanites, and the king of the Geshurites and the Maachathites lived among the Israelites until this day. Only no inheritance was given to the tribe of Levi, Lord the god of Israel is their inheritance, as the Lord told them. This is the division that Moses made to the Israelites in Araboth Moab, on the other side of Jordan, by Jericho. Moses gave the land to the tribe of Reuben according to their families. Their borders were from Aroer, which is opposite the brook of Arnon, and theirs is the city that is in the valley of Arnon; and all Misor, to Heshbon, and all the cities in Misor, and Debir, and Bamoth-Ba'al, and the house of Baal-Meon, and Bashan, and Bakedmoth, and Maephaad, and Kariathaim, and Shibmah, and Serada, and Sior on Mount Emak,[2] and the House of Peor,[3] and Azzah Phasga, and the House of Jeshi-moth, and all the cities of Misor, and all the kingdom of Sihon king of the Amorites, who Moses killed, both he and the princes of Midian,[4] Evi,[5] Petra,[6] Zur,[7] and Hur,[8] and Prince Reba of the remnants of Sihon, and the inhabitants of the land.

Balaam the son of Beor the prophet they killed in the battle. The borders of Reuben were at the Jordan, which was the boundary. This is the inheritance of the children of Reuben according to their families, these were their cities and their villages. Moses gave an inheritance to the sons of Gad according to their families. Their borders were Jazer, all the cities of Gilead, and half the land of the Ammonites to Arabah, which is before Arad. From Heshbon to Araboth by Massepha, and Betonim, and Mahanaim to the borders of Debir, and Enadom, and Othargai, and the House of Nimrah, and Succoth, and Zaphon, and the rest of the kingdom of Sihon king of Heshbon, and Jordan will be the boundary as far as part of the Sea of Galilee,[9] beyond Jordan to the east. This is the inheritance of the children of Gad according to their families and according to their cities. According to their families, they will turn their backs before their enemies, because their cities and their villages were according to their families.

Moses gave to half the tribe of Manasseh according to their families. Their borders were from Mahanaim, and all the kingdom of Bashan, and all the kingdom of Og king of Bashan, and all the villages of Jair, which are in the region of Bashan, sixty cities, and the half of Gilead, and in Ashteroth, and in Edrei, royal cities of Og in the land of Bashan, Moses gave to the sons of Machir the sons of Manasseh, including to the half-tribe sons of Machir the sons of Manasseh, according to their families. These are those who Moses allowed to inherit beyond the Jordan, in Araboth Moab, and beyond Jordan east of Jericho.

# Joshua: Chapter 13 Notes

**1** Codex Vaticanus: Phylistiim (ⲫⲨⲗⲓⲥⲧⲓⲓⲙ). Translation: Philistines (or Pelesets, Pelesets)

• Aleppo Codex: Plštym (פלשתים). Translation: Philistines (or Palestinians, Pelesets)

• Leningrad Codex: Pelishtim (פְּלִשְׁתִּים). Translation: Philistines (or Palestinians, Pelesets)

• Targum Jerusalem: Pelishta'ei (פְּלִשְׁתָּאֵי). Translation: Philistines (or Palestinians, Pelesets)

The Pelesets were an ancient people based in the region of the modern Gaza Strip of the Palestinian Territories. The earliest surviving mention of them is from the reliefs of the Temple of Ramses III at Medinet Habu in Egypt that dates back to some time between 1186 and 1155 BC, in which they were called Pwrảsảtj (𓊪𓅱𓂋𓄿𓈒𓏏𓀁), commonly anglicized as Pelesets. They were also known in Middle Babylonian as the ᵏᵘʳPalastu (𒆳𒉺𒆷𒀸𒌈).

It is unclear where they came from, however, one theory is that they were the Pala, a Luwian people from the Black Sea coast of Anatolia. The region was an independent country called Palaa (𒉺𒆷𒀀) in the Neshite (Hittite) records from the 1600s BC, however, have become part of the Nesite Empire by the 1500s BC. Around the time the Pelesets invaded Canaan, the Pala were driven from their homeland by the neighboring Kaskians from northeast Anatolia, which supports the connection between the groups, however, it has yet to be proven conclusively.

The presence of the Pelesets in Southern Canaan during the time of Joshua is anachronistic, as the Egyptians recorded the Pelesets arriving in the 1200s BC. At the time, the Egyptians recorded that the Hanubu were the dominant population in Sinai, which is believed to have been a reference to the Minoans, however, they disappeared from the region shortly after the Minoan erruption. Therefore this section of text, describing the origin of the Semitic tribes, found in both the Septuagint and the Masoretic text, likely dates to the original Phoenician translation in the early Iron Age, by which time the name Hanubu was no longer recognized.

**2** Codex Vaticanus: Emac (ЄΜΑΚ)

• Aleppo Codex: ômq (עמק). Translation: valley (or vale, lowland, open country)

• Leningrad Codex: emek (עֵמֶק). Translation: valley (or vale, lowland, open country)

• Targum Jerusalem: meishra (מֵישְׁרָא). Translation: plain (or valley)

**3** Codex Vaticanus: Baethphogôr (ΒΑΙΘΦΟΓωΡ)

• Aleppo Codex: Byt Pôwr (בית פעור). Translation: House (or Temple) of Pwr

• Leningrad Codex: Veit Pe'ovr (בֵית פְּעֹור). Translation: House (or Temple) of Peor

• Targum Jerusalem: Veit Pe'or (בֵית פְּעֹור). Translation: House (or Temple) of Peor

This verse has not survived among the Dead Sea Scrolls. There are no known locations associated with the name Peor, which implies the location was abandoned after the events of Joshua. Other Israelite texts, such as Micah refer to the Lord of Peor in association with the Shittim Valley, however, this name appears to have been an insult directed towards Lord Hammon who was worshiped at Tell el-Hammam in the 800s BC.

There is no clear link between Hammon and Peor, implying the worshipers of Peor disappeared around the time the Israelites passed through the Shittim Valley. The major ruins in the Shittim Valley, are found at Tell el-Hammam, which was occupied from at least 3600 BC until the beginning of the Late Bronze Age (1550 to 1200) when the site was abandoned for unknown reasons. It was rebuilt in the 900s BC as a Samaritan city. As Tell el-Hammam is in the Shittim Valley and was destroyed or abandoned when the Israelites moved through the region, using either the traditional Christian dating or the Minoan Eruption and collapse of the Hyksos Dynasty from the Book of Exodus, it is likely that the Bronze-Age city was Peor (Φαγωρ). The exact dating of the abandonment of the bronze-age city is unclear, and there is some evidence of occupation for a few decades after 1550 BC, but the site does appear to have been abandoned around 1500 BC, meaning Joshua would have had to have destroyed it around them.

**4** Codex Vaticanus: Madiam (ΜΑΔΙΑΜ). Translation: Midian

• Aleppo Codex: Mdyn (מדין). Translation: Midian

• Leningrad Codex: Midyan (מִדְיָן). Translation: Midian

• Targum Jerusalem: Midyan (מִדְיָן). Translation: plain (or valley)

**5** Codex Vaticanus: Eui (ЄΥΙ)

• Aleppo Codex: Åwy (אוי)

• Leningrad Codex: Evi (אֱוִי)

• Targum Jerusalem: Evi (אֱוִי)

**6** Codex Vaticanus: Rocom (ΡΟΚΟΜ)

• Aleppo Codex: rqm (רקם). Translation: Petra

• Leningrad Codex: reqem (רֶקֶם). Translation: Petra

• Targum Jerusalem: reqem (רֶקֶם). Translation: Petra

Raqmu was the ancient name of Petra, in modern southwest Jordan. By the era of the kingdoms of Judah and Samaria, the region was known as Sela (סֶלַע), suggesting this section of text is older.

**7** Codex Vaticanus: Sour (ⲥⲟⲩⲣ)

• Aleppo Codex: Ṣwr (צור). Translation: Zur (or rock)

• Leningrad Codex: Tzur (צֻּוׁר). Translation: Zur (or rock)

• Targum Jerusalem: Tzur (צוּר). Translation: Zur (or rock)

Based on the other locations in southern Canaan, this is probably a reference to Beth-Zur, in the West Bank, south of Jerusalem.


**8** Codex Vaticanus: Oyr (ⲟⲩⲣ)

• Aleppo Codex: ḥwr (חור). Translation: white

• Leningrad Codex: chur (חֻּוׁר). Translation: white

• Targum Jerusalem: chur (חוּר). Translation: watch (or look)

This appears to be a reference to Tell es-Safi near Hebron, an ancient fortress from the Bronze Age, built on a hill composed of white cliffs. The site has been occupied continuously since the 5th millenium BC.


**9** Codex Vaticanus: thalassês Chenereth (ⲐⲀⲗⲁⲤⲤⲎⲤ ⲬⲈⲚⲈⲣⲉⲐ). Translation: Sea of Chinnereth

• Aleppo Codex: ym Knrt (יס כנרת). Translation: Sea of Chinnereth

• Leningrad Codex: yam-Kinneret (יֵס־כִּנֶּרֶת). Translation: Sea of Chin-nereth

• Targum Jerusalem: yam Ginosar (יַם גִּינוֹסַר). Translation: sea of Ginosar

These are all alternate names for the Sea of Galilee, also known as Lake Tiberius.

# Joshua: Chapter 14

These are those of the Israelites that received their inheritance in the land of Canaan, to who Eleazar the priest, and Joshua the son of Nun, and the heads of the families of the tribes of the Israelites, gave inheritance. They inherited according to their lots, as the Lord commanded by the hand of Joshua to the nine tribes and the half-tribe, on the other side of Jordan. But to the Levites, he gave no inheritance among them. For the sons of Joseph were two tribes, Manasseh and Ephraim, and there was no inheritance in the land given to the Levites, only cities to live in, and their suburbs separated for the livestock, and their livestock. As the Lord commanded Moses, so the Israelites did when they divided the land.

The children of Judah came to Joshua at the circle, and Caleb the son of Jephunneh the Kenezite said to him, "You know the word that the Lord spoke to Moses the man of God concerning me and you in Kadesh Barnea. For I was forty years old when Moses the servant of God sent me out of Kadesh Barnea to spy out the land, and I returned him an answer according to his mind."

"My brothers that went up with me turned away the heart of the people, but I chose to follow the Lord, my God. Moses swore on that day, 'The land on which you have gone up, it will be your inheritance and your children's forever, because you have chosen to follow Lord the god.' Now the Lord has kept me alive as he said."

"This is the forty-fifth year since the Lord spoke that word to Moses, and Israel journeyed in the wilderness, and now look, I am on this day eighty-five years old. I am still strong this day, like when the Lord sent me. Just as strong am I now to go out and to come in for war. Now I ask of you this mountain, as the Lord said on that day, for you heard this word on that day, and now the Anaks are there, cities great and strong. If then the Lord should be with me, I will completely destroy them, as the Lord told me."

Joshua blessed him and gave Hebron to Caleb the son of Jephunneh the son of Kenez for an inheritance. Therefore Hebron became the inheritance of Caleb the son of Jephunneh the Kenezite until this day because he followed the commandment of Lord the god of Israel. The name of Hebron was previously the city Argob, it was the mother city of the Anaks, and the land rested from war.

# Joshua: Chapter 15

The borders of the tribe of Judah according to their families were from the borders of Edom from the Wilderness of Zin, as far as Kadesh to the south. Their borders were from the south as far as a part of the salt sea from the high country that extends to the south. They follow from the ascent of Akrabbim, and go out around Zenan, and go up from the south to Kadesh Barnea, and go out to Hezron, and proceed up to Adar, and go out by the way that is west of Karkaa. They go out to Zalmonah and start at the valley of Egypt, and the end of its boundaries will be at the sea. These are their boundaries to the south.

Their boundaries to the east are along the salt sea and the Jordan.

The borders in the north are from the seacoast, and part of the Jordan, the borders go up to the House of Hoglah, and continue along the north to the House of Arabah, and up to the stone of Bohan the son of Reuben. The borders continue on to the quarter of the valley of Achor, and go down to the circle which is at the approach to Adummim, which is to the south in the valley, and terminate at the water of the Fountain of Shemesh,[1] and from there go to the Fountain of Rogel. The borders go up to the valley of Hinns,[2] behind Jebus to the south (this is Jerusalem). The borders terminate at the top of the mountain, which is before the valley of Hinns towards the west, (which is next to the land of the Raphites of the north). The border going out from the top of the mountain terminates at the fountain of the water of Nephtoah and terminates at Mount Ephron, and the border will lead to Baalah (this is the city of Jarim).

The border will go around Baalah to the sea and will go on to Mount Seir behind the city of Jearim to the north (this is

Chesalon). It will come down to the Temple of Shemesh and will go on to the south. The border terminates behind Ekron to the north, and the borders will terminate at Booths, and the borders will go on to the south and will terminate at Libnah, and the start of the borders will be at the sea. Their borders will be at the sea, the great sea will be the boundary. These are the borders of the children of Judah according to their families.

To Caleb the son of Jephunneh, he gave a portion in the middle of the children of Judah by the command of God. Joshua gave him the city of Arboc the mother-city of Anaks (this is Hebron). Caleb the son of Jephunneh destroyed the three sons of the Anaks there: Susi, and Tholami, and Achima.

Caleb went up there to the inhabitants of Debir. (The name of Debir was previously the City of Letters before.)[3]

Caleb offered, "Whoever will take and destroy the City of Letters, and conquer it, to him will I give my daughter Acsah as a wife."

Othniel the son of Kenaz the brother of Caleb took it, and he gave Acsah his daughter to him as a wife. As she left she counseled him, "I will ask of my father a field, and she called from her donkey."

Caleb asked her, "What do you have to say?"

She answered him, "Give me a blessing, as you have set me to the land of Negev. Give me Botthanis."

He gave her Upper Gonaethla, and Lower Gonaethla. This is the inheritance of the tribe of the children of Judah.

The cities belonging to the tribe of the children of Judah on the borders of Edom by the wilderness where: Kabzeel, Ara, Hazor, Icam, Regma, Aruel, Kadesh, Asorionain, Maenam, Balmaenan, and their villages, and the cities of Hezron: Hazor, Sen, Salmaa, Molada, Seri, Bethpalet, Hazarshual, and Beersheba, and their villages, and their hamlets: Baalah, Bacoc, Hushim, Eltolad, the Temple of El, Hormah, Ziklag, Macharim, Sethennac, Lebaoth, Sale, and Eromoth. Twenty-nine cities, and their villages.

In the plain country: Eshtaol, Raa, Assa, Ramen, Tano, Iluthoth, Maeani, Jermuth, Adullam, Membra, Socoh, Jazeca, Sharaim, and Gederah and its villages; fourteen cities and their villages.

Zenan, Hadashah, Migdalgad, Dilean, Mizpeh, Joktheel, Bozkath, Ideadalea, Chabra, Maches, Maachos, Gederoth, Temple of Dagon, Naamah, Makkedah; sixteen cities, and their villages.

Libnah, Ether, Anoch, Jana, Nezib, Keilah, Achzib, Kezib, Bathesar, and Elon; ten cities and their villages.

Ekron and her villages, and their hamlets. From Ekron: Gemna and all the cities that are near Azzah, and their villages.

Asiedoth, and her villages and hamlets.

Gaza, and its villages and hamlets as far as the river of Egypt, and the Mediterranean Sea[4] is the boundary.

In the hill country: Shamir, Jetheth, Socha, Renna, and the City of Letters (this is Debir),[5] and Anon, Es, Anim, Aesam, Goshen, Chalu, Channa, Giloh; eleven cities, and their villages.

Aerem, Remna, Soma, Janum, Bethtappuah, Aphekah, Humtah, and the city Arboc, (this is Hebron) and Zior; Nine cities and their villages.

Maon, Carmel, Ozib, Itan, Jezreel, Aricam, Zacanaim, Gibeah, and Thimnathah; nine cities, and their villages.

Halhul, House of Zur, Gedor, Maarath, the Temple of Anat, Eltekon; six cities, and their villages.

Theco, Ephrath, this is House of Lehem, Phagor, Aetan, Culon, Tatam, Thobes, Carem, Galem, Thether, and Manocho; eleven cities, and their villages.

The Town of Baal (this is the city of Jarim), and Sotheba; two cities and their villages.

Baddargeis, Tharabaam, Aenon, Aeochioza, Naphlazon, and the cities of Sadon, and Ancades, seven cities, and their villages.

The Jebusite lived in Jerusalem, and the children of Judah could not destroy them. (The Jebusites live in Jerusalem to this day.)

# Joshua: Chapter 15 Notes

**1** Codex Vaticanus: Êliou (ΗΛΙΟΥ). Translation: Helios (or sun)

- Aleppo Codex: šmš (שמש). Translation: Shemesh (or sun)

- Leningrad Codex: shemesh (שֶׁמֶשׁ). Translation: Shemesh (or sun)

- Targum Jerusalem: shemesh (שְׁמֶשׁ). Translation: Shemesh (or sun)

Shemesh was the Canaanite sun god, whose worship was later banned by King Josiah.


**2** Codex Vaticanus: pharanga Onom (ΦΑΡΑΓΓΑΟΝΟΜ). Translation: abyss (or ravine) of Onom

- Aleppo Codex: gy vn hnm (גי בן הנם). Translation: Valley of the sons of Hnm

- Leningrad Codex: gei ven-Hinnom (גֵּי בֶן־הִנֹּם). Translation: Valley of the sons of Hinnom

- Targum Jerusalem: lecheilat bar Hinom (לְחֵילַת בַּר הִנֹם). Translation: the stength of the sons of Hinom

The Septuagint includes a different name in chapter 18, reading 'Forest of Sonnam' (ναπης Σονναμ) where the Masoretic text reads Valley of the Sons of Hinnom (גֵּי בֶן־הִנֹּם). The misreading of an H (ה) for a S (ש) indicates a transcription error when a Samaritan or Judahite version of the book was translated into Aramaic, however, the substitution of 'forest' for 'valley of the sons...' is clearly not a translation error. The combination of 'valley/abyss' and 'forest' suggests it is a reference to a gravesite, and not a physical valley. At the time, Canaanites marked gravesites by planting trees, usually oak, which was known as the 'Asherah' tree, because it could self-pollinate, and was therefore seen as a 'virgin' tree.

The origin of the word is likely a plural of hinn (حِنّ), a reference to an ancient extinct type of being that once lived on the Earth in Semitic folklore. The hinns continue to be part of the Islamic and Druze religions, although their roles in the religions vary. It is agreed that they are extinct, however, it isn't clear what they were. Many sources describe the hinn and binn as powerful, gigantic primordial creatures, suggesting they were influenced by finding the bones of extinct animals. Conversely, the Revelations of 'Abdullah Al-Sayid Muhammad Habib claims the hinns were air creatures, and their enemies the binns were water creatures, while the medieval Islamic historian al-Tabari claimed they were created from poisonous fire (سموم). In most versions of the stories, they fought in part of a series of wars for control of the earth before the creation of humanity, and most of the ancient species became extinct, including the hinns.

In the context of a gravesite, it is likely that the term 'sons of hinns' did not refer to some known people, but an ancient gravesite of a by then unknown people. Oak trees are known to live over 1000 years, and reproduce, so the gravesite in question could have already been thousands of years old. Later during the reforms of King Josiah, ancient graves and Asherah groves near Jerusalem were destroyed, and he was specifically recorded as destroying a statue in the valley of the sons of Hinns, implying that this was the gravesite he destroyed.

**3** Codex Vaticanus: Dabir an to proteron Polis grammatôn (ⲆⲀⲂⲓⲣ ⲎⲚ ⲦⲞ ⲠⲢⲞⲦⲈⲢⲞⲚ ⲠⲞⲗⲓⲥ ⲅⲣⲀⲙⲙⲀⲦⲱⲚ). Translation: Dabir it was previously City of Letters (or writing)

• Aleppo Codex: dbr lpnym qryt spr (**דבר לפנים קרית ספר**). Translation: Dbr was formerly Village Book (or scroll)

• Leningrad Codex: dəbir lefanim kiryat-sefer (דְּבִר לְפָנִים קִרְיַת־סֵפֶר). Translation: Debir was formerly Village of Book (or scroll)

• Targum Jerusalem: dəbar milkadmin kiryat archei (דְבַר מִלְקַדְמִין קִרְיַת אַרְכֵי). Translation: Debar was in old days village of chief

The location of this city is unclear, however, it is often identified with Khirbet Rabud in the West Bank of Palestinian Territories.

**4** Codex Vaticanus: thalassa ê megalê (ΘΑΛΑϹϹΑΗΜΕΓΑΛΗ). Translation: sea the great

- Aleppo Codex: hym hgbwl [hgdwl] (הים הגבול [הגדול]). Translation: sea the edge [the great]

- Leningrad Codex: hayyam haggavovl K [haggadovl Q] (הַיָּם הַגְּבוֹל כ [הַגָּדוֹל ק]). Translation: sea the edge (K) [the great (Q)]

- Targum Jerusalem: yama Rabbah (יְמָא רַבָּה). Translation: sea great

The Great Sea was a name for the Mediterranean.


**5** Codex Vaticanus: polis grammatôn autê estin Dabir (ΠΟΛΙϹ ΓΡΑΜΜΑΤΩΝ ΑΥΤΗ ΕϹΤΙΝ ΔΑΒΙΡ). Translation: city of letters this is Dabir

- Codex Alexandrinus: Polis grammatôn hautê Dabir (ΠΟΛΙϹ ΓΡΑΜΜΑΤΩΝ ΑΥΤΗ ΔΑΒΙΡ). Translation: city of letters it's Dabir

- Aleppo Codex: qryt snh hyå dbr (קרית סנה היא דבר). Translation: village of bush (or bramble) it is Debir

- Leningrad Codex: kiryat-sannah hi devir (קִרְיַת־סַנָּה הִיא דְבָר). Translation: village of bush (or bramble) it is Debir

- Targum Jerusalem: kiryat sanah hi devir (קִרְיַת סָנָה הִיא דְבִיר). Translation: village of bush (or bramble) it's Debir

# Joshua: Chapter 16

The borders of the children of Joseph were from the Jordan by Jericho to the east, and they went up from Jericho to the hill country, to the wilderness, to the Temple of El in Luza,[1] and they will go out to the Temple of El and continue to the borders of the Archites. They go across to the sea to the borders of Japhletites, as far as the borders of Lower House of Horon, and from there the border will be the sea. The sons of Joseph, Ephraim, and Manasseh took their inheritance.

The borders of the children of Ephraim were according to their families, and the borders of their inheritance were to the east of Ataroth, and Eroc as far as Upper House of Horon, and Gazara. The borders continue to the sea to Icasmon north of Therma, and they go east to Taanath and Sellesa and pass on eastward to Janohah, and to Macho, and Ataroth, these are their villages, and they will come to Jericho and will start at Jordan. The borders will proceed from Tappuah to the sea by Kanah, and the end will be at the sea. This is the inheritance of the tribe of Ephraim according to their families.

The cities separated to the Ephramites were among the inheritance of the sons of Manasseh, all the cities and their villages. Ephraim did not destroy the Canaanites who lived in Gezer, and the Canaanites lived in Ephraim until Pharaoh the king of Egypt went up and took it, and burnt it with fire. The Canaanites and Perizzite, and the residents in Gaza were destroyed, and Pharaoh gave them as a dowry to his daughter.

# Joshua: Chapter 16 Notes

**1** Codex Vaticanus: Baethêl Louza (ΒΑΙΘΗΛΛΟΥΖΑ)

- Aleppo Codex: Byt Âl lwzh (בית אל לוזה). Translation: House (or Temple) of El (or God) in Luza

- Leningrad Codex: Veit-Ēl lûzâ (בֵּית־אֵל לוּזָה). Translation: House (or Temple) of El (or God) in Luza

- Targum Jerusalem: Veit Ēl (בֵּית אֵל). Translation: House (or Temple) of El

# Joshua: Chapter 17

The borders of the tribe of the children of Manasseh, (as he was the firstborn of Joseph,) assigned to Machir the firstborn of Manasseh the father of Gilead, as he was a warrior, were the lands of Gilead and of Bashan. There was land assigned to the other sons of Manasseh according to their families. To the sons of Jezi and to the sons of Kelez, and to the sons of Asriel, and to the sons of Shechem, and to the sons of Symarim, and to the sons of Hepher, these are the males according to their families.

Zelophehad the sons of Hepher had no sons but daughters, and these are the names of the daughters of Zelophehad: Maala, Noah, Hoglah, Milcah, and Tirzah. They stood before Eleazar the priest, and before Joshua, and before the rulers, and said, "God gave an order by the hand of Moses, to give us an inheritance among our brothers," so there was given to them by the command of the Lord an inheritance among the brothers of their father. Their lot fell to them from Manasseh, and to the plain of Labec of the land of Gilead, which is beyond Jordan. For the daughters of the sons of Manasseh inherited a portion among their brothers, and the land of Gilead was assigned to the remainder of the sons of Manasseh.

The borders of the sons of Manasseh were Delanath, which was before the sons of Anath, and it proceeded to the borders even to Jamin and Jassib to the Fountain of Tappuah. It belonged to Manasseh, and Tappuah on the borders of Manasseh belonged to the Ephramites. The borders went down to the valley of Kanah southward by the valley of Jezreel (there is a turpentine tree belonging to Ephraim between that and the city of Manasseh), and the borders of Manasseh are north to the brook, and the sea will be its end. To the south, the land belonged to Ephraim, and north to Manasseh and the sea was their border. To the north, they bordered Asher, and to the east Issachar.

Manasseh had in the portion of Issachar: Asher, the House of Shean and their villages, and the inhabitants of Dor, and its villages, and the inhabitants of Megiddo, and its villages, and the third part of Mapheta, and its villages. The sons of Manasseh were not able to destroy these cities, and the Canaanites began to live in that land. It happened that when the Israelites were strong, they made the Canaanites subject, but they did not completely destroy them. The sons of Joseph asked Joshua, "Why have you caused us to inherit one inheritance and one line? We are a great people, and God has blessed us."

Joshua replied to them, "If you are a great people, go up to the forest, and clear the land for yourself, if Mount Ephraim is too little for you."

They answered, "Mount Ephraim does not please us, and the Canaanites living in it in the House of Shean, and in its villages, and in the valley of Jezrael, have the best cavalry and iron."

Joshua said to the sons of Joseph, "If you are a great people, and have great strength, you will not have only one inheritance. For you have the wood, for there is a forest and you will clear it, and the land will be yours. Then you will completely destroy the Canaanites, for they have the best cavalry, yet you are stronger."

# Joshua: Chapter 18

All the congregation of the Israelites was assembled at Shiloh, and there they pitched the tabernacle of witness, and the land was subdued by them. The sons of Israel remained, all those who had not received their inheritance, seven tribes.

Joshua said to the sons of Israel, "How long will you wait to inherit the land that Lord the god has given you? Appoint for yourselves three men from each tribe, and let them rise up and go through the land, and let them describe it to me, as it would be best to divide it. They came to him and he divided to them seven portions, saying, "Judah will be for them a southern border, and the sons of Joseph will be for them a northern border. Divide the land into seven parts, and bring the description here to me, and I will bring your lot before Lord the god. The Levites have no part among you, for the priesthood of the Lord is his portion. Gad, Reuben, and the half-tribe of Manasseh have received their inheritance beyond the Jordan to the east, which Moses the servant of the Lord gave to them.

The men rose and went out, and Joshua ordered the men who went to walk through the land, saying, "Go and explore the land and come to me, and I will bring your lot here before the Lord in Shiloh."

They went and explored the land, and they viewed it, and described it according to the cities, seven parts in a book, and brought the book to Joshua. Joshua cast the lot for them in Shiloh before the Lord. The lot of the tribe of Benjamin came out first according to their families, and the borders of their lot came out between the children of Judah and the children of Joseph. Their borders were to the north from the Jordan near Jericho to the mountain in the west, and the start of it will be the Temple of An[1] of the desert-dwellers.[2]

The borders will go out there to Luz, to the south of Luz, (this is the Temple of El). The borders will go down to Ataroth Addar, to the hill country, which is southward of Lower House of Horon. The borders will pass through and proceed to the part that looks towards the sea, on the south, from the mountain in front of House of Horon southward, and its termination will be at the town of Ba'al, this is the town of Jearim, a city of the children of Judah towards the west.

The south side on the part of the town of Ba'al and the borders will go across to Gasin, to the fountain of the water of Nephtoah. The borders will extend down on one side, this is in front of the Forest of Hinns[3] (which is the Valley of Raphites of the north),[4] and go down the Valley of Hinns[5] south of the Jebusites. It will come down to the Fountain of Rogel. The borders will go across to the Fountain of the Temple of Shemesh, and will proceed to Geliloth, which is on the way to Adummim, and they will come down to the stone of Bohan of the sons of Reuben, and will pass to the north of the House of Arabah, and will go down to the borders to the north of the sea. The termination of the borders will be at the creek of the salt sea northward to the south side of the Jordan. These are their southern borders. The Jordan will be their boundary on the east. This is the inheritance of the children of Benjamin, these are their borders according to their families.

The cities of the children of Benjamin according to their families were Jericho, the House of Hoglah, the Valley of Keziz, the House of Arabah, Sarai, Besana, Avim, Phara, Ophrah, Carapha, Cephira, Moni, Geba; twelve cities and their villages.

Gibeon, Ramah, Beeroth, Mizpah, Miron, Amoke, Phira, Caphan, Nacan, Selecan, Taralah, Jebus (this is Jerusalem), Gibeah; thirteen cities, and their villages.

This is the inheritance of the sons of Benjamin according to their families.

# Joshua: Chapter 18 Notes

**1** Codex Vaticanus: Baethôn (ΒΑΙΘΩΝ)

- Aleppo Codex: Byt Åwn (בית און)

- Leningrad Codex: Veit Aven (בֵּית אָוֶן)

- Targum Jerusalem: Veit Aven (בֵּית אָוֶן)

The Temple of Ôn / Aven was still being used in the time of Hosea, in the 700s BC, as he warned Israelites not to worship there. On was also the name of Moses' god in the Septuagint's book of Exodus, which claims that Ôn (Ων) was the name that he was known to by Abram, Isaac, and Jacob. This implies that the original name of Abram's god was Anu (✳), the Mesopotamian version of El, which would support his origin story in the city of Ur.

**2** Codex Vaticanus: Madbaritis (ΜΑΔΒΑΡΙΤΙC). Translation: Madbarites

- Aleppo Codex: mdbr (מדבר). Translation: desert (or wilderness)

- Leningrad Codex: midbara (מִדְבָּר). Translation: desert (or wilderness)

- Targum Jerusalem: madbar (מִדְבַּר). Translation: desert (or wilderness)

Similar to the transliteration of Madbaritidi (Μαδβαρῖτις) in chapter 5, this a synthesis of the Aramaic mdbrå (מדברא) meaning 'desert' and the Greek '-itis' (-ῖτις), meaning 'people of,' the precursor to the modern English '-ites.' Again, the Greek appears to have translated the Aramaic word mdbråyn (מדבראין), meaning 'desert-dweller,' which is a deviation from the simpler term 'desert' found in the Hebrew and Judeo-Aramaic translations. The deviation likely occurred because the term desert-dwellers could be a reference to the Israelites themselves during the era, and the Hebrew translators wanted to clarify that it was a temple in the desert, not the temple in Samaria.

**3** Codex Vaticanus: napês Sonnam (ΝΑΠΗϹϹΟΝΝΑΜ). Translation: woodland (or grove) of Sonnam

- Aleppo Codex: gy vn hnm (גי בן הנם). Translation: Valley of the sons of Hnm

- Leningrad Codex: gei ven-Hinnom (גֵּי בֶן־הִנֹּם). Translation: Valley of the sons of Hinnom

- Targum Jerusalem: cheilat bar Hinom (חֵילַת בַּר הִנֹם). Translation: stength of the sons of Hinom

The Septuagint includes a different name in chapter 18, reading 'abyss of Onom' (φαραγγα ονομ) where the Masoretic text reads Valley of the Sons of Hinnom (גֵּי בֶן־הִנֹּם), indicating the Aramaic translation used shorter names than the Judahite and Samaritan versions. The difference between in the names Sonnam and Hinnom in this verse likely originated when the Aramaic translation was created, as the Canaanite's script, which was used for Samaritan and Judahite in the early iron age, had similar shapes for the H (ঀ) and the Ś (ᚹ). While the Aramaic script did not have a similar H (ℸ) and Ś (Ƨ), the early Greek alphabet did have a similar H (ε) and Š (ϲ), and therefore, the error could be interpreted as a Greek copying error. However, a virtually identical error is found in the Judahite Apocalypse of Ezra, which rendered the Sea of Edom as the Sea of Sodom. In that case, it was the word 'the/of' in between 'sea' and 'Edom' that was misread as an S, indicating the error took place in the Canaanite script.

The origin of the name Hnm (הנם) is likely a plural of hinn (حِنّ), a reference to an ancient extinct type of being that once lived on the Earth in Semitic folklore. The hinns continue to be part of the Islamic and Druze religions, although their roles in the religions vary. It is agreed that they are extinct, however, it isn't clear what they were. Many sources describe the hinns and binns as powerful, gigantic primordial creatures, suggesting they were influenced by finding the bones of extinct animals. Conversely, the Revelations of 'Abdullah Al-Sayid Muhammad Habib claims the hinns were air creatures, and the binns were water creatures, while the medieval Islamic historian al-

Tabari claimed they were created from poisonous fire (سموم). In most versions of the stories, they fought in part of a series of wars for control of the earth before the creation of humanity, and most of the ancient species became extinct, including the hinns.

The substitution of 'forest' or 'woodland' for 'valley of the sons...' is clearly not a translation error. The combination of 'valley/abyss' and 'forest/woodland' suggests it is a reference to a gravesite, and not a physical valley. At the time, Canaanites marked gravesites by planting trees, usually oak, which was known as the 'Asherah' tree, because it could self-pollinate, and was therefore seen as a 'virgin' tree. In the context of a gravesite, it is likely that the term 'sons of hinns' did not refer to some known people, but an ancient gravesite of a by then unknown people. Oak trees are known to live over 1000 years, and reproduce, so the gravesite in question could have already been thousands of years old. Later during the reforms of King Josiah, ancient graves and Asherah groves near Jerusalem were destroyed, and he was specifically recorded as destroying a statue in the valley of the sons of Hinns, implying that this was the gravesite he destroyed.

**4** Codex Vaticanus: merous Emecraphaen apo borrha (ΜΕΡΟΥϹ ΕΜΕΚΡΑΦΑΕΙΝΑΠΟΒΟΡΡΑ). Translation: region of Emecraphaen of the north

• Aleppo Codex: åshr vômk rfåm tzfvnh (אשר בעמק רפאיס צפונה). Translation: exists the valley of Raphaim northern

• Leningrad Codex: asher be'emek refa'im tzafovnah (אֲשֶׁר בָּעֵמֶק רְפָאִים צָפוֹנָה). Translation: exists the valley Raphaim northern

• Targum Jerusalem: bemeishar gibbaraya tzifuna (בְּמֵישַׁר גִבָּרַיָא צְפוּנָא). Translation: straight of the husband of the north

As the Greek includes a transliteration of the Hebrew, the Hebrew is imported. This scribal note seems to confirm that the 'Forest of Hinns' was the 'valley of the Raphiam,' supporting the term 'valley/abyss of hinns' referring to a graveyard. The two terms translated as 'Hinns' and

'Raphites' are not generally found in the same ancient literature, with hinns being mostly found in Arabic literature, and Raphites being mostly found in Canaanite literature. This scribal note, in both the Greek and Hebrew translations, indicates the scribe was trying to let a northern reader understand that a Hinn was a Raphite. This shows that the original language of the text was more influenced by Arabic than Canaanite, supporting the claims that the people following Joshua had previously been in the Arabian desert. The scribal note must date back to an earlier copy of the text, as there would have been no reason to add it to both the Aramaic and Judahite translations, which later served as the basis for the Greek and Hebrew. The Aramaic translators would have simply used the correct Aramaic term, and left the Judahite text unaltered. It probably originated in the Samaritan version of the text, as at its height, the Kingdom of Israel was reported to have spanned the Levant from Edom to Hama.

At other points in the Septuagint, the Valley of Raphim is translated as the Valley of Gigantes (κοιλαδι των γιγαντων), indicating that the Greeks were not clear on who the sons of the Raphim were. It is likely that this was not being used as a reference to a tribe by the time the scribal note was added, as the Raphites (𐤓𐤐𐤀𐤌) were already viewed as residing in the underworld in Ugaritic Texts from the mid-1300s BC.

**5** Codex Vaticanus: Gaeenna (ⲅⲁⲓⲉⲛⲛⲁ). Translation: Gaeenna

• Aleppo Codex: gy hnm (גי הנם). Translation: valley Hnm

• Leningrad Codex: gei Hinnom (גֵּי הִנֹּם). Translation: valley Hinnom

• Targum Jerusalem: lecheilat bar hinom (לְחֵילַת בַּר הִנֹם). Translation: the army (or strength, force) of the sons of Hinom

As the Greek includes a transliteration of the Hebrew 'valley of Hinns,' the Hebrew is imported.

# Joshua: Chapter 19

The second lot came out for the children of Simeon, and their inheritance was in the middle of the lots of the children of Judah. Their lot was Beersheba, Sheba, Caladam, Arsola, Balah, Jason, Erthula, the Temple of El, Hormah, Ziklag, the House of Marcaboth, the Yard of Susah, the House of Lebaoth, and their fields; thirteen cities, and their villages.

Rimmon, Thalcha, Jetheth, and Ashan; four cities and their villages around the cities as far as Balec as men go south to Bameth.

This is the inheritance of the tribe of the children of Simeon according to their families. The inheritance of the tribe of the children of Simeon was a part of the lot of Judah, for the portion of the children of Judah was greater than theirs, and the children of Simeon inherited in the middle of their lot.

The third lot came out to Zebulun according to their families. The borders of their inheritance will be: Esedekgola will be their border, the sea, and Magelda, and it will reach towards the House of Arabah in the valley, which is opposite Jokneam. The border returned from Sedduc in a contrary direction eastward from the Temple of Shemesh, to the borders of Chisloth Tabor, and will pass on to Daberath, and will proceed upward to Phangai. There it will come around in the opposite direction eastward to Gebere to the city of Kazin, and will go on to Rimmon Ammatharim Annoua.[1] The borders will come north to Hannathon, and will continue on to Jiphthah El, Kattath, Nahalal, Shimron, Jericho, and the House of Lehem. This is the inheritance of the tribe of the sons of Zebulun according to their families, these cities and their villages.

The fourth lot came out to Issachar. Their borders were Jezreel, Chesulloth, Shunem, Agin, Shion, Reeroth, Anaharath,

Dabiron, Kishion, Abez, Remeth, Jeon, Tomman, Aemarec, and Bersaphes. The boundaries will border on Gaethbor, and on Salim westward, and the Temple of Shemesh, and the extremity of his border will be the Jordan. This is the inheritance of the tribe of the children of Issachar according to their families, the cities and their villages.

The fifth lot came out to Asher according to their families. Their borders were Helkath, Hali, Bathok, Achshaph, Alamm-elech, Ammi-El, and Maasa, and the lot bordered on Carmel in the west, and on Sihon and Libnath. It will return westward from the Temple of Dagon, and will join Zebulun and the valley of Iphtah-El to the north, and the borders will come to the north Beth Emek, and Neiel, and will go on to Cabul on the left, including Ebron, Rehob, Hammon, and Kanah to Sidon the Great. The borders will turn back to Ramah, and to the Fountain of Masphassat, and the Tyrians and the borders will return to Hosah, and their end will be the sea by Apoleb, Achzib, Archob, Aphek, and Rehob. This is the inheritance of the tribe of the sons of Asher according to their families, the cities and their villages.

The sixth lot came out to Naphtali. Their borders were Moolam, Mola, Besemiin, Arme, Nekeb, Jephthamai, as far as Dodam, and ended at the Jordan. The coasts returned westward by Athabor, and go out from there to Jacana, and border on Zebulun to the south, and Asher will join it to the west, and the Jordan to the east. The walled cities of the Tyrians: Tyre, Omath-adaketh, Kenereth, Armaith, Areal, Hazor, Kadesh, Assari, the well of Hazor, Iron, Migdal El, the Temple of Anath, and the Temple of Shemesh. This is the inheritance of the tribe of the children of Naphtali.

The seventh lot came out to Dan. Their borders were Zorah, Asa, the City of Shemesh, Salamin, Ammon, Jethlah, Elon,

Timnah, Ekron, Eltekeh, Begethon, and Gebeelan, Azor, Bene-berak, and Gath Rimmon. West of Hieracon the border was near to Jaffa. This is the inheritance of the tribe of the children of Dan, according to their families, these are their cities and their villages.

The children of Dan did not drive out the Amorites who attacked them in the mountains, and the Amorites would not allow them to come down into the valley, but they forcibly took from them the border of their portion. The sons of Dan went and fought against Leshem, and took it, and slaughtered it with the edge of the sword, and they lived in it and called the name of it Leshem Dan. The Amorites continued to live in Edom and in Salamin, and the hand of Ephraim prevailed against them, and they became a tribute for them.

They proceeded to take possession of the land according to their borders, and the Israelites gave an inheritance to Joshua the son of Nun among them, by the command of God, and they gave him the city which he asked for, Timnath Serah, which is on Mount Ephraim, and he built the city and lived in it. These are the divisions which Eleazar the priest divided by lot, and Joshua the son of Nun, and the heads of families among the tribes of Israel, according to the lots, in Shiloh before the Lord by the doors of the tabernacle of testimony, and they went to take possession of the land.

# Joshua: Chapter 19 Notes

**1** Codex Vaticanus: Remmôn Ammatharim Annoua (ремми͡ɴ ᴀммᴀѳᴀꝑᴍᴀɴɴоγᴀ)

- Aleppo Codex: Rmwn hmtår hnôh (רמון המתאר הנעה)

- Leningrad Codex: Rimmovn hammeto'ar hanne'ah ( רִמּוֹן הַמְּתֹאָר הַנֵּעָה)

- Targum Jerusalem: Rimon dimto'ar umittaman mistechar lene'ah (רמון דְמְתוֹאַר וּמִתַּמָן מְסְתְּחַר לְנֵעָה). Translation: desert (or wilderness)

In this case, the Greeks transliterated a word similar to hammeto'ar (הַמְתֹאָר) as Ammatharim (Αμμαθαριμ). As 'hammesoor' translates as 'that describes' it is possible that the text originated by the scribal note "(which is Annoua)" however, that cannot be known for sure. As it is, neither the Greek nor Hebrew translations make sense in this verse.

# Joshua: Chapter 20

The Lord said to Joshua, "Tell the Israelites, 'Assign the cities of refuge, of which I told you through Moses. A refuge for the slayer who has struck a man unintentionally. The cities will be refuges for you, and the slayer will not be put to death by the avenger of blood until he has stood before the congregation for judgment.'"

Joshua separated Kadesh in Galilee on Mount Naphtali, and Shechem on Mount Ephraim, and the city of Arba (this is Hebron), in the mountains of Judah. Beyond the Jordan, he appointed Bezer in the wilderness in the plain out of the tribe of Reuben, and Ramoth in Gilead out of the tribe of Gad, and Golan in the country of Bashan out of the tribe of Manasseh.

These were the cities selected for the sons of Israel, and for the stranger living among them, that everyone who kills a mind unintentionally should flee there, that he should not die by the hand of the avenger of blood until he should stand before the congregation for judgment.

# Joshua: Chapter 21

The heads of the families of the Levites approached Eleazar the priest and Joshua the son of Nun, and to the heads of families of the tribes of Israel. They said to them in Shiloh in the land of Canaan, "The Lord gave commandment by Moses to give us cities to live in, and the country around it for our livestock."

The Israelites gave the Levites their inheritance by the command of the Lord, the cities, and the country around them. The lot came out for the Kohathites, and the sons of Aaron, the priests the Levites, had by lot thirteen cities out of the tribes of Judah, Simeon, and Benjamin. To the sons of Kohath that were left were given by lot ten cities, out of the tribes of Ephraim and Dan, and out of the half-tribe of Manasseh. The sons of Gershon had thirteen cities, out of the tribes of Issachar, Asher, Naphtali, and out of the half-tribe of Manasseh in the land of Bashan. The sons of Merari according to their families had by lot twelve cities, out of the tribes of Reuben, Gad, and Zebulun. The Israelites gave to the Levites the cities and their suburbs by lot, as the Lord commanded Moses.

The tribe of the children of Judah, and the children of Simeon, and part of the tribe of the children of Benjamin gave these cities, and they were assigned to the sons of Aaron of the family of Kohath of the Levites, for the lot fell to these. And they gave to them the town of Arba, the mother-city of the sons of Anaks (this is Hebron), in the mountainous country of Judah, and the suburbs around it. But the lands of the city and its villages Joshua gave to the sons of Caleb the son of Jephunneh for a possession. To the sons of Aaron, he gave the city of refuge for the slayer, Hebron, and the suburbs belonging to it, and Libnah, and the suburbs belonging to it, and Elon and its suburbs, and Teman and its suburbs, Gella and its suburbs, and Debir and its suburbs, and Asa and its suburbs, and Tany and its suburbs, and the Temple of Shemesh and its suburbs; nine cities from these two tribes.

From the tribe of Benjamin, Gibeon and its suburbs, Geba and its suburbs, Anathoth and its suburbs, Almon and its suburbs; four cities. All the cities of the sons of Aaron the priests, thirteen. To the families, including the sons of Kohath the Levites, that were left of the sons of Kohath, there was given their priests' city, out of the tribe of Ephraim, and they gave them the slayer's city of refuge Shechem, and its suburbs, and Gezer and its suburbs, and House of Horon and its suburbs; four cities. From the tribe of Dan: Eltekeh and its suburbs, Gibbethon and its suburbs, Ayalon and its suburbs, Gath Rimmon and its suburbs; four cities.

Out of the half-tribe of Manasseh: Taanach and its suburbs, and Jebatha and its suburbs; two cities. In all were given ten cities, and the suburbs of each belonging to them, to the families of the sons of Kohath that remained. Joshua gave to the sons of Gershon the Levites out of the other half-tribe of Manasseh cities set apart for the slayers, Golan in the country of Bashan, and its suburbs, and Bosora and its suburbs; two cities.

Out of the tribe of Issachar: Kishion and its suburbs, Daberath and its suburbs, Remmath and its suburbs, and the Well of Letters, and its suburbs; four cities.

Out of the tribe of Asher: Basella and its suburbs, and Abdon and its suburbs, and Helkath and its suburbs, and Rehob and its suburbs; four cities.

Of the tribe of Naphtali: the city set apart for the slayer, Kadesh in Galilee, and its suburbs, and Hammoth Dor, and its suburbs; and Themmon and its suburbs; three cities. All the cities of the Gershonites according to their families were thirteen cities. To the family of the sons of Merari the Levites that remained, he gave out of the tribe of Zebulun, Mahanaim and its suburbs, Kadesh and its suburbs, and Zillah and its suburbs: three cities.

Beyond the Jordan near Jericho, out of the tribe of Reuben: the city of refuge for the slayer, Bezer in the wilderness, Miso and its suburbs, Jahaz and its suburbs, Kedemoth and its suburbs, Mephaath and its suburbs; four cities.

Out of the tribe of Gad the city of refuge for the slayer, both Ramoth in Gilead, and its suburbs, Mahanaim and its suburbs, Heshbon and its suburbs, Jazer and its suburbs: the cities were four in all. All these cities were given to the sons of Merari according to the families of them that were left out of the tribe of Levi, and their limits were the twelve cities. All the cities of the Levites among the possession of the Israelites, were forty-eight cities, and their suburbs around these cities, a city and the suburbs round about the city to all these cities: and Joshua ceased dividing the land by their borders: and the Israelites gave a portion to Joshua because of the commandment of the Lord: they gave him the city which he asked: they gave him Timnath Serah on Mount Ephraim, and Joshua built the city and lived in it. Joshua took the knives of stone, which he circumcised the Israelites that were born in the desert along the way, and put them in Timnath Serah. So the Lord gave to Israel all the land which he swore to give to their fathers: and they inherited it, and lived in it. The Lord gave them the rest around at, as he swore to their fathers: not one of all their enemies maintained his ground against them. The Lord delivered all their enemies into their hands. Not one of the good things which the Lord said to the Israelites failed. All happened.

# Joshua: Chapter 22

Then Joshua called together the sons of Reuben, and the sons of Gad, and the half-tribe of Manasseh, and said to them, "You have heard all that Moses the servant of the Lord commanded you, and you have listened to my voice in all that he commanded you. You have not deserted your brothers these many days. Until this day you have kept the commandment of Lord the god. Now Lord the god has given our brothers rest, as he told them. Now then, return and leave to your homes, and to the land of your possession, which Moses gave you on the other side of the Jordan. But take great heed to do the commands and the law, which Moses the servant of the Lord commanded you to do: to love Lord the god, to walk in all his ways, to keep his commands, and to cling to him, and serve him with all your mind, and with all your mind."

Joshua blessed them and dismissed them, and they went to their homes. To one half of the tribe of Manasseh Moses gave a portion in the land of Bashan, and to the other half, Joshua gave a portion with his brothers on the west side of the Jordan. When Joshua sent them away to their homes, then he blessed them. They departed with much wealth to their houses, and they divided the spoil of their enemies with their brothers, a great deal of livestock, silver, gold, iron, and many clothes. So the sons of Reuben, and the sons of Gad, and the half-tribe of Manasseh, departed from the Israelites in Shiloh in the land of Canaan, to go away into Gilead, into the land of their possession, which they inherited by the command of the Lord, by the hand of Moses.

They came to Gilead of Jordan, which is in the land of Canaan. The children of Reuben, and the children of Gad, and the half-tribe of Manasseh built an altar there by the Jordan, a great altar to look at. The Israelites were heard to say, "Look, the sons of Reuben, Gad, and the half-tribe of Manasseh have built an altar at the borders of the land of Canaan at Gilead of Jordan, on the opposite side as the Israelites." All the Israelites gathered together to Shiloh, to go up and fight against them. The Israelites sent to the sons of Reuben, Gad, and the half-tribe of Manasseh in the land of Gilead, both Phinehas the son of Eleazar the son of Aaron the priest, and ten of the chiefs with him, one chief of every household out of all the tribes of Israel, (the heads of families are the captains of thousands in Israel.)

They came to the sons of Reuben, Gad, and the half-tribe of Manasseh in the land of Gilead, and said to them, "The whole congregation of the Lord says, 'What is this transgression that you have done before the God of Israel, to turn away today from the Lord, in that you have built for yourselves an altar so that you should be apostates from the Lord? Is the sin of Peor too little for you, whereas we have not been cleansed from it until this day, though there was a plague among the congregation of the Lord? You have this day rebelled from the Lord. It will come to pass if you revolt this day from the Lord, that tomorrow there will be anger on all Israel."

"Now if the land of your possession is too little, cross over to the land of the possession of the Lord, where the tabernacle of the Lord lives, and receive your inheritance among us. Do not become apostates from God, neither become apostates from the Lord, because of your having built an altar apart from the altar of Lord the god. Look! did not Achan the son of Zerah commit a trespass taking of the cursed thing, and there was anger on the whole congregation of Israel? Yet he himself died alone in his own sin."

The sons of Reuben, Gad, and the half-tribe of Manasseh answered the captains of the thousands of Israel, "The god of gods is Lord, and the god of gods, Lord himself knows[1] and judges Israel. If we have transgressed before the Lord by apostasy, let him not save us this day. If we have built for ourselves an altar, to apostatize from Lord the god, to offer on it a sacrifice of whole burnt offerings, to offer on it a sacrifice of peace offering, the Lord will require it. But we have done this for the sake of precaution concerning this thing, saying, 'In case from now on your sons should say to our sons, 'What have you to do with Lord the god of Israel? The Lord has set boundaries between us and you, even the Jordan, and you have no portion in the Lord,' and your sons will alienate our sons, that they should not worship the Lord.'"

"We gave orders to do this, to build this altar, not for burnt offerings, nor for meat-offerings, but that this may be a witness between you and us, and between our posterity after us, that we may do service to the Lord before him, with our burnt offerings and our meat-offerings and our peace offerings. So your sons will not say to our sons, from now on, 'You have no portion in the Lord.' We said, 'If ever it should come to pass that they should speak so to us, or to our posterity from now on, then will they say, 'Look the likeness of the altar of the Lord, which our fathers made, not for the sake of burnt offerings, nor for the sake of meat-offerings, but it is a witness between you and us, and between our sons.' Far be it from us therefore that we should turn away from the Lord this day to apostatize from the Lord, so that we should build an altar for burnt offerings, and for peace offerings, besides the altar of the Lord which is before his tabernacle."

Phinehas the priest and all the chiefs of the congregation of Israel who were with him heard the words which the children of Reuben, Gad, and the half-tribe of Manasseh spoke, and it pleased them. Phinehas the priest said to the sons of Reuben, Gad, and to the half-tribe of Manasseh, "Today we know that the Lord is with us, because you have not trespassed grievously against the Lord, and because you have delivered the Israelites out of the hand of the Lord."

So Phinehas the priest and the princes departed from the children of Reuben, Gad, and the half-tribe of Manasseh, out of Gilead to the land of Canaan to the Israelites, and reported the words to them. It pleased the Israelites, and they spoke to the Israelites, and blessed the God of the Israelites, and told them to not go up to war against the others and destroy the land of the children of Reuben, Gad, and the half-tribe of Manasseh. Joshua gave a name to the altar of the children of Reuben, Gad, and the half-tribe of Manasseh, and said, "It is a testimony among them, that the Lord is their God."

# Joshua: Chapter 22 Notes

**1** Codex Vaticanus: o t̄h̄s̄ t̄h̄s̄ estin c̄s̄, cae o t̄h̄s̄ t̄h̄s̄ c̄s̄ autòs oĩden (Ο Θ͞C Θ͞C ΕCΤΙΝ Κ͞C ΚΑΙ Ο Θ͞C Θ͞C Κ͞C ΑΥΤΟC ΟΙΔΕΝ). Translation: the god god is lord, and the god god lord himself knows

- Aleppo Codex: ål ålhym yhwh ål ålhym yhwh hwå ydô (**אל אלהים יהוה אל אלהים יהוה הוא ידע**). Translation: the (or god, El) gods (or elohim) Yhwh the (or god, El) gods (or elohim) Yhwh he knows

- Leningrad Codex: el | elohim | Yehvah el | elohim | Yehvah hu yodea' (אֵל ׀ אֱלֹהִים ׀ יְהוָה אֵל ׀ אֱלֹהִים ׀ יְהוָה הוּא יֹדֵעַ). Translation: god (or El) – gods (or elohim) – Yehwah god (or El) – gods (or elohim) – Yehwah he knows

- Targum Jerusalem: el elohim Yeyah el elohim Yeyah kodamohi yedia' (אֵל אֱלֹהִים יְיָ אֵל אֱלֹהִים יְיָ קֳדָמוֹהִי יְדִיעַ). Translation: god (or El) gods Yahw god (or El) gods Yahw he knows

As neither the Greek nor Hebrew text makes sense here, and clearly were not understood by the Masoretes due to their punctuation marks, it is assumed that the Greeks translated both 'el' and elohim as 'god,' as they did in other sections of the Septuagint. If the term elohim originally meant 'gods' in this verse, which is its Aramaic meaning, then the Aramaic precursor text would have read 'the god of gods is Lord (possibly Adonay or Ba'al), and the god of gods, Lord himself, knows..."

# Joshua: Chapter 23

Many days after the Lord had given Israel rest from all his enemies, when Joshua was old and advanced in years. Joshua called together all the Israelites, and their elders, and their chiefs, and their judges, and their officers, and said to them, "I am old and advanced in years. You have seen all that Lord the god has done to all these nations before us. It is Lord the god who has fought for you. See, that I have given to you these nations that are left to you by lots to your tribes, all the nations beginning at the Jordan. Some I have destroyed, and the boundaries will be at the great sea to the west."

"The Lord the god, will destroy them before us until they completely perish, and he will send against them the wild beasts until he has completely destroyed them and their kings from before you, and you will inherit their land, as Lord the god promised you. Therefore strive diligently to observe and do all things written in the book of the law of Moses, that you do not turn to the right or to the left, that you do not go in among these nations that are left, and the names of their gods will not be named among you. Neither will you serve them, neither will you bow down to them. But you will cling to Lord the god, as you have done until this day. The Lord will destroy them before you, even great and strong nations. No one has stood before us until this day. One of you has chased a thousand, because Lord the god, he fought for you, as he said to us."

"Pay close attention to love Lord the god. For if you will turn aside and attach yourselves to these nations that are left with you, and make marriages with them, and become mingled with them and they with you, know that the Lord will no longer destroy these nations from before you, and they will be to you snares and stumbling blocks, and nails in your heels, and darts in your eyes until you are destroyed from off this good land, which Lord the god has given you. But I quickly go the way of death, as all that are on the earth also do, and you know in your heart and in your mind, that not one word has fallen to the ground of all the words which Lord the god has spoken respecting all that concerns us".

"There has not one of them failed. It will come to pass, that as all the good things have come on us which Lord the god will bring on you all the evil things until he has destroyed you from off this good land, which the Lord has given you, when you transgress the covenant of Lord the god, which he has ordered us, and go and serve other gods, and bow down to them."

# Joshua: Chapter 24

Joshua gathered all the tribes of Israel to Shiloh, and assembled their elders, and their officers, and their judges, and set them before God. Joshua said to all the people, "Lord the god of Israel says, 'Your fathers at first stayed beyond the river, including Terah, the father of Abraham and the father of Nahor, and they served other gods. I took your father Abraham from the other side of the river, and I guided him through all the land, and I multiplied his seed, and I gave to him Isaac, and to Isaac Jacob and Esau. I gave to Esau Mount Seir for him to inherit, and Jacob and his sons went down to Egypt and became a great and populous and mighty nation there, and the Egyptians attacked them. I struck Egypt with the wonders that I worked among them.'"

"Afterward God brought out our fathers from Egypt, and you entered into the Papyrus Sea, and the Egyptians pursued after our fathers with chariots and horses into the Papyrus Sea. We cried aloud to the Lord, and he put a cloud and darkness between us and the Egyptians, and he brought the sea on them and covered them. Your eyes have seen all that the Lord did in the land of Egypt, and you were in the wilderness many days. He brought us into the land of the Amorites that lived beyond the Jordan, and the Lord delivered them into our hands, and you inherited their land, and completely destroyed them from before you. Balak, king of Moab, son of Zippor, rose, and made war against Israel, and sent and called Balaam to curse us. But Lord the god would not destroy you, and he greatly blessed us, and rescued us out of their hands, and delivered them to us. You crossed across the Jordan and came to Jericho, and the inhabitants of Jericho fought against us, the Amorites, Canaanites, Perizzites, Mitanni, Jebusites, Cypriots, and Girgasite, but the Lord delivered them into our hands. He sent out hornets before you, and he drove them out from before you, all twelve kings of the Amorites, not with your sword, nor with your bow."

"He gave you a land on which you did not labor and cities which you did not build, and you were settled in them. You eat of vineyards and olive yards which you did not plant. Now fear the Lord, and serve him in righteousness and justice, and remove the strange gods, which our fathers served beyond the river, and in Egypt, and serve the Lord. But if it does not seem good to you to serve the Lord, choose for yourselves today who you will serve, whether the gods of your fathers that were on the other side of the river, or the gods of the Amorites, among whose land you live in, but I and my house will serve the Lord, for he is holy."

The people answered and said, "Far be it from us to forsake the Lord, to serve other gods. Lord the god, he is God. He brought us and our fathers out from Egypt and protected us along the roads on which we walked, and among all the nations through which we passed. The Lord threw out the Amorites and all the nations that inhabited the land from before us. Yes, we will serve the Lord, for he is our god."

Joshua said to the people, "Indeed you will not be able to serve the Lord, for God is holy, and he being jealous will not forgive your sins and your transgressions. Whenever you will forsake the Lord and serve other gods, then he will come on you and afflict you, and consume you, because he has done good for you."

The people said to Joshua, "No, but we will serve the Lord."

Joshua said to the people, "You are witnesses against yourselves, that you have chosen the Lord to serve him. Now take away the strange gods that are among you, and set your heart right towards Lord the god of Israel."

The people replied to Joshua, "We will serve the Lord, and we will listen to his voice."

So Joshua made a covenant with the people on that day and gave them a law and an ordinance in Shiloh before the tabernacle of the God of Israel. He wrote these words in the book of the laws of God. Joshua took a great stone and set it up under the turpentine tree before the Lord. Joshua said to the people, "Look, this stone will be among you as a witness, for it has heard all the words that have been spoken to it by the Lord. He has spoken to you today, and this stone will be among you as a witness in the last days, whenever you will deal falsely with Lord the god."

Joshua dismissed the people, and they went every man to his place. It happened after these things that Joshua the son of Nun the servant of the Lord died, at the age of a hundred and ten years. They buried him by the borders of his inheritance in Timnath Serah on Mount Ephraim, north of Mount Gilead. There they put with him into the tomb in which they buried him, the knives of stone with which he circumcised the Israelites at the circle, when he brought them out of Egypt, as the Lord appointed them, and there they are to this day.

Israel served the Lord all the days of Joshua and all the days of the elders that lived as long as Joshua, and all that knew all the works of the Lord which he worked for Israel. The Israelites brought up the bones of Joseph out of Egypt, and buried them in Shechem, in the portion of the land which Jacob bought of the Amorites who lived in Shechem for a hundred ewe-lambs, and he gave it to Joseph for a portion. It happened afterward that Eleazar the high-priest the son of Aaron died and was buried in the hill of Phinehas his son, which he gave him on Mount Ephraim.

On that day the Israelites took the box of God and carried it around among them, and Phinehas exercised the priest's office in place of Eleazar his father until he died, and he was buried in his own place Gabaar, but the Israelites departed every one to their place, and to their own city, and the Israelites worshiped Asherah and Astarte,[1] and the gods of the nations around them, and the Lord delivered them into the hands of Eglom king of Moab and he ruled over them eighteen years.[2]

# Joshua: Chapter 24 Notes

**1** Codex Vaticanus: Astartên cae Astarôth (ᴀᴄᴛᴀρᴛʜɴκᴀɪ ᴀᴄᴛᴀρⲱⲑ). Translation: Asherah and Astarte

This verse, is not found in the Masoretic text. The two goddesses mentioned are the wives of El from the Ugaritic Texts: Åṯrt (𐎀𐎘𐎗𐎚), later called Asherah (אשרה) by the Israelites; and Ôṯtrt-ym (𐎓𐎘𐎚𐎗𐎚𐎊𐎎), later called Ôštrt (𐤏𐤔𐤕𐤓𐤕) by the Phoenicians, Astarte (Ἀστάρτη) by the Greeks, and Ashtoret (עַשְׁתֹּרֶת) by the Israelites. The names in the Septuagint are transliterations of the Aramaic names, not the Greek names, indicating that they were in the Aramaic version of Joshua. The more common English names are used.

**2** This verse is not found in the Masoretic text, indicating that the Septuagint's Joshua was made from a Samaritan text, and not a Judahite text, as Eglom king of Moab only conquered Gilead and Samaria, not Judah or Edom.

# Forward to Judges

It is generally accepted that there were several versions of Judges written in Samaritan, Judahite, and Aramaic before the translation of the Septuagint. Fragments of the book of Judges have been found among the dead sea scrolls, however, only in the Assyrian script of the Hasmonean Dynasty, and dated to between 140 and 37 BC.

The God of the book of Judges in the Septuagint is called 'the Lord the god' (τον Κύριον τὸν θεὸν), or simplified to 'the Lord' (τοῦ Κυρίου). These terms are mirrored in the Masoretic version of Judges with 'the Yehwah god' (אֶת־יְהוָה אֱלֹהֵי), and the name Yhvah (יהוה). One explanation for the difference between the texts is the Christian redaction of the 3rd century AD, when the name Iaô (Ιαω) was removed from the Septuagint, replaced by Lord (Κύριοσ). Fragments of older Septuagint manuscripts still exist that contain the name Iaô (Ιαω), transliterated from the Aramaic Yhw (יהו^), however, none of the fragments of the Book of Judges include the name. The name Yhwh (יהוה) is found in a couple of fragments of Judges found among the Dead Sea Scrolls, however, they date to the Hasmonean dynasty, and therefore date to over 85 years after the Septuagint's version of Judges was translated.

The Aramaic sections of Masoretic Daniel that were not translated into Hebrew maintain the term adonai ha'elohim (אֲדֹנָי הָאֱלֹהִים), meaning the 'Lord the gods' where the Septuagint has 'Lord the god' (Κύριον τὸν θεὸν), however, the Hebrew sections have Yehwah elohim (יְהוָה אֱלֹהִים) where the Septuagint has 'Lord the god,' suggesting the Greek more accurately reflects the Aramaic source texts than the Hebrew translation. According to some records from the time, this was to repair the damage King

Manasseh had done 600 years earlier when he removed the name Yhwh from the Israelite Texts, however, no evidence has survived from the era of Manasseh or earlier that proves the name was originally in the text, suggesting it was an attempt by the first Hasmonean High-Priest/King Simon the Zealot to create a national Judean religion with a god having a name similar to the Roman god Jove.

The Greek terms in the Septuagint's Judges are translations of well-known terms related to Canaanite god El, the Canaanite creator-god. El translates in Canaanite, Aramaic, and Hebrew as 'God,' and was the primary god worshiped in ancient Canaan in the era Abraham, Isaac, and Jacob were reported to have passed through the area. El was also the patron god of the Temple of El, built by Jacob near the modern city of Nablus in the Palestinian West Bank, which featured in many of the early Hebrew scriptures before Samaria was conquered by the Assyrian Empire.

In the Book of Micah, the Temple of El was referred to as Jacob's Temple of El, which confirms that the Israelites in the 8th century BC considered the Temple of El at Shiloh to be the Temple of El that Jacob built in Genesis chapter 35. In Judges, the Temple of El in Shechem is called the fortified Temple of the God of the Covenant, and the Temple of the Lord of the Covenant in both the Septuagint and the Masoretic text, which supports the identification of El with the covenant in the early Israelite religion.

The Book of Judges also includes many other gods, which the ancient Israelites are repeatedly accused of worshiping, including Ba'al, Asherah, and the Lords (Baalim) and Ashteroths of the Canaanites. Several of the Canaanite gods are mentioned incidentally, such as the fertility god Lord Lahem, the god of dusk Lord Shalim, the solar-god Lord Shemesh, and the grain-god Dagon. All these gods are part of the old Canaanite religion, in which El (God) and his wife Asherah (commonly called Qetesh) were the parents of the Canaanite gods. The term ba'al translates as lord, however, when used as a name, it generally represented Lord Hadad, the storm god of the Ba'al Cycle literature of the ancient Ugaritic texts in ancient Canaan. The Ugaritic Texts continued to be used well into the era of the ancient kingdoms of Samaria and Judah, as the prophet Jeremiah quoted them circa 630 BC. Additionally, the name of the Egyptian god Aten appears to have been in the Book of Judges before Aten was forgotten as a god. The name appears twice, once in the Song of Deborah, in chapter 5, and later as part of the name of a town in chapter 12:

> "You who move as Aten the sun god at midday, sitting in judgment, and following the path, and riding the pathway, declare from the noise of disturbers among the drawers of water, and retell the righteous acts of the Lord. Increase righteous acts in Israel, then the people of the Lord will go down to the cities."

> "After him, Abdon the son of Hillel, a Per-Atenite, judged Israel. He had forty sons, and thirty grandsons, that rode on seventy colts, and he judged Israel eight years. Abdon the son of Hillel, the Per-Atenite, died and was buried in Per-Aten in the land of Ephraim in the mountains of Amalek."

In both cases, a word that appears to be a transliteration of Aten survives in the Masoretic text, although is considered an unknown term, and has been viewed that way for thousands of years. The Book of Judges contains more unknown terms than any other book in the Masoretic text and the most archaic form of Canaanite other than in the Book of Job. Judges is considered by most biblical scholars to be the oldest book in the Masoretic text, composed earlier than the surviving versions of the Torah, or Joshua.

Nevertheless, the version in the Masoretic text still suffers from the damage done by the Hasmonean dynasty and therefore does not align with the recorded history of the Egyptians, Assyrians, or Babylonians, causing many historians to consider it to be a collection of very ancient fictional stories. On the other hand, the Septuagint's version of Exodus, Joshua, and Judges, contain a different chronology from the Masoretic text, covering 460 years from the time of the Exodus, circa 1550 BC, to the era of chaos that started in 1090 BC, and would later end in 1037 BC when Saul became the first king of the independent Kingdom of Israel.

Saul was not the first king of the Israelites, as Abimelech had previously been recognized as King of Israel a couple of centuries earlier. Abimelech's reign had only been for three years and seems to have only controlled the region around Shechem, the city that would later become the capital of Saul's Israel. This earlier attempt at an independent kingdom took place between 1267 and 1264 BC, according to the Septuagint, at the same time that the Egyptian records report that King Ramesses II had lost control over Canaan. The fact that the Egyptians dominated Canaan throughout the era of the Judges is not in doubt; Egyptian, Babylonian, Assyrian, and Nesite records all confirm this, as do the archaeological ruins of Egyptian cities spread through the region. The curious thing is that they are not mentioned in the book of Judges.

There is a reference to what appears to be a transliteration of 'Egypt' found in the Masoretic text, however, it is for some reason assumed to be a village called 'Egypt' somewhere in Canaan. Like one of the earlier references to Aten, this reference to 'Egypt' is found in the Song of Deborah, in chapter 5:

> "My mighty mind will trample him down. When the hoofs of the horse were entangled, his mighty ones earnestly rushed to curse Southern Egypt. Curse it," said the messenger of the lord.

The place that was cursed in this verse is generally transliterated as Meroz from the Masoretic text, which is not new, as the Greeks transliterated it as Mêrôz (Μηρωζ) circa 225 BC, and Lucian of Antioch transliterated it as Marôz (Μαρωζ) circa 300 AD.

The question of what Meroz was, has resulted in a great deal of speculation. The commentary in the Talmud (Moed Katan 16a) claims that Meroz is a planet that refused to help the Israelites in their time of trouble, however, the name Meroz does not correlate with the Semitic name of any planet in this star system, and was likely an error based on the misidentification of the Latin name of the planet Mars during the Roman era. In the later school of Merkabah mysticism, Meroz became a class of angels that lived on the planet Meroz who refused to help the Israelites, instead of the planet itself, meaning in modern terms, Yahweh was cursing a group of extraterrestrials.

Modern scholarship has focused on the idea that there was a village in Israel called Misr, which is the Arabic name for Egypt. This village of Egyptians would then have been the focus of the curse, however, there is no known village called Misr dating to that time period, nor an explanation for the Arabic name. There is a village called Misr in northern modern Israel, however, it appears to have been founded much later.

The connection between Meroz and Misr is generally based on the assumption that Meroz (מרוז) was a scribal error, a transcription error of Misr (מצר), however, it is difficult to see how that could have happened. Egypt was known as ᵐᵃᵗMuṣru (𒆳𒈬𒋔𒊒) in Akkadian, Miṣriâi (𒆳𒈬𒌅𒊑) in Babylonian, Mṣrm (𐎎𐎕𐎗𐎎) in Ugaritic, Mṣryn (𐡌𐡑𐡓𐡍) in Aramaic, Miṣrayim (מִצְרַיִם) in Hebrew, and Miṣr (مِضر) in Arabic. The Mycenaean Greeks also used the adopted Semitic name as Misarajo (𐀖𐀩). None of the known variants of the Semitic name of Egypt are a close match to

Meroz/Maroz, however, the Egyptian name Marēs, is almost phonetically identical.

Mâôresi (𓇋𓇋𓃀𓈖) was an ancient Egyptian name for Southern Egypt, which translates as approximately 'Southern Place.' It continued to be used until the Classical era, when it was spelled as Marēs (Ⲙⲁⲣⲏⲥ) in Coptic, the Classical form of Egyptian. The exact pronunciation of ancient Egyptian names is debated before the development of the Demotic script in the early Iron Age, and therefore it cannot be known how the Egyptians pronounced Mares during the era of Deborah, however, it is documented in Demotic as being Mâôrs (𐦠/𐦣), supporting the New Kingdom era pronunciation as being very similar to the term used by Deborah.

Nevertheless, the Song of Deborah does not curse a 'village of Meroz,' but 'Meroz' itself, meaning Southern Egypt. Meroz is cursed for not sending troops to help the Israelites during the era when King Jabin of Hazor was dominating the land, which according to the timeline of the Septuagint was a 20 year period between 1334 and 1314 BC. This was the era between the collapse of Egyptian power at the end of the Amarna Period, and the resurgence of Egyptian power under Pharaoh Horemheb. At the time, the capital of the Egyptian Empire was in Thebes, the capital of southern Egypt.

The Amarna Period, as Egyptologists call it, is the era when Pharaoh Amenhotep IV changed his name to Akhenaten, moved the capital of Egypt to a new city he built called Amarna, and instituted a national religion in Egypt today called Atenism. Under his rule, the various temples of the old gods of Egypt were systematically shut down, and a new national priesthood was created focused on the one god that all Egyptians could see every day, the sun, then known as Aten. His reign left the Empire in chaos, and when he died in 1336 BC, the empire rapidly shifted between the Pharaohs Smenkhkare (1335-1334 BC), Neferneferu-aten (1334-1332 BC), and Tutankhamen (1334-1325 BC). Pharaoh Tutankhamen was a boy when he assumed the throne, and the real power at the time appears to have Ay, who would later become Pharaoh himself after Tutankhamen's young death left no heirs. Tutankhamen and Ay restored the priesthoods of the old gods, and abandoned Amarna, returning the imperial capital to Thebes. The priesthood of Aten quickly faded away, and Aten disappeared from the list of Egyptian gods, forgotten entirely until Egyptologists rediscovered him in the late 1800s. Ay ruled for just over a decade (1332-1319 BC), and managed to restore some semblance of normality to Upper and Lower Egypt, however, Kush and Canaan remained in chaos until Horemheb (1319-1292 BC) reestablished Egyptian control early in his reign.

This matches what is recorded in the book of Judges, where 80 years of peace under the Judges Ehud and Shamgar ended in 1334 BC when King Jabin of Hazor seized control of Canaan, supported by the Chief-of-the-army Siazara, who lived in the Forge-of-the-Foreigners, and commanded a force of 900 iron chariots. Based on both the Canaanite texts and Egyptian records Jabin was a common Canaanite name, however, Siazara appears to be the Egyptian name Siazårô (⟨𓂝𓄿𓇋𓋴𓇳⟩), meaning 'recognized son of Ra.' This specific name would have denoted a king from either southern Egypt or Nubia, however, Siazara is otherwise unknown from regal records, suggesting he attempted to seize control of the empire after Akhenaten died, however, ultimately failed, and was left out of the regal history of Egypt.

The 900 iron chariots are generally assumed to be an exaggeration, or a flat lie by scholars studying the book of Judges, as no petty Canaanite chieftain could have raised a force of 900 chariots at that time, and iron was generally not in use by armies until much later, after 1200 BC. This is, however, not exactly true. Tutankhamen was buried with an iron dagger in 1325 BC, and that dagger was of very high quality. Modern analysis indicates it may have been meteoric iron, however, it may have simply been made of the iron-nickel residue produced from the gold smelting in southeast Egypt.

Iron smelting was in use across the ancient world by the era of the Amarna Period, including in Anatolia, where the Hattic civilization had been smelting iron since at least 2500 BC, and in Uttar Pradesh, in India, where iron had been smelted since at least 1800 BC, however, in Egypt the high-quality iron-nickel weapons and jewelry found by Egyptologists are believed to have been made from the residue of gold smelting and bronze production. The gold mines of southeast Egypt produced a gold-silver ore with trace amounts of iron and nickel, which the Egyptians may have called djôm (𓇋𓅓𓏏).

Djôm is commonly translated as 'electrum' by Egyptologists, however, was recorded as a metal that the New Kingdom era Egyptians made weapons from, including chariots. The translation of djôm as 'electrum' is not new, the Classical era Greeks didn't know what djôm was either, and translated the word as electon (ἤλεκτρον), the name of a mythical metal that shone like the sun. As the early European Egyptologists knew little about Egyptian mineralogy, they adopted the term as 'electrum,' however, it is unlikely that the Egyptians would have built their weapons out of a soft metal, like gold, or a valuable metal, like gold, and no gold-silver alloy weapons have ever been found, suggesting that djôm was in fact the iron-nickel metal residue left over when the gold and silver was smelted from the gold ore.

The fact that the Egyptian General Siazara was stationed at a place called the Forge-of-the-Foreigners, implies the Egyptians were using something they had conquered from a group of foreigners to build the iron chariots he was reported to have had. The term Forge-of-the-Foreigners, is, unfortunately, not usually translated, but transliterated in most Bibles, and therefore the meaning of the name is lost. This is not a new practice, as the Greeks transliterated the name as Arisôth tôn ethnôn (Αρισωθ των εθνων), meaning: Arisoth of Nations. The Masoretic text contain charoshet haggovyim (חֲרֹשֶׁת הַגּוֹיִם), which translates as 'The forge of the gentiles' or 'The forge of the foreigners,' however, this is generally transliterated as Harosheth Hagoyim, or partially translated as Harosheth of the Gentiles.

The Egyptians themselves are known to have produced smelted iron since at least the Old Kingdom era as a by-product of gold and bronze production, however, the quantities were very minimal, and the value of the iron produced was greater than the value of gold until the New Kingdom era.

Iron was used in Egypt in greater quantities during the Hyksos Dynasty, however, an iron industry never became established in Egypt under their rule, indicating they were using one or more forges in Canaan to produce their iron weaponry. One iron smelting site is known from the New Kingdom era, Site 200, in the Timna Valley, in Jordan, however, it is unclear if it was in use during the Hyksos Dynasty. The main reason that iron production was never established in Egypt under the Hyksos, was because the source of iron that would later be used in the Late Period was in the mountains of southern Egypt, near the gold mines, which the Hyksos never gained control over, however, there was likely also another reason.

Even after iron became the primary metal being used across the Middle East and the Mediterranean, between 1200 and 1000 BC, the Egyptians did not widely adopt it, instead, continuing to develop better forms of bronze that could compete with iron. This did not end until the Empire of Kush conquered the Egyptians, and instituted wide-scale iron production between 744 and 656 BC.

By the time the Kushites conquered Egypt, Egypt was centuries behind the metallurgical technology of its neighbors. There is no obvious political or religious reason for Egypt having not adopted iron a thousand years earlier, implying an economic reason, likely an agreement between bronze working guilds that dated back thousands of years to the Old Kingdom or earlier. The Egyptians did not accept change easily, and it appears neither the Hyksos, who conquered them from Canaan nor the Libyans who later conquered them from the Sahara could convince them to implement iron production. Unlike the previous invaders, the Kushites did not depend on their conquest for economic stability as Kush provided all the food and iron they needed to rule their empire. Under the pressure of having to compete with Kushite metallurgists, the Egyptians finally acquiesced, and Egypt finally joined the iron age.

The Forge-of-the-Foreigners referred to in the Judges, was most likely a forge left over from the Hyksos dynasty, some-where along the Kishion river, in northern Israel. The alliance between the renegade King Jabin and Egyptian General Siazara, which in the Septuagint's chronology seized control of Canaan in 1334 BC, a year when Egypt had three pharaohs: Smenkhkare, Neferneferuaten, and Tutankhamen, implies that Siazara and his army did not accept any of the Pharaohs as legitimate. If Siazara's name was any indicator, he was a Ra worshiper, and as the worship of Ra had been banned by Akenaten, he likely saw the bond between the monarchy and the gods as having been severed, meaning the entire royal family would have been invalidated. This view could only have been validated by meeting Tutankhamen himself, as the boy was the product of generations of inbreeding, and suffered from several hereditary diseases. Even as a child, he could not walk without a cane. His young death, at 18 years of age, has been a matter of wide debate, with historians once having accused Ay of assassinating him. Based on the study of his remains, it appears he died of natural causes related to his genetic diseases.

According to Judges, an Israelite named Barak defeated Siazara and restored peace to Canaan in 1314 BC, when Deborah sang her song that referred to the sun as Aten, implying that the Israelites had remained loyal to the Egyptian monarchy throughout the insurrection of Jabin and Siazara. This would have been five years into the reign of Horemheb, when Egypt restored control over southern Canaan, however, did so without using the Egyptian military. The exact means that Horemheb used has traditionally been a mystery within Egyptology, however, the Book of Judges states it was the Israelites themselves that restored Egyptian control over the region, as Barak became the judge of Israel after defeating Siazara, and the land was peaceful for 40 years, until 1274 BC, which was the same year that Ramesses II marched his army north to attack the Nesite Empire according to Egyptologists.

The synchronizations between the Book of Judges and the records of Egypt are far too many to be overlooked or ignored. As almost all denominations of Christians and Jews agree that King Saul established his kingdom in 1037 BC, and the Septuagint's version of Judges includes 460 years of the land being ruled by

Judges, or foreign kings, followed by an era of chaos when there was no king, the latest possible date the Exodus could have taken place was the 1500s BC, which supports the idea that the 10 plagues of Egypt were descriptions of the fallout and effects of the Minoan eruption which Egyptologists date to 1550 BC. According to Joshua, 42 years later the Israelites invaded Samaria, (northern modern Israel and the Palestinian West Bank) under the leadership of Joshua, which would have been 1508 BC. The plan was already laid out in the Book of Joshua to occupy the entire land of Canaan, yet just three years later, when Joshua was 85 years old, the Israelites stopped their campaign, after having only occupied the cities in Samaria, this would have been in 1505 BC.

The reason they stopped their invasion is not given, however, Egyptian records do explain it, as in the same year, 1505 BC, Pharaoh Thutmose I marched his army through Canaan to reconquer it for the Egyptian Empire. It had previously been under the control of the Hyksos Dynasty whose empire collapsed in the aftermath of the Minoan eruption. In 1550 BC, the Hyksos capital fell to the rival southern dynasty of Pharaoh Ahmose I, and the Hyksos retreated to their fortress of Sharuhen, near modern Gaza in the Palestinian Gaza Strip. This suggests the Hyksos maintained control over Canaan until Sharuhen fell to Ahmose I in 1540 BC. Ahmose I led an invasion of southern Canaan a few years later in an attempt to root out any remaining Hyksos. Egyptologists are not sure when this campaign was, placing it sometime between 1537 and 1527 BC. This campaign is not believed to have reached farther north than Byblos, in modern Lebanon, and did not result in any long-term political control over Canaan. Ahmose I's main goal seems to have been to destroy any remaining Hyksos in the region to ensure they did not try to recapture Egypt.

# FORWARD TO JUDGES

For decades after the conquest of Avaris, the new 18ᵗʰ Dynasty struggled to control Egypt, with numerous insurrections reported in the Nile Delta and Nubia, and does not appear to have tried to re-exert control over Canaan until Thutmose I's armies occupied the region in 1505 BC. Thutmose I marched his army all the way north to the Euphrates River in Syria, and reported all the peoples of Canaan surrendered to him without conflict, he then returned to Egypt and marched his army south to Nubia to suppress an insurrection there later that year. This means his army was only briefly in Canaan and did not have time to conquer any of the cities there, so either they did surrender without conflict, or, he lied. While the Book of Judges does not mention the Egyptian army passing through, this seems to have been redacted at a later point, as Joshua did stop his campaign in 1505 BC, and did not declare himself king, instead taking the subservient role of judge. Joshua's becoming a judge, means he ruled over a group of people but was under the authority of a king. The people were obviously the Israelites, and the king could only have been Thutmose I. This is an anticlimactic end to the tail of escape from Egypt and was likely redacted during the era of the two kingdoms when Egypt was again a foreign enemy.

According to Judges, Joshua judged the Israelites until he was 110 years old and then died in what would have been 1480 BC, following which Kushan Rishatayim ruled the Israelites. While the Hebrew term Kush (כּוּשׁ) referred to the land of Kush, south of Egypt, whose people were known as the Kushi (כּוּשִׁי), Kushan (כּוּשׁן) was a different term, which the Greeks did not recognize, and therefore transliterated it as Chousa (Χουσα). As the term referred to someone who was the king in the rivers of Aram (Syria), the origin of the word was almost certainly Kasium (𒅗𒀸𒋗), today translated as Kassite. The Kassites were the rulers of Babylonia in the late bronze age from some time in the

1500s BC, until 1155 BC, when they were conquered by the Elamites.

The Hebrew term rishatayim (רִשְׁעָתַיִם) is not proper Hebrew, Canaanite, or Aramaic, however, may be a the ancient Canaanite spelling of the name of king Parshatatar (𒉺𒅕𒊭𒋫𒋫𒅈), king of the Mitanni Empire circa 1485 BC. Parshatatar is recorded as occupying northern Canaan during the reign of Hatsheput by establishing a series of puppet states across the region, and gaining access to the Mediterranean Sea.

In circa 1479 BC, the Egyptian king Thutmose II died, and his former queen Hatsheput seized the throne in the name of his two year old son Thutmose III. Hatsheput was not the mother of Thutmose III, another wife Iset was, whom Hatsheput married after officially changing her sex to male. After changing genders Hatsheput declared himself to be Thutmose III's regent, although later assumed the role of king himself until his death, when Thutmose III inherited the throne. While Hatsheput was a very unpopular king, his rule established the dominant architectural style of the New Kingdom.

The entire concept of a female king was rejected by many, with graffiti mocking King Hatsheput's gender appearing in the archaeological record of the era. Most of Kush appears to have rejected Hatsheput, and rebelled against his rule. After inheriting the throne in circa 1458 BC, Thutmose III attempted to erase Hatsheput's rule from Egyptian records, claiming to have ruled continuously from the death of Thutmose II in circa 1479 BC. While her role as queen of Thutmose II was never erased, the era when Hatsheput ruled Egypt was, and his era as king was not rediscovered until the 1800s.

It is clear that there was a rebellion against King Hatsheput in Syria, backed by the Mitanni, and control of all territory north of Megiddo was lost, as the first thing Thutmose III did after assuming the throne was march north into Canaan, where he fought the battle of Megiddo against the rebelling Syrian kings, and their Mitanni allies. The Battle of Megiddo was the largest battle recorded in Egyptian records up until that time, with both the Egyptians and Canaanite rebels estimated to have fielded around 1,000 chariots and 10,000 infantry. After defeating the Canaanites in the initial battle, the Egyptians plundered 924 chariots and 200 suits of armor. The Canaanite kings fell back to the fortified city of Kadesh, which the Egyptians then besieged for seven months. According to the records at Karnak, when the city surrendered the Egyptians captured 340 Canaanite and Mitanni princes, 2,041 mares, 191 foals, 6 stallions, 924 chariots, 200 suits of armor, 502 bows, 1,929 cattle, and 22,500 sheep.

Between 1458 and 1425 BC, Thutmose III fought a series of campaigns in Canaan, pushing Egyptian control north to the Euphrates River, and then crossed it into the Mitanni empire, where he plundered the country, which apparently had not rebuilt its defenses after the loss at Megiddo. After securing Canaan, Thutmose III marched his army south into Nubia, recapturing territory as far as the fourth cataract, all of which had been lost under the rule of Hatsheput.

It is unclear why the author would have referred to Parshatatar as a Kassite unless it was actually written at the time. The Mitanni rulers are often linked to the Kassites culturally, however, the peoples they ruled were not culturally similar. During the wars of Thutmose III in Canaan, the term Mitanni become common, however, earlier records simply called the land Naharin, meaning 'Rivers,' and called the people Hurrians. While the Hurrians were the primary population of the Mitanni Empire, the rulers were an unrelated group of Indo-Aryans, who spoke a language similar to Sanskrit, and worshiped the Vedic gods. They appear to have seized power over the Hurrians in the Khabur river region in the 1550s BC, from which they expanded in every direction until the Battle of Megiddo.

The Mitanni relationship with the Kassites is unclear, as the Kassites are not viewed as being Indo-Aryans, however, may have been Hurrians. The two cultures were close at the time, and it is plausible that the earliest Mitanni to arrive in the region were viewed as being Kassites by the Canaanites. Nevertheless, by 1457 BC the term would have already been anachronistic, as the term Mitanni would have replaced it, suggesting this verse was written between 1472 and 1457 BC.

In Judges, after the Kassite Parshatatar was deposed, the land was peaceful for 40 years under Judge Othniel, which would have been between 1472 and 1432 BC. This era corresponds to the reign of the Kings Hatsheput (1479-1458 BC) and Thutmose III (1458-1425 BC). Thutmose III fought 17 campaigns in northern Canaan during the era, however, southern Canaan appears to have been peaceful throughout most of the era under the protection of the Egyptian army.

According to Judges, this era of peace in southern Canaan ended in 1432 BC when Eglon the king of Moab conquered the Israelites east of the Jordan River. These Israelites appear to have never been under Egyptian governance, and the war east of the Jordan appears to have been separate from, yet inspired by the general insurrection against Egypt in northern Canaan. This conquest of the eastern Israelites by Eglon the Moabite is referred to at the end of Joshua, right after the death of Joshua, implying the book of Joshua originated with the eastern tribes, who lived in peace between 1480 and 1432 BC. After 18 years of domination by the Moabites, King Eglon was killed by an Israelite named Ehud, which began a period of 80 years of peace, during which Eglon and then Shamgar were the Judges of Israel. This time span would have been 1414 to 1334 BC, ending when the Egyptian monarchical power collapsed at the end of the Amarna period, and King Jabin of Hazor and General Siazara rebelled.

After Jabin and Siazara were defeated the land had another peaceful era of forty years under Judge Barak, who had defeated Siazara. Barak's wife was the prophet Deborah, to whom the Song of Deborah is attributed. The Song of Deborah, which is chapter 5 of Judges, is generally considered by scholars to be the oldest piece of Israelite literature to survive more or less intact to the present. While Barak was the leader who defeated the army of Siazara, it was Jael, the wife of Eber the blacksmith who killed Siazara after taking him to her bed-chamber and then driving a stake through his temple.

The significance of the blacksmiths in Judges is often also over-looked, as the word blacksmith is generally transliterated as Kenite, implying a tribe. This is not a new practice, as the Greeks did the same thing when they translated the Septuagint, translit-erating the Hebrew word for blacksmith: qêni (קֵינִ) as Cinaeou (Κιναιου). The significance of the metal-smiths, especially iron-smiths, which is what the word qêni likely meant in Judges, was lost in the millennium between the age of Deborah, and the age of the Ptolemies, likely because by then metallurgy was universal, including iron-working. These 'Kenites' were so significant at the time, that even Moses appears to have married his daughter to one, named Jobab. This story has been lost, however, the refer-ence to Jobab the 'groom of Moses' has survived in both the Septu-agint and Masoretic text.

# FORWARD TO JUDGES

The connection between Siazara's army being based at the Forge-of-the-Foreigners, and him being killed by the wife of a blacksmith cannot be ignored. The fact that he was listed as commanding 900 iron war-chariots also cannot be overlooked, as that would have been a major division within the Egyptian army at the time, and likely the entire Egyptian army stationed in Canaan.

After the defeat of Siazara and Jabin, Judges states that the land was peaceful for 40 years under Judge Barak, which would have been between 1314 and 1274 BC. This era of peace ended when the Midianites, Amalekites, and the 'sons of the east' conquered the Israelites in 1274 BC. 1274 BC is also the year that Egyptologists claim that Pharaoh Ramesses II launched his disastrous First Syrian Campaign. The Egyptian army was soundly defeated by the Nesites, allowing nomadic groups like the Amalakites and Midianites to plunder Canaan as described in the Book of Judges. The 'sons of the East' in the Book of Judges are likely none other than the Nesites, commonly misidentified as Hittites, as they came from the region north of the Euphrates, which while being geographic nonsense in the modern mindset, was considered to be the east by the ancient Canaanites, as one had to head north to the Euphrates before heading east into Mesopotamia. It's likely the Israelites did not know where exactly the Nesites were from and assumed it was the east in Mesopotamia, like the Babylonians and Assyrians.

According to Judges, the Midianites ruled Israel for 7 years, between 1274 and 1267 BC, however, it is not clear if these Israelites were east or west of the Jordan, and therefore, they may not have been the Israelites in Egyptian-ruled Canaan. Ramesses II's Second Syrian Campaign, in 1273 BC was equally disastrous, and his army was defeated again, although did make it to the outskirts of Kadesh. His Third Syrian Campaign, in 1271 BC, was focused on reconsolidating Egyptian authority outside of Nesite-controlled areas, and he marched his army from city to city in Canaan demanding tribute. Cities that offered tribute were considered loyal to Egypt, and left alone, while those that refused were sacked. Edom, Seir, Moab, Jerusalem, Jericho, Heshbon, and Damascus are all listed as cities or lands that were visited by the army, although it is not clear which were loyal and which were sacked.

In 1270 and 1267 BC, Ramesses II's armies marched against Kadesh again and managed to drive the Nesites from the region. The Book of Judges claims that the Shechemite leader Abimelech defeated the Midianites and their Amakaite and Nesite (sons of the East) allies in 1267 BC, and became the King of Israel, however, his kingdom appears to have been rejected by most Israelites, and he was described in the Book of Judges as a real bastard, the son of a prostitute. His kingdom only lasted 3 years, until 1264 BC, when the other Israelites under the leadership of Judge Tola overthrew him.

There were 23 peaceful years under Judge Tola, followed by 22 under Judge Jair, which would have been between 1264 and 1219 BC. During this era, King Ramesses was focused on defending Egypt from a naval power called the 'Sea Peoples' by Egyptologists. It is unclear where they were based, however, Sardinia and Greece are the two dominant theories. Ramesses signed a peace treaty with the Nesite King Hattusili III in 1258 BC, and Canaan does appear to have been peaceful throughout the era of Judges Tola and Jair. During that era, Ramesses built a series of forts along the Mediterranean coast of modern Egypt, for the first time in recorded history attempting to protect the desert-routes from the invasions of these Sea Peoples.

# FORWARD TO JUDGES

This peaceful era in southern Canaan ended abruptly in 1219 BC according to Judges, when the Pelesets and Ammonites seized control of the region. Egyptian records depict this as a time of great unrest, as the war with the Sea Peoples was still going on, and Ramesses II died in 1213 BC, after being Pharaoh for 66 years. In 1208 and 1207 BC, the Sea People launched a major invasion of Egypt, and control of the Nile Delta was briefly lost. Pharaoh Merneptah (1213-1203 BC) appears to have negotiated an agreement with the Sea Peoples in 1207 BC which allowed them to settle in Canaan if they returned the Nile Delta, and the following year, 1206 BC, Canaanite towns and tribes were listed in open revolt against Egyptian authority, with the list of rebels including Gaza, Ashkelon, Yenoam, Israel, and the Arameans. It is unclear what level of authority the Egyptian New Kingdom exerted over Canaan after 1206 BC, however, the Book of Judges reports that Judge Jephthah defeated the Moabites in 1201 BC, and judged the Israelites for 6 years. He was followed by the judges Ibzan, Elon, and Abdon, who judged the Israelites until 1170 BC when the Pelesets (also called Philistines or Palestinians) seized control of southern Canaan.

This occupation of southern Canaan by the Pelesets, recorded in Judges, is also recorded by the Egyptians, carved into the walls of the mortuary temple of Pharaoh Ramesses III at Medinet Habu. According to the Egyptian records from the era, several groups of Sea Peoples attacked Egypt in waves between 1179 and 1174 BC, including groups known as the Peleset, Denyen, Shardana. Peleset is the Egyptian name for the Pelesets, while the Denyen are believed to have been the Danoi tribe of ancient Greece, and the Shardana were the Egyptians' main antagonists of the previous century, generally thought to have been Sardinians.

These attacks during the reign of Ramesses III were the worst Egypt had seen, with allied over land attacks by the Meshwesh tribes of Libya, and the Tjekker, a group of Sea Peoples that had occupied and fortified the town of Dor, on the northern coast of modern Israel a few decades earlier. While Ramesses III's records report that he graciously allowed the Pelesets to live in southern Canaan after he defeated them, it appears that all his forces could do was defend the Nile Delta, and the Pelesets captured Egypt's northern-most territory.

Based on the records in Judges, the Israelites recognized the authority of the Pelests in 1170 BC, four years after their last battle against Egypt. This appears to have been the end of the New Kingdom's authority in southern Canaan, however, after 40 years of Peleset rule, Samson rose as a Judge of Israel under Peleset rule. He was described as judging Israel for 20 years during the Peleset era, before leading a failed revolt against them and being captured by his favorite prostitute. After Samson's heroic suicide, the Book of Judges indicates that his father Manoah judged Israel for another 20 years, before the era of chaos, when there was no king.

This era of chaos in Canaan would have begun in 1090 BC, shortly before the same thing happened in Egypt in 1077 BC. Egyptologists call this the Third Intermediate Period, as there are few records from the era. In Greece, where civilization collapsed at approximately the same time, it would later be called the Dark Age, which then inspired the name of the Dark Age that followed the collapse of the Roman Empire in Western Europe. During this Dark Age of ancient Canaan, the book of Judges records that there was no king, however, a lot did happen during this era implying it lasted several decades. During this era, the Danites conquered Laish and renamed it Dan, and the Benjamite genocide took place. The Danites had been described as living on boats until this era, which some modern historians have taken as evidence that they were new arrivals in Canaan, likely related to the Danoi tribe of Greece. This is most likely not correct, as the name Dan appears in many ancient Canaanite texts, and appears to have been common in ancient Canaan.

The Benjaminite genocide was a strange story set in this era as well and likely tied to the downfall of Lord Lahem, the fertility god of ancient Canaan that Bethlehem was named after. The story involved the Benjaminites in the town of Gibeah attempting to gang-rape a young man who had stopped there for the night. He had been taken in by an old man that lived in the city, and when the men of the city demanded the old man hand over the young man so they could rape him, the old man gave them his daughter and the young man's concubine instead, who were raped to death. When the other Israelite tribes heard of this event, they virtually wiped out the Benjaminites. It is a strange story to have been simply made up and added to the historical narrative of Judges, which up until this dark age had been fairly consistent with Egyptian records of their rule of Canaan, indicating the story was likely based on something that had happened.

The Benjaminite genocide took a number of years and resulted in most of the tribe being destroyed. During the genocide the other tribes vowed to not allow Benjaminites to marry their daughters, however, by the end, the other tribes took pity on them, and allowed their daughters to be abducted by Benjaminites to become their wives. While every aspect of the story is odd, the strangest aspect of the story is the part not found in Judges, but in 1st Kingdoms (Masoretic Samuel), the fact that King Saul was a Benjaminite. As this genocide took place sometime between 1090 and 1037 BC, it is strange that a Benjaminite could have become king in 1037 BC. A lot of this story has been lost in the past 3000 years.

The story of the rape itself appears to have simply been a catalyst for the Benjaminite genocide, as the murder of an entire tribe seems excessive punishment for any crime committed by a few members of the tribe. The genocide of Benjamin was likely related to the fall of the Egyptian Empire, as the tribe was the most Egyptianized of the Israelite tribes. Even their name was Egyptian: Pen-Amen ( ⬚𓆓𓏏𓊹, Middle Egyptian transliteration pån-jômån), which meant Son of Amen. Amen (𓆓𓏏𓊹), also transliterated into English as Amun or Amon, was the father god of the Theban triad, and supreme god of Egypt throughout the New Kingdom era, other than during the brief Amarna Period. The Egyptian tale, the Voyage of Wenamen, set during the same era as King Saul, described the journey of a Theban priest of Amen's travels in Canaan, and his shock that everyone in Canaan had lost respect for Amen after the Egyptian Empire had collapsed.

The Book of Judges itself is very old, and the Song of Deborah may be the oldest surviving piece of Israelite literature, as it uses some of the most archaic forms of Canaanite in the Masoretic text. Within the book of Judges, the spoken dialect was part of the division between the Israelites during the battle between the Gileadites from east of the Jordan, and the Ephraimites from west of the Jordan. The spelling of šblt (שבלת) in the Masoretic text is not the Hebrew spelling of šybwlt (שיבולת), but the older Canaanite spelling, recorded as šblt (𐎌𐎁𐎍𐎚) in Ugaritic Canaanite, and šblt (𐤔𐤁𐤋𐤕) in Phoenician Canaanite.

This older Canaanite spelling developed into the Hebrew spelling during the Persian era, under the influence of Imperial Aramaic. The older Akkadian cuneiform term was šubulta

(𝌆𝌍 𝌎𝌏), indicating that the division among the Israelites was already between those speaking Canaanite versus Aramaic. Arameans appeared in Mesopotamian records centuries earlier than the Habirus, and the two cultures were generally described as inhabiting the same regions, although the Arameans were more urban, and the Habirus were more nomadic.

There is evidence that the book was either assembled or redacted in the Kingdom of Samaria, as the book includes the name of the Canaanite sun-god Shemesh, whose worship was later banned in Judah by King Josiah in circa 625 BC. The region of the book also generally corresponds with the territory of the northern kingdom, both the region that had once been under Egyptian authority west of the Jordan and the region east of the Jordan which had generally been independent of Egypt. Conversely, the Aramaic book of Judges which was used as a source text by the Greeks appears to have been translated into Aramaic during the Persian era, as the Greek translation includes Persian loanwords the Greeks would not have used, such as satrap, the title of Persian governors.

Judges is a continuation of the story found in Joshua, but not a seamless one, as Joshua includes the Moabites occupying Samaria after the death of Joshua, which skips past 48 years of history recorded in Judges. This gap in Joshua reflects the fact that none of that 48 years of history affected the eastern Israelites who were outside the sphere of Egypt. This shows that the two books had different origins, Joshua from the eastern Israelites, and Judges from the western Israelites. The two books were likely united as part of a historical narrative along with Deuteronomy in the Kingdom of Samaria between 930 and 720 BC. As Deuteronomy is a collection of amendments to the laws found in Exodus that generally repeats the amendments and stories of Leviticus and

Numbers, it is likely it was composed in Samaria to serve the same function as Leviticus-Numbers would later serve in Judah. Deuteronomy and Joshua flow together seamlessly, implying that Joshua was once a part of Deuteronomy, however, Judges does not flow seamlessly from Joshua and is composed in an older dialect, implying the book was already very old by the time Deuteronomy-Joshua was organized into its pre-Hasmonean state by the Levites of Samaria.

The presence of the name Aten in the Song of Deborah proves that at least Chapter 5 dates back to the time it describes, the late 1300s BC. Only a few fragments of Judges have survived among the Dead Sea Scrolls, and all date to the Herodian Dynasty or later, meaning they all date to after the Hasmonean redaction of circa 140 BC. If some of the songs and stories found in the book of Judges were written in the 1300s BC, they could not have been written in the Phoenician script that emerged in the 1100s BC, suggesting an older script was used.

The Ugaritic script was being used in northern Canaan at the time, however, there is no evidence of it being used in southern or central Canaan. At the time, the Egyptian court was corresponding with the governors and judges throughout Canaan using the Akkadian cuneiform script, suggesting that was the script used, however, no clear evidence exists to support any of Judges being written in cuneiform, unlike Exodus and Joshua, which each include Akkadian loanwords. Nevertheless, there are terms related to Egypt that suggest a cuneiform precursor to the Phoenician version of Judges. The presence of the 'unknown' terms Aten and Meroz in the song of Deborah proves it must have been written in some script, and the spelling of the terms prh nôrk (פרה נערך), and prôwt (פרעות) in the Masoretic text supports this as having been in cuneiform.

Both prh nôrk (פרה נערך) and prôwt (פרעות) are also considered 'unknown' terms, resulting in some strange translations. The translators at the Library of Alexandria translated the term as 'Phara the child (or servant)' (Φαρα το παιδαριον), while the Hebrew translates as 'carrying-boy,' or 'cow-servant,' or possibly even 'cow-boy.' Based on the context, this strange sentence appears to be a reference to an Egyptian overseer stationed by Pharaoh among the Tribe of Manasseh.

The Phoenician spelling of 'pharaoh' was prôh (𐤓𐤏𐤓𐤐), while the Aramaic spelling was prôwn (פרעון), neither of which is an exact match for the transliterated words prh (פרה) and phara (Φαρα), indicating that neither the Paleo-Hebrew nor Aramaic texts included the word 'pharaoh' but a similar sounding word. This indicates that the word, along with the Song of Deborah, was transliterated from another script, likely Akkadian Cuneiform or Egyptian.

The Akkadian Cuneiform spelling of 'pharaoh' was pirôû (𒉺𒊑) during the late Bronze Age, which would have been pronounced the same as the Masoretic word, while the Egyptian spelling was per-ôå (𓉐𓉻), which would have been pronounced slightly differently, supporting the Song of Deborah having been written in cuneiform.

# Judges: Chapter 1

After the death of Joshua, the Israelites asked the Lord,[1] "Who will go up for us first against the Canaanites, to fight against them?"

The Lord answered, "Judah will go up. Watch, I have delivered the land into his hand."

Judah said to his brother Simeon, "Come up with me into my allotted territory and let us ally ourselves against the Canaanites, and I also will go with you into your allotted territory," and Simeon went with him. Judah went up, and the Lord delivered the Canaanite and the Perizzite into their hands, and they slaughtered ten thousand men in Bezek.[2] They defeated the Lord of Bezek[3] in Bezek and fought against him, and they attacked the Canaanites and the Perizzites. The Lord of Bezek fled, and they chased after him, and caught him, and cut off his thumbs and his big toes.

The Lord of Bezek said, "Seventy kings collected their food from my table after I cut their thumbs and their big toes off. As I have done, God has repaid me."

They brought him to Jerusalem, and he died there.

The children of Judah attacked Jerusalem and plundered it, and slaughtered by the edge of the sword, and burnt the city with fire. Afterward, the children of Judah went down to fight with the Canaanites living in the hill country, and the Negev, and the plain country.

Judah went to the Canaanites who lived in Hebron and Hebron came out against him. (Previously, Hebron was called the village of Arbaseifer.) They slaughtered Sheshai, Ahiman, and Tamlai, the descendants of Anaks.

They went up from there to the inhabitants of Debir. (Debir was previously called the village of Seifer [City of Letters.])[5]

Caleb said, "Whoever will attack the village of Seifer, and will capture it first, I will give him my daughter Acsah as a wife."

Othniel the younger son of Kenez the brother of Caleb captured it, and Caleb gave him his daughter Acsah as a wife. It happened as she went in, that Othniel urged her to ask for a field from her father, and she whined and cried from her donkey, "You have sent me out into a southern land."

Caleb asked her, "What is your request?"

Acsah answered him, "Give me a blessing, I beg of you, for you have sent me out to a southern land, and you will give me the prize of water," and Caleb gave her according to her heart the prize of the upper springs and the low springs.

The children of Jobab the blacksmith[6] the son-in-law of Moses went up from the city of palm-trees[7] with the children of Judah, to the wilderness that is to the south of Judah, which is at the descent of Arad, and they lived with the people. Judah went with Simeon his brother and slaughtered the Canaanites that inhabited Zephath, and they completely destroyed them, and they called the name of the city Anathema.[8] But Judah did not inherit Gaza and her coast, or Ashkelon and her coast, or Ekron and her coast, or Ashdod and the lands around it. The Lord was with Judah, and he inherited the mountain, as they were not able to destroy the inhabitants of the valley, for Rechab[9] prevented them. They gave Hebron to Caleb, as Moses said, and there he inherited the three cities of the children of Anaks. But the Benjaminites did not take the inheritance of the Jebusites who lived in Jerusalem, and the Jebusites lived with the Benjaminites in Jerusalem until this day.

The sons of Joseph also went up to the Temple of El[10] and the Lord was with them. They camped and surveyed the Temple of El (the name of the town was Luz[11] then). The spies looked and saw a man go out of the city, and they captured him, and said, "Show us the way into the city, and we will deal mercifully with you."

He showed them the way into the city, and they slaughtered the city with the edge of the sword, but they let the man and his family go. The man went into the land of the Cypriots,[12] and built a city there called Luz,[13] and this is its name until this day.

Manasseh did not drive out the inhabitants of the House of She'an[14] (which is Scythopolis), or her towns and her suburbs, nor Ti'inik[15] and her towns, nor the inhabitants of Dor[16] and her suburbs and towns, or the inhabitants of Balak[17] and her suburbs and her towns, or the inhabitants of Megiddo[18] and her suburbs and towns, or the inhabitants of Belameh[19] and her suburbs and towns. The Canaanites began to live in this land. It happened when Israel was strong, that he made the Canaanites tributary, but did not completely drive them out.

Ephraim did not drive out the Canaanites that lived in Gezer, and the Canaanites lived among them in Gezer and became tributary.

Zebulun did not drive out the inhabitants of Kitron, nor the inhabitants of Domana,[20] and the Canaanites lived among them and became tributary to them.

Asher did not drive out the inhabitants of Acco who became tributary to him, or the inhabitants of Dor,[21] Sidon,[22] Ahlab,[23] Achazib,[24] Helbah, Nai,[25] or Ereo.[26] Asher lived among the Canaanites who inhabited the land, for they could not drive them out.

Naphtali did not drive out the inhabitants of House of Shemesh,[27] or the inhabitants of House of Anat,[28] and Naphtali lived among the Canaanites who inhabited the land, but the inhabitants of House of Shemesh and House of Anat became tributary to them.

The Amorites drove out the children of Dan into the mountains, and they did not allow them to come down into the valley. The Amorites began to live in the clay mountains,[29] where there are bears and foxes, in Myrsinoni[30] and Sha'alvim.[31] The hand of the house of Joseph was heavy on the Amorites, and they became tributary to them. The border of the Amorites was from the ascent of Akrabbim,[32] from the Petra[33] and upwards.

# Judges: Chapter 1 Notes

**1** Codex Vaticanus: tou cyriou (ΤΟΥΚΥΡΙΟΥ). Translation: the Lord

• Codex Alexandrinus: en cyriô (ЄΝΚΥΡΙѠ). Translation: of Lord

• Aleppo Codex: byhwh (בִיהוה). Translation: in (or with, while, among, on) Yhwh

• Leningrad Codex: baYhvah (בַּיהֹוָה). Translation: in (or with, while, among, on) Yhvah

• Targum Jerusalem: daYeyah (דְיֵי). Translation: of (or from) Yahw

This chapter does not survive among the Dead Sea Scrolls, however, the name Yhwh does survive in later sections of Judges that have survived among the Dead Sea Scrolls.

• Dead Sea Scroll 4QJudgᵃ: Yhwh (𐤉𐤄𐤅𐤄)

• Dead Sea Scroll 4QJudgᵇ: Yhwh (𐤉𐤄𐤅𐤄)

The Septuagint's version of the Judges was translated before 200 BC, as it was carried south by the Beta Israel community, who left Egypt for Kush (modern Sudan) during the Jewish Rebellion against the Ptolemys in 200 BC. This means it predates the Hasmonean redaction and contains the term Lord (Κύριος) instead of Iaw (Ιαω), which, if correctly translated from the Aramaic source texts, would have read ådny (אדני). The Greeks are believed to have transliterated Yhw (יהו), the Aramaic version of the name Yhvah/Yehvah, as Iaô (Ιαω) in the Book of Leviticus, published circa 250 BC, as evidenced by the Dead Sea Scroll Septuagint fragment 4QpapLXXLevᵇ, which dates from Hasmonean era Judea. 4QpapLXXLevᵇ could be interpreted as a Hasmonean redaction of the Septuagint, however, Leviticus appears to have been written during the rule of King Josiah, and his God was Yahw, supporting the existence of Yahw in the Book of Leviticus. The Aramaic sections of Masoretic Daniel that were not translated into Hebrew maintain the term adonai ha'elohim (אֲדֹנָי הָאֱלֹהִים), meaning the 'Lord the gods' where the Septuagint has 'Lord the god' (Κύριον τὸν θεὸν), however, the Hebrew sections have Yehvah elohim (יְהֹוָה אֱלֹהִים)

where the Septuagint has 'Lord the god,' suggesting the Greek more accurately reflects the Aramaic source texts than the Hebrew translation. According to the Talmud, this was to repair the damage King Manasseh had done 600 years earlier when he removed the name Yehvah from the Israelite Texts, however, no evidence has survived from the era of Manasseh or earlier that proves the name was originally in the text, suggesting it was an attempt by the first Hasmonean High-Priest/King Simon the Zealot to create a national Judean religion with a god having a name similar to the Roman god Jove.

In the 3rd century AD, the Christians redacted the Septuagint removing the name Iaô, both in Greek, and in Latin translations which transliterated Ιαω as Iaw, replacing it with 'Lord.' This resolved the debate with the Gnostics about whether Iaw was the devil or not. Before that, the various versions of the early Christian-era Septuagint books that included the name, either used Ιαω, or the name written in Hebrew or Phoenician (Paleo-Hebrew) scripts. According to Origen of Alexandria in the late 2nd century AD, the Phoenician (most ancient script) was the most accurate. According to Theodoret of Cyprus in the 5th century, the Samaritans, who never switched to the Assyrian block letter 'Hebrew,' pronounced the name as Iabe (Ιαβε) or Iabae (Ιαβαι). Hebrews substitute the word 'hasheim,' meaning 'the name,' in all non-scriptural contexts since the Hasmoneans banned the pronunciation of the names of God. Christians have traditionally translated several ways including Jehovah, Jehova, and Jova. As the original Greek translation of Joshua does not appear to have included the name, the term Lord is used in this translation.

**2** Codex Vaticanus: Bezec (ʙεzεκ)

- Aleppo Codex: bzq (בֶזֶק)

- Leningrad Codex: bezeq (בֶּזֶק)

- Targum Jerusalem: bezeq (בֶזֶק)

The location of Bezek is debated. Currently, the majority of scholars believe it was at the village of Ibziq in the northern Palestinian West Bank, while others had suggested it was at the nearby village of Salhab.

**3** Codex Vaticanus: Adônibezec (ΑΔωΝΙΒΕΖΕΚ)

- Aleppo Codex: ådny bzq (אדני בזק). Translation: Lord of Bezek

- Leningrad Codex: adoni bezeq (אֲדֹנִי בֶזֶק). Translation: Lord of Bezek

- Targum Jerusalem: adoni bezeq (אֲדֹנִי בֶזֶק). Translation: Lord of Bezek

While the Septuagint treats Adonibezec as a proper name, it is clear from the Masoretic text that is was simply his title. The fact that this 'Lord' who had defeated 70 kings was not considered a king himself, supports the dating for the invasion of southern Canaan circa 1500 BC, after Pharaoh Thutmose's armies had passed through the territory, and the local chieftains had sworn allegiance to him. As the region was in chaos between the collapse of the Hyksos Dynasty circa 1540 BC, and the Pharaoh Thutmose's army pacifying the region in 1505 BC, it is entirely possible that a would-be successor to the Hyksos may have captured and mutilated 70 other would-be kings, before submitting to the Egyptians and consolidating his position within the new empire as a local lord.

**4** Codex Vaticanus: Cariatharboxepher (ΚΑΡΙΑΘΑΡΒΟΞΕΦΕΡ)

- Codex Alexandrinus: Cariatharbocsepher (ΚΑΡΙΑΘΑΡΒΟΚΣΕΦΕΡ)

- Aleppo Codex: qryt årbô (קרית ארבע). Translation: Village of Labor

- Leningrad Codex: kiryat arba (קִרְיַת אַרְבַּע). Translation: Village of Labor

- Targum Jerusalem: kiryat arba (קִרְיַת אַרְבַּע). Translation: Village of four

The Greek καριαθαρβοξεφερ and καριαθαρβοκσεφερ are not transliterations of kiryat arba (קִרְיַת אַרְבַּע), but a transliteration of kiryat arba sefer (קִרְיַת אַרְבַּע סָפֶר), meaning 'village of working books,' or 'village of the library.' As the word was removed from the text after 200 BC, the Hasmoneans are the most likely redactors.

**5** Codex Vaticanus: Cariathsôphar polis grammatôn (ΚΑΡΙΑΘϹѠΦΑΡ ΠΟΛΙϹΓΡΑΜΜΑΤѠΝ). Translation: Cariathsôphar, city of letters

• Codex Alexandrinus: Polis grammatôn (ΠΟΛΙϹΓΡΑΜΜΑΤѠΝ). Translation: City of Letters

• Aleppo Codex: qryt spr (קרית ספר). Translation: Village Book (or scroll)

• Leningrad Codex: kiryat-sefer (קִרְיַת־סֵפֶר). Translation: Village Book (or scroll)

• Targum Jerusalem: kiryat archei (קִרְיַת אַרְכֵי). Translation: Village of Arke

The Greek καριαθσωφαρ is a transliteration of the Hebrew term found in the Masoretic text. The Greeks added a translation 'city of the letters,' meaning they considered the name of the town to imply a communications hub. These two cities being burnt imply that the Judeans and Simeonites were targeting centers for higher learning within Canaan. These towns would have likely served as the main communications centers, as, prior to telegraphs being invented in the 1800s AD, the primary form of long-distance communication was letters. Cities where scribes studied writing and pigeon handling were found throughout the Middle East and the Mediterranean, such as Sumerian (and later Babylonian) Zimbar (later Sippar), a name also translating a 'Letters,' in Babylonian, although originally meaning 'birds' in Sumerian.

**6** Codex Vaticanus: Iothor tou Cinaeou tou gambrou Môyseôs (ΙΟΘΟΡ ΤΟΥ ΚΙΝΑΙΟΥ ΤΟΥ ΓΑΜΒΡΟΥ ΜѠΥϹΕѠϹ). Translation: Jethro the Kenite the son-in-law of Moses

• Codex Alexandrinus: Iôbab tou Cinaeou pentherou Môysê (ΙѠΒΑΒ ΤΟΥ ΚΙΝΑΙΟΥ ΠΕΝΘΕΡΟΥ ΜѠΥϹΗ). Translation: Jobab the Kenite father-in-law of Moses

• Aleppo Codex: qyny htn mšh (קיני חתן משה). Translation: smith (or metalworker) son-in-law (or brother-in-law) of Moses

• Leningrad Codex: keini choten Mosheh (קֵינִי֙ חֹתֵ֣ן מֹשֶׁ֔ה). Translation: smith (or metalworker) son-in-law (or brother-in-law) of Moses

• Targum Jerusalem: Shalma'ah chamuhi deMosheh (שַׁלְמָאָה חֲמוּהִי דְמֹשֶׁה). Translation: Shalmaite (Arabic tribe) of the house of (or his daughter's father-in-law) of Moses

Three variations of this text are known, two in the Septuagint codices, and one in the Masoretic text. The two Septuagint versions name the man in question as either Jethro (Ιοθορ) or Jobab (Ιωβαβ), while the Masoretic text omits the name. The one version of the Septuagint and the Masoretic text agree that he was Moses' son-in-law or brother-in-law (Γαμβρου / חֹתֵ֣ן), while the other Septuagint version claims father-in-law (Πενθερου). Of all these sources, the Codex Vaticanus is the oldest, dating to the 4th century AD, which calls him Jethro the blacksmith son-in-law of Moses. The Codex Alexandrinus dates to the 5th century AD and is believed to be based on the revision made by Lucian the Martyr circa 300 AD, who redacted the Septuagint to make it more like the Hebrew texts that were then in circulation. Strangely, the Codex Alexandrinus claims Jobab was Moses' father-in-law, while the Masoretic text claims the unnamed blacksmith was Moses' son-in-law. As the Masoretic text omit the name, there were likely different versions of Judges in circulation at the time the Masorites began copying the text, and they omitted the name in order to not pass on the wrong name. Regardless of what the Masoretic text state, almost all English translations of them, refer to this blacksmith as Moses's father-in-law.

As two of the sources, Codex Vaticanus and the Masoretic text agree he was Moses's son-in-law, the term son-in-law is used in this translation. Additionally, Moses' father-in-law Jethro was not a blacksmith, but a shepherd, and therefore it seems clear that Moses married his daughter to a blacksmith, although that story has not survived to the present. The man is named both Jethro and Jobab in this chapter of the surviving

Septuagint codices, however, all three source texts call him 'Jobab the son-in-law of Moses' in Judges chapter 4.

**7** Codex Vaticanus: poleôs tôn phoenicôn (ΠΟΛΕWC ΤWN ΦΟΙΝΙΚWN). Translation: city the Phoenicians (or palm trees, dates, Phoenix)

• Aleppo Codex: môyr htmrym (**מְעִיר הַתְּמָרִים**). Translation: dates (or date palm trees in Hebrew), or blinking (in Aramaic)

• Leningrad Codex: me'ir hattemarim (מֵעִיר הַתְּמָרִים). Translation: dates (or date palm trees)

• Targum Jerusalem: karta Yericho (קַרְתָּא יְרִיחוֹ). Translation: city of Jericho

As this flows from the Judahites capturing the 'city of letters,' suggesting that 'city of palm trees' was an alternate translation of the same location. The term used in the Masoretic text is Hebrew, however, the word was adopted into Hebrew from the Aramaic word tmrâ (תַּמְרָא) in the Iron Age, meaning it cannot have been the name used in the text before the Phoenician translation was made in the Kingdom of Samaria or Israel in the early Iron Age. The translator of the Targum Jerusalem seems to have recognized the anachronism, and substituted 'Jericho.' If 'palm' was the alternate translation of 'letters,' it suggests the Phoenician translation of Judges was made from an Egyptian language text, as 'book,' 'scroll,' 'papyrus,' and 'palm plants' was the same word in Egyptian: bât ( 𓃀𓄿𓈖𓏏 ), while the words were not synonyms in Semitic languages.

**8** Codex Vaticanus: Anathema (ΑΝΑΘΕΜΑ)

• Codex Alexandrinus: Hexolethreusis (ΕΞΟΛΕΘΡΕΥCΙC)

• Aleppo Codex: ḥrmh (**חרמה**). Translation: the highlands (or the heights)

• Leningrad Codex: charemah (חָרְמָה). Translation: the highlands (or the heights)

- Targum Jerusalem: charemah (חָרְמָה). Translation: destruction

As all three source texts use a different name, the name Anathema is used from the Codex Vaticanus, the oldest of the surviving translations.

**9** Codex Vaticanus: Rêchab (ⲢΗⲭⲀⲃ)

- Aleppo Codex: rkb brzl (רכב ברזל). Translation: chariots of iron

- Leningrad Codex: rekeb barzel (רֶכֶב בַּרְזֶל). Translation: chariots of iron

- Targum Jerusalem: detichin devarzela (דְתִיכִין דְבַרְזְלָא). Translation: in the judgment of iron

The Greek translation, Masoretic text, and Targum Jerusalem each interpret this sentence quite differently. The Greek translation interpreted Rechab as the name of a town or people, and is likely the same town or people mentioned in Psalms chapter 86 as Raab (Ρααβ), which was listed alongside other lands and cities that had defeated the Israelites, including Babylon, Tyre, Kush, and the Philistines. The term shows up in the parallel verse in the Masoretic text as rhb (רהב), generally transliterated as Rahob, which was also the name of a sea monster in ancient Israelite myths. The prophet Isaiah, who lived around the time that the Phoenician translation of Judges was probably made, also used the term to refer to Egypt, suggesting the original text read that 'Egypt' had stopped Judah from destroying the people living in the valley. The translators of the Septuagint also translated rhb (רהב) as Cetus (Κητη) in Job chapter 9, indicating that they viewed Rechab as the ancient Israelite asterism of Cetus. Another term also translated as Cetus was Tanninim (תַנִּינִם) in Genesis which was also translated as dragons (δρακοντα) in Psalms, while the term Livyatan (לִוְיָתָן), generally transliterated as Leviathan was also translated as a dragon (δρακων).

The term Leviathan was used in the book of Isaiah, in a reference to the Ugaritic Texts which substituted the name Leviathan for Lotan. As such, this verse could the read either as the people of a town named Rêchab (Ρηχαβ) repulsing the Israelite attack, or the Egyptians forbidding the attack, or the god-monster itself defeating them, and presumably their god. Clearly, the Hasmonean redactors did not like this implication, and so changed this to read rkb brzl (רכב ברזל), meaning either chariots of iron, or the Egyptian's iron, depending on the interpretation of rekeb (רֶכֶב). The translator of the Targum Jerusalem seemed to have recognized the double meaning of rekeb, and therefore substituted 'the judgment of iron' (דְתִיכִין דְבַרזְלָא), however, iron is generally not viewed as being in wide use before the beginning of the iron age, and so these 'iron chariots,' are often viewed as an anachronism. If the 'iron chariots' were part of an older version of the story which had been lost in the Aramaic translation that the Greeks worked from, the 'iron' was probably the metal the ancient Egyptians called djôm (𓎡𓏭𓏤), which they recorded building chariots from during the New Kingdom era. Egyptologists generally believe this metal was electrum, as it is reported as coming from the 'gold' mines of southeast Egypt, where the 'gold' veins are rich in silver. The Egyptians had separate terms for both gold and silver, and referred to djôm as if it was some other kind of metal.

As the gold veins in the region also contain small amounts of iron and nickle, it is possible that djôm was the residue left over from smelting the gold and sliver out of the raw metal, meaning that 'iron' would be an appropriate translation. The New Kingdom king Tutankhamen was buried with an iron-nickel dagger, indicating that the residue from the gold and silver processing was being used to make weaponry during the New Kingdom era, however, it has not been proven that this was the metal known as djôm which was used to make chariots. Additionally, the Egyptians were smithing iron mined at Site 200 in the Timna Valley, in southern Israel's Arabah region during the New Kingdom era, presumably for weaponry. Nevertheless, it is more likely that the original reference was simply to Egypt itself, and the term 'iron' was an addition made in the early classical era, as the Greeks certainly knew what iron was, and would have translated it if it was in the texts they worked from, and it is improbable that the Aramaic translator would have removed the word.

**10** Codex Vaticanus: Baethêl (ⲃⲁⲓⲑⲏⲗ)

- Aleppo Codex: byt âl (בֵית אֵל). Translation: house (or temple) of El (or god), Baitylos (or meteorite)

- Leningrad Codex: beit-El (בֵּית־אֵל). Translation: house (or temple) of El (or god), Baitylos (or meteorite)

- Targum Jerusalem: veit El (בֵית אֵל). Translation: house (or temple) of El

The term Bethel meant several things in ancient Canaan. The term translates as 'house of god,' which can be translated as either 'Temple of God/El' or 'sky/heaven.' Bethel was worshiped as a god by the ancient Canaanites, the brother of El and Dagon according to Sanchuniathon, who referred to him as Baitylos, which is the name used in this translation when the god. The term can also be translated as 'meteorite' as meteorites were believed to be parts of the god Baitylos that had fallen to the Earth, and shrines were built around them.

**11** Codex Vaticanus: Louza (ⲗⲟⲩⲍⲁ)

- Aleppo Codex: Lwz (לוז)

- Leningrad Codex: Luz (לוּז)

- Targum Jerusalem: Luz (לוּז)

The Samaritan city at the foot of Mount Gerizim is still known as Luza.

**12** Codex Vaticanus: Chettiin (ⲭⲉⲧⲧⲓⲓⲛ)

- Codex Alexandrinus: Chettiim (ⲭⲉⲧⲧⲓⲓⲙ)

- Aleppo Codex: Htym (חתים). General Translation: Cypriots

- Leningrad Codex: Chittim (חִתָּים). Translation: Cypriots

- Targum Jerusalem: Chitta'ei (חִתָּאֵי). Translation: Cypriots

This term has created a great deal of confusion since the misidentification of the ruins of the Neshites as being 'Hittite' in the 1800s. The modern archaeological name 'Hittite,' is not derived from an ancient name for the culture applied by themselves, or anyone else, but rather adopted from the biblical reference to a then-unknown civilization somewhere in the region. There was an ancient culture in the region called the Hattians, however, they were conquered by the Nesites before 1700 BC, and subsequently disappeared from the historic records. The name was applied to culture today referred to as 'Hittites,' before the 'Hittite' language had been translated, and is incorrect. Since 1906, excavations at Boğazköy, the ancient 'Hittite' capital Hattusa have uncovered more than 10,000 'Hittite' texts, including the royal achieve. The actual name of the 'Hittite' language and people was Nešili (𒉈𒅖𒇷), which is now rendered in some academic literate as Nesite or Neshite. As early as the mid-1800s some scholars disputed the identification of the Nesites as the Biblical Hittites, including the Orientalist Max Müller, who was one of many claiming the Biblical Hittites were ancient Greeks or some other Mediterranean people.

Later in the Septuagint's translation of the Maccabees, the similar term Chettiim (Χεττιιμ) as a reference to all Greek-speaking lands, and therefore the Biblical Hittites were likely the Minoans or the Achaean Greeks. In the 1st century AD, the Jewish historian Josephus reported that Cethima was the name of Cyrus in Aramaic, and the Chettim were the descendants of Noah's grandson Chethimus, who had settled on Cyprus. Josephus reported that the name was preserved in the Greek name of the town Cition (Κίτιον). Most historians view it as more likely that the Aramaic name was derived from the city-state of Cition, which was known as Kåtjåy (𓊖𓏤𓈖𓏤) in Egyptian records from the New Kingdom Era in the late Bronze Age, and Kt (𐤊𐤕) or Kty (𐤊𐤕𐤉) in Phoenician records from the early Iron Age. While this may be the origin of the term, by the era of the Neo-Assyrian era, the term must have also referred to other Greek islands, as both the prophets Isaiah and Ezekiel used the term 'Islands of Kittim.' As the term referred to the entire island of Cyprus in Aramaic, the translations of 'Cyprus' and 'Cypriots' are used here.

**13** Codex Vaticanus: Louza (ⲗOYZⲁ)

- Aleppo Codex: Lwz (לוז)

- Leningrad Codex: Luz (לוּז)

- Targum Jerusalem: Luz (לוז)

The Greek spelling of Louza (Λουζα) is a transliteration of the Aramaic spelling of the name, Lwzå (לוזא), indicating the Greek translation was made from an Aramaic source text. It is not clear which city of Luz/Louza the man built. There are a number of ancient cities across the Mediterranean bearing the name, including the Minoan city of Liso/Lissus (Λισο/Λισσος) on Crete, the ancient Greek city of Laüs (Λαος) in southern Italy, and the ancient Portuguese town of Lousã, as well as ancient records of towns with similar names in Carthaginian Tunisia and Algeria. The town of Liso in Crete is believed to date back to late Minoan times, before 1100 BC, making it the most likely city being referred to.

The Canaanites (Phoenicians and Carthaginians) were present in southern Italy, northwest Africa, and Iberia long before the Greeks, however, it is not clear that any of the other settlements date back to before 1000 BC. The Greeks had occupied Laüs before 500 BC, however, it is not clear who founded the city or when. Ruins of the Portuguese town of Lousã have been found dating back to the Roman era, and the locations of the towns in Tunisia and Algeria are no longer known.

**14** Codex Vaticanus: Baethsan (ⲃⲁⲓⲑⲥⲁⲛ)

- Aleppo Codex: byt šăn (בית שאן). Translation: House (or temple) of She'an

- Leningrad Codex: beit-She'an (בֵּית־שְׁאָן). Translation: House (or temple) of She'an

- Targum Jerusalem: beit She'an (בֵּית שְׁאָן). Translation: House (or temple) of wishes

# Judges: Chapter 1 Notes

The city of Beth She'an was officially annexed by the Egyptians around 1457 BC, when the army of Thutmose III occupied Canaan en route to Syria. The city was an Egyptian city in Canaan until the collapse of the Egyptian New Kingdom, circa 1150 BC, when the city was burnt down. It was rebuilt a few decades later as a Canaanite city and the ruins of the new city show no evidence of being culturally connected to Egypt. The Assyrians burnt down the city again when they occupied Samaria circa 732 BC, and it remained largely unoccupied until sometime in the Persian era, when Scythians settled at the site, resulting in the Greek name Scythopolis.

While the Greeks added the reference to the contemporary name of Scythopolis, the Masoretic text does not include that reference, and the city in question is the city of Beth She'an that was burned down in 1150 BC. The book of Judge's claims that Beth She'an was not occupied by the Israelites is true, the Egyptians recorded that the city was under their control and there are no records of it being attacked. These Egyptian records are found on the monuments in Karnak and are supported by the archaeological evidence of an Egyptian city at the site between 1450 and 1150 BC. Based on the Egyptian records, the main god worshiped at the Beth She'an was a god called Mekal, which appears to be a precursor to the Jewish messenger Michael.

**15** Codex Vaticanus: Thanak (ΘΑΝΑΚ).

• Codex Alexandrinus: Ecthanaad (ΕΚΘΑΝΑΑΔ)

• Aleppo Codex: Tônk (תַעֲנַךְ)

• Leningrad Codex: Ta'nach (תַּעְנַךְ)

• Targum Jerusalem: Ta'anach (תַּעֲנַךְ)

As the Codex Vaticanus and Masoretic text agree, most translations of the Septuagint prefer the name Thanak (or Taanach) over Ecthanaad. The modern village is called Ti'inik, and is located in the northern-most region of the Palestinian West Bank. Ti'inik was occupied by the Egyptians between 1457 and 1150 BC.

**16** Codex Vaticanus: Dôr (ⲇⲱⲣ)

- Aleppo Codex: Dwr (דור)

- Leningrad Codex: Dor (דוֹר)

- Targum Jerusalem: Dor (דוֹר)

The city of Dor was occupied by the Egyptians during the New Kingdom era, between 1457 and 1150 BC. The city of Djr (𓈖𓍯𓇋𓀭⊛) was mentioned in several Egyptian texts from the New Kingdom era, and featured in the Voyage of Wenamen set circa 1050 BC, after the city had broken away from Egyptian control. The city was located as the mound today called Tel Dor on the Mediterranean coast of Israel between Haifa and Hadera.

**17** Codex Vaticanus: Balak (ΒΑΛΑΚ)

- Codex Alexandrinus: Balaam (ΒΑΛΑΑΜ)

- Aleppo Codex: Yblôm (יבלעם)

- Leningrad Codex: Yivle'am (יִבְלְעָם)

- Targum Jerusalem: Yivle'am (יִבְלְעָם)

The Septuagint's list of cities also includes Ieblaam (Ιεβλααμ) at the end, which also appears to be a transliteration of Yivle'am (יִבְלְעָם) from the Masoretic text As Belameh (Βαλααμ / בְּלְעָם) also appears at the end of the list, Balak is used in this translation. The name Balak (Βαλακ) appears to be a translation of the Hebrew name Balak (בָּלָק), which was the name of the Moabite king in Numbers, which implies the land of Balak was Moab. Moab was occupied by the Egyptians during the New Kingdom, however, does not appear in their records until the Canaanite campaigns of Ramesses II circa 1275 BC. By the time of Ramesses II, Moab was a petty kingdom allied to Egypt, however, it is likely that it was officially annexed in 1457 BC when Thutmose III's armies annexed the rest of Canaan.

**18** Codex Vaticanus: Magedô (ΜΑΓΕΔω)

- Codex Alexandrinus: Magedôn (ΜΑΓΕΔωΝ)

- Aleppo Codex: Mgdw (מגדו)

- Leningrad Codex: Megiddov (מְגִדּוֹ)

- Targum Jerusalem: Megido (מְגִדוֹ)

The town of Megiddo was listed as a town occupied by the armies of Thutmose III's army in 1457 BC. Some records from Megiddo have survived among the Amarna Letters. Amarna Letter EA245 mentioned the governor Biridiya, from circa 1350 BC.

**19** Codex Vaticanus: Ieblaam (ΙΕΒΛΑΑΜ)

The Masoretic text does not contain another name after Meggido in this list, however, the Greek Ieblaam (Ιεβλααμ), which is found in both the Vaticanus and Alexandrinus versions of Judges, appears to be a translation of yiVle'am (יִבְלְעָם), meaning 'of Vle'am,' which is listed earlier in the Masoretic text. The city of Balaam is generally accepted as the city of Belameh, listed as one of the towns occupied by Pharaoh Thutmose III's army circa 1450 BC. The town was occupied throughout Israelite and Judahite history, and was known as Belemoth during the Greco-Roman era.

**20** Codex Vaticanus: Dômana (ΔωΜΑΝΑ)

- Codex Alexandrinus: Enaala (ΕΝΑΑΛΑ)

- Aleppo Codex: Nhll (נהלל)

- Leningrad Codex: Nahalol (נַהֲלֹל)

- Targum Jerusalem: Nahalol (נַהֲלֹל)

The Codex Alexandrinus' Enaala appears to be a transliteration of the Hebrew Nahalal, however, was most likely part of Lucian's redaction circa 300 AD, meaning the original Septuagint probably used the name

Domana. There is an Israeli community called Nahalal in northern Israel today, however, there is no archaeological evidence connecting it to the ancient settlement.

**21** Codex Vaticanus: Dôr (ܕܘܪ)

The Masoretic text does not mention Dor a second time here, however, it was previously listed among the cities that Manasseh did not drive the inhabitants out of.

**22** Codex Vaticanus: Sidôna (ⲥⲓⲆⲱⲚⲀ)

- Aleppo Codex: Ṣydwn (צִידוֹן)

- Leningrad Codex: Tzidovn (צִידוֹן)

- Targum Jerusalem: Tzidovn (צִידוֹן)

- Sidon (𐤑𐤃𐤍) was one of the most ancient Canaanite cities, and arguably the mother-city of all of Canaanite culture. Tyre also claimed to be Phoenicia's mother-city, however, it was originally a colony of Sidon. Egyptian records from the 1300s BC listed the city as Djedunå (𓂧𓏤𓈖𓈗) while it was part of the Egyptian New Kingdom. It was likely occupied by Thutmose III with the rest of Canaan in 1457 BC.

**23** Greek: Aalaph (ⲀⲀⲀⲀⲫ)

- Aleppo Codex: Åhlb (אַחְלָב)

- Leningrad Codex: Achlav (אַחְלָב)

- Targum Jerusalem: Achlav (אַחְלָב)

**24** Codex Vaticanus: Aschazi (ⲀⲤⲭⲀⲌⲓ)

- Codex Alexandrinus: Achazib (ⲀⲭⲀⲌⲓⲃ)

- Aleppo Codex: Åkzyb (אַכְזִיב)

193

• Leningrad Codex: Achziv (אַכְזִיב)

• Targum Jerusalem: Achziv (אַכְזִיב)

Achzib was a major Canaanite city during the Egyptian New Kingdom Era. It was originally built between two rivers, however, by the Middle Bronze Age, the city extended from one river to the other, and the Canaanites dug a moat between the two rivers, effectively making the city into an island. The city was later transferred to King Hiram of Tyre by King Solomon and appears to have been independent of Israelite (Samaritan and Judahites) control until the Assyrians conquered it in 701 BC under King Sennacherib. The city of Achzib was located along the Mediterranean coast of modern Israel, north of Acre.

**25** Codex Vaticanus: Nai (ΝΑΙ)

• Codex Alexandrinus: Aphec (ΑΦΕΚ)

• Aleppo Codex: Åpyq (אפיק)

• Leningrad Codex: Afik (אֲפִיק)

• Targum Jerusalem: Afik (אֲפִיק)

The Codex Alexandrinus' Aphec appears to be a transliteration of the Hebrew åpyq, however, was most likely part of Lucian's redaction circa 300 AD, meaning the original Septuagint probably used the name Nai.

**26** Codex Vaticanus: Ereô (ΕΡΕΩ)

• Codex Alexandrinus: Roôb (ΡΟΩΒ)

• Aleppo Codex: Rhb (רחב)

• Leningrad Codex: Rechov (רְחֹב)

• Targum Jerusalem: Rechov (רְחוֹב)

This location is not known today. There are the remains of another place called Rehob near Beth She'an, however, the ruins in question are not believed to be associated with this Rehob. There is also not an ancient site known as Ereo. The general assumption is that the location of this Rehob (or Ereo) was in Lebanon somewhere. As the name Roôb found in the Codex Alexandrinus is likely part of Lucian's redaction, and Ereo was likely the original name in the Septuagint, Ereo is used in this translation.

**27** Greek: Baethsamys (ΒΑΙΘCΑΜΥC)

• Aleppo Codex: Byt Šmš (בית שמש). Translation: house (or temple) of Shemesh (or sun)

• Leningrad Codex: veit-Shemesh (בֵּית־שֶׁמֶשׁ). Translation: house (or temple) of Shemesh (or sun)

• Targum Jerusalem: veit Shemesh (בֵּית שֶׁמֶשׁ). Translation: house (or temple) of Shemesh (or sun)

The modern city of Beit Shemesh (בֵּית שֶׁמֶשׁ / بيت شيمش) is located near the ancient site of the town, today called Tel Beit Shemesh. Shemesh was the Canaanite sun god, influenced by the Mesopotamian solar-god Shamesh. King Josiah of Judah banned the worship of Shemesh in circa 625 BC, along with the other Canaanite and early Israelite gods.

**28** Codex Vaticanus: Baethanath (ΒΑΙΘΑΝΑΘ)

• Codex Alexandrinus: Baetheneth (ΒΑΙΘΕΝΕΘ)

• Aleppo Codex: Byt ônt (בית ענת). Translation: house (or temple) of Anat

• Leningrad Codex: veit-Anat (בֵית־עֲנָת). Translation: house (or temple) of Anat

• Targum Jerusalem: veit Anat (בֵּית עֲנָת). Translation: house (or temple) of Anat

# JUDGES: CHAPTER 1 NOTES

The location of Beth Anat is unknown today. Sites have been suggested in Lebanon, Galilee, and at the foot of Mount Hermon. Anat (𐤏𐤍𐤕) was a war goddess, and one of the major deities of Canaan. Anat was one of the key motivators of her brother Baʻal Hadad's rebellion against Yam (Sea) in the Canaanite Baʻal Cycle literature, dated to between 1450 and 1200 BC. She was also central to Baʻal's resurrection during his conflict with Mot (Death). Her worship had already been imported to Egypt during the Second Intermediate Period, currently dated to between 1650 and 1580 BC, and was part of Pharaoh Anat-Har's name, showing how important she was at the time.

She was integrated into the Egyptian pantheon as the daughter of Ptah, the creator-god. It is unclear which dynasty Anat-Har was a Pharaoh of, however, his name suggests he was a Canaanite or Hyksos Pharaoh. There are remains of temples dedicated to her dating from the Hyksos Dynasty in the ruins of Avaris (later Pi-Ramesses, and then Ramesses) and Memphis (now Cairo) in Egypt, and Beth She'an (later called Scythopolis) in Israel. The Temple of Anat in Avaris was taken over by later dynasties and expanded within the renamed city of Pi-Ramesses, and she continued to be a major Egyptian goddess throughout the New Kingdom. Anat later became synonymous with her Canaanite title Qetesh in Canaan, although Qetesh was adopted as a separate Goddess by the Egyptians. Qetesh was widely worshiped by the Israelites before King Josiah banned her worship in Judah circa 625 BC. The name Anat continued to be used by the Israelites in addition to her title Qetesh (Holiness), and was treated as the wife of Yahw (Yehvah) until at least the 5th century BC, as evidenced by the Elephantine papyri, which listed her as Anat-Yahw.

---

**29** Codex Vaticanus: ori tô ostracôdi (ΟΡΕΙΤѠΟϹΤΡΑΚѠΔΕΙ). Translation: Mountains of earth (or pottery)

- Codex Alexandrinus: ori tou Myrsinônos (ΟΡΕΙΤΟΥ ΜΥΡϹΙΝѠΝΟϹ). Translation: Mountains of Myrsinônos (or myrtle)

- Aleppo Codex: bhr hrs (כהר חרס). Translation: mountain of destruction (or clay)

- Leningrad Codex: behar-cheres (בְּהַר־חֶרֶס). Translation: mountain of destruction (or clay)

- Targum Jerusalem: tur cheres (טוּר חֶרֶס). Translation: Mount Heres

As the name Codex Vaticanus is similar to the 'Mount Heres' of the Masoretic text, that name is imported. However, it is not entirely clear what the name Heres means, as it is sometimes a reference to the underworld in Canaanite literature, but sometimes a reference to the sun or a sun-god in early Israelite literature. This may be an alternate or earlier translation of the northern Mount Hor from the Book of Joshua.


**30** Codex Vaticanus: Myrsinôni (ΜΥΡϹΙΝѠΝΙ)

- Codex Alexandrinus: does not mention the Μυρσινωνι Mountains a second time, however, does mention the name earlier in the verse.

- Aleppo Codex: Åylwn (אילון)

- Leningrad Codex: Ayyalovn (אַיָּלוֹן)

- Targum Jerusalem: Ayalon (אַיְלוֹן)

Ajalon was listed by Governor Adbi-Heba of Jerusalem as a town destroyed by invaders in the El-Amarna Letters circa 1330 BC. Prior to this, the town was considered Egyptian territory, however, this attack on Ayalon appears to be part of an ongoing process of territorial losses by the New Kingdom. Pharaoh Sheshonk I recaptured the region in 925 BC after the collapse of the United Kingdom of Israel.


**31** Codex Vaticanus: Thalabin (ΘΑΛΑΒΙΝ).

- Codex Alexandrinus: does not mention the name Thalabin, Shaalbim, or any other variation in this verse.

- Aleppo Codex: Šôlbym (שעלבים)

- Leningrad Codex: Sha'alvim (שַׁעַלְבִים)

• Targum Jerusalem: Sha'alvim (שַׁעֲלְבִים)

The ruins near the modern Israeli town of Šôlbym are believed to be the ruins of Shaalbim. As the Greek Thalabin appears to be a transliteration of Shaalbim, and the modern town is called Sha'alvim, that name is used in this translation.

**32** Codex Vaticanus: Acrabin (ΑΚΡΑΒΙΝ)

• Aleppo Codex: ôqrbym (עקרבים). Translation: scorpions

• Leningrad Codex: akrabbim (עַקְרַבִּים). Translation: scorpions

• Targum Jerusalem: akra bim (עֲקָר בִּים). Translation: barren (or sterile) among

The location of the Ascent of Akrabbim has been debated for over 2000 years. The 1ˢᵗ century AD Jewish historian Flavius Josephus described the Ascent of Akrabbim as lying between Judea and Galilee in Samaria in *The Wars of the Jews* circa 75 AD:

> Now as to the country of Samaria, it lies between Judea and Galilee; it begins at a village that is in the great plain called Ginea, and ends at the Acrabbene toparchy, and is entirely of the same nature with Judea; for both countries are made up of hills and valleys, and are moist enough for agriculture, and are very fruitful.

**33** Codex Vaticanus: Petras (ΠΕΤΡΑC). Translation: Petra (or stone)

• Aleppo Codex: Slô (סלע). Translation: stone

• Leningrad Codex: Sela (סֶלַע). Translation: stone

• Targum Jerusalem: keifa (כֵּיפָא). Translation: pressure

It is not clear from the Masoretic text if the original author intended the city of Petra or not, however, the Greek translators did translate the term as the name of the city. The 1ˢᵗ century AD Jewish historian Flavius Josephus located the Torah's Kadesh Barnea at Petra, which would mean that Petra was in the Hebrew texts before the era of Judges. A town called Sela was listed in the Amarna Letters from circa 1330 BC, which appears to be Petra. In the Amarna Letters, Sela was occupied by the Egyptians, however, does not appear to have been part of the Egyptian Empire before that time.

# Judges: Chapter 2

The messenger of the lord[1] went up from the circle[2] to Bokim,[3] the Temple of El, and to the Temple of Israel,[4] and said to them, "The Lord says, 'I brought you up out of Egypt, and I brought you into the land which I swore to your fathers and I promised, "I will never break my covenant that I have made with you. You will make no covenant with those that live in this land, neither will you worship their gods. Instead, you will destroy their carved images, you will pull down their altars." But, you did not listen to my voice, and you did these things, and I said, "I will not drive them out from before you, but they will be distresses to you, and their gods will be an offense to you."'"

When the messenger of the lord spoke these words to the Israelites, the people raised their voices and wept. They renamed that place Bokim. They sacrificed to the Lord there, and Joshua dismissed the people, and they went each man to his inheritance, to inherit the land. The people served the Lord all the days of Joshua, and all the days of the elders that lived many days with Joshua, as many as knew all the great works of the Lord, what things he had worked in Israel. Joshua the son of Nun, the servant of the Lord, died at a hundred and ten years old. They buried him in the border of his inheritance, in Timnath Heres, in the mountains of Ephraim, on the north side of Mount Gaash. All that generation was laid with their fathers, and another generation rose up after them, who did not know the Lord, nor the work which he did for Israel. The Israelites worked evil before the Lord and served the Ba'als.[5] They forgot the Lord God[6] of their fathers, who brought them out of the land of Egypt, and followed other gods, the gods of the nations around them, and they worshiped them. They provoked the Lord, and forgot him, and served Ba'al[7] and Astarte.[8] The Lord was very angry with Israel, and he gave them into the hands of plunderers, and they ruined them. He sold them into the hands of their enemies around them, and they could no longer resist their enemies, among whoever they went, and the hand of the Lord was evilly against them. As the Lord had promised, and as the Lord had sworn to them, he punished them greatly. Then the Lord raised up judges, and the Lord saved them out of the hands of those that plundered them, and yet they did not listen to the judges, and they went whoring after other gods and worshiped them. They turned quickly from how their fathers walked when they listen to the words of the Lord. The Lord raised judges among them, and the Lord was with the judges and saved them out of the hand of their enemies all the days of the judges because the Lord was moved by their moaning caused by those that besieged them and attacked them. When the judges died, they went back and again corrupted themselves worse than their fathers, going after other gods to serve them and to worship them. They did not abandon their devices or their stubborn ways. The Lord was very angry with Israel, and said, "Since this nation has forgotten my covenant which I commanded their fathers, and has not listened to my voice, I will never again drive out a man from the nations in front of them, which Joshua the son of Nun left in the land."

The Lord left them to see if Israel would keep the way of the Lord, and follow it like their fathers had or not. So the Lord left these nations and did not drive them out suddenly, and he did not deliver them into the hand of Joshua.

# Judges: Chapter 2 Notes

**1** Codex Vaticanus: angelos cyriou (ΑΓΓΕΛΟΣΚΥΡΙΟΥ). Translation: messenger lord

- Aleppo Codex: mlåk Yhwh (מלאך יהוה). Translation: messenger Yhwh

- Leningrad Codex: mal'ach-Yehvah (מַלְאַךְ־יְהוָה). Translation: messenger Yehwah

- Targum Jerusalem: kodam Yeyah (קֳדָם יְיָ). Translation: advance of Yahw

**2** Codex Vaticanus: Galgal (ΓΑΛΓΑΛ)

- Aleppo Codex: glgl (גלגל). Translation: circle

- Leningrad Codex: gilgal (גִּלְגָּל). Translation: circle

- Targum Jerusalem: gilgela (גִּלְגְּלָא)

Gilgal (גִּלְגָּל) is the Hebrew word for circle. Archaeologists have discovered several ceremonial stone circles in Canaan that were used between 1200 and 1000 BC for gatherings that are assumed to be religious in nature. As these stone circles are found down in the valleys, unlike the altars at the tops of hills where the Canaanites worshiped, and 'circles' (גלגל) are mentioned throughout the old Hebrew texts, it is assumed they are early Israelite religious centers from before the First Temple was built. According to the Book of Joshua, the Israelites built a stone circle in Samaria after invading Canaan in approximately 1508 BC.

**3** Codex Vaticanus: Clauthmôna (ΚΛΑΥΘΜΩΝΑ). Translation: weepings

- Aleppo Codex: bkym (בכים). Translation: cryings

- Leningrad Codex: bochim (בֹּכִים). Translation: cryings

- Targum Jerusalem: Bochim (בּוֹכִים)

As the Greek translation appears to be a translation of the Hebrew name, the Hebrew name is used in this translation.

**4** Codex Vaticanus: oecon Israêl (ΟΙΚΟΝΙϹΡΑΗΛ). Translation: home (or house, or temple) of Israel

This reference is missing from the Masoretic version of Judges, however, as it was referring to the Samaritan temple on or near Mount Gerizim, it would have been removed. Assuming this is part of the original text of Judges, it supports the Samaritan claim that the original Israelite temple built in Canaan was on Mount Gerizim, before the building of King Solomon's Temple. Conversely, this may be viewed as evidence that the Greeks translated a Samaritan copy of Judges, however, it is unlikely that any Samaritan copies have been translated into Aramaic, as the Samaritans never abandoned the old Canaanite dialect of Samaria or the Phoenician script.

**5** Greek: Baalim (ΒΑΑΛΙΜ)

- Aleppo Codex: bôlym (בעלים). Translation: the lords (or the masters, the husbands)

- Leningrad Codex: be'alim (בְּעָלִים). Translation: the lords (or the masters, the husbands)

- Targum Jerusalem: ba'alaya (בַּעֲלַיָּא). Translation: lords

The term Ba'al was an ancient Semitic term that was used to denote lords or gods of Canaan.

**6** Codex Vaticanus: ton c͞n ton t͞h͞n (ΤΟΝΚ͞ΝΤΟΝΘ͞Ν). Translation: the Lord the God

- Codex Alexandrinus: ton cyrion theon (ΤΟΝΚΥΡΙΟΝΘΕΟΝ). Translation: the Lord God

- Aleppo Codex: ât yhwh âlhy (אֶת יהוה אלֹהִי). Translation: the Yhwh god

- Leningrad Codex: et-Yehvah | elohei (אֶת־יְהֹוָה \ אֱלֹהֵי). Translation: the Yehwah. God

- Targum Jerusalem: daYeyah elaha (דַיְיָ אֱלָהָא). Translation: from Yahw god

The name Yahw (𐤉𐤄𐤅) was transliterated as Iaô (Ιαω) in some books of the Septuagint, which was later transliterated as Iaw by the Pre-Christian Romans. In later copies of the Septuagint, the name was replaced by the name written in Canaanite (𐤉𐤄𐤅𐤄) or Assyrian script (יהוה). There are no early surviving copies of the Septuagint's version of Judges which have the name Iaô (Ιαω) in it, like some of the other books of the Septuagint, and therefore it cannot be proven conclusively if the name was in the Septuagint's Judges or not, however, a number of other books in the Septuagint appear to retain older versions of the Hebrew scriptures that pre-date the redaction during the Hasmonean dynasty, which replaced many older names of gods with Yehvah or Yehvah tzeva'ovt, the national god of Hasmonean Judea. The Aramaic sections of Masoretic Daniel that were not translated into Hebrew maintain the term adonai ha'elohim (אֲדֹנָי הָאֱלֹהִים), meaning the 'Lord the gods' where the Septuagint has 'Lord the god' (Κύριον τὸν θεὸν), however, the Hebrew sections have Yehvah elohim (יְהֹוָה אֱלֹהִים) where the Septuagint has 'Lord the god,' suggesting the Greek more accurately reflects the Aramaic source texts than the Hebrew translation.

According to tractate Sanhedrin (103b) in the Talmud, King Manasseh was blamed for removing the name, however, as his grandson Josiah 'restored' the Torah circa 625 BC, one would expect that he would have restored the name as well, if it had have been in Exodus to begin with. Furthermore, the early Torah appears to have already been translated into Aramaic during the era of Manasseh's father king Hezekiah, suggesting that he removed the name during his religious reforms.

**7** Codex Vaticanus: Ba'al (ΒΑΑΛ)

• Aleppo Codex: bôl (בֹּעַל). Translation: lord (or master, or husband)

• Leningrad Codex: ba'al (בָּעַל). Translation: lord (or master, or husband)

• Targum Jerusalem: va'ala (בְעָלָא). Translation: lord (or master, or husband)

While Ba'al was a title applied to many Canaanite gods, when used as a name, it referred to Ba'al Hadad, the storm god, and hero of the Ba'al Cycle literature of ancient Canaan.


**8** Codex Vaticanus: Astartaes (ΑϹΤΑΡΤΑΙϹ)

• Aleppo Codex: Ôštrwt (עשתרות)

• Leningrad Codex: Ashtarovt (עַשְׁתָּרֹות)

• Targum Jerusalem: Ashtarata (עֲשָׁתְּרָתָא)

Astarte was the Greek name the Canaanite of Ashtoreth and Mesopotamian Ishtar. Ashtoreth was the Canaanite goddess of love, sex, war, and the planet Venus. Local versions of her were worshiped throughout the Middle East and the Mediterranean Sea. In Akkadian, he was a god known as Asdartu, while in Babylonia she was known as Ishtar, in Ugaritic she was known as 'Athtart, and in Etruscan, she was known as Uni-Astre. The Greek goddess Aphrodite appears to be derived from an early version of her, while the Roman goddess appears to be derived indirectly through the Etruscan Uni-Astre. The Aramean transgender deity Atargatis appears to be another early offshoot that maintained the early male aspect of the god from the Akkadian era while accepting that the god had become a goddess. During the New Kingdom era of Egyptian history, circa 1549 tom 1077 AD, Astarte was incorporated into the Egyptian pantheon as one of the daughters of Ra, as she appeared in the book entitled the 'Contest between Horus and Set.' According to the Phoenician scholar Sanchuniathon, who suppos-edly lived circa 1200 BC, Astarte's sister was Asherah, who was also known as Anat. The word Asherah also appears in the Septuagint many times and appears to be widely worshiped by the early Israelites.

# Judges: Chapter 3

These are the nations which the Lord left to test Israel with, all that had not known the wars of Canaan, for the sake of the generations of Israel, to teach them war. The men before them did not know them. The five lords of the foreigners,[1] and all the Canaanites, Sidonians, and Mitanni[2] who lived in Lebanon from Mount Hermon[3] to the entrance of Hama.[4] This was done to test Israel, to know whether they would obey the commands of the Lord, which he ordered their fathers through the hand of Moses. The Israelites lived among the Canaanites, Cypriots, Amorites, Perizzites, Mitannians, and Jebusites. They took their daughters as wives for themselves, and they gave their daughters to their sons and served their gods.

The Israelites did evil in the sight of the Lord, and forgot the Lord God, and served Ba'als and Asherahs.[5] The Lord was very angry with Israel and sold them into the hand of the Kassite Barattarna,[6] king of the Syrian rivers,[7] and the Israelites served the Kassite Barattarna eight years. The Israelites cried to the Lord, and the Lord raised a savior for Israel, and he saved them, Othniel the son of Kenez, the younger brother of Caleb. The spirit of the Lord came on him, and he judged Israel, and he went out to war against the Kassite Barattarna, and the Lord delivered into his hand the Kassite Barattarna king of the Syrian rivers, and his hand prevailed against the Kassite Barattarna. The land was peaceful for forty years, and Othniel the son of Kenez died.

The Israelites continued to do evil before the Lord, and the Lord strengthened Moab against Israel because they had done evil before the Lord. He gathered to himself all Ammonites and Amalekites, and went and attacked Israel, and occupied the city of palm-trees. The Israelites served Eglon the king of Moab for eighteen years. The Israelites cried to the Lord, and he raised for them a savior, Ehud the son of Gera, a Benjamite, a man who used both hands alike, and the Israelites sent gifts by his hand to Eglon king of Moab. Ehud made himself a double-edged dagger a span long, and he hid it under his cloak on his right thigh. He went and brought the presents to Eglon king of Moab, and Eglon was a very fat man.[8] When Ehud had finished offering his gifts, he dismissed those that brought the gifts. He returned from the quarries that were by the circle, and Ehud said, "I have a secret message for you, king!"

Eglon replied to him, "Be quiet, and he sent away from his presence all who waited on him."

Ehud went to him, and they sat in his upper summer chamber all alone, and Ehud said, "I have a message from God for you, my king," and Eglon rose up from his throne near him. As he arose, Ehud stretched out his left hand, and took the dagger from his right thigh, and plunged it into his stomach, and drove in also the haft behind the blade, and the fat closed in on the blade, as he did not pull out the dagger from his belly. Ehud went out to the porch, and collapsed out by the guards stationed there, and shut the doors of the chamber on him, and locked them. He went out, and Eglon's servants came and saw, and the doors of the upper chamber were locked, and they asked, "Does he not uncover his feet in the summer chamber? They waited until they were embarrassed, and no one opened the doors of the upper chamber. They took the key, and opened them, and found their lord had fallen dead on the ground.

Ehud escaped while they were in chaos, and no one paid attention to him, and he passed the quarries and escaped to Seirah.[9] It happened when Ehud came into the land of Israel, that he blew the horn on Mount Ephraim, and the Israelites came down with him from the mountain. He led them and said, "Come down after me, for the Lord God has delivered our enemies, Moab, into our hands!"

They went down after him and occupied the fords of the Jordan en route to Moab, and he did not allow a man to pass over. They slaughtered about ten thousand Moabites on that day, every lusty person and every mighty man, and not a man escaped. Moab was humbled on that day under the hand of Israel, and the land had peace for eighty years, and Ehud judged them until he died.

After him rose up Shamgar the son of Anat, and slaughtered six hundred Pelesets with a plowshare, like one drawn by oxen, and he too saved Israel.

# Judges: Chapter 3 Notes

**1** Greek: allophylôn (ⲁⲗⲗⲟⲫⲩⲗⲱⲛ). Translation: foreigners (or strangers, aliens)

- Aleppo Codex: plštym (פלשתים). Translation: Philistines (or Palestinians, Peleset)

- Leningrad Codex: Felishtim (פְּלִשְׁתִּים). Translation: Philistines (or Palestinians, Peleset)

- Targum Jerusalem: Pelishta'ei (פְּלִשְׁתָּאֵי). Translation: Philistines (or Palestinians, Peleset)

The Pelesets were an ancient people based in the region of the modern Gaza Strip of the Palestinian Territories. The earliest surviving mention of them is from the reliefs of the Temple of Ramses III at Medinet Habu in Egypt that dates back to some time between 1186 and 1155 BC, in which they were called Pelesets (𓂋𓏤𓊪𓏲𓏭𓈖𓀀𓏥). They were also known in Middle Babylonian as the ᵏᵘʳPalastu (𒆳𒉺𒆷𒅖𒌅). It is unclear where they came from, however, one theory is that they were the Pala, a Luwian people from the Black Sea coast of Anatolia. The region was an independent country called Palaa (𒉺𒆷𒀀) in the Neshite (Hittite) records from the 1600s BC, however, have become part of the Nesite Empire by the 1500s BC. Around the time the Pelesets invaded Canaan, the Pala were driven from their homeland by the neighboring Kaskians from northeast Anatolia, which supports the connection between the groups, however, it has yet to be proven conclusively.

The presence of the Pelesets in Southern Canaan during the time of Abraham and Isaac is anachronistic, and therefore this section of text, describing the origin of the Semitic tribes, found in both the Septuagint and the Masoretic text, likely dates to the original Phoenician translation in the early Iron Age.

**2** Greek: Euaion (ΕΥΑΙΟΝ)

- Aleppo Codex: Hwy (חוי)

- Leningrad Codex: Chivvi (חִוִּי)

- Targum Jerusalem: Chiva'ei (חִוָּאֵי). Translation: farmer

The term is believed to have been derived from the name of the Hurrians, however, is derived separately from the other term Chori (חֹרִי). As the Hivites are routinely reported to be rulers, the term appears to represent the Mitanni-Aryan nobility or Vedic priests. As the Mitanni Empire lost its Canaanite territory circa 1350 BC, the original text of Judges must date back to before that time.

**3** Codex Vaticanus: orous tou Aermôn (ΟΡΟΥΣΤΟΥΑΕΡΜΩΝ). Translation: mountain of Hermon

- Codex Alexandrinus: orous tou Balaermôn (ΟΡΟΥΣΤΟΥ ΒΑΛΑΕΡΜΩΝ). Translation: mountain of Balaermon

- Aleppo Codex: hr Bôl Hrmwn (הר בעל חרמון). Translation: mountain of Lord Hermon

- Leningrad Codex: har Ba'al Chermovn (הַר בַּעַל חֶרְמוֹן). Translation: mountain of Lord Hermon

- Targum Jerusalem: tur meishar Chermovn (טוּר מֵישַׁר חֶרְמוֹן). Translation: mountain of the prince (or commander) of Hermon

The location of Ba'al-Hermon in the Masoretic text and Codex Alexandrinus is unclear, however, the Codex Vaticanus indicates it was Mount Hermon, on the modern Israeli-Lebanese-Syrian border. Mount Hermon was the location where the Watchers descended to Earth in the Enochian Book of the Watchers. It is also the location of the Anaks in the Book of Joshua, which appears to be a reference to the descendants of the Watchers. The Egyptians listed a people known as the Anaq living in the region between 2300 and 1700 BC, which are accepted as being the same people the Israelites called the Anaks. The ruins of over 30 temples have been discovered on Mount Hermon, including a rock-cut temple of the summit called Qasr Antar, which may date back to the Anak civilization.

**4** Codex Vaticanus: Labôemath (ⲗⲁⲃⲱⲉⲙⲁⲑ)

• Codex Alexandrinus: Lobôêmath (ⲗⲟⲃⲱⲏⲙⲁⲑ)

• Aleppo Codex: lbwå Hmt (**לבוא חמת**). Translation: entrance to Hama

• Leningrad Codex: levov Chamat (לְבֹוא חֲמָת). Translation: entrance to Hama

• Targum Jerusalem: ma'alana daChamat (מַעֲלָנָא דַחֲמָת). Translation: gateway of Hama

The Greeks transliterated the word meaning 'entrance' as part of the name, and therefore the Masoretic version of the name is used in this translation. Hama is a major city in western Syria north of Lebanon that had been inhabited since around 6000 BC. It was under the control of the Mitanni Empire between 1500 and 1350 BC.

**5** Codex Vaticanus: toes alsesin (ⲧⲟⲓⲥ ⲁⲗⲥⲉⲥⲓⲛ). Translation: the sacred groves

• Aleppo Codex: åšrwt (**אשרות**). Translation: Asherahs

• Leningrad Codex: Asherovt (אֲשֵׁרֹות). Translation: Asherahs

• Targum Jerusalem: Asharata (אֲשֵׁרָתָא). Translation: Asherahs

Asherah was the wife of the Canaanite god El, and Mesopotamian god An (Anu), and the mother of the Canaanite gods. The Asherahs in question were likely sacred oak trees dedicated to Asherah, similar to the sacred acacia trees dedicated to Iusaaset in Egypt. Iusaaset was the wife of Atum, the Egyptian creator god of Heliopolis that served as the basis of Moses' creator god, and Egyptian equivalent of Ba'al Shalim, the Canaanite god that Jerusalem was named after.

**6** Codex Vaticanus: Chousarsathaem (ΧΟΥϹΑΡϹΑΘΑΙΜ)

• Codex Alexandrinus: Chousarsathôm (ΧΟΥϹΑΡϹΑΘѠΜ)

• Aleppo Codex: kwšn ršôtym (כושן רשעתים)

• Leningrad Codex: kushan rish'atayim (כּוּשַׁן רִשְׁעָתָ֫יִם)

• Targum Jerusalem: Kushan chayava (כּוּשַׁן חַיָּבָא). Translation: Kushan sinner (or debtor, stammerer, legal heir)

While the Hebrew term Kush (כוש) referred to the land of Kush, south of Egypt, whose people were known as the Kushi (כּוּשִׁי), Kushan (כּוּשַׁן) was a different term, which the Greeks did not recognize, and therefore transliterated as Chousa (Χουσα). As the term referred to someone who was the king in thee rivers of Aram (Syria), the origin of the word was almost certainly Kasium (𒆕𒀸𒋛𒅎), today translated as Kassite. The Kassites were the rulers of Babylonia in the late bronze age from some time in the 1500s BC, until 1155 BC, when they were conquered by the Elamites. The Hebrew term rishatayim (רִשְׁעָתָ֫יִם) is not proper Hebrew, Canaanite, or Aramaic, however, may be a corruption of the term resha'im (רְשָׁעִים), meaning 'criminals.' Alternatively, this may be the ancient Canaanite spelling of the name of king Paarshataar (𒌓𒀀𒈾𒉺𒀜𒋫𒈾), more commonly transliterated as Barattarna today, king of the Mitanni Empire circa 1485 BC. Barattarna is recorded as occupying northern Canaan during the reign of Hatsheput by establishing a series of puppet states across the region, and gaining access to the Mediterranean Sea. In circa 1479 BC, the Egyptian king Thutmose II died, and his former queen Hatsheput seized the throne in the name of his two year old son Thutmose III.

Hatsheput was not the mother of Thutmose III, another wife Iset was, whom Hatsheput married after officially changing her sex to male. After changing genders Hatsheput declared himself to be Thutmose III's regent, although later assumed the role of king himself until his death, when Thutmose III inherited the throne. While Hatsheput was a very unpopular king, his rule established the dominant architectural style of the New Kingdom. The entire concept of a female king was rejected by many, with graffiti mocking King Hatsheput's gender appearing in archaeological records of the era. Most of Kush appears to have rejected Hatsheput, and rebelled against his rule. After inheriting the throne in circa 1458 BC, Thutmose III attempted to erase Hatsheput's rule from Egyptian records, claiming to have ruled continuously from the death of Thutmose II in circa 1479 BC. While her role as queen of Thutmose II was never erased, the era when Hatsheput ruled Egypt was, and his era as king was not rediscovered until the 1800s.

It is clear that there was a rebellion against King Hatsheput in Syria, backed by the Mitanni, and control of all territory north of Megiddo was lost, as the first thing Thutmose III did after assuming the throne was march north into Canaan, where he fought the battle of Megiddo against the rebelling Syrian kings, and their Mitanni allies. The Battle of Megiddo was the largest battle recorded in Egyptian records up until that time, with both the Egyptians and Canaanite rebels estimated to have fielded around 1,000 chariots and 10,000 infantry. After defeating the Canaanites in the initial battle, the Egyptians plundered 924 chariots and 200 suits of armor. The Canaanite kings fell back to the fortified city of Kadesh, which the Egyptians then besieged for seven months. According to the records at Karnak, when the city surrendered the Egyptians captured 340 Canaanite and Mitanni princes, 2,041 mares, 191 foals, 6 stallions, 924 chariots, 200 suits of armor, 502 bows, 1,929 cattle, and 22,500 sheep.

Between 1458 and 1425 BC, Thutmose III fought a series of campaigns in Canaan, pushing Egyptian control north to the Euphrates River, and then crossed it into the Mitanni empire, where he plundered the country, which apparently had not rebuilt its defenses after the loss at Megiddo. After securing Canaan, Thutmose III marched his army south into Nubia, recapturing territory as far as the fourth cataract, all of which had been lost under the rule of Hatsheput.

It is unclear why the author would have referred to Barattarna as a Kassite unless it was actually written at the time. The Mitanni rulers are often linked to the Kassites culturally, however, the peoples they ruled were not culturally similar. During the wars of Thutmose III in

Canaan, the term Mitanni become common, however, earlier records simply called the land Naharin, meaning 'Rivers,' and called the people Hurrians. While the Hurrians were the primary population of the Mitanni Empire, the rulers were an unrelated group of Indo-Aryans, who spoke a language similar to Sanskrit, and worshiped the Vedic gods. They appear to have seized power over the Hurrians in the Khabur river region in the 1550s BC, from which they expanded in every direction until the Battle of Megiddo.

The Mitanni relationship with the Kassites is unclear, as the Kassites are not viewed as being Indo-Aryans, however, may have been Hurrians. The two cultures were close at the time, and it is plausible that the earliest Mitanni to arrive in the region were viewed as being Kassites by the Canaanites. Nevertheless, by 1457 BC the term would have already been anachronistic, as the term Mitanni would have replaced it, suggesting this verse was written between 1472 and 1457 BC. As the actions of King Barattarna correlate with what Rishatayim is described as doing in the verse, his name is used in this translation, however, it is plausible it was simply a reference to the rebels.

**7** Codex Vaticanus: basileôs Syrias potamôn (ΒΑϹΙΛΕѠϹϹΥΡΙΑϹ ΠΟΤΑΜѠΝ). Translation: king of the Syrian rivers

- Aleppo Codex: mlk Årm nhrym (מלך ארס נהרים). Translation: king of Aram's rivers

- Leningrad Codex: melech Aram naharayim (מֶלֶךְ אֲרַם נַהֲרָיִם). Translation: king of Aram's rivers

- Targum Jerusalem: malka da'Aram di al Perat (מַלְכָּא דַאֲרָם דִי עַל פְּרָת). Translation: king of Aram (or Syria) on the Euphrates

The region in question is northern-most modern Syria, and south-east Turkey north of Syria, which was occupied by the Egyptians between 1505 and 1480 BC, and again between 1457 and 1350 BC. The Egyptian name was Naharin, which had been adopted from the local Aramaic word meaning 'rivers.' At the time specified in the Septuagint's chronology, between 1480 and 1472 BC, this was the Mitanni king Barattarna.

**8** Codex Vaticanus: Eglôm anêr astios sphodra (ⲈⲄⲀⲰⲘ ⲀⲚⲎⲢ ⲀⲤⲦⲈⲒⲞⲤ ⲤⲪⲞⲆⲢⲀ). Translation: Elgom was a very handsome (or cosmopolitan, elegant) man

- Aleppo Codex: ôglwn åyš bryå måd (**עגלון איש בריא מאד**). Translation: Eglon was a very healthy (or very fat, lusty) man

- Leningrad Codex: Eglovn ish bari me'od (עֶגְלוֹן אִישׁ בָּרִיא מְאֹד). Translation: Eglon was a very healthy (or very fat, lusty) man

- Targum Jerusalem: Eglon gevar fatim lachada (עֶגְלוֹן גְבַר פַּטִים לַחֲדָא). Translation: Eglon was a powerful (or strong) perfumed (or fat) one

The Greeks appear to have translated fat (בָּרִיא) as handsome (αστειος) assuming this was a homosexual encounter, however, the Hebrew term implies the man was either healthy or fat or lusty, and later he is confirmed as being very fat.

**9** Codex Vaticanus: Setirōtha (ⲤⲈⲦⲒⲢⲰⲐⲀ)

- Codex Alexandrinus: Sirôtha (ⲤⲈⲒⲢⲰⲐⲀ)

- Aleppo Codex: Šôyrth (שְׂעִירָתָה)

- Leningrad Codex: Se'iratah (שְׂעִירָתָה)

- Targum Jerusalem: Se'irata (שְׂעִירָתָא)

The Greek and Hebrew names appear to be transliterations of the same name, assumed to be an ancient town in the mountains of Ephraim.

# Judges: Chapter 4

The Israelites continued to do evil against the Lord after Ehud was dead. The Lord sold the Israelites into the hand of Jabin the king of Canaan who ruled from Hazor,[1] and the chief of the army was Siazara,[2] who lived in the Forge-of-the-Foreigners.[3] The Israelites cried to the Lord because he had nine hundred iron chariots, and he mightily oppressed Israel twenty years. Deborah was a prophetess and the wife of Lapidoth who judged Israel at that time. She sat under the Palm Tree of Deborah between Ramah[4] and Bethel in the mountains of Ephraim, and the Israelites went up to her for judgment.

Deborah sent and called Barak the son of Abinoam out of Kadesh Naphtali, and she asked him, "Has not the Lord God of Israel commanded you, 'Go to Mount Tabor, and take ten thousand men of the Naphtalites and Zebulonites. I will bring to you to the Kishion river, where Siazara the captain of the army of Jabin and his chariots and his multitude are, and I will deliver them into your hands?'"

Barak answered her, "If you will go with me, I will go, and if you will not go, I will not go, as I don't know the day to which the Lord sends his messenger to me."

She replied, "I will certainly go with you, but know that your victory will not depend on the expedition you undertake, for the Lord will sell Siazara into the hands of a woman."

Deborah left Kadesh with Barak. Barak called the Zebulonites and Naphtalites out of Kadesh, and 10,000 men went up with him, and Deborah also went up with him. Eber the blacksmith[5] who remained of the blacksmiths,[6] descended from the sons of Jobab, the son-in-law of Moses,[7] pitched his tent by the oak of the covetous ones, which is near Kedesh. Siazara was told that Barak

219

the son of Abinoam had gone up to Mount Tabor. Siazara summoned all his chariots, nine hundred iron chariots, and all the people with him from the Forge-of-the-Foreigners to the Kishion river.

Deborah said to Barak, "Rise, for this is the day on which the Lord has delivered Siazara into your hand. The Lord will go out before you," and Barak went down from Mount Tabor and 10,000 men with him.

The Lord discomfited Siazara, and all his chariots, and army, with the edge of the sword before Barak, and Siazara fell off his chariot and fled on foot. Barak chased after the chariots and army, to the Forge-of-the-Foreigners, and the whole army of Siazara fell by the edge of the sword, and there was no one left. Siazara fled on foot to the tent of Jael the wife of Eber the blacksmith his friend, for there was peace between Jabin king of Hazor and the house of Eber the blacksmith. Jael went out to meet Siazara, and said to him, "Turn aside my lord, turn aside to me, don't be afraid."

He turned aside to her into the tent, and she covered him with a mantle. Siazara said to her, "Give me, I beg you, a little water to drink, for I am thirsty," and she opened a jug of milk, and gave it to him drink, and covered him.

Siazara told her, "Stand now by the door of the tent, and it will come to pass if any man comes to you, and asks, 'Is there a man here?' Then answer, 'There is not.'"

Jael the wife of Eber took a tent spike and a hammer in her hands, and went secretly to him and held the spike to his temple and drove it through into the ground, and he collapsed, and darkness fell on him and he died. Barak was chasing Siazara, and Jael went out to meet him, and said to him, "Come, and I will take you to the man who you are looking for."

He went with her and saw Siazara was dead, and the spike was in his temple. So God destroyed Jabin king of Canaan on that day before the Israelites. The hand of the Israelites prevailed more and more against King Jabin of Canaan until they completely destroyed King Jabin of Canaan.

# Judges: Chapter 4 Notes

**1** Codex Vaticanus: Asôr (ᴀᴄⲱⲣ)

- Aleppo Codex: Hswr (חצור)

- Leningrad Codex: Chatzovr (חָצֹור)

- Targum Jerusalem: Chatzovr (חָצֹור)

Hazor was a major town north of the Sea of Galilee for thousands of years, from at least 2700 BC to the Greek era. The town was mentioned in the Egyptian Execration Texts from the 1700s BC, the Mari Archive of the 1600s BC, the Annals of Thutmoses III in the 1400s BC, the Amarna Letters of the 1300s, and the Papyrus Anastasi I from the 1200s BC. Between 1800 and 1550 BC, the town was a vassal of the city of Qatna, in modern Syria. Hazor was officially annexed by the New Egyptian Empire in 1457 BC when Pharaoh Thutmose III's armies passed through Canaan en route to Syria, however, continued to be governed by local kings subject to the empire. The Amarna Letters include correspondence between the King of Hazor and Pharaoh Akhenaten, specifically EA227 and EA228, the second one mentioning the name of the King of Hazor as being Abdi-Tirshi of 'Hasura.'

These Letters are broadly dated with the rest as being written between 1350 and 1330 BC. According to the chronology of the Septuagint, the era that Jabin of Hazor ruled the Israelites was 1334 to 1314 BC, implying he was appointed by Smenkhkare, Neferneferuaten, or Tutankhamen in the aftermath of Akhenaten's reign (1351 to 1334 BC), or by Siazara when he claimed the throne. This implies that the Judges Ehud and Shamgar were close to the Egyptian crown during their periods as Judge, which would have taken place during the reigns of Amenhotep II, Thutmose IV, Amenhotep III, and Akhenaten.

**2** Codex Vaticanus: Sisara (ⲥⲓⲥⲁⲣⲁ)

- Aleppo Codex: Sysrå (סיסרא)

- Leningrad Codex: Sisra (סִיסְרָא)

- Targum Jerusalem: Sisra (סִיסְרָא)

This name appears to have been the Egyptian name Siazårô
(𓂝𓈎𓇳𓇗𓇋), meaning 'recognized son of Ra,' however, this specific
name would have denoted a king from either southern Egypt or Nubia,
and Siazara is otherwise unknown from regal records. As Siazara is
described as commanding an army with 900 iron chariots, this appears to
be the Egyptian army stationed in Canaan. Based on the chronologies in
the Septuagint's Exodus, Joshua, and Judges, Siazara would have been
the commander of the Egyptian forces in Canaan sometime between
1334 to 1314 BC. Iron weapons and chariots had been introduced by the
Hyksos dynasty, and the Egyptians of the New Kingdom did use some
iron weapons for their military, however, it is not clear if they were
still using iron chariots, or have reverted to bronze chariots. It is not
known where they were smithing their iron weapons, however, it was
not in Egypt and believed to have been somewhere in Canaan or Nubia.
This may have been at Site 200 in the Timna Valley, in southern Israel's
Arabah region. Site 200 is an iron smelting site worked by Egyptians
during the Egyptian New Kingdom era.


**3** Codex Vaticanus: Arisôth tôn ethnôn (ΑΡΙϹΩΘΤΩΝΕΘΝΩΝ).
Translation: Arisoth the Nations

- Aleppo Codex: ḥršt hgwym (חרשת הגוים)

- Leningrad Codex: charoshet hagGovyim (חֲרֹשֶׁת הַגּוֹיִם). Translation:
the forge of the foreigners

- Targum Jerusalem: tekof kerakkei ammaya (תְּקוֹף כְּרַכֵּי עַמְמַיָא).
Translation: fortified (or strong) large city of the commoners (or peoples)

The term govyim (גּוֹיִם), translated as 'tribes' (εθνων) in Greek and
'commoners' (עַמְמַיָא) in the Targum Jerusalem, was originally adopted
from the Akkadian name of the Gutium (𒆳𒋗𒁴𒆠) tribe who lived in
the Zagros mountains during the Akkadian and Neo-Sumerian eras.
During the Middle Babylonian era, the setting of Judges, the term
began being applied to the Indo-European tribes that entered

Mesopotamia from the Zagros mountains, including the Kassites, who seized control of Babylon, and then ruled Babylonia for centuries. The only peoples in Canaan likely to be identified as Gutium were the Hyksos and Mitanni. The Smith of the Gutium is described as being the fortress that Siazara's army was based out of. It seems likely the fortress was inherited from the Hyksos Dynasty which built several fortresses in Canaan.

**4** Codex Vaticanus: Rama (ᴘᴀᴍᴀ)

• Aleppo Codex: Rmh (רמה)

• Leningrad Codex: Ramah (רָמֶה)

Targum Jerusalem: Yricho pardesin beramata zeitin avedin meshach bevik'ata beit shakya (יְרִיחוֹ פַּרְדְּסִין בְּרָמָתָא זֵיתִין עָבְדִין מְשַׁח בְּבִקְעָתָא בֵּית שָׁקְיָא). Translation: Jericho's orchards (or walled gardens) and Ramah's olives, creators of perfume in the valley of Beth Shakya. A town called Ramah was located near Gibeah in the Book of Joshua.

**5** Codex Vaticanus: Chaber o Cinaeos (ᴄᴀʙᴇᴘᴏᴋɪɴᴀɪᴏᴄ). Translation: Chaber the Cinaeos

• Codex Alexandrinus: plêsion tou Cinaeou (ᴨᴧʜᴄɪᴏɴ ᴛᴏʏ ᴋɪɴᴀɪᴏʏ). Translation: near the Cinaeou

• Aleppo Codex: Hbr hqyny (חבר הקיני). Translation: Hbr the Kenite (or smith)

• Leningrad Codex: Chever hakkeini (חֶבֶר הַקֵּינִי). Translation: Heber the Kenite (or smith)

• Targum Jerusalem: Chever Shalma'ah (חֶבֶר שַׁלְמָאָה). Translation: Heber Shalmaite

As the term Kenite means blacksmith, he is referred to him as 'Heber the blacksmith' in this translation. The Shalmaites mentioned in the Jerusalem Targum were a tribe of arabs from the late Classical era, 2000 years after the era the book is set in.

**6** Codex Vaticanus: Caena (ΚΑΙΝΑ)

• Codex Alexandrinus: the term is omitted from the verse

• Aleppo Codex: qyn (קֵין). Translation: smith, metalworker, blacksmith

• Leningrad Codex: kayin (קָיִן). Translation: smith, metalworker, blacksmith

• Targum Jerusalem: Shalma'ei (שַׁלְמָאֵי). Translation: Shalmaites

**7** Codex Vaticanus: Iôbab gambrou Môysê (ΙΩΒΑΒΓΑΜΒΡΟΥ ΜΩΥCΗ). Translation: Jobab bridegroom of Moses

• Aleppo Codex: Ḥbb ḥtn Mšh (חבב חתן משה). Translation: Ḥbb groom Moses

• Leningrad Codex: Chovav choten Mosheh (חֹבָב חֹתֵן מֹשֶׁה). Translation: Hobab groom Moses

• Targum Jerusalem: Chovav chamuhi deMosheh (חוֹבָב חֲמוּהִי דְמֹשֶׁה). Translation: Hobab in the house of Moses

# Judges: Chapter 5

Deborah and Barak ben Abinoam, sang on that day:

A revelation was made in Israel when the people were made willing!

Praise you, Lord!

Listen you kings! Listen governors,[1] and I will sing!

I will sing to the Lord! I will!

I will sing a psalm to the Lord God of Israel!

Lord, in your going out on Seir, when you went out of the land of Edom, the earth quaked and the sky dropped dew, and the cloud rained.

The mountains were shaken before the face of the Lord, the Sinai before the face of the Lord God of Israel.

In the days of Shamgar son of Anath, in the days of Jael, they deserted the ways and became perverse.

The mighty men in Israel failed, they failed until Deborah arose as a mother for Israel.

They chose new gods, then the rulers of cities fought, and there was no shield or spear seen among forty thousand Israelites.

My heart listens to the orders given in Israel, you that are willing among the people, bless the Lord.

You who move as Aten the sun god at midday,[2] sitting in judgment, and following the path, and riding the pathway, declare from the noise of disturbers among the drawers of water and retell the righteous acts of the Lord. Increase righteous acts in Israel, then the people of the Lord will go down to the cities.

Awake, awake, Deborah! Awake, awake, sing a song!

Rise, Barak, and catch captives, son of Abinoam.

Then the survivors went down against the nobles, the people of the Lord went down for him among the mighty ones from me. Ephraim rooted them out in Amalek, then Benjamin with your people from Machir came down with me hunting out the enemy, and from Zebulun came those that write with the scribe's pen to record.

Princes of Issachar were with Deborah and Barak, so she sent Barak on foot into the valley to the portions of Reuben. Great pangs reached the heart.

Why did they sit between the sheepfolds to hear the bleating of flocks for the divisions of Reuben? There was great searching of hearts. Gilead is on the other side of Jordan where he pitched his tents. Why does Dan remain in ships? Asher sat down on the sea-coasts, and he will camp at his ports. The people of Zebulun exposed their mind to death, and Naphtali went to the high places of their land.

Kings set themselves in formation, and then the kings of Canaan fought in Ti'inik at the water of Megiddo, and they took no bribe of money. The stars from the sky set themselves in formation, they left their paths to fight with Siazara. The brook of Kishion swept them away, the ancient brook, the brook Kishion.

"My mighty mind will trample him down. When the hoofs of the horse were entangled, his mighty ones earnestly rushed to curse Southern Egypt.[3] Curse it," said the messenger of the lord, "Cursed is everyone who dwells in it, because they did not come to help the Lord, to help him among the mighty."

"Blessed among women be Jael the wife of Eber the black-smith. Let her be blessed above women in tents. He asked for water, and she gave him milk in a dish, she brought butter of princes, she stretched out her left hand to the spike, and her right to the hand workman's hammer and she struck Siazara with it, she nailed through his head and murdered him!"

"She nailed through his temples! He rolled down between her feet, and he fell and lay between her feet. He collapsed and fell, where he collapsed, there he fell dead."

"The mother of Siazara looked down through the window out of the loophole, saying, 'Why was his chariot ashamed? Why did the wheels of his chariots wait?'"

"Her wise ladies answered her, and she returned answers to herself, 'Won't they find him dividing the plunder? He will certainly be gracious to every man! There are spoils of dyed garments for Siazara, spoils of various dyed garments, dyed embroidered garments, they are the spoils for his neck.'"

"So let all your enemies perish, Lord! They who love him will be like the sun[4] coming in his strength."

The land had peace for forty years.[5]

# Judges: Chapter 5 Notes

**1** Codex Vaticanus: satrapae (**ϹΑΤΡΑΠΑΙ**). Translation: satraps

• Codex Alexandrinus: satrapae dynatoe (**ϹΑΤΡΑΠΑΙΔΥΝΑΤΟΙ**). Translation: satraps of power (or forces)

• Aleppo Codex: rznym {s} ånky {r} ({ר}) (רֹזְנִים {ס} אָנֹכִי)

• Leningrad Codex: rozenim anochi (רֹזְנִים אָנֹכִי)

• Targum Jerusalem: shiltonaya (שִׁלְטֹנַיָּא). Translation: sultans

The Greeks transliterated the word in the old Aramaic text as 'satraps,' the Persian word for governors, however, that is not a translation of the term in the Hebrew translation. Likewise, the translator of the Targum Jerusalem substituted 'sultans.' The Aleppo Codex indicates that the terms 'rznym' and 'ånky' were found in two different source texts, however the Leningrad Codex later treats them as continuous string of words. Neither term is actually Hebrew, however, rznym (רזנים) is generally assumed to be scribal error of rbnym (רבנים), meaning 'great ones' which may be the source of the Greek 'satraps,' however, it is more likely that 'satraps' was already added to the Aramaic text the Greeks translated, as they had no reason to substitute a Persian word.

Assuming that rznym is a scribal error of rbnym, this error must have taken place when the cuneiform text of Judges, or possibly just a book of Deborah and Barak was translated into Canaanite. The Akkadian cuneiform BÈ (𒁀) was part of the ZÁ (𒍝), along with the UD (𒌓). As the UD also held the phonetic value of U, it would have simply meant the original Canaanite cuneiform word in the text was a plural of rabbu (𒊏𒁀𒌓), which mirrors the reconstructed pronunciation of the word rabbu (𒊏𒁀), the in Ugaritic Canaanite version of the word from the same era.

None of the other scripts that the book could have been written in had similar letters for B and Z, including Egyptian hieroglyphics as used to spell Canaanite words: B (𓃀) and Z (𓏤), Paleo-Canaanite: B (𐤁) and Z (=), Phoenician Canaanite: B (𐤁) and Z (𐤆), and Aramaic: B (𐡁) and Z (𐡆). The translation of 'satraps of power,' found in the Codex Alexandrinus, indicates that the two words were already in a combined form of the text by the 5th century, and that the Greeks interpreted Ånky (אנכי) as a reference to the Anaki (עֲנָקִי). The Ånâkj (𓂝𓈖𓆥) were also recorded in Egyptian records from the Middle Kingdoms as having lived in the region of mount Hermon and mount Carmel, however, they do not appear to have still been around in the New Kingdom era, suggesting it was an attempt to interpret the word rznym after the script had been translated into Proto-Canaanite or Canaanite. As the original term in the text was probably 'rabbu' which is essentially the bronze age version of the Septuagint's 'satrap,' and Targum Jerusalem's 'sultan,' the term 'governor' is used in this translation.

**2** Codex Vaticanus: epibebêcotes epi onou thêlias mesêmbrias cathêmenoe epi critêriou cae poreuomenoe epi odous synedrôn eph odô (ΕΠΙΒΕΒΗΚΟΤΕϹ ΕΠΙ ΟΝΟΥ ΘΗΛΕΙΑϹ ΜΕϹΗΜΒΡΙΑϹ ΚΑΘΗΜΕΝΟΙ ΕΠΙ ΚΡΙΤΗΡΙΟΥ ΚΑΙ ΠΟΡΕΥΟΜΕΝΟΙ ΕΠΙ ΟΔΟΥϹ ϹΥΝΕΔΡΩΝ ΕΦ ΟΔΩ). Translation: "You who rides on a single female at noon, sitting in judgment, and following the path, and riding the pathway."

• Codex Alexandrinus: epibebêcotes epi ypozygiôn cathêmenoe epi lampênôn (ΕΠΙΒΕΒΗΚΟΤΕϹ ΕΠΙ ΥΠΟΖΥΓΙΩΝ ΚΑΘΗΜΕΝΟΙ ΕΠΙ ΛΑΜΠΗΝΩΝ). Translation: "You who ride on a beast of burden and covered chariots."

• Aleppo Codex: rkby åtnwt shrwt {s} yšby {r} ôl mdyn whlky ôl drk--šyhw {s} (רכבי אתנות צחרות {ס} ישבי {ר} על מדין והלכי על דרך--שיחו {ס}). Translation: "You who mount tribes [S] inhabitants [R] in Midian and travel along the path, speak [S]"

• Leningrad Codex: rochevei atonovt tzechorovt yoshevei al-middin veholechei al-derech sichu (רֹכְבֵי אֲתֹנוֹת צְחֹרוֹת יֹשְׁבֵי עַל-מִדִּין וְהֹלְכֵי עַל-דֶּרֶךְ שִׂיחוּ). Translation: "You who ride on white donkeys, and sit in Midian and travel along the path, speak."

The verse had been a mystery for thousands of years, as God should not be described as riding a 'female at noon,' 'beasts of burden and covered chariots,' or 'white donkeys.' Ȧtnwt (אתנות) appears to be an ancient attempt to transliterate Aten (𓇼𓈖𓇳) into Aramaic and then Hebrew via the Akkadian Cuneiform Iaati ᵃⁿUtu (𒁹𒌓𒌝𒌓 ✳𒊩), meaning 'Aten god of the Sun.' This would mean the verse was something like: "You who move as Aten the sun god at midday, sitting in judgment, and following the path, and riding the pathway."

Aten was the Egyptian solar-god during the reign of Akhenaten (1353 to 1336 BC), whose name translates in Egyptian as 'disk.' The name Aten fell out of use in Egypt during the restoration of the old gods by Pharaoh Horemheb (1319-1292 BC), implying the Song of Deborah and Barak date to before the end of this era. Based on the dating of the Book of Judges found in the Septuagint, the song would have been sung in 1314 BC, five years into Horemheb's reign.

**3** Codex Vaticanus: Mêrôz (ΜΗΡѠΖ)

- Codex Alexandrinus: Marôz (ΜΑΡѠΖ)

- Aleppo Codex: Mrwz (מרוז)

- Leningrad Codex: Meroz (מֵרוֹז)

- Targum Jerusalem: Meroz (מֵרוֹז)

Interpretations of what Merez was, differ wildly. Some associate it with the village of Mitzr (כָּפַר מְצָר) in northern Israel, southwest of the Sea of Galilee. The Village of Misr was founded at some point by Egyptian settlers in Canaan, however, it is unclear when. The oldest ruins discovered in the village only date back to the Roman era, however, the name is Arabic, indicating that this community was founded long after the time of Deborah.

A commentary in the Talmud (Moed Katan 16a) claims that Meroz is a planet that refused to help the Israelites in their time of trouble, however, the name Meroz does not correlate with the Canaanite name of any planet. The author of Moed Katan was probably conflating the Hebrew word from Judges with the Roman name Mars, which would have been anachronistic, as even if a precursor to the Latin language existed in the late Bronze Age, there is no reason an Israelite would have used the proto-Latin name.

None of the known variants of the Semitic name of Egypt are a close match to Meroz/Maroz, however, the Egyptian name Marēs, is almost phonetically identical. Mâôresi (𓄿𓂋𓇳𓏤) was an ancient Egyptian name for Southern Egypt, which translates as approximately 'Southern Place.' It continued to be used until the Classical era, when it was pronounced as Marēs (Μαρης). The exact pronunciation of ancient Egyptian names is debated before the development of the Demotic script, and therefore it cannot be known how the Egyptians pronounced Maaresi during the era of Deborah, however, it is documented in Late Egyptian Demotic as being Mâôrs (𓏭/ⲁⲣⲥ), supporting the New Kingdom era pronunciation as being very similar to the term used by Deborah.

The simplest explanation is that the word Mrwz (מרוז) referred to Southern Egypt itself, and not the village named 'Egypt.' At the time, the Egyptian imperial capital was in Thebes, the capital of Southern Egypt. Therefore, the implication is that King Jabin and the Egyptian General Siazara, were rebelling against Egypt, and the Egyptians did not send relief into Canaan to help their subjects. As the Septuagint dates their rule over Canaan to between 1334 and 1314 BC, this means they seized control when Akenhaten died, and ruled throughout the brief reigns of Smenkhkare (1335-1334 BC), Neferneferuaten (1334-1332 BC), Tutankhamen (1334-1325 BC), and Ay (1332-1319 BC), as well as the first five years of Horemheb (1319-1292 BC). This was a chaotic period in Egyptian history, and it is possible the entire Egyptian army in Canaan rebelled, as it wasn't entirely clear who the Pharaoh actually was during most of this period. General Siazara may have not seen his army as being in rebellion if he did not see the government in Egypt as valid.

By year five of Horemheb's reign, it would have been clear that the government had been restored in Egypt, and his position in Canaan would have become a clear case of rebellion, which would explain why his army had become so ineffective as his troops abandoned him to return to Egypt. As the word does appear to be s reference to Southern Egypt, that name is restored in this translation.

**4** Codex Vaticanus: Êliou (ΗΛΙΟΥ). Translation: Helios

• Codex Alexandrinus: tou Êliou (ΤΟΥΗΛΙΟΥ). Translation: the sun

• Aleppo Codex: hšmš (השמש). Translation: the sun

• Leningrad Codex: hashemesh (הַשֶּׁמֶשׁ). Translation: the sun

• Targum Jerusalem: shimsha (שִׁמְשָׁא). Translation: sun

Shemesh was the Canaanite sun god, whose worship was later banned by King Josiah. The presence of a sun-god in the text supports the earlier reading of åtnwt (אתנות) as Aten, as Aten was the dominant Egyptian solar-god at the time, and Canaan was part of the Egyptian Empire at the time.

**5** Based on the chronology of the Septuagint, these forty years of peace ended in 1279 BC, when Ramesses II launched his first campaign against Syria.

# Judges: Chapter 6

The Israelites did evil in the sight of the Lord, and the Lord gave them into the hand of Midian for seven years. The hand of Midian prevailed against Israel, and the Israelites made for themselves the caves in the mountains, and the dens, and the holes in the rocks because of Midian. It happened when the Israelites sowed, that the Midianites, Amalekites, and Nesites[1] went up together. They camped against them and destroyed their fruits as far as Gaza, and they did not leave the support of life in the land of Israel, and not even an ox or donkey among the herds. They brought their animals and came with their tents in great numbers like the locusts, and there was no counting them and their camels. They came to the land of Israel and laid waste to it.

Israel was greatly impoverished because of Midian and the Israelites cried to the Lord because of Midian. The Lord sent a prophet to the Israelites, and he said to them, "The Lord God of Israel says, 'I am he who brought you up out of the land of Egypt, and I brought you up out of the house of your slavery. I delivered you out of the hands of Egypt, and out of the hands of all that attacked you, and I drove them out before you, and I gave you their land. I said to you, 'I am the Lord God, you will not fear the gods of the Amorites in whose land you live,' but you did not listen to my voice."

The messenger of the lord came and sat down under the fir tree, which was in Ephrath in the land of Joash the father of Esdri. Gideon his son was threshing wheat in a wine press to escape from the face of Midian. The messenger of the lord appeared to him and said to him, "The Lord is with you, and you are mighty in strength."

Gideon replied to him, "Be gracious with me, my lord, but if the Lord is with us, why have these evils found us? Where are all his miracles, which our fathers have told us about, when they said, 'Did not the Lord bring us up out of Egypt?' Now he has abandoned us and given us into the hand of Midian."

The messenger of the lord turned to him and said, "Go in your strength, and you will save Israel out of the hand of Midian. Look, I have sent you."

Gideon asked him, "Be gracious with me, my lord. How will I save Israel? Look, my thousand² are weak among Manasseh, and I am the least in my father's house."

The messenger of the lord answered him, "The Lord will be with you, and you will slaughter Midian like one man."

Gideon said to him, "If I have found mercy in your eyes, and you will do for me all that you have said to me today, don't leave here until I come to you, and I will bring an offering and offer it to you."

He replied, "I will remain until you return."

Gideon went and prepared a goat-kid and a bushel of fine unleavened flour, and he put the meat in the basket, and poured the broth into the pot, and brought them out to him under the turpentine tree, and approached.

The messenger of God said to him, "Take the meat and the unleavened cakes, and put them on that rock, and pour out the broth nearby," and he did so. The messenger of the lord stretched out the end of the wand that was in his hand and touched the flesh and the unleavened bread, and fire came up out of the rock and consumed the flesh and the unleavened bread, and the messenger of the lord vanished from his sight.

Gideon understood that he was the messenger of the lord, and Gideon said, "Oh my Lord God! I have seen the messenger of the lord face to face!"

The Lord said to him, "Peace be to you, and don't be afraid, as you will not die."

Gideon built an altar there to the Lord, and called it Lord Shalim.[3] Until this day, as it is still in Ephrath of the father of Esdri. It happened that night, that the Lord said to him, "Take the young bull which your father has, the second bull which is seven years old, and destroy the altar of Ba'al which your father has, and the Asherah which is by it, you will also destroy. You will build an altar to the Lord God on the top of the rocky mountain[4] in the appointed place, and you will take the second bull and will offer up whole burnt offerings with the wood of the grove, which you will destroy."

Gideon took ten men from his servants and did as the Lord had told him, and as he was afraid of what the house of his father and the men of the city would do if he did it in the daytime, so he did it at night. The men of the city rose up early in the morning and saw the altar of Ba'al had been demolished, and the Asherah next to it had been destroyed, and they saw the second bull which Gideon offered on the altar that had been built. Men asked their neighbors, "Who has done this?" and they inquired and searched, and learned that Gideon the son of Joash had done this thing.

The men of the city demanded of Joash, "Bring out your son, and let him die because he has destroyed the altar of Ba'al and because he has destroyed the Asherah that was by it."

Gideon the son of Joash said to all the men who rose up against him, "Do you now plead for Ba'al? Will you save him? Whoever will plead for him, let him be murdered this morning! If he is a god, let him plead for himself, because someone has torn down his altar."

He called it on that day Jerubbaal, saying, "Let Ba'al plead because his altar has been overthrown."

All Midian and Amalek, and the Nesites themselves together and camped in the valley of Jezreel.[5] The wind of the Lord came on Gideon, and he blew with the horn, and Abiezer came to follow him. Gideon sent messengers to all Manasseh, Asher, and Zebulun, and Naphtali, and he went up to meet them. Gideon said to God, "If you will save Israel by my hand, as you have promised, I have put the fleece of wool in the threshing floor, and if there is dew on the fleece only, and the rest of the ground is dry, I will know that you will save Israel by my hand, as you have said."

It was so, and he rose up early in the morning and wrung the fleece, and dew dropped from the fleece, filling a full bowl of water.

Gideon said to God, "I beg you, don't become angry with me, and I will speak again. I will  make one more test with the fleece. Let the fleece only be dry, and let there be dew on all the ground."

God made it so that night, and only the fleece was dry, and on all the ground there was dew.

# Judges: Chapter 6 Notes

**1** Codex Vaticanus: uioe anatolôn (ΥΙΟΙΔΝΔΤΟΛωΝ). Translation: sons of the east

• Aleppo Codex: bny qdm (בני קדם). Translation: sons of the east (or ancients)

• Leningrad Codex: venei-kedem (בְנֵי-קֶדֶם). Translation: sons of the east (or ancients)

• Dead Sea Scroll 4QJudgᵃ: bny qdm (בגי קדם). Translation: sons of the east (or ancients)

• Targum Jerusalem: venei madincha (בְנֵי מַדִינְחָא). Translation: sons of the country (or city, Medina)

The 'East' in ancient Canaan referred to Mesopotamia, meaning that the Israelites were referring to a Mesopotamian people plundering the land with the support of the Midianites and Amalekites. The Septuagint's chronology places this 7-year period in approximately 1274 to 1267 BC. This time period corresponds to Ramesses II's campaigns in Canaan against the Nesites (𐤍𐤀⸗𐤉⸗ 𐤀𐤍⸗𐤀⸗𐤉), often misidentified as Hittites, between 1274 and 1269 BC. By Ramesses II's reign, the Egyptians had lost control of northern Canaan to the Nesites, and in 1274 BC Ramesses launched an invasion of northern Canaan, attempting to recapture Kadesh. The first campaign, in 1274 BC, was a failure, although Egypt did weaken the Nesite army in the south. The second campaign, in 1273 BC, was also a failure, although the Egyptians did reach the outskirts of Kadesh. The third campaign, in 1271 BC, successfully captured Kadesh, and pushed the Nesites out of Canaan.

In the following years, Egypt consolidated control over Canaan, occupying Edom, Seir, Moab, Jerusalem, Jericho, Heshbon, and Damascus, most of which submitted to Egypt peacefully. This consolidation of Egyptian authority in Canaan is believed to have only taken until 1269 BC according to Egyptologists, however, the Book of Judges reports it took until 1267 BC. The conflict with the Nesites did continue after 1269 BC, and the peace treaty between Egypt and the Nesites was not signed until 1258 BC. This indicates the people referred to in Judges as 'sons of the East,' were Nesites, which is the term used in this translation.

**2** Codex Vaticanus: chilias (ⲭⲓⲗⲓⲁⲥ). Translation: thousand

• Aleppo Codex: ålpy (אלפי). Translation: thousands

• Leningrad Codex: alpi (אֲלָפַי). Translation: thousands

• Targum Jerusalem: zar'iti (זַרְעִיתִי). Translation: families

**3** Codex Vaticanus: eirênê c̄u (ⲈⲓⲢⲎⲚⲎⲕⲨ̄). Translation: peace lord

• Aleppo Codex: Yhwh šlwm (יהוה שלום). Translation: Yhwh peace

• Leningrad Codex: Yehvah shalovm (יְהוָה שָׁלוֹם). Translation: Yehwah peace

• Targum Jerusalem: Yeyah da'avad leih shelam (יְיָ דְעָבַד לֵיה שְׁלָם). Translation: Yahw serves the Yah to be complete (or to be Shalim, until evening)

As the Greek translation predates the Hasmonean redaction of circa 140 BC that inserted Yehvah, it reads 'Lord' instead of Yehvah. The Aramaic version of Judges likely read ådny šlmå (𐡍𐡋𐡔 𐡀𐡃𐡍), meaning 'Lord Peace,' which was both the Greek translation and the Masoretic interpretation of the Hebrew translation. The Hebrew term šlwm (שלום) is a transliteration of the Phoenician term šlm (𐤔𐤋𐤌), which can be translated as either 'peace' or 'Shalim,' the name of the god of the evening, known as Atum in Egyptian, and the name of the god that Jerusalem was named after. As Shalim was one of the ancient Canaanite Lords at the time, it is likely that the earlier Phoenician text read Ba'al Shalim (𐤔𐤋𐤌 𐤁𐤏𐤋). The Hasmoneans redacted most instances of Adon and Ba'al to Yehvah around 140 BC, resulting in the strange expression 'Yehvah Peace' in the Masoretic text, however, there is no evidence of a community named after 'Yehvah Peace' in Canaan in the 1200s BC.

**4** Codex Vaticanus: Maouec (ΜΑΟΥЄΚ)

• Codex Alexandrinus: Maôz (ΜΑѠΖ)

• Aleppo Codex: môwz (מעוז). Translation: rock (or stone)

• Leningrad Codex: ma'ovz (מָעֹוז). Translation: rock (or stone)

• Targum Jerusalem: tukefa (תּוּקְפָא). Translation: power

The Greeks transliterated the Aramaic word for 'rock' which is used in this translation.


**5** Codex Vaticanus: Ezereel (ЄΖЄΡЄЄΛ)

• Codex Alexandrinus: Iezrael (ΙЄΖΡΑЄΛ)

• Aleppo Codex: Yzrôâl (יזרעאל)

• Leningrad Codex: Yizre'el (יִזְרְעֶאל)

• Targum Jerusalem: Yizre'el (יִזְרְעֶאל)

The Jazreel Valley is in northern Israel and was along the over land route between Egypt and Syria. Some scholars believe the name Jezreel was the origin of the name Israel, as the valley runs through ancient Samaria. If the Nesites pushed as far south as Jazreel, it would have likely been between Ramesses II's first Syrian campaign in 1273 BC, and the Battle of Kadesh in 1269 BC when Ramesses II pushed the Nesites out of Canaan.

# Judges: Chapter 7

Jerubbaal rose early, as did Gideon and all the people with him, and camped at the Fountain of Arad. The camp of Midian was to the north of him, reaching from the Hill of Moreh, in the valley.

The Lord said to Gideon, "The people with you are many, so many that I may not deliver Midian into their hand, in case at any time Israel boasts against me, saying, 'My own hand has saved me.' Now tell the people, 'Whoever is afraid and fearful? Let him turn and leave Mount Gilead,'" and twenty-two thousand people left, leaving ten thousand.

The Lord said to Gideon, "The people are still too numerous, bring them down to the water, and I will purge them there for you. It will happen that whoever I will say to you, 'This one will go with you,' he will go with you, and of whoever I will say to you, 'This one will not go with you,' he will not go with you."

He brought the people down to the water, and the Lord said to Gideon, "Whoever will lap of the water with his tongue like a dog, you will set him apart, and also whoever will kneel on his knees to drink."

The count of those that lapped with their hand to their mouth was three hundred men, and all the rest of the people knelled on their knees to drink water. The Lord said to Gideon, "I will save you by the three hundred men that lapped, and I will give Midian into your hand, and all the rest of the people will go everyone to his home."

They took the provisions of the people in their hands and their horns, and he sent away every man of Israel each to his tent, and he strengthened the three hundred, and the army of Midian was beneath him in the valley. In that night the Lord said to him, "Rise, go down into the camp, for I have delivered it into your hand. If you are afraid to go down, go down with Pharaoh's servant[1] to the soldiers' camp. You will hear what they will say, and afterward, your hands will be strong, and you will go down into the camp."

He and Pharaoh's servant went down to the extremity of the companies of fifty, which were in the camp. Midian and Amalek and all the Nesites were scattered in the valley like locusts in multitude, and there was no counting their camels, and they were like the sand of the seashore for multitude. Gideon came and heard a man describing a dream to his neighbor. He said, "Look, I have dreamed a dream, in which a cake of barley bread rolled into the camp of Midian, and it came as far as a tent and hit it, and it fell, and it turned over, and the tent fell."

His neighbor replied, "This is none other than the sword of Gideon, son of Joash, an Israelite. God has delivered Midian and all the army into his hand."

When Gideon heard the account of the dream and the interpretation of it, he worshiped the Lord and returned to the camp of Israel, and said, "Rise, for the Lord has delivered the camp of Midian into our hand."

He divided the three hundred men into three companies and put horns in the hands of all, and empty pitchers, and torches in the pitchers, and he said to them, "You will watch me, and this is what you will do. I will go into the army, and as I do, you will also do. I will blow with the horn, and all you with me will blow with the horn around the whole camp, and you will shout, "For the Lord and Gideon."

Gideon and the hundred men that were with him came to the outskirts of the army at the beginning of the midnight watch, and they completely roused the guards and sounded with the horns, and they broke the pitchers that were in their hands, and the three companies sounded with the horns, and broke the pitchers, and held the torches in their left hands, and in their right hands their horns to sound with. They cried out, "A sword for the Lord and Gideon."

Every man stood in his place around the army, and all the army ran, and sounded an alarm, and fled. They sounded with the three hundred horns, and the Lord set every man's sword in all the army against his neighbor. The army fled as far as the Temple of Seth in Garagatha,[2] Abel-meholah,[3] and Tabbath, and the Israelites from Naphtali, Asher, and Manasseh came to help and chased after Midian. Gideon sent messengers into all the mountains of Ephraim, saying, "Come down to meet Midian, and capture for yourselves the water as far as the House of Barah on the Jordan."

Every Ephraimite cried out, and they captured the water all the way to the House of Barah on the Jordan. They captured the princes of Midian, including Oreb and Zeeb. They killed Oreb in Sur Oreb, and killed Zeeb at the winepress of Zeeb,[4] and they crushed Midian and brought the heads of Oreb and Zeeb to Gideon from beyond the Jordan.

# Judges: Chapter 7 Notes

**1** Codex Vaticanus: Phara to paedarion (ΦΑΡΑΤΟΠΑΙΔΑΡΙΟΝ).
Translation: Phara the child (or servant)

- Aleppo Codex: prh nôrk (פרה נערך). Possible translation: carrying (or cow, Purah) boy (or servant, youth)

- Leningrad Codex: furah na'archa (פֻּרָה נַעַרְךָ). Possible translation: carrying (or cow, Purah) boy (or servant, youth)

- Targum Jerusalem: furah ulemach (פוּרָה עוּלֶמָךְ). Translation: framework (or wine press) the world

Based on the context, this strange sentence appears to be a reverence to an Egyptian overseer stationed by Pharaoh among the Tribe of Manasseh. The Phoenician spelling of 'pharaoh' was prôh (𐤐𐤓𐤏𐤄), while the Aramaic spelling was prôwn (𐡐𐡓𐡏𐡍), neither of which is an exact match for the transliterated words prh (פרה) and phara (φαρα), indicating that neither the Paleo-Hebrew nor Aramaic texts included the word 'pharaoh' but a similar sounding word. This suggests that the word, along with the Song of Deborah, was transliterated from another script, likely Akkadian Cuneiform or Egyptian.

The Akkadian Cuneiform spelling of 'pharaoh' was pirôû (𒉿𒊑𒌋) during the late Bronze Age, while the Egyptian spelling was pr-ôå (𓉐𓉻) during the late Bronze era and early Iron Age. While either script could have been used at the time, the cuneiform name is pronounced almost exactly like the term found in the Hebrew translation, while the Egyptian is pronounced slightly differently, suggesting the original text was in cuneiform.

**2** Codex Vaticanus: Bêthseedta Garagatha (ΒΗΘCΕΕΔΤΑ ΓΑΡΑΓΑΘΑ)

- Codex Alexandrinus: Baethasetta (ΒΑΙΘΑCΕΤΤΑ)

- Aleppo Codex: byt hšth srrth (בית השטה צררתה)

- Leningrad Codex: beit hashittah tzereratah (בֵּית הַשִּׁטָּה צְרֵרָתָה)

- Targum Jerusalem: beit shitah litzreirat (בֵּית שִׁיטָה לְצָרִירַת)

The term vyt hoshth (בית השטה) translates as House of 'sth,' which appears to be a transliterated name, possibly Seth, the Egyptian god that had been widely worshiped by the Hyksos. Shth (שטה) could also be a spelling error of shvth (שוטה), meaning 'fool,' or shyth (שיטה), meaning 'system.' As Seth is a direct translation, the term 'House of Seth in Garagatha,' is used. Zererah is spelled in various ways in the Masoretic text and transliterated in various ways, including Zaretan, Zarethan, Zeredathah, Zartanah, or Zarthan. It is believed the town was in the Jordan valley, south of the Sea of Galilee. It is unclear if Garagatha was an alternate name for Zererah or another location, however, as the names are noticeably different the Greek term is used.


**3** Codex Vaticanus: Abômeoula (ΑΒѠΜΕΟΥΛΛ)

- Codex Alexandrinus: Abelmeoula (ΑΒΕΛΜΕΟΥΛΛ)

- Aleppo Codex: Åbl mhwlh (אבל מחולה)

- Leningrad Codex: Avel mechovlah (אָבֵל מְחוֹלָה)

- Targum Jerusalem: Avel mechovlah (אָבֵל מְחוֹלָה)

Abel-meholah would later be the birth town of the prophet Elisha. It was described as being near the Jordan River, south of the House of She'an (Beit She'an), which would seem to confirm that Zererah was somewhere in the area.


**4** Codex Vaticanus: Iacephzêph (ΙΛΚΕΦΖΗΦ)

- Codex Alexandrinus: Iacephzêb (ΙΛΚΕΦΖΗΒ)

- Aleppo Codex: byqb zåb (ביקב זאב). Translation: wine press of Zeeb

- Leningrad Codex: veyekev-Ze'ev (בְיֶקֶב זְאָב). Translation: wine press of Zeeb

- Targum Jerusalem: meishar Ze'ev (מֵישַׁר זְאֵב). Translation: level (or upright) of Zeeb

As the Greeks transliterated the word 'wine press of Zeeb' as Ιακεφζηφ or Ιακεφζηβ, the Hebrew translation is imported from the Masoretic text.

# Judges: Chapter 8

The Ephraimites said to Gideon, "What is this that you have done to us, in that you did not call us when you went to fight with Midian?"

They rebuked him sharply, and later when their spirit calmed towards him, he replied to them, "What have I now done in comparison to you? Is not the gleaning of Ephraim better than the vintage of Abiezer? The Lord has delivered into your hand the princes of Midian, both Oreb and Zeeb, and what could I do in comparison to you?"

Gideon came to Jordan, and went over, himself and the three hundred with him, hungry, yet still chasing. He said to the men of Succoth, "Give, I beg you, bread to feed these people that follow me, because they are tired, and look, I am chasing after Zebah and Zalmunna, the kings of Midian."

The princes of Succoth asked, "Are the hands of Zebah and Zalmunna now in your hand, that we should give bread to your army?"

Gideon answered, "When the Lord gives Zebah and Zalmunna into my hand, then I will scourge your flesh with the thorns of the wilderness, and briers.

He went up from there to Penuel and spoke to them the same way, and the men of Penuel answered him as the men of Succoth had answered him. Gideon said to the men of Penuel, "When I return in victory, I will break down this tower."

Zebah and Zalmunna were in Karkor, and their army was with them, about fifteen thousand, all that were left of the army of the Neshites,[1] and they that fell were a hundred and twenty thousand men that drew the sword. Gideon went up by the way of them that lived in tents, east of Nobah and Jogbehah, and he struck the army, and the army was secure. Zebah and Zalmunna fled, and he chased after them, and took the two kings of Midian, Zebah, and Zalmunna, and discomfited all the army.

Gideon the son of Joash returned from the battle, from the Ascent of Heres.[2] He took as prisoner a boy from Succoth and questioned him, and he wrote for him the names of the princes of Succoth and their elders, seventy-seven men. Gideon came to the princes of Succoth, and said, "Look Zebah and Zalmunna, who you teased me about, saying, 'Are the hands of Zebah and Zalmunna now in your hand, that we should give bread to your men that are faint?'"

He took the elders of the city and he scourged them with the thorns of the wilderness and the briers. He torn down the tower of Penuel and killed the men of the city. He asked Zebah and Zalmunna, "Where are the men who you killed in Tabor?"

They answered, "Like you, they were in the ranks of the sons of the king."[3]

Gideon said, "They were my brothers and the sons of my mother. As the Lord lives, if you had kept them alive, I would not murder you."

He said to Jetheth his firstborn, "Rise and kill them," but the boy did not draw his sword, for he was afraid, as he was still very young.

Zebah and Zalmunna said, "Rise and attack us, for your strength is like that of a man," and Gideon rose, and killed Zebah and Zalmunna, and he took the round ornaments that were on the necks of their camels.

The men of Israel said to Gideon, "Rule, my lord, over us. Both you, and your son, and your son's son, for you have saved us out of the hand of Midian."

Gideon said to them, "I will not rule, and my son will not rule over you. The Lord will rule over you."

Gideon said to them, "I will make a request of you, that you each give me an earring out of your plunder, as they had golden earrings because they were Ishmaelites."

They said, "We will certainly give them," and he opened his garment, and each man tossed into it an earring from his plunder. The weight of the golden earrings which he asked, was a thousand and seven hundred pieces of gold, besides the crescents, and the chains, and the garments, and the purple cloths that were on the kings of Midian, and besides the chains that were on the necks of their camels. Gideon made a vest from it and set it in his city in Ephrath.

All Israel went whoring after it there, and it became a stumbling block to Gideon and his house. Midian, was straightened before the Israelites, and they did not lift their head anymore, and the land had rest forty years in the days of Gideon. Jerubbaal the son of Joash went and sat in his house. Gideon had seventy sons begotten of his body, for he had many wives. His concubine in Shechem carried him a son and gave him the name Abimelech.

Gideon son of Joash died in his city, and he was buried in the sepulcher of Joash his father in Ephrath of Abi-Esdri. It happened when Gideon was dead, that the Israelites turned, and went whoring after Ba'als, and made for themselves a covenant with Ba'al that he should be their god. The Israelites did not remember the Lord God who had delivered them out of the hand of all that attacked them. They did not deal mercifully with the house of

Jerubbaal (this is Gideon), according to all the good which he did for Israel.

# Judges: Chapter 8 Notes

**1** Codex Vaticanus: allophylôn (ΑΛΛΟΦΥΛΩΝ). Translation: foreigners (or aliens, gentiles)

- Codex Alexandrinus: huiôn anatolôn (ΥΙΩΝΑΝΑΤΟΛΩΝ). Translation: sons of the easterners

- Aleppo Codex: bny qdm (בני קדם). Translation: sons of the east (or easterners)

- Leningrad Codex: venei-kedem (בְנֵי־קֶדֶם). Translation: sons of the east (or easterners)

- Targum Jerusalem: benei madincha (בְּנֵי מַדְנְחָא). Translation: sons of east (or Medina)

As the sons of the east in this story are the Neshites, that name is used in the translation.


**2** Codex Vaticanus: parataxeôs Ares (ΠΑΡΑΤΑΞΕΩΣΑΡΕΣ). Translation: phalanx (or side by side) of Ares

- Codex Alexandrinus: anabaseôs Ares (ΑΝΑΒΑΣΕΩΣΑΡΕΣ). Translation: ascent of Ares

- Aleppo Codex: mlmôlh hḥrs (מלמעלה החרס). Translation: from above the destruction (or demolished, destroyed)

- Leningrad Codex: milma'aleh heChares (מִלְמַעֲלֵה הֶחָרֶס). Translation: from above the Chares

- Targum Jerusalem: me'al shimsha (מֵעַל שִׁמְשָׁא). Translation: upper (or fraudulent) sun (or servant, minister)

The Greeks transliterated Ḥrs as Ares, however, the Semitic term meant variations of 'destruction.' The Hebrew and Aramaic term also referred to pottery, clay, or ceramic, as did the cuneiform word ḥarši (𒄩) used in Nesite. In this case, the Greek translations and Masoretic interpretation seem consistent, as each of them interpreted the term as a proper name, suggesting a town named Heres, or if the Codex Alexandrinus is correct: Ascent of Heres. It is possible that Heres was the name of a god of destruction worshiped in Canaan, in which case it may have been the origin of the Greek Ares, whose origin is unclear.

As the sources do not agree on the word before Ares/Heres, the term 'Ascent of' is used from the Codex Alexandrinus, as that does seem consistent with the naming conventions of Canaanite towns.

**3** Codex Vaticanus: ôs su ôs autoi eis omoiôma uiou basileôs (ⲱⲥ ⲥⲩ ⲱⲥ ⲁⲩⲧⲟⲓ ⲉⲓⲥ ⲟⲙⲟⲓⲱⲙⲁ ⲩⲓⲟⲩ ⲃⲁⲥⲓⲗⲉⲱⲥ). Translation: like you like himself (or he, she, it) into effigy son (or child) king (or chief, master lord)

• Codex Alexandrinus: ôsi sy omoeos soe, omoeos autôn, ôs idos morphê uiôn basileôn (ⲱⲥⲉⲓ ⲥⲩ ⲟⲙⲟⲓⲟⲥ ⲥⲟⲓ ⲟⲙⲟⲓⲟⲥ ⲁⲩⲧⲱⲛ ⲱⲥ ⲉⲓⲇⲟⲥ ⲙⲟⲣⲫⲏ ⲩⲓⲱⲛ ⲃⲁⲥⲓⲗⲉⲱⲛ). Translation: just as you resembling (or equal to) you resembling (or equal to) himself (or he, she, it), like the appearance (or kind, species, image) form (or appearance, kind, type) son (or child) king (or chief, master lord)

• Aleppo Codex: kmwk kmwhm åhd ktår bny hmlk (כמוך כמוהם אחד כתאר בני המלך). Translation: as like one of like the title (or rank, appearance) of the sons (or children, boys) of the king

• Leningrad Codex: kamovcha chemovhem echad keto'ar benei hammelech (כְּמוֹךָ כְּמוֹהֶם אֶחָד כְּתֹאַר בְּנֵי הַמֶּלֶךְ). Translation: as like one of like the title (or rank, appearance) of the sons (or children, boys) of the king

• Targum Jerusalem: me'al shimsha (מְעַל שִׁמְשָׁא). Translation: upper (or fraudulent) sun (or servant, minister)

# Judges: Chapter 9

Abimelech the son of Jerubbaal went to Shechem to his mother's brothers, and he said to them and all the families of the house of his mother's father, "Speak, I beg you, in the ears of all the men of Shechem, and say, 'Which is better for you? That seventy men, even all the sons of Jerubbaal, should reign over you, or that one man should reign over you? And remember that I am your bone and your flesh."

His mother's brothers spoke about him to all the men of Shechem, and their hearts turned towards Abimelech, and they said, "He is our brother. They gave him seventy pieces of silver out of the Temple of the Lord of the Covenant,[1] and Abimelech hired vain and cowardly men, and they followed him. He went to the house of his father in Ephrath and executed his brothers, the sons of Jerubbaal, seventy men on one stone. Jotham the youngest son of Jerubbaal was not executed, as he hid. All the men of Shechem and all the House of Millo were gathered together, and they made Abimelech king by the Oak of Sedition, which was at Shechem.

It was reported to Jotham, and he went and stood on the top of Mount Gerizim, and shouted to them, "Hear me, you men of Shechem, and God will hear you. The trees went out once on a time to anoint a king over them, and they said to the olive, 'Reign over us.' But the olive replied to them, 'Will I leave my fatness, with which men will glorify God, and go to be promoted over the trees?' The trees said to the fig tree, 'Come, reign over us.' But the fig tree replied to them, 'Will I leave my sweetness and my good fruits, and go to be promoted over the trees?' The trees said to the vine, 'Come, reign over us.' The vine replied to them, 'Will I leave my wine that gladdens God and men, and go to be promoted over the trees?' Then all the trees said to the bramble, 'Come, and reign over us.' The bramble replied to the trees, 'If you in truth anoint me to reign over you, come, stand under my shadow, and if not, let fire come out from me and devour the cedars of Lebanon.'"

"Now, if you have done it in truth and integrity, and have made Abimelech king. If you have worked well with Jerubbaal, and with his house. If you have done to him according to the reward of his hand, as my father fought for you, and put his life in jeopardy, and delivered you out of the hand of Midian, and you are risen up this day against the house of my father, and have slain his sons, being seventy men, on one stone, and have made Abimelech the son of his slave-woman king over the men of Shechem, because he is your brother. If then you have done truly and faithfully with Jerubbaal, and with his house today, rejoice in Abimelech, and let him also rejoice over you. But, if not, let fire come out from Abimelech, and devour the men of Shechem, and the House of Millo, and let fire come out from the men of Shechem and the House of Millo, and devour Abimelech."

Jotham fled, and ran away and went as far as Beer, and lived there, out of the way of his brother Abimelech. Abimelech reigned over Israel for three years. God sent an evil spirit between Abimelech and the men of Shechem, and the men of Shechem dealt treacherously with the house of Abimelech, to bring the injury done to the seventy sons of Jerubbaal, and to lay their blood on their brother Abimelech, who killed them, and on the men of Shechem because they strengthened his hands to kill his brothers. The men of Shechem set men to lay in wait against him on the top of the mountains and robbed everyone who passed by them on the way, and it was reported to King Abimelech. Gaal the son of Jabal came, and his brothers, and passed by Shechem, and the men of Shechem trusted in him. They went out into the field, and gathered their grapes, and crushed them, and had a part, and they brought the grapes into the house of their god, and ate and drank, and cursed Abimelech.

Gaal the son of Jabal asked, "Who is Abimelech, and who is the son of Shechem, that we should serve him? Is he not the son of Jerubbaal, and is not Zebul his steward, his servant with the son of Hamor the father of Shechem? Why should we serve him? If only these people were under my hand! I would then remove Abimelech, and I would say to him, 'Multiply your army, and come out.'"

Zebul the ruler of the city heard the words of Gaal the son of Jabal, and he was very angry. He sent messengers to Abimelech secretly, saying, "Look, Gaal the son of Jabal and his brothers have come to Shechem, and they have besieged the city against you. Now rise by night, you and the people with you, and lay wait in the field. It will come to pass in the morning at sunrise, you will rise early and approach the city, and he and the people with him will come out against you, and you will do to him according to your power."

Abimelech and all the people with him rose up by night and formed an ambuscade against Shechem in four companies. Gaal the son of Jabal went out and stood by the door of the gate of the city, and Abimelech and the people with him rose up from the ambuscade. Gaal the son of Jabal saw the people, and said to Zebul, "Look, people come down from the top of the mountain."

Zebul replied to him, "You see the shadow of the mountain as men."

Gaal continued and said, "Look, people come down from the west, from the area bordering the middle of the land, and another company comes by the road to the Oak of Visions."[2]

Zebul asked him, "Where is your mouth as you said, 'Who is Abimelech that we should serve him?' Are not these the people you despised? Go out now, and set the battle formation against him."

Gaal went out before the men of Shechem and set the battle formation against Abimelech. Abimelech pursued him, and he fled from before him, and many fell slain as far as the door of the gate. Abimelech entered into Arumah, and Zebul drove out Gaal and his brothers so that they should not live in Shechem. On the second day, people went out into their field, and one brought word to Abimelech. He took the people, and divided them into three companies, and formed an ambush in the field, and he looked, and the people went out of the city, and he rose up against them and struck them.

Abimelech and the chiefs of companies that were with him rushed forward and stood by the door of the gate of the city, and the two other companies rushed forward on all that were in the field and slaughtered them. Abimelech fought against the city all that day, and captured the city, and killed the people that were in it, and destroyed the city, and sowed it with salt.

All the men of the tower of Shechem heard and came to the gathering at the fortified Temple of the Lord of the Covenant.[3] It was reported to Abimelech, that all the men of the tower of Shechem were gathered together. Abimelech went up to Mount Zalmon, and all the people that were with him, and Abimelech took an ax in his hand, and cut down a branch of a tree, and took it, and laid it on his shoulders. He said to the people that were with him, "Follow my example, quickly,"

They cut down branches, each man, and followed Abimelech, and laid them against the place of gathering, and burnt the place of gathering with fire, and they died, all the men of the tower of Shechem, about a thousand men and women. Abimelech went out of the fortified temple of the covenant, and camped in Tubas[4] and captured it. There was a fortified tower in the middle of the city, where all the men and the women of the city fled and shut the door and went up on the roof of the tower. Abimelech approached the tower and besieged it.

When Abimelech approached the door of the tower to burn it with fire, a woman threw a piece of a millstone on his head and broke his skull. He cried out quickly to the young man, his armorbearer, saying, "Draw your sword and kill me, so they should never say, 'A woman killed him,'" and the young man stabbed him through, and he died. The men of Israel saw that Abimelech was dead, and they went each to his place. So God repaid the wickedness of Abimelech, which he worked against his father, in slaying his seventy brothers. All the wickedness of the men of Shechem, God repaid on their head and also the curse of Jotham, the son of Jerubbaal.

# Judges: Chapter 9 Notes

**1** Codex Vaticanus: oecou Baalberith (**OIKOYBAAABEPIΘ**). Translation: house of Ba'al-Berith

• Codex Alexandrinus: oecou Ba'al diathêcês (**OIKOYBAAA ΔIAΘHKHC**). Translation: house of Ba'al of the testament

• Aleppo Codex: byt bôl bryt (**בית בעל ברית**). Translation: Temple of the Lord of the Covenant

• Leningrad Codex: beit ba'al berit (**בֵּית בַּעַל בְּרִית**). Translation: Temple of the Lord of the Covenant

• Targum Jerusalem: beit ba'eil keyam (**בֵּית בָּעֵיל קְיָם**). Translation: Temple of the Lord of establishment

As Ba'al translates as 'Lord,' and berith translates as 'covenant' or 'testament,' the translation 'Temple of the Lord of the Covenant' is used.


**2** Codex Vaticanus: êlônmaônenim (**HΛωNMAωNENIM**)

• Codex Alexandrinus: dryos apoblepontôn (**ΔPYOC ATTOBΛETTONTωN**). Translation: oak of visions

• Aleppo Codex: âlwn môwnnym (**אלון מעוננים**). Translation: oak of clouds (or diviners)

• Leningrad Codex: elovn me'ovnnim (**אֵלוֹן מְעוֹנְנִים**). Translation: oak of clouds (or diviners)

• Targum Jerusalem: meishar me'onenaya (**מֵישַׁר מְעוֹנְנַיָּא**). Translation: straight from Onnaya

The Greeks transliterated the words for 'oak of diviners' as ηλωνμαωνενιμ at the Library of Alexander, and later translated is as δρυος αποβλεποντων in the early Christian Era. While the term was a proper name, the name also had a meaning, and therefore this translation uses the later translation found in the Codex Alexandrinus. It is possible that this oak was one of the Asherah trees that were later banned by King Josiah in circa 625 BC.

**3** Codex Vaticanus: syneleusin Baethêlberith (ϹΥΝΕΛΕΥϹΙΝ ΒΑΙΘΗΛΒΕΡΙΘ). Translation: meeting place (or coming together) Baethêlberith

• Codex Alexandrinus: to ochyrôma oecou tou Ba'al diathêcês (ΤΟ ΟΧΥΡѠΜΑ ΟΙΚΟΥ ΤΟΥ ΒΑΑΛ ΔΙΑΘΗΚΗϹ). Translation: the fortified house (or temple) the Ba'al covenant

• Aleppo Codex: sryh byt ål bryt (צריח בית אל ברית). Translation: fortified house (or temple) god covenant

• Leningrad Codex: tzeriach veit El berit (צְרִיחַ בֵּית אֵל בְּרִית). Translation: fortified temple god covenant

• Targum Jerusalem: veit El lemigzar keyam (בֵּית אֵל לְמִגְזַר קְיָם). Translation: temple god of the separation of establishment

The Codex Vaticanus and Masoretic text are phonetically similar here, however, the 5th century AD Codex Alexandrinus has a significant deviation. The earlier Greek translation from the Library of Alexandria appears to have transliterated the term preserved in the Masoretic text as byt ål bryt (בית אל ברית) as Baethêlberith (Βαιθηλβεριθ), indicating it was viewed as a proper name. The later Codex Alexandrinus translation, from the 5th century AD, which was based on the Hebrew translation in circulation at the time, refers to the Ba'al of the Covenant instead of the god of the Covenant. As the Greeks could not have transliterated a word that was not in the Hebrew text, the term must have been present at the time, however, the earlier Vaticanus Codex supports the text found in the Masoretic text as having also been in the Aramaic version of Judges that the Greeks translated in the 3rd century BC.

It isn't clear where the version of the verse preserved in the Codex Alexandrinus came from, however, must have been Aramaic, suggesting the verse was edited to change the 'Temple of the God of the Covenant' to a temple of some ba'al. As this temple was in Shechem, it was likely part of the Hasmonean anti-Samaritan propaganda between 113 and 69 BC. The fact that the Temple of the God of the Covenant already existed in Shechem before the time of Solomon supports the Samaritan claim that Solomon's Temple was not the original temple of their God, as Shechem was the ancient capital of Samaria.

**4** Codex Vaticanus: Thêbês (ΘΗΒΗC)

- Codex Alexandrinus: Thebes (ΘΕΒΕC)

- Aleppo Codex: Tbs (תבץ)

- Leningrad Codex: Tevetz (תֵבֵץ)

- Targum Jerusalem: Tevetz (תֵבֵץ)

This is believed by some to be a reference to the city of Tubas (طوباس) in the northern area of the modern Palestinian West Bank, which is near Mount Gerizim, and so the name Tubas is used in this translation.

# Judges: Chapter 10

After Abimelech, Tola the son of Puah rose up to save Israel, being the son of his father's brother, an Issacharite, and he lived in Samaria[1] in the mountains of Ephraim. He judged Israel twenty-three years, and died, and was buried in Samaria. After him arose Jair of Gilead, and he judged Israel twenty-two years. He had thirty-two sons riding on thirty-two colts, and they had thirty-two cities, and they called them Jair's towns until this day in the land of Gilead. Jair died and was buried in Ramnon.[2] The Israelites did evil again in the sight of the Lord and served the Lords and Ashteroths, the gods of Arameans, Sidonians, Moabites, Ammonites, and Pelesets, and they forgot the Lord and did not serve him. The Lord was very angry with Israel and sold them into the hands of the Pelesets and the hands of the Ammonites. They afflicted and bruised all the Israelites beyond Jordan in the land of the Amorites in Gilead at that time and for eighteen years. The Ammonites crossed the Jordan to attack Judah, Benjamin, and Ephraim, and the Israelites were greatly afflicted. The Israelites cried to the Lord, "We have sinned against you because we have forgotten God and served the Lords."

The Lord said to the Israelites, "Didn't I save you from Egypt and the Amorites, and from the sons of Ammon (and Moab),[3] and from the Pelesets, and from the Sidonians, Amalekites, and Midianites[4] who afflicted you? And you cried to me, and I saved you out of their hands? Yet you forgot me and served other gods, therefore I will not save you anymore. Go, and pray to the gods who you have chosen for yourselves, and let them save you in the time of your affliction."

The Israelites said to the Lord, "We have sinned. Do to us whatever is good in your eyes, but save us this day."

They put away the foreign gods from among them and served only the Lord, and his mind was pained for the trouble of Israel. The Ammonites went up and camped in Gilead, and the Israelites were gathered together and camped on the hill. The people and the princes of Gilead said each man to his neighbor, "Who is he that will begin to fight against the Ammonites? He will be the head over all that live in Gilead."

# Judges: Chapter 10 Notes

**1** Codex Vaticanus: Samir (ϲΑΜΙΡ)

• Codex Alexandrinus: Samaria (ϲΑΜΑΡΕΙΑ)

• Aleppo Codex: Šmyr (שמיר). Translation: dill, emery-stone, brier, flint, thistle, adamant, fennel, batch, aggregate, bribe

• Leningrad Codex: Shamir (שָׁמִיר). Translation: dill, emery-stone, brier, flint, thistle, adamant, fennel, batch, aggregate, bribe

• Targum Jerusalem: Shamir (שָׁמִי). Translation: dill, emery-stone, brier, flint, thistle, adamant, fennel, batch, aggregate, bribe

Lucian's version of the Septuagint deviates from both the Codex Vaticanus and Masoretic text at this point, however, it is not clear if he had a Hebrew or Aramaic copy of Judges which included the word Samaria (שומרון), or simply interpreted Šmyr (שמיר) as Samaria. The term may be a relic of the Akkadian version of Judges, as the land was known as ᵏᵘʳSamerina (𒆳𒊮𒈨𒊑𒈾) in Cuneiform, meaning 'land Samerina.' In any event, Shamir does appear to be a reference to the land that would later be called Samaria, and therefore the Codex Alexandrinus is followed.


**2** Codex Vaticanus: Ramnôn (ΡΑΜΝΩΝ)

• Codex Alexandrinus: Rammô (ΡΑΜΜΩ)

• Aleppo Codex: Qmwn (קמון)

• Leningrad Codex: Kamovn (קָמוֹן)

• Targum Jerusalem: Kamovn (קָמוֹן)

This location is unknown today, however, would have been in northwest Jordan. As both versions of the Septuagint generally agree, the Greek name is retained.

**3** Codex Vaticanus: cai apo uiôn Ammôn (ΚΑΙΑΠΟΥΙѠΝ ΑΜΜѠΝ). Translation: and from sons of Ammon

• Codex Alexandrinus: cae oe uioe Ammôn cae Môab (ΚΑΙ ΟΙ ΥΙΟΙ ΑΜΜѠΝ ΚΑΙ ΜѠΑΒ). Translation: and of the sons of Ammon and Moab

• Aleppo Codex: wmn bny Ômwn (וּמִן בְּנִי עמון). Translation: and from the sons of Ammon

• Leningrad Codex: umin-benei Ammovn (וּמִן־בְּנֵי עַמּוֹן). Translation: and from the sons of Ammon

• Targum Jerusalem: umin emora'ah umin benei Amon (וּמִן אֱמוֹרָאָה וּמִן בְּנֵי עַמּוֹן). Translation: and from the speakers and the sons of Ammon

As Moab is only mentioned in the Codex Alexandrinus, is may be a later scribal note, and is therefore placed in parentheses. It is unclear if it was the source of the Targum Jerusalem's 'speakers' as the words are similar. It is possible that the term Moabite was mistranslated from the term 'speaker' in the targums of the era.

**4** Codex Vaticanus: Sidôniôn cae Amalêc cae Madiam (ϹΙΔѠΝΙѠΝ ΚΑΙ ΑΜΑΛΗΚ ΚΑΙ ΜΑΔΙΑΜ). Translation: Sidonians and Amalakites and Midianites

• Codex Alexandrinus: Sidônioe cae Madiam cae Amalêc (ϹΙΔѠΝΙΟΙ ΚΑΙΜΑΔΙΑΜΚΑΙΑΜΑΛΗΚ). Translation: Sidonians and Madianites and Amakites

• Aleppo Codex: sydwnym wômlq wmôwn (צידונים ועמלק ומעון). Translation: Sidonians and Amalakite and abode (or dwelling)

• Leningrad Codex: Tzidovnim va'Amalek uma'ovn (צִידוֹנִים וַעֲמָלֵק וּמָעוֹן). Translation: Sidonians and Amalakites and abode (or dwelling)

• Targum Jerusalem: Tzidona'ei va'Amalka'ei ve'enashei (צִידוֹנָאֵי וַעֲמַלְקָאֵי וֶאֱנָשֵׁי). Translation: Sidonians and Amalakites and people

The Hebrew term ma'ovn (מָעוֹן) in the Masoretic text is not the same as the name Midian (Μαδιαμ) in the Septuagint, however, is likely a transcription error from Midyan (מִדְיָן), as it only appears once in Masoretic Judges.

# Judges: Chapter 11

Jephthah the Gileadite was a mighty man, but he was the son of a prostitute who carried Jephthah for Gilead. The wife of Gilead carried his sons, and the sons of his wife grew up, and they drove out Jephthah, and said to him, "You will not inherit from the house of our father as you are the son of a concubine!"

Jephthah fled from the face of his brothers and lived in the land of Tob, and vain men gathered around Jephthah and went out with him. It happened when the Ammonites prepared to fight with Israel, that the elders of Gilead went to fetch Jephthah from the land of Tob.[1]

They said to Jephthah, "Come, and be our leader, and we will fight with the Ammonites."

Jephthah said to the elders of Gilead, "Did you not hate me, and drive me out of my father's house, and banish me from you? And now you have come to me when you need me?"

The elders of Gilead said to Jephthah, "We have now turned to you that you should go with us and fight against the Ammonites, and be our head over all the inhabitants of Gilead."

Jephthah said to the elders of Gilead, "If you turn back to me to fight with the Ammonites and the Lord should deliver them before me then will I be your leader."

The elders of Gilead said to Jephthah, "The Lord be a witness between us if we do not do according to your word."

Jephthah went with the elders of Gilead, and the people made him head and ruler over them, and Jephthah spoke before the Lord in Mizpeh. Jephthah sent messengers to the king of Ammon, saying, "What have I to do with you, that you have come against me to fight in my land?"

The king of Ammon said to the messengers of Jephthah, "Israel took my land when he went up out of Egypt, from Arnon to Jabbok, and to the Jordan, now then, return it peaceably and I will leave."

Jephthah again sent messengers to the king of Ammon, who said to him, "Jephthah says, 'Israel did not take the land of Moab, or the land of Ammon, in their going up out of Egypt, Israel went in the wilderness as far as the Papyrus Sea[2] and came to Kadesh. Israel also sent to the king of Moab, and he did not consent, and Israel stayed in Kadesh. They journeyed in the wilderness and circumnavigated the land of Edom and the land of Moab. They traveled to the east of the land of Moab, and camped in the country beyond Arnon, and did not enter into the borders of Moab, as Arnon is the border of Moab. Israel sent messengers to Sihon king of the Amorites and the king of Heshbon, and Israel said to him, 'Let us pass, we beg you, through your land to our place.' Sihon did not trust Israel to pass by his borders, and Sihon gathered all his people, and they camped at Jahaz, and he set the battle formation against Israel."

"Lord the god of Israel delivered Sihon and all his people into the hand of Israel, and they slaughtered him, and Israel inherited all the land of the Amorites who lived in that land, from Arnon and to Jabbok, and from the wilderness to the Jordan. Now Lord the god of Israel has removed the Amorites from before his people Israel, and will you inherit his land? Won't you inherit the possessions which Chemosh your god will cause you to inherit? Won't we inherit the land of all those who Lord the god has removed from before you? Now, are you any better than Balak son of Zippor, king of Moab? Did he not fight with Israel and make war with them when Israel lived in Heshbon and in its borders, and in the land of Aroer and in its borders, and in all the cities by the

Jordan for three hundred years? And did you recover them at that time? Now I have not sinned against you, but you wrong me in preparing war against me. Now decide, Lord Judge,[3] today between the Israelites and the Ammonites."

But the king of Ammon did not listen to the words of Jephthah, which he sent to him. The spirit of the Lord came on Jephthah and he passed through Gilead and Manasseh and passed by the watch-tower of Gilead to the other side of the Ammonites. Jephthah vowed a vow to the Lord, saying, "If you will indeed deliver the Ammonites into my hand, then it will come to pass that whoever will first come out of the door of my house to meet me when I return in peace from the Ammonites, he will be the Lord's, and I will offer him up for a whole burnt offering."

Jephthah advanced to meet the Ammonites to fight against them, and the Lord delivered them into his hand. He slaughtered them from Aroer all the way to Arnon,[4] in twenty cities, and as far as Abel's vineyard[5] with massive great destruction. The Ammonites were straightened before the Israelites, and Jephthah returned to his house in Mizpeh and saw his daughter come out to meet him dancing with tambourines. She was his only child, he had no other son or daughter. When he saw her, he tore his clothes, and said, "Oh, oh, my daughter! You have indeed troubled me, and you are the cause of my trouble! I have vowed against you to the Lord, and I will not be able to return from it!"

She said to him, "Father, have you vowed to the Lord? Do to me accordingly as the words of your mouth, in that the Lord has worked vengeance for you on your enemies of the Ammonites. Let my father now do this thing. Leave me alone for two months, and I will go up and down in the mountains, and I will mourn my virginity with my friends."

He said, "Go," and he sent her away for two months. She went with her friends, and mourned her virginity in the mountains. It happened at the end of the two months that she returned to her father, and he performed her his vow which he vowed, and she had known no man. It was an ordinance in Israel, that the daughters of Israel went from year to year to mourn the daughter of Jephthah the Gileadite for four days in a year.

# Judges: Chapter 11 Notes

**1** Codex Vaticanus: Tôb (ⲧⲱⲃ)

- Aleppo Codex: Twb (טוֹב)

- Leningrad Codex: Tovv (טֽוֹב)

- Targum Jerusalem: tava (טָבָא). Translation: rumor

The town of Tob is believed to have been in Amman southeast of the Sea of Galilee. It is generally accepted that it is the town of Tubu (𒌝𒁍) mentioned in the Amarna Letter EA205 from circa 1350 BC.

**2** Codex Vaticanus: thalassês Siph (ⲑⲁⲗⲁⲥⲥⲏⲥ ⲥⲓⲫ). Translation: Siph Sea

- Codex Alexandrinus: thalassês erythras (ⲑⲁⲗⲁⲥⲥⲏⲥⲉⲣⲩⲑⲣⲁⲥ). Translation: Erythrean Sea

- Aleppo Codex: ym swp (יט סוף). Translation: Papyrus (or reed) Sea

- Leningrad Codex: yam-Suf (יַם־סֽוּף). Translation: Papyrus (or reed) Sea

- Targum Jerusalem: yama deSuf (יַמָא דְסוּף). Translation: sea of papyrus (or reeds)

The older Codex Vaticanus maintains the Greek transliteration of the name the Suf (סֽוּף) Sea as Siph (Σιφ) Sea, while the later Codex Alexandrinus uses the more common Greek translation of Erythrean (Ἐρυθρᾶσ) Sea. The confirms that the Aramaic text the Greeks translated included the name Swf Sea. Both the Aramaic swf (𐡎𐡅𐡐) and Phoenician term swf (𐤎𐤅𐤐), meaning papyrus plants, were adopted from the Egyptian term tjufi (𓆄𓏲𓈖𓈗), which referred to papyrus, papyrus plants, and papyrus marshes. The Egyptian term continued to be used into the Classical era as the Coptic words čoouf (ϫⲟⲟⲩϥ), conf (ϭⲟⲛϥ), and comf (ϭⲟⲙϥ), all meaning papyrus. Conversely, the Egyptian name of the Red Sea was the Sea of Ḥeḥ (𓎛), meaning 'very large sea' from the Middle Kingdom era onward, however, it is believed to have originally been named after the ancient Egyptian frog god Heh (𓆐). As the Greek translation of Erythrean Sea is anachronistic, the translation of Papyrus Sea is imported from the Masoretic text.

**3** Codex Vaticanus: crinae c̄s̄ crinôn (**КΡΙΝΑΙΚ͞СΚΡΙΝѠΝ**). Translation: decide Lord Judge

- Codex Alexandrinus: crinae cyrios o crinôn (**КΡΙΝΑΙΚΥΡΙΟСΟ КΡΙΝѠΝ**). Translation: decide lord the judge

- Aleppo Codex: yšpt Yhwh hšpt (**ישפט יהוה השפט**). Translation: will decide Yhwh the judge

- Leningrad Codex: yishpot Yehvah hashofet (יִשְׁפֹּט יְהוָה הַשֹּׁפֵט). Translation: will decide Yehvah the judge

- Targum Jerusalem: yedin Yeyah da'avad dina (יְדִין יְיָ דְעֲבַד דִינָא). Translation: powers of Yahw the slave (or servant) of law (or judgment)

As Shofet does not appear to be the name of a Canaanite god, in the Septuagint's version of Judges Jephthah is recognizing the King of Amman as a Lord Judge, implying the King of Amman is one of Egypt's local magistrates under Ramesses II and Merneptah. As Amman was one of the few Canaanite cities not listed as being in revolt during the reign of Merneptah, while Israel was listed as being in revolt, it seems this story of Jephthah's revolt against Amman was the Israelite revolt listed in Egyptian records.

**4** Codex Vaticanus: Arnôn (**ΑΡΝѠΝ**)

- Codex Alexandrinus: Semôith (**СЕМѠΙΘ**)

- Aleppo Codex: Mnyt (**מנית**)

- Leningrad Codex: Minnit (מִנִּית)

- Targum Jerusalem: Minit (מְנִית)

As none of the sources agree, the oldest source-text, the Codex Vaticanus' Arnon is used in this translation. The Arnon stream is generally accepted as being the Wadi Mujib river canyon in Jordan, approximately 90 km (56 miles) south of Amman.

**5** Codex Vaticanus: Ebelcharmin (ЄΒЄΛΧΑΡΜΙΝ).

• Codex Alexandrinus: Abel ampelônô (ΑΒЄΛΑΜΠЄΛΩΝΩ). Translation: Abel's vineyard

  • Aleppo Codex: Åbl krmym (אבל כרמים). Translation: Abel's vineyard

  • Leningrad Codex: Avel keramim (אָבֵל כְּרָמִים). Translation: Abel's vineyard

  • Targum Jerusalem: yshar keramaya (יְשַׁר כְּרָמַיָא). Translation: directly to (or even) vineyard

As the Codex Vaticanus includes a transliteration of the name found in the Masoretic text, and the Codex Alexandrinus includes a translation of the name found in the Masoretic text, the Masoretic name is imported.

# Judges: Chapter 12

The Ephraimites assembled and went to the north, and said to Jephthah, "Why did you go and fight Amman, and did not call us to go with you? We will burn your house!"

Jephthah answered them, "I and my people and Amman were engaged in war, and I called for you, and you did not save me out of their hand. I saw that you were no ally, and I took my life in my own hand and invaded Amman, and the Lord delivered them into my hand. Why have you come up against me today to fight with me?" Jephthah gathered all the men of Gilead and fought with Ephraim, and the men of Gilead slaughtered Ephraim, because they that escaped of Ephraim said, "You are of Gilead among Ephraim and among Manasseh."

Gilead took the fords of the Jordan near Ephraim, and they who escaped among the Ephraimites said to them, "Let us go across," and the men of Gilead asked, "Are you an Ephraimite?"

He answered, "No."

Then they said to him, "Now say, 'stalk of grain,'"[1] and he did not pronounce it right, so they captured him and killed him at the fords of the Jordan. Forty-two thousand Ephraimites died there at that time. Jephthah judged Israel six years, and Jephthah the Gileadite died and was buried in his city in Gilead.

After him, Ibzan of the Temple of Lehem[2] judged Israel. He had thirty sons, and thirty daughters, who he sent out, and he brought in thirty daughters for his sons from outside, and he judged Israel seven years. Ibzan died and was buried at the Temple of Lehem. After him, Elon of Zebulun judged Israel for ten years. Elon of Zebulun died and was buried in Aijalon in the land of Zebulun.

After him, Abdon the son of Hillel, a Per-Atenite, judged Israel. He had forty sons, and thirty grandsons, that rode on seventy colts, and he judged Israel eight years. Abdon the son of Hillel, the Per-Atenite, died and was buried in Per-Aten[3] in the land of Ephraim in the mountains of Amalek.

# Judges: Chapter 12 Notes

**1** Codex Vaticanus: stachys (ⲥⲧⲁⲭⲩⲥ). Translation: stalk of grain (or progeny)

• Codex Alexandrinus: synthêma (ⲥⲨⲚⲐⲎⲘⲀ). Translation: anything agreed upon

• Aleppo Codex: šblt (שבלת). Translation: stalk of grain

• Leningrad Codex: shibbolet (שִׁבֹּלֶת). Translation: stalk of grain

• Targum Jerusalem: shubbalta (שׁוּבַּלְתָּא). Translation: stalk of grain (or branch of river)

The spelling of šblt (שבלת) in the Masoretic text is not the Hebrew spelling of šybwlt (שיבולת), but the older Canaanite spelling, recorded as šblt (𐎌𐎁𐎍𐎚) in Ugaritic Canaanite, and šblt (𐤔𐤁𐤋𐤕) in Phoenician Canaanite. This older Canaanite spelling developed into the Hebrew spelling during the Persian era, under the influence of Imperial Aramaic. The Aramaic spelling found in the Targum Jerusalem is virtually identical to the older Akkadian cuneiform term šubulta (𒋗𒁍𒌌𒋫), indicating that the division among the Israelites was already between those speaking Canaanite versus Aramaic. Arameans appeared in Mesopotamian records centuries earlier than the Habirus, and the two cultures were generally described as inhabiting the same regions, although the Arameans were more urban, and the Habirus were more nomadic.

**2** Codex Vaticanus: Baethleem (ⲃⲀⲓⲐⲖⲉⲉⲘ)

• Aleppo Codex: byt lhm (בית לחם). Translation: house (or temple) of Lehem (or grain)

• Leningrad Codex: beit Lachem (בֵּית לָחֶם). Translation: house (or temple) of Lehem (or grain)

• Targum Jerusalem: beit Lechem (בֵּית לֶחֶם). Translation: house (or temple) of Lehem (or grain)

Lehem was an ancient Canaanite god of grain, rebirth, and life, similar in nature to the Egyptian god Osiris, and Greek god Dionysus. Lehem was also the word meaning 'grain,' meaning the name could be interpreted as anything from the 'Temple of Lehem' to the 'grain silo,' however, the ancient Samaritan city of Bethlehem is being referenced, which was named after the Temple of Lehem, and so the name is translated directly from the Masoretic text.

**3** Codex Vaticanus: Pharathôm (ⲪⲀⲢⲀⲐⲰⲘ).

- Codex Alexandrinus: Phraathôn (ⲪⲢⲀⲀⲐⲰⲚ)

- Aleppo Codex: prôtwn (פרעתון)

- Leningrad Codex: Fir'atovn (פִּרְעָתוֹן)

- Targum Jerusalem: Fir'atovn (פִּרְעָתוֹן)

The Hebrew name is a translation of an Egyptian name, Per-Aten. It is unknown where the town of Per-Aten (or Per-Atum) in the land of Ephraim was located, however, it seems evident that it started as an Egyptian colony during the New Kingdom era. As it was named Per-Aten (𓉐𓇋𓈖𓆄𓇳) the foundation of the colony would have almost certainly taken place during the Amarna Period, between 1353-1336 BC. During that era, Ephraim was ruled by the Judges Ehud and Shamgar, and the land was described as being at peace until the end of the era.

# Judges: Chapter 13

The Israelites again committed iniquity before the Lord, and the Lord delivered them into the hands of the Pelesets for forty years. There was a man of Zorah, of the family of the Danites whose name was Manoah, and his wife was barren and did not become pregnant.

The messenger of the lord appeared to the woman, and said to her, "Look, you are barren and have not carried, yet you will conceive a son. Now be very cautious, and drink no wine or strong drink, and eat nothing unclean, as you are with child, and will give birth to a son. No iron must touch his head, for the child will be a Nazarite to God from the womb, and he will begin to save Israel from the hand of the Pelesets."

The woman went in, and told her husband, "A man of God came to me, and he looked like a messenger of God, very dreadful, and I did not ask him from where he was, and he did not tell me his name. He said to me, 'Look, you are with child and will give birth to a son, and now drink no wine or strong drink, and eat nothing unclean, for the child will be holy to God from the womb until the day of his death."

Manoah prayed to the Lord, "If you, Lord, sent to me a man of God, let him now come to us once more, and teach us what we will do to the child about to be born."

The Lord heard the voice of Manoah, and the messenger of God came again to the woman, as she sat in the field, and Manoah her husband was not with her. The woman rushed, and ran to bring word to her husband, and said to him, "Look the man who came to me the other day has appeared to me."

Manoah arose and followed his wife, and came to the man, and said to him, "Are you the man that spoke to the woman?"

The messenger answered, "I am."

Manoah said, "Now your word will come to pass. How will we judge the child and our dealings with him?"

The messenger of the lord said to Manoah, "Of all things concerning which I spoke to the woman, she will beware. She will eat nothing that comes of the vine yielding wine, and let her not drink wine or strong liquor, and let her not eat anything unclean. All the things that I have ordered her she will observe."

Manoah said to the messenger of the lord, "Let us keep you here, and prepare for you a kid of the goats."

The messenger of the lord replied to Manoah, "If you should detain me, I will not eat of your bread, and if you would offer a whole burnt offering, to the Lord you will offer it."

Manoah did not know that he was the messenger of the lord. Manoah said to the messenger of the lord, "What is your name, that when your word will come to pass, we may glorify you?"

The messenger of the lord said to him, "Why do you ask my name when it is wonderful?"

Manoah took a kid of the goats and its meat offering and offered it on the rock to the Lord, and the messenger worked a distinct work, and Manoah and his wife were looking on. It happened when the flame went up above the altar towards the sky, that the messenger of the lord went up in the flame, and Manoah and his wife were looking, and they fell on their face to the earth. The messenger did not appear again to Manoah or his wife. Then Manoah knew that this was the messenger of the lord. Manoah said to his wife, "We will certainly die because we have seen God."

But his wife said to him, "If the Lord wanted to kill us, he would not have received from our hand a whole burnt offering and a meat offering. He would not have shown us all these things, and he would have made us hear all these things."

The woman gave birth to a son, and she called his name Samson, and the child grew, and the Lord blessed him. The spirit of the Lord began to go out with him in the camp of Dan and between Zorah and Esthaol.

# Judges: Chapter 14

Samson went down to Timnah and saw a woman in Timnah from the daughters of the Pelesets. He returned and told his father and his mother, and said, "I have seen a woman in Timnah of the daughters of the Pelesets, and now procure her for me as a wife."

His father and his mother replied to him, "Are there no daughters of your brothers, and is there not a woman of all my people, that you go to take a wife instead of from the uncircumcised Pelesets?"

Samson said to his father, "Take her for me, as she is good-looking."

His father and his mother did not know that it was of the Lord. That he wanted to take revenge on the Pelesets. At that time the Pelesets lorded over Israel. Samson and his father and mother went down to Timnah, and he came to the vineyard of Timnah. A young lion roared in meeting him. The spirit of the Lord came powerfully over him, and he crushed him as he would have killed a kid of the goats, barehanded. He did not tell his father and his mother what he had done.

They went down and spoke to the woman, and she was beautiful in the eyes of Samson. After some time he returned to take her, and he turned aside to see the carcass of the lion, and in the mouth of the lion was a hive of bees with honey. He collected some and ate some, and he took some to his father and mother and gave it to them, and they also ate, but he did not tell them that he took the honey out of the mouth of the lion. His father went down to the woman, and Samson made a banquet there for seven days, as the young men used to. When they saw him they took thirty guests and joined him. Samson said to them, "I propound a riddle for you. If you will answer it for me, and solve it within the seven days of the feast, I will give you thirty sheets and thirty changes of clothing. If you can't answer it for me, you will give me thirty sheets and thirty changes of clothing."

They answered him, "Propound your riddle, and we will hear it."

He said to them, "Meat came out of the eater, and sweetness out of the strong."

They could not answer the riddle for three days. On the fourth day, they said to the wife of Samson, "Deceive now your husband and let him tell you the riddle, in case we burn you and your father's house with fire. Did you invite us to do violence?"

Samson's wife wept in front of him, and said, "You hate me, and don't love me! The riddle which you have propounded to my people, you have not told me."

Samson said to her, "If I have not told it to my father and my mother, will I tell it to you?"

She wept in front of him seven days, during which their banquet lasted, and on the seventh day, he told her because she troubled him, and she told it to her people. The men of the city said to him on the seventh day, before sunrise, "What is sweeter than honey, and what is stronger than a lion?"

Samson said to them, "If you had not plowed with my heifer, you would not have known my riddle."

The Spirit of the Lord came on him powerfully, and he went down to Ashkelon, and murdered thirty of the men that lived there, and took their clothes, and gave the changes of clothing to those that answered the riddle. Samson was very angry and went back to the house of his father. The wife of Samson was given to one of his friends that he was close with.

# Judges: Chapter 15

In the days of wheat harvest, Samson visited his wife with a kid, and said, "I will go to my wife to the bed-chamber, but her father did not allow him to go."

Her father said, "I said that you did certainly hate her, and I gave her to one of your friends. Is not her younger sister better than she? Let her be for you instead of her."

Samson said to them, "For once am I blameless among the Pelesets, even though I cause problems among them."

Samson went and caught three hundred foxes, and took torches, and turned tail to tail, and put a torch between two tails, and fastened it. He set fire to the torches and sent the foxes into the grain of the Pelesets, and everything was burnt from the threshing floor to the standing grain, including the vineyard and olives.

The Pelesets inquired, "Who has done these things?"

They answered, "Samson the son-in-law of the Timnahite, because he has taken his wife, and given her to one of his friends.

The Pelesets went up and burnt her and her father's house with fire. Samson said to them, "Though you may have dealt so with her, verily I will be avenged against you, and afterward I will stop."

He knocked them down, and ran down and hid in a cave of the rock Etam. The Pelesets went up, and camped in Judah, and spread themselves abroad in Lehi. The men of Judah asked, "Why have you come up against us?"

The Pelesets answered, "We have come up to catch Samson, and to do to him as he has done to us."

The three thousand men of Judah went down to the cave in the rock Etam, and they said to Samson, "Don't you know that the Pelesets rule over us? What is this that you have done to us?"

Samson answered to them, "As they did to me, so have I done to them."

They said to him, "We have come down to catch you and deliver you into the hand of the Pelesets."

Samson replied to them, "Swear to me that you will not kill me yourselves."

They answered him, "No, we will only tie you tight, and deliver you into their hand, and will not kill you," and they tied him with two new ropes, and brought him from that rock.

They came to Lehi, and the Pelesets shouted, and ran to meet him, and the Spirit of the Lord came mightily on him, and the ropes that were on his arms became as kindling which is burnt with fire, and his bonds were consumed from off his hands. He found the jaw-bone of a donkey that had been thrown away, and he took it in his hand and killed a thousand men with it.

Samson said, "With the jaw-bone of a donkey I have completely destroyed them, for with the jaw-bone of a donkey I have slaughtered a thousand men!"

When he stopped speaking, then he threw the jaw-bone from his hand, and he called that place Raising-the-Jaw-Bone. He was very thirsty, and wept before the Lord, and said, "You were willing to grant this great deliverance by the hand of your servant, but now I will die from thirst, and fall into the hand of the uncircumcised?" He was very thirsty, and wept before the Lord, and said, "You were willing to grant this great deliverance by the hand of your servant, but now will I die from thirst, and fall into the hand of the uncircumcised?"

God broke open a hollow place in the jaw, and there came out water, and he drank, and his spirit returned and he revived. Therefore the name of the fountain was called The Well of the Invoker, which is in Lehi until this day. He judged Israel in the days of the Pelesets twenty years.

# Judges: Chapter 16

Samson went to Gaza, and visited a prostitute there, and went into her. It was reported to the Gazites, saying, "Samson has come here," and they surrounded him and laid wait for him all night at the gate of the city, and they were quiet all the night, saying, "Let's wait until the dawn, and we'll kill him."

Samson slept until midnight, and rose up at midnight, and took hold of the doors of the gate of the city with the two posts, and lifted them up with the bar, and laid them on his shoulders, and he went up to the top of the mountain that is before Hebron and laid them there. After this, he loved a woman in Sorek, and her name was Delilah. The princes of the Pelesets came up to her, and said to her, "Seduce him, and see where his great strength comes from, and how we will prevail against him, and bind him to humble him, and we will give you each eleven hundred pieces of silver."

Delilah said to Samson, "Tell me, I beg you, what is your great strength, and how will you be bound that you may be humbled?

Samson said to her, "If they tie me with seven moist cords that have not been stretched, then I will be as weak as one of the ordinary men."

The princes of the Pelesets brought her seven moist cords that had not been stretched, and she tied him with them. The men were hiding in her chamber, and she said to him, "The Pelesets are on you, Samson!"

He broke the cords like anyone would break a thread when it has touched the fire, and his strength was unknown. Delilah said to Samson, "Look, you have cheated me, and told me lies. Now then tell me how you will be tied."

He said to her, "If they should tie me fast with new ropes with which work has not been done, then will I be as weak as another man."

Delilah took new ropes and tied him with them, and the men that were hiding, came out of the chamber, and she said, "The Pelesets are on you, Samson,' and he broke them off his arms like a thread."

Delilah said to Samson, "Look, you have deceived me, and told me lies. Tell me, I demand of you, how you may be tied."

He said to her, "If you should braid the seven locks of my head with a braid, and should fasten them with the pin into the wall, then I will be weak as another man."

When he was asleep, Delilah took the seven locks of his head, and braided them into a braid, and fastened them with the pin into the wall, and she shouted, "The Pelesets are on you, Samson!"

He awoke out of his sleep and pulled the pin of the braid out of the wall. Delilah said to Samson, "How can you say, 'I love you,' when your heart is not with me? This third time you have deceived me, and have not told me where your great strength is."

She hurt him with her words and chastised him so much that his spirit failed almost to death. Then he told her all his heart, and said to her, "A razor has not come on my head, because I have been a holy one of God from my mother's womb. If then I should be shaven, my strength will leave from me, and I will be weak, and I will be like all other men."

Delilah saw that he told her all his heart, and she sent and called the princes of the Pelesets, saying, "Come up one more time, as he has told me all his heart."

The chiefs of the Pelesets went up to her and brought the money in their hands. Delilah made Samson sleep on her knees, and she called a man, and he shaved the seven locks of his head, and she began to humble him, and his strength departed from him. Delilah yelled, "The Pelesets are on you Samson!"

He woke out of his sleep and said, "I will go out as I did before, and shake myself," and he did not know that the Lord was departed from him. The Pelesets took him, and cut out his eyes, and brought him down to Gaza, and bound him with brass shackles, and he ground grain in the prison-house. The hair of his head began to grow as before it was shaven.

The chiefs of the Pelesets met to offer a great sacrifice to their god Dagon, and to celebrate, and they said, "God has given into our hand our enemy Samson." The people saw him, and sang praises to their god, "Our god," they said, "has delivered into our hand our enemy, who destroyed our land, and who murdered many of us."

When their heart was happy, they said, "Call Samson out of the prison-house, and let him play before us," and they called Samson out of the prison-house, and he played before them. They slapped him with the palms of their hands and tied him between the pillars.

Samson said to the young man that guided him, "Allow me to feel the pillars on which the house rests, so I can lean on them."

The house was full of men and women and all the chiefs of the Pelesets were there, and on the roof were about three thousand men and women looking at the sports of Samson. Samson wept before the Lord, and said, "Lord, my lord! Remember me, I beg you, and strengthen me, God, just this once, and I will repay the Pelesets for my eyes."

Samson took hold of the two pillars which supported the house, and leaned on them, and laid hold of one with his right hand, and the other with his left. Samson yelled, "Let me die with the Pelesets!" and he put his back into it, and the house fell on the princes, and on all the people that were in it. The dead who Samson killed in his suicide was more than those he murdered during his life. His brothers and his father's house went down, and they took him, and they went up and buried him between Zorah and Esthaol in the sepulcher of his father Manoah, and he judged Israel twenty years.

# Judges: Chapter 17

There was a man from the mountains of Ephraim, and his name was Micah. He said to his mother, "The eleven hundred pieces of silver which you took of yourself, and about which you cursed me, and spoke in my ears, look, the silver is with me. I took it."

His mother said, "Blessed be my son of the Lord."

He restored the eleven hundred pieces of silver to his mother, and his mother said, I had wholly consecrated the money to the Lord out of my hand for my son, to make a graven and a molten image, and now I will restore it to you. But he returned the silver to his mother, and his mother took two hundred pieces of silver and gave them to a silversmith, and he made from it a molten idol, and it was in the house of Micah. The house of Micah was for him, a Temple of God, and he made a vest and teraphim, and he consecrated one of his sons, and he became to him a priest.

In those days there was no king in Israel, and every man did that which was right in his own eyes. There was a young man in the House of Lehem of the tribe of Judah, and he was a Levite, and he was traveling there. The man departed from House of Lehem in a town of Judah to stay in whatever place he might find, and he came as far as Mount Ephraim and stopped at the house of Micah. Micah asked him, "From where have you come?"

He answered him, "I am a Levite from the Temple of Lehem in Judah, and I go to stay in any place I may find."

Micah offered him, "Live with me and be for me a father and a priest, and I will give you ten pieces of silver each year, and a change of clothing, and your living."

The Levite began to live with the man, and the young man was to him as one of his sons. Micah consecrated the Levite, and he became for him a priest, and he was in the house of Micah. Micah said, "Now I know that the Lord will do good for me because a Levite has become my priest."

# Judges: Chapter 18

In those days there was no king in Israel, the tribe of Dan wanted for itself an inheritance to inhabit because no inheritance had fallen to it until that day among the tribes of Israel. The sons of Dan sent from their families five men of valor, from Zorah and Esthaol, to spy out the land and to search it. They said to them, "Go and search out the land."

They came as far as the mountains of Ephraim to the house of Micah and they lodged there, in the house of Micah, and they recognized the voice of the young man the Levite, and turned in there, and asked him, "Who brought you in here? And what are you doing in this place? And what have you here?"

He answered them, "Micah hired me, and I became his priest."

They said to him, "Inquire of God, now, whether the path in which we are going will be prosperous."

The priest answered them, "Go in peace. Your way in which you go is before the Lord."

The five men traveled on, and arrived at Laish and saw the people in it living peacefully, and at ease like the Sidonians. There was no one perverting or shaming anything in the land, and no heir extorting their wealth, yet they were far from the Sidonians, and they had no trade with anyone. The five men went to their brothers, to Zorah and Esthaol, and asked their brothers, "Why do you sit here idle?"

They said, "Get up, and let us go up against them, for we have seen the land, and, saw it is very good. Yet you are idle. Don't delay leaving. Enter in and seize the land. When you will go, you will come to a peaceful people, and the land is extensive, but God has given it into your hand. A place where nothing is lacking that the earth provides. They departed there from the families of Dan, from Zorah and Esthaol, six hundred men, equipped with weapons of war. They went up and camped in the village of Ye'arim in Judah. (Therefore that place was called the Camp of Dan, until this day. Look, it is near the village of Ye'arim.)

They went on from there to the mountains of Ephraim and came to the house of Micah. The five men who went to spy out the land of Laish answered, and said to their brothers, "You know that there is in this place, a vest and teraphim, and a molten idol, and now consider what you will do."

They turned aside there, and went into the house of the young man, the Levite, into the Temple of Micah, and asked him how he was. The six hundred Danites who were equipped with their weapons of war stood by the door of the gate. The five men who went to spy out the land went up and entered into the Temple of Micah, and the priest stood. They took the idol, and the vest and teraphim, and the priest asked them, "What are you doing?"

They answered him, "Be silent, lay your hand on your mouth, and come with us, and be for us a father and a priest. Is it better for you to be the priest of the house of one man, or to be the priest of a tribe and house for a family of Israel?"

The heart of the priest was glad, and he took the vest, and teraphim, and molten idol, and went among the people. So they turned and departed, and put their children and their property and their baggage before them. They went some distance from the Temple of Micah, and Micah, and the men in the houses near Micah's Temple, called out, and chased after Dan. Dan turned around, and asked Micah, "What is the matter with you that you have called out?"

Micah said, "You have taken my molten idol which I made, and my priest is gone, and what have I remaining? Yet you ask me, 'Why do you call out?"

The children of Dan said to him, don't let your voice be heard by us, in case angry men attack you, and take away your life, and the lives of your house. The children of Dan went their way, and Micah saw that they were stronger than he was, and he returned to his house. The children of Dan took what Micah had made, and the priest that he had, and they came to Laish, to a quiet and peaceful people, and they slaughtered them with the edge of the sword and burnt the city with fire. There were no survivors, because the city was far from the Sidonians, and they had no trade with other men. It was in the valley of the house of Ereo, that they built the city, and lived in it. They called the name of the city Dan, after the name of Dan their fore-father, who was born to Israel.

(The name of the town had been Hall of the Lion[1] before.)

The children of Dan set up the molten idol for themselves, and Jonathan son of Gershom son of Manasseh, he and his sons were priests to the tribe of Dan until the time the nation was taken away captive. They set up for themselves the molten idol which Micah made, all the days that the Temple of God was in Shiloh. It was so in those days that there was no king in Israel.

# Judges: Chapter 18 Notes

**1** Codex Vaticanus: Oylamaes (ΟΥλΑΜΑΙΟ)

- Codex Alexandrinus: an Laes (ΗΝλΑΙΟ). Translation: it was Laes

- Aleppo Codex: åwlm lyš (**אוּלם ליש**). Translation: but (or Hall of) or lion (or wealth)

- Leningrad Codex: ulam layish (אוּלָם לָיִשׁ). Translation: but (or Hall of) lion (or wealth)

- Targum Jerusalem: veram layish (בְרַם לָיִשׁ). Translation: besides lion (or Leo)

The translators at the library of Alexandria, or the earlier translators of the Aramaic version they worked from interpreted the name differently from the Hebrew translators. The term åwlm (אולם) can be interpreted as 'but,' as the Hebrew translators rendered it, or as 'hall,' or 'salon' as the early Aramaic translators interpreted it. As the Greeks considered it part of the name they transliterated it, meaning they interpreted the Aramaic text as reading 'Hall of Aes.' Either they missed the L (Λ / ל) at the beginning of the name Lysh, or it had been dropped in the Aramaic translation. Reading åwlm lyš (אולם ליש) the way it was read at the Library of Alexandria renders the old name of the town as 'Hall of the Lion' using the unusual but documented translation of lyš (ליש) as 'lion,' or 'Hall that's there,' using the more common interpretation of lyš (ליש). The term lyš does not appear to have had meant 'lion' in early Aramaic, and was probably interpreted as 'the aesh' by the Aramaic translator, who also interpreted Aesh as a proper name, resulting in the translation of 'Hall of Aesh' instead of 'Hall of the Aesh.' As Hall of the Lion is probably the origin of the name, however, that name is imported from the Aleppo Codex.

# Judges: Chapter 19

A Levite was traveling along the sides of Mount Ephraim, and he took for himself a concubine from the House of Lehem in Judah. His concubine left him and traveled from him to the house of her father, in the House of Lehem in Judah, and she was there four months. Her husband rose up and went after her, to speak kindly to her, and to restore her to himself. He had a young man with him, and a pair of donkeys. She brought him into the house of her father, and the father of the woman saw him and was very pleased to meet him. His father-in-law, the father of the woman, detained him, and he stayed with him for three days, and they ate and drank, and lodged there. It happened on the fourth day, that they rose early, and he stood up to leave, and the father of the woman said to his son-in-law, "Strengthen your heart with a morsel of bread, and afterward you will go."

They two sat down together and ate and drank, and the father of the woman said to her husband, "Wait now the night, and let your heart be happy."

The man rose to leave, but his father-in-law detained him, and he stayed and lodged there. He rose early in the morning on the fifth day to leave, and the father of the woman said, "Strengthen your heart, and equip yourself as a soldier until the evening, and the two ate."

The man rose up to leave, he and his concubine, and his young man, but his father-in-law the father of the woman said to him, "Look now, it's late in the day, almost evening, stay here and let your heart rejoice, and you will rise early tomorrow for your journey and you will leave to your home."

But the man would not lodge there, he rose and departed, and came to the area opposite Jebus, (this is Jerusalem,) and there was with him a pair of donkeys saddled, and his concubine was with him. They came as far as Jebus, and the day had advanced, and the young man said to his master, "Come, I beg you, and let us turn aside into this city of the Jebusites, and let us lodge in it."

His master said to him, "We will not turn aside into a strange city, where there are none one of the Israelites. We will pass on as far as Gibeah." He said to his young man, "Come, and let's approach one of the places, and we will lodge in Gibeah or Ramah."

They continued and went on, and the sun set on them near Gibeah, which is in Benjamin. They turned aside there to go into a lodge in Gibeah, and they went in and sat down in the street of the city, and no one took them into a house to lodge. An old man came out of the field from his work in the evening, and the man was from Mount Ephraim, and he stayed in Gibeah, and the men of the place were Benjaminites. He lifted his eyes and saw a traveler in the street of the city, and the old man said to him, "To what place go you, and from where come you?"

He answered him, "We are passing by from House of Lehem in Judah to the sides of Mount Ephraim. I am from there, and I went as far as House of Lehem in Judah, and I am going home, and there is no man to take me into his house. Yet is there straw and food for our donkeys, and bread and wine for me and my handmaid and the young man with your servants, there is no lack of anything."

The old man said, "Peace be to you, only do by no means lodge in the street." He brought him into his house and made room for his donkeys, and they washed their feet and ate and drank.

They were comforting their heart, when look, the lawless men of the city surrounded the house and knocked at the door. They spoke to the old man, the owner of the house, saying,

"Bring out the man who came into your house, that we may rape him."

The master of the house came out to them, and said, "No, brothers, do not do wrong, I beg you. After this man has come into my house, do not do this foolishness. Look my daughter a virgin, and the man's concubine, I will bring them out, and humble you them, and do to them that which is good in your eyes, but to this man do not this folly."

But the men would not consent to listen to him, so the man grabbed hold of his concubine, and threw her out to them, and they raped her, and abused her all night until the morning, and let her go when the morning dawned. The woman came back in the early morning and fell at the door of the house where her husband was until it was light. Her husband rose up in the morning, and opened the doors of the house, and went out to go on his journey, and look, the woman his concubine had fallen by the doors of the house, and her hands were on the threshold. He said to her, "Rise, and let us go."

She did not answer, as she was dead. He took her on his donkey and went to his place. He took his sword, and laid hold of his concubine, and divided her into twelve parts, and sent them to every coast of Israel. It was so, that everyone who saw it said, "Such a day as this has not happened nor has been seen from the day of the going up of the Israelites out of the land of Egypt until this day. Take counsel concerning it, and speak."

# Judges: Chapter 20

All the Israelites went out, and all the congregation was gathered as one man, from Dan to Beersheba, and in the land of Gilead, to the Lord at Mizpeh. All the tribes of Israel stood before the Lord in the assembly of the people of God, four hundred thousand men who drew a sword. The Benjaminites heard that the Israelites had gone up to Mizpeh, and the Israelites came and said, "Tell us, where did this wickedness take place?"

The Levite, the husband of the woman that was slain, answered and said, "I and my concubine went into Gibeah in Benjamin to lodge. The men of Gibeah rose against me and surrounded the house at night against me. They wished to kill me, and they abused my concubine, and she is dead. I took hold of my concubine, and cut her into pieces, and sent the parts to every border of the inheritance of the Israelites, as they have worked immorally and an abomination in Israel. Look, all you are Israelites. Consider and take counsel here among yourselves."

All the people rose up as one man, saying, "Not one of us will return to his tent, and not one of us will return to his house. Now this is what will be done in Gibeah, we will go up against it by lot. Moreover, we will take ten men for a hundred for all the tribes of Israel, and a hundred for a thousand, and a thousand for ten thousand, to take provisions, for them to come to Gibeah of Benjamin, to do to it according to all the abomination, which they worked in Israel."

All the men of Israel were gathered to the city as one man. The tribes of Israel sent men through the whole tribe of Benjamin, saying, "What is this wickedness that has been worked among you? Now then give up the lawless men that are in Gibeah, and we will put them to death, and purge out wickedness from Israel, but the Benjaminites did not agree to listen to the voice of their brothers the Israelites. The Benjaminites were gathered from their cities to Gibeah, to go out to fight with the Israelites. The Benjaminites from their cities were numbered on that day, twenty-three thousand, every man drawing a sword, besides the inhabitants of Gibeah, who numbered seven hundred chosen men of all the people able to use both hands alike.

All these, could sling stones at a rabbit, and not miss. The men of Israel, other than Benjamin, numbered four hundred thousand men that drew a sword, all these were men of war. They rose and went up to the Temple of El, and asked God, "Who will lead us to fight with the Benjaminites?"

The Lord said, "Judah will go up first as a leader."

The Israelites rose up in the morning and camped near Gibeah. They went out, all the men of Israel, to fight with Benjamin, and engaged with them at Gibeah. The Benjaminites went out from Gibeah, and they destroyed in Israel on that day twenty-two thousand men. The men of Israel strengthened themselves and again engaged in battle in the place where they had engaged on the first day. The Israelites went up, and cried out to the Lord until evening, and inquired of the Lord, saying, "Will we enter battle again with our brothers the Benjaminites?"

The Lord said, "Go up against them."

The Israelites advanced against the Benjaminites on the second day. The Benjaminites went out to meet them from Gibeah on the second day and destroyed another eighteen thousand of the Israelites of those who drew a sword. The Israelites and all the people got up, and went to the Temple of El, and they wept and sat there, before the Lord. They fasted on that day until evening, and offered whole burnt offerings and perfect sacrifices to the

Lord, for the box of Lord the god was there in those days. Phinehas the son of Eleazar the son of Aaron stood before it in those days, and the Israelites inquired of the Lord, "Will we again go out to fight with our brothers, the Benjaminites?"

The Lord answered, "Go up, tomorrow and I will give them into your hands."

The Israelites set an ambush near Gibeah, and the Israelites went up against the Benjaminites on the third day and formed up against Gibeah as before. The Benjaminites went out to meet the people, and were all drawn out of the city, and began to attack and kill the people as before in the roads, which go up to the Temple of El, and each from Gibeah was outnumbered by about thirty men of Israel. The Benjaminites said, "They'll fall before us like before."

The Israelites said, "Let us flee, and draw them out from the city into the roads," and they did so. All the men rose up out of their places and engaged in Ba'al Tamar,[1] and those laying in wait of Israel advanced from their place, the cave of Geba.[2] There came against Gibeah ten thousand men were chosen out of all of Israel, and the fight was severe, and they did not know that evil was coming on them. The Lord slaughtered Benjamin before the Israelites, and the Israelites destroyed 25,100 Benjaminites on that day, all those that drew a sword. The Benjaminites saw that they were slaughtered.

The men of Israel gave place to Benjamin because they trusted in the ambuscade which they had prepared against Gibeah. When they retreated, then the layers in wait rose up, and they moved towards Gibeah, and the whole ambush came out, and they struck the city with the edge of the sword. The Israelites had a signal of battle with the layers in wait, that they should send up a signal of smoke from the city. The Israelites saw that the layers in wait had seized Gibeah, and they stood in battle formation, and Benjamin began to kill the wounded ones among the men of Israel, about thirty men, as they said, "Certainly they will fall again before us, as in the first battle."

The signal went up increasingly over the city as a pillar of smoke, and Benjamin looked behind him and saw the destruction of the city rose to the sky. The men of Israel turned back, and the men of Benjamin rushed because they saw that evil had come on them. They ran to the wilderness from before the Israelites and fled, but the battle caught up to them, and they from the cities and destroyed them in the middle of them. They cut down Benjamin, and put an end to them, stopping and trampling them[3] until they came near Gibeah on the east. There fell from Benjamin eighteen thousand men, all these were men of might.

The rest turned and fled to the wilderness to the rock of Rimmon, and the Israelites picked off another five thousand men, and the Israelites chased after them as far as Gedan, and they slaughtered another two thousand of them. All that fell of Benjamin were twenty-five thousand men that drew a sword on that day; all these were men of might. The rest turned and fled to the wilderness to the rock of Rimmon, only six hundred men, and they stayed four months in the rock of Rimmon. The Israelites returned to the Benjaminites and slaughtered them with the edge of the sword from the city of Methla,[4] including the livestock and everything that was found in all the cities, and they burnt with fire the cities they found.

# Judges: Chapter 20 Notes

**1** Codex Vaticanus: Baalthamar (ΒΑΑΛΘΑΜΑΡ)

- Aleppo Codex: bôl tmr (כעל תמר)

- Leningrad Codex: ba'al Tamar (בַּעַל תָּמָר)

- Targum Jerusalem: Yericho (יְרִיחוֹ). Translation: Jericho

Eusebius reported the existence of a Beth-Tamar in Roman Judea as late as the 4th century AD, however, nothing is known about Ba'al Tamar or Beth-Tamar today. Apparently, nothing was known about is when the Targum Jerusalem was translated as well, as the translator substituted Jericho.

**2** Codex Vaticanus: Maaragabe (ΜΑΑΡΑΓΑΒΕ)

- Codex Alexandrinus: dysmôn tês Gabaa (ΔΥCΜΩΝΤΗCΓΑΒΑΑ). Translation: setting the Gabaa

- Aleppo Codex: môrh gbô (מערה גבע). Translation: cave Geba

- Leningrad Codex: ma'areh-Gava (מַעֲרֵה־גָבַע). Translation: cave of Gava

- Targum Jerusalem: meishar Giv'ata (מֵישַׁר גִּבְעָתָא). Translation: strength (or flat) of Givata

As the Codex Vaticanus includes a transliteration of the term found in the Masoretic text, that term is imported into this translation as 'cave of Geba.'

**3** Codex Vaticanus: cae ediôxan auton apo Noua cata poda autou (ΚΑΙ ΕΔΙΩΞΑΝΑΥΤΟΝΑΠΟΝΟΥΑΚΑΤΑΠΟΔΑΑΥΤΟΥ). Translation: and chased them from Noua and against them

- Codex Alexandrinus: catapausae auton catapausin cae catepatêsan auton (ΚΑΤΑΠΑΥCΑΙΑΥΤΟΝΚΑΤΑΠΑΥCΙΝΚΑΙΚΑΤΕΠΑΤΗCΑΝ ΑΥΤΟΝ). Translation: put an end to them stopped and trampled them

• Aleppo Codex: hrdyphw mnwhh hdrykhw (הרדיפהו מנוחה הדריכהו).
Translation: persecuted them easily guided (or directed, commanded)

• Leningrad Codex: hirdifuhu menuchah hidrichuhu (הִרְדִיפֻהוּ מְנוּחָה
הִדְרִיכֻהוּ). Translation: persecuted them easily guided (or directed,
commanded)

• Targum Jerusalem: redafunun mibbeit neyachahon teradunun
(רְדָפוּנוּן מִבֵּית נְיָחֲהוֹן טְרָדוּנוּן). Translation: chased them away from inside
their inheritance

The translation in the Codex Vaticanus appears to have an error,
which was fixed in the Codex Alexandrinus. The Greek translators
appear to have mistranslated menuchah (מְנוּחָה), meaning 'easily,' as
'from Noua' (from Noua), therefore the Codex Alexandrius is followed
here.

**4** Codex Vaticanus: Methla (ΜΕΘΛΑ)

• Codex Alexandrinus: hexês (ΕΞΗΣ). Translation: following

• Aleppo Codex: mtm (מתם). Translation: men

• Leningrad Codex: metom (מְתֹם). Translation: men

• Targum Jerusalem: mikirveihon (מְקִרְוֵיהוֹן). Translation: original
wealth

As all three sources have a different term here, the Codex Vaticanus is
followed as it is the oldest.

# Judges: Chapter 21

The Israelites swore in Mizpeh, "None of us will give his daughter to a Benjamin as a wife."

The people came to the Temple of El, and sat there until evening before God, and they lifted their voice and cried with a great voice, and said, "Lord the god of Israel! Has this come to pass, That today one tribe should be missing from Israel?"

In the morning the people rose up early, and built an altar, and offered up whole burnt offerings and peace offerings. The Israelites said, "Who of all the tribes of Israel, did not go up in the congregation to the Lord?" as there was a great oath concerning those who did not go up to the Lord in Mizpeh, saying, "He will certainly be put to death."

The Israelites relented towards Benjamin their brothers, and said, "Today one tribe is cut off from Israel. What will we do for wives for the rest that remain? We have sworn by the Lord, not to give them of our daughters as wives."

They asked, "Which man is there of the tribes of Israel, who did not go up to the Lord in Mizpeh?"

No man came to the camp from Jabin Gilead to the assembly. The people were counted, and there was not a man there from the inhabitants of Jabin Gilead. The congregation sent twelve thousand of the strongest men, and they ordered, "Go and slaughter the inhabitants of Jabin Gilead with the edge of the sword. Do this to every male, and you will murder every woman that has laid with a man, but the virgins you will keep alive," and they did so.

They found among the inhabitants of Jabin Gilead four hundred young virgins, who had not known a man by lying with him, and they brought them to Shiloh in the land of Canaan. All the congregation sent and spoke to the Benjaminites in the rock Rimmon, and invited them to make peace. Benjamin returned to the Israelites at that time, and the Israelites gave them the women who they had not murdered from the daughters of Jabin Gilead, and they were content. The people repented for Benjamin because the Lord had made a breach in the tribes of Israel.

The elders of the congregation said, "What will we do for wives for those who remain? For the women of Benjamin have been slaughtered."

They said, "There must be an inheritance for them that escaped of Benjamin, or a tribe will be destroyed out of Israel. We will not be able to give them wives from our daughters, because we swore among the Israelites, saying, 'Cursed is he that gives a wife to Benjamin.'"

They said, "Look! Now there is a feast of the Lord from year to year in Shiloh, which is to the north of Bethel, eastward on the road that goes up from Bethel to Shechem, and from the south of Libnah."

They ordered the Benjaminites, saying, "Go and lie in wait in the vineyards, and you will see, and if the daughters of the inhabitants of Shiloh come out to dance in dances, then you will go out of the vineyards and kidnap for yourselves every man a wife of the daughters of Shiloh, and return to the land of Benjamin. When their fathers or their brothers come to dispute with us, then we will say to them, 'Grant them freely to us, for we have not taken each man his wife in battle. Because you did not give to them at the time, you transgressed.'"

The Benjaminites did so, and they took wives according to their number from the dancers who they kidnapped and they went and returned to their inheritance, and built the cities, and lived in them. The Israelites went home at that time every man to his tribe and his families, and they went every man to his inheritance.

In those days there was no king in Israel, every man did that which was right in his own sight.

# Forward to Ruth

Fragments of the book of Ruth have been found among the dead sea scrolls, however, only in the Assyrian script of the Hasmonean Dynasty, and dated to between 140 and 37 BC. The God of the book of Ruth in the Septuagint is called Lord God (Κυριω Θεω) or simplified to Lord (Κυριοσ). These terms are mirrored in the Masoretic text by Yehwah (יְהוָֹה) and Yhvah (יהוָֹה). The name Yhwh (יהוה) survives in one fragment of Ruth found among the Dead Sea Scrolls, however, it dates to the Hasmonean dynasty, and therefore dates to over 85 years after the Septuagint's version of Ruth was translated.

The Greek terms in the Septuagint's Ruth are translations of well-known terms related to Canaanite god El, the Canaanite creator-god. El translates in Canaanite dialects, including Judahite, Samaritan, Moabite, Edomite, and Sidonian, as well as in Hebrew as 'God,' and was the primary god worshiped in ancient Canaan in the era Abraham, Isaac, and Jacob were reported to have passed through the area. El was also the patron god of the Temple of El, built by Jacob near the modern city of Nablus in the Palestinian West Bank, which featured in many of the early Israelite scriptures before Samaria was conquered by the Assyrian Empire. In the Book of Micah, the Temple of El was referred to as Jacob's Temple of El, which confirms that the Israelites in the 8th century BC considered the Temple of El at Shiloh to be the Temple of El that Jacob built, in Genesis chapter 35. In Judges, the Temple of El in Shemchem is called the fortified Temple of the God of the Covenant, and the Temple of the Lord of the Covenant in both the Septuagint and the Masoretic text, which supports the identification of El with the covenant in the early Israelite religion.

If the Greeks translated the Septuagint accurately, which everything other than the names of God indicates, then the term

God (Θεοσ) would have been Ȧl (𐤋𐤀) in the texts they translated. Likewise, Lord God (Κυριω Θεω) would have been Ȧdn Ȧlm (𐤟𐤋𐤀 𐤉𐤀𐤟), the title of El, which translates as 'Father of the gods,' and Lord (Κυριοσ) would have been Ȧdn, meaning lord, master, or father. Ȧdn Ȧlm was a Canaanite title for El, found in the Ugaritic Texts. The word ȧl (אל), meaning 'god,' is used throughout the Masoretic text, but generally in relation to other gods, or as a part of a name, such as Israel, or Beth-El, proving El was of primary importance throughout the early era of the Israelite religion, before Yhwh became dominant under King Hezekiah.

The Masoretic Book of Ruth also includes a reference to the god Šdy (שדי), who was described as having 'dealt very bitterly' with Naomi when she was in Moab. In the Septuagint, the name was translated as ikanós (ικανοσ), meaning 'capable,' which indicates that the word Šdy (𐤔𐤃𐤅) was not in the Aramaic text the Greeks translated, however, a similar name was. Shaddai was in several of the books that ended up in both the Septuagint and the Masoretic text, and in other books was translated into Greek as 'omnipotent' (παντοκρατοροσ) or transliterated directly in Greek as Saddai (Σαδδαι). This indicates that the god that dealt bitterly with Naomi was the Moabite god Shaddayin.

Šdyn (𐤔𐤃𐤉𐤍), generally anglicized as Shaddayin, was a Moabite god in the 800s BC, as evidenced by the Deir Alla Inscription (or KAI 312), which was found during an excavation at Deir 'Alla, Jordan, and described Balaam as the prophet of the Elohin and Shaddayin, believed to be Moabite translations of 'Elohim' and 'Shaddai.' In the Book of Ruth, Šdy is placed in opposition to the Lord God of Israel, which implies the name was left in the Judahite version of Ruth after the Hasmonean redaction, as it was viewed as a reference to the Moabite god, who 'dealt very bitterly' with Naomi when she was in Moab.

The Greek and Hebrew translations often differ in regards to the name or title Shaddai, suggesting that the Aramaic and Canaanite (Judahite or Samaritan) source texts they worked from differed in regards to this word. The term was omitted throughout Cosmic Genesis, suggesting that when the word was first encountered the Greeks did not know how to interpret it. It is equally possible that it was the Aramaic translator who had omitted it, however, it was almost certainly in the Canaanite version the translator worked from, as it is used consistently in the rest of the Torah, and is mentioned again when Moses god's name Ān is introduced in the Septuagint's Exodus. The cause of the confusion over the term Shaddai, is likely due to the difference between the meaning of the word in Canaanite versus Aramaic.

In Akkadian cuneiform, which was adopted as the written script by many cultures, the term was <sup>deity</sup>Šēdu (✳⊏⊑⫲), however, it referred to a 'protective spirit' or 'lesser god.' In the later Aramaic language, the word became šydå (𐡍𐡉𐡀𐡔), meaning 'demon' in the classical sense, as a type of muse or nymph. Whereas in Canaanite, šd (𐤀𐤔) took on a different meaning, generally interpreted as 'powerful' by the Early Classical Era, which is likely where the Greeks ultimately derived the term 'omnipotent' (παντοκράτοροσ), which was used later in the Septuagint where the Masoretic text generally uses the term Shaddai.

This alternate interpretation of the šd (𐤀𐤔) in Canaanite is likely due to the Egyptian New Kingdom era rule over Canaan, when Shed (𓍷𓂝𓈖𓏭, transliteration: šd), was worshiped in the region. Shed, who was often referred to as 'the savior,' was virtually identical to the earlier Canaanite god Resheph who was largely suppressed after the fall of the Hyksos dynasty. In the Masoretic Book of Job, Eliphaz referred to humanity as the 'sons of Resheph' (בני-רשף) instead of the 'sons of Adam,' and then refers god as šdy (שדי). This usage is consistent throughout Masoretic Job, indicating that at some point the name Resheph was updated to Shaddai, likely during the New Kingdom era, when Resheph worship was suppressed due to his associated with the earlier Hyksos dynasty. During the early New Kingdoms era, holy texts about Resheph would have been updated to Shed (𓈙𓂞𓏏𓀭), which would have been transliterated into Canaanite using the Akkadian Cuneiform script in the late New Kingdom era as [deity]Šēdu (𒀭𒂄), before being translated into Canaanite using the Phoenician script in the early iron age as šdy (𐤔𐤃𐤉), resulting in the confusing 'god of demons' (שׁידא) in Aramaic. In this particular verse, 'capable' (ικανοσ) appears to be a translation of a word similar to šdy (שדי), but not actually šdy, or 'omnipotent' (παντοκράτοροσ) would have been used, as in other books of the Septuagint, and therefore the Moabite version of the name, Shaddayin, is used in this translation.

The Septuagint and Masoretic text have different names for Naomi's husband. He is called Abimelech (αβιμελεχ) in the Codex Vaticanus, but Elimelech (אֱלִימֶלֶךְ) in the Masoretic text. It is not clear why the Hasmoneans would have changed the name of this minor character, however, it may have been to disassociate King David from the first King of Israel, King Abimelech, who led an insurrection against Egypt and declared himself king in 1267 BC. Other than the name and the fact that both were Ephriamites, the two Abimelechs seem to have nothing in common. King Abimelech was the son of Gideon in the Book of Judges, who was so unpopular the Israelites overthrew him and restored the judges after 3 years, in 1264 BC, following which he was killed.

# FORWARD TO RUTH

The book of Ruth appears to be part of a Samaritan story designed to splice the Moabites into the royal genealogy. The Book of Deuteronomy, which was likely written in Samaria, uses Moabite names of locations instead of Judahite names, indicating that a Moabite priesthood was active in Samaria before the kingdom fell to the Assyrians.

The Book of Judges refers to King Abimelech as the bastard son of Gideon by a prostitute, which speaks volumes about his memory, however, he was an Ephraimite, as was the Abimelech in the Book of Ruth, indicating that he could not have been viewed that badly a century after his death, when Ruth's father in law would have been born. Ruth, the step-daughter of Abimelech in the Book of Ruth, ultimately became an ancestor of King David, meaning it is possible that some Israelites were connecting the two Abimelechs in the Second Temple era, claiming that David was a descendant of King Abimelech.

The setting of the Ruth is the lands of Judah and Moab in the early 1000s BC, when the Book of Judges claimed there was no king. The last judge under the Pelesets in the books of Judges was Samson's father Manoah, who ruled until 1090 BC when the Peleset Kingdom apparently collapsed. This was just over a decade before the collapse of the Egyptian New Kingdom in 1077 BC, which began the Third Intermediate Period, when Egyptian records became sparse. This collapse of civilization in Canaan and Egypt was mirrored by collapses across the Mediterranean, sparking what the Greeks would later call the Dark Age. This Dark Age is not in doubt, however, is poorly understood due to the sparse records from the era. The story would have taken place around the same era as the Benjaminite genocide in the Book of Judges, which is likely the reason the book of Ruth was placed directly behind the book of Judges in the Septuagint.

# Forward to Ruth

It is not clear when the Book of Ruth was written, however, it is not generally considered to date back to the era it is set in. Based on the connection between the Book of Ruth and King David, it seems likely that the book was written no earlier than the era of King David, however, the book is generally dated to the time of Ezra the Scribe circa 350 BC. It is generally interpreted as an attempt to bridge the older books of Joshua and Judges with the newer books of the Kingdoms (Masoretic Samuel and Kings), which are generally accepted as having been compiled during the time of Ezra the scribe.

# Ruth: Chapter 1

In the time when the judges ruled, there was a famine in the land, and a man went from the House of Lehem[1] in Judah[2] to stay in the land of Moab[3] with his wife and his two sons. The man's name was Abimelech,[4] and his wife's name Naomi, and the names of his two sons Mahlon and Chilion, Ephrathites[5] from the House of Lahem in Judah who also traveled to the land of Moab and remained there. Abimelech the husband of Naomi died, and she was left with her two sons. They took for themselves as wives, Moabite women. The name of the one was Orpah, and the name of the second Ruth. They lived there for about ten years. Both Mahlon and Chilion also died, and the woman was left without her husband and her two sons.

She rose up with her two daughters-in-law, and they left out of the land of Moab, for she heard in the country of Moab that the Lord[6] had visited his people to give them bread. She left the place where she was, and her two daughters-in-law with her, and they traveled by road to return to the land of Judah. Naomi said to her daughters-in-law, "Return now, return each to the house of her mother. The Lord deal mercifully with you, as you have dealt with the dead, and with me. The Lord grant you that you may find rest, each of you in the house of her husband," and she kissed them.

They lifted their voice and wept. They said to her, "We will return with you to your people."

Naomi said, "Return now, my daughters. Why do you go with me? Have I more sons in my womb to be your husbands? Turn now, my daughters, for I am too old to be married. As I said, 'Suppose I were married and should carry sons, would you wait for them until they should be grown? Or would you refrain from being married for their sake?' No, my daughters, I am sad for you, that the hand of the Lord has gone out against me."

They lifted their voice and wept again, and Orpah kissed her mother-in-law and returned to her people, but Ruth continued to follow her. Naomi said to Ruth, "Look, your sister-in-law has returned to her people and to her gods, now turn also and follow after your sister-in-law."

Ruth replied, "Don't ask me to leave you, or to turn from following you. Wherever you go, I will go, and wherever you lodge, I will lodge. Your people will be my people, and your god will be my god. Wherever you die, I will die, and there I will be buried. The Lord do so for me, and more also, if I leave you. Only death will divide me and you."

Naomi, seeing that she was determined to go with her, stopped speaking to her about it. They both traveled until they came to the Temple of Lahem, and it came to pass, when they arrived at the Temple of Lahem, that all the city rang with them, and they asked, "Is this Naomi?"

She said to them, "No, do not call me Naomi. Call me Bitter, as Shaddayin[7] has dealt very bitterly with me. I went out full, and the Lord has brought me back empty. Why do you call me Naomi, when the Lord has humbled me and Shaddayin has afflicted me?"

So Naomi and Ruth the Moabitess, her daughter-in-law, returned from the country of Moab, and they arrived at the Temple of Lahem at the beginning of barley harvest.

# Ruth: Chapter 1 Notes

**1** Codex Vaticanus: Baethleem (ΒΑΙΘΛΕΕΜ)

• Codex Alexandrinus: Bêthleem (ΒΗΘΛΕΕΜ)

• Septuagint ms. 376: Bithleem (Βιθλεεμ)

• Septuagint ms. 131: Bêthlaeem (Βηθλαεεμ)

• Aleppo Codex: byt lhm (בית לחם). Translation: house (or temple, abode) of Lehem (or bread)

• Leningrad Codex: beit Lechem (בֵּית לֶחֶם). Translation: house (or temple, abode) of Lehem (or bread)

• Vetus Latina: Bethlem

• Targum on Ruth: beit Lechem (בֵּית לֶחֶם). Translation: house (or temple, abode) of Lehem (or bread)

**2** Codex Vaticanus: Iouda (ΙΟΥΔΑ). Translation: Judah

• Septuagint ms. 119: Ioudaeas (ιουΔΑφΑc). Translation: Judea

• Aleppo Codex: Yhwdh (יהודה). Translation: Judah

• Leningrad Codex: Yehudah (יְהוּדָה). Translation: Judah

• Targum on Ruth: Yehudah (יְהוּדָה). Translation: Judah

Judah was an iron age kingdom in southern modern Israel and the Palestinian West Bank between approximately 930 and 586 BC, which indicates the story was likely written during this era. The time period mentioned when the judges ruled, dates the story to earlier. Based on the later reference to Naomi being the mother of Obed, the grandfather of King David, the story is set around 1100 BC.

**3** Codex Vaticanus: Môab (ᴍⲱⲟⲁʙ). Translation: Moab

• Aleppo Codex: Mwåb (מואב). Translation: Moab

• Leningrad Codex: Mo'av (מוֹאָב). Translation: Moab

• Targum on Ruth: Mo'av (מוֹאָב). Translation: Moab

Moab was a kingdom in modern Jordan, on the east shore of the Dead Sea from sometime before King Ramesses II of Egypt, who recorded them as a country he conquered during his third Syrian campaign in 1291 BC.


**4** Codex Vaticanus: Abimelech (ⲁʙⲉⲓⲙⲉⲗⲉⲭ)

• Codex Alexandrinus: Alimelec (ⲁⲗⲓⲙⲉⲗⲉⲕ)

• Codex Basiliano-Vaticanus: Elimelech (ⲉⲗⲓⲙⲉⲗⲉⲭ)

• Septuagint ms. 241: Alimelech (ⲁλιμɞλɞχ)

• Septuagint ms. 243: Ailimelech (ⲁιλιμɞλɞχ)

• Aleppo Codex: Ålymlk (אלימלך)

• Leningrad Codex: Elimelech (אֱלִימֶלֶךְ)

• Targum on Ruth: Elimelech (אֱלִימֶלֶךְ)

This name does not survive in this verse among the Dead Sea Scrolls, however, has survived in later verses.

• Dead Sea Scroll 4QRuthᵃ: ålymlk (אלימלך)

There is no obvious reason the Hasmoneans would have changed the name of Abimelech to Elimelech, unless it was to disassociate King David's house from circa 1000 BC, from the earlier house of King Abimelech, the first King of Israel, circa 1267 to 1264 BC. These two Abimelechs cannot be the same person, as their stories have nothing in common, and they lived a century apart, nevertheless, the names are different in the Septuagint's version of Ruth, translated circa 225 BC and the oldest pre-Masoretic version of Ruth, the Dead Sea Scroll 4QRuthᵃ, dates to the Hasmonean Dynasty (140-37 BC). It is possible that the Hasmoneans did not change the name and there were two versions of the texts in circulation before the Greeks translated the text, or, that the Greeks mistranslated the name.

**5** LXX 236: Ephraam (Ἐφρααμ)

- LXX: Ephrathaeoe (Ἐφραθαιοι)

- LXX: Ephranthaeoe (Ἐφρανθαιοι)

- Aleppo Codex: Åfrtym (אפרתים)

- Leningrad Codex: Efratim (אֶפְרָתִים)

- Targum on Ruth: Efratin rabbanin (אֶפְרָתִין רַבָּנִין). Translation: Ephramite nobles

- Dead Sea Scroll 4QRuthᵃ: Åfrtym (אגרתים)

- Vetus Latina: euphratei

Ephratha (Εφραθα) / Efratah (אֶפְרָתָה) was listed as the former name of Bethlehem in the Torah. The name appears to be the Egyptian name, erperte (𓉐𓏤𓂋𓏏𓏏), which translates as 'temple of bread, a direct translation of the Canaanite name byt lhm (𐤁𐤉𐤕 𐤋𐤇𐤌). The same region is later known as the land of Ephriam (אֶפְרַיִם) during the early iron age, and part of the Kingdom of Samaria until it was conquered by Assyrian war in 723 BC. While LXX 236 reads Ephriam, the rest of the sources support the reading or Ephrathiam, indicating that these were the remnants of the Egyptized Bethlehemites that would have still been present in the region in the era the book is set in. This suggests the book of Ruth dates back to the early iron age.

**6** Greek: c̄s (ⲕ̄ⲥ̄). Translation: lord

- Dead Sea Scroll 4QRuthª: Yhwh (יהוי).

- Aleppo Codex: Yhwh (יהוה)

- Leningrad Codex: Yehvah (יְהוָה)

- Targum on Ruth: Yeyah (?‎?). Translation: Yahw

The Septuagint's version of the Ruth was translated before 200 BC, as it was carried south by the Beta Israel community, who left Egypt for Kush (modern Sudan) during the Jewish Rebellion against the Ptolemys in 200 BC. This means it predates the Hasmonean redaction and contains the term Lord (Κύριος) instead of Iaw (Ιαω).

There are no surviving early fragments of the Septuagint's Ruth that include the name, suggesting the word in the Aramaic version of Exodus was Ădōnāy, which meant 'lord' and was also the name of a god in the Canaanite religion, especially in the region around Baalbek, in modern Lebanon. Like the Samaritan Yahw, Adonay was the son of Asherah, suggesting that the Aramaic term in the text the Greek translation was made from used the name Adonay.

The Aramaic sections of Masoretic Daniel that were not translated into Hebrew maintain the term adonai ha'elohim (אֲדֹנָי הָאֱלֹהִים), meaning the 'Lord the gods' where the Septuagint has 'Lord the god' (Κύριον τὸν θεὸν), however, the Hebrew sections have Yehvah elohim (יְהוָה אֱלֹהִים) where the Septuagint has 'Lord the god,' suggesting the Greek more accurately reflects the Aramaic source texts than the Hebrew translation. According to Sanhedrin (103b) tractate in the Talmud, King Manasseh was blamed for removing the name, however, as his grandson Josiah 'restored' the Torah circa 625 BC, one would expect that he would have restored the name as well, if it had have been in Exodus to begin with. Furthermore, the early Torah appears to have already been translated into Aramaic during the era of Manasseh's father king Hezekiah, suggesting that he removed the name during his religious reforms.

# RUTH: CHAPTER 1 NOTES

As the original translation of Ruth does not appear to have included the name, the term 'Lord' is used in this translation. Lord (Ba'al and Adon) were commonly used in ancient Canaan as titles of the various Canaanite gods, and early Israelites appear to have used the terms the same way themselves. In this context, the Lord in question is Lord Lehem, the Canaanite god of fertility, grains, and rebirth. The limited amount of information that survives about him, suggests he was similar to Osiris and Dionysus, meaning he would have been a precursor to Lord Sabaoth.

**7** Greek: icanos (ικanoc). Translations: capable (or able, competent, skillful, fit, potent, efficient, apt, shifty)

• LXX 29: ischyros (ισχυβοc). Translations: strong (or powerful, mighty)

• Aleppo Codex: šdy (שדי). Translation: demons (or phantoms, demonic, ghoulish, devilish)

• Leningrad Codex: Shaddai (שַׁדַּי). Translation: (or demons, phantoms, demonic, ghoulish, devilish)

• Targum on Ruth: Shaddai (שַׁדַּי). Translation: (or powerful)

• Vetus Latina: deus. Translation: god

In the Septuagint, the term El Shaddai was directly transliterated as theos Saddai (θεος Σαδδαι) once in Ezekiel, and therefore the term must have been in the Aramaic texts the Greeks used to translate Ezekiel, however, in the other books of the Septuagint, the term 'almighty' (παντοκρατορος) appears where the Masoretic texts have Shaddai. Šdyn (𐤔𐤃𐤉𐤍), generally anglicized as Shaddayin, was a Moabite god in the 800s BC, as evidenced by the Deir Alla Inscription (or KAI 312), which was found during an excavation at Deir 'Alla, Jordan, and described Balaam as the prophet of the Elohin and Shaddayin, believed to be Moabite translations of 'Elohim' and 'Shaddai.'

In the Book of Ruth, Shaddai is placed in opposition to the Lord God of Israel, which implies the name was left in the Judahite version of Ruth after the Hasmonean redaction as it was viewed as a reference to the Moabite god, who 'dealt very bitterly' with Naomi when she was in Moab. The Greek and Hebrew translations often differ in regards to the name or title Shaddai, suggesting that the Aramaic and Canaanite (Judahite or Samaritan) source texts they worked from differed in regards to this word. The term was omitted throughout Cosmic Genesis, suggesting that when the word was first encountered the Greeks did not know how to interpret it. It is equally possible that it was the Aramaic translator who had omitted it, however, it was almost certainly in the Canaanite version the translator worked from, as it is used consistently in the rest of Genesis, and is mentioned again when Moses god's name Ān is introduced in the Septuagint's Exodus. The cause of the confusion over the term Shaddai, is likely due to the difference between the meaning of the word in Canaanite versus Aramaic.

In Akkadian cuneiform, which was adopted as the written script by many cultures, the term was <sup>deity</sup>Šēdu (✳ 𒁲), however, it referred to a 'protective spirit' or 'lesser god.' In the later Aramaic language, the word became šydå (𐡔𐡉𐡃𐡀), meaning 'demon' in the classical sense, as a type of muse or nymph. Whereas in Canaanite, šd (𐤔𐤃) took on a different meaning, generally interpreted as 'powerful' by the Early Classical Era, which is likely where the Greeks ultimately derived the term 'omnipotent' (παντοκράτορος), which was used later in the Septuagint where the Masoretic text generally uses the term Shaddai.

This alternate interpretation of the šd (𐤔𐤃) in Canaanite is likely due to the Egyptian New Kingdom era rule over Canaan, when Shed (𓆑𓂝𓂧𓀭, transliteration: šd), was worshiped in the region. Shed, who was often referred to as 'the savior,' was virtually identical to the earlier Canaanite god Resheph who was largely suppressed after the fall of the Hyksos dynasty. In the Masoretic Book of Job, Eliphaz referred to humanity as the 'sons of Resheph' (בני-רשף) instead of the 'sons of Adam,' and then refers god as šdy (שדי).

This usage is consistent throughout Masoretic Job, indicating that at some point the name Resheph was updated to Shaddai, likely during the New Kingdom era, when Resheph worship was suppressed due to his associated with the earlier Hyksos dynasty. During the early New Kingdoms era, holy texts about Resheph would have been updated to Shed (𓇋𓃀𓏏), which would have been transliterated into Canaanite using the Akkadian Cuneiform script in the late New Kingdom era as <sup>deity</sup>Šēdu (𒀭𒁲), before being translated into Canaanite using the Phoenician script in the early iron age as šdy (𐤔𐤃𐤉), resulting in the confusing 'god of demons' (ܫܐܕܐ) in Aramaic. In this particular verse, 'capable' (ικανος) appears to be a translation of a word similar to šdy (שׁדי), but not actually šdy, or 'omnipotent' (παντοκράτορος) would have been used, as in other books of the Septuagint, and therefore the Moabite version of the name, Shaddayin, is used in this translation.

# Ruth: Chapter 2

Naomi had a friend, an acquaintance of her husband, and the man was a mighty man of the families of Abimelech. His name was Boaz. Ruth the Moabitess said to Naomi, "Let me go now to the field, and I will glean from the ears behind whichever man will let me."

She replied to her, "Go, daughter."

She went and gleaned in the field behind the reapers and she happened by chance to come on a portion of the land of Boaz of the families of Abimelech, and Boaz came from the Temple of Lahem and said to the reapers, "The Lord be with you."

They said to him, "The Lord bless you."

Boaz asked his servant who was in charge of the reapers, "Whose is this girl?"

His servant who was in charge of the reapers answered and said, "It is the Moabite girl who returned with Naomi out of the land of Moab. She asked, 'I beg you, let me glean and gather among the sheaves after the reapers,' and she came and worked from morning until evening, and did not rest even a little in the field."

Boaz said to Ruth, "Have you not heard, my daughter? Don't go to glean in another field and don't leave here. Stay close with my girls, and watch the field where my men reap, and go after them. Look, I have ordered the young men not to touch you, and when you thirst, then you may go to the vessels, and drink of that which the young men will have drawn."

She fell on her face, and did reverence to the ground, and said to him, "How is it that I have found grace in your eyes, that you should take notice of me, when I am a foreigner?"

Boaz answered her, "It has been told to me how you have dealt with your mother-in-law after the death of your husband, and how you left your father and your mother, and the land of your birth, and came to a people who you did not know before. The Lord repay your work, may a full reward be given you of the Lord God of Israel, to whom you have come to trust under his wings."

She said, "Let me find grace in your sight, my lord, because you have comforted me, and because you have spoken kindly to your handmaid, and look, I will be one of your servants."

Boaz said to her, "Now it is time to eat. Come here, and you will eat of the bread, and you will dip your food in the vinegar."

Ruth sat by the side of the reapers, and Boaz handed her a meal and she ate until she was satisfied and left. She rose up to glean and Boaz ordered his young men, "Let her even among the sheaves, and do not reproach her. You, carry it for her and drop for her some of that which is piled up. Let her eat and glean, and don't rebuke her."

So she gleaned in the field until evening and beat out all that she had gleaned, and it was about a bushel of barley. She picked it up and went into the city. Her mother-in-law saw what she had gleaned, and Ruth brought out and gave her the food which she had left after she had been satisfied. Her mother-in-law said to her, "Where have you gleaned today, and where have you worked? Blessed be he that took notice of you."

Ruth told her mother-in-law where she had worked, and said, "The name of the man with who I worked today is Boaz."

Naomi said to her daughter-in-law, "Blessed is he by the Lord because he has not failed in his mercy with the living and with

the dead. The man is a close relative to us, he is one of our relations."

Ruth said to her mother-in-law, "Yes, he also told me, 'Keep
close to my girls, until the men will have finished all my
reaping.'"

Naomi said to Ruth her daughter-in-law, 'It is well, daughter,
that you went out with his girls, so they will not meet you in
another field."

Ruth joined herself to the girls of Boaz to glean until they had
finished the barley harvest and the wheat harvest.

# Ruth: Chapter 3

She lodged with her mother-in-law, and Naomi her mother-in-law said to her, "My daughter, should I not seek rest for you, that it may be well with you? Now is not Boaz our relative, with whose girls you were? Look, he winnows barley this night on the floor. Wash and anoint yourself, and get dressed and go up to the threshing floor. Do not show yourself to the man until he has done eating and drinking. It will come to pass when he lies down, that you will watch the place where he lies down, and will come and lift up the covering of his feet, and will lie down. He will tell you what to do."

Ruth said to her, "I will do all that you say, She went down to the threshing floor, and did according to all that her mother-in-law told her. Boaz ate and drank, and his heart was glad, and he came to lie down by the side of the heap of grain, and she sneaked to him and lifted the covering off his feet. It was past midnight and the man was amazed, and troubled, and saw a woman laying at his feet."

He asked, "Who are you?"

She answered, "I am your handmaid Ruth, spread your skirt over your handmaid, for you are a near relative."

Boaz said, "Blessed are you by the Lord God,[1] my daughter, for you have made your latter kindness greater than the former, in that you don't chase after young men, whether they are poor or rich. Now don't be afraid, my daughter, whatever you will say I will do to you, for all the tribe of my people know that you are a virtuous woman. Now I am truly related to you, nevertheless, there is a relative nearer than I. Lodge here for the night, and it will be in the morning, if he will do the duty of a relative to you, well let him do it, but if he will not do the duty of a relative to you, I will do the relative's duty to you, as the Lord lives. Lie down until the morning."

She lay at his feet until the morning, and she rose up before the sun rose, and Boaz said, "Let it not be known that a woman came into the floor."

He said to her, "Bring the apron that is on you," and she held it, and he measured six measures of barley and put them on her, and she went into the city. Ruth went to her mother-in-law, and she said to her, "My daughter!" and Ruth told her all that the man had done to her.

She said to her, "He gave me these six measures of barley, as he said to me, 'Don't go empty to your mother-in-law.'"

She replied, "Sit still, my daughter, until you will know how the matter will fall out. The man will not rest today until the matter is accomplished.

# Ruth: Chapter 3 Notes

**1** Codex Vaticanus: cô thô (ܟ‎ܘܘ‎). Translation: Lord God

• Codex Alexandrinus: cyriô (ⲔⲨⲣⲒⲱ). Translation: Lord

• LXX 106: Cyriô tô theô (Ⲕⲩⲣϥⲱ ⲧⲱ ⲑⲉⲱ). Translation: Lord the god

• LXX 29: Theô (Ⲑⲉⲱ). Translations: God

• Aleppo Codex: Yhwh (יהוה)

• Leningrad Codex: Yhvah (יְהֹוָה)

• Targum on Ruth: Yeyah (יי). Translation: Yahw

The Septuagint's version of the Ruth was translated circa 225 BC, before the Hasmonean redaction, and contains the term Lord God (Κυριω Θεω) instead of the name Yhvah / Yahw. The Aramaic sections of Masoretic Daniel that were not translated into Hebrew maintain the term adonai ha'elohim (אֲדֹנָי הָאֱלֹהִים), meaning the 'Lord the gods' where the Septuagint has 'Lord the god' (Κύριον τὸν θεὸν), however, the Hebrew sections have Yehvah elohim (יְהוָה אֱלֹהִים) where the Septuagint has 'Lord the god,' suggesting the Greek more accurately reflects the Aramaic source texts than the Hebrew translation. According to the Sanhedrin (103b) tractate in the Talmud, King Manasseh was blamed for removing the name, however, as his grandson Josiah 'restored' the Torah circa 625 BC, one would expect that he would have restored the name as well, if it had have been in Exodus to begin with. Furthermore, the early Torah appears to have already been translated into Aramaic during the era of Manasseh's father king Hezekiah, suggesting that he removed the name during his religious reforms.

As the original text of Ruth was almost certainly written in Phoenician (Judahite), the original term was probably Ådn Ålm (𐤟𐤋𐤀 𐤉𐤀𐤟). Ådn Ålm was a Canaanite epithet for El, found in the Ugaritic Texts from the 1300s BC. In the polytheistic Canaanite religion, the term translates as 'Father of the gods' as El was the father of the 70 Elohim (gods) and creator of the world in the Canaanite religion. The term 'father of the gods' subsequently became Lord God in the Aramaic trans-lation made in the Babylonian or Persian era, before being replaced by Yehvah in the Hasmonean dynasty. According to several ancient Hebrew scriptures, El had a major temple in Shiloh, the capital of ancient Samaria, which Jacob built in the Book of Genesis. El is also mentioned in later books of the Septuagint and appears to have been one of the main gods worshiped by the ancient Israelites, as well as other Canaanites. As Κυριω Θεω translates directly as Lord God, that term is used in this translation.

# Ruth: Chapter 4

Boaz went up to the gate and sat there, and watched until the relative passed by, of whom Boaz had spoken. Boaz said to him, "Turn aside, and sit here," and he turned aside and sat down. Boaz called ten men of the elders of the city, and said, "Sit here," and they sat down.

Boaz said to the relative, "The matter regards the portion of the field which was our brother Abimelech's which was given to Naomi when she returned out of the land of Moab. I said, 'I will inform you. Buy it before those who sit, and before the elders of my people. If you will redeem it, redeem it, but if you will not redeem it, tell me, and I will know, for there is no one beside you to do the duty of a relative, and I am next after you."

He replied, "I am here, and I will redeem it."

Boaz said, "In the day of your buying the field of the hand of Naomi and of Ruth the Moabitess the wife of the deceased, you must also buy her, to raise up the name of the dead on his inheritance."

The relative said, "Will I not be able to redeem it for myself, in case I damage my own inheritance? You redeem my right for yourself, as I will not be able to redeem it."

This was the ordinance in Israel for redemption in former times, and for a bargain, to confirm every word, a man removed his shoe and gave it to his neighbor that redeemed his right. This was a testimony in Israel. The relative said to Boaz, "Buy my right for yourself, and he took off his shoe and gave it to him."

Boaz said to the elders and to all the people, "You are this day witnesses, that I have bought all that was Abimelech's, and all that belonged to Chilion and Mahlon, of the hand of Naomi. Moreover,

I have bought for myself as wife Ruth the Moabitess, the wife of Mahlon, to raise up the name of the dead on his inheritance, so the name of the dead will not be destroyed from among his brothers, and from the tribe of his people. You are on this day witnesses."

All the people who were in the gate said, "We are witnesses," and the elders said, "The Lord make your wife who goes into your house, as Rachel and as Leah, who both together built the house of Israel, and worked mightily in Ephrath, and there will be a name for you in the Temple of Lahem. Let your house be as the house of Pharez, who Tamar carried for Judah, of the seed which the Lord will give you of this handmaid. Boaz took Ruth, and she became his wife, and he went into her, and the Lord gave her conception, and she carried a son.

The woman said to Naomi, "Blessed is the Lord, who has not allowed a redeemer to fail you this day, even to make your name famous in Israel. He will be for you a restorer of your mind, and one to cherish your old age. For your daughter-in-law which has loved you, who is better to you than seven sons, has born him."

Naomi took the child and laid it on her chest, and became a nurse to it. The neighbors gave it a name, saying, "A son has been born to Naomi," and they called his name Obed. This is the father of Jesse the father of David.

These are the generations of Pharez:

Pharez fathered Hezron,

Hezron fathered Ram,

Ram fathered Amminadab,

Amminadab fathered Nahshon,

Nahshon fathered Salmon,

Salmon fathered Boaz,

Boaz fathered Obed.

Obed fathered Jesse,

and Jesse fathered David.

# Forward To Kingdoms

The four books of the Kingdoms are generally believed to have been written during the time of Ezra the scribe, compiled from the now-lost books of the Chronicles of the Kingdoms of Samaria and Judah. The authors of the Kingdoms repeatedly refer to the Chronicles as sources for more detailed information, suggesting the books of the Kingdoms were an abridged version and certainly written from a specific theological perspective missing from the Chronicles. However, the books have transliterated Neo-Babylonian loanwords indicating that either they were compiled in cuneiform, or the older Chronicles had been translated into Cuneiform before the books of the Kingdoms quoted them. If they were written in Neo-Babylonian, they likely date to the Neo-Assyrian through early-Persian era, and were probably compiled in Babylonia. By the mid-Persian era, Imperial Aramaic had replaced cuneiform throughout the western half of the empire, and there would have been no reason to compile books in cuneiform.

The four books of the kingdoms and two Masoretic books of Samuel and Kings are remarkably inconsistent when it comes to the primary god of the text. Samuel and Kings themselves used the terms Yehwah 'forces' (יְהֹוָה צְבָאֹות), Yhvah 'god forces' (יהוה אֱלֹהֵי צְבָאֹות), and Yehwah (יְהֹוָה) fairly consistently, however, the four books of the kingdoms use 'lord god' Sabaôth (Κυρίῳ Θεῷ Σαβαωθ), Adônae 'Lord' Elôae Sabaôth (Αδωναι Κύριε Ελωαι Σαβαωθ), 'lord omnipotent' (κυριοσ παντοκρατωρ), 'lord the forces' (κυριου των δυναμεων), and 'Lord' Sabaôth (Κυρίῳ Σαβαωθ), with these terms rarely mirroring their Hebrew counterparts.

In 1ˢᵗ Kingdoms, the Greek text reads Lord God Sabaôth (Κυρίῳ Θεῷ Σαβαωθ) where the Masoretic text uses Yhwah tzeva'ovt (יְהֹוָה צְבָאֹות), meaning 'Yahweh of forces.' The term Adônae Lord Elôae Sabaôth (Αδωναι Κύριε Ελωαι Σαβαωθ) is also used in

1st Kingdoms, which is mirrored by Yehwah tzeva'ovt (יְהֹוָ֣ה צְבָא֗וֹת) in the Masoretic text, indicating that the Aramaic text the Greeks used as source material was not exactly the same as the later Hebrew translation.

Adônae (αδωναι) was the Greek transliteration of the Canaanite word ådny (𐤀𐤃𐤍𐤉), meaning 'my lord,' indicating that the Cuneiform translator had interpreted the word as a proper name and transliterated it directly into cuneiform as aduni (𒀀𒁺𒉌), which was later transliterated into Aramaic as ådny (𐡀𐡃𐡍𐡉). The term is used extensively in the Aramaic sections of Masoretic Daniel, where the Greeks translated 'Lord' (κύριε), mirrored by Yehwah (יְהֹוָ֣ה) in the Hebrew sections of Daniel, which the Greeks also translated as 'Lord,' indicating that the Hebrew translators viewed ådny (𐡀𐡃𐡍𐡉) as an Aramaic substitute for the name Yehwah ( יְהֹוָ֣ה). The other word the Greeks transliterated in this phrase was the Aramaic word ålh (𐡀𐡋𐡄), meaning 'god,' which the translator rendered as elôae (ελωαι), meaning the Aramaic text would have read 'Ådny Lord God Sabaôth.'

While the name Sabaoth (Σαβαωθ) is clearly related to the Hebrew word tzeva'ovt (צְבָא֗וֹת), it is not interpreted as meaning 'of forces' in 1st Kingdoms, however, is interpreted as 'the forces' (των δυναμεων) in 2nd, 3rd, and 4th Kingdoms, yet not exclusively, as 4th Kingdoms also includes the name Lord Sabaôth (Κυρίω Σαβαωθ). This suggests that the Aramaic text the Greeks translated included both the terms ṣbåt (𐡑𐡁𐡀𐡕), which the Greek translators interpreted as 'the forces' (των δυναμεων), and another similar word which was interpreted as the proper name of Lord Sabaôth (Σαβαωθ).

Considering that the Hasmonean Dynasty 'restored' the name Yhwh when they translated the texts into Classical Hebrew, the term Adônae Lord Elôae Sabaôth (Αδωναι Κύριε Ελωαι Σαβαωθ)

344

is similar to the term Yhvah ĕlōhê tzeva'ovt (יהוָה אֱלֹהֵי צְבָאֹות) used in the second half of Samuel, and first half of Kings, however, that is mirrored by 'Lord omnipotent' (Κυριοσ παντοκρατωρ) in the Septuagint's 2$^{nd}$ and 3$^{rd}$ Kingdoms. In the older books of the Septuagint, 'omnipotent' (παντοκρατωρ) is the translation of Shaddai (שַׁדַּ֣י).

The Greek and Hebrew translations often differ in regards to the name or title Shaddai, suggesting that the Aramaic and Canaanite (Judahite, Samaritan, Moabite, and Edomite) source texts they worked from differed in regards to this word. The term was omitted throughout Cosmic Genesis, suggesting that when the word was first encountered the Greeks did not know how to interpret it. It is equally possible that it was the Aramaic translator who had omitted it, however, it was almost certainly in the Canaanite text the translator worked from, as it is used consistently in Bereshít (the Masoretic version of Cosmic Genesis), and is mentioned again in the Masoretic version of Exodus when Moses god's name Ān is introduced in the Septuagint's Exodus. The cause of the confusion over the term Shaddai, is likely due to the difference between the meaning of the word in Canaanite versus Aramaic.

In Akkadian cuneiform, which was adopted as the written script by many cultures, including the Babylonian and Assyrian cultures, the term was $^{ilu}$šēdu (✳⊏彐), however, it referred to a 'protective spirit' or 'lesser god.' In the later Aramaic language, the word became šydå ( NϤ^Ʋ), meaning 'demon' in the classical sense, as a type of muse or nymph. Whereas in Canaanite, šd (ᴀʷ) took on a different meaning, generally interpreted as 'powerful' by the Early Classical Era, which is likely where the Greeks ultimately derived the term 'omnipotent' (παντοκράτορος), which

was used later in the Septuagint where the Masoretic text generally uses the term shadday.

This alternate interpretation of šd (⊿ᵂ) in Canaanite is likely
due to the Egyptian New Kingdom era rule over Canaan, when
Shed (☌⊑◻, transliteration: šd), was worshiped in the region.
Shed, who was often referred to as 'the savior,' was virtually
identical to the earlier Canaanite god Resheph who was largely
suppressed after the fall of the Hyksos dynasty.

In the Masoretic Book of Job, Eliphaz referred to humanity as
the 'sons of Resheph' (בני-רשף) instead of the 'sons of Adam,' and
then refers to his god as šdy (שדי). This usage is consistent
throughout Masoretic Job, indicating that at some point the name
Resheph was updated to Shaddai, likely during the New
Kingdom era, when Resheph worship was suppressed due to his
association with the earlier Hyksos dynasty. During the early
New Kingdom era, holy texts about Resheph would have been
updated to Shed (☌⊑◻), which would have been transliterated
into Canaanite using the Akkadian Cuneiform script in the late
New Kingdom era as $^{ilu}$šēdu (✳⊏⧩), before being translated into
Canaanite using the Phoenician script in the early iron age as šdy
(ᴢ⊿ᵂ), resulting in the confusing 'god of demons' (Ͷᐟᐱᐺ) in
Aramaic.

It would have been impossible to translate šdy (ᴢ⊿ᵂ) back into
cuneiform without using the term $^{ilu}$šēdu (⊢⊦⊨⊩⊣), which by the
Neo-Assyrian era referred to a type of protective griffin, and
therefore, the translator appears to have substituted the word
Sebittu (⊣⫟⊳⧩⧫). In the Old Akkadian language, the Sebittu
(⫞⧓⊳⧨) had been the seven gods (planets) that ruled the sky,
however, this usage had disappeared by the late bronze age,
leaving only the vague concept of cosmic authority by the Neo-

Babylonian era. The related Neo-Assyrian name Sebitti (𒄊𒑖𒀭) was viewed as the god of war, which is ultimately the origin of the name of the Phrygian god of war Sabazdiôs (𐤔𐤀𐤁𐤀𐤕𐤙𐤏𐤎), which was later reinterpreted as Sabazios (Σαβάζιος) in the Greco-Roman era, who was viewed as the Phrygian version of Sabaoth.

Sabazios and Sabaoth were both interpreted as local variants of Dionysus by the Greeks before the Maccabean Revolt, and one of the high priest/governors of the temple in Jerusalem was a Phrygian named Phillip. The worship of Dionysus (Sabazious, Sabaoth) at the temple in Jerusalem was one of the reasons for the Maccabean Revolt, which led to the independent Hasmonean Dynasty of Judea. This dynasty needed to replace the Judean god Sabaoth with another god, and 'restored' the name Yahweh to the ancient texts, even those that had been written in Aramaic and Babylonian, and which originally had nothing to do with Yahweh.

With the exception of 1st Kingdoms, there is a consistent pairing of 'Lord Omnipotent' in the Septuagint, with 'Yahweh god of forces' in the Masoretic text, and 'Lord the Forces' in the Septuagint with 'Yahweh of forces' in the Masoretic text, suggesting that while the names of the god were not the same in the Aramaic text as the later Hebrew translation, the placement of the names was consistent. The translation of Yhwh (יהוה) in Dead Sea Scroll 4QSamᵃ, where the Masoretic text reads Yhvah god of forces (יהוה אֱלֹהֵי צְבָאוֹת), and the Septuagint reads 'Lord Omnipotent' proves that the alteration of the name took place in the Hebrew translation after the Greek translation was made, and the Hebrew translations still weren't stabilized by the Herodian dynasty. A similar later redaction of the Hebrew text is probably the reason for the Septuagint's 'Lord Sabaoth' being mirrored by

'Yahweh' once in 4<sup>th</sup> Kingdoms, as the Hasmonean redaction should have produced 'Yahweh of forces.'

While the Aramaic text the Greeks translated appears to have used a mixture of 'Lord Shaddai,' 'Lord Sabaoth,' and 'Lord of forces,' this translation standardizes all three terms to Lord Sabaoth, as all three are clearly references to the same god. Shaddai was probably the original term in the Chronicles of Samaria, however, after Samaria fell to Assyria, King Hezehkiah's anti-Mosaic reforms attempted to replace Shaddai with Yahweh, and therefore Shaddai was probably not included in the Chronicles of Judah, which accounts for 4<sup>th</sup> Kingdoms having no mention of Lord Omnipotent.

Shaddai was mentioned in most of the Masoretic books set earlier than the Neo-Assyrian era, including Bereshít, Exodus, Numbers, Ruth, Job, and Psalms, as well as in some of the prophets' writings of the era, such as Isaiah, Ezekiel, and Joel, and yet is not mentioned at all in Samuel and Kings, which describe the history of the era. Likewise, tzeva'ovt (צְבָאוֹת) was not used as a name or epithet of god in Bereshít, Exodus, Numbers, Deuteronomy, Ruth or Job, first appearing in Samuel and Kings, indicating it was introduced during the Neo-Assyrian era. Both the terms Shaddai and tzeva'ovt were used in Isaiah's writing, suggesting that the transition took place during the era of Hezekiah's reforms, roughly between 716 and 697 BC.

Lord Sabaoth was the Aramaic name of the Judean god under Greek rule, who the Greeks regarded as the Judean version of Dionysus, the Phrygians viewed as the Judean version of Sabazios, and the Romans viewed as the Judean version of Bacchus. Therefore, the term was viewed as the name of the Judean god when the Septuagint was translated at the Library of Alexandria, explaining why it was used as a proper name.

348

The origin of the books of the Kingdoms, along with the books of the Paralipomena, is a matter of great debate among scholars. The Bava Basra tractate of the Talmud, reports that the first 25 chapters of Samuel, and therefore the first 25 chapters of 1$^{st}$ Kingdoms, were written by the prophet Samuel, and the rest of Samuel, which would be chapter 26 through 31 of 1$^{st}$ Kingdoms and the entire book of 2$^{nd}$ Kingdoms was written by the prophets Gad and Nathan.

Samuel, Gad, and Nathan are all mentioned in 1$^{st}$ and 2$^{nd}$ Kingdoms, however, most biblical scholars have rejected the idea that they had anything to do with the authorship of these books, for hundreds of years. Almost all scholars, in every era, have agreed with the idea that the six books were based on the older, now lost, Chronicles of the Kings of Samaria and Chronicles of the Kings of Judah mentioned in the books of Kingdoms. The lost Chronicles of the Kings of Samaria would have been compiled in the kingdom of Samaria before it fell to Assyria, while the Chronicles of the Kings of Judah would have been compiled in the kingdom of Judah, before it fell to the Babylonians. The author of Kingdoms (Masoretic Samuel and Kings) makes repeated references to the chronicles, however, it is unlikely the chronicles would have been widely published, suggesting Kingdoms was intended for people that had access to the chronicles, likely the Israelite intelligentsia in Babylon.

The Masoretic books of the Samuel and Kings maintain some of the more archaic linguistic elements of the Tanakh, suggesting a Judahite or Samaritan translation was created long before it was translated into Hebrew. The early sections of 1$^{st}$ Kingdoms (Masoretic Samuel) dealing with Eli and Samuel read like a continuation of Judges, implying the original book of Judges continued until Saul seized power in 1037 BC.

If Eli and Samuel were originally part of Judges, it would explain the conflicting pro-republican and pro-monarchist views expressed by Samuel, who was against the appointing of a king, but then did anoint both Saul and David as kings of Israel. The logical explanation of the conflicting views of Samuel is that they originate in different texts, written from different perspectives. Samuel's pro-republican view is almost certainly the view that would have originally been part of Judges, as the Israelites only had one king in Judges, King Abimelech, who ruled briefly for 3 years between 1267 in 1264 BC. Abimelech was described as being both a heroic warrior of the Israelites, and the worst possible tyrant. Judges describes him as being the bastard son of Gideon, mothered by a prostitute, which is about as bad as a description as anyone had in the Israelite scriptures.

The anointment of Saul would undoubtedly have originated in the original book about King Saul, while the anointment of David would have undoubtedly originated in the original book about King David. These three sources would also explain the conflicting introductions between Saul and David in the Masoretic Book of Samuel, as these stories came from somewhere. In Masoretic Samuel, David became the armor-bearer of Saul in chapter 16, because Saul wanted an armor-bearer that was good at playing a harp, and Saul 'loved him greatly.' Then a few verses later he was the shepherd son of Jesse, who Samuel found and anointed, clearly a separate story from the previous one, which appears to come from the Davidic source. The story continues with David visiting his older brothers who were serving in Saul's army, where he met Saul for the first time again, and Saul tried to get David to wear his armor when he went to fight Goliath, but it was too heavy. Then after defeating Goliath, Saul again met David, for the first time. Saul also promised to give his daughter Ahinoam to David, but then married her to someone else, twice in the Masoretic version, however, this only happened once in the Septuagint's version. In one Masoretic version, Saul is depicted as being duplicitous, while in the other version, found in both the Masoretic text and Septuagint, Saul chose to give his other daughter Michal to David as she loved him, which paints Saul's action in a noble light.

These conflicting views of the events are written from different perspectives, Republican, Saulic, and Davidic perspectives, however, the root of these stories likely run deeper than that. Saul was a Samaritan, while David was a Judahite, two nations that were each described as having separate armies. The nations were described as sharing the same king, Saul and then David, followed by Solomon and Rehoboam before the kingdoms split in 931 BC, however, other than being united against common enemies the two nations were generally described as being divided. When David's son Solomon assumed the throne, there was a brief civil war in which the Samaritans supported his older brother Adonijah, while the Judahites and Jebusites supported Solomon, who ultimately took the throne. When his son Rehoboam took the throne, the Samaritans rebelled and he was left with only Judah and Edom. Saul was the first Samaritan king since Abimelech, while David was the first Judahite king, therefore, these conflicting stories of Saul and David were likely sourced from the Chronicles of the Kings of Samaria, and the Chronicles of the Kings of Judah, both lost long before the Greek era.

The setting of 1$^{st}$ Kingdoms was the era between 1077 BC when Eli became Judge, and 1010 BC when David became king. The first 40 years of this era were the reigns of the judges Eli and Samuel, who judged the Israelites between the time the Egyptian New Kingdom collapsed, and when Saul was declared king of the

Israelites in 1037 BC. The Egyptians had effectively lost control of southern Canaan circa 1150 BC when the House of She'an was destroyed, and according to the Book of Judges, the Pelesets ruled the land after that, until Saul's revolt in 1037 BC. Saul was depicted as a complex conflicted character in 1st Kingdoms, which can either be read as a description of a crazy person or conflicting views from two or more sources. Saul both banned mediums and wizards from his kingdoms, and then tracked one down to channel Samuel's ghost.

The setting of 2nd Kingdoms was the era of King David's rule of Samaria and Judah, between 1010 and 970 BC. Few records of this era have survived to the present, as it took place during the Egyptian Third Intermediate Period, and the Greek Dark Age. According to 2nd Kingdoms, an Egyptian king named Sousacim (Σουσακιμ) invaded the region. In Masoretic Samuel, the king's name was not mentioned, and while it does appear to have been in Dead Sea Scroll 4QSamª, it is in a damaged section of text. This king was called Shishak (שׁישׁק) later in 3rd Kingdoms (Masoretic Kings), which, based on the era when he lived and the records of him invading Judah, is generally accepted as Shoshenq I (𓇓𓈙𓈙𓐍) who campaigned in Canaan during the era of King Rehoboam. The damaged section of text in Dead Sea Scroll 4QSamª indicates that the longer version of the verse found in the Septuagint was once in Hebrew translations, however, the following verse which discusses the brass that David captured in war, and which Solomon later used in the temple, is missing from both the Masoretic text and appears to have not been included in Dead Sea Scroll 4QSamª.

The setting of 3rd Kingdoms was the era of King Solomon's rule of Samaria, Judah, Edom, and Aram, between 970 and 931 BC, and the era of his son King Rehoboam of 931 to 913 BC, who ruled over the collapsing kingdom. Few records of this era have survived to the present, as it took place during the Egyptian Third Intermediate Period, and the Greek Dark Age. According to 2<sup>nd</sup> and 3<sup>rd</sup> Kingdoms, an Egyptian king named Sousacim (Σουσακιμ) invaded the region. In Masoretic Kings, the king's name is Shishak (שׁישַׁק), which, based on the era when he lived and the record of him invading Judah, is generally accepted as Shoshenq I (𓍿𓈙𓈙𓆷) who campaigned in Canaan during the era of King Rehoboam.

The Septuagint's 4<sup>th</sup> Kingdoms tells the history of the kingdoms of Samaria and Judah from circa 850 BC until the Babylonians conquered Judah around 600 BC. This era of history is well documented in the historical records of the Assyrians, Egyptians, and Babylonians, and unlike the earlier books of the Kingdoms, is generally accepted by historians. This era included the rise and fall of the Aramean Empire based in Damascus, the rise and fall of the Assyrian Empire farther north, the Assyrian wars against Egypt, and the sack of Thebes, and ultimately the rise of the Babylonian Empire. During this tumultuous time, the kingdoms of Israel, Judah, and Aram, which appears to have been considered an Israelite kingdom by the prophet Ezekiel, struggled for survival and fell one by one to the expanding empires around them.

Before the era of 4<sup>th</sup> Kingdoms, Samara had established an empire, occupying the Aramean kingdoms of Damascus and Hama in modern Syria, which had ended suddenly when an earthquake had leveled Samaria. The earthquake was mentioned in the Book of Amos, and archaeological evidence of it is found throughout modern northern Israel and the Palestinian West Bank. It is estimated to have been between 7.8 and 8.2 on the Richter Scale, and aftershocks likely lasted around 6 months. In the aftermath, Damascus rose to form its own Aramean empire, occupying Hama, and northern Samaria, as well as Gilead in southern modern Syria, which had been part of Samaria since the division of Israel into Samaria and Judah. However, as Assyria began to expand to the north, Samaria and Aram formed an anti-Assyrian alliance, and the Samarian forces were stationed in Aram to help defend the northern border from the Assyrians. Judah was invited to join the alliance, but instead formed an alliance with the Assyrians and invaded and pillaged Samaria and southern Aram.

Judah continued to be an ally of Assyria as the Assyrians conquered Aram, Samaria, and Sidon which had also allied with them. Fortunately, as Samaria finally fell to the Assyrians after a three-year campaign, the king of Assyria died, sparking a civil war between rival heirs. This civil war bought Judah almost twenty years to build up defenses, and King Hezekiah built extensively across his kingdom. Archaeological evidence of Hezekiah's construction projects is common in the region around Jerusalem, and the southern region of the Palestinian West Bank, including the Broad Wall in Jerusalem, and the Siloam Tunnel, which connected Jerusalem with a water source outside the walls of the city. Ancient records of anti-siege artillery on the walls of Jerusalem also exist, likely ballistas or catapults, so, it is clear the Judahites knew they would be next. While the Assyrians did lay siege to Jerusalem according to 4th Kingdoms, they were not able to conquer the city. The Assyrian Annals record the campaign against Judah and record the cities they captured, which did not include Jerusalem, and so historians accept the general account of what happened found in 4th Kingdoms.

The defeat of the Assyrian army was not recorded in the Assyrian Annals, however, the Egyptians recorded the Assyrian army was besieged by a plague of mice. The Septuagint's 4th Kingdoms reports that the messenger of the Lord (ἄγγελοσ

Κυρίου) wiped out the Assyrian army, while the Masoretic texts claim it was Yahweh (יְהֹוָה). In some places where the Septuagint refers to the angel of the Lord, the Masoretic texts refers to the 'messenger Yahweh' (מַלְאָךְ יְהֹוָה) which could also be interpreted as 'messenger of Yahweh,' showing the fingerprints of the Hasmonean redactors.

Like the earlier books of the Septuagint, the Kingdoms were set in the early Israelite polytheistic culture, and several gods are mentioned in the book. Qetesh Asherah is referred to by both her Hebrew name Asherah (אֲשֵׁרָה), and her title Qetesh (קְדוֹשׁ), in 4th Kingdoms, and was by all accounts a major Israelite goddess before King Hezekiah, and later King Josiah's reforms banned her worship. The ban on Asherah's worship was very effective in Judah, as the translators working at the Library of Alexandria didn't recognize the names just 350 years later, and translated Asherah as 'groves' (ἄλσοσ) and Qetesh and 'saint' (ἅγιον). While the meaning of these words clearly changed during the intermediate period, the names of the other ancient Canaanite gods the Israelites were worshiping were still understood by the Greeks, as many of the old names were still in use by the Phoenicians and Babylonians. Her sister Astarte (Ἀστάρταισ / עֲשְׁתָּרֹת) is also mentioned in passing during Josiah's reforms when she was banned.

The Septuagint has several transliterated Semitic names, as well as direct translations of the names of Canaanite gods into the Greek language that show the text they translated was generally the same, but specifically different in some places. The Greeks translated Shemesh (שֶׁמֶשׁ), the Canaanite and Israelite solar-god, as Helios (Ἡλίω), the Greek solar-god, proving that they did understand that Shemesh was the name of the early Israelite solar-god, which was proven conclusively by Josiah banning Shemesh in

Judah. Obviously, he was not banning the sun from shining on Judah. He also destroyed the chariot of the Shemesh and the horses that pulled it, which is iconically identical to Helios's chariot and the four horses that pulled it across the sky. The four horses are a reference to what are commonly called sundogs today, the refracted light that appears 22° to the left and right of the Sun, and in rare cases again at 44°, when there are ice crystals in the atmosphere.

Kings Hezekiah and Josiah also banned other gods from being worshiped in Judah, including the armies of Shamayim (δυνάμει τοῦ Οὐρανοῦ / צְבָא הַשָּׁמָיִם). The Hebrew term translates as 'skies,' and is documented as an ancient Canaanite god, which the Greeks translated as Uranus (Οὐρανοῦ), the name of their sky-god. This term is often translated as 'hosts of heaven' or 'forces of heaven,' however, chapter 23 implies the armies of Shamayim were a reference to astrology:

> "The king commanded Hilkiah the high priest, and the priests of the second order, and those who kept the door, to bring out of the temple of the Lord all the vessels that were made for Ba'al, and for Asherah, and all the army of Shamayim, and he burnt them outside of Jerusalem in the fields of Kidron, and took the ashes of them to the Temple of El. He burnt the sacred male prostitutes, who the kings of Judah had appointed, and those who burnt incense in the Bamahs and in the cities of Judah, and the places around Jerusalem, and those who that burnt incense to Ba'al, Shemesh, Yarikh, the Zodiac, and the power of the armies of Shamayim."

The term Ba'al, which translates as 'Lord' is accepted by archaeologists as a reference to the god Hadad, the storm-god of the Canaanite pantheon, while Shemesh was the sun-god, and Yarikh (Σελήνη / יָרֵחַ) was the moon-god. The term translated as Zodiac (Μαζουρωθ / מַזָּלוֹת) is almost certainly based on the Aramaic mzrwt (לאזרות), itself derived from the Babylonian mazraåtu (𒂍𒀸𒊏𒀀𒌈), meaning 'mansions' or 'manors.' The Hebrew translators appear to have made a transliteration error, replacing an R (ר) with an L (ל). The Jewish interpretation of the Hebrew word has traditionally been a reference to the zodiac, which does appear to be what the cuneiform word would mean in this context.

In any event, the sixteen-year-old King Josiah, who had been advised by Levites from Libnah since they killed his father when he was 8 and placed him on the throne, authorized the slaughter of all other priesthoods, and for the priests to be sacrificed on their altars before the various temples across Judah were torn down, forcing the majority of the population to effectively become atheists, as only the royal temple in Jerusalem was allowed to continue existing. They also authorized the slaughter and sacrifice of the astrologers and healers, as well as the sacred prostitutes of Qetesh, and dug up the bones of the old kings and priests and desecrated them as well. He was the greatest king Israel ever had, even greater than Saul, David, or Solomon, at least according to the author of 4th Kingdoms. Apparently, the God he worshiped didn't agree as he was killed by Pharaoh, and Judah became a satellite state of the Egyptian Empire. When Judah rebelled against Egypt, the Babylonians conquered them, ending the existence of the last Israelite kingdom.

# 1st Kingdoms: Chapter 1

There was a man from Armathaem Sipha[1] of Mount Ephraim, whose name was Elkanah, a son of Jeremeel, the son of Elihu, the son of Tohu in Nezib Ephraim. He had two wives, one named Hannah and the other named Peninnah. Peninnah had children, but Hannah had none. The man went annually from Armathaem to worship and sacrifice to Lord God Sabaoth[2] in Shiloh,[3] where Eli and his two sons Hophni and Phinehas, were the priests of the Lord. The day came, and Elkanah sacrificed and gave portions to his wife Peninnah and her children. To Hannah, he gave a prime portion, because she had no child, yet Elkanah loved Hannah more than the other, however, the Lord had kept her from having children. The Lord gave her no child in her suffering, and in her depression due to her suffering she was miserable because the Lord stopped her from conceiving. Therefore she went every year to the Temple of the Lord, and she was depressed and cried, and did not eat.

Elkanah her husband called to her, "Hannah."

She answered him, "I am here, my lord."

He asked her, "Why are you so sad and crying? Why don't you eat? Why does your heartache? Am I not better to you than ten children?"

Hannah rose after they had eaten in Shiloh, and stood before the Lord, and Eli the priest was on a seat by the lintels of the Temple of the Lord. She was very sad in her mind, and prayed to the lord and cried greatly. She vowed to the Lord, "My lord, Lord God Sabaoth,[4] if you will indeed look on the humiliation of your slave-woman and remember me, and give to your slave-woman the seed of a man, then will I indeed dedicate him to you until the day of his death. He will drink no wine or strong drink, and no iron will touch his head."

While she was praying before the Lord, Eli the priest noticed her mouth. She was speaking in her heart, and her lips moved, but her voice was not heard, and Eli assumed she was a drunken woman. The servant of Eli said to her, "How long will you be drunk? Take your wine with you, and leave the presence of the Lord!"

Hannah answered and said, "No, my lord, I have had a hard day, and I have not drunk wine or strong liquor, and I pour out my mind before the Lord. Don't see your servant as a daughter of wickedness, because of my many complaints, and the grief that I have spoken of to the Lord."

Eli answered and said to her, "Go in peace. The god of Israel will grant you all you have asked of him."

She replied, "Your servant has found favor in your eyes."

The woman left and returned to her lodging, and ate and drank with her husband, and she was no longer sad. They rose early in the morning, and worship the Lord, and then went their way. Elkanah returned to his house at Armathaem and knew his wife Hannah, and the Lord remembered her and she conceived. When the time had come, she gave birth to a son, and called his name Samuel,[5] and said, "Because I asked Lord God Sabaoth for him."

The man Elkanah and all his house went back to offer the annual sacrifice in Shiloh, and make his vows, and pay the tithes of his land. But Hannah did not go up with him, as she said to her husband, "I will not go up until the child goes up after I have weaned him, and he will be presented before the Lord, and he will stay there permanently."

Elkanah her husband replied to her, "Do that which is good in your eyes, and stay until you have weaned him. May the Lord establish that which comes from your mouth."

The woman stayed and suckled her son until she had weaned him, and then she went up with him to Shiloh with a three-year-old calf, loaves, a ephah[6] of fine flour, and a waterskin[7] of wine. She entered into the Temple of the Lord in Shiloh, along with the child. They brought him before the Lord, and his father killed his offering which he offered to the Lord each year, and he brought the child near and killed the calf, and Hannah the mother of the child brought him to Eli and said, "I beg you, my lord, as your mind lives! I am the woman that stood in your presence with you while praying to the Lord. This child I prayed for, and the Lord has given me what I requested of him. I lend him all his days that he lives, as a loan to the Lord."

# 1st Kingdoms: Chapter 1 Notes

**1** Codex Vaticanus: Armathaem Sipha (ⲀⲢⲘⲀⲐⲀⲓⲘⲥⲓⲫⲀ)

• Codex Alexandrinus: Armathaem Sôphim (ⲀⲢⲘⲀⲐⲀⲓⲘⲥⲱⲫⲓⲙ)

• Codex Basiliano-Vaticanus: Armathaem Sêpha (ⲀⲢⲘⲀⲐⲀⲓⲘⲥⲏⲫⲀ)

• LXX 707: Armathaem Sipha (Ⲁβμⲁθⲁιμ ⲥιϨⲀ)

• LXX 127: Armathaem ek Sipha (Ⲁβμⲁθⲁιμ Ꝺⲓ ⲥιϨⲀ)

• Aleppo Codex: hrmtym ṣwpym (הרמתים צופים)

• Leningrad Codex: haramatayim tzovfim (הָרָמָתַיִם צוֹפִים)

• Targum Jerusalem: meramata mittalmidei (מֵרָמָתָא מִתַּלְמִידֵי)

This site is generally believed to be Nahbi Samwil, in the West Bank of the Palestinian Territories.


**2** Codex Vaticanus: Cô Thô Sabaôth (Κ̅Ꙍ̅Θ̅Ꙍ̅ⲤⲀⲂⲀⲰⲐ). Translation: Lord God Sabaoth

• Codex Basiliano-Vaticanus: Cyriô tô theô pantocratori Sabaôth (ⲔⲨⲢⲓⲱ ⲐⲈⲱ ⲠⲀⲚⲦⲞⲔⲢⲀ́ⲦⲞⲢⲓ ⲤⲀⲂⲀⲰⲐ). Translation: Lord god omnipotent Sabaoth

• LXX 56: Cyriô Sabaôth (Ⲕυβιⲟⲟ ⲥⲁⲩⲁ∞θ). Translation: Lord Sabaoth

• LXX 107: Cyriô tô theô pantocratori Sabaôth (Ⲕυβιⲟⲟ ⲧⲟⲟ θⲟ̅ⲟ̅ⲟ πⲀⲚⲦⲟⲩβⲁⲅⲅⲧⲟβⲓ ⲥⲁⲩⲁ∞θ). Translation: Lord the omnipotent god Sabaoth

• LXX 19: Cyriô Sabaôth theô pantocratori (Ⲕυβιⲟⲟ ⲥⲁⲩⲁ∞θ θⲟ̅ⲟ̅ⲟ πⲀⲚⲦⲟⲩβⲁⲅⲅⲧⲟβⲓ). Translation: Lord Sabaoth omnipotent god

• Aleppo Codex: lyhwh ṣbảwt (ליהוה צבאות). Translation: to Yhwh armies

• Leningrad Codex: laIhvah tzeva'ovt (לַיהוָה צְבָאוֹת). Translation: to Yhwah armies

• Targum Jerusalem: Yeyah tzeva'ovt (יְיָ צְבָאוֹת). Translation: Yhw desires

This name has not survived in the fragments of 1st Kingdoms (the first half of Masoretic Samuel) found among the Dead Sea Scrolls, however, it found within the fragments of 2nd Kingdoms (the second half of Masoretic Samuel).

• Dead Sea Scroll 4QSamᵃ equivalent in other lines of text: yhwh sbåwt (𐤉𐤄𐤅𐤄 𐤑𐤁𐤀𐤅𐤕). Translation: Yahweh armies

**3** Codex Vaticanus: Sêlô (ⲤⲎⲀⲰ). Translation: Shiloh

• Codex Basiliano-Vaticanus: Sêlôm (ⲤⲎⲀⲰⲘ)

• LXX 127: Silôm (Ⲥιλωμ)

• LXX 93: Sinaen (ⲤιⲛⲀιⲛ)

• Aleppo Codex: šlh (שלה). Translation: Shiloh

• Leningrad Codex: Shiloh (שִׁלֹה). Translation: Shiloh

• Targum Jerusalem: Shiloh (שִׁלֹה). Translation: Shiloh

Shiloh was the town where the tabernacle was established after the Israelites entered Canaan, believed to be in or near the Samaritan town of Shiloh, in the modern West Bank of the Palestinian Territories, approximately 10 km south of Bethel. While the earliest codices agree the name was Sêlô (Σηλω), many of the later codices use the name Sêlôm (Σηλωμ), and some refer to the city as Silôm (Σιλωμ) or Sinain (Σιναιν). The name Sêlôm (Σηλωμ) is also used later in the major codices, suggesting there may have been a spelling error in the Aramaic texts, and the town was not Shiloh but Salem. Jeremiah recorded there was a town called Salem in Samaria during his lifetime, however, this was later incorrectly re-identified by a scribe during Ezra's time as being the archaic name of Jerusalem. Egyptian records used the name Uru-Shalim during the bronze age, meaning it was not known as Salem before David conquered the Jebusites that lived in it.

363

# 1st KINGDOMS: CHAPTER 1 NOTES

**4** Codex Vaticanus: Adônae C̄e Elôe Sabaôth (ᴀᴅꞶⲚᴀⲓⲔⲈⲈᴧꞶⲈ ⳭᴀʙᴀꞶⲐ). Translation: Adonai Lord Elôe Sabaôth

• Codex Alexandrinus: Adônae Cyrie cae Elôae Sabaôth (ᴀᴅꞶⲚᴀⲓ ⲔⲨⲢⲓⲈ Ⲕᴀⲓ ⲈᴧꞶᴀⲓ ⳭᴀʙᴀꞶⲐ). Translation: Adonai Lord and Elôae Sabaôth

• LXX 707: Adônae Cyrie Elôi Sabaôth (ᴀᴧⲟⲟⲛⲀⲓ ⲔⲁⲂⲣⲓⲋ Ⲉλⲟⲟⲓ ⳭⲀⲩⲁⲟⲟⲐ). Translation: Adonai Lord Ellôi Sabaôth

• LXX 245: Adonae Cyrie Ellôi Sabaôth (ᴀᴧⲟⲛⲀⲓ ⲔⲁⲂⲣⲓⲋ Ⲉλλⲟⲟⲓ ⳭⲀⲩⲁⲟⲟⲐ). Translation: Adonai Lord Ellôi Sabaôth

• LXX 242: Adônae Cyrie Ellôi Sabaôth (ᴀᴧⲟⲟⲛⲀⲓ ⲔⲁⲂⲣⲓⲋ Ⲉλλⲟⲟⲓ ⳭⲀⲩⲁⲟⲟⲐ). Translation: Adonai Lord Ellôi Sabaôth

• LXX 92: Adônae Cyrie Ellôi Sabôôth (ᴀᴧⲟⲟⲛⲀⲓ ⲔⲁⲂⲣⲓⲋ Ⲉλλⲟⲟⲓ ⳭⲀⲩⲟⲟⲟⲟⲐ). Translation: Adonai Lord Ellôi Sabôôth

• Aleppo Codex: Yhwh ṣbåwt (**יהוה צבאות**). Translation: Yhwh armies

• Leningrad Codex: Yehvah tzeva'ovt (יְהֹוָה צְבָאֹות). Translation: Yehwah armies

• Targum Jerusalem: Yeyah tzeva'ovt (יְיָ צְבָאֹות). Translation: Yahw desires

Three different transliterations of the Semitic words survive in the various Septuagint manuscripts, yet they are not found in the Masoretic text, or Targum Jerusalem. The two missing Semitic words were the Canaanite ådny (𐤀𐤃𐤍𐤉), meaning 'my lord,' and the Aramaic word ålh (𐡀𐡋𐡄), meaning 'god,' meaning the Aramaic text would have read as 'my lord Lord god of desires,' and the earlier Canaanite text would have read as 'my lord Ba'al god of war.' The substitution of Adony with Yahweh was common under the Hasmonean dynasty, however, the Hasmoneans had no reason to alter the rest of the phrase, suggesting it was altered by Phillip the Phrygian when he was the High Priest at the temple, shortly before the Maccabean revolt. Phillip believed that the Judean god Sabaoth was the local version of the Phrygian god Sabazious, a common view among the Greeks as well, who called both gods Dionysus.

**5** Codex Vaticanus: Samouêl (ϹΑΜΟΥΗΛ)

• Aleppo Codex: Šmwål (שמואל). Translation: name of El (or god)

• Leningrad Codex: Shemu'el (שְׁמוּאֵל). Translation: name of El (or god)

• Targum Jerusalem: Shemu'el (שְׁמוּאֵל). Translation: name of El

This verse does not survive intact among the Dead Sea Scrolls, however, the name does survive later verses among the Dead Sea Scrolls.

• Dead Sea Scroll 4QSamᵃ: Šmwål (שמואל). Translation: name of El (or god)

The presence of El's name in both Samuel's name and Elkanah's name indicates his parents worshiped El, the Canaanite and early-Israelite creator-God.

**6** Codex Vaticanus: oephi (ΟΙΦΙ)

• LXX 489: yphi (υφι)

• LXX 125: iphi (ιφι)

• LXX 74: yphê (υφη)

• LXX 247: yphên (υφην)

• Aleppo Codex: åyph (איפה). Translation: ephah

• Leningrad Codex: eifah (אֵיפָה). Translation: ephah

• Targum Jerusalem: chilta (כֵּילְתָא). Translation: measurement

The Septuagint includes a Greek transliteration of the Hebrew term åyph (איפה). The ephah was a unit of measurement adopted by the Canaanites and Arabs from the Egyptian ipet (𓁹𓏤𓂝𓏤). It continued to be used in Egypt during the classical era, where the word was spelled in Coptic as aeipe (ⲁⲉⲓⲡⲉ) in Akhmimic, aipi (ⲁⲓⲡⲓ) in Fayyumic, oeipe (ⲟⲉⲓⲡⲉ) in Sahidic, and ōipi (ⲱⲓⲡⲓ) in Bohairic. The ephah was a dry measurement equaling approximately 19.2 liters, and therefore the measurement was around 1.9 liters (½ gallon).

**7** Codex Vaticanus: nebel (ΝⲉΒⲉⲗ)

- LXX 82: nebal (ⲛⲟⲩⲁⲗ)

- LXX 376: ebel (ⲟⲩⲟⲗ)

- Aleppo Codex: nbl (נבל)

- Leningrad Codex: nevel (נֵבֶל)

- Targum Jerusalem: gerav (גְרַב). Translation: bottle

Nebel was neither a Greek nor Canaanite word, but a transliteration of the Akkadian Cuneiform word, nādu (𒃻𒈾𒁺), meaning waterskin, suggesting that the book of 1ˢᵗ Kingdoms was originally composed in cuneiform, likely during the Neo-Babylonian era.

# 1st Kingdoms: Chapter 2

She continued, "My heart is established in the Lord, my horn is exalted in my god. My mouth is enlarged over my enemies. I have rejoiced in your salvation. For there are none as holy as the Lord, and there is none righteous as our god! There is none holy beside you. Don't brag, and don't speak of high things! Don't let high-sounding words come out of your mouth, for the Lord is a god of knowledge, and god prepares his own designs. The bow of the powerful has become feeble, and the weak have girded themselves with strength."

"They who were full of bread are brought low, and the hungry have forgotten the land. The barren has born seven, and she who abounded in children has become feeble. The Lord kills and makes live. He brings down to the grave and brings up. The Lord makes poor and makes rich. He brings low and lifts up. He lifts up the poor from the earth, and raises the needy from the dunghill, to seat him with the princes of the people, and causes them to inherit the throne of glory, granting the petition to he who prays. He blesses the years of the righteous, for man can't prevail by strength alone."

"The Lord will weaken his adversary! The Lord is holy! Don't let the wise man boast of his wisdom, or let the mighty man boast of his strength, or let the rich man boast of his wealth. Instead, let he who boasts, boast of understanding and knowing the Lord, and to executing judgment and justice on the earth. The Lord has gone up to the heavens and has thundered. He will judge the extremities of the earth, and he gives strength to our kings and will exalt the horn of his anointed."[1]

She left him there before the Lord and departed to Armathaem, and the child ministered in the presence of the Lord before Eli the priest. The sons of Eli the priest were evil, not knowing the Lord. The priest heard the claim from all of the people that sacrificed, that the servant of the priest came with a three-pronged flesh-hook in his hand when the meat was boiling. He struck it into the great cauldron, or the bronze vessel, or into the pot, and whatever came up with the flesh-hook, the priest took for himself, and so they did to all Israel that came to sacrifice to the Lord in Shiloh. Before the fat was burned for a sweet savor, the servant of the priest would come, and say to the man that sacrificed, "Give meat to roast for the priest, and I will not take from you soaked flesh out of the cauldron."

If the man that sacrificed said, "First let the fat be burnt, as is fit, and take for yourself of all things which your mind desires."

Then he would say, "No, give it to me now or I will take it by force."

So the sin of the young men was very great before the Lord, for they set nothing of the sacrifice before the Lord. Samuel ministered before the Lord, a child girded with a linen vest. His mother made him a little shirt and brought it to him each year when she went there with her husband to offer the yearly sacrifice. Eli blessed Elkanah and his wife, saying, "The Lord repaid you the seed of this woman, in return for the loan which you have lent to the Lord," and the man returned to his place.

The Lord visited Hannah, and she gave birth to another three sons and two daughters. The child Samuel grew before the Lord. Eli was very old when he heard what his sons did to the Israelites, and he asked them, "Why do you do this, which I hear from the mouths of all the people of the Lord? No my sons, for the report which I hear is not good. Do not do it, for the reports which I hear are not good, and so the people do not serve God. If a sinner sins against a man, then he can pray to the Lord, but if a man sins against the Lord, who will he pray to?"

They did not listen to the voice of their father, because the Lord would, by all means, destroy them. The child Samuel grew older and was in favor with God and with men. A prophet came to Eli, and said, "The Lord says, 'I revealed myself to the house of your father when they were servants in Egypt to the house of Pharaoh. I chose the house of your father out of all the tribes of Israel to minister to me in the priest's office, to go up to my altar, and to burn incense, and to wear a vest. I gave to the house of your father all the offerings by fire of the Israelites for food. However, you have looked on my incense-offering and my meat-offering with a shameless eye, and have honored your sons above me, so that they should bless themselves with the first-fruits of every sacrifice of Israel before me.'"

"Therefore Lord the god of Israel,² said, 'Your house and the house of your father will pass before me forever,' but now the Lord says, 'That has nothing to do with me, and I will only honor those that honor me, and he that disregards me I will despise.' Look, the days will come when I will destroy your seed and the seed of your father's house."

"You will not have an old man in my house forever. If I do not destroy a man of you from my altar, it will be that his eyes may fail and his mind may perish, and everyone that remains in your house will fall by the sword of men. This will come on your two sons Hophni, and Phinehas which will be a sign for you, and they will both die on one day. I will raise for myself a faithful priest, who will do all that is in my heart and my mind. I will build him a sure house, and he will walk as my anointed forever. It will come to pass that he who survives in your house, will come to do obeisance before him for a little piece of silver, saying, 'Put me into one of your priest's offices to eat bread.'"

# 1ˢᵗ Kingdoms: Chapter 2 Notes

**1** Codex Vaticanus: christou (ⲭⲣⲓⲥⲧⲟⲩ). Translation: anointed (singular form)

• Codex Coislinianus: christôn (χριστων). Translation: anointed (plural form)

• LXX 93: chrêstou (χρηστου). Translation: good (or useful)

• Dead Sea Scroll 4QSamª: mšyh (משיח). Translation: anointed (singular form)

• Aleppo Codex: mšyh (מָשִׁיח). Translation: anointed (masculine singular form)

• Leningrad Codex: meshicho (מְשִׁיחֹ). Translation: anointed (masculine singular form)

• Targum Jerusalem: meshicheih (מְשִׁיחֵיה). Translation: anointed (feminine singular form)


**2** Codex Vaticanus: c̄s o t̄h̄s Israêl (ⲕⲥ ⲟ ⲑⲥ ⲓⲥⲣⲁⲏⲗ). Translation: Lord the god of Israel

• LXX 19: cyrios Israêl (ⳙⲟⳙ ⲓⲟⲣⲇⲁⲏ λ). Translation: lord of Israel

• Aleppo Codex: Yhwh âlhy Yšrâl (יהוה אלהי ישראל). Translation: Yahweh god Israel

• Leningrad Codex: Yehvah elohei Yisra'el (יְהוָה אֱלֹהֵי יִשְׂרָאֵל). Translation: Yahweh god of Israel

• Targum Jerusalem: Yeyah elaha deYisra'el (יְיָ אֱלָהָא דְיִשְׂרָאֵל). Translation: Yahw god of Israel

The Aramaic sections of Masoretic Daniel that were not translated into Hebrew maintain the term adonai ha'elohim (אֲדֹנָי הָאֱלֹהִים), meaning the 'Lord the gods' where the Septuagint has 'Lord the god' (Κυριον τον θεον). As most books of the Septuagint were translated from Aramaic

371

texts, the Aramaic text almost certainly used the term adonai ha'elaha Yisra'el where the Septuagint has 'Lord the god Israel.' The name Yahweh appears to have been added to most of the books in the Masoretic text when the texts were translated to Hebrew during the Hasmonean Dynasty of Judea, between 140 and 37 BC. According to the the Talmud, this was to repair the damage King Manasseh had done 600 years earlier when he removed the name Yahweh from the Israelite Texts, however, no evidence has survived from the era of Manasseh or earlier that proves the name was originally in the text, suggesting it was an attempt by the first Hasmonean High-Priest/King Simon the Zealot to create a national Judean religion with a god having a name similar to the Roman god Jove.

The name Yahweh, in the Aramaic form of Yahw (𐤉𐤄𐤅^) does appear to have originally been in some of the books of the Septuagint, such as Leviticus, which originated under the rule of King Josiah or later, and Yahw was a popular god among Judeans and Israelites under Persian and Greek rule. The translators at the Library of Alexandria transliter-ated this name as Iaw (Ιαω) in the books it was originally in, however, under the Hasmonean Dynasty it seems to have been added to all the books translated into Hebrew, creating some confusion among early Christians.

There were debates in the early Christian era about which version of the Israelite scriptures to use, the Greek, Hebrew, Samaritan, or Syriac translations, resulting in different versions of the scriptures being used by different churches. Some versions replaced the name Lord with Iaw in the Greek texts, either in the Greek form as Ιαω, or by copying in the Hebrew form of the name Yhwh (יהוה) or the older Phoenician form of Yhwh (𐤉𐤄𐤅𐤄), or by mocking the Hebrew with Greek letters as ΠΙΠΙ.

This created a great deal of confusion among Christians, and ultimately the books of the Septuagint that had the name Iaw in them were redacted so all the books used the term Lord (Κυριος). Most Christian translations, as well as Jewish translations, have continued to use the term 'Lord' in place of the name Yahweh, due to the prohibition on using any names of God that was introduced during the Hasmonean dynasty. There are no early surviving copies of the Septuagint's version of Genesis which have the name Iaw (Ιαω / יהו‎) in them, like some of the other books of the Septuagint, and therefore it cannot be proven if the name was in the Septuagint's Genesis or not, however, the terms used in Septuagint's Genesis are consistent with the surviving Aramaic sections of Masoretic Daniel, strongly suggesting the Aramaic source text the Greek translators used, included the term adonai ha'elaha Yisrael, and not Yahw ha'elaha Yisrael. The Aramaic term likely meant 'Lord the god of Israel.'

# 1ˢᵗ Kingdoms: Chapter 3

The child Samuel ministered for the Lord before Eli the priest, and the word of the Lord was precious in those days, as there was no distinct vision. It happened at that time that Eli was sleeping in his place, and his eyes began to fail, and could not see. The lamp of God was burning before it was trimmed, and Samuel slept in the Temple where the box of the god[1] was. The Lord called, "Samuel! Samuel?"

He answered, "Look, I am here," and then ran to Eli, and said, "Here I am. Did you call me?

He replied, "I did not call you. Go back to sleep, and he returned and went to sleep."

The Lord called again, "Samuel! Samuel?"

He went to Eli a second time, and said, "Look I am here, as you did call me."

He replied, "I did not call you. Go back to sleep." (This was before Samuel knew the Lord, and before the word of the Lord was revealed to him.)

The Lord called Samuel again for the third time, and he rose and went to Eli, and said, "Look, I am here. You did call me."

Eli realized that the Lord had called the child. He said, "Go back to sleep, and if he calls you, say, 'Speak, because your servant hears.'"

Samuel went and lay down in his place. The Lord came, and stood, and called him like before, and Samuel answered, "Speak, because your servant hears."

The Lord said to Samuel, "Look, I execute my words in Israel. Whoever hears them, both his ears will tingle. In that day I will raise up against Eli all things that I have said against his house. I will start, and I will finish. I have told him that I will be avenged on his house perpetually for the iniquities of his sons, because his sons spoke evil against God, and he did not admonish them. It will not go on. I have sworn to the house of Eli, the iniquity of the house of Eli will not be atoned for with incense or sacrifices forever."

Samuel rose early in the morning and opened the doors of the Temple of the Lord, and Samuel was afraid to tell Eli the vision. Eli called Samuel, "Samuel, my son?"

He answered, "Look, I am here."

He asked, "What was told to you? I beg you, don't hide it from me. May God do these things to you, and even more if you withhold from me any of the words that were spoken to you in your ears."

Samuel reported all the words and did not hide them from him, and Eli said, "He is the Lord. He will do that which is good in his sight."

Samuel grew and the Lord was with him, and not one of his words fell to the ground. All Israel knew from Dan even to Beersheba, that Samuel was faithful like a prophet to the Lord. The Lord manifested himself again in Shiloh, and the Lord revealed himself to Samuel. Samuel was recognized in all Israel as a prophet of the Lord from one end of the land to the other. Eli was very old, and his sons kept advancing in wickedness, and their way was evil before the Lord.

# 1st Kingdoms: Chapter 3 Notes

**1** Codex Vaticanus: cibôtos tou t̄h̄u̅ (ΚΙΒШΤΟϹΤΟΥΘΥ). Translation: box of the god

- Aleppo Codex: årwn ålhym (ארון אלהים). Translation: box (or coffin) gods (in Aramaic, or goddesses in Hebrew, god in Neo-Assyrian)

- Leningrad Codex: arovn elohim (אֲרוֹן אֱלֹהִים). Translation: box (or coffin) gods (in Aramaic, or goddesses in Hebrew, god in Neo-Assyrian)

- Targum Jerusalem: arona da'Yay (אֲרוֹנָא דַיְיָ). Translation: coffin (or box) of Yahw

# 1st Kingdoms: Chapter 4

In those days, the Pelesets[1] allied themselves together to make war against Israel, and Israel went out to meet them and camped at Ebenezer, and the Pelesets camped in Aphek. The Pelesets were prepared to fight with Israel, and the war turned against them, and the Israelites fell before the Pelesets. Four thousand men were slaughtered on the battlefield, and the people came to the camp, and the elders of Israel asked, "Why has the Lord caused us to fall today before the Pelesets? Let's take the box of God out of Shiloh, and let it travel among us, and it will save us from the hand of our enemies."

The people sent to Shiloh, and they took the box of the Lord who lived between the sphinxes.[2] Both the sons of Eli, Hophni, and Phinehas, traveled with the box. When the Lord's box entered into the camp, all Israel cried out with a loud voice, and the earth vibrated. The Pelesets heard the cry, and asked, "What is this great cry in the camp of the Habirus?"[3]

They learned that the box of the Lord has come into the camp. The Pelesets were afraid, and said, "These are the gods[4] that have come with them into the camp. "Woe to us! Save us today Lord,[5] from what happened yesterday, and before. Drive away from us, the hand of these cruel gods who defeated the Egyptians with every plague! Strengthen yourselves and behave like men, you Pelesets, so you may not serve the Hebrews as they have served us, but be men and fight against them."

They fought against them, and the Israelites fell, and every man fled to his ten. There was a massive slaughter, and thirty thousand Israelite warriors died there. The box of God was captured, and both the sons of Eli, Hophni and Phinehas died. A Benjaminite ran from the battle that day to Shiloh. His clothes were torn and dirt was on his face. He saw Eli was on the seat by the gate watching the road, as he was greatly concerned for the box of God. The man entered the city to bring greetings, and the city cried out. Eli heard the sound of the cry, and asked, "What is the meaning of this noise?"

The men rushed and went in, and reported to Eli. Now Eli was ninety years old, and his eyes were blind, and he couldn't see. Eli asked those who stood around him, "What is the meaning of this noise?"

The man rushed and approached Eli, and said to him, "I have come from the camp, and I have fled from the battle today."

Eli asked, "What is the situation, my son?"

The young man answered, "The Israelites fled from before the Pelesets. There was a great slaughter of our people. Both your sons are dead and the box of God has been captured."

When he mentioned the box of God, he fell from the seat backward near the gate, and his back broke, and he died as he was an old man and overweight. He had judged Israel for twenty years. His daughter-in-law the wife of Phinehas was pregnant, and about to give birth. She heard that the box of God was taken and that her father-in-law and her husband were dead, and she cried and gave birth, and her pains came on her. She died while giving birth, and the midwives that stood by her, told her, "Don't be afraid, for you have birthed a son," but she did not hear it as her heart had stopped. She had named the child Oy-bar-Kabod,[6] because of the box of God, and because of her father-in-law, and because of her husband.

They said, "The glory of Israel is departed, as the box of God is captured."

# 1st Kingdoms: Chapter 4 Notes

**1** Codex Vaticanus: allophyloe (ΑΛΛΟΦΥΛΟΙ). Translation: tribals (or foreigners)

- Aleppo Codex: plštym (פלשתים). Translation: Pelesets (or Palestinians)

- Leningrad Codex: Pelishtim (פְּלִשְׁתִּים). Translation: Pelesets (or Palestinians)

- Targum Jerusalem: Pelishta'ei (פְּלִשְׁתָּאֵי). Translation: Pelesets (or Palestinians)

The Pelesets, also translated as Philistines or Palestinians, were an ancient people based in the region of the modern Palestinian Gaza Strip and southern Israel. The earliest surviving mention of them is from the reliefs of the Temple of Ramses III at Medinet Habu in Egypt that dates back to some time between 1186 and 1155 BC, in which they were called Pwråsåtj ([illegible]), commonly anglicized as Pelesets. Based on biblical chronology, this story is set in approximately 1057 BC, twenty years before Saul becomes king.

It is unclear where they came from, however, one theory is that they were the Pala, a Luwian people from the Black Sea coast of Anatolia. The region was an independent country called Palaa (𒉺𒆷𒀀) in the Hittite records from the 1600s BC, however, have become part of the Nesite Empire by the 1500s BC. Around the time the Pelesets invaded Canaan, the Pala were driven from their homeland by the neighboring Kaskians from northeast Anatolia, which supports the connection between the groups, however, it has yet to be proven conclusively.

**2** Codex Vaticanus: cheroubim (ΧΕΡΟΥΒΙΜ)

- Codex Alexandrinus: cheroubin (ΧΕΡΟΥΒΕΙΝ)

- LXX 19: cheroubêm (χέρουβημ)

- LXX 158: chaeroubêm (χαιρουβημ)

- Aleppo Codex: krbym (כרבים). Translation: cherubs (or sphinxes, griffins)

- Leningrad Codex: keruvim (כְּרֻבִים). Translation: cherubs (or sphinxes, griffins)

- Targum Jerusalem: keruvaya (כְּרוּבַיָא). Translation: griffin

The word 'cherub' (ܟܪܘܒ / כרוב / 𐤊𐤓𐤁 / 𓐠) was the West Semitic term for the mythical creature generally called a 'griffin' today. Based in the archaeological record of Canaan, it appears that the concept of the cherub was based on the Egyptian sphinx, as the earliest cherub statues found in Canaan were Egyptian statues of sphinxes. Archaeologists are not sure if the sphinxes of Anatolia were based on the Canaanite cherub, or the Egyptian sphinxes directly, however, all three mythical beings are closely related in the archaeological record. The term cherub was for some reason reinterpreted as 'baby angels' by Christians, although in the Books of the Kingdoms God was described as riding on cherubs, and it is not clear why any god would ride around on 'baby angels,' therefore the alternate translation of 'sphinxes' is used in this translation.


**3** Codex Vaticanus: Ebraeôn (ЄΒΡΑΙΩΝ). Translation: Hebrews (or Arameans, Judahites, Samaritans)

- LXX 92: hiereôn (ιϵρϵ͞ων). Translation: clergymen (or priest, minister)

- LXX 509: huiôn HIÊL ( υιων ΙΗΛ). Translation: son (or child) of Israel

- Aleppo Codex: ôbrym (עברים). Translation: Eberites (or Hebrews, Habirus)

- Leningrad Codex: Ivrim (עִבְרִים). Translation: Eberites (or Hebrews, Habirus)

- Targum Jerusalem: Yhuda'ei (יְהוּדָאֵי). Translation: Judahites (or Judeans, Jews)

The Greek and Hebrew terms are translations of the Aramaic word ôbryn (ᗌᐱᎮᎮᵁ), meaning 'crossers,' referring to the descendants of those who left Mesopotamia and crossed the Euphrates to settle in Canaan. The Akkadian cuneiform logogram of habiru was ⤛⫩, while the word was also spelled phonetically as ḫabiru (𒌷𒄯𒁀𒊏). The term had several meanings in cuneiform, including 'crosser,' 'transgressor,' 'sinner,' 'criminal,' and 'husband.' The earliest records of the Habiru used the word interchangeably with the Sumerian word sagaz (𒊕𒂵𒍣), meaning 'murderer.'

The earliest surviving mention of the Ḫabiru, was from the time of King Rim-Sin I of Larsa between approximately 1822 and 1763 BC, who reported they were an Aramean tribe living in southern Iraq. Over the next 600 years, they were reported in hundreds of surviving documents ranging across the Middle East and Egypt, generally as marauders, although some were reported to be mercenaries, and those in Egypt were generally slaves. The Egyptian records of Canaan during the New Kingdom era record the Ôprw (𓂝𓄿𓏤) settling in Samaria and Aram, in the same cities that the Ebraeôn / ôbrym settled in, in the books of Joshua and Judges, supporting the Aramaic term as being a continuation of the Akkadian term, and therefore the term Habiru is used in this translation.

**4** Codex Vaticanus: oe theoe (ΟΙΘΕΟΙ). Translation: the gods

• LXX 554: ho theos (ο θϵ́oc). Translation: the god

• LXX 245: ho S (ο c). Translation: the Sabaoth

• LXX 19: ho S autôn (ο c ἀυτοoν). Translation: the Sabaoth himself (or itself)

• Aleppo Codex: hålhym (הָאלהיס). Translation: the gods (in Aramaic, or the goddesses in Hebrew, god in Neo-Assyrian)

• Leningrad Codex: ha'elohim (הָאֱלֹהִים). Translation: the gods (in Aramaic, or the goddesses in Hebrew, god in Neo-Assyrian)

• Targum Jerusalem: arona daYyah (אֲרוֹנָא דַיְיָ). Translation: box of Yahw

There are several places in the Septuagint where the word 'elohim' was translated as 'gods,' meaning the word still was considered a plural form when the Greeks translated the Septuagint in the 3rd and 2nd centuries BC.


**5** Codex Vaticanus: exelou êmas c̄e (ΕΞΕΛΟΥΗΜΑCK̄Ε). Translation: rescue us lord

• Aleppo Codex: my ysylnw myd hålhym (מִי יַצִילֵנוּ מִיד הָאלֹהִים). Translation: who will rescue us from the hand of the gods

• Leningrad Codex: mi yatzilenu miyyad ha'elohim ( מִי יַצִּילֵנוּ מִיַּד הָאֱלֹהִים). Translation: who will rescue us from the hand of the gods

• Targum Jerusalem: yesheizvinana miyad meimra daYya ( יְשֵׁיזְבִינָנָא מִיַד מֵימְרָא דַיְיָ). Translation: who will rescue us from the hand commanded by Yahw

The Greek and Hebrew verses are significantly different, as the Greek translation has the Palestinians calling out to a Lord to save them, while in the Hebrew translation they ask who can save them from the gods of the Israelites. As the books of the Kingdoms were probably complied during the late Persian era in Aramaic, this indicates that there was a more significant redaction of 1st Kingdoms than just changing replacing Adonai with Yhwh when the Hebrew translation was prepared. As the Palestinians did worship the Lord Dagon, as reported later in the book, as well as other ancient sources, and as proven by the archaeological record, this is almost certainly the Lord they calling out to.


**6** Codex Vaticanus: Oyae Barchabôth (ΟΥΑΙΒΑΡΧΑΒΩΘ)

• Codex Alexandrinus: Ouae Chabôth cae Ipan (ΟΥΑΙΧΑΒΩΘΚΑΙ ΕΙΠΑΝ). Translation: Ouae Chaboth and Ipan

• Codex Basiliano-Vaticanus: Ouae Bary Barchabôd (ΟΥΑΙΒΑΡΥ

ⲂⲀⲢⲭⲀⲂⲱⲆ)

- LXX 19: Oyae Bariôchabêl (Ⲟⲩⲁⲓ ⲃⲁⲣⲓⲟⲟⲭⲁⲩⲗⲗ)

- LXX 158: Oyaeb Barchabôd (Ⲟⲩⲁⲓⲩ ⲃⲁⲣⲭⲁⲩⲟⲟⲆ)

- LXX 246: Oyli i bary Barchamôth (Ⲟⲩⲗⲓⲓ ⲩⲁⲣⲩ ⲃⲁⲣⲭⲁⲩⲟⲟⲑ)

- LXX 247: ou Echaôth (ⲟⲩ ⳟⲭⲁⲟⲟⲑ). Translation: not Echaoth

- LXX 376: ouc Echaôth (ⲟⲩⲩ Ⲉⲭⲁⲟⲟⲑ). Translation: not Echaoth

- LXX 554: Oyae Bariochabêl (Ⲟⲩⲁⲓ ⲃⲁⲣⲓⲟⲭⲁⲩⲗⲗ)

- LXX 82: Oyae Barôichabêl (Ⲟⲩⲁⲓ ⲃⲁⲣⲟⲟⲓⲭⲁⲩⲗⲗ)

- LXX 55: Oyae Bary Barchamôth (Ⲟⲩⲁⲓ ⲃⲁⲣⲩ ⲃⲁⲣⲭⲁⲩⲟⲟⲑ)

- Aleppo Codex: åykbwd (**אִיכבוֹד**). Translation: No dignity

- Leningrad Codex: i-chavovd (אִי־כָבוֹד). Translation: island of Dignity

- Targum Jerusalem: i chavod (אִי כָבוֹד). Translation: no dignity

The Greek text appears to be a transliteration of the Hebrew words oy bar chavovd (אוֹי בַּר כָבוֹד), meaning 'Woe! Son of dignity.'

# 1ˢᵗ Kingdoms: Chapter 5

The Pelesets took the box of God from Ebenezer to Ashdod and placed the box of the Lord in the Temple of Dagon,[1] and set it next to Dagon. The people of Ashdod rose early and entered into the Temple of Dagon, and found Dagon had fallen on his face before the box of God, and so they lifted Dagon and set him in his place. The hand of the Lord was heavy on the Ashdodites, and he plagued them, and he infected them in their genitals, in both Ashdod and her lands. When they rose early in the morning they found Dagon had fallen on his face before the box of the covenant of the Lord, and the head of Dagon and both the palms of his hands were cut off each severed, and both the wrists of his hands had fallen on the floor. Only the stump of Dagon was left. Therefore the priests of Dagon and everyone that entered into the Temple of Dagon did not tread on the threshold of the Temple of Dagon in Ashdod until today, they step over it.

The hand of the Lord was heavy on Ashdod, and he brought evil on them, and it burst out on them into the ships, and mice sprang up among their country, and there was great and indiscriminate death in the city. The men of Ashdod saw that it was so, and they said, "The box of the god of Israel will not stay with us, because his hand is heavy against us and Dagon our god!"

They summoned and gathered the lords of the Pelesets to them, and asked, "What will we do with the box of the god of Israel?"

The Gathites said, "Let the box of God come to us," and the box of God of Israel was taken to Gath.

After it went to Gath, the hand of the Lord came on the city with very great confusion, and he killed the men of the city both small and great and infected them in their genitals, and the Gathites developed hemorrhoids. They sent away the box of God to Ashkelon, and when the box of God went into Ashkelon, the men of Ashkelon cried out, "Why have you brought back the box of the god of Israel to us, to kill us and our people?"

They summoned and gathered the lords of the Pelesets, and said, "Send away the box of the gods of Israel and let it return to its place, and let it not kill us and our people." There was great confusion in all the cities when the box of God of Israel entered there. Those who lived, and did not die were infected with hemorrhoids, and the cry of the city went up to the sky.

# 1st Kingdoms: Chapter 5 Notes

**1** Codex Vaticanus: oecon Dagôn (ΟΙΚΟΝ∆ΑΓωΝ). Translation: house (or room, hall) of Dagon

- Aleppo Codex: byt dgwn (בית דגון). Translation: house (or temple) of Dagon

- Leningrad Codex: beit Dagovn (בֵּית דָּגוֹן). Translation: house (or temple) of Dagon

- Targum Jerusalem: beit Dagovn (בֵּית דָּגוֹן). Translation: house (or temple) of Dagon

Dagon was an ancient Semitic god worshiped by several cultures since at least 2500 BC. His Akkadian name was [an]Dagana (𒀭𒁕𒂵𒈾), his Ugaritic name was Dgn (𐎄𐎂𐎐), and his Phoenician name was Dgn (𐤃𐤂𐤍). He was later considered to be the equivalent of the Greek Titan Cronus, who was worshiped by the Achaean Greeks at the time.

# 1ˢᵗ Kingdoms: Chapter 6

The box was in the country of the Pelesets for seven months, and their land produced swarms of mice. The Pelesets call their priests, and their prophets, and their enchanters, saying, "What will we do to the box of the Lord? Tell us where to send it to."

They answered, "If you send away the box of the covenant of the god of Israel, do not send it away empty, but sacrifice an offering to it for the plague, and then you will be healed, and atonement will be made for you in case his hand is not lifted off of you!"

They asked, "What is the offering for the plague which we will sacrifice to it?"

They answered, "According to the number of the lords of the Pelesets, five golden statues of mice,[1] for the plague on you, your rulers and the people, and golden mice like the mice that destroy your land. You will praise to the god, that he may lighten his hand from off you, and from off your gods, and from off your land. Why do you harden your hearts, like Egypt and Pharaoh hardened their hearts? Was it not so when he mocked them, that they let the people go, and they departed? Now take wood, and make a new wagon, and take two cows that have calved for the first time, away from their calves. Yoke the cows to the wagon, but take the calves away from them, and home. You will take the box and put it on the wagon, and you will restore to it the golden articles for the trespass-offering in a coffer by the side of it. You will let it go, and send it away, and you will leave. Watch if it travels the road to the House of Shemesh,[2] who has brought on us this great affliction. If not, then we will know that his hand has not touched us, but this is a chance which has happened to us."

The Pelesets did this. They took two cows that had calved for the first time, and harnessed them to the wagon, and shut up their calves at home. They set the box of God, and the coffer, and the golden mice, on the wagon. The cows went straight on the road to House of Shemesh, they went along one track, and labored, and did not turn aside to the right hand or the left, and the lords of the Pelesets followed it as far as the frontier of the House of Shemesh. The men of the House of Shemesh were reaping the wheat harvest in the valley, and they lifted their eyes, and saw the box of God, and rejoiced and meet it. The wagon entered into the field of Joshua, which was in House of Shemesh, and they stopped it there by a great stone, and they split the wood of the wagon and offered up the cows as a whole burnt offering to the Lord.

The Levites brought up the box of God, and the coffer with it, and the golden statues on it, and placed them on the great stone, and the men of Temple of Shemesh offered whole burnt offerings and meat offerings on that day to the Lord. The five lords of the Pelesets saw and returned to Ashkelon on that day. These are the golden hemorrhoids which the lords of the Pelesets gave as a trespass-offering to the Lord, one each for Ashdod, Gaza, Ashkelon, Gath, and Ekron. The golden mice according to the number of all the cities of the Pelesets, belonging to the five lords, from the fenced city to the village of the Perizzites, and to the great stone, on which they placed the box of the covenant of the Lord, that was in the field of Joshua the Bethshemite. The sons of Jechonias were not pleased with the men of the House of Shemesh, because they saw the box of God, and God slaughtered 50,070 men among them, and the people mourned because the Lord had inflicted on the people, a terrible plague.

The men of the House of Shemesh asked, "Who will be able to pass before the Lord of the holy?[3] Who will take the box of God up from us? They sent messengers to the inhabitants of the village of Ye'arim, saying, "The Pelesets have brought back the box of the Lord, come down and take it home to yourselves."

# 1st Kingdoms: Chapter 6 Notes

**1** Codex Vaticanus: omoeôma tôn myôn (ΟΜΟΙѠΜΑΤѠΝΜΥѠΝ). Translation: statues of the mice

- LXX 19: omoeômata tôn myôn (ομοιῶμᾱτᾱ τοον μυοον). Translation: effigies of the mice

- LXX 107: homoeôma toutôn (ομοφοομᾱ τοῦτοον). Translation: statues here

- LXX 52: homoeôma tôn muiôn (ομοφοομᾱ τοον μυφοον). Translation: statues of the flies

- LXX 489: omoeômata tôn muiôn (ομοιῶμᾱτᾱ τοον μυφοον). Translation: statues of the flies

- LXX 247: muiôn (μυφοον). Translation: flies

- Dead Sea Scroll 4QSamᵃ: ṣlmy ôkbrykm (צלמי עכבריכם). Translation: images of your mice.

- Aleppo Codex: ṣlmy ôkbrykm (צַלְמֵי עכבריכם). Translation: images of your rats

- Leningrad Codex: tzalmei achbereichem (צַלְמֵי עַכְבְּרֵיכֶם). Translation: images of your rats

- Targum Jerusalem: achberei dahava (עַכְבְּרֵי דַהֲבָא). Translation: mice of gold

The Pelesets creating statues of mice to appease the god causing the plagues supports the idea that they viewed the Israelite god as being a southern Canaanite version of Apollo, who in the late bronze age was known as Ablu (𒀸𒇻) in Syria. This roughly translates as the 'son,' and is generally accepted as a shortened version of aplu ^iluEllil (𒀸𒇻 ✶ 𒀭𒂗𒆤), an epithet of Nergal, the son of the Old Babylonian god Ellil. Like Resheph and Nergal, Ablu was a god of both plague and healing. He was also imported to the Neshite (Hittite) and Trojan civilizations, as the god Apaliunas (𒀀𒉺𒇷𒌋𒈾𒀸) was mentioned in a peace treaty between the civilizations in 1280 BC. Homer reported in the Illiad that Apollôn (Απολλων) was the god that built the wall of Troy, which confirms that the Greeks did view Apaliunas as Apollo. In the Illiad, a priest of Apollo called Chryses, referred to Apollo as the 'Lord of Mice' as he was believed to protect from plagues of mice. The southern Canaanite version of Aplu during the late bronze age had been Shed (𓈖𓏤�), another god of plagues and healing, which supports the Israelites referring to their god as Shaddai in the time of David.

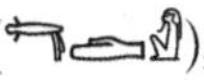

**2** Codex Vaticanus: Baethsamys (ΒΑΙΘϹΑΜΥϹ)

• Codex Alexandrinus: Beththamys (ΒΕΘΘΑΜΥϹ)

• Codex Basiliano-Vaticanus: Bethsamys (ΒΕΘϹΑΜΥϹ)

• LXX 509: Bessamys (βϵσσαμυϲ)

• LXX 56: Bethsamoes (βϵθσαμοιϲ)

• LXX 74: Baethsamous (βαιθσαμουϲ)

• LXX 247: Bethsamous (βϵθσαμουϲ)

• LXX 245: Baenousamys (βαινουσαμυϲ)

• Aleppo Codex: byt šmš (**בית שמש**). Translation: House (or Temple) of Shemesh (or the sun)

• Leningrad Codex: beit Shemesh (בֵּית שֶׁמֶשׁ). Translation: House (or Temple) of Shemesh (or the sun)

• Targum Jerusalem: beit Shemesh (בֵּית שְׁמָשׁ). Translation: House (or Temple) of Shemesh (or the sun)

• Shemesh was the Canaanite sun-god, whose worship was later banned by King Josiah.

**3** Codex Vaticanus: c̄u tou agiou (ΚΥΤΟΥΑΓΙΟΥ). Translation: lord of the holy (or saint, sacred)

• Codex Alexandrinus: ȳ tou ȳ tou agiou (ΥΤΟΥΥΤΟΥΑΓΙΟΥ). Translation: Son the Son of the holy (or saint, sacred)

• Codex Codex Basiliano-Vaticanus: y tou agiou (ΥΤΟΥΑΓΙΟΥ). Translation: Son of the holy (or saint, sacred)

• Dead Sea Scroll 4QSamᵃ: Yhwh hqdwš (ש׳דקה הוהי). Translation: Yhwh of Kadesh (or the holiness, the Qetesh)

• Aleppo Codex: Yhwh hålhym hqdwš (שודקה היהלאה הוהי). Yehvah the godessess (or gods in Aramaic, god in Neo-Assyrian) of Kadesh (or the holiness)

• Leningrad Codex: Yehvah ha'elohim hakKadovosh (הָאֱלֹהִים יְהוָה הַקָּדוֹשׁ). Translation: Yehvah the godessess (or gods in Aramaic, god in Neo-Assyrian) of Kadesh (or the holiness)

Qetesh, meaning Holiness, was the title of the goddess Asherah, who was widely worshiped by the Israelites before King Josiah banned her worship circa 625 BC. Dead Sea Scroll 4QSamᵃ, is closer to the Septuagint's translation than the Masoretic text's version, which indicates the term 'the gods' (הָאֱלֹהִים) was added to the Masoretic version after the Herodian era to shift the interpretation from 'Lord of Kadesh' to the 'holy god Yahweh.'

# 1st Kingdoms: Chapter 7

The men of the village of Ye'arim came and brought the box of the testament of the Lord to the house of Aminadab in the hills. They sanctified Eleazar his son, to keep the box of the covenant of the Lord. Many days passed after the box arrived in the village of Ye'arim, adding up to twenty years, and all the house of Israel turned their back on the Lord. Samuel spoke to all the house of Israel, saying, "If you with all your heart return to the Lord, take away your alien gods[1] from among, you and sacred groves,[2] and prepare your hearts to serve the Lord, and serve him only, he will save you from the hand of the Pelesets."

The Israelites took away the Ba'als[3] and trees of Astarte,[4] and served only the Lord, and Samuel said, "Gather all Israel to Mizpeh, and I will pray to the Lord for you."

They gathered together in Mizpeh, and they drew water and poured it out on the earth before the Lord. They fasted on that day, and said, "We have sinned before the Lord."

Samuel judged the Israelites in Mizpeh. The Pelesets heard that all the Israelites were gathered together to Mizpeh, and the lords of the Pelesets went up against Israel, and the Israelites heard, and they were afraid of the Pelesets. The Israelites said to Samuel, "Don't stop calling out to Lord the god for us, and he will save us out of the hand of the Pelesets!"

Samuel took a suckling lamb and offered it up as a whole burnt offering with all the people to the Lord. Samuel cried to the Lord for Israel, and the Lord heard him. Samuel was offering the whole burnt offering, and the Pelesets drew near to attack Israel. The Lord thundered with a mighty sound in that day against the Pelesets, and they were confused and overthrown before Israel. The Israelites went out from Mizpeh, and chased the Pelesets, and slaughtered them to the region around the House of Car. Samuel took a stone, and set it up between Mizpeh and the old city, and he called the name of it Ebenezer, the stone of the helper, and he said, "Until now the Lord has helped us."

The Lord humbled the Pelesets, and they did not cross the frontier into Israel again, and the hand of the Lord was against the Pelesets all the days of Samuel. The cities which the Pelesets took from Israel were captured and they restored them to Israel from Ashkelon to Azob, and they took the coast of Israel out of the hand of the Pelesets. There was peace between Israel and the Amorites. Samuel judged Israel all the days of his life. He went year by year and traveled to the Temple of El,[5] the circle,[6] and Mizpeh, and he judged Israel in all these consecrated places. He returned to Armathaem, because his house was there, and he judged Israel there and built an altar to the Lord there.

# 1st Kingdoms: Chapter 7 Notes

**1** Codex Vaticanus: theous allotrious (ΘΕΟΥΣΑΛΛΟΤΡΙΟΥΣ). Translation: gods of foreigners

• Codex Alexandrinus: theous tous allotrious (ΘΕΟΥΣΤΟΥΣ ΑΛΛΟΤΡΙΟΥΣ). Translation: gods of the foreigners

• LXX 107: theous tous allophylous (θεοὺς τους ἀλλοφῦλους). Translation: gods of foreigners

• Aleppo Codex: ålhy hnkr (אלהי הנכר). Translation: god the foreigners (or aliens, recognized, recognizable)

• Leningrad Codex: elohei hannechar (אֱלֹהֵי הַנֵּכָר). Translation: god of the foreigners

• Targum Jerusalem: ta'avat ammaya (טַעֲוַת עַמְמִיָא). Translation: errors (or idols) of commoners


**2** Codex Vaticanus: alsê (ΑΛϹΗ). Translation: sacred groves

• Aleppo Codex: ôštrwt (עשתרות)

• Leningrad Codex: ashtarot (עַשְׁתָּרוֹת)

• Targum Jerusalem: ashterata (עֲשְׁתְּרָתָא)

Ôštrwt (עשתרות) is a variation of ôštrt (עשתרת), which the Greek translators interpreted as a reference to the sacred trees Canaanites planted as grave markers. The goddess Asherah was worshiped by planting oak trees, and the way that the Greeks translated this verse suggests that Astarte was as well.


**3** Codex Vaticanus: baalim (ΒΑΑΛΙΜ)

• LXX 247: baalêm (μΔΔΛΣμ)

• LXX 52: balim (βΔΛϭιμ)

- LXX 82: ballim (βαλλόιμ)

- LXX 74: baallim (υλλλλιμ)

- Aleppo Codex: bôlym (בְעלִיס). Translation: lords (or owners, masters, husbands)

- Leningrad Codex: be'alim (בְּעָלִים). Translation: lords (or owners, masters, husbands)

- Targum Jerusalem: be'alaya (בְּעָלְיָא). Translation: husbands

The Greek term Baalim (βααλιμ) is a transliteration of the Hebrew word be'alim (בְּעָלִים), meaning 'lords.' The term ba'al was an ancient Semitic term that was used to denote lords or gods that ruled various cities or regions.

**4** Codex Vaticanus: alsê Astarôth (ᴀᴀсʜᴀстᴀрⲱθ). Translation: grove (or wooded park) of Astaroth (or Astarte)

- Codex Codex Basiliano-Vaticanus: alsê astarôm (ᴀᴀсʜᴀстᴀрⲱм). Translation: grove (or wooded park) of Astarom

- Aleppo Codex: Ôštrt (עשתרת). Translation: Astarte

- Leningrad Codex: Ashtarot (עֶשְׁתָּרֹת). Translation: Astarte

- Targum Jerusalem: Ashterata (עַשְׁתְּרָתָא)

Ôštrt (עשתרת) was the Hebrew spelling of the name of the goddess Astarte. She was known as ᵃⁿAsdartú (✳ 🐟 🗃 ◁) in Akkadian Cuneiform and Ôṭtrt-Ym (◁◁—▭—᷿) in Ugaritic Cuneiform during the late Bronze Age. She was known as Ôštrt (𐤏𐤔𐤕𐤓𐤕) by the Phoenicians during the Iron Age, which was translated as Ôštrt (עשתרת) in Hebrew and Astartên (Ασταρτην) in Greek.

The Romans translated the Greek version as Astarte, resulting in most European variants of the name written in the Latin alphabet. During the New Kingdom era of Egyptian history, circa 1549 tom 1077 BC, Astarte was incorporated into the Egyptian pantheon as one of the daughters of Ra, as she appeared in the book entitled the 'Contest between Horus and Set.' According to the Phoenician scholar Sanchuniathon, who supposedly lived circa 1200 BC, Astarte's sister was Asherah. The names Astarte and Asherah both appear in the Septuagint and Masoretic text, and both appear to be widely worshiped by the early Israelites.

Archaeologists have found that household shrines of statues of Asherah were common in Israel until the 6ᵗʰ century BC. The goddess Asherah was worshiped by planting oak trees, and the way that the Greeks translated this verse suggests that Astarte was as well.

**5** Codex Vaticanus: Baethêl (ΒΑΙΘΗΛ)

- LXX 247: Bethêl (βεθιλ)

- Aleppo Codex: byt âl (בית אל). Translation: Temple (or house) of El

- Leningrad Codex: veit-El (בֵּית־אֵל). Translation: Temple (or house) of El

- Targum Jerusalem: veit El (בֵית אֵל). Translation: Temple (or house) of El

The Temple of El was built by Jacob in the Book of Genesis, circa 2000 BC.

**6** Codex Vaticanus: Galgala (ΓΑΛΓΑΛΑ)

- LXX 19: Galgal (Γαλγαλ)

- LXX 74: Galga (Γαλγα)

- LXX 119: Galala (Γαλαλα)

- LXX 376: Galaad (Γαλααδ)

- Aleppo Codex: glgl (גלגל). Translation: circle

- Leningrad Codex: gilgal (גִּלְגָּל). Translation: circle

- Targum Jerusalem: Gilgala (גִּלְגָּלָא)

The circle in question was likely the stone circle built by Joshua in the Book of Joshua, circa 1500 BC, although several stone circles have been documented in ancient Canaan.

# 1st Kingdoms: Chapter 8

When Samuel was old, he made his sons judges over Israel. They were named Joel (the firstborn), and Abiah (the second-born), and they were judges in Beersheba. His sons did not walk in his way, and they turned aside after profit, and took bribes and perverted judgments. The Israelites gathered themselves together, and come to Armathaem to Samuel, and they said to him, "Look, you have grown old, and your sons do not follow in your way. Now place over us a king to judge us, as the other nations have."

The idea was evil in the eyes of Samuel, when they said, "Give us a king to judge us," and Samuel prayed to the Lord.

The Lord said to Samuel, "Listen to the voice of the people, in whatever they will ask you. They have not rejected you, but they have rejected me from reigning over them. All their actions, which they have done to me from the day that I brought them out of Egypt until today, even when they deserted me and served other gods, likewise they do also to you. Now listen to their voice, but solemnly testify to them, and describe to them the manner of the king who will reign over them."

Samuel spoke the words of the Lord to the people who asked of him a king. He said, "This will be the kind of king that will rule over you, he will take your sons, and put them in his chariots, and among his cavalry, and running before his chariots, and his way will be to make them captains of hundreds and captains of thousands, and to reap his harvest, and gather his vintage, and prepare his weapons of war and the implements of his chariots. He will take your daughters to be perfumers, and cooks, and bakers. He will take your fields, and your vineyards, and your good olive yards, and give them to his servants. He will tax your seeds and your vineyards and give it to his eunuchs and his slaves. He will take your slaves and your slave-women, and your good herds and your donkeys, and will take the tenth of them for his works. He will tax your flocks, and you will be his slaves. You will cry out on that day because of your king, whom you have chosen for yourselves, and the Lord will not hear you in those days, because you have chosen for yourselves a king."

But the people would not listen to Samuel, and they said to him, "No! There will be a king over us, and we will be like all the nations, and our king will judge us, and will go out before us, and fight our battles."

Samuel heard all the words of the people and spoke them in the ears of the Lord, and the Lord said to Samuel, "Listen to their voice, and appoint them a king."

Samuel said to the Israelites, "Let each man go back to his city."

# 1st Kingdoms: Chapter 9

There was a man of the Benjaminites whose name was Kish, the son of Abiel, the son of Zeror, the son of Bachir, the son of Aphek, the son of a Benjamite, and a man of strength. This man had a son whose name was Saul, a good man of great height, and there was none among the sons of Israel bigger than he, high above all the people from his shoulders and upward.

The donkeys of Kish, the father of Saul, were lost and Kish said to Saul his son, "Take one of the young men with you. Rise and go seek the donkeys."

They went through Mount Ephraim, and they went through the land of Shalisha,[1] and did not find them. They passed through the land of Shechem,[2] and they were not there. They passed through the land of Benjamin and did not find them. When they came to Zuph, Saul said to the young man that was with him, "Come and let's return, in case my father has stopped looking for the donkeys and has started worrying about us."

The young man answered him, "See now, a prophet[3] in this city, a man of high repute. All that he will state will certainly happen. So let's go, and he may tell us our way on which we have set out."

Saul said to the young man that was with him, "We'll go, but what will we bring the prophet? The loaves are spent out of our vessels, and we have nothing left with us that belongs to us to bring to the prophet."

The young man answered Saul, "Look, I have in my hand a quarter of a shekel of silver. Give it to the prophet, and he will tell us our way."

(In previous times in Israel, everyone going to inquire of God said, "Come and let's go to the seer," as the people previously called the prophet a seer.)

Saul said to his servant, "Well said, come and let's go," and they went into the city where the prophet was.

As they went up the hill to the city, they found girls coming out to draw water, and they asked them, "Is the seer here?"

The virgins answered them, "He is. Look, he is ahead of you now. He is returning to the city, because of the day, as today there is a sacrifice for the people on the bamah.⁴ As soon as you enter the city, you will find him in the city before he goes up to the bamah to eat. The people will not eat until he comes in, as he blesses the sacrifice, and afterward, the guests eat. Now then go up, as you will find him because of the holiday."

They went up to the city, and as they were entering into the city, Samuel came out to meet them, on his way up to the bamah. The Lord uncovered the ears of Samuel one day before Saul came to him, "At this time tomorrow I will send to you a man out of the land of Benjamin, and you will anoint him to be ruler over my people Israel, and he will save my people out of the hand of the Pelesets. I have looked on the humiliation of my people, as their cry is heard by me."

Samuel saw Saul, and the Lord told him, "See the man that I told you of, this one will rule over my people."

Saul approached Samuel inside the city and asked, "Tell me now, which is the house of the seer?"

Samuel answered Saul, "I am he. Go up with me to the bamah, and eat with me today, and I will send you away in the morning, and I will tell you all that is in your heart. Concerning your donkeys that have been lost for the last three days, don't worry about them as they were found. To whom does the kingship of Israel belong? Isn't it you and your father's house?"

Saul answered, "I am a Benjamite, the smallest tribe of the Israelites, and the smallest family of the whole tribe of Benjamin. Why have you said this to me?"

Samuel took Saul and his servant, and brought them to the inn, and seated them there among the chiefs of those that were called, about seventy men. Samuel said to the cook, "Give me the portion which I gave you, which I told you to set aside."

Now the cook had boiled the shoulder, and he set it before Saul, and Samuel said to Saul, "Look that which is left, sits before you, eat. It is set before you as a testimony in preference to the others. Take it."

Saul ate with Samuel on that day. He went down from the bamah into the city, and they prepared lodging for Saul on the roof, and he slept. When the morning dawned, Samuel called Saul on the roof, "Rise, and I will dismiss you."

Saul arose, and he and Samuel went out. As they went down through the city, Samuel said to Saul, "Speak to the young man, and let him leave us, but you stay the day, and listen to the word of God."

# 1st Kingdoms: Chapter 9 Notes

**1** Codex Vaticanus: Selcha (ceʌxʌ)

- Codex Alexandrinus: Salissa (cʌʌiccʌ)

- Codex Codex Basiliano-Vaticanus: Elcha (eʌxʌ)

- LXX 707: Segalim (c6ɣʌλιμ)

- LXX 120: Salisa (cʌλιoʌ)

- LXX 247: Salêssa (cʌλhooʌ)

- LXX 376: Salêga (cʌλhɣʌ)

- LXX 120: Salisa (cʌλιoʌ)

- LXX 106: Saalisa (cʌʌλιoʌ)

- Aleppo Codex: Šlšh (שלשׁ)

- Leningrad Codex: Shalishah (שָׁלִשָׁה)

- Targum Jerusalem: Roma (רוֹמָא). Translation: Rome

Selcha, also called Baʿal-Shalisha, was an ancient city that was listed as being in Gilead in Deuteronomy chapter 3.


**2** Codex Vaticanus: gês Easacem (ⲅⲏⲥeʌcʌⲕeⲙ). Translation: land of Easacem

- Codex Alexandrinus: gês Saalim (ⲅⲏⲥcʌʌʌιⲙ). Translation: land of Saalim

- Basiliano-Vaticanus: gês Segalim (ⲅⲏⲥceⲅʌʌιⲙ). Translation: land of Segalim

- LXX 707: Saamin (cʌʌμιɴ)

- LXX 19: gês Gaddi tês poleôs Segalim (ɣhc ⲅʌʌʌι ⲧhc πⲟⲗⲟⲟc c6ɣʌλιμ). Translation: land of Gaddi the town of Segalim

- LXX 121: gês Seasacem (ⲅⲗⲥ Cⲟ̄ⲁⲥⲁⲗⲓⲟ̄ⲙ). Translation: land of Seasacem

- LXX 509: gês Elsacim (ⲅⲗⲥ Ελⲥⲁⲗⲓⲙ). Translation: land of Elsacim

- LXX 246: gês Beniamin (ⲅⲗⲥ Bⲟ̄ⲛⲓⲁⲙⲛ). Translation: land of Beniamin

- LXX 244: gês Egalim (ⲅⲗⲥ Eⲅⲁⲗⲓⲙ). Translation: land of Egalim

- LXX 242: gês Egalim (ⲅⲗⲥ ⲓⲁⲙⲛ). Translation: land of Iamin

- LXX 158: gês Segalêm (ⲅⲗⲥ Cⲟ̄ⲅⲁⲗⲏⲙ). Translation: land of Segalem

- LXX 55: gês Segallim (ⲅⲗⲥ Cⲟ̄ⲅⲁⲗⲗⲓⲙ). Translation: land of Segallim

- LXX 44: gês Saalisa (ⲅⲗⲥ Cⲁⲁⲗⲓⲥⲁ). Translation: land of Saalisa

- LXX 247: gês Salim (ⲅⲗⲥ Cⲁⲗⲓⲙ). Translation: land of Salim

- LXX 376: gês Salêm (ⲅⲗⲥ Cⲁⲗⲏⲙ). Translation: land of Salem

- Aleppo Codex: ârs Šôlym (ארץ שעלים). Translation: land of Shalim (or dusk)

- Leningrad Codex: eretz-Sha'alim (אֶרֶץ־שָׁעֲלִים). Translation: land of Shalim (or dusk)

- Targum Jerusalem: ara matbera (אֲרַע מַתְבְּרָא). Translation: land of breakers

The land of Shalim is probably the region around Jerusalem, which was named after the Canaanite god of dusk, Shalim (𐤔𐤋𐤌 / 𐤔𐤋𐤌). The city was known as Åwšåmm (𓂝𓃀𓈙𓄿𓄿𓅓) in the Egyptian execration texts of the Middle Kingdom era, and ᵗᵒʷⁿÙrušalim (𒌷𒋛𒌝𒊏) in the Amarna Texts from the New Kingdom Era.

The oldest surviving Greek translation of 'land Easacem' is clearly a reference to a different location. The name appears to be a transliteration of y shecham (אִי שְׁכֶם), meaning the 'land of Shechem,' suggesting the word 'land' was both translated and transliterated when the Greek translation was made. Shechem was mentioned in the Egyptian Middle Kingdom Sebek-khu Stele, and later in the Amarna Letters of the New Kingdom era, which mentions that it had been taken over by Habirus. Around the same time Shechem became the first capital of the Hebrews according to the author of Judges. As the books of the Kingdoms appear to have been organized in the Late Persian Era in Aramaic, the most probable reason for the difference between the two versions is a redaction of the old Samaritan capital city by High-Priest/King Simon the Zealot when the Hebrew translation was made, and therefore, Shechem is used in this translation.

**3** Codex Vaticanus: anthrôpos tou t͞h͞u (ⲀⲚⲐⲢⲰⲠⲞⲤⲦⲞⲨⲐⲨ̄). Translation: man of god

• Aleppo Codex: âyš âlhym (אִישׁ אלהים). Translation: prophet (or man of gods)

• Leningrad Codex: ish-elohim (אִישׁ־אֱלֹהִים). Translation: prophet (or man of gods)

• Targum Jerusalem: neviya daYyah (נְבִיָא דְיָי). Translation: prophet of Yahw

**4** Codex Vaticanus: bama (ⲂⲀⲘⲀ)

• Aleppo Codex: bmh (במה). Translation: bamah

• Leningrad Codex: bamah (בָּמָה). Translation: bamah (or heights)

• Targum Jerusalem: beit Ascharuta (בֵּית אַסְחָרוּתָא). Translation: house (or temple) of Ashurtah (or feasting)

Bamahs were stone platforms built at the tops of hills, where sacrifices were made to gods in ancient Canaan and Assyria. These Bamahs generally included an altar for barbecuing the sacrifices, a stele, a seat for the god (which the priest would sit in), an oaktree representing Asherah or Astarte, and a cistern for water. These Bamahs were also generally accompanied by a banquet hall, and a 'low stone' used for slaughtering and butchering the animal. Bamahs were the main religious centers used by the Israelites until King Josiah banned and destroyed them circa 625 BC.

# 1st Kingdoms: Chapter 10

Samuel took a vial of oil, and poured it on his head, and kissed him, and asked him, "Has not the Lord anointed you as a ruler over his people, over Israel? You will rule among the people of the Lord, and you will save them out of the hand of their enemies. This will be the sign for you that the Lord has anointed you as a ruler over his inheritance."

"As soon as you have left me today, you will find two men by the burial-place of Rachel on Mount Benjamin celebrating greatly, and they will say to you, 'The donkeys are found which you went to look for, and, see, your father has given up the matter of the donkeys, and he is anxious for you, saying, "What will I do about my son?"' You will leave there, and will go beyond that as far as the oak of Tabor where you will find three men there on their way to worship God at the Temple of El, one carrying three goat-kids, and another carrying three vessels of bread, and another carrying a bottle of wine. They will ask you how you do and will give you two gifts of bread, and you will receive them from their hand."

"Afterward you will go to the Hill of God where the Pelesets are camped, where the commanders of the Pelesets[1] are. When you have entered into the city, you will meet a band of prophets coming down from the bamah, and before them will be lutes, and a drum, a pipe, and a harp, and they will prophesy. The spirit of the Lord[2] will come over you, and you will prophesy with them and will be turned into a different man. When these signs will happen, then do whatever your hand wants because God is with you. Go down to the stone circle and I will come down to you to offer a whole burnt offering and peace-offerings. Then you will wait seven days until I will come to you, and I will make tell you what you will do."

When he turned to leave Samuel, God gave him another heart, and all these signs came to pass in that day. He came to the hill and found a band of prophets coming the opposite way, and the spirit of God came on him, and he prophesied among them. All that had known him before came and saw him among the prophets, and the people asked each other, "What is this that has happened to the son of Kish? Is Saul a prophet?"

One of them answered and said, "Who is his father?" and therefore it became a saying, "Is Saul a prophet?"

He stopped prophesying and returned to the hill. His relative asked him and his servant, "Where did you go?"

They answered, "To look for the donkeys. We saw that they were lost, and we went to Samuel."

His relative asked Saul, "Tell me, I beg you, what did Samuel say to you?"

Saul answered his relative, "He told me that the donkeys were found," but he did not tell him about the kingdom.

Samuel summoned all the people before the Lord at Mizpeh. He said to the Israelites, "The Lord God of Israel has said, 'I brought up the Israelites out of Egypt, and I rescued you out of the hand of Pharaoh king of Egypt, and out of all the kingdoms that attacked you. You have today rejected the god who saved you from all your evils and plagues, and you said, 'No, but you will set a king over us.' Now stand before the Lord according to your tribes, and according to your families."

Samuel brought near all the tribes of Israel, and the tribe of Benjamin was chosen by lot. He brought near the tribe of Benjamin by families, and the family of Matri was chosen by lot. They brought near the family of Matri, man by man, and Saul the son of Kish was chosen, and he searched for him, but he was not found. Samuel asked the Lord, "Will the man come here?"

The Lord answered, "Look, he is hiding among the equipment."

He ran and grabbed him, and he brought him among the people, and he was higher than all the people by ahead. Samuel said to all the people, "Have you seen who the Lord has chosen for himself, that there is none like to him among you all?"

All the people took note, and said, "Let the king live!"

Samuel told the people the description of the king, and wrote it in a book, and set it before the Lord. Samuel sent away all the people, and each returned to his home. Saul departed to his house in Gibeah, and mighty men whose hearts God had touched went with him, but evil men said, "Who is this man that will save us?" and they hated him, and brought him no gifts.

# 1ˢᵗ Kingdoms: Chapter 10 Notes

**1** Codex Vaticanus: Nasib o allophylos (ΝΑϹΙΒΟΑΛΛΟΦΥΛΟϹ). Translation: Nasib the foreigner

• LXX 489: Nasim ho allophylos (Νασϭιμ ο ἀλλϡϕυλοc). Translation: Nasim the foreigner

• LXX 52: Nasêm ho allophylos (Νασῑμ ο ἀλλϡϕυλοc). Translation: Nasem the foreigner

• LXX 246: Asim ho allophylos (Ασϭιμ ο ἀλλϡϕυλοc). Translation: Asim the foreigner

• LXX 82: Nasiph ho allophylos (Νασϭιϸ ο ἀλλϡϕυλοc). Translation: Nasiph the foreigner

• LXX 19: Nassib ho allophylos (Νασσιμ ο ἀλλϡϕυλοc). Translation: Nassib the foreigner

• LXX 245: Asib ho allophylos (Ασιμ ο ἀλλϡϕυλοc). Translation: Asib the foreigner

• Aleppo Codex: nsby plštym (נצבי פלשתים). Translation: commanders of the Pelesets (or Palestinians)

• Leningrad Codex: netzivei Pelishtim (וְנִצְבֵי פְלִשְׁתִּים). Translation: commanders of the Pelesets (or Palestinians)

• Targum Jerusalem: istartinei Felishta'ei (אִסְטְרַטִינֵי פְלִשְׁתָּאֵי). Translation: soldiers of Pelesets

As the Greeks appear to have transliterated the Aramaic word for 'commanders' the Aramaic term is translated directly in this translation.


**2** Codex Vaticanus: pneuma c̄u (ΠΝΕΥΜΑΚῩ). Translation: air (or breath, spirit, wind) lord

• Aleppo Codex: rwh yhwh (רוח יהוה). Translation: wind (or spirit, wind) Yhwh

- Leningrad Codex: ruach Yehvah (רוּחַ יְהוָֹה). Translation: wind (or spirit, wind) Yehwah

- Targum Jerusalem: Yeyah (??). Translation: Yahw

# 1ˢᵗ Kingdoms: Chapter 11

About a month after this, Nahash the Ammonite[1] went up and laid siege to Jabesh in Gilead, and all the Jabeshites said to Nahash the Ammonite, "Make a covenant with us, and we will serve you."

Nahash the Ammonite said to them, "I will make a covenant with you on these terms. I will cut out all your right eyes, and I will lay a reproach on Israel."

The men of Jabin said to him, "Allow us seven days, and we will send messengers to all the frontiers of Israel. If there should be no one to save us, we will come out to you."

The messengers came to Saul in Gibeah, and they spoke words into the ears of the people, and all the people raised their voices and cried. Saul came out of the field late in the morning, and asked, "Why do the people cry?" and they told him the words of the Jabeshites. The spirit of God came on Saul when he heard these words, and his anger was great against them. He took two cows, and cut them in pieces, and sent them into all the frontiers of Israel in the hands of messengers, saying, "Whoever does not follow after Saul and Samuel, they will do this to his oxen!"

The ecstasy of the Lord came over the people of Israel, and they came out to battle as one man. He reviewed them from the bamah at Bezek, every man of Israel numbering 600,000, and another 70,000 from Judah. He told the messengers that came, "Go tell the Jabeshites, 'Tomorrow you'll have deliverance when the sun is hot,' and the messengers returned to the city and told the Jabeshites, and they celebrated.

The Jabeshites said to Nahash the Ammonite, 'Tomorrow we will come out to you, and you can do to us whatever you think is right."

In the morning, Saul divided the people into three companies, and they went into the middle of the camp in the morning watch, and they slaughtered the Ammonites until the day was hot. Those who were left were scattered and there was not left among them two together. The people said to Samuel, "Who has said that Saul will not reign over us? Give up the men, and we will put them to death."

Saul replied, "No man will die today, as today the Lord has worked deliverance in Israel."

Samuel said the people, "Let us go to the stone circle, and renew the kingdom there."

All the people went to the stone circle, and Samuel anointed Saul there to be king before the Lord in the stone circle, and there he offered meat-offerings and peace-offerings before the Lord, and Samuel and all Israel celebrated.

# 1ˢᵗ Kingdoms: Chapter 11 Notes

**1** Codex Vaticanus: Ammanitês (ΑΜΜΑΝΙΤΗϹ)

- Codex Alexandrinus: Amanitês (ΑΜΑΝΙΤΗϹ)

- LXX 52: Thamanitês (ΘΑμΑΝϕΤλϹ)

- LXX 245: Manitês (ΜΑΝϕΤλϹ)

- Aleppo Codex: Ômwn (עָמוֹן)

- Leningrad Codex: Ammon (עָמֹון)

- Targum Jerusalem: Amon (עָמֹון)

Ammonites are people from the land of Amman, which is today the capital city of the Kingdom of Jordan. Ammonites are called descendants of Esau in the Torah.

# 1st Kingdoms: Chapter 12

Samuel said to all Israel, "Look, I have listened to your voice and all the things that you have said to me, and I have set a king over you. Now, look, the king leads you, and I have grown old and will rest, and see, my sons are among you. I have led you from my youth until today. Here I am, report against me before the Lord and his anointed, whose calf have I taken? Whose donkey have I taken? Who among you have I oppressed? From whose hand have I taken a bribe, or even a sandal? Witness against me, and I will make restitution to you."

They replied to Samuel, "You have not injured us, and you have not oppressed us. You have not afflicted us, and you have not taken anything from anyone's hand."

Samuel said to the people, "The Lord is a witness among you, and our witness today that you have not found anything in my hand."

They answered, "He is a witness."

Samuel said to the people, "The Lord, who appointed Moses and Aaron is witness, who brought our fathers up out of Egypt. Now stand still, and I will judge you before the Lord, and I will tell you all the righteousness of the Lord, the things which he has worked among you and your fathers. When Jacob and his sons went into Egypt, and Egypt humbled them, then our fathers cried to the Lord, and the Lord sent Moses and Aaron, and they brought our fathers out of Egypt and made them live in this place."

"They forgot Lord the god, and he sold them into the hands of Sisera captain of the army and King Jabin in Hazor, and the hands of the Pelesets, and into the hands of the king of Moab, and he fought with them. They cried to the Lord, 'We have sinned, for we have forgotten the Lord, and have served the Lords and the Ashteroth. Now deliver us out of the hand of our enemies, and we will serve you.' He sent Jerubbaal, Barak, Jephthah, and Samuel, and rescued us out of the hands of our enemies all around, and you lived in security. You saw that Nahash king of the Ammonites came against you, and you said, 'No! None but a king will reign over us,' yet Lord the god was your king."

"Now look to the king who you have chosen, and see, the Lord has set a king over you. If you should fear the Lord, and serve him, and listen to his voice, and not resist the word of the Lord, and you and your king that reign over you should follow the Lord. But if you should not listen to the voice of the Lord, and you should resist the word of the Lord, then the hand of the Lord will be against you and on your king. Now stand still, and see this great thing, which the Lord will do before your eyes. Is it not wheat harvest today? I will call on the Lord, and he will send thunder and rain, and you will see, that your wickedness is great which you have worked before the Lord, having asked for a king for yourselves. Samuel called on the Lord, and the Lord sent thunders and rain on that day, and all the people were afraid of the Lord and Samuel. All the people said to Samuel, "Pray for your servants to Lord God, and don't let us die, as we have added to all our sins this iniquity, in asking for us a king."

Samuel said to the people, "Don't be afraid, you have indeed worked all this iniquity. Only don't turn from following the Lord, and serve the Lord with all your heart. Don't follow after the gods that are nothing, who will do nothing, and will not deliver you, because they are nothing. The Lord will not throw away his people for his great name's sake, because the Lord graciously took you to himself as a people. Far be it from me to sin against the

Lord in ceasing to pray for you. I will serve the Lord, and show you the good and the right way. Only fear the Lord, and serve him in truth and with all your heart, for you see what great things he has worked with you, if you continue to do evil, then you and your king will be consumed.

# 1st Kingdoms: Chapter 13

Saul chose for himself three thousand Israelites. There were with Saul two thousand who were from Michmash and the Mountain of the Temple of El, and a thousand were with Jonathan in Gibeah of Benjamin, and he sent the rest of the people everyone back to his own tent. Jonathan attacked the commander of the Pelesets that lived in the hills, and the Pelesets heard of it, and Saul sounded the trumpet through all the land, saying, "Break your word slaves!"[1]

All Israel was heard to say, "Saul has killed the commander of the Pelesets! Until now Israel has been put to shame before the Pelesets," and the Israelites went up to Saul in the stone circle.

The Pelesets gathered together to make war against Israel and came up against Israel with 30,000 chariots, 6,000 cavalry, and people as numerous as the sand of the seashore. They come up, and camped in Michmash, south of the Temple of Horon.[2] The Israelites saw that they were in trouble and that they could not approach, and the people hid in caves, sheepfolds, rocks, ditches, and pits. They who crossed the Jordan to the land of Gad and Gilead. Saul remained in the stone circle, and all the people watched him in amazement. He continued seven days for the appointed testimony, as Samuel told him, and Samuel did not come to the stone circle, and his people were dispersed from him. Saul said, "Bring me, victims, that I may offer whole burnt offerings and peace-offerings," and he offered the whole burnt offering.

When he had finished offering the whole burnt offering Samuel arrived, and Saul went out to meet him, and to bless him, but Samuel asked, "What have you done?"

Saul answered, "I saw how the people were scattered from me, and you did not arrive on the day you said you were coming, and the Pelesets were gathered at Michmash. I wondered, 'Will the Pelesets come down to meet me at the stone circle now? I have not sacrificed before the Lord yet! So I made myself do it and offered the whole burnt offering."

Samuel rebuked Saul, "You have done foolishly! You have not kept my command, which the Lord commanded you, or by now the Lord would have confirmed your kingdom over Israel forever. But now your kingdom will not stay with you, and the Lord will seek for himself a man after his own heart, and the Lord will appoint him to be a ruler over his people because you have not kept all that the Lord commanded you."

Samuel rose and left the stone circle, and the remnant of the people went with Saul to meet him with the soldiers when they come out of the stone circle to Gibeah of Benjamin. Saul counted the people who were found with him, about six hundred men. Saul and Jonathan his son, and the people who were found with them stopped in Gibeah of Benjamin, and they cried. The Pelesets had camped in Michmash. Men came out to destroy the land of the Pelesets in three companies, one company turning on the road at Ophrah towards the land of Shual, and another company turning on the road at the Temple of An, and another company turning on the road of Gibeah that turned aside to Ai of Zeboim.

There was not found a blacksmith in all the land of Israel, as the Pelesets said, "In case the Hebrews make themselves swords or spears."

All Israel went down to the land of the Pelesets to forge, every one with his reaping-hook and his tools, and everyone with his ax and his sickle. It was near the time of vintage, and their tools were valued at three shekels per plowshare, and there was the same rate for the ax and the sickle. It came to pass in the days of the war of Michmash, that there was neither a sword nor spear found in the hand of all the people, that were with Saul and Jonathan, except Saul and Jonathan his son. Some of the Pelesets went out of their camps to the place beyond Michmash.

# 1st Kingdoms: Chapter 13 Notes

**1** Codex Vaticanus: êthetêcasin oe douloe (ΗΘΕΤΗΚΑϹΙΝΟΙ ΔΟΥΛΟΙ). Translation: break trust (or your word) slave

• LXX 19: êthetêcasan hoe douloe (ἠθέτρμλσᾶν οι Δουλοι). Translation: break trust (or your word) slave

• Aleppo Codex: yšmôw hÔbrym (**יִשְׁמְעוּ הָעִבְרִים**). Translation: listen the Hebrews

• Leningrad Codex: yishme'u ha'Ivrim (יִשְׁמְעוּ הָעִבְרִים). Translation: listen the Hebrews

• Targum Jerusalem: yishme'un Yehuda'ei (יִשְׁמְעוּן יְהוּדָאֵי). Translation: listen Judahites

In the Greek translation from before the Hasmonean dynasty, Saul was calling on the Palestinians' slaves to revolt, however, the Hasmoneans redacted that line as slaves were one of Judea's major exports during the Hasmonean dynasty.


**2** Codex Vaticanus: Baethôrôn (ΒΑΙΘΩΡΩΝ)

• Codex Alexandrinus: Baethôn (ΒΑΙΘΩΝ)

• LXX 707: Baethôrnôn (βαιθωρνοον)

• LXX 52: Baethôron (βαιθωρον)

• LXX 92: Baethorôn (βαιθορων)

• LXX 56: Bethôrôn (βεθωρων)

• LXX 509: Bethaerôn (βεθαιρων)

• LXX 158: Baethôrrhôn (βαιθωρρων)

• LXX 376: Bethôr (βεθωρ)

• Aleppo Codex: Byt Åwn (**בית און**). Translation: Temple (or House) of

Awn

• Leningrad Codex: beit Aven (בֵּית אָוֶן). Translation: Temple (or House) of Aven

• Targum Jerusalem: beit Aven (בֵּית אָוֶן). Translation: Temple (or House) of Aven

The various Septuagint manuscripts vary at this point, with the majority including a variation of a Greek translation of Bet Horon (Βαιθωρων, Βαιθωρον, Βαιθορων, Βεθωρων, Βεθαιρων, Βεθωρ, Βαιθωρρων, or Βαιθωρνων), which indicates that the Aramaic version of the texts must have read Bet Horon. A large minority of the manuscripts follow the Greek translation of Bet Awen (Βαιθων) found in the Masoretic text, however, this almost certainty resulted from attempts to 'correct' the Greek by synchronizing it with the Hebrew in the late Classical era.

Both Bet Horon and Bet Awen were mentioned in various Israelite texts, and both have been identified in the region around Ramallah, in the modern Palestinian West Bank, which is approximately 10 km (6 miles) north of Jerusalem. Beth Horon has been identified as the twin villages of Beit Ur al-Fauqa and Beit Ur al-Tahta, 11 and 14 km (7 and 9 miles) west of Ramallah, while Bet Awen, continues to be the name of the Palestinian village of Beitin (بيتين), 5 km (3 miles) northeast of Ramallah. Beitin has been identified as the site of ancient Bet El, indicating that the name was changed from Bet El to Bet Awen at some point, likely during the era of the prophet Hosea, who mentioned them together in the 8th century BC. The shift likely took place as a result of the Assyrians occupying the region, as the Neo-Assyrian translation of the Canaanite word El (𐎛𐎍) was An (𐎀𐎐).

This suggests that an early Samaritan book of Samuel or Saul used the name Bet El, which the Judahite scribes updated to Bet Awen, while the Aramaic translators replaced with Bet Horon. Both Beitin and Beit Ur al-Tahta existed at the time, however, Beit Ur al-Fauqa (Upper Bet Horon) was apparently founded by Solomon several decades later. Bet Horon was mentioned in Egyptian records from the era this story is set in, as Båtå Ḥwårwn (𓂺𓆓𓈖𓉐 𓆑𓈖𓃭𓈖𓏲𓈗), proving the town was known by that name at the time, however, the name of Beitin in the era is unclear; Cosmic Genesis claims it was known as Luz before being renamed Bet El, while the Book of Joshua claims Luz was near Bet El. The town probably was not commonly known as Bet Awen until the late 8ᵗʰ century BC or later, suggesting it was known as Bet El at the time of Saul.

The substitution of Bet Horon for Bet El likely took place in the aftermath of the Assyrian war against Samaria, when the city of Bet El was destroyed, while the Judahite city of Bet Horon survived. Later the city was rebuilt by Assyria as Bet Awen, suggesting the Judahite update took place after the Aramaic translation. It the Judahite book of Samuel was updated at the same time as Cosmic Genesis, it would have been in the late 8ᵗʰ century, during the reign of King Hezekiah.

# 1st Kingdoms: Chapter 14

On a certain day, Jonathan the son of Saul said to the young man that carried his armor, "Come and let's go to the commander of the Pelesets who is over there," but did not tell his father.

Saul sat on the top of the hill under the pomegranate tree that is in Migron, and there were about six hundred men with him. Ahiah son of Ahitub, the brother of Ichabod the son of Phinehas, the son of Eli, was the priest of God in Shiloh wearing a vest, and the people did not know that Jonathan was gone. Along the passage that Jonathan wanted to pass over to the encampment of the Pelesets, there were sharp rocks on both sides. The name of the one was Bozez and the name of the other Seneh. The one road ran north to Michmash, and the other road ran south to Gibeah. Jonathan said to the young man that carried his armor, "Come, let us go to the garrison of these uncircumcised, and perhaps the Lord may do something for us, as the Lord is not restricted to save by many or by few."

His armor-bearer replied to him, "Do all that your heart wants. I am with you, my heart is like your heart."

Jonathan said, "Look, we will go over to the men, and will come down suddenly on them. If they should say to us, 'Stand over there until we send you word,' then we will remain still by ourselves, and will not go up against them. But if they should say to us, 'Come up to us,' then we will go up, for the Lord has given them into our hands. This will be a sign for us."

They both went to the commander of the Pelesets and the Pelesets said, "Look, the Hebrews come out of their caves, where they were hiding."

The men of the garrison called to Jonathan and his armor bearer, and said, "Come up to us, and we will show you something."

Jonathan said to his armor bearer, "Come up with me, for the Lord has delivered them into the hands of Israel."

Jonathan and his armor bearer sneaked up on their hands and feet. They saw the face of Jonathan, and he attacked them along with his armor bearer. They slaughtered twenty men with arrows and slings, and there was dismay in the camp and the field. All the people in the garrison and the destroyers were amazed. They could not act as the earth quaked, and there was panic sent from God.

The watchmen of Saul saw from Gibeah in Benjamin, that the army was thrown into confusion on every side. Saul said to the people with him, "Count yourselves now, and see who has gone out from you," and they counted themselves, and found Jonathan and his armor bearer were missing. Saul said to Ahiah, "Bring the vest," as he wore a vest in those days before Israel. While Saul was speaking to the priest, the sound in the camp of the Pelesets continued to increase greatly, and Saul said to the priest, "Withdraw your hands."

Saul went up and all the people who were with him, and they came to the battle and found every man's sword was against his neighbor, a complete confusion. The slaves who had previously been with the Pelesets, who had been forced into the army switched sides to the Israelites who were with Saul and Jonathan. All the Israelites who were hidden in Mount Ephraim heard also that the Pelesets fled, and they also gather themselves after them to battle. The Lord saved Israel on that day, and the war passed by the Temple of An, and all the people with Saul were about ten thousand men. The battle extended itself to every city in the Mountains of Ephraim. Saul committed a great trespass of ignorance in that day, and he laid a curse on the people, saying, "Cursed is the man who will eat bread before the evening, because I will avenge myself on my enemy," and none of the people tasted bread, though all the land was dining.

Jaal was a forest abounding in swarms of bees covering the ground. The people went into the place of the bees, and they continued speaking, and none put his hand to his mouth, as the people were afraid of the oath of the Lord. Jonathan had not heard when his father cursed the people, and he reached out to the end of the staff that was in his hand, and dipped it into the honeycomb, and returned his hand to his mouth, and looked up with his eyes.

One of the people said, "Your father solemnly cursed the people, saying, 'Cursed is the man who will eat bread today.'"

The people were very hungry, and Jonathan knew it, and said, "My father has destroyed the land, see how my eyes have received sight now that I have tasted a little of this honey. Certainly, if the people had today eaten freely of the spoils of their enemies which they found, the slaughter among the Pelesets would have been greater!"

On that day he slaughtered some of the Pelesets in Michmash and the people were very tired. The people turned to plunder and took flocks, and herds, and killed calves on the ground, and the people ate with the blood. It was reported to Saul, "The people have sinned against the Lord, eating with the blood."

Saul said, "Roll a great stone to me here from Getthaim. Disperse yourselves among the people, and tell them each to bring a calf here, and a sheep, and let them kill it on this stone and not sin against the Lord in eating with the blood."

The people brought each one that which he had, and they killed them there. Saul built an altar there to the Lord. This was the first altar that Saul built to the Lord. Saul said, "Let us go down after the Pelesets this night, and let us maraud among them until the daybreak, and let's not spare a man among them."

They said, "Do all that is good in your sight."

The priest said, "Let's consult God."

Saul inquired of God, "If I go down after the Pelesets, will you deliver them into the hands of Israel?"

He did not answer him that day, and so Saul said, "Bring all the chiefs of Israel here, and know and see who has committed this sin today. As the Lord lives, who has saved Israel, if the answer should be against my son Jonathan, he will certainly die."

No one answered out of all the people, and he said to all the Israelites, "You will be under subjection, and I and Jonathan my son will be under subjection, and the people said to Saul, "Do that which is good in your sight."

Saul asked, "Lord the god of Israel, why have you not answered your servant today? Is the iniquity in me, or Jonathan my son? Lord the god of Israel, give clear manifestations. If the lot should declare this, I beg you, give to your people of Israel, I pray, give holiness."

Jonathan and Saul were set aside, and the people escaped. Saul said, "Cast lots between me and my son Jonathan, whoever the Lord will cause to be taken by lot, let him die."

The people said to Saul, "This cannot be done!"

Saul prevailed against the people, and they cast lots between him and Jonathan his son, and Jonathan was chosen by lot, and Saul asked Jonathan, "Tell me what you have done?"

Jonathan told him, "I did indeed taste a little honey, with the end of the staff that was in my hand. So am I to die?"

Saul said to him, "God do so to me, and more also, you will certainly die today!"

The people said to Saul, "Will he who has worked this great salvation for Israel be put to death today? As the Lord lives, there will not fall to the ground one of the hairs of his head! The people of God have worked successfully today!"

The people prayed for Jonathan that day, and he did not die. Saul chased the Pelesets, and the Pelesets departed to their homes. Saul received the kingdom, and by lot he inherited the office of ruling over Israel. He fought against all his enemies around it, against Moab, Amman, Edom, the House of Eor, Zobah, and against the Pelesets. Wherever he went, he was victorious. He valiantly slaughtered, and killed the Amalekites, and saved Israel out of the hand of those that trampled on them.

The sons of Saul were Jonathan, Ishwi,[1] Malchi-shua, (Ishbaal, Melchizedek, and Iesioud)[2] and the names of his two daughters were Merab the firstborn, and Michal the second born. The name of his wife was Ahinoam, the daughter of Ahimaaz. The name of the captain of his army was Abner, the son of Ner, son of a relative of Saul. Kish was the father of Saul, and Ner, the father of Abner, the Benjaminite, son of Abiel. The war was vehement against the Pelesets all the days of Saul, and when Saul saw any mighty man and any valiant man, then he recruited them for himself.

# 1ˢᵗ Kingdoms: Chapter 14 Notes

**1** Codex Vaticanus: Iessioul (ιεccιOΥⲗ)

- Codex Alexandrinus: Isoui (ιⲥOΥι)

- Codex Basiliano-Vaticanus: Iessoui (ιεccOΥι)

- LXX 19: Iessiou (ιϬϭϭιου)

- LXX 509: Iessioud (ιϬϭϭιουⲗ)

- LXX 554: Iesioud (ιϬϭιουⲗ)

- LXX 82: Iessêou (ιϬϭϭλου)

- LXX 245: Iesoui (ιϬϭουι)

- LXX 314: Iessou (ιϬϭϭου)

- LXX 52: Iesou (ιϬϭου)

- LXX 158: Esoui (Εϭουι)

- LXX 107: Iêsoui (ιλϭουι)

- LXX 71: Iasour (ιⲗϭουβ̰)

- LXX 74: Iêsoue (ιλϭουϬ)

- Aleppo Codex: Yšwy (יִשְׁוִי)

- Leningrad Codex: Yishvi (יִשְׁוִי)

- Targum Jerusalem: Yishvi (יִשְׁוִי)

The name of this son of Saul has different names in different Hebrew texts, including Ish-bosheth (אִישְׁבֹּשֶׁת), Ish-baal (אֶשְׁבַּעַל), implying it was redacted several times. The version found in the Codex Vaticanus suggests the Aramaic translator used the name Ishwi-El. As the Greek translations disagree, a transliteration of Yšwy (יִשְׁוִי), Ishwi is used in this translation.

**2** Codex Vaticanus: Melchisa (ⲙⲉⲗⲭⲓⲥⲁ)

- Codex Alexandrinus: Melchisoue (ⲙⲉⲗⲭⲓⲥⲟⲩⲉ)

- Basiliano-Vaticanus: Melchosoue (ⲙⲉⲗⲭⲟⲥⲟⲩⲉ)

- LXX 19: Melchiseddi cae Eisbaal (Μόλχισόδδι ⳤδι Εισυλλλ). Translation: Melchiseddi and Eisbaal

- LXX 52: Melisa cae Iesbaal (Μόλισδ ⳤδι ιόσυλλλ). Translation: Melisa and Iesbaal

- LXX 509: Melchisad (Μόλχισδδ)

- LXX 376: Melchisoue cae Iesphal (Μόλχισουό ⳤδι ιόσ$δλ). Translation: Melchisoue and Iesphal

- LXX 158: Melchisoue cae Isbaal (Μόλχισουό ⳤδι ιουλλλ). Translation: Melchisoue and Isbaal

- LXX 121: Melchisa cae Iesphaal (Μόλχισδ ⳤδι ιόσ$δλλ). Translation: Melchisa and Iesphaal

- LXX 127: Melchisedde cae Eisbaal (Μόλχισόδδό ⳤδι Εισυλλλ). Translation: Melchisoue and Iesphal

- LXX 544: Melchisedec cae Eisbaan cae Iêsoui cae Melchisoue (Μόλχισόδόⳤ ⳤδι Εισυλλν ⳤδι ιℏσουι ⳤδι Μόλχισουό). Translation: Melchisedec and Eisbaan and Iêsoui and Melchisoue

- Septuagint ms. 44: Melchisoni (Μόλχισονι)

- Dead Sea Scroll 4QSamª: Mlkyšô (מלכישׁ). Translation: my king ascends (in Aramaic)

- Aleppo Codex: Mlkyšwô (מלכישוע). Translation: My king helps

- Leningrad Codex: Malki-shua' (מַלְכִּי־שׁוּעַ). Translation: My-king-helps

- Targum Jerusalem: Malkishua' (מַלְכִּישׁוּעַ). Translation: My-king-helps

The various Hebrew forms of the first name are generally anglicized as: Malchi-shua. As the Greek transliterations appear to be based on the Hebrew (or Aramaic) name, the name is rendered as Malchi-shua. The transliteration in the Codex Vaticanus appears to be a transliteration of the Aramaic variation of the name found in Hebrew language Dead Sea Scroll 4QSamᵃ, suggesting that the name may have originally been Aramaic, not Canaanite. An alternate interpretation, is that this section of the Judahite version of Samuel was based on an Aramaic translation, which would also help explain the variations of the name of Malchi-shua brother Ishwi's name.

Many Greek versions of the verse include a second name, which as transliterations of Eshbaal (אֶשְׁבַּעַל), who was also listed as a son of Saul in 1ˢᵗ Paralipomenon (Masoretic Dīvrē-hayYāmīm), in chapters 8 and 9. Manuscript 554 also includes the names of two other sons, Melchizedek and Iesioud, while 1ˢᵗ Paralipomenon mentions another son named Abinadab. As the name lists are not consistent, the additional names are listed in parentheses.

# 1st Kingdoms: Chapter 15

Samuel said to Saul, "The Lord sent me to anoint you king over Israel, and now hear the voice of the Lord. Lord Sabaoth said, 'Now I will take vengeance for what Amalek did to Israel when he met him along the road as he came up out of Egypt.' Now go, and you will slaughter Amalek and Hermon[1] and all that belongs to them. You will not leave anything alive, you will completely destroy them, and you will devote them and all their property to destruction, and you will spare nothing that belonged to him. You will kill both man and woman, and infant and toddler, and calf and sheep, and camel and donkey."

Saul summoned the people, and he counted them in the circle, 400,000 regular troops, and from Judah 30,000 regular troops. Saul came to the cities of Amalek and laid wait in the valley. Saul said to the blacksmiths,[2] "Go, withdraw from among the Amalekites, or I'll consider you with them, for you dealt mercifully with the Israelites when they left of Egypt."

So the blacksmiths departed from among the Amalekites, and Saul slaughtered Amalek from Havilah to Shur bordering Egypt. He took Agag the king of Amalek alive, and he killed all the people and confiscated with the edge of the sword. Saul and all the people left Agag alive, and the best of the flocks, and the herds, and of the fruits, of the vineyards, and all the good things, and they would not destroy them, but every worthless and garbage thing they destroyed. The word of the Lord came to Samuel, saying, "I regret that I have made Saul the king, as he has turned away from following me, and has not followed my orders."

Samuel was saddened and cried to the Lord all night. Samuel rose early and went to meet Israel in the morning, and Saul was told, "Samuel has come to Carmel, and he has raised help for himself, and he turned his chariot," and came down to the stone circle to Saul, and look, he was offering up a whole burnt offering to the Lord, the chief of the spoils which he brought out of Amalek.

Samuel came to Saul, and Saul said to him, "Blessed are you of the Lord. I have performed all that the Lord commanded."

Samuel asked, "What then is the bleating of this flock in my ears, and the sound of the oxen which I hear?"

Saul answered, "I have brought them out of Amalek, that which the people saved, including the best of the sheep and other livestock, so they might be sacrificed to the Lord your god, and the rest I have destroyed."

Samuel said to Saul, "Stay, and I will tell you what the Lord says to me this night."

He replied to him, "Continue speaking."

Samuel asked Saul, "Were you not small in his eyes, though a leader of one of the tribes of Israel? Yet the Lord anointed you to be king over Israel. The Lord sent you on a journey, and said to you, 'Go and destroy. You will kill the sinners against me, all the Amalekites, and you will war against them until you have consumed them.' Why didn't you listen to the voice of the Lord, but rushed to take plunder, and did that which was evil in the sight of the Lord?"

Saul answered Samuel, "Because I listened to the voice of the people. Yet I followed the path that the Lord sent me, and I captured Agag the king of Amalek, and I destroyed Amalek. But the people took plunder from the best flocks and herds out of that which was destroyed, to sacrifice before the Lord our god in the stone circle."

Samuel said, "Does the Lord take as much pleasure in whole burnt offerings and sacrifices, as in following the words of the Lord? Look, obedience is better than a good sacrifice, and listening than the fat of rams. For sin is like divination, and idols bring on pain and grief. Because you have rejected the word of the Lord, the Lord also will reject you from being king over Israel."

Saul said to Samuel, "I have sinned, in that I have transgressed the word of the Lord and your orders, as I was afraid of the people and I listened to their voice. Now, I beg you, remove my sin, and return with me, and I will worship Lord your god."

Samuel said to Saul, "I will not return with you, for you have rejected the word of the Lord, and the Lord will reject you from being king over Israel."

Samuel turned his face to leave, and Saul caught hold of his skirt and tore it. Samuel said to him, "The Lord has torn your kingdom of Israel out of your hand today, and will give it to your neighbor who is better than you. And Israel will be divided into two, and God will not turn nor repent, for he is not like a man to repent."

Saul said, "I have sinned, yet honor me, I beg you, before the elders of Israel, and before my people, and return with me, and I will worship the Lord your god."

So Samuel returned with Saul, and he worshiped the Lord. Samuel said, "Bring me Agag the king of Amalek," and Agag came to him trembling.

Agag asked, "Is death this bitter?"

Samuel answered Agag, "As your sword has bereaved women of their children, so will your mother be made childless among women," and Samuel killed Agag before the Lord in the stone circle. Samuel departed to Armathaem, and Saul went up to his house at Gibeah. Samuel did not see Saul again until the day of his death, for Samuel mourned after Saul, and the Lord regretted that he had made Saul king over Israel.

# 1st Kingdoms: Chapter 15 Notes

**1** Codex Vaticanus: cae Ierim cae (ΚΛΙΙΕΡΙΜΚΛΙ). Translation: and Ierim and

• Codex Alexandrinus: cae Ieerim cae (ΚΛΙΙΕΕΡΙΜΚΛΙ). Translation: and Ieerim and

• Basiliano-Vaticanus: cae Iarim cae (ΚΛΙΙΑΡΙΜΚΛΙ). Translation: and Iarim and

• LXX 121: cae Erim cae (ιιλι εℓιμ ιιλι). Translation: and Erim and

• LXX 52: cae Iarem cae (ιιλι ιλℓ6μ ιιλι). Translation: and Iarem and

• LXX 707: cae Iarin cae (ιιλι ιλℓιν ιιλι). Translation: and Iarin and

• Aleppo Codex: whhrmtm (וְהַחֲרַמְתֶּם). Translation: 'and then consecrate completely'

• Leningrad Codex: vehacharamtem (וְהַחֲרַמְתֶּם). Translation: 'and then consecrate completely'

• Targum Jerusalem: utegamar (וּתְגָמַר). Translation: and finish

This verse has been translated several ways over the millennia. The common medieval translation of 'finish,' as found in the Targum Jerusalem is still the common interpretation, as reflected in the King James bible's 'and utterly destroy.' The Greek translators instead viewed this as a reference to another group of people, with variations of the name including Ierim (Ιεριμ), Ieerim (Ιεεριμ), Erim (Εριμ), Iarim (Ιαριμ), Iarem (Ιαρεμ), and Iarin (Ιαριν). The Greek variations indicate that at least some of the Aramaic translations used a variant of this name, and that it was missing the final syllable found in the Masoretic text, the tm (תם). This suggests that the Aramaic translator viewed the tm (𐤉𐤕) in the old Samaritan text as an equivalent of the Assyrian tum (𒌈) and Babylonian tum (𒌈), used in Eastern Semitic plural forms, and therefore dropped it, as was common when translating from east Semitic languages to Aramaic.

If so, the original Samaritan word would have been something that could be read as the plural form of Hrm (חרמ), which in Hebrew would be Hrmwn (חרמון), the name Mount Hermon.

**2** Codex Vaticanus: cinaeon (ΚΙΝΑΙΟΝ)

• LXX 19: Cinnaeon (Κιννᾱιον)

• Aleppo Codex: qyny (קיני)

• Leningrad Codex: keini (קֵינִי)

• Targum Jerusalem: Shalma'ah (שְׁלְמָאָה). Translation: Shalmaite (an Arab tribe)

This appears to be an alternate transliteration of kayin (קַיִן), meaning blacksmith.

# 1st Kingdoms: Chapter 16

The Lord asked Samuel, "How long will you mourn for Saul when I have rejected him from reigning over Israel? Fill your horn with oil, and come, I will send you to Jesse in the House of Lehem,[1] for I have seen a king for me among his sons."

Samuel said, "How can I go? If Saul hears of it, he'll kill me."

The Lord said, "Take a heifer in your hand say, 'I am coming to sacrifice to the Lord.' You will call Jesse to the sacrifice, and I will tell you what you will do. You will anoint him who I indicate to you."

Samuel did all that the Lord told him, and he came to the House of Lehem. The elders of the city were amazed at meeting him, and asked, "Do you come peaceably, you Seer?"

He answered, "Peaceably. I have come to sacrifice to the Lord. Sanctify yourselves, and rejoice with me today, and he sanctified Jesse and his sons, and he called them to the sacrifice. When they came in, he saw Eliab and said, "Certainly the Lord's anointed is before him."

But the Lord said to Samuel, "Look not at his appearance, or at his height, as I have rejected him. God does not see like a man, because man looks at the outward appearance, but the Lord looks at the heart."

Jesse called Aminadab, and he passed before Samuel, and he said, "God has not chosen this one either."

Jesse had Sama pass by, and he said, "God has not chosen this one either."

Jesse had his seven sons pass before Samuel, and Samuel said, "The Lord has not chosen these."

Samuel asked Jesse, "Have you no more sons?"

Jesse answered, "There is a little one, but he is tending the flock."

Samuel said to Jesse, "Send and fetch him as we may not sit down until he comes."

He sent and fetched him, and he was red-haired, with beautiful eyes, and very good looking. The Lord said to Samuel, "Rise and anoint David, for he is good."

Samuel took the horn of oil and anointed him among his brothers, and the spirit of the Lord came over David from that day forward. Samuel rose and departed to Armathaem. The spirit of the Lord departed from Saul, and an evil spirit from the Lord tormented him. Saul's servants said to him, "See now, an evil spirit from God torments you. Let now your servants speak before you and let them seek for our lord a man skilled to play on the harp, and it will come to pass when an evil spirit comes on you and he will play on his harp, that you will be well, and he will refresh you."

Saul said to his servants, "Look for a skillful player for me, and bring him to me."

One of his servants answered and said, "I have seen a son of Jesse the Bethlehemite, and he understands playing the harp, and the man is prudent, and a warrior, and wise in speech, and the man is handsome, and the Lord is with him."

Saul sent messengers to Jesse, saying, "Send to me your son David who is with your flock."

Jesse took bread, and a bottle of wine, and one goat kid, and sent them by the hand of his son David to Saul. David went to Saul and stood before him, and he loved him greatly and he became his armor bearer. Saul sent word to Jesse, "Let David, I beg you, stay with me, for he has found grace in my eyes."

When the spirit of God was on Saul, David took his harp and played with his hand, and Saul was refreshed, and it was well with him, and the evil spirit departed from him.

# 1<sup>st</sup> Kingdoms: Chapter 16 Note

**1** Codex Vaticanus: Iessae eôs is Bêthleem (ιⲉⲥⲥⲀιⲉⲱⲥⲉιⲥ ⲃⲏⲐⲗⲉⲉⲙ). Translation: Iessae who was in Bethlehem

• LXX 19: heôs Bêthleem pros Iessae (ϭⲱⲥ ⲃⲗⲑⲗϭϭμ πϱⲟⲥ ιϭⲟⲟⲀι). Translation: until Bethlehem near Iessae

• LXX 92: Iesae heôs Bêthleem (ιϭⲟⲀι ϭⲱⲥ ⲃⲗⲑⲗϭϭμ). Translation: Iesae who was Bethlehem

• LXX 376: Iessae heôs is Bithleem (ιϭⲟⲟⲀι ϭⲱⲥ ϭιⲥ ⲃιⲑⲗϭϭμ). Translation: Iessae who was in Bethlehem

• Aleppo Codex: yšy byt hlhmy (יִשַׁי בֵּית הלחמי). Translation: Yisay from House (or Temple) of the Lahem

• Leningrad Codex: Yishai beit-hallachmi (יִשַׁי בֵּית־הַלַּחְמִי). Translation: Yisay from House (or Temple) of the Lahem

• Targum Jerusalem: Yishai demibbeit Lechem (יִשַׁי דְּמִבֵּית לֶחֶם). Translation: Yasay who was from House (or Temple) of the Lahem

# 1st Kingdoms: Chapter 17

The Pelesets gathered their armies for battle and assembled themselves at Sochoh in Judea, and camped between Sochoh and Azekah in Ephes Dammim. Saul and the Israelites gathered together, and they camped in the valley and set the battle formation against the Pelesets. The Pelesets positioned themselves on the mountain to one side, and Israel positioned themselves on the mountain to the other side, with the valley between them. A mighty man came out from the army of the Pelesets named Goliath, who was from Gath. He was four cubits[1] and a half[2] tall.[3] He had a helmet on his head, and he wore a breastplate of chain armor. The weight of his breastplate was five thousand shekels[4] of brass and iron. He wore brass armor on his legs, and a bronze shield was between his shoulders. The staff of his spear was like a weaver's beam, and the spear's head was made of six hundred shekels of iron.[5] His armor bearer went ahead of him.

He stood and shouted to the army of Israel, "Why have you come out and set yourselves in battle formation against us? Am not I a Peleset, and you Habirus of Saul? Choose for yourselves a man, and let him come down to me. If he will be able to fight against me and will kill me, then we will be your slaves. If I should prevail and kill him, you will be our slaves and serve us."

The Peleset shouted, "Look! I have defied the armies of Israel this very day. Give me a man, and we will fight in single combat!"

Saul and all Israel heard these words of the Peleset, and they were both depressed and terrified. David was the son of an Ephrathite. This Ephrathite was from the House of Lehem in Judah, named was Jesse, who had eight sons. The man was an old man among the men in the days of Saul. The three elder sons of

Jesse followed Saul to the war, and their names were, Eliab his first-born, and his second Aminadab, and his third son Sama. David himself was the younger son, and the three elders followed Saul. David departed and returned from Saul, to feed his father's sheep near the House of Lehem.

The Peleset came forward morning and evening, and stood up for forty days. Jesse told David, "Take now to your brothers a bushel of this meal, and these ten loaves, and run to the camp and give them to your brothers. Take to the captain of the thousand these ten wheels of cheeses, and see how your brothers fare and learn what they are short of. Saul himself and all the Israelites were in the valley of the Oak, warring with the Pelesets. David rose early in the morning, and left the sheep to a keeper, and went as Jesse commanded him, and he came to the trench and the army as it was going out to combat, and they shouted for the battle. The Israelites and the Pelesets formed their lines one oppo-site the other.

David left what he was carrying in the hands of a keeper, and ran to the line, and went and asked his brothers how they were. While he was speaking with them, the hero named Goliath advanced between the armies. He was a Peleset from Gath, from among the armies of the Pelesets, and he shouted like before, and David heard. All the Israelites, when they saw the man ran from him, and they were terrified. The Israelites said, "Have you seen this man that comes up? He has insulted Israel and has come up, and whoever kills him, the king will enrich him with great wealth and will give him his daughter, and will set his father's house free in Israel."

David spoke to the men who stood with him saying, "Will this really be done to the man who kills that Peleset, and removes the insult from Israel? Who is this uncircumcised Peleset, that he has defied the phalanx of the living god?"[6]

The people answered him, "It will be done for the man who will kill him."

Eliab his older brother heard him speaking to the men, and Eliab was very angry with David and said, "Why have you come down, and with who did you leave those few sheep in the wilderness? I know your pride and the naughtiness of your heart! You have come down to see the battle!"

David replied, "What have I done now? Have I no business here?" He left him, and he asked the same question, and the people answered him as before.

The words that David asked were heard and were reported to Saul, and he brought him to himself. David asked Saul, "I beg you, don't let the heart of my lord be depressed within him. Your servant will go, and fight with this Peleset."

Saul said to David, "You will not be able to go against this Peleset to fight with him, for you are a mere youth and he a warrior since his youth."

David said to Saul, "Your servant was tending the flock for his father, when a lion came and a bear, and took a sheep out of the flock. Then I chased after him, and hit him, and took the plunder out of his mouth. As he rose up against me, I caught hold of his throat, and struck him, and killed him. Your servant struck both the lion and the bear. The uncircumcised Peleset will be like one of them. I will go and kill him and remove the insult from Israel today! Who is this uncircumcised one, who has defied the army of the god Lehem? The Lord who delivered me out of the paw of the lion and out the paw of the bear, will deliver me out of the hand of this uncircumcised Peleset."

Saul said to David, "Go, and the Lord will be with you."

Saul clothed David with a military coat and put his bronze helmet on his head. He girded David with his sword over his coat, and he tested him walking back and forth with them on. David said to Saul, "I will not be able to go with these, as I am not used to them," so they remove them from him.

He took his staff in his hand, and he chose for himself five smooth stones out of the brook and put them in the shepherd's bag which he had for his belongings, and with a sling in his hand, he approached the Peleset. The Peleset advanced and approached David, and a man carrying his shield went before him, and the Pelesets watched. Goliath saw David, and hated him, as he was a boy, and red-haired, with fair skin. The Peleset said to David, "Am I a dog that you come against me with a staff and stones?"

David said, "No! Less than a dog."[7]

The Peleset cursed David by his gods. The Peleset said to David, "Come at me, and I will give your flesh to the birds of the air, and the beasts of the earth."

David replied to the Peleset, "You come to me with a sword, a spear, and a shield, but I come to you in the name of Lord Sabaoth, god of the phalanx of Israel,[8] which you have defied today. The Lord will deliver you today into my hand, and I will kill you, and cut your head from off you, and will give your limbs and the limbs of the army of the Pelesets today to the birds of the sky, and the wild beasts of the earth and all the earth will know that there is a god in Israel. All this assembly will know that the Lord delivers not by sword or spear, for the battle is the Lord's, and the Lord will deliver you into our hands."

The Peleset rose and approached David. David reached into his bag, and took a stone, and shot it from his sling, and struck the

Peleset in his forehead, and the stone penetrated through the helmet into his forehead, and he fell to the ground on his face. And so David defeated the Peleset with a sling and a stone and killed the Peleset without a sword in his hand. David ran, and stood on him, and took his sword, and cut off his head.

The Pelesets saw that their champion was dead and they fled. The Israelites and Judahites rose and shouted, and pursued them as far as the gates of Gath, and as far as the gate of Ashkelon. The Pelesets hid behind the gates, both in Gath and in Ekron. The Israelites turned from chasing after the Pelesets, and they destroyed their camp. David took the head of the Peleset and brought it to Jerusalem,[9] but he put his armor in his tent.

# 1ˢᵗ Kingdoms: Chapter 17 Note

**1** Codex Vaticanus: pêcheôn (ΠΗΧΕѠΝ). Translation: cubits

- Aleppo Codex: åmwt (אמות). Translation: cubits

- Leningrad Codex: ammovt (אַמּוֹת). Translation: cubits

- Targum Jerusalem: amin (אַמִּין). Translation: cubits

The length of the cubit changed from culture to culture and through time. Around the time the Septuagint was translated into Greek, the Greek cubit was approximately 46 cm (18 inches), while the Judean cubit is believed to have been around 51 cm (21 inches).


**2** Codex Vaticanus: spithamês (ϹΠΙΘΑΜΗϹ). Translation: span

- Aleppo Codex: zrt (זרת). Translation: half-cubit

- Leningrad Codex: zaret (זֶרֶת). Translation: half-cubit

- Targum Jerusalem: zeirta (זְיִרְתָא). Translation: hand-span

A span was a half cubit in length.


**3** Based on the length of the Judean cubit at the time when the Septuagint was translated into Greek, Goliath would have been 234 cm (7'8") tall.


**4** Codex Vaticanus: siclôn (ϹΙΚΛѠΝ)

- LXX 509: sitlôn (σϕτλωͶ)

- LXX 242: siclou (σϕιλου)

- Aleppo Codex: šqlym (שקלים). Translation: shekels

- Leningrad Codex: shekalim (שְׁקָלִים). Translation: shekels

- Targum Jerusalem: tiklei (תִּקְלֵי). Translation: weight

The silver coin used in Judea during the Second Temple period of approximately 6.87 grams of silver. The weight of Goliath's armor would be 34.35 kg (72.73 lbs).

**5** The weight of the spearhead would be 4.12 kg (9.08 lbs).

**6** Codex Alexandrinus: theou zôntos (ΘЄΟΥ ΖѠΝΤΟϹ). Translation: god living

• Aleppo Codex: âlhym ḥyym (אלהים חיים). Translation: gods living

• Leningrad Codex: elohim chayyim (אֱלֹהִים חַיִּים). Translation: gods living

• Targum Jerusalem: daYah kayama (דַיְיָ קַיְמָא). Translation: the Yahw exists

**7** Codex Alexandrinus: cae ipen Dauid ouchi all ê chirô cynos (ΚΑΙ ЄΙΠЄΝ ΔΑΥΙΔ ΟΥΧΙ ΑΛΛΗ ΧЄΙΡѠ ΚΥΝΟϹ). Translation: and said David, "No, but as lower than a dog

This line is found in approximately half of the Septuagint manuscripts, but not in the Masoretic text.

**8** Codex Vaticanus: t̄h̄u sabaôth parataxeôs Israêl (ΘῩ ϹΑΒΑѠΘ ΠΑΡΑΤΑΞЄѠϹ ΙϹΡΑΗΛ). Translation: god Sabaoth phalanx of Israel

• Codex Alexandrinus: cyriou sabaôth theou parataxeôs Israêl (ΚΥΡΙΟΥ ϹΑΒΑѠΘ ΘЄΟΥ ΠΑΡΑΤΑΞЄѠϹ ΙϹΡΑΗΛ). Translation: Lord Sabaoth god of phalanx of Israel

• LXX 247: cyriou SAÔTH theou parataxeôs Israêl (ιυβϕου ϹΑѠΘ θϐου παϕατaⱳξϐωϲ ιϛϕλ λ). Translation: Lord Sabaoth god of phalanx of Israel

- Aleppo Codex: Yhwh sbåwt ålhy môrkwt Yšrål (**יהוה צבאות אלהי מערכות ישראל**). Translation: Yhwh armies god of the campaigns of Israel

- Leningrad Codex: Yehvah tzeva'ovt elohei ma'archovt Yisra'el (יְהוָה צְבָאוֹת אֱלֹהֵי מַעַרְכוֹת יִשְׂרָאֵל). Translation: Yehwah armies god of the campaigns of Israel

- Targum Jerusalem: daYyah tzeva'ovt elaha desidrei (דַיְיָ צְבָאוֹת אֱלָהָא דְסִדְרֵי). Translation: the Yahw desires (or wishes) god of arrangement

**9** Codex Vaticanus: Ierousalêm (ΙΕΡΟΥϹΑΛΗΜ). Translation: Jerusalem

- Aleppo Codex: Yrwšlm (**ירושלם**). Translation: Jerusalem

- Leningrad Codex: Yerushaliam (יְרוּשָׁלִָם). Translation: Jerusalem

- Targum Jerusalem: Yrushelem (יְרוּשְׁלֵם). Translation: Jerusalem

Both the Septuagint and Masoretic text agree that Goliath's head was taken to Jerusalem, which suggests that Saul was based in Jerusalem. The Book of Joshua claimed Jerusalem was within Benjaminite territory, although according to other books it remained a predominantly Jebusite city. The extended text of this chapter and the following chapter found in the Masoretic text is also set in Jerusalem.

# 1st Kingdoms: Chapter 18

Women came out dancing to meet David from all the cities of Israel, with timbrels, and with rejoicing, and with cymbals. The women began to say, "Saul has struck his thousands, but David his ten thousand."

This seemed evil in the eyes of Saul concerning and he said, "To David, they have given ten thousand, and to me, they have given thousands? What more can he have but the kingdom?"

Saul watched David from that day onward. He left the court and became captain of a thousand of his men, and he went out and came in before the people. David was prudent in all his ways, and the Lord was with him.

Saul saw that he was very wise, and he was afraid of him. All Israel and Judah loved David because he came in and went out before the people.

Michal the daughter of Saul loved David, and it was told to Saul, and the thing was pleasing in his eyes. Saul said, "I will give her to him, and she will be a stumbling block for him."

The hands of the Pelesets were against Saul at the time, and Saul ordered his servants, "Speak privately to David, saying, 'Look, the king loves you, and all his servants love you, and you should become the king's son-in-law.'"

The servants of Saul spoke these words to David, and David replied, "Is it a minor thing in your eyes to become son-in-law to the king? I am a humble man, and not honorable."

The servants of Saul reported to him the words of David. Saul said, "Say this to David, 'The king wants no gift but a hundred foreskins of the Pelesets, to avenge himself on the king's enemies.'"

Now Saul thought to throw him into the hands of the Pelesets. The servants of Saul repeated these words to David, and David was very happy to become the son-in-law of the king. David rose, and went with his men, and slaughtered a hundred Peleset men, and brought their foreskins, and he became the king's son-in-law, and Saul gave him Michal his daughter as wife.

Saul saw that the Lord was with David and that all Israel loved him. Yet he was more afraid of David.

# 1st Kingdoms: Chapter 19

Saul told Jonathan his son and all his servants to kill David. Jonathan, Saul's son, chose David, and Jonathan said to David, "Saul wants to kill you, be careful tomorrow morning and hide, and stay in hiding. I will go out and stand near my father in the field where you are, and I will ask my father about you. I will see what his answer is, and I will tell you."

Jonathan spoke favorably concerning David to Saul his father, and said to him, "Don't let the king sin against your servant David, for he has not sinned against you, and his deeds are very good. He took his life in his hand attacked the Pelesets, and the Lord worked a great deliverance, and all Israel saw and celebrated. Why then do you sin against innocent blood, and kill David without a cause?"

Saul listened to the voice of Jonathan, and Saul swore, "As the Lord lives, he will not die."

Jonathan called David and told him all these words, and Jonathan brought David to Saul, and he was before him as he had been previously. Again there was a war against Saul, and David did valiantly, and fought against the Pelesets, and slaughtered them in great numbers, and they fled from before him. An evil spirit from God was on Saul, and he was resting in his house, and a spear was in his hand, and David was playing on the harp with his hands. Saul wanted to murder David with the spear, and David ran suddenly from the presence of Saul, and he drove the spear into the wall. David ran away and escaped. In that night, Saul sent messengers to the house of David to watch him, to kill him in the morning, and Michal, David's wife told him, "Unless you save your life this night, tomorrow you will be murdered."

Michal let David down out the window and he escaped. Michal took idols and laid them on the bed, and she put the liver of a goat as his head and covered them with clothes. Saul sent messengers to take David, and they were told that he was sick. He sent a messenger to David, saying, "Bring him to me on the bed, that I may kill him."

The messengers came, and saw that idols were on the bed and the goat's liver as his head. Saul asked Michal, "Why have you deceived me like this, and allowed my enemy to leave, and he has escaped?"

Michal answered Saul, "He said, let me go or I will kill you."

David fled and traveled to Samuel in Armathaem, and told him all that Saul had done to him, and Samuel and David went and lived in Naioth in Ramah.

Saul was told, "Look, David is in Naioth in Ramah," and so Saul sent messengers to take David, and they saw the assembly of the prophets, and Samuel stood as appointed over them, and the spirit of God came on the messengers of Saul, and they prophesied. It was told to Saul and he sent other messengers and they also prophesied, and Saul sent a third group of messengers and they also prophesied. Saul was very angry and went to Armathaem, and he came as far as the well of the threshing floor that is in Sechu, and he asked, and "Where are Samuel and David?"

They answered, "Look, in Naioth in Ramah."

As he travelled to Naioth in Ramah, and the spirit of God came on him there also, and he went on prophesying until he arrived at Naioth in Ramah. He took off his clothes, and prophesied before them, and lay down naked all that day and all that night. Therefore they asked, "Is Saul also a prophet?"

# 1ˢᵗ Kingdoms: Chapter 20

David fled from Naioth in Ramah, and went to Jonathan, and asked, "What have I done? What is my error? How have I sinned before your father that he wants my life?"

Jonathan answered him, "Don't be concerned, you will not die. Look, my father will not do anything great or small without telling it to me, and why would my father hide this matter from me? This thing is not so."

David replied to Jonathan, "Your father knows certainly that I have found grace in your sight, and he said, 'don't let Jonathan know this, in case he refuses his consent,' but as the Lord lives and your mind lives, as I said, 'the space is filled up between me and death.'"

Jonathan said to David, "What do you want from me, and what can I do for you?"

David said to Jonathan, "Look, tomorrow is the new moon, and I will not on any account sit down to eat, but you will let me go and I will hide in the field until the evening. If your father asks about me, then you will say, 'David earnestly asked permission from me to run to the House of Lehem, his town, for there is an annual sacrifice there for all the family.' If he replies well, all is safe for your servant, but if he will answer harshly to you, know that he has evil intent. You will deal mercifully with your servant, for you have brought your servant into a covenant of the Lord with yourself, and if there is iniquity in your servant, kill me yourself, but why would you bring me to your father?"

Jonathan replied, "That is far from you, for if I certainly know that evil is determined by my father to come on you, although it should not be against your cities, I will tell you."

David asked Jonathan, "Who can tell me if your father should answer roughly?"

Jonathan answered David, "Go, and wait in the field."

They both went out into the field, and Jonathan said to David, "The Lord the god of Israel knows that I will question my father when I have an opportunity three times, and if good should be determined about David, and I do not send to you to the field, God do to Jonathan also and more as well. I will also report the evil to you, and make it known to you, and I will let you go, and you will leave in peace, and the Lord will be with you, as he was with my father. If indeed I continue to live, then you will deal mercifully with me, and if I indeed die, you will not withdraw your mercy from my house forever, and if you do not, when the Lord cuts off the enemies of David each from the face of the earth, should it happen that the name of Jonathan be discovered by the house of David, then let the Lord seek out the enemies of David."

Jonathan swore further to David because he loved the mind of him that loved him. Jonathan said, "Tomorrow is the new moon, and you will be asked for because your seat will be seen as vacant. You will stay three days, and watch an opportunity, and will come to your place where you may hide in the day of your business, and you will wait by the former mines.¹ I will shoot three arrows, aiming them at a mark. Watch, I will send a boy, saying, 'Go find the arrow for me.' If I should expressly say to the boy, 'The arrow is here, and on this side of you, take it,' then return as it is well with you, and there is no reason for fear, as the Lord lives. If I should say to the young man, 'The arrow is on that side of you, and beyond,' leave, as the Lord has sent you away.' As for the word which you and I have spoken, look, the Lord is a witness between me and you forever."

David hid in the field, and the new month arrived. The king came to the table to eat. He sat on his seat as in former times, his seat by the wall next to Jonathan. Abner sat on one side of Saul, and the place of David was empty. Saul said nothing on that day, for he thought, 'Something must have happened and he is not clean, because he has not purified himself.' In the morning on the second day of the month, the place of David was empty again, and Saul asked Jonathan his son, "Why has the son of Jesse not been at the table both yesterday and today?"

Jonathan answered Saul, and said to him, "David asked me to let him go to the House of Lehem, his city. He said, 'Let me go, I beg you, for we have a family sacrifice in the city, and my brothers have sent for me. If now I have found grace in your eyes, I will go and see my brothers,' therefore he is not present at the table of the king."

Saul was extremely angry with Jonathan, and said to him, "You son of a traitorous woman! I did not know that you were an accomplice of the son of Jesse! The shame of your mother's nakedness! As long as the son of Jesse lives on the earth, your kingdom will not be established! Now then send and take the young man, for he must certainly die."

Jonathan answered Saul, "Why must he die? What has he done?"

Saul raised his spear against Jonathan to kill him, so Jonathan knew that his father had decided to kill David. Jonathan ran from the table in great anger and did not eat on the second day of the month, for he grieved bitterly for David as his father decided on evil against him. Morning came, and Jonathan went out to the field, as he planned to do as a signal for David, and a little boy was with him. He said to the boy, "Run, find the arrows which I shot," and the boy ran, and Jonathan shot an arrow and sent it beyond him. The boy came to the place where the arrow was which Jonathan had shot, and Jonathan cried out after the boy, "The arrow is on that side of you and beyond you."

Jonathan shouted at the boy, "Rush and don't remain still!"

Jonathan's boy gathered up the arrows and brought the arrows to his master. The boy knew nothing, and only Jonathan and David knew. Jonathan gave his weapons to his boy, and said to his boy, "Go, enter into the city."

When the boy went in, then David arose from the south, and fell on his face, and paid respect to him three times, and they kissed each other, and cried for each other, for a great while. Jonathan said to "David, Go in peace, and as we have both sworn in the name of the Lord, 'the Lord will be a witness between me and you, and between my seed and your seed forever,' and so let it be. David arose and departed, and Jonathan went into the city.

# 1st Kingdoms: Chapter 20 Notes

**1** Codex Vaticanus: ergab ecino (ЄΡΓΑΒЄΚЄΙΝΟ). Translation: ergab that was

• Codex Alexandrinus: ergon ecino (ЄΡΓΟΝЄΚЄΙΝΟ). Translation: works (or labor, enclosure) that was

• LXX 19: lithô ecinô (λϕθω ϭμϭϕνω). Translation: stone there

• Aleppo Codex: åbn håzl (אבן האזל). Translation: stone exhausted

• Leningrad Codex: eben ha'azel (אֶבֶן הָאָזֶל). Translation: stone exhausted

• Targum Jerusalem: eben ata (אֶבֶן אָתָא). Translation: stone (or stone chamber) offering (or Ursa)

# 1st Kingdoms: Chapter 21

David traveled to Nob to meet Ahimelech the priest, and Ahimelech was amazed at meeting him, and asked, "Why are you alone, and nobody travels with you?"

David answered the priest, "The king commanded me today, 'Let no one know the matter on which I send you, and concerning which I have ordered you. I have ordered my servants to be in the place that's named for the god Amen, the beautiful temple.[1] Now if there are in your hands five loaves, give into my hand what is ready."

The priest answered David, "There are no common loaves in my hands, for I have none but holy loaves. If the young men have been kept at least from women, then they may eat them."

David answered the priest, "Yes, we have been kept from women for three days, when I came out for the journey all the young men were purified, but this expedition is unclean, therefore it will be sanctified today because of my weapons."

So Ahimelech the priest gave him the showbread for there were no loaves there, but only the presence loaves which had been removed from the presence of the Lord, so that hot bread should be set on, on the day on which he took them. On that day, one of Saul's servants was there remaining before the Lord named Doec the Syrian,[2] tending the mules of Saul.

David asked Ahimelech, "See if there is here in your hands a spear or sword, for I have not brought my sword or weapons, for the word of the king was urgent."

The priest said, "See the sword of Goliath the Peleset, whom you struck in the valley of Elah. It is wrapped in a cloth. If you want it, take it for yourself, as it is the only sword."

David said, "Look, there is none like it. Give it to me."

He gave it to him, and David rose and fled on that day from the presence of Saul. David traveled to King Achish of Gath. The servants of Achish said to him, "Is not this David, the king of the land? Did not the dancing women begin the song to him, saying, 'Saul has struck his thousand, and David his ten thousand?'"

David felt the words in his heart and was terrified of King Achish of Gath. He changed his appearance before him, and pretended to be someone else on that day, and drummed on the doors of the city, and used extravagant gestures with his hands, and fell against the doors of the gate, and his spittle ran down on his beard. Achish said to his servants, "Look! See the man is mad. Why have you brought him to me? Do I have a shortage of madmen, that you have brought him to me to play the fool? He will not come into the house."

# 1st Kingdoms: Chapter 21 Notes

**1** Codex Vaticanus: tô topô tô legomenô t̄h̄u̅ pistis Phellani Alemôni (ⲦⲰ ⲦⲟⲠⲰ ⲦⲰ ⲗⲉⲅⲟⲙⲉⲚⲰ ⲠⲨ ⲡⲓⲥⲧⲓⲥ ⲪⲉⲗⲗⲁⲚⲒ ⲁⲗⲉⲙⲰⲚⲒ). Translation: the place that's named for God Faith: Phellani Alemoni

- Codex Alexandrinus: tô topô tô legomenô theou pistis Phelmôni Almôni (ⲦⲰ ⲦⲟⲠⲰ ⲦⲰ ⲗⲉⲅⲟⲙⲉⲚⲰ ⲐⲉⲟⲨ ⲡⲓⲥⲧⲓⲥ ⲪⲉⲗⲙⲰⲚⲒ ⲁⲗⲙⲰⲚⲒ). Translation: the place that's named for God Faith: Phelmôni Almôni

- LXX 71: tô topô tô legomenô Phellani Emaniim theou pistis (ⲧⲟⲟ ⲧ⳿ⲩⲡⲟⲟ ⲧⲟⲟ ⲗⲟⲅⲟⲙⲅ̄ⲛⲟⲟ ⲪⲟⲗⲗⲁⲇⲛⲒ Ⲉⲙⲇⲛⲓϭⲓⲙ Ⲑⲟⲟⲩ ⲡ⳽ⲫⲟⲧⲓⲥ). Translation: the place that's named for Phellani Emaniim, god of faith

- LXX 44: tô topô tô legomenô Theou pistis Phelôni Alemôni (ⲧⲟⲟ ⲧ⳿ⲩⲡⲟⲟ ⲧⲟⲟ ⲗⲟⲅⲟⲙⲅ̄ⲛⲟⲟ Ⲑⲟⲟⲩ ⲡ⳽ⲫⲟⲧⲓⲥ ⲪⲟϭⲗⲟⲟⲛⲒ ⲁⲗⲟϭⲙⲟⲟⲛⲒ). Translation: the place that's named for God of faith Phelôni Alemôni

- LXX 509: topô legomenou Theou pistis Phellamin Memônim (ⲧ⳿ⲩⲡⲟⲟ ⲗⲟⲅⲟⲙⲅ̄ⲛⲟⲩ Ⲑⲟⲟⲩ ⲡ⳽ⲫⲟⲧⲓⲥ ⲪⲟϭⲗⲗⲁⲇⲙⲚ ⲘⲟϭⲙⲟⲟⲛⲒⲙ). Translation: place named for God of faith Phellamin Memonim

- LXX 52: tô topô tô legomenô Phellani Emmônim (ⲧⲟⲟ ⲧ⳿ⲩⲡⲟⲟ ⲧⲟⲟ ⲗⲟⲅⲟⲙⲅ̄ⲛⲟⲟ ⲪⲟϭⲗⲗⲁⲇⲛⲒ Ⲉⲙⲙⲟⲟⲛⲟϭⲓⲙ). Translation: the place that's named for Phellani Emmonim

- LXX 158: tô topô tô legomenô theou pistis (ⲧⲟⲟ ⲧ⳿ⲩⲡⲟⲟ ⲧⲟⲟ ⲗⲟⲅⲟⲙⲅ̄ⲛⲟⲟ Ⲑⲟⲟⲩ ⲡ⳽ⲫⲟⲧ⳽ⲓⲥ). Translation: the place that's named for god of faith

- LXX 376: tô topô tô legomenô Theou pistis Phelloni Almoni (ⲧⲟⲟ ⲧ⳿ⲩⲡⲟⲟ ⲧⲟⲟ ⲗⲟⲅⲟⲙⲅ̄ⲛⲟⲟ Ⲑⲟⲟⲩ ⲡ⳽ⲫⲟⲧⲓⲥ ⲪⲟϭⲗⲗⲟⲛⲒ ⲁⲗⲙⲟⲛⲒ). Translation: the place that's named for god of faith Phelloni Almoni

- LXX 107: topô legomenô Theou pistis Phellôni Almôni (ⲧ⳿ⲩⲡⲟⲟ ⲗⲟⲅⲟⲙⲅ̄ⲛⲟⲟ Ⲑⲟⲟⲩ ⲡ⳽ⲫⲟⲧⲓⲥ ⲪⲟϭⲗⲗⲟⲟⲛⲒ ⲁⲗⲙⲟⲟⲛⲒ). Translation: place named for god of faith Phelloni Almoni

• LXX 107: tô topô tô legomenô Theou pistis Phellanim Lemônim (τοω τỡπω τοω λϭγομϥₙοω Θϭου πϕοτιϲ ΦϬλλλνϬτμ λϬμοωνϬτμ). Translation: the place that's named for god of faith Phellanim Lemonim

• LXX 92: tô topô tô legomenô Emmonim (τοω τỡπω τοω λϭγομϥₙοω Єμμονιμ). Translation: the place that's named for Emmonim

• Dead Sea Scroll 4QSamᵇ: ål mqwm plny ålmwn- (אל מקום פלני אלמונ-). Translation: the place Plny Ålmwn-. The phrase is identical to the Aleppo codex, except for the final letter, which is damaged.

• Aleppo Codex: ål mqwm plny ålmwny (אל מקום פלני אלמוני). Translation: the place Plny Ålmwny

• Leningrad Codex: el-mekovm Peloni Almovni (אֶל־ מְקוֹם פְּלֹנִי אַלְמוֹנִי). Translation: the place Peloni Almovni

• Targum Jerusalem: la'atar kasi vetamir (לְאָתַר כַּסִי וְטָמִיר). Translation: the place covered and hidden

The Hebrew versions of the verse are all shorter than the Greek translations. It is unclear if the version found in the Dead Sea Scroll 4QSamᵇ was originally shorter, as the parchment is damaged near the end of the phrase and the following verse is entirely missing.

The Hebrew verse is accepted as a nonsense phrase, equivalent to 'so and so,' or 'such and such,' which the translator of the Targum Jerusalem took as a redaction of the original name in the verse. The Greek transliteration renders one of the words in the name as Alemôni, which is also a direct transliteration of the term ål åmwnh (אל אמונה) found in Deuteronomy chapter 32. The term ål åmwnh is generally translated as 'god of faith,' however, åmwnh (אלמונה) is the Aramaic spelling of the Egyptian god Amen's name, indicating that the Aramaic text referred to a place named after the 'god Amen.'

If plny (פלני) also originated in Egyptian, the term was simply the Egyptian term per-ôni (𓉐𓈖𓏌), meaning 'beautiful temple,' as a shift from the Egyptian R to the Canaanite L sounds was common in the early iron age, after Egypt lost control of Canaan. This means the original phrase would have meant 'the place that's named for the god Amen, the beautiful temple.' By the era the Aramaic translation took place the Egyptian origin of the name was probably forgotten, as the pronunciation would have shifted to Pelôny. This translation restores the Egyptian meaning of the 'nonsense' words as the verse is nonsense otherwise.

**2** Codex Vaticanus: Dôêc o Syros (ⲇⲱⲏⲕⲟⲥⲩⲣⲟⲥ). Translation: Doec the Syrian

- LXX 134: Doêc ho Syros (ⲇⲟⲏⲕ ⲟ ⲥⲣⲟⲥ). Translation: Doec the Syrian

- LXX 93: Doêc ho Idoumaeos (ⲇⲟⲏⲕ ⲟ ⲓⲆⲟⲩⲙⲆⲓⲟⲥ). Translation: Doec the Judean

- Aleppo Codex: dåg hådmy (**דאג האדמי**). Translation: Dag the Edomite

- Leningrad Codex: Do'eg ha'Adomi (דֹּאֵג הָאֲדֹמִי). Translation: Doeg the Edomite

- Targum Jerusalem: Do'eg Edoma (דוֹאֵג אֲדוֹמָא). Translation: Doeg Edomite

The replacement of the term 'Syrian' with 'Edomite' is consistent with the Hasmonean Dynasty's (140 to 37 BC) view of Edom as a land that was to be conquered by Judea, which it was in 125 BC, which supports the redaction as having been part of the Hasmonean redaction circa 140 BC.

# 1st Kingdoms: Chapter 22

David left there and escaped, and he traveled to the cave of Adullam. His brothers heard, and the house of his father and they went down to him there. Around him gathered everyone that was in distress, and everyone that was in debt, and everyone that was disturbed in mind, and he became a leader of them, and there were with him about four hundred men. David traveled from there to Mizpeh in Moab, and said to the king of Moab, "Let, I beg you, my father and my mother stay with you until I know what God will do to me."

He persuaded the King of Moab, and they stayed with him while David was in the hold. The prophet Gad told David, "Don't live in the hold, go, and enter the land of Judah." So David went and lived in his forest lookout.[1]

Saul heard that David had been seen along with his men with him. Saul lived in the hill below the field that is in Ramah, and his spear was in his hand, and all his servants stood near him. Saul said to his servants that stood by him, "Listen now, you Benjaminites! Will the son of Jesse indeed give all of you fields and vineyards? Will he make you all captains of hundreds and captains of thousands, so now you are conspiring against me, and no one informs me that my son made an alliance with the son of Jesse? None of you are is sorry for me, or inform me that my son has stirred up my servant against me as an enemy, as it is today?"

Doec the Syrian who was in charge of the mules of Saul answered and said, "I saw the son of Jesse as he came to Nob to visit the priest Ahimelech the son of Ahitub. The priest inquired of God for him, and gave him provision, and gave him the sword of Goliath the Peleset."

The king sent for Ahimelech the son of Ahitub and all his father's sons, the priests that were in Nob, and they all came to the king.

Saul said, "Hear now, you son of Ahitub."

He replied, "See, I am here! Speak, my lord."

Saul asked him, "Why have you and Jesse's son conspired against me? You gave him bread and a sword, and inquired of God for him, to raise him up against me as an enemy, as he is today?"

He answered the king, "Who is there among all your servants as faithful as David? He is a son-in-law of the king, and he is the executor of all your commands, and is honorable in your house! Have I begun today to inquire of God for him? By no means! Don't let the king bring an order against his servant, and against the whole of my father's house, as your servant did not know anything great or small about this."

King Saul said, "You and your whole family are going to die, Ahimelech!"

The king said to the footmen that attended on him, "Approach and kill the priests of the Lord, because their hand is with David, and because they knew that he fled, and they did not inform me," but the servants of the king would not lift their hands against the priest of the Lord.

The king said to Doec, "You! Turn and kill the priests," and Doec the Syrian turned and killed the priests of the Lord in that day, all 305 men wearing a vest.

He slaughtered Nob, the town of the priest with the edge of the sword, both man, and woman, infant and toddler, and calf, and ox, and sheep. Only one son of Ahimelech the son of Ahitub escaped. His name was Abiathar, and he fled to David. Abiathar told David that Saul had slain all the priests of the Lord.

David said to Abiathar, "I knew it on that day, that Doec the Syrian would certainly tell Saul. I am guilty of the death of the house of your father. Live with me and don't be afraid, for wherever I will seek a place of safety for my life, I will also seek a place for your life, for you are safely guarded while with me."

# 1st Kingdoms: Chapter 22 Note

**1** Codex Vaticanus: poli Saric (ΠΟΛΕΙCΑΡΙΚ). Translation: city of Saric

• Codex Alexandrinus: poli Ariath (ΠΟΛΕΙΑΡΙΑΘ). Translation: city of Ariath

• LXX 544: polin Sarich (π8λιν cΑβιχ). Translation: city of Sarich

• LXX 489: poli Sarêch (π8λ6ι cΑβℓχ). Translation: city of Sarêch

• LXX 121: poli Saricha (π8λ6ι cΑβ6τχλ). Translation: city of Saricha

• LXX 247: poli Arith (π8λ6ι Αβιθ). Translation: city of Arith

• Aleppo Codex: yôr hrt (**יַעַר חרת**). Translation: Forest of engraving

• Leningrad Codex: ya'ar charet (יַעַר חֶרֶת). Translation: Forest of engraving

• Targum Jerusalem: churesha decharet (חוּרְשָׁא דְחָרֵת). Translation: thicket of digging

The Greek term Saric / Sarich (Σαρικ / Σαριχ) could not have been transliterated from the Hebrew hrt (חרת), and instead appears to be a translation of the Aramaic word Shryq (ₚ^ₗＶ), which was not an Aramaic term, and likely treated as a proper name, as the Greeks translated it. It appears to have originated in a scribal error that copied shr yt (ₚ^ ₗＶ) as shryq (ₚ^ₗＮ), meaning the original Samaritan term would have been shr åyt (ϯ乙4 ٩Ｗ), meaning David returned to where 'he ruled.' The Greek term town (πολει), probably also originated in an early Aramaic scribal error that copied 'forest' (ₗᵁ^), as "town" (ₗᵁ), suggesting the old Samaritan text read 'forest that he ruled.' The difference between the Hebrew and likely old Samaritan versions of hrt (חרת) and shr åyt (ϯ乙4 ٩Ｗ) are not obvious, unless the original text read hwr åyt (ϯ乙4 ٩Ｙ⊟), meaning 'his lookout' in early Canaanite, however, meaning 'his hole,' in later forms of Samaritan and Judahite. This term would not have made sense by the era of the two kingdoms, resulting in both the Samaritan 'forest he ruled,' and Hebrew 'forest of engravers.'

# 1st Kingdoms: Chapter 23

David was told, "See the Pelesets war against Keilah, and they raid and trample on the threshing-floors."

David asked the Lord, "Will I go and kill these Pelesets?"

The Lord said, "Go, and you will slaughter these Pelesets and will save Keilah."

The men of David said to him, "Look, we are afraid here in Judah, and how will it be if we go to Keilah? How will we go and plunder the Pelesets?"

David asked again of the Lord, and the Lord answered him, "Rise and go down to Keilah, for I will deliver the Pelesets into your hands."

So David and his men with him went to Keilah and fought with the Pelesets, and they fled from before him, and he carried off their livestock and slaughtered them in great numbers, and David rescued the inhabitants of Keilah. Abiathar the son of Achimelech who had fled to David, also went down with David to Keilah with his vest in hand.

Saul was told that David had traveled to Keilah, and Saul said, "The gods have sold him into my hands, as he is shut in, having entered into a city that has gates and bars." Saul ordered all the people to go down to war at Keilah to besiege David and his men.

David knew that Saul spoke openly of evil against him, and David said to Abiathar the priest, "Bring the vest of the Lord."

David said, "The Lord God in Israel, your servant has indeed heard that Saul seeks to come against Keilah to destroy the city on my account. Will the place be besieged? Will Saul come down, as your servant has heard? Lord God in Israel, tell your servant!"

The Lord answered, "It will be besieged."

David rose and the men with him, numbering about four hundred, and they left Keilah and went wherever they could go, and it was told to Saul that David had escaped from Keilah, and he refrained from traveling to Keilah. He lived in strongholds in the wilderness, in the narrow passes, and lived in the wilderness in Mount Ziph in the dry country. Saul searched for him continuously, but God did not deliver him to his hands. David saw that Saul went out to search for him, and David was on the dry mountain of blacksmiths in Ziph. Jonathan the son of Saul rose and went to David among the blacksmiths,[1] and strengthened the hands of the Lord. He said to him, "Don't be afraid, for the hand of Saul my father will not find you, and you will be king over Israel, and I will be second to you. Saul my father knows it."

So they made a covenant before the Lord, and David lived among the blacksmiths, and Jonathan returned to his home. The Ziphites came up out of the dry country to the hill to Saul, saying, "Look, David is hidden with us in the strong-hold, in the narrows among the blacksmiths in the hill of Hachilah, which is on the right of Jeshimon. Now according to all the king's desires, come down and let him come down to us." They had offered him up into the hands of the king.

Saul said to them, "Blessed be you by the Lord, for you have been grieved on my account. Go, I beg you, and make preparations quickly, and watch his place where his foot will be, in that place which you spoke of, in case by any means he should be sneaky. Take note, then, and learn, and I will go with you. If he is in the land, I will search him out among all the thousands of Judah."

The Ziphites rose and went before Saul, and David and his men were in the wilderness of Maon, to the west, to the right of Jeshimon. Saul and his men went hunting for him, and they brought word to David, and he went down to the rock that was in the wilderness of Maon. Saul heard, and followed after David to the wilderness of Maon. Saul and his men went along one side of the mountain, and David and his men along the other side of the mountain. David was hiding to escape from Saul, and Saul and his men hunted David and his men, in order to capture them.

A messenger came there to Saul, saying, "Return quickly! The Pelesets have invaded the land."

So Saul returned from chasing David and went to meet the Pelesets. Therefore that place was called The divided rock.

# 1ˢᵗ Kingdoms: Chapter 23 Notes

**1** Codex Vaticanus: caenên (ⲕⲁⲓⲛⲏⲛ). Translation: new (or fresh, strange)

- Basiliano-Vaticanus: cenên (ⲕⲉⲛⲏⲛ). Translation: empty (or void)

- LXX 247: caenên pros dhad (ⲗⲁⲓⲛ̄ⲗ̄ⲛ ⲡⲣⲟⲥ ⲁⲇⲇ). Translation: strange regarding firebrand

- LXX 376: cenên pros dhad (ⲗⲟ̄ⲛⲗ̄ⲛ ⲡⲣⲟⲥ ⲁⲇⲇ). Translation: empty from firebrand

- Aleppo Codex: ḥršh (חרשה). Translation: grove (or woods, forest)

- Leningrad Codex: choreshah (חֹרְשָׁה). Translation: grove (or woods, forest)

- Targum Jerusalem: churesha (חוּרְשָׁא). Translation: thicket

As the Greek term caenên (καινην) could neither be translated of translated from choreshah (חֹרְשָׁה), and the Greek word 'new' makes no sense for the name of a mountain in the desert, the Greek word was likely a transliteration of the Hebrew word qynym (קינים), which translates as 'blacksmiths.' Additionally, some manuscripts use the alternate Greek transliteration of Cenên (Κενην), meaning 'empty' on Greek, another odd name for a mountain. The Greeks likely transliterated it believing it was a proper name, however, there is no known evidence for the existence of a 'Mountain of Cainen/Cenên,' so the original text was probably referring to a mountain that blacksmiths lived at, likely where iron or copper ore was mined.

# 1ˢᵗ Kingdoms: Chapter 24

David rose up from there and lived in the narrow passes of the Eye of Gedi.[1] When Saul returned from chasing the Pelesets, it was reported to him, "David is in the wilderness of the Eye of Gedi."

He took with him three thousand men chosen out of all Israel and went hunting David and his men led by demons.[2] He came to the flocks of sheep that were along the way, and there was a cave there, and Saul went in to make preparation, and David and his men were sitting inside the cave. The men of David told him, "Look, this is the day of which the Lord spoke to you, that he would deliver your enemy into your hands, and you will do to him as it is good in your sight."

David rose and secretly cut off the skirt of Saul's garment. After this David's heart ached, because he had cut off the skirt of his garment. David said to his men, "The Lord forbid that I should do this to my lord, the anointed Lord, to lift my hand against him as he is the anointed Lord."

So David persuaded his men by his words and did not allow them to rise and kill Saul, and Saul arose and went his way. David rose up and went after him out of the cave, and David called to Saul, "My lord, king!"

Saul looked behind him, and David bowed with his face to the ground and paid respect to him. David asked Saul, "Why do you listen to the words of the people, saying, 'Look, David seeks your life?' Look, your eyes have seen today how the Lord has delivered you today into my hands, in the cave. I would not kill you, but spared you, and said, 'I will not lift up my hand against my lord, for he is the Lord's anointed.' See the skirt of your mantle is in my hand, I cut off the skirt but did not kill you. Know and see today, there is no evil in my hand, nor impiety, nor rebellion. I have not sinned against you, yet you lay traps for my mind to kill it. The Lord judge between me and you, and the Lord requite you on yourself, but my hand will not be on you. As the old proverb says, 'Transgression will proceed from the wicked ones, but my hand will not be on you.' Now, who do you hunt, King of Israel? Who do you chase? After a dead dog, or after a flea? The Lord is judge and juror between me and you, the Lord looks on and judges my cause, and rescues me out of your hand."

When David had finished saying this, Saul replied, "Is this your voice, my son David?"

Saul lifted his voice and cried, and said to David, "You are more righteous than I am, for you have rewarded me good, but I have repaid you with evil. You have told me today what good you have done me, how the Lord trapped me in your hands today, and you did not kill me. If anyone should find his enemy in distress and should send him away in good health, then the Lord will reward him well, as you have done today. Now, understand, I know that you will certainly reign, and the kingdom of Israel will be established in your hand. Now then swear to me by the Lord, that you will not destroy my seed after me, and that you will not blot out my name from the house of my father."

So David swore to Saul, and Saul left to his home, and David and his men went up to the narrow strong-hold.³

# 1<sup>st</sup> Kingdoms: Chapter 24 Note

**1** Codex Vaticanus: Engaddi (ϵΓΓΛΔΔΙ)

- LXX 509: Engaaddi (ЄΝγΔΔΔΛϬ1)

- LXX 376: Engaddioes (ЄΝγΔΔΔΙΟΙϹ)

- Septuagint ms. 82: Gaddi (ΓΔΔΔΙ)

- Aleppo Codex: ôyn Gdy (**עֵין גדי**). Translation: eye of Gedi

- Leningrad Codex: ein-Gedi (עֵין־גֶּדִי). Translation: eye of Gedi

- Targum Jerusalem: ein Gedi (עֵין גֶדִי). Translation: eye of Gedi


**2** Codex Vaticanus: Eddaeem (ЄΔΔΛΙЄΜ)

- Codex Alexandrinus: Aimin (ΛЄΙΜЄΙΝ)

- Codex Basiliano-Vaticanus: Saden (ϹΛΔЄΜ)

- LXX 19: Elaphôn (ЄλαΛΛϑοοΝ)

- LXX 121: Saddaeem (ϹΔΔΔΛΙϬμ)

- LXX 245: Saddaem (ϹΔΔΔΛΙμ)

- LXX 52: Sadiem (ϹΔΔΙϬμ)

- LXX 106: Saden (ϹΔΔϬΝ)

- LXX 376: Abialim (ΛШΙΔλϬμ)

- LXX 236: Sadeem (ϹΔΔϬϬμ)

- LXX 244: Sadaeem (ϹΔΔΔΙϬμ)

- Aleppo Codex: ṣwry hyôlym (**צוּרֵי הַיְעֵלִים**). Translation: rock the ibexes (or mountain goats)

• Leningrad Codex: tzurei hayye'elim (צוּרֵי הַיְּעֵלִים). Translation: rock the ibexes (or mountain goats)

• Targum Jerusalem: shekifei cheifaya (שְׁקִיפֵי כֵיפַיָא). Translation: cliff rocks

The common Greek transliterations are clearly of Hebrew and Canaanite word šdyym (שדיים), meaning demons (or devils, phantoms). The name should have almost certainly been redacted by the Hasmoneans as the Moabites worshiped Šdyym and the Hasmoneans did not want foreign gods in their holy books.

**3** Codex Vaticanus: Messara stenên (ΜΕССΑΡΑСΤΕΝΗΝ). Translation: Messara narrow

• Codex Alexandrinus: Mesaras stenên (ΜΕСΑΡΑССΤΕΝΗΝ). Translation: Mesaras narrow

• Codex Basiliano-Vaticanus: Messêra stenên (ΜΕССΗΡΑСΤΕΝΗΝ). Translation: Messera narrow

• LXX 243: Messaram tên stenên (Μόσσαβαμ τὴν στένᾳρν). Translation: Messeram the narrow

• LXX 127: Messera tên stenên (Μόσσόβα τὴν στένᾳρν). Translation: Messera the narrow

• LXX 158: Mesira is stenên (Μόσιβα ὅις στένᾳρν). Translation: Mesira in narrow

• LXX 509: Messar stenên (Μόσσαβ στένᾳρν). Translation: Messar narrow

• LXX 121: Messaran stenên (Μόσσαβαν στένᾳρν). Translation: Messaran narrow

• LXX 247: Mesara Stelên (Μόσαβα стέλᾳρν). Translation: Messaran Stelen

- LXX 52: Mesaran stenên (Μϭσάβλν στϭνρν). Translation: Mesaran narrow

- LXX 55: Mesera stenên (Μϭσϭβλ στϭνρν). Translation: Mesera narrow

- LXX 245: Mesêra tên stenên (Μϭσλβλ τλν στϭνρν). Translation: Mesera the narrow

- LXX 489: Masara stenên (Μλσλβλ στϭνρν). Translation: Masara narrow

- Aleppo Codex: mṣwdh (מצודה). Translation: citadel (or strong-holds)

- Leningrad Codex: metzudah (מְצוּדָה). Translation: citadel (or strong-holds)

- Targum Jerusalem: metzadta (מְצָדְתָּא). Translation: fort (or trap)

As the Greeks translated both metzudah (מְצוּדָה) and metzadot (מְצָדוֹת) as messara (μεσσαρα) and maserem (μασερεμ), the Hebrew terms strong-hold and strong-holds are translated from the Masoretic texts.

# 1st Kingdoms: Chapter 25

Samuel died, and all Israel assembled and mourned him, and they buried him in his house in Armathaem. David rose and went down to the wilderness of Maon. There was a man in Maon, and his flocks were in Carmel. He was a very rich man who had three thousand sheep and a thousand she-goats, and he happened to be shearing his flock in Carmel. The man's name was Nabal, and his wife's name was Abigail, and his wife had an understanding nature and was very beautiful, but the man was harsh, and evil in his actions and the man was difficult.

David heard in the wilderness that Nabal the Carmelite was shearing his sheep. David sent ten young men, and he said to the young men, "Go up to Carmel, and go to Nabal, and ask him in my name how he is. Tell him, 'May you and your house seasonably prosper, and all yours be prosperous. Now, look, I have heard that your shepherds who were with us in the wilderness are shearing your sheep, and we did not bother them, neither did we demand anything from them all the time they were in Carmel. Ask your servants, and they will tell you. Let your servants find grace in your eyes, for we have come on a good day. We beg you, give whatever your hand may find, to your son David.'"

So the servants went and spoke these words to Nabal, in the name of David. Nabal sprang up, and answered the servants of David, "Who is David? Who is the son of Jesse? Nowadays there is an abundance of slaves who have run away from their masters. Will I take my bread, and my wine, and my animals that I have slain for my shearers, and give them to men when I don't know where they are from?"

The servants of David returned and reported to David his response. David said to his men, "Every man grab your sword!"

About four hundred men followed David, and two hundred stayed with their belongings. One of the servants reported to Abigail the wife of Nabal, "Look, David sent messengers out of the wilderness to salute our lord, but he turned away from them. The men were very good to us. They did not hinder us, or demand from us anything all the days that we were with them. When we were in the field, they were as a wall round about us, both by night and by day, all the days that we were with them feeding the flock. Now you consider, and see what you will do, for evil is determined against our lord and against his house, and he is a vile character, and one can't speak to him."

Abigail rushed and took two hundred loaves, and two vessels of wine, and five sheep already dressed, and five ephahs[1] of fine flour, and one omer[2] of dried grapes, and two hundred cakes of figs, and put them on donkeys. She told her servants, "Go before me and see, I will follow you," but she did not tell her husband. When she had mounted her donkey and was going down by the cover of the mountain, She saw David and his men coming down to meet her, and she met them.

David said, "I could have kept all his possessions in the wilderness that he should wrong me, and we did not order the taking any of all his goods, yet he has rewarded me evil for good. So, God punish David, if I leave one man alive of all that belongs to Nabal until the morning."

Abigail saw David, and she rushed and dropped off of her donkey, and she felt before David on her face, and paid respect to him, bowing to the ground, even to his feet, and said, "On me, my lord, be my wrong. I beg you, let your servant speak in your ears, and hear the words of your servant. I beg you, Don't let my lord take to heart this pestilent man. Nabal is his name and folly is with him, but I, your slave-woman didn't see the servants of my lord who you sent. Now Lord, as Lord lives your mind lives, the Lord has kept you from coming against innocent blood, and from executing vengeance for yourself. Now, therefore, let your enemies, and those that seek evil against my lord, become as Nabal."

"Now accept this token of goodwill, which your servant has brought to my lord, and you will give it to the servants that wait on my lord. Remove, I beg you, the trespass of your servant, for the Lord will certainly make for my lord a sure house, for the Lord fights the battles of my lord, and there will be no evil ever found in you. If a man will rise up persecuting you and seeking your life, yet will the life of my lord be bound up in the bundle of life with Lord the god, and you will whirl the life of your enemies as among a sling. It will be when the Lord has worked for my lord all the good things he has spoken concerning you and will appoint you to be ruler over Israel, then this will not be an abomination and offense to my lord, to have shed innocent blood outside cause, and for my lord to have avenged himself, and so may the Lord do good to my lord, and you will remember your slave-woman and do good for her."

David said to Abigail, "Blessed be Lord the god of Israel, who sent you this very day to meet me. Blessed be your conduct, and blessed be you, who have hindered me this very day from coming to shed blood, and from avenging myself. Certainly, as Lord the God in Israel lives, who hindered me today from doing you harm, if you had not rushed and come to meet me, then I said, 'There will certainly not be left alive one male of Nabal until the morning.'" David took from her hand all that she brought to him, and said to her, "Go in peace to your house, see, I have listened to your voice, and accepted your petition."

Abigail came to Nabal, and look, he had a banquet in this house, like the banquet of a king, and the heart of Nabal was happy within him, and he was very drunken. She told him nothing great or small until the morning light. In the morning, when Nabal sobered from his wine, his wife told him these actions, and his heart died within him, and he became like a stone. After about ten days, the Lord killed Nabal.

David heard it and said, "Blessed is the Lord, who has judged the cause of my reproach at the hand of Nabal and has delivered his servant from the power of evil. The Lord has returned the evil of Nabal on his own head."

David sent for Abigail and offered to take her as a wife for himself. The servants of David went to Abigail at Carmel, and said to her, "David has sent us to you, to take you for himself as a wife."

She rose, and did reverence with her face to the earth, and said, "Look, your servant is but a slave-woman to wash the feet of your servants."

Abigail rose and mounted her donkey, and took five women with her, and followed the servants of David, and became his wife. David took Ahinoam of Jezreel, and they were both his wives. Saul gave Michal his daughter, David's wife, to Palti the son of Laish who was from Romma.

# 1ˢᵗ Kingdoms: Chapter 25 Note

**1** Codex Vaticanus: alphitou (ⲁⲗ̄ⲫⲓⲧⲟⲩ)

- LXX 19: alphitôn (ἀλⲫ̄ⲫⲧⲟⲟⲛ)

- Aleppo Codex: såym (סָאִים). Translation: s'ahs

- Leningrad Codex: se'im (סְאִים). Translation: s'ahs

- Targum Jerusalem: s'ah (סְאִין). Translation: s'ahs

The Greek term is a transliteration of the Hebrew ephah (עֵיפָה) which was three times the s'ah. The ephah was a Judean and Samaritan unit of measure was approximately 23 liters (6.1 gallons). The s'ah was a later Aramean and Judean measurement of volume which had a more varied value, however, generally viewed in Judea as being approximately 7.7 liters (2 gallons).


**2** Codex Vaticanus: gomor (ⲅⲟⲙⲟⲣ)

- LXX 245: gômôr (ⲅⲟⲟⲙⲟⲟⲫ)

- LXX 236: gomon (ⲅⲟ̄ⲙⲟⲛ)

- Aleppo Codex: måh (מָאה). Translation: hundred

- Leningrad Codex: me'ah (מֵאָה). Translation: hundred

- Targum Jerusalem: me'ah (מְאָה). Translation: hundred

The ôwmr (עומר) was a Judean and Samaritan unit of measure was approximately 2.3 liters (0.6 gallons). The measurement must have been in the Aramaic text the Greeks translated, but does not appear in the Hebrew translation, which substitutes the number 100. The measurement of 'gomer' was likely a simplification by the Aramaic translator.

# 1st Kingdoms: Chapter 26

The Ziphites came out of the dry country to Saul at the hill, saying, "Look, David hides with us in the hill of Hachilah, opposite Jeshimon. Saul rose and went down to the wilderness of Ziph, and with him went three thousand men chosen out of Israel, to hunt David in the wilderness of Ziph. Saul camped in the hill of Hachilah near Jeshimon, along the way. David lived in the wilderness and David saw that Saul came after him into the wilderness. David sent spies and learn that Saul had come prepared out of Keilah. David arose secretly and went into the place where Saul was sleeping, and there was Abner the son of Ner, the captain of his army. Saul was sleeping in a chariot, and the people had camped around him.

David spoke to Ahimelech the Cypriot,[1] and Abishai the son Zeruiah the brother of Joab, "Who will go in with me into Saul's camp?"

Abishai said, "I will go in with you." So David and Abishai went in among the people by night and found Saul was fast asleep in his chariot, and his spear was stuck in the ground near his head, and Abner and his people slept round about him. Abishai said to David, "God has trapped your enemy in your hands today, and now I will pierce him into the ground with the spear once for all, and I will not strike him again."

David said to Abishai, "Do not kill him, for who will lift his hand against the anointed Lord, and be guiltless?"

David said, "As the Lord lives if the Lord does not kill him, or his day comes and he dies, or he goes down to battle and is added to his fathers, do not do it. The Lord forbids me to lift my hand against the anointed Lord, and I beg you, take the spear from his holster, and the pitcher of water, and let us return home."

David took the spear, and the pitcher of water from his holster and they went home, and no one saw, and no one that knew, and no one woke, all being asleep, as a stupor from the Lord had fallen on them. So David went to the far side and stood on the top of a hill far off, and there was a good distance between them. David called to the people, and spoke to Abner, "Will you not answer, Abner?"

Abner answered and said, "Who are you that call?"

David said to Abner, "Aren't you a man? And who is like you in Israel? Why then do you not guard your lord the king? For one out of the people went in to destroy your lord the king. This thing is not good which you have done. As the Lord lives, you are worthy of death, you who guards your lord the king, the anointed Lord. Now look, I beg you, the spear of the king, and the cruse of water, where are the articles that should be at his head?"

Saul recognized the voice of David, and said, "Is this your voice, son David?"

David said, "I am your servant, my lord, king. Why does my lord pursue his servant? How have I sinned? What unrighteousness has been found in me? Now let my lord the king hear the word of his servant. If God stirs you up against me, let your offering be acceptable, but if the sons of men, they are cursed before the Lord, for they have thrown me out today so that I should not be established in the inheritance of the Lord, saying, 'Go, serve other gods.' Now don't let my blood fall to the ground before the Lord, for the king of Israel has come forth to seek your life, as the night hawk pursues its prey in the mountains."

Saul replied, "I have sinned. Turn back my son David, for I will not hurt you, as my life was precious in your eyes. Today I have been foolish and have erred greatly."

David answered and said, "Look, the spear of the king. Let one of the servants come over and take it. The Lord will repay each according to his righteousness and his truth since the Lord delivered you today into my hands, and I would not lift my hand against the Lord's anointed. And, look, as your life has been precious this very day in my eyes, so let my life be precious before the Lord, and may he protect me, and deliver me out of all affliction."

Saul said to David, "Blessed be you, my son, and you will certainly do valiantly, and certainly prevail."

David went on his way, and Saul returned to his place.

# 1st Kingdoms: Chapter 26 Notes

**1** Codex Vaticanus: Chettaeon (ΧΕΤΤΑΙΟΝ)

- LXX 489: Getthaeon (Γόттθλιον)

- Aleppo Codex: Ḥty (חתי). Translation: Cypriot

- Leningrad Codex: Chitti (חִתִּי). Translation: Cypriot

- Targum Jerusalem: Chitta'ah (חִתָּאָה)

This term has created a great deal of confusion since the misidentification of the ruins of the Neshites as being 'Hittite' in the 1800s. The modern archaeological name 'Hittite,' is not derived from an ancient name for the culture applied by themselves, or anyone else, but rather adopted from the biblical reference to a then-unknown civilization somewhere in the region. There was an ancient culture in the region called the Hattians, however, they were conquered by the Nesites before 1700 BC, and subsequently disappeared from the historic records.

The name was applied to culture today referred to as 'Hittites,' before the 'Hittite' language had been translated, and is incorrect. Since 1906, excavations at Boğazköy, the ancient 'Hittite' capital Hattusa have uncovered more than 10,000 'Hittite' texts, including the royal achieve. The actual name of the 'Hittite' language and people was Nešili (𒉌𒅆𒇷), which is now rendered in some academic literate as Nesite or Neshite. As early as the mid-1800s some scholars disputed the identification of the Nesites as the Biblical Hittites, including the Orientalist Max Müller, who was one of many claiming the Biblical Hittites were ancient Greeks or some other Mediterranean people.

Later in the Septuagint's translation of the Maccabees, the similar term Chettiim (Χεττιιμ) as a reference to all Greek-speaking lands, and therefore the Biblical Hittites were likely the Cypriots or the Achaean Greeks. In the 1st century AD, the Jewish historian Josephus reported that Cethima was the name of Cyrus in Aramaic, and the Chettim were the descendants of Noah's grandson Chethimus, who had settled on Cyprus. Josephus reported that the name was preserved in the Greek

name of the town Cition (Κίτιον). Most historians view it as more likely
that the Aramaic name was derived from the city-state of Cition, which
was known as Kâtjåy (𓈖𓃀𓇋𓈖𓊖) in Egyptian records from the New
Kingdom Era in the late Bronze Age, and Kt (𐤊𐤕) or Kty (𐤊𐤕𐤉) in
Phoenician records from the early Iron Age. While this may be the
origin of the term, by the era of the Neo-Assyrian era, the term must
have also referred to other Greek islands, as both the prophets Isaiah and
Ezekiel used the term 'Islands of Kittim.' As the term referred to the
entire island of Cyprus in Aramaic, the translations of 'Cyprus' and
'Cypriots' are used here.

# 1st Kingdoms: Chapter 27

David said in his heart, "One day, I will be delivered for death into the hands of Saul. There is nothing good for me unless I escape into the land of the Pelesets, and Saul should stop searching for me through every frontier of Israel. Therefore, I will escape out of his hand."

David rose, and the 600 men that were with him, and he went to Achish, son of Maoch, king of Gath. David lived with Achish with his men, each man with his family and David with both his wives, Ahinoam, the Jezraelitess, and Abigail the wife of Nabal the Carmelite. It was told to Saul that David had fled to Gath and he no longer hunted after him. David said to Achish, "If your servant has found grace in your eyes, let them give me, I beg you, a place in one of the cities in the country, and I will live there. Why does your servant live with you in a royal city?"

He gave him Ziklag on that day, therefore Ziklag came into possession of the king of Judea even to today. The number of days that David lived in the country of the Pelesets was four months. David and his men went up and attacked all the Geshurites and the Amalekites, and the land was abandoned, (including the land from Gelampsur) by those who come from the fortified cities even to the land of Egypt. He slaughtered the land, and left neither man nor woman alive. They took flocks and herds, donkeys, camels, and clothing, and they returned and came to Achish, and Achish demanded of David, "Who have you attacked today?"

David said to Achish, "The south of Judea, the south of Iesmega, and the south of the Kenizzites. I have not left man or woman alive to bring them to Gath," as I thought, "In case they carry a report to Gath against us," saying, "These things David does." This was his manner all the days that David lived in the country of the

Pelesets. So David had the full confidence of Achish, who said, "He is thoroughly disgraced among his people in Israel and he will be my servant forever."

# 1st Kingdoms: Chapter 28

In those days the Pelesets gathered themselves together with their armies to go out to fight with Israel, and Achish said to David, "Know certainly, that you will go out to battle with me, you, and your men."

David said to Achish, "Now you will know what your servant will do."

Achish said to David, "I will make you the captain of my bodyguard forever."

Samuel died, and all Israel mourned for him, and they buried him in his city of Armathaem, and Saul drove those with divining spirits in them, and the wizards, out of the land. The Pelesets assembled themselves and camped in Shunem, and Saul gathered all the Israelites, and they camp in Gilboa. Saul saw the camp of the Pelesets and was alarmed, and his heart was greatly depressed. Saul inquired of the Lord, and the Lord did not answer him in his dreams, or by Urim,[1] or through prophets. Then Saul instructed his servants, "Seek for me a woman who has in her a divining spirit, and I will go to her, and inquire of her."

His servants said to him, "Look there is a woman who has in her a divining spirit in the Eye of Dor."[2]

Saul disguised himself in other clothing and traveled with two men to visit the woman by night, and he said to her, "Divine for me, I beg you, by the divining spirit within you, and channel for me the one I name."

The woman said to him, "Look now, you know what Saul has done, how he has cut off those who had in them divining spirits, and driven the wizards from the land. Why do you set a trap for my life to destroy it?"

Saul swore to her, "As the Lord lives, no injury will come to you on this account."

The woman said, "Who will I channel for you?"

He answered, "Channel Samuel for me."

The woman saw Samuel, and cried out with a loud voice, and said to Saul, "Why have you lied to me? You are Saul!"

The king said to her, "Don't be afraid, just tell me who you have seen."

The woman said to him, "I saw gods[3] ascending out of the earth."

He asked her, "What did you see?"

She answered him, "An upright man ascending out of the earth, and he was clothed with a mantle."

Saul knew that this was Samuel, and he bowed with his face to the earth and paid respect to him. Samuel asked, "Why have you bothered me, that I should come up?"

Saul answered, "I am greatly distressed, and the Pelesets war against me and God has departed from me, and no longer listens to me, either by the hand of the prophets or in dreams. So, now I have called you to tell me what to do."

Samuel said, "Why do you ask me when the Lord has departed from you and joined with your neighbors? The Lord has done to you as the Lord spoke through me, and the Lord will rip your kingdom out of your hand and will give it to your neighbor David. You did not listen to the voice of the Lord and did not execute his fierce anger against Amalek, and therefore the Lord has done this thing to you today. The Lord will deliver Israel and you into the hands of the Pelesets, and tomorrow you and your sons with you will fall, and the Lord will deliver the army of Israel into the hands of the Pelesets."

Saul instantly fell flat to the earth and was terrified because of the words of Samuel, and there was no longer any strength in him, for he had eaten no bread that day and all night. The woman went to Saul and saw that he was greatly depressed, and said to him, "Look now, your slave-woman has listened to your voice, and I have put my life in my hand, and have heard the words which you have spoken to me. Now listen, I beg you, to the voice of your slave-woman, and I will set before you a morsel of bread, and eat, and you will be strengthened, and you will be going on your way." But he would not eat, so his servants and the woman compelled him, and he listened to their voice, and rose up from the earth and sat on a bench. The woman had a fat heifer in the house and she rushed and killed it. She took meal and kneaded it, and baked unleavened cakes. She brought the meat before Saul, and his servants and they ate, and rose up, and departed that night.

# 1ˢᵗ Kingdoms: Chapter 28 Notes

**1** Codex Vaticanus: dêloes (ⲆⲎⲖⲞⲓⲥ). Translation: manifestations

- Aleppo Codex: åwrym (אורים). Translation: lights

- Leningrad Codex: urim (אוּרִים). Translation: lights

- Targum Jerusalem: uraya (אוּרַיָא). Translation: evening

Whatever the åwrym were, they were originally mentioned in the Torah, in Exodus, along with the thummim as something that was used for fortune telling by Aaron, the first high priest of the Lord.


**2** Codex Vaticanus: Aeldôr (ⲀⲈⲖⲆⲱⲣ)

- Codex Alexandrinus: Nêndôr (ⲚⲎⲚⲆⲱⲣ)

- LXX 71: Aendôps (Ⲁ𝑔ⲚⲀⲟⲟⲯ)

- LXX 509: Dôr (Ⲇⲟⲟ𝑝)

- LXX 119: Naendôr (ⲚⲀ𝑔ⲚⲀⲟⲟ𝑝)

- LXX 121: Aerdôn (Ⲁ𝑔𝑝ⲀⲟⲟⲚ)

- LXX 376: Êndôr (ⲎⲚⲀⲟⲟ𝑝)

- LXX 247: Indôr (ⲓⲚⲀⲟⲟ𝑝)

- Aleppo Codex: ôyn Dwr (עין דור). Translation: eye of Dor

- Leningrad Codex: ein Dovr (עֵין דֹּור). Translation: eye of Dor

- Targum Jerusalem: ein Dor (עֵין דֹור). Translation: hole (or opening, eye, sight) of Dor

The location is assumed to be near the southern end of the Jezreel Valley, however, the location is debated as no physical evidence has been found. The alternate hypothesis is that it was the spring that the Dalya river flowed from in the modern Horshan Mountain Reserve. The Dalya flows from the mountains to the former swamp lands on the

Israeli Mediterranean coast directly south of the ruins of Tel Dor. The city of Djr (⬭ⵀⵀⵀⵀ⊛) was a major port in the region from at least the Egyptian New Kingdom era, and featured in the Voyage of Wenamen set in the same era as Saul and David, after the city had broken away from Egyptian control.

**3** Codex Vaticanus: theous (ⲐⲈⲞⲨⲤ). Translation: gods

• Aleppo Codex: ålhym (אלהים). Translation: gods (Aramaic), goddesses (Hebrew)

• Leningrad Codex: elohim (אֱלֹהִים). Translation: gods (Aramaic), goddesses (Hebrew)

• Targum Jerusalem: Yyah (?'). Translation: Yahw

The word in the Masoretic text is commonly translated as God, but is a plural form of the Aramaic ålhå (𐡍𐡈𐡋𐡍), meaning 'gods,' or a plural form of the Hebrew elah (אֱלָה) meaning 'goddesses.' The term ålhym (𐤓𐤆𐤀𐤋𐤟), and ålhym (𐡊𐡀𐡈𐡋𐡍), are also direct transcriptions of the Assyrian word elium (𒄿𒇷𒌝), which by the Iron Age meant 'god,' indicating that text had previously been written in cuneiform, and was translated into Aramaic or Phoenician during the iron age. During the bronze age, the earlier form of the word alium (𒁹𒈨𒌷𒌝) referred to a specific god, ᵈᵉⁱᵗʸAn (✳✳) the highest god, and father of the other gods. His Akkadian name was derived from the word elûm (𒁹𒐊), meaning 'higher,' as the term was intended to convey the meaning of 'highest.'

He was believed to live in the polar region of the sky, where the modern constellation of Draco is located, making him the highest in the sky, around which all the gods (stars) circled. During the Old Babylonian and Old Assyrian eras, the gods Marduk and Ashur, the national gods of Babylon and Assyria, replaced the Akkadian Alium as the primary god of the Mesopotamian pantheons, and by the iron age, the word elium had came to mean 'god,' explaining why the Aramaic term ålhym (𐡊𐡀𐡈𐡋𐡍) would have sometimes been interpreted as 'god,' by the Greeks, and sometimes in its Aramaic meaning as 'gods.' For some reason the translator of the Targum Jerusalem thought the god in question was Yahweh, although Yahweh was not generally associated with the underworld, other than in early 2ⁿᵈ Christianity.

# 1st Kingdoms: Chapter 29

The Pelesets gathered all their armies at Aphek, and Israel camped at the Eye of Dor, which is in Jezreel. The lords of the Pelesets went in by hundreds and thousands, and David and his men traveled at the rear with Achish. The lords of the Pelesets asked, "Who are these that pass by?"

Achish said to the captains of the Pelesets, "Is not this David the servant of Saul king of Israel? He has been with us some time, this is his second year, and I have not found any fault in him from the day that he attached himself to me even until today."

The captains of the Pelesets were displeased at him, and they said to him, "Send the man away, and let him return to his place, where you did set him, and don't let him come with us to the war and don't let him be a traitor in the camp when he becomes reconciled to his master. Won't it be with the heads of those men? Is not this David whom they celebrated in dances, saying, "Saul has struck his thousands, and David his ten thousand?"

Achish called David, and said to him, "As the Lord lives, you are right and approved in my eyes, and so is your going out and your coming in with me in the army, and I have not found any evil to charge against you from the day that you came to me until today, however, you are not approved in the eyes of the lords. Now then return and go in peace, so you will not do evil in the sight of the lords of the Pelesets."

David asked Achish, "What have I done to you? What have you found in your servant from the first day that I was before you until today, that I should not come and war against the enemies of the lord my king?"

Achish answered David, "I know that you are good in my eyes, but the lords of the Pelesets say, 'He will not come with us to the war.' Now then rise early in the morning, you and the servants of your lord that have come with you, and go to the place where I appointed you, and entertain no evil thought in your heart, for you are good in my sight. Rise early for your journey when it is light, and leave."

Therefore, David rose early, he and his men, to leave and guard the land of the Pelesets, and the Pelesets went up to Jezreel to battle.

# 1st Kingdoms: Chapter 30

On the third day that David and his men were returning to Ziklag, Amalek invaded from the south and attacked Ziklag, and slaughtered Ziklag, and burnt it with fire. The women and all things that were in it, both great and small they did not kill. They took both men and women as captives and went on their way. David and his men came into the city and found it was burnt with fire, and their wives, and their sons, and their daughters were taken as captives. David and his men lifted their voice and cried until there was no longer any power within them to cry. Both the wives of David were carried captive, Ahinoam, the Jezraelitess, and Abigail the wife of Nabal the Carmelite.

David was greatly distressed because the people spoke of stoning him, and the mind of all the people was grieved, each for his sons and his daughters, but David strengthened himself in Lord the god. David said to Abiathar the priest, the son of Achimelech, "Bring the vest near."

David asked the Lord, "Will I pursue after these troops? Will I overtake them?"

He answered him, "Pursue, for you will certainly overtake them, and you will certainly rescue the captives."

David and the six hundred men with him, gave chase, and they traveled as far as the Brook of Besor, and the extra ones stopped. He continued with four hundred men, but two hundred remained behind and waited on the other side of the Brook of Besor. They found an Egyptian in the field, and they captured him and brought him to David. They gave him bread and he ate, and they made him drink water. They gave him a piece of a fig cake and he ate, and his spirit was restored in him, for he had not eaten bread, and had not drunk water three days and three nights.

David asked him, "Whose, are you? Where are you from?"

The young Egyptian man answered, "I am the slave of an Amalekite, and my master left me because I had taken ill three days ago. We invaded to the south of the Cherethites, and in the parts of Judea, and to the south of Caleb, and we burnt Ziklag with fire."

David asked him, "Will you lead me down to these troops?"

He answered, "Swear now to me by God that you will not kill me, and that you will not return me to the hands of my master, and I will bring you down to his troops."

He brought him down there, and they were scattered across the land, eating and drinking, and feasting because of the great plunder which they had taken out of the land of the Pelesets, and out of the land of Judah.

David attacked them and slaughtered them from the morning until the evening, and on the following day, and only four hundred young men escaped, who fled mounted on camels. David recovered all that the Amalekites had taken, and he rescued both his wives. Nothing was missing of theirs either great or small, either from the plunder, or the sons and daughters, or anything that they had taken of theirs. David recovered it all. He took all the flocks, and the herds, and led them away as plunder, and it was said of this plunder, "These are the spoils of David."

David returned to the two hundred men who were left behind and had not followed David, as he had ordered them to remain by the Brook of Besor. They came out to meet David, and to meet the people with him. David approached the people, and they asked him how he did. Then every ill-disposed and bad man of the soldiers who had gone with David answered and said, "Because they did not pursue together with us, we will not give them of the plunder which we have recovered, only let each one leave with him his wife and his children, and let them return."

David said, "You will not do so after the Lord has delivered the enemy to us, and guarded us, and the Lord has delivered into our hands the troop that came against you. Who will listen to these your words? They are not inferior to us, for according to the portion of him that went down to the battle, so will be the portion of him that waited with the baggage, they will share equally."

From that day forward, it became an ordinance and a custom in Israel until today. David returned to Ziklag and sent some of the plunder to the elders of Judah, and to his friends, saying, "Look some of the plunder of the enemies of the Lord, to those in the House of Rock,¹ and Ramah in the Negev, Jattir, Aroer, Ammadi, Saphi, Esthie, Gath, Cimath, Saphec, Themath, Carmel, the cities of Jeroham, the cities of the blacksmiths, and Jarmuth, Beersheba, Nombe, Hebron, and to all the places which David and his men had passed through.

# 1ˢᵗ Kingdoms: Chapter 30 Notes

**1** Codex Vaticanus: Baethsour (ΒΑΙΘΣΟΥΡ)

- Codex Alexandrinus: Baethêl (ΒΑΙΘΗΛ)

- Codex Basiliano-Vaticanus: Bethsour (ΒΕΘΣΟΥΡ)

- LXX 246: Basor (Βασορ)

- LXX 509: Beessour (Βεεσσουρ)

- LXX 245: Baeosour (Βαιοσουρ)

- LXX 92: Baethsor (Βαιθσορ)

- LXX 107: Bethsor (Βεθσορ)

- LXX 489: Bethsôr (Βεθσωρ)

- LXX 82: Baethour (Βαιθουρ)

- LXX 93: Bethour (Βεθουρ)

- LXX 134: Baethor (Βαιθορ)

- LXX 247: Bethêl (Βεθηλ)

- Aleppo Codex: byt Ål (בית אל)

- Leningrad Codex: veit-El (בֵית־אֵל)

- Targum Jerusalem: veit El (בֵית אֵל)

The Codex Vaticanus, and more Septuagint manuscripts use a translation is of the name Bet-Zur (בית צור) not the name Bet-El which is found in the Masoretic text. Bet-Zur translates as House of Rock, or House of Flint, and is believed to have been the ancient town at the Khirbet et-Tubeiqa ruins in the southern modern Palestinian West Bank. The substitution of Beth-El for Beth-Zur is consistent with the other Hasmonean redactions, as Beth-El was a Samaritan city, and the Samaritans refused to accept the Hasmonean changes to their holy books.

# 1ˢᵗ Kingdoms: Chapter 31

The Pelesets fought with Israel, and the Israelites fled from before the Pelesets, and they fell wounded on the mountain in Gilboa. The Pelesets advanced closely towards Saul and his sons, and the Pelesets killed Jonathan, Abinadab, and Malchi-shua sons of Saul. The battle moved against Saul, and the archers hit him with arrows and he was wounded under the ribs. Saul said to his armor bearer, "Draw your sword and pierce me through with it, in case these uncircumcised come and pierce me through, and mock me."

But his armor bearer would not, as he was terrified, so Saul took his sword and fell on it. His armor bearer saw that Saul was dead, and he also fell on his sword and died with him. So Saul died, and his three sons, and his armor bearer, all on that day. The Israelites who were on the other side of the valley, and those beyond the Jordan, saw that the Israelites fled and that Saul and his sons were dead, and they left their cities and fled, and the Pelesets entered and lived in them. It came to pass on the morning that the Pelesets went out to strip the dead, and they found Saul and his three sons fallen in the mountains of Gilboa. They turned him over, and stripped off his armor, and sent it back to the land of the Pelesets, sending it around with glad tidings to their idols and the people. They set up his armor at the Temple of Astarte,[1] and they fastened his body on the wall of the House of She'an.[2] The inhabitants of Jabesh in Gilead heard what the Pelesets did to Saul, and they rose up, including every strong man, and marched all night, and took the body of Saul and the body of Jonathan his son from the wall of the House of She'an, and they brought them to Jabesh and burnt them there. They took their bones, and buried them in the field that is in Jabesh, and fasted seven days.

# 1ˢᵗ Kingdoms: Chapter 31 Notes

**1** Codex Vaticanus: Astartion (ΑϹΤΑΡΤΕΙΟΝ). Translation: Astarte

• Aleppo Codex: Ôštrwt (עשתרות). Translation: Ashtoreth (or Astarte)

• Leningrad Codex: Ashtarot (עַשְׁתָּרֹות). Translation: Ashtoreth (or Astarte)

• Targum Jerusalem: Ashterata (עֲשְׁתְּרָתָא)


**2** Codex Vaticanus: Baethem (ΒΑΙΘΕΜ)

• Codex Sinaiticus: Baethem (ΒΑΙΘϹΑΝ)

• Codex Coislinianus: Baethsam (ΒΑΙΘϹΑΜ)

• Aleppo Codex: byt Šn (בית שן). Translation: House of She'an

• Leningrad Codex: beit Shan (בֵּית שָׁן). Translation: House of She'an

• Targum Jerusalem: beit Shan (בֵּית שָׁן). Translation: House of She'an

Beth She'an was an Egyptian colony in central Canaan, in northern modern Israel. The city was founded sometime before 5000 BC, and was annexed by Thutmoses III in the mid-1400s BC. The Egyptian colony was destroyed circa 1150 BC when the Egyptians lost control of Canaan. The city was rebuilt sometime before 1000 BC, and was a Samaritan city until the Assyrians destroyed the city during the conquest of Samaria in 732 BC. The Persians later settled Scythians at the site during their rule of Judea, resulting in the new city of Scythopolis.

# 2nd Kingdoms: Chapter 1

David returned from slaughtering the Amalekites after Saul was dead, and David stayed two days in Ziklag. On the third day, a man came from the camp of Saul's people. His garments were torn and dirt was on his face. When he went to David, he fell on the ground and paid respect to him. David asked him, "Where have you come from?"

He answered him, "I have escaped from the camp of Israel."

David asked him, "What is the matter? Tell me."

He answered, "The people fled from the battle, and many of the people have fallen and are dead, and Saul and Jonathan his son are dead."

David asked the young man who brought him the news, "How do you know that Saul and Jonathan his son are dead?"

The young man that brought the news, said to him, "I happened to be on Mount Gilboa, and saw Saul was leaning on his spear, and, the chariots and captains of horse pressed hard on him. He looked behind him, and saw me, and called me, and I said, 'Look, here I am'. He asked me, 'Who are you?' and I answered, 'I am an Amalekite.' He said to me, 'Stand, I beg you, over me, and kill me, for a dreadful darkness has come on me, for all my life is in me.' So I stood over him and killed him because I knew he would not live after he had fallen, and I took the crown that was on his head, and the bracelet that was on his arm, and I have brought them here to my lord."

David grabbed his garments and tore them, and all the men who were with him tore their garments. They lamented, and wept, and fasted till evening, for Saul and Jonathan his son, and the people of Judah, and the house of Israel, because they were slaughtered with the sword.

David asked the young man who brought the news to him, "Where are you from?"

He answered, "I am the son of an Amalekite immigrant."

David asked him, "How is it you were not afraid to lift your hand to destroy the anointed lord?"[1]

Then David called one of his young men, and said, "Go and kill him," and he killed him.

David said to him, "Your blood is on your own head, for your mouth has testified against you, saying, 'I have slain the Anointed Lord.'"

David mourned over the death of Saul and Jonathan his son, and he gave orders to teach it to the sons of Judah, as it is written in the Book of the Righteous,[2] "set up a stele, Israel, for the slain that died in your bamahs."[3]

How the mighty have fallen.

Don't tell it in Gath, and don't tell it as good news in the streets of Ashkelon, in case the daughters of the Pelesets rejoice, in case the daughters of the uncircumcised celebrate. You mountains of Gilboa, don't let dew or rain fall on you, or fields from first-fruits are for you, for there, the shield of the mighty ones have been grievously assailed, the shield of Saul was not anointed with oil. From the blood of the slain, and the fat of the mighty, the bow of Jonathan did not return empty, and the sword of Saul did not return empty. Saul and Jonathan, the beloved and the beautiful were not divided. Beautiful they were in life, and in their death, they were not divided. They were swifter than eagles, and they were stronger than lions. Daughters of Israel, cry for Saul, who clothed you with scarlet together with your adorning, who added golden ornaments to your apparel.

How the mighty have fallen in battle, Jonathan, even the slain ones on your bamahs.

I am grieved for you, my brother Jonathan, you were very lovely to me. Your love for me was wonderful beyond the love of women.

How the mighty have fallen, and the weapons of war perished.

# 2nd Kingdoms: Chapter 1 Notes

**1** Codex Vaticanus: ton christon c̄ū (ⲧⲟⲛⲭⲣⲓⲥⲧⲟⲛⲕ̄ⲩ̄). Translation: the anointed (or messiah) lord (or master)

- Codex Alexandrinus: ton christon c̄n cyriou (ⲧⲟⲛ ⲭⲣⲓⲥⲧⲟⲛ ⲕ̄ⲛ̄ ⲕⲩⲣⲓⲟⲩ). Translation: the anointed (or messiah) Lord lord (or master)

- LXX 247: ton chrêston cyriou (ⲧⲟⲛ χρ̂ⲗⲟⲧⲟⲛ ⲗⲩβⲓⲟⲩ). Translation: the good (or useful) lord (or master)

- Aleppo Codex: åt mšyḥ yhwh (**אֵת מְשִׁיחַ יהוה**). Translation: the anointed Yehwah

- Leningrad Codex: et-meshiach Yehvah (אֶת־מְשִׁיחַ יְהֹוָה). Translation: the anointed Yehwah

- Targum Jerusalem: yat meshicha daYahy (יַת מְשִׁיחָא דַיְיָ). Translation: the anointed of Yahw

Based on the Greek translations, the Aramaic text they translated must have read åt mšyḥ ådn (𐤀𐤕 𐤌𐤔𐤉𐤇 𐤀𐤃𐤍), meaning that Saul was being referred to the 'anointed lord.' This indicates that when the Hasmonean redactors added 'Yhwh' to the Hebrew translation they created, they replaced ådn (𐤀𐤃𐤍) somewhat indiscriminately.


**2** Codex Vaticanus: bibliou tou euthous (ⲃⲓⲃⲗⲓⲟⲩ ⲧⲟⲩ ⲉⲩⲑⲟⲩⲥ). Translation: papyrus (or tablet, writing, letter) of the righteous

- Codex Coislinianus: bibliou tou euthous cae ipen (ⲃⲓⲃⲗⲓⲟⲩ ⲧⲟⲩ ⲉⲩⲑⲟⲩⲥⲕⲁⲓⲉⲓⲡⲉⲛ). Translation: papyrus (or tablet, writing, letter) of the straight and said...

- LXX 127: biblou tou chthous cae ipen (ⲙⲓⲙⲗⲟⲩ ⲧⲟⲩ χⲑⲟⲩⲥ ⲗⲁⲓ ⲟⲓⲡⲟ̄ⲛ). Translation: papyrus (or tablet, writing, letter) of the land (or earth, world), and said...

- LXX 108: bibliou tou euthous (ⲙⲓⲙⲗ̄ⲫⲟⲩ ⲧⲟⲩ ⲟⲩⲑⲟⲟⲥ). Translation: papyrus (or tablet, writing, letter) of the immediate

- LXX 376: biblion tou euthys (ѡѡλιον του Ϭυθυc). Translation: papyrus (or tablet, writing, letter) of the straight

- LXX 127: bibliou tou penthous cae ipen (ѡѡλϕου του πϬνθουc ѹѹ ϬιπϬν). Translation: papyrus (or tablet, writing, letter) of the misfortune (or grief), and said...

- Aleppo Codex: spr hyšr (ספר הישר). Translation: writing (or book) the correct (or justice)

- Leningrad Codex: sefer hayyashar (סֵפֶר הַיָּשָׁר). Translation: writing (or book) the correct (or justice)

- Targum Jerusalem: sifra de'orayta (סְפְרָא דְאוֹרָיְתָא). Translation: scroll (or scribe) of the Orit (or Torah)

The Septuagint's "Set up a stele, Israel, for the slain that died in your bamahs." is not found in the Masoretic text, and is incompatible with Judaism after King Josiah's reforms, indicating that 2nd Kingdoms must have been written in Aramaic, or translated into Aramaic, earlier than circa 625 BC, when Josiah began his reforms. This book, like many others that are mentioned in the Tanakh (Old Testament), is considered lost. A book titled the Book of Jasher was published in the 1700s by Jacob Ilive, claiming to have been discovered in Persia, however, the original is undocumented, and the content is incompatible with all known versions of Judaism, and all forms of Christianity other than Catholic and Protestant Christianity. It is generally accepted as having been written in the 1700s, by Jacob Ilive, in England.

The title 'Book of the correct' might be a reference to the latter half of the Book of Exodus, in which Moses wrote the laws, and described the building of the steles on hill tops, however, does not appear to be a direct quote from any surviving copy. It could also reference a lost Hieratic, Paleo-Canaanite, or Cuneiform book about Isaac and Jacob, as Yshr (ישר) is also the beginning of the title 'Israel' (ישראל), which they both bore in early Israelite beliefs.

**3** Codex Vaticanus: ta ypsê (ΤΑΥϯΗ). Translation: the heights

• Aleppo Codex: bmwtyk (בְּמוֹתִין). Translation: your bamahs

• Leningrad Codex: bamoteicha (בָּמוֹתֶין). Translation: your bamahs

• Targum Jerusalem: beit tokefeichon itremeitun (בֵּית תּוֹקְפֵיכוֹן אִתְרְמֵיתוּן). Translation: house (or temple) of your drumming (or timbreling) places

Bamahs were stone platforms built at the tops of hills, where sacrifices were made to gods in ancient Canaan and Assyria. These Bamahs generally included an altar for barbecuing the sacrifices, a stele, a seat for the god (which the priest would sit on), an oak tree representing Asherah, and a cistern for water. These Bamahs were also generally accompanied by a banquet hall, and a 'low stone' used for slaughtering and butchering the animal. Bamahs were the main religious centers used by the Israelites until King Josiah banned and destroyed them circa 625 BC. After that, all Jews were required by law to worship at the temple in Jerusalem.

# 2nd Kingdoms: Chapter 2

After this David inquired of the Lord, "Will I go up into one of the cities of Judah?"

The Lord answered him, "Go up."

David asked, "Which place will I go to?"

He answered, "To Hebron."

David went up to Hebron with both his wives, Ahinoam the Jezraelitess, and Abigail the former wife of Nabal the Carmelite, and the men that were with him, everyone with his family. They lived in the cities of Hebron. The men of Judea came and anointed David there to reign over the house of Judah, and they reported to David, "The men of Jabesh of the country of Gilead have buried Saul."

David sent messengers to the rulers of Jabesh of the country of Gilead, and David said to them, "You are blessed by the Lord, because you have worked this mercy towards your lord, to Saul the anointed Lord, and you have buried him and Jonathan his son. Now may the Lord deal in mercy and truth towards you, and I also will repay you for this good deed, because you have done this. Now let your hands be made strong, and be valiant, for your master Saul is dead, and moreover, the house of Judah has anointed me to be king over them."

However, Abner the son of Ner, the commander-in-chief of Saul's army, took Ish-bosheth the son of Saul, and brought him up from the camp to Mahanaim and made him king over the lands of Gilead, the Ashurites, Jezreel, Ephraim, Benjamin, and over all Israel. Ish-bosheth, Saul's son was forty years old when he began to reign over Israel, and he reigned two years, but not over the house of Judah, who followed David. The days which David reigned in Hebron over the house of Judah were seven years and six months. Abner the son of Ner went out, and the servants of Ish-bosheth the son of Saul, from Mahanaim to Gibeah. Joab the son of Zeruiah, and the servants of David went out from Hebron, and met them at the fountain of Gibeah, at the same place, and these sat down by the fountain on this side and those by the fountain on that side.

Abner said to Joab, "Let the young men rise now, and play before us."

Joab said, "Let them rise."

Twelve of the children of Benjamin rose and passed by, belonging to Ish-bosheth the son of Saul, and twelve of the servants of David. Everyone seized the head of his neighbor with one hand and thrust his sword into the side of his neighbor, and they fell down together. And the name of that place was called 'The Portion of the Treacherous Ones,' which is in Gibeah. The battle was very severe on that day, and Abner and the men of Israel were defeated before the servants of David. There were three sons of Zeruiah: Joab, Abishai, and Asahel, and Asahel was swift on his feet as a doe in the field. Asahel followed after Abner, and did not turn to the right or to the left from following Abner.

Abner looked behind him, and asked, "Are you Asahel himself?"

He answered, "I am."

Abner said to him, "Turn to the right hand or to the left, and lay hold for yourself on one of the young men, and take for yourself his armor," but Asahel would not turn back from following him. Abner warned Asahel, "Stand a distance from me, in case I strike you to the ground! How could I lift up my face to Joab?"

"What does this mean?"

"Return to Joab your brother."

But he would not stand apart, and Abner hit him with the rear end of the spear on the loins, and the spear went through him, and he fell there and died on the spot, and it came to pass that every one that came to the place where Asahel fell and died, stood still. Joab and Abishai chased after Abner, until the sun went down. They went as far as the hill of Amman, which is near to Ai, by the desert road to Gibeah. The children of Benjamin who followed Abner gather themselves together, and they formed themselves into one body and stood on the top of a hill. Abner called Joab, "Will the sword devour perpetually? Don't you know that it will be bitter in the end? How long will you refuse to tell the people to turn from following our brothers?"

Joab said, "Living Lord!¹ If you had not spoken this morning, the people would have gone up every one from following his brother."

Joab sounded the trumpet, and all the people departed, and did not pursue after Israel, and did not fight any longer. Abner and his men departed in the evening, and traveled all that night, and crossed the Jordan, and traveled along the whole adjacent country, and they came to the camp. Joab returned from following Abner, and he assembled all the people, and there were missing of the people of David, nineteen men, and Asahel. The servants of David slaughtered the children of Benjamin, of the men of Abner, three hundred and sixty men belonging to him. They carried up Asahel and buried him in the tomb of his father in the Temple of Lehem. Joab and the men with him went all night, and the morning rose on them in Hebron.

# 2nd Kingdoms: Chapter 2 Notes

**1** Codex Vaticanus: zê c̄s (ᴢнᴋ̄ᴄ) Translation: ze lord (or owner)

• Dead Sea Scrolls 4QSamᵃ: Yhwh (יהוה)

• Aleppo Codex: hy hålhym (חי האלהים). Translation: life the god (in Neo-Assyrian, or gods in Aramaic, goddesses in Hebrew)

• Leningrad Codex: chai ha'elohim (חֵי הָאֱלֹהִים). Translation: life the god (in Neo-Assyrian, or gods in Aramaic, goddesses in Hebrew)

• Targum Jerusalem: hu Yeyah (הוּא יְ֞). Translation: he is (or it is, exists as) Yahw

The differences between the Masoretic text and Dead Sea Scroll 4QSamᵃ prove the text of 2ⁿᵈ Kingdoms (Samuel) was not standardized by era of the Herodian dynasty, and was still undergoing attempts to splice the name Yhwh into it.

# 2nd Kingdoms: Chapter 3

The war lasted a long time between the house of Saul and the house of David, and the house of David continually grew stronger, while the house of Saul continually grew weaker. Sons were born to David in Hebron, and his firstborn was Amnon the son of Ahinoam the Jezraelitess. His second son was Daluia, the son of Abigail the Carmelitess, and the third, Absalom the son of Maacah the daughter of Talmai the king of Geshur. The fourth was Ornia, the son of Haggith, and the fifth was Shephatiah, the son of Abital. The sixth was Ithream, the son of Eglah the wife of David. These were born to David in Hebron.

While there was a war between the houses of Saul and David, Abner was governing the house of Saul. Saul had a concubine, Rizpah, the daughter of Jol, and Ish-bosheth the son of Saul asked Abner, "Why have you gone to my father's concubine?"

Abner was very angry with Ish-bosheth for asking this, and Abner answered him, "Am I a dog's head? I have worked for the house of Saul your father, and with his brothers and friends, and have not gone over to the house of David, and you seek an order against me concerning injury to a woman? God[1] do to Abner and even more than the Lord swore to David, as I do to him this day, also take away the kingdom from the house of Saul and to raise up the throne of David over Israel and over Judah from Dan to Bathsheba."

Ish-bosheth could not rely on Abner because he was afraid of him. Abner immediately sent messengers to David at Thaelam where he was, "Make your covenant with me, and, look, my hand is with you to bring back to you all the house of Israel."

David said, "I will gladly make a covenant with you, only I demand one condition of you, 'You will not see my face unless you bring Michal the daughter of Saul when you come to see me.

David also sent messengers to Ish-bosheth the son of Saul, saying, "Restore to me my wife Michal, who I bought for a hundred foreskins of the Pelesets.

Ish-bosheth sent, and took her from her husband, from Paltiel the son of Selle. Her husband followed her weeping as far as Bahurim. Abner ordered him, "Go, return," and he returned.

Abner said to the elders of Israel, "In former days you wanted David to reign over you, and now make it happen, as the Lord has said concerning David, 'By the hand of my servant David, I will save Israel out of the hand of all their enemies.'"

Abner spoke to Benjamin, and then Abner went to speak to David at Hebron, all that seemed good in the eyes of Israel and in the eyes of the house of Benjamin. Abner came to David to Hebron, with twenty men, and David made for Abner and his men a banquet of wine.

Abner said to David, "I will rise now, and go, and gather to my lord the king all Israel, and I will make with him a covenant, and you will reign over all whom your mind² desires."

David sent away Abner, and he departed in peace. The servants of David and Joab arrived from their raids, and they brought a great deal of spoil with them. Abner was not with David in Hebron, because he had sent him away, and he had departed in peace. Joab and all his army came, and it was reported to Joab, "Abner the son of Ner has come to David, and David has let him go, and he has departed in peace."

Joab went to the king, and asked, "What is this that you have done? Look, Abner came to you! Why have you let him go, and he has departed in peace? Don't you know that it is for the evil that Abner the son of Ner has come to you, to deceive you, and to know your coming and goings, and to know all things that you do?" Joab returned from David and sent messengers to Abner after him, and they brought him back from the well of Seiram, but David did not know it. He brought back Abner to Hebron, and Joab caused him to turn aside from the gate to speak to him, laying in wait for him, and he stabbed him there in the loins, and he died for the blood of Asahel the brother of Joab.

David heard of it afterward, and said, "I and my kingdom are guiltless before the Lord even forever of the blood of Abner the son of Ner. Let it fall on the head of Joab, and on all the house of his father, and let there not be lacking the house of Joab one that has an issue, or a leper, or that leans on a staff, or that falls by the sword or starves. As Joab and Abishai, his brother laid wait continually for Abner, because he killed Asahel their brother at Gibeah in the battle."

David said to Joab and to all the people with him, "Rip your clothes, and gird yourselves with sackcloth, and mourn before Abner."

King David followed the bier, and they buried Abner in Hebron. The king lifted his voice and wept at his tomb, and all the people wept for Abner. The king mourned over Abner, and said, "Will Abner die because of the death of Nabal? Your hands were not bound, and your feet were not put in shackles. One did not bring you near Nabal, you fell before children of iniquity."

All the people assembled to mourn for him. All the people wanted David to eat bread while it was yet day, and David swore,

"May God kill me if I eat bread or anything else before the sun goes down."

All the people took notice, and all the things that the king did before the people were pleasing in their sight. So all the people and all Israel saw in that day, that it was not the king who killed Abner the son of Ner. The king said to his servants, "Don't you know that a great prince has fallen this day in Israel? That I am this day a mere relative of his, and as it were a subject, but these men the sons of Zeruiah are too hard for me. The Lord repays the evil-doer according to his wickedness."

# 2<sup>nd</sup> Kingdoms: Chapter 3 Notes

**1** Codex Vaticanus: o t̄h̄s̄ (ο θ̄ς̄). Translation: the god

• Aleppo Codex: ålhym (אלהים). Translation: goddesses (in Hebrew, or gods in Aramaic, or god in Neo-Assyrian)

• Leningrad Codex: elohim (אֱלֹהִים). Translation: goddesses (in Hebrew, or gods in Aramaic, or god in Neo-Assyrian)

• Targum Jerusalem: Yeyah (??). Translation: Yahw


**2** Codex Vaticanus: psychê sou (ψΥΧΗϹΟΥ). Translation: mind (or psyche, personality) yours

• Aleppo Codex: npšk (נפשך). Translation: your mind (or psyche, life, person, will)

• Leningrad Codex: nafshecha (נַפְשֶׁךָ). Translation: your mind (or psyche, life, person, will)

• Targum Jerusalem: nafshach (נַפְשָׁךְ). Translation: your mind (or psyche, life, person, will)

# 2ⁿᵈ Kingdoms: Chapter 4

Ish-bosheth the son of Saul heard that Abner the son of Ner had died in Hebron, and his hands were paralyzed, and all the men of Israel grew faint. Ish-bosheth the son of Saul had two men that were captains of bands, the name of the one was Baanah, and the name of the other Rechab, sons of Rimmon the Beerothite of the children of Benjamin, for Beeroth were considered among the children of Benjamin. The Beerothites ran away to Gethaim, and were immigrants there until this day. Jonathan, Saul's son, had a son with lame feet, and he was five years old when the news of Saul, and Jonathan his son, came from Jezreel, and his nurse picked him up to flee, and it happened that as he rushed to retreat, that he fell, and was injured. His name was Mephi-bosheth.

Rechab and Baanah the sons of Rimmon the Beerothite went to the house of Ish-bosheth in the heat of the day, and he was sleeping on a bed at noon, while the porter of the house winnowed wheat. He slumbered and slept, and the brothers Rechab and Baanah went secretly into the house. Ish-bosheth was sleeping on his bed in his chamber, and they stabbed him, and killed him, and cut off his head. They took his head and traveled all night by the western road. They brought the head of Ish-bosheth to David in Hebron, and they said to the king, "Look the head of Ish-bosheth the son of Saul your enemy, who wanted your life. The Lord has executed for my lord the king's vengeance on his enemies. It is this day, against Saul your enemy, and on his seed."

David replied to Rechab and Baanah his brother, the sons of Rimmon the Beerothite, "As the Lord lives, who has redeemed my spirit out of all affliction. He who reported to me that Saul was dead, even though he thought he was bringing good news to me,

I seized him and killed him in Ziklag. He, who thought I should have given a reward for his news. Now evil men have slain a righteous man in his house, and on his bed. Now then, I will require his blood from your hand, and I will destroy you from off the earth." David commanded his young men, and they kill them and cut off their hands and their feet, and they hung them up at the fountain in Hebron. They buried the head of Ish-bosheth in the tomb of Ebenezer the son of Ner.

# 2nd Kingdoms: Chapter 5

All the tribes of Israel came to David in Hebron, and said to him, "Look, we are your bone and your flesh. And until now Saul was our king, and you were the one that led in Israel, and the Lord said to you, 'You will feed my people Israel, and you will be a leader for my people Israel.'"

All the elders of Israel came to the king in Hebron, and King David made a covenant with them in Hebron before the Lord, and they anointed David king over all Israel. David was thirty years old when he began to reign, and he reigned forty years. Seven years and six months he reigned in Hebron over Judah, and thirty-three years he reigned over all Israel and Judah in Jerusalem. David and his men, departed to Jerusalem, to the Jebusites that inhabited the land, and it was told to David, "You will not come in here, for the blind and the lame outside, saying, "David will not come in here." David was the first to capture the hold of Zion,[1] (this is the City of David.) David said on that day, "Everyone that kills the Jebusite, let him attack with daggers both the lame and the blind, and all those that hate the spirit of David, and say, 'The lame and the blind will not enter into the house of the Lord.'"

David lived in the hold, and it was called the City of David, and he built the city itself around the citadel, and he built his own palace. David advanced and became great, and Lord Sabaoth[2] with him. Hiram king of Tyre sent messengers to David, and cedarwood, and carpenters, and stonemasons, and they built a palace for David. David knew that the Lord had prepared him to be king over Israel and that his kingdom was exalted for the sake of his people Israel. David took more wives and concubines from Jerusalem after he came from Hebron, and David had even more sons and daughters born to him.

These are the names of those that were born to him in Jerusalem: Shammua, Shobab, Nathan, Solomon, Ibhar, Elishua, Nepheg, Japhia, Elishama, Eliada, Eliphalet, Samae, Jessibath, Nathan, Galamaan, Jebaar, Theesus, Eliphalat, Naged, Nepheg, Jonathan, Leasamys, Baalimath, and Eliphaath. The Pelesets heard that David was the anointed king over Israel, and all the Pelesets went up to find David. When David heard of it and went down to the stronghold. The Pelesets came and assembled in the Valley of the Raphites.[3] David asked the Lord, "Will I attack the Pelesets? Will you deliver them into my hands?"

The Lord answered David, "Attack, and I will certainly deliver the Pelesets into your hands."

David traveled from the lord of the Perezites[4] and slaughtered the Pelesets there, and David said, "The Lord has destroyed the hostile Pelesets before me, like water is dispersed," therefore the name of that place was called Ba'al Peretzim. They left their gods there and David and his men took them. The Pelesets came up yet again and assembled in the Valley of Raphites. David inquired of the Lord, and the Lord said, "You will not go up to meet them, turn from them, and you will meet them near the place of weeping. It will come to pass when you hear the sound of a clashing together from the grove of weeping, then you will go down to them, for then the Lord will go out before you to make havoc in the battle with the Pelesets."

David did as the Lord commanded him, and slaughtered the Pelesets from Gibeah as far as the land of Gazer.

# 2<sup>nd</sup> Kingdoms: Chapter 5 Notes

**1** Codex Vaticanus: Siôn (ⲥⲉⲓⲱⲛ)

- Codex Alexandrinus: Siôn (ⲥⲓⲱⲛ)

- LXX 74: Sêôn (ⲥⳑⲟⲟⲛ)

- Aleppo Codex: Sywn (צִיּוֹן)

- Leningrad Codex: Tziyyon (צִיּוֹן)

- Targum Jerusalem: Tziyon (צִיוֹן)


**2** Codex Vaticanus: c̄s pantocratôr (ⲕⲥⲡⲁⲛⲧⲟⲕⲣⲁⲧⲱⲣ). Translation: lord omnipotent (or almighty)

- Codex Alexandrinus: c̄s o t̄hs o pantocratôr (ⲕⲥ ⲟ ⲑⲥ ⲟ ⲡⲁⲛⲧⲟⲕⲣⲁⲧⲱⲣ). Translation: lord the god the omnipotent (or almighty)

- Dead Sea Scroll 4QSam<sup>a</sup>: Yhwh ṣbåwt (יהוה צבאות). Translation: Yhwh of forces (or armies in Hebrew)

- Aleppo Codex: Yhwh ålhy ṣbåwt (יהוה אלהי צבאות). Translation: Yhwh god of forces (or armies in Hebrew)

- Leningrad Codex: Yhvah elohei tzeva'ovt (יְהוָה אֱלֹהֵי צְבָאוֹת). Translation: Yhwah god of forces (or armies in Hebrew)

- Targum Jerusalem: daYyah elaha tzeva'ovt (דַיְיָ אֱלָהָא צְבָאוֹת). Translation: Yahw god of desires


**3** Codex Vaticanus: Titanôn (ⲧⲓⲧⲁⲛⲱⲛ). Translation: Titans

- Aleppo Codex: Rpåym (רפאים). Translation: long dead

- Leningrad Codex: Refa'im (רְפָאִים). Translation: long dead

- Coptic manuscripts: Rafain (Ⲣⲁϥⲁⲉⲛ)

- Targum Jerusalem: gibbaraya (גִּבָּרַיָא). Translation: men (or husbands)

• The name of this valley was transliterated as Emecraphaen (Εμεκραφαειν) in the Septuagint's Joshua chapter 18, which was identified in a scribal note as the then current name of the former Forest of Sonnam (Ναπης Σονναμ). The Masoretic version of the verse uses the alternate name of Valley of the sons of Hinns (גי בן הנם) for the Forest of Sonnam, however, this means the Valley of the sons of Hinns was right next to the Hollows of the Raphites (עמק רפאים).

The Titans were a group of ancient deities that correlate to the Canaanite Elohim. The Rephaites may have been an ancient tribe that once lived in the region of Canaan, however, by the time the Ugaritic Texts were translated, circa 1350 BC, the Raphites were ghost-like 'long dead' ancestors in the underworld. As the Greeks appear to have translated 'Raphites' as 'Titans,' the term 'Valley of Raphites' is used in this translation.

**4** Codex Vaticanus: epanô diacopôn (ЄΠΑΝѠⲆΙΑΚΟΠⲦѠΝ). Translation: above (or on, up) breaks (or disruptions)

• LXX 707: epanô diacoptôn (ЄΠΑΝѠⲆΙΑΚΟΠⲦѠΝ). Translation: above (or on, up) breakers (or disrupters)

• LXX 246: epanô ANÔ diacopôn (ⲋΠαⲛⲛοο ⲀΝѠ ⲆιⲆⲗιοποοⲛ). Translation: above (or on, up) King breaks (or disruptions)

• Aleppo Codex: bôl prsym (**בעל פרצים**). Translation: the Lord of Perezites (or violent, murderers, robbers)

• Leningrad Codex: baal Peratzim (בְּעַל פְּרָצִים). Translation: the Lord of Perezites (or violent, murderers, robbers)

• Targum Jerusalem: meishar Peratzim (מֵישַׁר פְּרָצִים). Translation: plain of the violent (or murderers, robbers)

The Perezites (פְּרָצִים) in question were likely the Perezite clan of Judah, the descendants of the Perez (פֶּרֶץ), the son of Judah. Therefore, the term 'lord of the Perezites' is used in this translation.

# 2<sup>nd</sup> Kingdoms: Chapter 6

David again gathered all the young men of Israel, about seventy thousand. David rose and went with all the people that were with him, and some of the rulers of Judah on an expedition to a distant place, to bring back the ark of God.[1] (Who is known by the name of Lord Sabaoth[2] riding on the sphinxes.)[3] They put the ark of God on a new wagon and took it out of the house of Abinadab who lived on the hill, and Uzzah and his brothers, the sons of Abinadab drove the wagon with the ark, and his brothers traveled before the ark. David and the Israelites were playing mightily before the Lord on well-tuned instruments, and with songs, and with harps, lutes, drums, cymbals, and pipes.

They came as far as the threshing floor of Nachon, and Uzzah reached out his hand to the ark of God to keep it steady, and took hold of it, as the calf shook it out of its place. The Lord was very angry with Uzzah, and God killed him there, and he died there by the ark of the Lord in front of God. David was angry because the Lord had killed Uzzah, and that place was called the breach of Uzzah to this day. David was afraid of the Lord in that day, and said, "How will the ark of the Lord come to me?"

David would not bring the ark of the covenant of the Lord to himself in the City of David, and David stopped at the house of Obededom the Gethite. The ark of God stayed in the house of Obededom the Gethite three months, and the Lord blessed all the house of Obededom, and all his possessions. It was reported to King David, "The Lord has blessed the house of Obededom, and all that he has, because of the ark of God."

David went and brought up the ark of God from the house of Obededom in the City of David with celebration. There were with him seven hands carrying the ark, and for a sacrifice, a calf and lambs. David sounded with well-tuned instruments before the Lord, and David was clothed with a fine long robe. David and all the house of Israel brought up the ark of God with shouting, and with the sound of a trumpet. It came to pass as the ark arrived at the City of David, that Michal the daughter of Saul looked through the window, and saw king David dancing and playing before the Lord, and she despised him in her heart. They brought the ark of God and set it in its place in the middle of the tabernacle which David pitched for it, and David offered whole burnt offerings before the Lord and peace-offerings. David finished offering the whole burnt offerings and peace-offerings and blessed the people in the name of the Lord Sabaoth. He distributed to all the people, even to all the army of Israel from Dan to Bathsheba, both men, and women, to every one a cake of bread, and a joint of meat, and a cake from the frying-pan, and all the people departed every one to his home.

David returned to bless his house. Michal the daughter of Saul came out to meet David and saluted him, and said, "How was the king of Israel glorified today, who was today uncovered in the eyes of the handmaids of his servants, as one of the dancers wantonly uncovers himself!"

David said to Michal, "I will dance before the Lord. Blessed be the Lord who chose me before your father, and before all his house, to make me head over his people, even over Israel. Therefore I will play, and dance before the Lord. I will again unclothe myself, and I will be vile in your eyes, and with the maidservants by whom you said that I was not held in honor."

Michal the daughter of Saul had no child till the day of her death.

# 2nd Kingdoms: Chapter 6 Notes

**1** Codex Vaticanus: cibôton tou t̄h̄u̅ (ΚΙΒѠΤΟΝΤΟΥΘΥ). Translation: box of the god

• Dead Sea Scroll 4QSamᵃ: the phrase is damaged, however, -l-m l (ל-מי אל) survives. The missing text is reconstructed by academics as årwn hålhym ål (ארון האלהים אל), meaning 'ark of the god(s) El.'

• Aleppo Codex: årwn hålhym (ארון האלהים). Translation: box of the gods

• Leningrad Codex: arovn ha'elohim (אֲרוֹן הָאֱלֹהִים). Translation: box of the gods

• Targum Jerusalem: arona daYyah (אֲרוֹנָא דַיְיָ). Translation: box of Yahw

**2** Codex Vaticanus: c̄u̅ tôn dynameôn (ΚΥΤѠΝΔΥΝΑΜΕѠΝ). Translation: Lord of the forces

• LXX 127: Sabaôth (Cαuλ∞θ)

• LXX 56: Thy tôn dynameôn (ΘΥ τοoν Δuɴαɴɴμ6ϭoоɴ). Translation: god of the forces

• Dead Sea Scroll 4QSamᵃ: Yhwh (יהוה)

• Aleppo Codex: Yhwh sbåwt (יהוה צבאות). Yehwah of forces (or armies)

• Leningrad Codex: Yehvah tzeva'ovt (יְהוָה צְבָאוֹת). Translation: Yehwah of forces (or armies)

• Targum Jerusalem: daYyah tzeva'ovt (דַיְיָ צְבָאוֹת). Translation: the Yahw of desires

The Greek translation and surviving Hebrew sources do not agree at this point, indicating that there were multiple versions of 2ⁿᵈ Kingdoms (Masoretic: Samuel) in the Herodian era. The Greek translations of the four books of Kingdoms also do not appear consistent at this point, with the term translated in 2ⁿᵈ and 3ʳᵈ Kingdoms as 'of forces' (των δυναμεων) being transliterated directly as Sabaoth (Σαβαωθ) in 1ˢᵗ and 4ᵗʰ Kingdoms, as well as in 1ˢᵗ Paralipomenon. This indicates that the surviving version of 2ⁿᵈ and 3ʳᵈ Kingdoms found in the Septuagint manuscripts was probably based on Origen of Alexandria's Hexapla, published circa 240 AD, which itself drew on both the Old Greek translation, and the translation made the Jewish scholar Theodotion circa 150 AD. Theodotion retranslated the Septuagint into Greek from the Hebrew texts being used by Jews in the 2ⁿᵈ century.

The surviving copies of 2ⁿᵈ and 3ʳᵈ Kingdoms include both text that appears to have been redacted by the Hasmoneans, and text that appears to be pre-Hasmonean, strongly indicating it originated in the Hexapla. It is unclear why only 2ⁿᵈ and 3ʳᵈ Kingdoms were replaced, however, given the inconsistencies in the stories of Saul and David in 1ˢᵗ Kingdoms, it is possible that there were more inconsistencies in 2ⁿᵈ and 3ʳᵈ Kingdoms which the Hasmonean redactors removed, creating a clearer narrative that would have appealed to the early Greek Christians. As both the Septuagint and Masoretic texts support the name Sabaoth having once been in this verse, it is restored in this translation, however, the evidence from 1ˢᵗ Kingdoms is that the name Iaw (יהוה) was not in Samuel until the Hasmonean redaction, several decades after the Greek translation at the Library of Alexandria, and therefore the translation of 'Lord Sabaoth' is used, as it appears in the Greek translations of 1ˢᵗ and 4ᵗʰ Kingdoms.


**3** Codex Vaticanus: cheroubin (χερογʙɛιɴ)

• Codex Basiliano-Vaticanus: cheroubim (χερογʙɛιм)

• LXX 158: chaeroubim (χᾱιβουμϭιμ)

• Dead Sea Scroll 4QSamᵃ: krwby- (כרובי-). The word is damaged and the final letter, presumably an m (ם) is missing.

- Aleppo Codex: krbym (כרבים). Translation: cherubs (or sphinxes, griffins)

- Leningrad Codex: keruvim (כְּרֻבִים). Translation: cherubs (or sphinxes, griffins)

- Targum Jerusalem: keruvaya (כְּרוּבַיָא). Translation: cherubs (or sphinxes, griffins)

The Greek term is a transliteration of the Aramaic krbyn (ᵏʳᵇʸⁿ), indicating the Greek translation of 2<sup>nd</sup> Kingdoms was made from an Aramaic source. The term found in the Masoretic text a transliteration of the Aramaic word, indicating the Hebrew translation of Samuel was based on an Aramaic copy of the book. The damaged term found in Dead Sea Scroll 4QSam<sup>a</sup> is the Hebrew word 'cherubs' with the final letter, an M (ם), damaged. Dead Sea Scroll 4QSam<sup>a</sup>, both in this sentence and many others, shows that the Hebrew version of Samuel was still being modified as late as the Herodian Dynasty, however, the Masoretes appear to have gone back to an earlier version for their source.

The word 'cherub' (כרוב / בּֿהֿכ / עֿזֿע / 𐤂𐤓𐤁) was the West Semitic term for the mythical creature generally called a 'griffin' today. Based in the archaeological record of Canaan, it appears that the concept of the cherub was based on the Egyptian sphinx, as the earliest cherub statues found in Canaan were Egyptian statues of sphinxes. Archaeologists are not sure if the sphinxes of Anatolia were based on the Canaanite cherub, or the Egyptian sphinxes directly, however, all three mythical beings are closely related in the archaeological record. As the term cherub was for some reason reinterpreted as 'baby angels' by Christians, although it is not clear why any god would ride around on 'baby angels,' the alternate translation of 'sphinxes' is used in this translation.

# 2ⁿᵈ Kingdoms: Chapter 7

When the king sat in his house, and the Lord had given him an inheritance on every side, free from all his enemies around him. The king said to Nathan, the prophet, "Look now, I live in a palace of cedar, and the ark of God remains in a tent."

Nathan said to the king, "Go and do all that is in your heart, for the Lord is with you."

That night, the voice of the Lord came to Nathan, "Go, and say to my servant David, the Lord says, 'You will not build me a temple to live in. For I have not lived in a temple from the day that I brought up the Israelites out of Egypt to this day, but I have been walking in a lodge and in a tent, wherever I went with all Israel. Have I ever spoken to any of the tribes of Israel, which I commanded to tend my people Israel, "Why have you not built a temple of Cedar for me?"'"

"Now you will say to my servant David, the Lord Sabaoth[1] says, 'I took you from the sheepfold, that you should be a prince over my people, over Israel. I was with you wherever you went, and I destroyed all your enemies before you, and I made you as famous as anyone who is famous among the great ones in the earth. I will appoint a place for my people Israel and will plant them, and they will live by themselves and will no longer be distressed. The son of iniquity will no longer afflict them, as he has done from the beginning, from the days when I appointed judges over my people Israel."

"I will give you peace from all your enemies, and the Lord will tell you when you will build a temple for him. It will come to pass when your days have been fulfilled, and you will sleep with your fathers, that I will raise up your seed after you, even your own issue, and I will establish his kingdom. He will build for a temple to my name, and I will set up his throne even forever. I will be to him a father, and he will be to me a son. When he happens to transgress, then will I chasten him with the wand of men, and with the stripes of the sons of men. But my mercy I will not take from him, as I took it from those whom I removed from my presence. His house will be made sure, and his kingdom forever before me, and his throne will be set up forever." All these words and this entire vision Nathan spoke to David.

King David came in, and sat before the Lord, and said, "Who am I, Ba'al my Lord,[2] and what is my house, that you have loved me until now? I was very little before you, Ba'al my Lord, yet you spoke concerning the house of your servant for a long time to come. Is this the ways of man, Ba'al my Lord? What will David yet say to you? And now you know your servant, Ba'al my Lord."

"You have worked for your servant's sake, and according to your heart you have worked all this greatness, to make it known to your servant, that he may magnify you, my lord, for there is no one like you, and there are no gods like you among all of whom we have heard of. Which other nation in the earth is like your people Israel? God was his guide, to redeem for himself a people to make you a name, to do mightily and nobly so that you should throw out nations and their tabernacles from the presence of your people, whom you did redeem for yourself out of Egypt? You have prepared for yourself your people Israel to be a people forever, and you, the Lord, have become their god."

"Now, Ba'al my Lord, the word spoken concerning your servant and his house, stated by you Lord Sabaoth the god of Israel, and now as you said, (Let your name be praised forever,) Lord Sabaoth, you have uncovered the ear of your servant, saying, 'I will build you a house, therefore your servant has found in his heart to pray this prayer to you. Now, Ba'al my Lord, and your words will be true, and you have spoken these good things concerning your servant. Now begin and bless the house of your servant, that it may continue forever before you, for you, Ba'al my Lord, have spoken, and the house of your servant will be blessed with your blessing to continue forever."

# 2<sup>nd</sup> Kingdoms: Chapter 7 Notes

**1** Codex Vaticanus: c̄s pantocratôr (ΚⲤΠⲀΝΤⲞ-ΚΡⲀΤⲰΡ). Translation: lord omnipotent (or almighty)

- Aleppo Codex: Yhwh ṣbȧwt (**יהוה צבאות**). Translation: Yhwh of forces (or armies)

- Leningrad Codex: Yehvah tzeva'ovt (יְהֹוָה צְבָאֹות). Translation: Yehwah of forces (or armies)

- Targum Jerusalem: Yeyah tzeva'ovt (צְבָאֹות יְיָ). Translation: Yahw of desires


**2** Codex Vaticanus: Cyrie mou Cyrie (ΚΥΡⲒⲈⲘⲞΥΚΥΡⲒⲈ). Translation: lord my Lord

- Dead Sea Scroll 4QSamᵃ: uses this expression a couple of lines later: Yhwh ȧdny (𐤉𐤄𐤅𐤄 𐤀𐤃𐤍𐤉). Translation: Yhwh my lord

- Aleppo Codex: ȧdny Yhwh (**אדני יהוה**). Translation: my lord Yhwh

- Leningrad Codex: adonai Yehvih (אֲדֹנָי יְהֹוִה). Translation: my lord Yehwih

- Targum Jerusalem: Yeyah elohim (אֱלֹהִים יְיָ). Translation: Yahw of gods

As the Greeks would have translated the phrase found in the Masoretic texts as 'my lord Iaw' (μου κυριε Ιαω), and the text in the 4QSamᵃ as 'Iaw my lord' (Ιαω μου κυριε), it is clear the Aramaic text they translated contained a different phrase. Assuming adonai was the word the Greeks translated as 'my lord' (μου κυριε), the original phrase would have been 'Ba'al my Lord' (𐤁𐤏𐤋 𐤀𐤃𐤍𐤉) in Aramaic.

As David named his son Solomon after Ba'al Shalim, the Canaanite god of the evening, and Solomon went on to build the temple in Jerusalem that David had envisioned, in which he erected Moses' bronze snake statute, which was worshiped as Ba'al until King Hezekiah's reforms, this was probably the Ba'al David was referring too. All references to the statue were removed from the Israelite texts at some point, other than its introduction in Numbers, and its destruction in 4<sup>th</sup> Kingdoms, two events 700 years apart in the chronology of the Septuagint. Therefore, the bronze statue must have been housed in the tabernacle with the box of elohim before being moved to the Temple of Shalim in Jerusalem. As David is described as sitting before the lord in the tabernacle, the statue must have been viewed as the lord during his era.

# 2ⁿᵈ Kingdoms: Chapter 8

After this, David slaughtered the Pelesets and made them flee, and David took the tribute from the hand of the Pelesets. David invaded Moab, and measured them out with lines, having laid them down on the ground, and there were two lines for murdering, and two lines he left alive, and Moab became subject to David, yielding tribute. David slaughtered Hadadezer the son of Rehob king of Zoba, as he went to extend his power to the Euphrates River. David took a thousand of his chariots, and seven thousand cavalry, and twenty thousand infantry, and David hamstrung all his chariot horses, and he reserved to himself a hundred chariots.

Damascus in Syria came to help Hadadezer king of Zoba, and David slaughtered twenty-two thousand men belonging to the Syrians. David placed a garrison in Syria near Damascus, and the Syrians became servants and tributaries to David, and the Lord preserved David wherever he went. David took the golden bracelets which were on the servants of Hadadezer king of Zoba and brought them to Jerusalem. (King Shoshenq[1] of Egypt took them when he went up to Jerusalem in the days of Rehoboam the son of Solomon.)

King David took from Metebac, and from the choice cities of Hadadezer, a great deal of brass, which Solomon made the bronze sea, and the pillars, and the lavers, and all the furniture.

The king of Hemath heard that David had struck all the army of Hadadezer. You sent Jedduram his son to king David, to ask him of his welfare, and to congratulate him on his fighting against Hadadezer and striking him, for he was an enemy to Hadadezer. In his hands were vessels of silver, and vessels of gold, and vessels of brass. These kings David consecrated to the Lord, with the silver and with the gold which he consecrated out of all the cities which he conquered, out of Edom, and Moab, and the Ammonites, and from the Pelesets, and Amalek, and from the spoils of Hadadezer son of Rehob king of Zoba.

David made himself a name, and when he returned he struck Edom in Gebelem to the number of eighteen thousand. He set garrisons in Edom, even in all Edom: and all the Edomites were servants to the king. The Lord preserved David wherever he went. David reigned over all Israel: and David worked judgment and justice over all his people. Joab the son of Zeruiah was over the army, and Jehoshaphat the son of Ahilud was the keeper of the records. Zadok the son of Ahitub, and Ahimelech son of Abiathar were priests, and Sasa was the scribe, and Benaiah son of Jehoiada was a councilor, and the Cherethite and the Pelethite, and the sons of David were princes of the court.

# 2ⁿᵈ Kingdoms: Chapter 8 Notes

**1** Codex Vaticanus: Sousacim (ⲥⲟⲩⲥⲁⲕⲉⲓⲙ)

- Codex Alexandrinus: Sousacim (ⲥⲟⲩⲥⲁⲕⲓⲙ)

- LXX 489: Sousacin (ⲥⲟⲩⲥⲁⲗⲓⲛ)

- Coptic manuscripts: pharao (ⲫⲁⲣⲁⲟ). Translation: pharaoh

- Vetus Latina: Susac

The king's name was not mentioned in this verse of the Masoretic text or Targum Jerusalem, however is later called Shishak / Šyšq (שִׁישַׁק / שִׁישָׁק). Dead Sea Scroll 4QSamᵃ includes a damaged Hebrew version of the Septuagint's verse, however, the name is in the damaged section. Based on the era when he lived, he is generally accepted as Shoshenq I (𓇓𓈙𓈙) who campaigned in Canaan during the era of King Rehoboam. The damaged section of text in Dead Sea Scroll 4QSamᵃ indicates that the longer version of the verse found in the Septuagint was once in Hebrew translations, however, the following verse, which is missing from the Masoretic text also appears to have not been included in Dead Sea Scroll 4QSamᵃ.

# 2ⁿᵈ Kingdoms: Chapter 9

David asked, "Is there still anyone left in the house of Saul, that I may deal kindly with him for Jonathan's sake?"

There was a servant of the house of Saul named Ziba. They called him to David, and the king asked him, "Are you Ziba?"

He answered, "I am your servant."

The king asked, "Is there still a man left of the house of Saul, that I may act towards him with the mercy of God?"

Ziba answered the king, "There is still a son of Jonathan, with lame feet."

The king asked, "Where is he?"

Ziba answered the king, "He is in the house of Machir, the son of Ammiel of Lodebar."

King David went and took him out of the house of Machir, the son Ammiel of Lodebar. Mephibosheth the son of Jonathan the son of Saul came to King David, and he fell on his face and paid respect to him, and David said to him, "Mephibosheth."

He answered, "See, your servant."

David said to him, "Don't be afraid, for I will certainly deal mercifully with you for the sake of Jonathan your father, and I will restore to you all the land of Saul the father of your father, and you will eat bread at my table forever."

Mephibosheth paid respect, and said, "Who am I, your servant? That you have looked on a dead dog like me?"

The king called Ziba the servant of Saul, and said to him, "All that belonged to Saul and to all his house have I given to the son of your lord. You, and your sons, and your servants will till the land for him, and you will bring in bread to the son of your lord, and he will eat bread. Mephibosheth the son of your lord will eat bread forever at my table."

Ziba had fifteen sons and twenty servants. Ziba said to the king, "All that my lord, the king, has commanded his servant, your servant will do."

Mephibosheth ate at the table of David, like one of the sons of the king. Mephibosheth had a young son, and his name was Micha, and all the household of Ziba were servants to Mephibosheth. Mephibosheth lived in Jerusalem, and he continually ate at the table of the king, and he was lame in both his feet.

# 2ⁿᵈ Kingdoms: Chapter 10

After this, the king of the Ammonites died, and Hanun his son reigned in his place. David said, "I will show mercy to Hanun the son of Nahash, as his father dealt mercifully with me."

David sent to comfort him concerning his father by the hand of his servants, and the servants of David came into the land of the Ammonites. The princes of the Ammonites asked Hanun their lord, "Is it to honor your father before you that David has sent comforters to you? Has David not instead sent his servants to you that they should search the city, and spy it out and examine it?"

Hanun took the servants of David, and shaved their beards, and cut off their garments in the middle as far as their haunches, and sent them away. They brought David word concerning the men, and he sent to meet them, for the men were greatly dishonored, and the king said, "Remain in Jericho until your beards have grown, and then return."

The Ammonites saw that the people of David were ashamed, and the Ammonites sent and hired the Syrians of Bethrehob, Zoba, and Rehob, twenty thousand infantry, and the king of Amalek with a thousand men, and Ishtob with twelve thousand men. David heard, and sent Joab and all his army of mighty men. The Ammonites went out and set the battle formation by the door of the gate. Those of Syria, and Zoba, and Rehob, and Ishtob, and Amalek, were by themselves in the field. Joab saw the formation of the battle before him, seperate groups to attack in front and from behind, and he chose out some of all the young men of Israel, and they set themselves in formation against Syria.

The rest of the people he turned over to Abishai his brother, and they set the battle formation opposite the Ammonites, and he said, "If Syria is too strong for me, then you will help me, and if the Ammonites are too strong for you, then we will be ready to help you. Be courageous, and let us be strong for our people, and for the sake of the cities of our gods, and the Lord will do that which is good in his eyes."

Joab and his people with him advanced to battle against Syria, and they fled from before him. The Ammonites saw that the Syrians had fled, and they fled from before Abishai, and entered into the city, and Joab returned from the Ammonites, and came to Jerusalem. The Syrians saw that they were ashamed before Israel, and they gathered themselves together. Hadadezer sent and gathered the Syrians from the other side of the river Chalamak, and they came to Helam, and Shobach the captain of the army of Hadadezer was at their head. It was reported to David, and he gathered all Israel, and went across the Jordan, and came to Helam, and the Syrians set the battle formation against David and fought with him. Syria fled from before Israel, and David destroyed in Syria seven hundred chariots and forty thousand cavalry, and he killed Shobach the captain of his army, and he died there. All the kings the servants of Hadadezer saw that they were ashamed before Israel, and they went over to Israel and served them, and Syria was afraid to help the Ammonites again.

# 2ⁿᵈ Kingdoms: Chapter 11

When the time of the year for kings going out to battle had come around, David sent Joab, and his servants with him, and all Israel, and they destroyed the Ammonites, and besieged Rabbah. David stayed in Jerusalem. One afternoon David rose off his couch, and walked on the roof of the king's palace, and saw from the roof a woman bathing, and the woman was very beautiful to look at. David sent and inquired about the woman, and someone said, "Isn't this Bathsheba the daughter of Eliab, the wife of Orion[1] the Cypriot?"[2]

David sent messengers, and took her, and went into her, and he lay with her, and she was purified from her uncleanness and returned to her house. The woman conceived, and she sent a message and told David, "I am with child."

David sent a message to Joab, saying, "Send me Orion the Cypriot," and Joab sent Orion to David.

Orion arrived and went to him, and David asked him how Joab was, and how the people were, and how the war went on. David said to Orion, "Go to your house, and wash your feet," and Orion departed from the house of the king, and a portion of meat from the king followed him.

Orion slept at the door of the king with the servants of his lord and did not go down to his house. They informed David, "Orion has not gone down to his house."

David asked Orion, "Have you not come from a journey? Why have you not gone down to your house?"

Orion answered David, "The ark, and Israel, and Judah live in tents, and my lord Joab, and the servants of my lord, are camped in the open fields, yet I will return to my house to eat and drink, and lie with my wife? How could I do this? As your spirit lives, I will not do this thing."

David said to Orion, "Stay here today also, and tomorrow I will let you go."

Orion remained in Jerusalem that day and the day following. David called him, and he ate with him and drank, and he got him drunk, and he went out in the evening to lie on his bed with the servants of his lord and did not return to his house. The morning came, and David wrote a letter to Joab and sent it by the hand of Orion. He wrote in the letter, "Station Orion in front of the severe part of the fight, and retreat from behind him, so he will be wounded and die."

While Joab was watching against the city, he set Orion in a place where he knew that valiant men were. The men of the city went out and fought with Joab, and some of the people of the servants of David fell, and Orion the Cypriot died also. Joab sent, and reported to David all the events of the war. He ordered the messenger, "When you have finished reporting all the events of the war to the king, then it will come to pass if the anger of the king will rise, and he will say to you, 'Why did you approach the city to fight? Did you not know that they would shoot from off the wall? Who struck Abimelech the son of Jerubbaal the son of Ner? Did a woman not throw a piece of a mill stone on him from above the wall, and he died in Thebez? Why did you go near to the wall?' Then you will say, 'Your servant Orion the Cypriot is also dead.'"

The messenger of Joab went to the king in Jerusalem, and he came and reported to David all that Joab told him, all the affairs of the war. David was very angry with Joab, and said to the messenger, "Why did you approach the wall to fight? Didn't you know that you would be wounded from off the wall? Who struck Abimelech the son of Jerubbaal? Didn't a woman throw a piece of the mill stone on to him from the wall, and he died in Thebez? Why did you approach the wall?"

The messenger answered David, "The men prevailed against us, and they came out against us into the field, and we came on them even to the door of the gate. The archers shot at your servants from off the wall, and some of the king's servants died, and your servant Orion the Cypriot is dead also."

David said to the messenger, "Tell Joab, 'don't let the matter be grievous in your eyes, for the sword devours one way at one time and another way at another, strengthen your formation against the city, and destroy it, and strengthen him."

The wife of Orion heard that Orion her husband was dead, and she mourned for her husband. The time of mourning expired, and David sent and took her into his house, and she became his wife and carried him a son. But the thing which David did was evil in the eyes of the Lord.

# 2ⁿᵈ Kingdoms: Chapter 11 Notes

**1** Codex Vaticanus: Oyrian (ΟΥΡΕΙΑΝ)

• Codex Alexandrinus: Oyrian (ΟΥΡΙΑΝ). Translation: fair winds (an epithet of Zeus)

• Aleppo Codex: Åwryh (אוריה). Translation: light of Yah

• Leningrad Codex: Uriyyah (אוּרִיָּה). Translation: light of Yah

• Targum Jerusalem: Uriyah (אוּרִיָה)

The differences between the Greek and Hebrew translations do not follow the norm for Aramaic terms transliterated into Greek. If the older Aramaic source texts included åwryh (אוריה), it would have been transliterated as Oyrios (Ουριος). The Greek transliteration indicates that the Aramaic name was Åwrôån (אורואן). This suggests that the Hebrew translators substituted 'Yah' (יה) for 'An' (אן), in this name, which is consistent with other changes made when the Hebrew translation was made. The Septuagint's Exodus includes Moses' god identifying himself as Ôn (Ων), a name later found in the Septuagint's Book of Hosea, which is mirrored in the Masoretic text by the name Aven (אָוֶן) / Åwn (און). Therefore, the original name of this person was likely the Akkadian name úru An (𒌓𒀭), meaning 'Light of An,' which was imported to Greece in the early Iron Age as Orion (Ωριων). As the name Orion is more common than Uru-An, it is used in this translation.

**2** Codex Vaticanus: Chettaeon (ΧΕΤΤΑΙΟΝ)

• LXX 55: Chetaeon (Χέται̣ον)

• Aleppo Codex: Hty (חתי). Translation: Cypriot

• Leningrad Codex: Chitti (חִתִּי). Translation: Cypriot

• Targum Jerusalem: Chitta'ah (חִתָּאָה)

As the term referred to the entire island of Cyprus in Aramaic, the translations of 'Cyprus' and 'Cypriots' are used here.

# 2nd Kingdoms: Chapter 12

The Lord sent Nathan, the prophet to David, and he said to him, "There were two men in one city, one rich and the other poor. The rich man had many flocks and herds. But the poor man had only one little ewe lamb, which he had purchased, and preserved, and reared, and it grew up with himself and his children in common, it ate of his bread and drank of his cup, and slept on his chest, and was for him as a daughter. A traveler came to the rich man, and he refused to take from his flocks and of his herds, to dress for the traveler that came to him, and he took the poor man's lamb, and dressed it for the man that came to him."

David was greatly angered against the man, and David said to Nathan, "As the Lord lives, the man that did this thing will certainly die. He will restore the lamb seven-fold because he has not spared."

Nathan said to David, "You are the man that has done this, according to Lord the god[1] of Israel. I anointed you to be king over Israel, and I rescued you out the hand of Saul, and I gave you the house of your lord and the wives of your lord into your bosom, and I gave to you the house of Israel and Judah, and if that had been little, I would have given you yet more. Why have you disregarded the word of the Lord, to do that which is evil in his eyes? You have slain Orion the Cypriot with the sword, and you have taken his wife to be your wife, and you have slain him with the sword of the Ammonites. Now, therefore, the sword will not leave from your house forever, because you have viewed me as nothing, and you have taken the wife of Orion the Cypriot, to be your wife. The Lord says, 'Look, I will raise up against you evil out of your house, and I will take your wives before your eyes, and will give them to your neighbor, and he will lie with your wives in the sight of the sun. For you did it secretly, but I will do this thing in the sight of all Israel, and before the sun.'"

David said to Nathan, "I have sinned against the Lord."

Nathan said to David, "The Lord has forgiven your sin, you will not die. Only because you have given great occasion of provocation to the enemies of the Lord by this thing, your son also that is born to you will certainly die." Then Nathan departed to his house.

The Lord infected the child, which the wife of Orion the Cypriot carried to David, and it was ill. David inquired of God concerning the child, and David fasted, and went in and lay all night on the ground. The elders of his house arose and went to him to raise him up from the ground, but he would not rise, nor did he eat bread with them. It came to pass on the seventh day that the child died, and the servants of David were afraid to tell him that the child was dead, as they said, "Look, while the child was yet alive we spoke to him, and he did not listen to our voice. If we should tell him that the child is dead, he would harm himself."

David understood that his servants were whispering, and David perceived that the child was dead, and David asked his servants, "Is the child dead?"

They answered, "He is dead."

Then David rose up from the earth, and washed, and anointed himself, and changed his clothing, and went into the Temple of God, and worshiped him, and went into his palace, and called for bread to eat, and they set bread before him and he ate. His servants asked him, "What is this thing that you have done concerning the child? While it was yet living you fasted, and cried, and watched, and when the child was dead you rose up and ate bread, and drank?"

David said, "While the child yet lived, I fasted and wept, for I said, 'Who knows if the Lord will pity me, and let the child live? But now it is dead, why should I fast more? Will I be able to bring him back again? I will go to him, but he will not return to me."

David comforted Bathsheba his wife, and he went to her and lay with her, and she conceived and carried a son, and he called his named Solomon, and the Lord loved him. He sent by the hand of Nathan the prophet, and called his name Jedidiah, for the Lord's sake.

Joab fought against Rabbah of the Ammonites and captured the royal city. Joab sent messengers to David, saying, "I have fought against Rabbah, and captured the city of waters. Now gather the rest of the people, and besiege the city, and capture it first, in case I capture the city first, and my name is called on it."

David gathered all the people, and went to Rabbah, and fought against it, and captured it. He took the crown of their king from off his head, and the weight of it was a talent of gold, with precious stones, and it was on the head of David, and he carried out great plunder from the city. He brought out the people that were in it, and put them under the saw, and under iron harrows, and axes of iron, and made them pass through the brick-kiln. He did this to all the cities of the Ammonites, then David and all the people returned to Jerusalem.

# 2nd Kingdoms: Chapter 12 Notes

**1** Codex Vaticanus: cs o ths Israêl (ΚϹΟΘϹΙϹΡΑΗΛ). Translation: Lord the god of Israel

- Codex Basiliano-Vaticanus: o theos Israêl (ΟΘΕΟϹΙϹΡΑΗΛ). Translation: the god of Israel

- LXX 243: cyrios (κυριος). Translation: Lord

- Aleppo Codex: Yhwh âlhy (יהוה אלהי). Translation: Yehwah goddess

- Leningrad Codex: Yehvah elohei (יְהוָה אֱלֹהֵי). Translation: Yehwah goddess

- Targum Jerusalem: Yeyah elaha (יְיָ אֱלָהָא). Translation: Yahw god

The Aramaic sections of Masoretic Daniel that were not translated into Hebrew maintain the term adonai ha'elohim (אֲדֹנָי הָאֱלֹהִים), meaning the 'Lord the gods' where the Septuagint has 'Lord the god' (Κυριον τον θεον), however, the Hebrew sections have Yahweh elohim (יְהוָה אֱלֹהִים) where the Septuagint has 'Lord the god,' suggesting the Greek more accurately reflects the Aramaic source texts than the Hebrew translation. According to some records from the time, this was to repair the damage King Manasseh had done 600 years earlier when he removed the name Yahweh from the Israelite Texts, however, no evidence has survived from the era of Manasseh or earlier that proves the name was originally in the text, suggesting it was an attempt by the first Hasmonean High-Priest/King Simon the Zealot to create a national Judean religion with a god having a name similar to the Roman god Jove.

# 2nd Kingdoms: Chapter 13

Absalom the son of David had a very beautiful sister, and her name was Tamar, and Amnon the son of David loved her. Amnon was distressed even to sickness, because of Tamar his sister, for she was a virgin, and it seemed very difficult for Amnon to do anything to her. Amnon had a friend, and his name was Jonadab, the son of Shimeah the brother of David, and Jonadab was a very cunning man. He said to him, "What sickens you that you are so weak, son of the king, morning after morning? Won't you tell me?"

Amman answered, "I love Tamar the sister of my brother Absalom."

Jonadab said to him, "Lie on your bed, and make yourself sick, and your father will come in to see you, and you will say to him, 'Let, I beg you, Tamar my sister come, and feed me with morsels, and let her prepare food before my eyes, that I may see and eat at her hands.'"

So Amman lay down and made himself sick, and the king came in to see him: and Amnon said to the king, "Let, I beg you, my sister Tamar come to me and make a couple of cakes in my sight, and I will eat them at her hand."

David sent to Tamar in the house, saying, "Go now to your brother's house, and prepare food for him."

Tamar went to the house of her brother Amnon, and he was lying down, and she took the dough and kneaded it, and made cakes in his sight, and baked the cakes. She took the frying pan and poured them out before him, but he would not eat. Amnon said, "Send out every man from around me."

They removed every man from around him, and Amnon said to Tamar, "Bring the food into the room, and I will eat from your hand."

Tamar took the cakes which she had made and brought them to her brother Amnon in the room. She brought them to him to eat, and he caught hold of her, and said to her, "Come, lie with me, my sister.'

She answered him, "No, my brother, do not humiliate me, for it should not be done so in Israel. Don't do this folly. How will I remove my shame? You will be seen as a fool in Israel. Now, speak, I beg you, to the king, for certainly he will not keep me from you."

But Amnon would not listen to her voice, and he prevailed against her, and humiliated her, and lay with her. Then Amnon hated her greatly as he hated her more than he loved her, as the last wickedness was greater than the first, and Amnon said to her, "Rise, and be gone."

Tamar said to him, "This is a great evil, greater than the other that you did me, to send me away," but Amnon would not listen to her voice.

He called his servant who was in charge of the house, and said to him, "Throw this woman out from my house, and shut the door behind her."

She had on her a variegated robe, as all of the king's daughters that were virgins wore the same clothes, and his servant led her out and shut the door after her. Tamar took ashes and threw them on her head, and she tore the variegated garment she was wearing, and she laid her hands on her head and went crying continually. Absalom her brother said to her, "Has your brother Amnon been with you? Now then, my sister, be silent, for he is your brother. Be careful not to mention this matter." So Tamar lived like a widow in the house of her brother Absalom.

King David heard of all these things and was very angry, but he did not grieve the spirit of his son Amnon, because he loved him, as he was his firstborn. Absalom spoke not to Amnon, good or bad, because Absalom hated Amnon, on account of his humbling his sister Tamar. It came to pass at the end of two whole years, that they were shearing sheep for Absalom in Belasor near Ephraim, and Absalom invited all the king's sons. Absalom came to the king, and said, "Look, your servant is shearing sheep. Now, let the king and his servants go with your servant."

The king said to Absalom, "No, my son, let us not all go, and let us not be burdensome to you."

He pressed him, but he would not go but blessed him. Absalom said to him, "If not, let I beg you, my brother Amnon go with us."

The king said to him, "Why should he go with you?"

Absalom pressed him, and he sent with him Amnon and all the king's sons, and Absalom made a banquet like the banquet of the king. Absalom ordered his servants, "Mark when the heart of Amnon will be merry with wine, and I will say to you, kill Amnon, and kill him, don't be afraid. Is it not what I command you? Be courageous, and be valiant." The servants of Absalom did to Amnon as Absalom commanded them, and all the sons of the king rose up, and they mounted every man his mule and fled.

It came to pass, when they were in the way, that a report came to David, "Absalom has slain all the king's sons, and there is not one of them left." Then the king arose, and tore his garments, and lay on the ground, and all his servants that were standing around him tore their garments.

Jonadab the son of Shimeah brother of David, answered and said, "Don't let my lord the king say that he has slain all the young men the sons of the king, for Amnon only of them all is dead. He was appointed to death by the mouth of Absalom from the day that he humiliated his sister Tamar. Now don't let my lord the king take the matter to heart, saying, 'All the king's sons are dead,' for Amnon only of them is dead."

Absalom escaped and the young watchman, lifted his eyes, and looked, and saw many people traveling the road behind him from the side of the mountain in the descent, and the watchman came and told the king, and said, "I have seen men on the road of Oronen, by the side of the mountain."

Jonadab said to the king, "Look, the king's sons are here, as your servant said, it has happened."

When he had finished speaking, the king's sons came, and lifted their voices and wept, and the king also and all his servants wept with a very great weeping. But Absalom fled and went to Talmai son of Ammihud the king of Geshur to the land of Chamaachad, and King David mourned for his son continually. So Absalom fled, and departed to Geshur, and was there three years. King David stopped pursuing Absalom, for he was comforted concerning Amnon, regarding his death.

# 2nd Kingdoms: Chapter 14

Joab the son of Zeruiah knew that the heart of the king was towards Absalom. Joab sent to Tekoah, and took there a cunning woman, and said to her, "Mourn, I beg you, and put on mourning apparel, and anoint you not with oil, and you will act like a woman mourning for one that has been dead for many days. You will go to the king, and speak to him according to this word."

Joab put the words in her mouth. So the woman of Tekoah went to the king and fell on her face to the earth, and did him obeisance, and said, "Help, O king, help."

The king asked her, "What is the matter with you?"

She answered, "I am a widow. My husband is dead. Moreover, your handmaid had two sons, and they fought together in the field, and there was no one to part them, and the one struck the other his brother, and killed him. Look the whole family rose up against your handmaid, and they said, 'Give up the one that struck his brother, and we will put him to death for the life of his brother, whom he killed, and we will take away even your heir,' so they will quench my coal that is left, so as not to leave my husband remnant or name on the face of the earth."

The king said to the woman, "Go in peace to your house, and I will give commandment concerning you."

The woman of Tekoah said to the king, "On me, my lord king, and on my father's house be the iniquity, and the king and his throne be guiltless."

The king said, "Who was it that spoke to you? You will even bring him to me, and one will not touch him anymore."

She said, "Let now the king remember concerning his god the Lord in that the avenger of blood is multiplied to destroy, and let them not take away my son."

He said, "As the Lord lives, not a hair of your son will fall to the ground."

The woman said, "Let now your servant speak a word to my lord the king."

He said, "Keep speaking."

The woman asked, "Why have you devised this thing against the people of God? Or is this word out of the king's mouth as a transgression, so that the king should not bring back his banished? For we will certainly die and be as water poured on the earth, which will not be gathered up, and God will take the life, even as he devises to thrust forth from him his outcast. Now whereas I came to speak this word to my lord the king, the reason is that the people will see me, and your handmaid will say, 'Let one now speak to my lord the king, if perhaps the king will perform the request of his handmaid, for the king will hear.' Let him rescue his handmaid out of the hand of the man that seeks to throw out me and my son from the inheritance of God."

The woman said, "If now the word of my lord the king be gracious, well, for as a messenger of God, so is my lord the king, to hear good and evil, and Lord the god will be with you."

The king answered, and said to the woman, "Hide not from me, I beg you, the matter which I ask you."

The woman said, "Let my lord the king by all means speak."

The king asked, "Is not the hand of Joab in all this matter with you?"

The woman answered the king, "As your spirit lives, my lord, king, there is no turning to the right hand or to the left from all that my lord the king has spoken, for your servant Joab himself ordered me, and he put all these words in the mouth of your handmaid. So that this speech might come about it was that your servant Joab has framed this matter, and my lord is as wise as the wisdom of a messenger of God, to know all things that are in the earth."

The king said to Joab, "Look now, I have done to you according to this your word. Go, bring back the young man Absalom."

Joab fell on his face to the ground, and paid respect, and blessed the king, and Joab said, "Today your servant knows that I have found grace in your sight, my lord, my king, for my lord the king has performed the request of his servant."

Joab rose, and went to Geshur, and brought Absalom to Jerusalem. The king said, "Let him return to his house, and not see my face."

Absalom returned to his house and didn't see the king's face. There was not a man in Israel so very handsome as Absalom, from the sole of his foot even to the crown of his head there was no imperfection in him. When he shaved his head, (and it was at the beginning of every year that he shaved it because it grew, heavy on him,) even when he shaved it, he weighed the hair of his head, two hundred shekels[1] according to the royal shekel. There were born to Absalom three sons and one daughter, and her name was Tamar. She was a very beautiful woman, and she becomes the wife of Rehoboam the son of Solomon, and she carried Abiah for him.

Absalom remained in Jerusalem for two full years, and he didn't see the king's face. Absalom sent to Joab to bring him to the king, and he would not come to him, and he sent a message to him the second time, and he would not come. Absalom said to his servants, "Look, Joab's portion in the field is next to mine, and he has in it barley, go and set it on fire."

The servants of Absalom set the field on fire, and the servants of Joab came to him with their clothes torn, and they said to him, "The servants of Absalom have set the field on fire."

Joab arose, and came to Absalom into the house, and said to him, "Why have your servants set my field on fire?"

Absalom said to Joab, "Look, I sent to you, saying, 'Come here, and I will send you to the king, saying, 'Why did I come out of Geshur?' It would have been better for me to have remained there, and now, look, I have not seen the face of the king, but if there is iniquity in me, then put me to death.'"

Joab went to the king and brought him word, and he called Absalom, and he went to the king, and did him obeisance, and fell on his face to the ground, even in the presence of the king, and the king kissed Absalom.

# 2ⁿᵈ Kingdoms: Chapter 14 Notes

**1** Codex Vaticanus: siclous (ⲥⲓⲕⲗⲟⲩⲥ)

- LXX 127: siclôn (σιιλοον)

- LXX 247: sitlous (σιτλουϲ)

- Aleppo Codex: šqlym (שקלים). Translation: shekels

- Leningrad Codex: shekalim (שְׁקָלִים). Translation: shekels

- Targum Jerusalem: sil'in (סִלְעִין). Translation: rocks

The shekel was a unit of weight used throughout the Middle East for thousands of years, weighing approximately 8.6 grams of silver.

# 2<sup>nd</sup> Kingdoms: Chapter 15

Absalom prepared for himself chariots and horses, and fifty men to run before him. Absalom rose early and stood by the side of the road of the gate. Every man who had a cause, came to the king for judgment, and Absalom called to him, "From what city are you?"

He said, "Your servant is of one of the tribes of Israel."

Absalom said to him, "See, your affairs are right and clear, yet you have no one appointed from the king to hear you." Absalom said, "If only one would make me a judge in the land, then every man who had a dispute or a cause would come to me, and I would judge him!" When a man came near to do him obeisance, he stretched out his hand, and took hold of him, and kissed him. Absalom did this to all Israel that came to the king for judgment, and Absalom gained the hearts of the men of Israel. It came to pass after forty years, that Absalom said to his father, I will go now, and pay my vows, which I vowed to the Lord in Hebron.

For your servant vowed a vow when I lived at Geshur in Syria, saying, "If the Lord should indeed return me to Jerusalem, then I will serve the Lord."

The king said to him, "Go in peace."

He arose and went to Hebron. Absalom sent spies throughout all the tribes of Israel, saying, "When you hear the sound of the trumpet, then will you say, Absalom has become king in Hebron."

Two hundred chosen men from Jerusalem went with Absalom, and they went in their simplicity and did not know anything. Absalom sent to Ahithophel the Theconite, the counselor of David, from his city, from Giloh, where he was sacrificing, and there was a strong conspiracy, and the people with Absalom were increasingly numerous.

A messenger to David, saying, "the heart of the men of Israel is gone after Absalom."

David said to all his servants who were with him in Jerusalem, "Rise and let us flee, for we have no refuge from Absalom. Rush to leave, in case he overtakes us quickly, and brings evil on us, and strikes the city with the edge of the sword. The king's servants said to the king, In all things which our lord the king chooses, look we are your servants. The king and all his house went out on foot, and the king left ten women of his concubines to keep the house. The king and all his servants went out on foot, and lived in a distant house."

All his servants passed on by his side, and every Cherethite, and every Pelethite, and they stood by the olive tree in the wilderness, and all the people marched near him, and all his court, and all the men of might, and all the men of war, six hundred, and they were present at his side, and every Cherethite, and every Pelethite, and all the six hundred Gittites that came on foot out of Gath, and they went on before the king.

The king said to Ittai, the Gittite, "Why do you also go with us? Return, and live with the king, for you are a stranger, and you have come as an immigrant out of your country. Whereas you came yesterday, will I today make you travel with us, and will you therefore change your place? You arrived yesterday, and will I set you in motion today to go along with us? I indeed will go wherever I may go, return then, and cause your brothers to return with you, and may the Lord deal mercifully and truly with you."

Ittai answered the king, and said, "As the Lord lives, and as my lord the king lives, in whatever place my lord will be, whether it is in death or life, there, your servant will be."

The king said to Ittai, "Come and travel with me."

So Ittai the Gittite and the king fled with his servants and all the multitude with him. All the country wept with a loud voice. All the people fled over the brook of Kidron, and the king crossed the brook Kidron, and all the people and the king fled towards the road through the wilderness. Zadok and all the Levites were with him, bearing the ark of the covenant of the Lord from Abiathar, and they set down the ark of God, and Abiathar went up until all the people had passed out of the city.

The king said to Zadok, "Carry the ark of God back into the city if I should find favor in the eyes of the Lord, then will he bring me back, and he will show me it and its beauty. But if he should say, 'I have no pleasure in you, look, here I am, let him do to me according to that which is good in his eyes.'"

The king said to Zadok the priest, "Look, you will return to the city in peace, and Ahimaaz your son, and Jonathan the son of Abiathar, your two sons with you. I'll continue in the arms of Araboth of the desert until you report the news to me."

So Zadok and Abiathar brought back the ark of God to Jerusalem, and it remained there. David went up by the ascent of the Mount of Olives, ascending and weeping, and had his head covered, and went barefooted, and all the people that were with him covered his head, and they went up, ascending and weeping. It was reported to David, saying, "Ahithophel also is among the conspirators with Absalom."

David said, "Lord, I beg you, turn the counsel of Ahithophel. David came as far as Rosh, where he worshiped God, and look,

Hushai the chief friend of David came out to meet him, having torn his garment, and the earth was on his head. David said to him, "If you flee with me, then you will be a burden to me, but if you will return to the city, and will say to Absalom, 'Your brothers are fleeing, and the king your father is fleeing: and now I am your servant, my king, allow me to live. At one time even recently I was the servant of your father, and now I am your humble servant, so will you disconcert for me, the counsel of Ahithophel.' And, look, there are there with you Zadok and Abiathar the priests, and it will be that every word that you will hear of the house of the king, you will report it to Zadok and Abiathar the priests. There are there with them their two sons, Ahimaaz the son of Zadok, and Jonathan the son of Abiathar, and by them, you will report to me every word which you will hear."

So Hushai the friend of David went into the city, where Absalom had recently returned to Jerusalem.

# 2nd Kingdoms: Chapter 16

David continued on a little way from Rosh, and look, Ziba the servant of Mephibosheth came to meet him, and he had a couple of donkeys loaded with two hundred loaves, and a hundred bunches of raisins, and a hundred cakes of dates, and a bottle of wine.

The king asked Ziba, "What do you mean by these?"

Ziba answered, "The donkeys are for the household of the king to ride on, and the loaves and the dates are for the young men to eat, and the wine is for them that are faint in the wilderness to drink."

The king asked, "Where is the son of your master?"

Ziba answered the king, "He remains in Jerusalem, for he said, 'today will the house of Israel restore to me the kingdom of my father.'"

The king said to Ziba, "Look, all Mephibosheth's property is yours."

Ziba paid respect and said, "My lord, my king, let me find grace in your eyes."

King David came to Bahurim, and a man came out from there of the family of the house of Saul, and his name was Shimea the son of Gera. He came out and cursed as he went, and threw stones at David, and all the servants of King David and all the people and all the mighty men were on the right and left hands of the king. Shimea cursed him, "Go out, go out, you bloody man, and man of sin. The Lord has returned on you all the blood of the house of Saul because you have reigned in his place, and the Lord has given the kingdom into the hand of Absalom your son, and, look, you are taken in your evil, because you are a bloody man."

Abishai the son of Zeruiah said to the king, "Why does this dead dog curse my lord the king? Let me go now and chop off his head."

The king said, "What have I to do with you, you sons of Zeruiah? Leave him alone, and let him curse, for the Lord has told him to curse David, and who will say, 'Why have you done this?'" David said to Abishai and all his servants, "Look, my son who came out of my bowels seeks my life, still more may the son of Benjamin. Let him curse because the Lord has told him. If by any means the Lord may look on my torment, he will he return for me his cursing this day."

David and all the men with him went on the way, and Shimea went by the side of the hill next to him, cursing as he went, and throwing stones at him, and tossing dirt at him. The king and all the people with him came away and refreshed themselves there. Absalom and all the men of Israel went into Jerusalem, and Ahithophel with him. It came to pass when Hushai the chief friend of David came to Absalom, that Hushai said to Absalom, "Let the king live."

Absalom said to Hushai, "Is this your kindness to your friend? Why did you not go out with your friend?"

Hushai said to Absalom, "No, but whoever the Lord, and these people, and all Israel have chosen, his will I will follow, and with him, I will live. Again, whom will I serve? Should I not in the presence of his son? As I served in the sight of your father, so will I be in your presence."

Absalom said to Ahithophel, "Decide among yourselves concerning what we should do."

Ahithophel said to Absalom, "Go into your father's concubines, whom he left to keep his house, and all Israel will hear that you have dishonored your father, and the hands of all that are with you will be strengthened. They pitched a tent for Absalom on the roof, and Absalom went to his father's concubines in the sight of all Israel. The counsel of Ahithophel, which he counseled in previously, was as if one should inquire of the word of God, so was all the counsel of Ahithophel both to David and also to Absalom.

# 2<sup>nd</sup> Kingdoms: Chapter 17

Ahithophel said to Absalom, "Let me now choose for myself twelve thousand men, and I will rise and follow after David this night, and I will come against him when he is weary and weak handed, and I will strike him with terror, and all the people with him will flee, and I will king only the king. I will bring back all the people to you, as a bride returns to her husband. Only you seek the life of one man, and all the people have peace. The saying was right in the eyes of Absalom, and in the eyes of all the elders of Israel."

Absalom said, "Call now also Hushai the Archite, and let us hear what he has to say."

Hushai went to Absalom, and Absalom said to him, "Ahithophel said, 'Will we do according to his word? But if not, speak."

Hushai said to Absalom, "This counsel which Ahithophel has counseled this one time is not good."

Hushai said, "You know your father and his men, that they are very mighty, and bitter in their spirit, as a bereaved carry in the field, and as a wild boar in the plain, and your father is a man of war, and will not give the people rest. Look, he is now hidden in one of the hills or some other place, and it will come to pass when he falls on them at the beginning, that someone will certainly hear, 'There has been a slaughter among the people that follow after Absalom.' Then even he that is strong, whose heart is as the heart of a lion, it will completely melt, for all Israel knows that your father is mighty, and they that are with him are mighty men. For thus I have certainly given counsel, that all Israel be generally gathered to you from Dan even to Bathsheba, as the sand that is on the sea-shore for multitude, and that your presence goes in the middle of them. We will come on him in one of the places where we will find him, and we will camp against him, as the dew falls on the earth, and we will not leave of him and his men so much as one. If he has taken refuge with his army in a city, then will all Israel take ropes to that city, and we will draw it even into the river, that there may not be left there even a stone."

Absalom and all the men of Israel said, "The counsel of Hushai the Archite is better than the counsel of Ahithophel. For the Lord ordained to disconcert the good counsel of Ahithophel, that the Lord might bring all evil on Absalom."

Hushai the Archite said to Zadok and Abiathar the priests, "Ahithophel counseled a certain way to Absalom and the elders of Israel, and what have I counseled. Now send quickly, and report, to David 'Don't lodge this night in Araboth of the wilderness. Rush to leave, in case one swallows up the king, and all the people with him.'"

Jonathan and Ahimaaz stood by the well of Rogel, and a woman slave went and reported to them, and they went to tell King David, so they might not be noticed as they entered into the city. But a young man saw them and told Absalom, and the two went quickly and entered into the house of a man in Bahurim, and he had a well in his court, and they went down into it. A woman took a covering, and spread it over the mouth of the well, and spread out ground grain on it to dry, and the thing was not known. The servants of Absalom came to the woman into the house, and said, "Where are Ahimaaz and Jonathan?"

The woman said to them, "They have gone a little way beyond the water."

They searched and did not find them, and returned to Jerusalem. After they were gone, they came up out of the pit, and went on their way, and reported to King David, and said to David, "Rise and go quickly over the water, for Ahithophel counseled concerning you."

David rose up and all the people with him, and they crossed the Jordan in the morning light. There was not one missing who did not cross the Jordan. Ahithophel saw that his counsel was not followed, and he saddled his donkey, and arose and departed to his house into his city, and he gave orders to his household, and hanged himself, and died. He was buried in the sepulcher of his father. David passed over to Mahanaim, and Absalom crossed across the Jordan, with all the men of Israel with him. Absalom appointed Amasa in place of Joab over the army. Amasa was the son of a man whose name was Jetheth of Jezreel. He went to Abigail the daughter of Nahash, the sister of Zeruiah the mother of Joab.

All Israel and Absalom camped in the land of Gilead. When David came to Mahanaim, that Shobi the son of Nahash of Rabbah of the sons of Amman, and Machir the son of Ammiel of Lodebar, and Barzillai the Gileadite of Rogelim, brought ten embroidered beds, (with double coverings,) and ten cauldrons, and earthenware, and wheat, and barley, and flour, and meal, and beans, and pulse, and honey, and butter, and sheep, and cheeses of cows. They brought them to David and to his people with him to eat, for one said, "The people are weak and hungry and thirsty in the wilderness."

# 2nd Kingdoms: Chapter 18

David counted the people with him and set over them captains of thousands and captains of hundreds. David sent away the people, a third under the command of Joab, and under the command of Abishai the son of Zeruiah, the brother of Joab, and a third under the command of Ittai the Gittite. David said to the people, "I also will certainly go out with you."

They said, "You will not go out, for if we should indeed flee, they will not care for us, and if half of us should die, they will not spirit us. You are like ten thousand of us, and now it is well that you will be to us an aid to help us in the city."

The king said to them, "Whatever will seem good in your eyes I will do." The king stood by the side of the gate, and all the people went out by hundreds and by thousands. The king commanded Joab and Abishai and Ittai, "Spare for my sake the young man Absalom."

All the people heard the king ordering all the commanders concerning Absalom. All the people went out into the forest against Israel, and the battle was in the forest of Ephraim. The people of Israel fell there before the servants of David, and there was a great slaughter on that day, even twenty thousand men. The battle there was scattered over the face of all the land, and the forest killed more of the people than the sword killed on that day.

Absalom went to meet the servants of David, and Absalom was mounted on his mule, and the mule came under the thick boughs of a great oak, and his head became caught in the oak, and he was suspended between the sky and earth, and the mule continued from under him. A man saw it, and reported to Joab, "Look, I saw Absalom hanging in an oak."

Joab said to the man who reported it to him, "You saw him? Why didn't you kill him there? I would have given you ten pieces of silver and a girdle."

The man said to Joab, "Were I even to receive a thousand shekels of silver, I would not lift my hand against the king's son, for the king ordered you and Abishai and Ittai, 'Take care of the young man Absalom for me, and don't harm his life,' and nothing of the matter will be concealed from the king, and you will set yourself against me."

Joab said, "I will take care of this. I will not detain you." Joab took three darts in his hand, and threw them into the heart of Absalom, while he was yet alive hanging in the oak tree. Ten squires that carried Joab's armor surrounded Absalom, and stabbed him and killed him. Joab blew the trumpet, and the people returned from pursuing Israel, as Joab spared the people. He took Absalom, and cast him into a great cavern in the wood, into a deep pit, and set up over him a very great heap of stones, and all Israel fled every man to his tent.

Absalom while yet alive had taken and set up for himself the stele near which he was taken, and set it up to have the stele in the king's dale, for he said he had no son to keep his name in remembrance. He called the stele, Absalom's hand, as it is until this day. Ahimaaz the son of Zadok said, "Let me run now and carry the good news to the king, for the Lord has delivered him from the hand of his enemies."

Joab said to him, "You will not be a messenger of good news this day, you will carry them another day. On this day you will carry no news because the king's son is dead."

Joab said to Hushai, "Go, report to the king all that you have seen." Hushai paid respect to Joab and went out. Ahimaaz the son of Zadok asked Joab, "No, let me also follow Hushai."

Joab said, "Why would you follow, my son? Attend, you have no news for profit if you go."

He asked, "Why shouldn't I follow?"

Joab said to him, "Follow."

Ahimaaz ran along the road of Kechar and outran Hushai. David was sitting between the two gates, and the watchman went up on the top of the gate of the wall, and looked, and saw a man running alone before him. The watchman cried out and reported to the king. The king said, "If he is alone, there is good news in his mouth."

The man came and drew near. The watchman saw another man running, and the watchman called to the gate, "Look, another man running alone."

The king said, "He also brings good news."

The watchman said, "I see the first messenger is Ahimaaz the son of Zadok."

The king said, "He is a good man, and will come to report good news."

Ahimaaz called out and said to the king, "Peace."

He paid respect to the king with his face to the ground, and said, "Blessed be Lord the god, who has delivered up the men that lifted their hands against my lord the king."

The king asked, "Is the young man Absalom safe?"

591

Ahimaaz answered, "I saw a great multitude at the time of Joab's sending the king's servant and your servant, and I did not know what was there."

The king said, "Turn aside and wait here."

He turned aside and stood, and Hushai came up, and said to the king, "Let my lord the king hear good news, for the Lord has avenged you this day on all them that rose up against you."

The king asked Hushai, "Is it well with the young man Absalom?"

Hushai answered, "Let the enemies of my lord the king, and all whoever has risen against him for evil, be like that young man."

The king was troubled, and went to the chamber over the gate, and wept, and he cried as he went, "My son Absalom, my son, my son Absalom, if only I had died instead of you, I would have died for you, Absalom, my son, my son!"

# 2nd Kingdoms: Chapter 19

They reported to Joab, "The king weeps and mourns for Absalom."

The victory was turned into mourning that day for all the people, as the people heard it said that day, "The king grieves for his son."

The people sneaked away that day to go into the city, as people sneak away when they are ashamed, like when they flee in the battle.

The king hid his face, and the king cried with a loud voice, "My son Absalom! Absalom my son!"

Joab went to the king, into the house, and said, "You have this day shamed the faces of all your servants that have delivered you this day, and have saved the lives of your sons and of your daughters, and the lives of your wives, and of your concubines, as you love them that hate you, and hate them that love you. You have today declared that your princes and your servants are nothing in your sight, for I know this day, that if Absalom were alive, and all of us dead today, then it would have been right in your sight. Now rise, and go out, and speak comfortably to your servants, for I have sworn by the Lord, that unless you will go out today, there will not be a man remaining with you tonight. Know for yourself, this thing will indeed be evil to you beyond all the evil that has come on you from your youth until now."

Then the king arose and sat in the gate, and all the people reported, "Look, the king sits in the gate."

All the people went in before the king at the gate, for Israel had fled every man to his tent. All the people argued among all the tribes of Israel, saying, "King David delivered us from all our enemies, and he rescued us from the hand of the Pelesets, and now he has fled from the land, and his kingdom, and Absalom. Absalom, whom we anointed over us, is dead in battle. Now, why are you silent about bringing back the king?"

The word of all Israel came to the king. King David sent messengers to Zadok and Abiathar the priests saying, "Ask the elders of Israel, 'Why are you the last to bring back the king to his house? When the word of all Israel has come to the king to his house. You are my brothers, you are my bones and my flesh. Why are you the last to bring back the king to his house?' You will say to Amasa, 'Are you not my bone and my flesh? May God strike me down if you will not be a commander of the army before me continually in place of Joab.'

He bowed the heart of all the men of Judah as that of one man, and they sent messengers to the king, saying "Return with all your servants."

The king returned and came as far as the Jordan. The men of Judah came to Gilgal on their way to meet the king, to cause the king to cross the Jordan. Shimea the son of Gera, the Benjamite, of Bahurim, rushed and went down with the men of Judah to meet king David. A thousand men of Benjamin were with him, and Ziba the servant of the house of Saul, and his fifteen sons with him, and his twenty servants with him, and they went directly down to the Jordan before the king, and they performed the service of bringing the king cross and there went over a ferryboat to move the household of the king, and to do that which was right in his eyes.

Shimea the son of Gera fell on his face before the king, as he went across the Jordan, and said to the king, "Don't let my lord now impute iniquity, and don't remember all the iniquity of your servant in the day in which my lord went out from Jerusalem, so that the king should spirit it. For your servant knows that I have sinned. Look, I have come today before all Israel and the house of Joseph, to go down and meet my lord the king."

Abessai the son of Zeruiah answered and said, "Will Shimea not be put to death, because he cursed the Anointed Lord?"

David said, "What have I to do with you, you sons of Zeruiah, that you as it was lying in wait against me this day? Today no man in Israel will be put to death, for I don't know if I reign over Israel today."

The king said to Shimea, "You will not die," and the king swore to him.

Mephibosheth the son of Saul's son went down to meet the king, and had not dressed his feet, or cut his nails, or shaved, neither had he washed his garments, from the day that the king departed, until the day when he returned in peace. When he went into Jerusalem to meet the king, the king asked him, "Why did you not go with me, Mephibosheth?"

Mephibosheth answered him, "My lord, king, my servant deceived me. Your servant said to him, 'Saddle a donkey for me, and I will ride it, and go with the king,' as your servant is lame. He has dealt deceitfully with your servant for my lord the king, but my lord the king is as a messenger of God, so do that which is good in your eyes. For all the house of my father were but as dead men before my lord the king, yet you have set your servant among them that eat at your table. What right have I any longer even to talk to the king?"

The king said to him, "Why do you continue to speak of these matters? I have said, 'You and Ziba will divide the land.'"

Mephibosheth said to the king, "Yes, let him take all since my lord the king has come in peace to his house."

Barzillai the Gileadite came down from Rogelim and crossed the Jordan with the king, that he might conduct the king across the Jordan. Barzillai was a very old man, eighty years old, and he had maintained the king when he lived in Mahanaim, as he was a very great man. The king said to Barzillai, "You will go over with me, and I will nourish your old age with me in Jerusalem."

Barzillai said to the king, "How many are the days of the years of my life, that I should go up with the king to Jerusalem? I am this day eighty years old, can I then distinguish between good and evil? Can your servant taste any longer what I eat or drink? Can I any longer hear the voice of singing men or singing women? Therefore will your servant any longer be a burden to my lord the king? Your servant will go a little way across the Jordan with the king, and why does the king return me this recompense? Let, I pray you, your servant remain, and I will die in my city, by the tomb of my father and my mother. And, look, your servant Chimham will go over with my lord the king, and do to him as it seems good in your eyes."

The king said, "Let Chimham go over with me, and I will do to him what is good in my sight, and whatever you will choose at my hand, I will do for you."

All the people crossed the Jordan, and the king went over, and the king kissed Barzillai and blessed him, and he returned to his place. The king went over to Gilgal, and Chimham went over with him, and all the men of Judah went over with the king, and also half the people of Israel. All the men of Israel came to the king, and said to the king, "Why have our brothers the men of

Judah stolen you away and caused the king and all his house to pass across the Jordan, and all the men of David with him?"

All the men of Judah answered the men of Israel, "The king is a near relative of us, and why were you so angry concerning this matter? Have we indeed eaten of the king's food? Or has he given us a gift, or has he sent us a portion? The men of Israel answered the men of Judah, and said, 'We have ten parts in the king, and we are older than you, we have also an interest in David above you. Why have you insulted us, and why was our advice not taken before that of Judah, to bring back our king?"

The speech of the men of Judah was sharper than the speech of the men of Israel.

# 2nd Kingdoms: Chapter 20

There was a so-called transgressor of the law there named was Sheba, a Benjamite, the son of Bichri, and he blew the trumpet, and said, "We have no portion in David, neither have we any inheritance in the son of Jesse! To your tents, Israel, everyone."

All the men of Israel went up from following David after Sheba the son of Bichri, but the men of Judah adhered to their king, from Jordan even to Jerusalem. David went into his house at Jerusalem, and the king took the ten women his concubines, whom he had left to keep the house, and he put them in a place of custody, and maintained them, and did not go into them, and they were kept living as widows, till the day of their death.

The king said to Amasa, "Call the men of Judah to me for three days, and be present here."

Amasa went to call Judah and delayed beyond the time which David appointed him. David said to Amasa, "Now will Sheba the son of Bichri do us more harm than Absalom. Take with you the servants of your lord, and follow him, in case he finds for himself strong cities, so will he blind our eyes."

There went out after him Amasa and the men of Joab, and the Cherethites, and the Phelethites, and all the mighty men, and they went out from Jerusalem to chase after Sheba the son of Bichri. They were by the great stone that is in Gibeah, and Amasa went in before them, and Joab had on his military cloak over his apparel, and over it, he was girded with a dagger fastened on his loins in its scabbard, and the dagger came out was lowered under his cloak.

Joab said to Amasa, "Are you in health, my brother?" and the right hand of Joab took hold of the beard of Amasa to kiss him. Amasa did not see the dagger that was in the hand of Joab, and

Joab stabbed him with it on the loins, and his bowels spilled out on to the ground, and he did not respond, as he died.

Joab and Abessai his brother chased after Sheba the son of Bichri. There stood over him one of the servants of Joab, and said, "Who is he that is for Joab, and who is on the side of David following Joab?"

Amasa was dripping with blood in the middle of the road. A man saw that all the people stood still, and he removed Amasa out of the road into a field, and he threw a garment on him because he saw everyone that came to him standing still. When he was quickly removed from the road, every man of Israel passed behind Joab chasing after Sheba the son of Bichri. He went through all the tribes of Israel to Abel, and Bethmaachah and all in Charri too were assembled and followed after him. They came and besieged him in Abel and Phermacha, and they raised a mound against the city and it stood close to the wall, and all the people with Joab proposed to throw down the wall. A wise woman cried from the wall, and said, "Hear, hear. Say, I beg you, to Joab, come near here, and I will speak to him."

He approached her, and the woman asked him, "Are you, Joab?"

He said, "I am."

She said to him, "Hear the words of your handmaid."

Joab answered her, "I will hear."

She said, "Of old time they said, 'Certainly one was asked in Abel and Dan, whether the faithful in Israel failed in what they purposed, they will certainly ask in Abel, even in like manner, whether they have failed. I am a peaceful one of the strong ones in Israel, but you seek to destroy a city and a mother city in Israel, why do you seek to ruin the inheritance of the Lord?"

Joab answered and said, "Far be it, far be it from me, that I should ruin or destroy. Is not it the case, that a man of Mount Ephraim, named Sheba the son of Bichri, has lifted his hand against king David? Give him to me, and I will leave the city."

The woman said to Joab, "Look, his head will be thrown to you over the wall. The woman went to all the people, and she spoke to all the city in her wisdom, and they cut off the head of Sheba the son of Bichri, and took it and threw it to Joab. He blew the trumpet, and the people left the city, every man to his tent. Joab returned to Jerusalem to the king. Joab was in command of all the forces of Israel, and Benaiah the son of Jehoiada was over the Cherethites and the Phelethites. Adoniram was in charge of the tribute, and Jehoshaphat the son of Ahilud was the recorder. Sheva was a scribe, and Zadok and Abiathar were priests. Additionally, Ira the son of Jair was a priest to David.

# 2<sup>nd</sup> Kingdoms: Chapter 21

There was a famine in the days of David for three consecutive years, and David wanted the face of the Lord. The Lord said, "There is guilt on Saul and his house because of his bloody murder of the Gibeonites."

King David called the Gibeonites and talked to them (now the Gibeonites are not the Israelites but are of the remnant of the Amorites, and the Israelites had sworn to them, but Saul wanted to slaughter them in his zeal for the Israelites and Judah.) David said to the Gibeonites, "What will I do for you? How will I make atonement, that you may bless the inheritance of the Lord?"

The Gibeonites answered him, "We have no question about silver or gold with Saul and with his house, and there is no man for us to put to death in Israel."

He said, "What do you want? Speak, and I will do it for you."

They said to the king, "The man who would have exterminated us, and persecuted us, who plotted against us to destroy us, let us destroy him so that he has no standing in all the frontiers of Israel. Let one give us seven men of his sons, and let us hang them up in the Sun to the Lord in Gibeah, Saul's chosen Lord."[1]

The king said, "I will give them." But the king spared Mephibosheth, son of Jonathan the son of Saul, because of the oath of the Lord that was between them, between David and Jonathan the son of Saul. The king took the two sons of Rizpah the daughter of Aiah, who had carried to Saul, Hermonoi and Mephibosheth, and the five sons of Michol the daughter of Saul, she who carried Esdriel the son of Barzillai the Moulathite.

He gave them into the hand of the Gibeonites, and they hanged them up to the sun in the mountain before the Lord, and they died, the seven together. They were put to death in the days of harvest, at the beginning of barley harvest. Rizpah the daughter of Aiah took sackcloth and fixed it for herself on the rock at the beginning of barley harvest until water dropped on them out of the sky, and she did not allow the birds of the air to rest on them by day, nor the beasts of the field by night.

It was told to David what Rizpah the daughter of Aiah the concubine of Saul had done, as they were scared of Dan, the son of Ioa of the descendants of the Raphites,[2] (and sent a messenger to David for a great festival to exchange a daughter of the land as a concubine as requested.)

David went and took the bones of Saul, and the bones of Jonathan his son, from the men of the sons of Jabesh-Gilead, who stole them from the street of Bethshan, for the Pelesets set them there in the day in which the Pelesets killed Saul in Gilboa. He carried up the bones of Saul and the bones of Jonathan his son and gathered the bones of them that had been hanged. They buried the bones of Saul and the bones of Jonathan his son, and the bones of them that had been hanged, in the land of Benjamin in the hill, in the sepulcher of Kish his father, and they did all things that the king commanded.

After this God listened to the prayers of the land. There was still a war between the Pelesets and Israel, and David went down and his servants with him, and they fought with the Pelesets, and David went. Jesbi, who was of the descendant of Rephaites, and the head of whose spear was three hundred shekels in weight of brass. He was also girded with a club and thought he would kill David. Abishai the son of Zeruiah helped him and attacked the Peleset, and killed him. Then the men of David swore, "You will no longer go out with us to battle, and you will not quench the lamp of Israel."

After this there was a battle again with the Pelesets in Gath, then Sibbechai the Astatothite killed Saph of the descendant of Rephaites. There was a battle in Rom with the Pelesets, and Elhanan son of Jaareoregim the Bethlehemite killed Goliath the Gittite, and the staff of his spear was as a weaver's beam. There was another battle in Gath, and there was a man of stature, and the fingers of his hands and the toes of his feet were six on each, four and twenty in number, and he also was born to Rephaites. He defied Israel, and Jonathan son of Shimea brother of David, killed him. These four were born descendants of the giants in Gath, the family of Rephaites, and they fell by the hand of David, and by the hand of his servants.

# 2<sup>nd</sup> Kingdoms: Chapter 21 Notes

**1** Codex Vaticanus: exêliasômen autous tô c̄ō en gabaôn saoul eclectous c̄u (ΕΞΗΛΙΑϹΩΜΕΝ ΑΥΤΟΥϹ ΤΩ Κ̄Ω̄ ΕΝ ΓΑΒΑΩΝ ϹΑΟΥΛ ΕΚΛΕΚΤΟΥϹΚ̄Ῡ). Translation: hang them up before the sun, the Lord in Gabaon, Saul's chosen Lord

• Codex Coislinianus: exêlasomen en autoes tô c̄ō en tô bounô tô saoul eclectous tô c̄ō (ΕΞΗΛΑϹΟΜΕΝ ΕΝ ΑΥΤΟΙϹ ΤΩ Κ̄Ω̄ ΕΝ ΤΩ ΒΟΥΝΩ ΤΩ ϹΑΟΥΛ ΕΚΛΕΚΤΟΥϹ ΤΩ Κ̄Ω̄). Translation: hang them in the sun, by the Lord on the hill (or altar, heap) of the Saul, elected of the Lord

• Codex Basiliano-Vaticanus: exêliasômen autous tô Cyriô en tô bounô Saoul eclectous Cyriou (ΕΞΗΛΙΑ-ϹΩΜΕΝ ΑΥΤΟΥϹ ΤΩ ΚΥΡΙΩ ΕΝ ΤΩ ΒΟΥΝΩ ϹΑΟΥΛ ΕΚΛΕΚΤΟΥϹ ΚΥΡΙΟΥ). Translation: hang them up before the sun, before the Lord on the hill (or altar, heap), Saul's chosen Lord

• LXX 121: exilasômen autous tô Cyriô en Gabaôn Saoul eclectous Cyriou (ἐξιλάσομἐν αυτους τοο Κυρίοο ἐν Γαϐαον ϹΑουλ ἐκλἐϰτουϲ Κυρίου). Translation: hang them out in of the sun, the Lord in Gabaon, Saul's chosen Lord

• LXX 127: exilasometha en autoes tô Cyriô en Gabaôn Saoul eclectous tô Cyriô (ἐξιλάσομἐθὰ ἐν αυτοιϲ τοο Κυρίοο ἐν Γαϐαον ϹΑουλ ἐκλἐϰτουϲ τοο Κυρίοο). Translation: propitiate before the Lord in Gabaon, Saul chosen of the Lord

• LXX 707: exaliasômen autous tô Cyriô en Gabaôn Saoul eclectos cyriou (ἐξὰλιάσομἐν αυτους τοο Κυρίοο ἐν Γαϐαον ϹΑουλ ἐκλἐϰτοϲ Κυρίου). Translation: hang them up in the sun, the Lord in Gabaon, Saul's chosen Lord

• LXX 56: exêliasomen autous tô Cyriô en Gabaôn Saoul eclecton Cyriou (ἐξὴλιάσομἐν αυτους τοο Κυρίοο ἐν Γαϐαον ϹΑουλ ἐκλἐϰτον Κυρίου). Translation: hang them up before the sun, the Lord in Gabaon Saul's selected Lord

• LXX 247: exêliasomae autous tô Cyriô en Gabaôn tou Saoul eclectos tô Cyriô (ϵ̔ξλ λιλσομλι λυτους τοο Κυριοο ϭν Γλιλοον του Cλουλ ϭιλϭιτος τοο Κυριοο). Translation: appease the Lord in Gabaon, the Saul, elected of the Lord

• LXX 370: exêliasomen autous tô Cyriô en Gabaôn Saoul eclectous Cyriou (ϵ̔ξλ λισομϭν λυτους τοο Κυριοο ϭν Γλιλοον Cλουλ ϭιλϭιτους Κυριου). Translation: hang them up in front of the sun, the Lord in Gabaon, Saul's chosen Lord

• LXX 44: exêliôsômen autous tô Cyriô en Gabaôn Saoul eclectous Cyriou (ϵ̔ξλ λιοοσοομϭν λυτους τοο Κυριοο ϭν Γλιλοον Cλουλ ϭιλϭιτους Κυριου). Translation: hang them out in front of the sun, the Lord in Gabaon, Saul's chosen Lord

• LXX 489: exilasomen autous tô Cyriô en Gabaôn Saoul eclectous Cyriô (ϵ̔ξιλλσομϭν λυτους τοο Κυριοο ϭν Γλιλοον Cλουλ ϭιλϭιτους Κυριοο). Translation: hang them out in of the sun, the Lord in Gabaon, Saul's chosen Lord

• LXX 19: exilasômetha autous tô Cyriô en Gabaôn tô Saoul eclectous Cyriou (ϵ̔ξιλλσοομϭθλ λυτους τοο Κυριοο ϭν Γλιλοον τοο Cλουλ ϭιλϭιτους Κυριου). Translation: conciliate the Lord in Gabaon, the Saul's chosen Lord

• LXX 92: exiliasomen autous tô Cyriô en Gabaô Saoul eclectous Cyriou (ϵ̔ξιλιλσομϭν λυτους τοο Κυριοο ϭν Γλιλλο Cλουλ ϭιλϭιτους Κυριου). Translation: hang them out in of the sun, the Lord in Gabao, Saul's chosen Lord

• LXX 314: exêliasômen autous en Gabaô bounô Saoul eclectous Cyriou (ϵ̔ξλ λιλσοομϭν λυτους ϭν Γλιλλο υουνοο Cλουλ ϭιλϭιτους Κυριου). Translation: hang them up in front of the sun, on Gabao hill (or mound, altar), Saul's chosen Lord

• Aleppo Codex: whwqônwm lYhwh bgbôt šåwl bḥyr Yhwh (וְהוֹקַעֲנוּס לִיהוָה בְּגִבְעַת שָׁאוּל בְּחִיר יהוה). Translation: and hang them up before Yhwh in Gibeah, Saul's (or underworld) chosen Yhwh

• Leningrad Codex: vehovka'anum laYhvah begiv'at Sha'ul bechir Yehvah (וְהוֹקַעֲנוּס לַיהוָה בְּגִבְעַת שָׁאוּל בְּחִיר יְהוָה). Translation: and hang them up before the Yhwah in Gibeah, Saul's (or underworld) chosen Yehwah

• Targum Jerusalem: venatzlevinun kodam Yeyah begiv'ata deSha'ul bechira daYyah (וְנִצְלְבִינוּן קֳדָם יְיָ בְּגִבְעָתָא דְשָׁאוּל בְּחִירָא דַיְיָ). Translation: impale them before Yahw hill, the Saul (or underworld) selected of the Yahw

The Greek translation clearly predates the current Hebrew version, as there is no way to translate the Masoretic version into the Greek version. Based on the rest of the Septuagint's books of Kingdoms, the original text was likely 'hang them up before Shemesh the Lord in Gibeah, Saul's chosen lord' which would explain the redaction to Yahweh in the Hebrew translation, as Shemesh was the sun-god banned by King Josiah circa 625 BC. The Dead Sea Scroll 4QSam[a] does includes the first one and a half words of the verse, however the rest are damaged. The only word that survives in full does not match it's counterpart in the Masoretic text, however, as it is the only word to survive it is unclear how much the Hebrew translations deviated in the 1st century.

**2** Codex Vaticanus: cae catelaben autous Dan uios Iôa ec tôn apogonôn tôn Gigantôn (ΚΑΙ ΚΑΤΕΛΑΒΕΝ ΑΥΤΟΥΣ ΔΑΝ ΥΙΟΣ ΙΩΑ ΕΚ ΤΩΝ ΑΠΟΓΟΝΩΝΤΩΝΓΙΓΑΝΤΩΝ). Translation: and seized (or comprehended, overtook) him Dan the sons of Ioa from the descendants (or offspring, progeny) of Gigantes

• LXX 127: cae catelaben autous Dan huios Iôas ec tôn apogonôn tôn Gigantôn (ⲖⲀⲓ ⲖⲀⲧⲅ̄ⲗⲀⲙ̄ⲋⲛ Ⲁⲩⲧⲟⲩⲥ ⲆⲀⲛ ⲩⲓⲟⲥ ⲓⲟⲟⲀⲥ ⲟ̄ⲗ ⲧⲟⲟⲛ Ⲁⲡⲟ/ⲅ̄ⲛⲟⲟⲛ ⲧⲟⲟⲛ ⲅⲓⲅⲁ/ⲛ̄ⲧⲟⲟⲛ). Translation: and seized (or comprehended, overtook) him

608

Dan the son of Ioas from the descendants (or offspring, progeny) of Gigantes.

• LXX 247: cae catelaben aútous dan huios Iôl ec tõn apogonôn tõn Gigantôn cae apêngelê tô Dauid osa epoeêsen respha thygatêr aea pallacê Saoul (ᒷᗅᒐ ᒷᗅᛐᡊᛌᗅᒷᏅᶰ ᗅᘈᡊᘈᏟ ᘈᗝᏟ ᥄Ꮯᗅᛌ Ꮭᒷ ᛐᗝᶰ ᥄ᛐᏗᏝᏘᶰᗝᗝᶰ ᛐᗝᶰ ᒿ᥄᥄ᗅᶰᶰᛐᗝᗝᶰ ᒷᗅᒐ ᥄ᛐᛌ᥄᥄ᏝᏅᒷᛌ ᛐᗝᗝ ᥄᥄ᘈ᥄᥄ ᗝᏟ᥄ Ꮭᛐᗝ᥄ᛌᏟᏅᶰ ᥄ᏝᏟᏘ᥄ ᕳ᥄᥄᥄ᛐᛌ᥄ ᥄᥄᥄ π᥄᥄᥄᥄ᛌᛌᛌ Ꮯ᥄ᗝ᥄᥄). Translation: and seized (or comprehended, overtook) him Dan the son of Iol from the descendants (or offspring, progeny) of Gigantes and sent a messenger to David for a great festival to exchange a daughter of the land as a concubine of Saul (or asked, borrowed, lent if translated from Canaanite or Aramaic)

The section of text is missing from the Masoretic text and a large minority of Septuagint manuscripts, including the Codex Coislinianus and Codex Basiliano-Vaticanus. Based on the interchangeable use of 'Gigante' and Rapha (Ραφα / רְפָה) later in the chapter, it appears that the Greeks translated Rapha as Gigante in this verse, as they did elsewhere in the Septuagint.

# 2ⁿᵈ Kingdoms: Chapter 22

David sang to the Lord this song in the day in which the Lord rescued him out of the hand of all his enemies, and out of the hand of Saul:

"The Lord, my rock, and my fortress, and my deliverer, my God, he will be for me my guard, I will trust in him. He is my protector, and the horn of my salvation, my helper, and my sure refuge, you will save me from the unjust man."

"I will call on the Lord who is worthy to be praised, and I will be saved from my enemies."

"For the troubles of death compassed me, the floods of iniquity amazed me. The pangs of death surrounded me, the agonies of death prevented me. When I am attacked I will call on the Lord and will cry to my God, and he will hear my voice out of his temple, and my cry will come into his ears."

"The earth was troubled and quaked, and the foundations of the sky were confounded and torn asunder because the Lord was angry with them."

"There went up smoke in his anger, and fire out of his mouth devours as coals were started in it."

"He lowered the sky, and came down, and there was darkness under his feet."

"He rode on the sphinxes and flew, and was seen on the wings of the wind."

"He made darkness his hiding-place, his tabernacle around him was the darkness of waters, he condensed it with the clouds of the air. At the brightness before him, coals of fire were started."

"The Lord thundered out of the sky, and the Highest uttered his voice."

"He sent forth arrows, and scattered them, and he flashed lightning, and dismayed them."

"The channels of the sea were seen, and the foundations of the world were discovered, at the rebuke of the Lord, at the blast of the breath of his anger."

"He sent from above and took me, he drew me out of many waters."

"He delivered me from my strong enemies, from them that hated me, for they were stronger than I."

"The days of my torment prevented me, but the Lord was my stay."

"He brought me into a wide place, and rescued me because he delighted in me."

"The Lord recompensed me according to my righteousness, even according to the purity of my hands did he recompense me."

"Because, I kept the ways of the Lord, and did not wickedly leave from my god."

"For all his judgments and his ordinances were before me, I did not depart from them."

"I will be blameless before him, and will keep myself from my iniquity."

"The Lord will recompense me according to my righteousness, and according to the purity of my hands in his eye-sight."

"With the holy, you will be holy, and with the perfect man you will be perfect, and with the excellent, you will be excellent, and with the perverse, be perverse."

"You will save the poor people, and will bring down the eyes of the haughty."

"For you, Lord, are my lamp, and the Lord will shine forth to me in my darkness."

"For by you will I run as a girded man, and by my god will I leap over a wall."

"El,[1] immaculate are your ways."

"The word of the Lord is strong and tried in the fire, he is a protector to all that put their trust in him."

"Who is a God besides the Lord?"

"Who will be a Creator except for our god?"

"El strengthens me with might, and has prepared my way without fault."

"He makes my feet like hart's feet, and sets me on the bamahs."

"He teaches war to my hands, and has broken a bronze bow through my arms."

"You have given me the shield of my salvation, and your propitious dealing has increased me, to make room under me for my going, and my legs did not totter."

"I will pursue my enemies, and will completely destroy them, and I will not turn again till I have consumed them."

"And I will crush them, and they will not rise, and they will fall under my feet."

"You will strengthen me with power for the war, you will cause them that rise up against me to bow down under me."

"You have caused my enemies to flee before me, even those who hated me, and you have killed them."

"They will cry, and there will be no helper but the Lord, but he does not listen to them."

"I ground them as the dust of the earth, I beat them small as the mire of the streets."

"You will deliver me from the struggle of the peoples, and you will keep me to be the head of the Pelesets, a people which I did not know served me."

"The strange children feigned obedience to me, they listened to me as soon as they heard."

"The strange children will be thrown away, and will be overthrown out of their hiding places."

"The Lord lives, and blessed be my guardian, and my gods, my strong keeper, will be exalted."

"The Lord who avenges me is strong, punishing the nations under me, and bringing me out from my enemies, and you will set me on high from among those that rise against me."

"You will deliver me from the violent man, and therefore will I confess to you, Lord among the Pelesets, and sing to your name."

"He magnifies the salvation of his king, and works mercy for his anointed, even for David and for his seed forever."

# 2ⁿᵈ Kingdoms: Chapter 22 Notes

**1** Codex Vaticanus: ischyros (ιϲⲭⲨⲢⲞⲤ). Translation: strength (or might, power)

- LXX 127: ischyros Ths (ιⲟⲭⲩβ̅ⲥ̅ ⲑⲥ). Translation: strength of god

- LXX 245: Isauros (ιⲟⲇⲩβⲟⲥ)

- Aleppo Codex: Ål (אֵל). Translation: god (or El)

- Leningrad Codex: El (אֵל). Translation: god (or El)

- Targum Jerusalem: elaha (אֱלָהָא). Translation: god

El (𒀭𒇷 / 𐤋𐤀) was the supreme god of the Canaanites, and the term El (אל) continues to serve as the word 'god' in the modern Hebrew language. The Greeks translated ål (𐤋𐤍) into Greek as 'strength' in Job as well, indicating that the term had been transliterated directly into Aramaic, and therefore the name El is restored in this translations.

# 2nd Kingdoms: Chapter 23

These are the last words of David, "Faithful is David the son of Jesse, and faithful the man whom God raised up to be the anointed of the God of Jacob, and beautiful are the psalms of Israel. The Spirit of the Lord spoke by me, and his word was on my tongue."

The god over Israel says, "A watchman out of Israel told me a parable, 'I said among men, 'How will you strengthen the fear of the anointed? In the morning light of God, let the sunrise in the morning, from the light of which the Lord passed on, and as it were from the rain of the tender grass on the earth. Therefore my house is not with Ishkur, for he has made an everlasting covenant with me, ready, guarded at every time, for all my salvation and all my desire is, that the wicked should not flourish.' All these are like a thorn thrust out, for they will not be taken with the hand, and a man will not labor among them, and one has that which is fully armed with iron, and the staff of a spear, and he will burn them with fire, and they will be burnt in their shame.'"

These are the names of the mighty men of David: Ish-bosheth the Canaanite is a captain of one third. Adino the Eznite, he drew his sword against eight hundred soldiers at once. After him, Elhanan the son of his uncle, son of Dodo who was among the three mighty men with David, and when he defied the Pelesets they were gathered there to war, and the men of Israel went up. He arose and attacked the Pelesets until his hand was weary, and his hand clung to the sword. The Lord worked great salvation on that day, and the people rested behind him only to strip the slain. After him Shammah the son of Agee the Archite.

The Pelesets were gathered to Theria, and there was there a portion of ground full of lentils, and the people fled before the Pelesets. He stood firm in the middle of the portion, and rescued it, and struck the Pelesets, and the Lord worked a great deliverance. Three out of the thirty went down, and came to Cason to David, to the cave of Adullam, and there was an army of the Pelesets, and they camped in the valley of Raphites.[1] David was then in the stronghold, and the garrison of the Pelesets was then in Bethlehem.

David longed, and said, "Who will give me water to drink out of the well that is in the Temple of Lehem by the gate?"

Now the band of the Pelesets was then in the Temple of Lehem.[2] The three mighty men broke through the army of the Pelesets and drew water out of the well that was in the Temple of Lehem in the gate, and they took it and brought it to David, and he would not drink it but poured it out before the Lord. He said, "Lord forbid that I should do this! That I should drink of the blood of the men who went and risked their lives," and he would not drink it. These three mighty men did these things. Abishai the brother of Joab the son of Zeruiah, was chief among the three, and he lifted his spear against three hundred whom he killed, and he had a name among the three.

Of those three he was most honorable, and he became chief over them, but he did not reach to the first three. Benaiah the son of Jehoiada, was abundant in mighty deeds, from Cabeseel, and he slaughtered the two sons of Areli of Moab, and he went down and struck a lion in the middle of a pit on a snowy day. He killed an Egyptian, an amazing man, and in the hand of the Egyptian was a spear like the side of a ladder, and he went down to him with a staff, and snatched the spear from the Egyptian's hand, and killed him with his own spear. These things did Benaiah the son of Jehoiada, and he had a name among the three mighty men. He was honorable among the second three, but he did not reach to the first three, and David made him his reporter.

These are the names of King David's mighty men. Asahel Joab's brother, he was among the thirty. Elhanan son of Dodo his uncle in the Temple of Lehem, Shammah the Rudaean, Selles the Kelothite, Ira the son of Ikkesh the Tekoite, Abiezer the Anethothite, of the sons of the Anethothites. Zalmon the Ahohite, Maharai the Netophathite, Esthai the son of Ribai of Gabaeth, sons of Benjamin the Ephrathite, Asmoth the Bardiamite, Emasu the Salabonite, Adroi of the brooks, Gadabiel son of the Arabothaeite, the sons of Ashan, Jonathan, Samnan the Arodite, Amnan the son of Arai the Saraurite, Aliphaleth the son of Asbites, the son of the Machachachite, Eliab the son of Ahithophel the Gelonite, Asarai the Carmelite the son of Uraeoerchi, Gaal the son of Nathana, the son of much valor, the son of Galaaddi, Elie the Ammonite, Gelore the Bethorite, armor-bearer to Joab, son of Zeruiah, Ira the Ethirite, Gerab the Ethenite, and Orion the Cypriot, thirty-seven in all.

# 2ⁿᵈ Kingdoms: Chapter 23 Notes

**1** Codex Vaticanus: Raphaem (ΡΑΦΑΕΙΜ)

• Codex Alexandrinus: Raphaen (ΡΑΦΑΕΙΝ)

• LXX 44: Raphin (Ραϐιν)

• LXX 127: Titanôn (Τιτανων). Translation: Titans

• LXX 246: Raphae cae ta thêria tôn allophylôn parenebalon en tê coeladi tôn Titanôn (Ραϐαι και τα θηρια των αλλοφυλων παρενϐαλον ϵν τη κοιλαδι των Τιτανων). Translation: Raphae and the animals (or Lupus) of the tribes (or foreigners) put in besides the valley of the Titans

• Aleppo Codex: Rpåym (רפאיס). Translation: long dead (or Raphites)

• Leningrad Codex: Refa'im (רְפָאִים). Translation: long dead (or Raphites)

• Targum Jerusalem: gibbaraya (גִבָּרַיָּא). Translation: men (or husbands)


**2** Codex Vaticanus: Baethleem (ΒΑΙΘΛΕΕΜ)

• Codex Alexandrinus: Bêthleem (ΒΗΘΛΕΕΜ)

• LXX 56: Bethleem (Βϵθλϵϵμ)

• LXX 92: Bithleem (Βιθλϵϵμ)

• Dead Sea Scroll 4QSamᵃ: -t lh- (-אֿל ֿת-). The letters that survive match the name Byt Lhm found in the Masoretic text.

• Aleppo Codex: byt lhm (בית לחס). Translation: House (or Temple) of Lahem

• Leningrad Codex: beit lachem (בֵּית לֶחֶם). Translation: House (or Temple) of Lahem

- Targum Jerusalem: beit lachem (בֵּית לֶחֶם). Translation: House (or Temple) of Lahem

Lehem was a Canaanite fertility and rebirth god, somewhat similar to the Egyptian Osiris and Greek Dionysus. The town of Bethlehem was build around the Temple of Lahem.

# 2nd Kingdoms: Chapter 24

The Lord caused his anger to burn out again in Israel, and moved[1] David against them, saying, "Go, count Israel and Judah."

The king said to Joab commander of the army, who was with him, "Go now through all the tribes of Israel and Judah, from Dan to Bathsheba, and count the people, and I will know the number of the people."

Joab said to the king, "May the Lord add to the people a hundred-fold as many as they are, and may the eyes of my lord the king see it, but why does my lord the king desire this thing?"

The word of the king prevailed against Joab and the captains of the army. Joab and the captains of the army went out from the king to count the people of Israel. They went across the Jordan, and camped in Aroer, on the right of the city which is in the middle of the valley of Gad and Jaazer. They came to Gilead, and into the land of Tahtimhodshi, which is Adasai, and they came to Danjaan and Udan, and compassed Sidon. They came to Mapsar of Tyre, and to all the cities of the Mitanni[2] and the Canaanites, and they went to the south of Judah to Bathsheba. They circled the whole land, and they arrived in Jerusalem at the end of nine months and twenty days. Joab gave the number of the census of the people to the king, and Israel consisted of eight hundred thousand men of might that drew the sword, and the men of Judah, five hundred thousand fighting men.

The heart of David struck him after he heard the number of the people, and David said to the Lord, "I have sinned grievously, the Lord, in what I have now done. Remove, I pray you, the iniquity of your servant, for I have been exceedingly foolish. David rose early in the morning, and the word of the Lord came to the prophet Gad, the seer, saying, "Go, and speak to David, and say, 'The Lord says, 'I bring one of three things on you, now choose from them, and I will do it to you.'

Gad went to David, and told him, and said to him, "Choose one of these things to befall you, whether there will come on you for three years famine in your land, or that you should flee three months before your enemies, and they should pursue you, or that there should be for three days mortality in your land. Now then decide, and see what answer I will return to him that sent me."

David said to Gad, "On every side, I am much straitened, let me fall now into the hands of the Lord, for his compassion is very much, and let me not fall into the hands of man."

So David chose for himself the mortality, and they were the days of wheat harvest, and the Lord sent a pestilence on Israel from morning until noon, and the plague began among the people, and there died among the people from Dan to Bathsheba seventy thousand men. The messenger of God[3] stretched out his hand against Jerusalem to destroy it, and the Lord repented his evil, and said to the messenger that destroyed the people, "It is enough now, withhold your hand."

The messenger of the lord[4] was by the threshing floor of Araunah the Jebusite. David said to the Lord when he saw the messenger killing the people, "Look, it is I that have done wrong, but what have these sheep done? I beg you, let your hand be on me and on my father's house."

Gad came to David in that day, and said to him, "Go up, and set up an altar to the Lord in the threshing floor of Araunah the Jebusite."

David went up according to the word of Gad, as the Lord commanded him. Araunah looked out and saw the king and his servants coming on before him, and Araunah went out and paid respect to the king with his face to the earth. Araunah asked, "Why has my lord the king come to his servant?"

David answered, "To buy of you the threshing floor, to build an altar to the Lord that the plague may be restrained from off the people."

Araunah said to David, "Let my lord the king take and offer to the Lord that which is good in his eyes. Look, here are oxen for a whole burnt offering, and the wheels and furniture of the oxen for wood."

Araunah gave all to the king, and Araunah said to the king, "Lord the god bless you."

The king said to Araunah, "No, but I will certainly buy it from you at a fair price, and I will not offer to the Lord my god a whole burnt offering for nothing."

David purchased the threshing floor and the oxen for fifty shekels of silver. David built an altar to the Lord there and offered up whole burnt offerings and peace-offerings. Solomon made an addition to the altar afterward, for it was little at first. The Lord listened to the land, and the plague was stopped from Israel.

# 2nd Kingdoms: Chapter 24 Notes

**1** Codex Vaticanus: epesisen (ⲈⲦⲦⲈⲤⲈⲓⲤⲈⲚ). Translation: shake at

• LXX 52: epise (ϭⲡϭⲓⲟϭ). Translation: convinced (or mislead, bribed, persuaded)

• LXX 242: epempse (ϭⲡϭⲙⲯϭ). Translation: sent (or dispatched)

• LXX 707: epesen (ϭⲡϭⲟϭⲛ). Translation: threw

• LXX 134: epesisen CS (ϭⲡϭⲟϭⲓⲟϭⲛ ⲔⲤ). Translation: shake at Lord

• Aleppo Codex: yst (יסת)

• Leningrad Codex: yaset (יָּסֶת)

• Targum Jerusalem: garei (גְּרִי). Translation: inflamed

The meaning of both the Greek and Hebrew verses are not clear, however, are generally interpreted as 'and he moved' in Christian translations. The Hebrew term appears to be a direct transliteration of something found in the Aramaic texts that were used as source, however, this does not appear to be an Aramaic term, but an Aramaic transliteration of the Neo-Babylonian ishatu (𒉿𒐀). It suggests the original phrase was something like '...and fired David against...' in the Cuneiform text that the Aramaic translation was based on.


**2** Codex Vaticanus: Euaiou (ⲈⲨⲀⲓⲟⲨ)

• LXX 107: Ebaeou (Ⲉⲩⲗⲓⲟⲩ)

• LXX 127: Enei (Ⲉⲩϭⲓ)

• LXX 108: Enein (Ⲉⲩϭⲓⲛ)

• Aleppo Codex: ḥwy (חוי)

• Leningrad Codex: Chivvi (חִוִּי)

• Targum Jerusalem: Chiva'ei (חִוָאִי). Translation: farmer

The term is believed to have been derived from the name of the Hurrians, however, is derived separately from the other term Chori (חֹרִי). Chori is accepted as referring to the Hurrians, which the Egyptians called Hårw (𓉔𓄿𓂋𓅱), and the Babylonians called Huurri (𒄷𒌨𒊑). The Hurrians were one of the oldest cultures in the Middle East, however, became largely a slave culture within the Akkadian and Old Babylonian empires. Under the Mitanni empire, they rose to a position of wealth, and formed the noble caste. The Greek transliteration of this term was variations of Chorrhaeous (Χορραιους), which, like the Hebrew term, was used interchangeably in the texts with Eyaeon (Ευαιον) / Chivvi (חִוִּי), although that term generally applied to the rules and priests.

The ultimate origin of the terms Eyaeon (Ευαιον) and Chivvi (חִוִּי), both appear to be the cuneiform word Éan (𒂍𒀭), meaning temple or sacred. In the Amarna Letters, which date to the 1330s BC, the term Éan (𒂍𒀭) was the name of a people, who appear to be the Mitanni, or the Mitanni-Aryan priesthood within the Mitanni. A similar correlation between the terms is found in the Septuagint's 1<sup>st</sup> Paralipomenon and Masoretic Divrei-hay Yamim, where the Greek translation uses Beithani (Βαιθανι), however, the Hebrew uses the term Mitni (מִתְנִי). This term also refers to a group of people, meaning the underlying Edomite text the Greeks translated would have been 'people of the House of Ån' (𐤁𐤕𐤀𐤍), a direct Canaanite translation of É An (𒂍𒀭).

While Mitni was the transliteration used in the Edomite text that formed the basis of the Hebrew translation of Divrei-hayYamim, it was replaced with Chivvi (חִוִּי) in the Judahite texts, which served as the basis of most of the Masoretic texts. This likely originated in a Judahite copy of the text, after the Aramaic translation had been made, where an n (𐤍) was replaced with a w (𐤅). The Aramaic translation would have already been made in the time of King Manasseh, were the term was transliterated as Hyån (חׁ𐡀𐡍), itself a transliteration of the early Canaanite Hyån (𐤄𐤉𐤀𐤍).

The term Ebaeôn (Εβαιων), which is found as a substitute for Eyaeon (Ευαιov) in some copies of the Septuagint for term, must have originated in an intentional alteration to the text, as there are no similar letters for b (ב ,ﬤ ,ﬡ) and y (י ,ﬡ ,ﬦ) in the Semitic alphabets the text was previously in. This probable origin was an Ebionite translation in the first century AD. The Ebionites were an early Judeo-Christian sect based in Judea before the First Jewish-Roman war. Many fled east to Mesopotamia with the Mandeans and other smaller Judahite religious groups, while others fled south into Arabia. The Arabian Ebionites are generally viewed as shaping the Islamic view of the prophet Jesus (عِيسَى).

**3** Codex Vaticanus: o angelos tou t̄h̄u̅ (ΟΑΓΓΕΛΟΣΤΟΥΘΥ). Translation: the messenger of the god

• LXX 245: o angelos tou c̄y̅ (ο Αγγѐλοc του ΚΥ). Translation: the messenger of the lord

• Dead Sea Scroll 4QSamᵃ: -hwh (ﬡﬢ-). The DSS 4QSamᵃ is quite damaged in this verse, however, does read differently from both the Masoretic and Septuagint's version. It appears that the verse either referred to the messenger of Yhwh or Yhwh himself killing the people of Jerusalem, although it is not clear which.

• Aleppo Codex: hmlåk (הַמַלְאָ). Translation: the messenger

• Leningrad Codex: hammal'ach (הַמַּלְאָךְ). Translation: the messenger

• Targum Jerusalem: mal'acha (מַלְאָכָא). Translation: messenger

**4** Codex Vaticanus: o angelos c̄u̅ (ΟΑΓΓΕΛΟΣΚΥ). Translation: the messenger lord

• LXX 707: ho angelos tou cyriou (ο Αγγѐλοc του Κυρ̄ριου). Translation: the messenger of the lord

- LXX 127: ho angelos tou THU (ο ἀγγόλοc του Θ Υ). Translation: the messenger of the god

- Aleppo Codex: wmlǎk yhwh (ומלאך יהוה). Translation: and messenger Yhwh

- Leningrad Codex: umal'ach Yehvah (וּמַלְאַךְ יְהוָה). Translation: and messenger Yehwah

- Targum Jerusalem: umal'acha daYyah (וּמַלְאָכָא דַיְיָ). Translation: and messenger of Yahw

# 3rd Kingdoms: Chapter 1

When King David was old and advanced in days, they dressed him in a lot of clothes because he was not warm. His servants said, "Let them seek for the king a young virgin, and she will wait on the king, and love him, and lie with him, and my lord the king will be warmed."

They searched for a beautiful girl from within the frontiers of Israel, and they found Abishag the Shunammite, and they brought her to the king. The girl was extremely beautiful, and she loved the king and ministered to him, but the king did not have relations with her.

Adonijah the son of Haggith exalted himself, saying, "I will be king!" He prepared for himself chariots and horses, and fifty men to run before him.

His father never at any time insulted him by asking, "Why have you done this?" He was also very handsome, his mother carried him after Absalom. He conspired with Joab the son of Zeruiah, and with Abiathar the priest, and they supported Adonijah. But Zadok the priest, and Benaiah the son of Jehoiada, and Nathan the prophet, and Shimei, and Rei, and the mighty men of David did not follow Adonijah.

Adonijah sacrificed sheep and calves and lambs by the stone of Zoheleth, which was near En Rogel, and he called all his brothers, and all the adult men of Judah, servants of the king. But Nathan the prophet, and Benaiah, and the mighty men, but Solomon his brother he did not call. Nathan asked Bathsheba the mother of Solomon, "Have you not heard that Adonijah the son of Haggith reigns, and our lord David does not know it? Now come, let me, I beg, give you counsel, and you will save your life, and the life of your son Solomon. Hurry, and go in to king David, and tell him,

'Have not you, my lord, my king, sworn to your handmaid, 'Your son Solomon will reign after me, and he will sit on my throne?' Why then does Adonijah reign?' Look, while you are still speaking there with the king, I also will come in after you, and will confirm your words.'

So Bathsheba went to the king into his room, and the king was very old, and Abishag the Shunammite was serving the king. Bathsheba bowed and paid respect to the king, and the king asked, "What is your request?"

She answered, "My lord, you swore by Lord the god[1] to your handmaid, saying, 'Your son Solomon will reign after me, and will sit on my throne.' Now, look, Adonijah reigns, and you, my lord, my king, do not know it. He has sacrificed calves and lambs and sheep in abundance and has called all the king's sons, and Abiathar the priest and Joab the commander-in-chief of the army, but Solomon your servant he has not called. You, my lord king, the eyes of all Israel are on you, tell them who will sit on the throne of my lord the king after him. It will come to pass when my lord the king will sleep with his fathers, that I and Solomon my son will not be offenders."

While she was still talking with the king, Nathan the prophet came. It was reported to the king, "Nathan the prophet is here," and he came to the king's presence, and paid respect to the king with his face to the ground.

Nathan said, "My lord, my king, did you command, 'Adonijah will reign after me, and he will sit on my throne?' For he has gone down today, and has sacrificed calves and lambs and sheep in abundance, and has called all the king's sons, and the chiefs of the army, and Abiathar the priest, and, look, they are eating and drinking before him, and they said, 'Long live King Adonijah.'

But he has not invited me, your servant, or Zadok the priest, nor Benaiah the son of Jehoiada, or Solomon your servant. Has this matter happened by the authority of my lord the king, and have you not made known to your servant who will sit on the throne of my lord the king after him?"

King David answered and said, "Call Bathsheba to me," and she came in before the king, and stood before him. The king swore, "As Lord lives, who redeemed my mind out of all allowing, as I swore to you by Lord god in Israel,² 'Solomon your son will reign after me, and he will sit on my throne in my place,' again I will do it today."

Bathsheba bowed with her face to the ground, and paid respect to the king, and said, "Let my lord king David live forever."

King David said, "Call me Zadok the priest, and Nathan the prophet, and Benaiah the son of Jehoiada," and they came in before the king. The king said to them, "Take the servants of your lord with you, and mount my son Solomon on my mule, and bring him down to Gihon. There let Zadok the priest and Nathan the prophet anoint him to be king over Israel, and do you sound the trumpet, and you will say, 'Let king Solomon live.' He will sit on my throne, and reign in my place, and I have given an order that he should be for a prince over Israel and Judah."

Benaiah the son of Jehoiada answered the king, "Let it be so! May Lord God of my lord the king confirm it. As Lord was with my lord the king, so let him be with Solomon, and let him magnify his throne above the throne of my lord king David."

Zadok the priest went down, with Nathan the prophet and Benaiah, the son of Jehoiada, and the Cherethites, and the Pelethites and they mounted Solomon on the mule of king David and led him away to Gihon. Zadok the priest took the horn of oil out of the tabernacle, and anointed Solomon, and blew the trumpet, and all the people shouted, "Let king Solomon live!" All the people followed him, and they danced in choirs and celebrated with great joy, and the earth shook with their voice.

Adonijah and all his guests heard. They had just finished eating, when Joab heard the sound of the trumpet, and asked, "What does the sound of the city in celebration mean?"

While he was yet speaking, Jonathan the son of Abiathar the priest came in, and Adonijah said, "Come in, for you are a mighty man, and you come to bring good news."

Jonathan answered and said, "Verily our lord king David has made Solomon king, and the king has sent with him Zadok the priest, Nathan the prophet, Benaiah the son of Jehoiada, and the Cherethites, and the Pelethites, and they have mounted him on the king's mule. Zadok the priest and Nathan the prophet have anointed him in Gihon, and have gone up there rejoicing, and the city resounded. This is the sound that you have heard. Solomon is seated on the throne of the kingdom. The servants of the king have gone to bless our lord King David, saying, God make the name of Solomon better than your name, and make his throne greater than your throne, and the king worshiped on his bed. Moreover, the king said, 'Blessed be Lord God in Israel, who has this day appointed one of my seed sitting on my throne, and my eyes see it.'"

All the guests of Adonijah were dismayed, and every man went his way. Adonijah was afraid of Solomon, and departed, and took the horns of the altar. It was reported to Solomon, "Look, Adonijah fears king Solomon, and holds the horns of the altar, saying, 'Let Solomon swear to me this day, that he will not kill his servant with the sword.'"

Solomon said, "If he is should a valiant man, there will not a hair of him fall to the ground, but if evil is found in him, he will die." King Solomon sent, and they brought him away from the altar, and he went in and paid respect to king Solomon, and Solomon said to him, "Go to your house."

# 3rd Kingdoms: Chapter 1 Notes

**1** Codex Vaticanus: cyriô tô theô (ΚΥΡΙѠΤѠѲΕѠ). Translation: Lord the god

• Codex Basiliano-Vaticanus: cyriô theô (ΚΥΡΙѠѲΕѠ). Translation: Lord God

• LXX 19: CU sou tou THU (ΚΥ σου του ΘΥ). Translation: my Lord the god

• Aleppo Codex: yhwh âlhyk (יהוה אלהין). Translation: Yhwah your god (in Aramaic, or goddess in Hebrew)

• Leningrad Codex: Yhvah eloheicha (יְהֹוָה אֱלֹהֶיךָ). Translation: Yhwah your god (in Aramaic, or goddess in Hebrew)

• Targum Jerusalem: daYyah elahach (דַיְיָ אֱלָהָךְ). Translation: the Yahw your god

Fragments of older Septuagint manuscripts still exist that contain the Aramaic version of the name, Yhw (𐤉𐤄𐤅), transliterated into Greek as Iaô (Ιαω), however, none of the fragments of the books of 3rd Kingdoms include the name.


**2** Codex Vaticanus: c̄s o t̄h̄s Israêl (Κ͞CΟ͞Θ͞CΙͼ𐤛ΑΗλ). Translation: Lord the god of Israel

• Codex Alexandrinus: Cyrios Theos Israêl (ΚΥΡΙΟCΘΕΟCΙͼ𐤛ΑΗλ). Translation: Lord God of Israel

• LXX 19: CS tou THS Israêl (ΚΥ του ΘΥ ιο𐤛λ). Translation: Lord the God of Israel

• Aleppo Codex: Yhwh âlhy Yšrâl (יהוה אלהי ישראל). Translation: Yhwh god (in Aramaic or goddess in Hebrew) of Israel

• Leningrad Codex: Yehvah elohei Yisra'el (יְהֹוָה אֱלֹהֵי יִשְׂרָאֵל). Translation: Yehwah god (in Aramaic or goddess in Hebrew) of Israel

- Targum Jerusalem: daYyah elaha deYisra'el (דְיִי אֱלָהָא דְיִשְׂרָאֵל).
Translation: the Yahw god of Israel

The original Septuagint's version of the 3<sup>rd</sup> Kingdoms was translated circa 160 BC, before the Hasmonean redaction, and contains the term Lord the god (Κύριος ο θεος) several times. The Aramaic sections of Masoretic Daniel that were not translated into Hebrew maintain the term adonai ha'elohim (אֲדֹנָי הָאֱלֹהִים), meaning the 'Lord the gods' where the Septuagint has 'Lord the god' (Κυριον τον θεον), however, the Hebrew sections have Yahweh elohim (יְהוָה אֱלֹהִים) where the Septuagint has 'Lord the god,' suggesting the Greek more accurately reflects the Aramaic source texts than the Hebrew translation.

According to some records from the time, this was to repair the damage King Manasseh had done 600 years earlier when he removed the name Yahweh from the Israelite Texts, however, no evidence has survived from the era of Manasseh or earlier that proves the name was originally in the text, suggesting it was an attempt by the first Hasmonean High-Priest/King Simon the Zealot to create a national Judean religion with a god having a name similar to the Roman god Jove.

# 3<sup>rd</sup> Kingdoms: Chapter 2

When the days of David were drawing so a close, he knew and told his son Solomon, "I go the way of all the earth, but you be strong, and prove yourself a man. Keep the orders of Lord the god, to follow in his ways, to keep the commandments and the ordinances and the judgments which are written in the law of Moses, that you may understand what you will do in all things that I command you."

"So that Lord may confirm his word when he said, 'If your children will pay attention to their way to walk before me in truth with all their heart, I promise you, 'There will not fail among you a man on the throne of Israel. Moreover you know all what Joab the son of Zeruiah did to me, what he did to the two captains of the forces of Israel, to Abner the son of Ner, and to Amasa the son of Jether, that he killed them, and shed the blood of war in peace, and put innocent blood on his girdle that was about his loins, and on his sandal that was on his foot. Therefore you will deal with him according to your wisdom, and you will not bring down his gray hair in peace to Hades. But you will deal kindly with the sons of Barzillai the Gileadite, and they will be among those that eat at your table, for they drew near to me when I fled from the face of your brother Absalom. And, look, there is with you Shimei the son of Gera, a Benjamite of Bahurim, and he cursed me with a terrible curse in the day when I went into the camp. He came down to the Jordan to meet me, and I swore to him by Lord, 'I will not put you to death with the sword.' You will by no means hold him guiltless, for you are a wise man, and will know what you will do to him, and will bring down his gray hairs with blood to the grave."

David slept with his fathers and was buried in the city of David. The days which David reigned over Israel were forty years, he reigned seven years in Hebron and thirty-three years in Jerusalem. Solomon sat on the throne of his father David, and his kingdom was developed greatly. Adonijah the son of Haggith came to Bathsheba the mother of Solomon and paid respect to her, and she answered, "Do you enter peaceably?"

He answered, "Peaceably. I have business with you."

She replied to him, "Speak."

He said to her, "You know that the kingdom was mine, and all Israel turned their face towards me like a king, but the kingdom was taken from me and became my brother's, as it was appointed to him from Lord. Now I make one request of you, do not turn away your face."

Bathsheba said to him, "Continue."

He said to her, "Speak, I beg you, to king Solomon, for he will not turn away his face from you, and let him give me Abishag the Shunammite as a wife."

Bathsheba said, "Well, I will ask the king for you."

Bathsheba went to King Solomon to speak with him concerning Adonijah, and the king rose up to meet her, and kissed her, and sat on the throne, and a throne was set for the mother of the king, and she sat on his right hand. She said to him, "I ask of you one little request, do not turn me away from you."

The king said to her, "Ask, my mother, and I will not reject you."

She said, "Let, I pray you, Abishag the Shunammite be given to Adonijah your brother as a wife."

King Solomon answered his mother, "Why have you asked Abishag for Adonijah? Ask for him the kingdom also, as he is my elder brother, and he has as his co-conspirators Abiathar the priest and Joab the son of Zeruiah the commander-in-chief." King Solomon swore by Lord, "God do so to me, and more also if Adonijah has not spoken this word against his own life. Now as Lord lives who has established me, and set me on the throne of my father David, and he has made me a house, as Lord spoke, this day will Adonijah be put to death."

So king Solomon sent by the hand of Benaiah the son of Jehoiada, and he killed him, and Adonijah died that day. The king said to Abiathar the priest, "Leave quickly to Anathoth, your farm, for you are worthy of death this day, but I will not kill you, because you have borne the box of the covenant of the Lord before my father, and because you allowed in all things in which my father allowed."

Solomon removed Abiathar from being a priest of Lord, that the word of Lord might be fulfilled, which he spoke concerning the house of Eli in Shiloh. The report came to Joab son of Zeruiah, for Joab had followed Adonijah, and did not go to Solomon. Joab fled to the tabernacle of Lord and caught hold of the horns of the altar. It was told to Solomon, "Joab has fled to the tabernacle of Lord, and he has taken hold of the horns of the altar."

King Solomon sent to Joab, asking "What bothers you, that you have fled to the altar?"

Joab answered, "I was afraid of you, and fled for refuge to Lord."

Solomon ordered Benaiah the son of Jehoiada, "Go and kill him, and bury him."

Benaiah son of Jehoiada went to Joab in the tabernacle of Lord, and said to him, "The king said, 'Come out.'

Joab replied, "I will not come out, for I will die."

Benaiah son of Jehoiada returned and said to the king, "Joab has spoken, and he has said this to me."

The king said to him, "Go, and do to him as he has said, and kill him and bury him, and you will remove this day the blood which he shed without cause, from me and from the house of my father. Lord has returned on his own head the blood of his unrighteousness, inasmuch as he attacked two men more righteous and better than himself, and killed them with the sword, and my father David did not know of their blood, even Abner the son of Ner the commander-in-chief of Israel, and Amessa the son of Jether the commander-in-chief of Judah. Their blood is returned on his head, and on the head of his seed forever, but to David, and his seed, and his house, and his throne, may there be peace for ever from Lord."

So Benaiah son of Jehoiada went up, and attacked him, and killed him, and buried him in his house in the wilderness. The king appointed Benaiah son of Jehoiada in his place over the army, and the kingdom was established in Jerusalem. As for Zadok the priest, the king appointed him to be a high priest in place of Abiathar. Solomon son of David reigned over Israel and Judah from Jerusalem, and Lord gave understanding to Solomon, and a great deal of wisdom, and largeness of heart, as the sand by the sea-shore.

The Wisdom of Solomon was far beyond the wisdom of all the ancients, and beyond all the wise men of Egypt. He took the daughter of Pharaoh, and brought her into the city of David, while he finished building his own house, and the Temple of Lord, and the walls around Jerusalem. For seven years he built and finished them.

Solomon had seventy thousand laborers and eight thousand stonemasons in the mountain. Solomon made the sea, and the bases, and the great lavers, and the pillars, and the fountain of the court, and the bronze sea, and he built the citadel as a defense above it, he made a breach in the wall of the city of David, so the daughter of Pharaoh went up out of the city of David to her house which he built for her. Then he built the citadel, and Solomon offered up three whole burnt offerings in the year, and peace-offerings on the altar which he built to Lord, and he burnt incense before Lord, and finished the house. These are the chief persons who presided over the works of Solomon: three thousand and six hundred masters of the people that worked the works. He built Asshur, Megiddo, and Gazer, and upper Bethhoron, and Ballath. After he had built the Temple of Lord, and the wall of Jerusalem around it, he built these cities.

When David was still living, he ordered Solomon, "Look, there is with you Shimei the son of Gera, of the seed of Benjamin out of Hebron. He cursed me with a terrible curse in the day when I went into the camp, and he came down to meet me at the Jordan, and I swore to him by Lord, 'He will not be slain with the sword.' But now don't you hold him guiltless, for you are a man of understanding, and you will know what you will do to him, and you will bring down his gray hairs with blood to Hades."

The king called Shimei, and said to him, "Build you a house in Jerusalem, and live there, and you will not go out there any to what place."

It will come to pass in the day that you will go out and cross over the brook Kidron, know assuredly that you will certainly die. Your blood will be on your head. The king caused him to swear on that day. Shimei said to the king, "Good is the word that you have spoken, my lord my king, so will your servant do."

Shimei lived in Jerusalem for three years. After the three years, that two servants of Shimei ran away to Achish son of Maacah king of Gath, and it was told to Shimei, "Look, your servants are in Gath."

Shimei rose up, saddled his donkey, and went to Gath to Achish to seek out his servants, and Shimei went and brought his servants out of Gath.

It was told to Solomon, "Shimei is gone out of Jerusalem to Gath, and has brought back his servants."

The king sent and called Shimei, and said to him, "Did I not adjure you by Lord, and testify to you, saying, 'In whatever day you will go out of Jerusalem, and go to the right or left, know certainly that you will assuredly die? Why have you not kept the oath of Lord and the commandment which I commanded you?'"

The king said to Shimei, "Your heart knows the evil, which you did to David my father, and Lord has recompensed your evil on your own head. King Solomon is blessed, and the throne of David will be established before Lord forever."

Solomon commanded Benaiah the son of Jehoiada, and he went out and killed him.

King Solomon was very prudent and wise, and the people of Judah and Israel were very many, as the sand which is by the sea for multitude, eating, and drinking, and rejoicing. Solomon was chief in all the kingdoms, and they brought gifts and served Solomon all the days of his life. Solomon began to open the domains of Lebanon, and he built Thermae in the wilderness. This was the daily provision of Solomon, thirty measures of fine flour, and sixty measures of ground meal, ten choice calves, and twenty oxen from the pastures, and a hundred sheep, besides stags, and does, and choice fed birds. For he ruled in all the country on this side the river, from Raphi to Gaza, over all the kings on this side the river, and he was at peace on all sides around it. Judah and Israel lived safely, everyone under his vine and under his fig tree, eating, drinking, and feasting, from Dan even to Bathsheba, all the days of Solomon.

These were the princes of Solomon: Azariu son of Zadok the priest, and Orniu son of Nathan chief of the officers, and he went to his house, and Zobah the scribe, and Basa son of Achithalam recorder, and Abi son of Joab commander-in-chief, and Ahira son of Edrai was over the levies, and Benaiah son of Jehoiada over the household and over the brickwork, and Cachur the son of Nathan was counselor.

Solomon had forty thousand broodmares for his chariots, and twelve thousand horses. He reigned over all the kings from the river and to the land of the foreigners, and to the borders of Egypt, so Solomon the son of David reigned over Israel and Judah from Jerusalem.

# 3rd Kingdoms: Chapter 3

The people burnt incense on the bamahs,[1] because a temple had not yet been built for the Lord. Solomon loved the Lord, and followed the ordinances of David his father, and he only sacrificed and burnt incense on the bamahs. He arose and went to Gibeon to sacrifice there, for that was the greatest bamah. Solomon offered a whole burnt offering of a thousand victims on the altar in Gibeon.

The Lord appeared to Solomon in a dream by night, and god said to Solomon, "Ask something for yourself."

Solomon said, "You have dealt very mercifully with your servant David my father when he walked before you in truth, and in righteousness, and in uprightness of heart with you, and you have kept for him this great mercy, to set his son on his throne, as it is this day. Now, Lord the god, you have appointed your servant in place of David my father. I am a little child and don't know my going out and my coming in. But your servant is among people, whom you have chosen, a great people, which on this day can't be counted. You will give therefore to your servant a heart to hear and to judge your people justly, and to discern between good and evil, for who will be able to judge your great people?"

It was pleasing before the Lord, that Solomon asked this thing and Lord said to him, "Because you have asked this thing of me, and have not asked for yourself long life, and have not asked wealth, nor have asked the lives of your enemies, but have asked for yourself understanding to hear judgment, I have done as you have asked. Look, I have given you an understanding and wise heart, there has not been anyone like you before you, and after you, there will not rise one like you. I have also given you what you have not asked, wealth and glory so that there has not been anyone like you among kings. If you will follow my ways, to keep my commandments and my ordinances, as David your father followed, then will I multiply your days."

Solomon woke from his dream, and he rose and went to Jerusalem, and stood before the altar that was in front of the box of the covenant of Lord in Zion. He offered whole burnt offerings, and sacrificed peace-offerings, and made a great banquet for himself and all his servants.

Then two prostitutes came before the king, and they stood before him. The one woman said, "Hear me, my lord, I and this woman lived in one house, and we gave birth in the house. It came to pass on the third day after I gave birth, this woman also gave birth. We were together, and there was no one with us besides us in the house. This woman's child died in the night, because she rolled over on to it, and she rose in the middle of the night, and took my son from my arms, and laid him in her bosom, and laid her dead son in my bosom. I arose in the morning to suckle my son, and he was dead. I looked at him in the morning, and it was not my son, who I carried."

The other woman said, "No, but the living is my son, and the dead is your son."

So they spoke before the king, and the king said to them, "You say, 'This is my son, even the living one, and this woman's son is the dead one,' and you say, 'No, but the living is my son, and the dead is your son.'"

The king ordered, "Fetch a sword." They brought a sword to the king, and he ordered, "Cut the live child, the infant, in two. Give half of it to one, and half of it to the other."

The woman whose child was living, answered the king, (as her heart yearned for her son) and she said, "I beg you, my lord, give her the child, and do not kill it."

But the other said, "Let it be neither mine nor hers, kill it."

Then the king answered and said, "Give the child to her that said, 'Give it to her, and by no means kill it,' she is its mother." And all Israel heard this judgment which the king judged, and they were afraid of the king because they saw that the wisdom of the gods was in him, to execute judgment.

# 3ʳᵈ Kingdoms: Chapter 3 Notes

**1** Codex Vaticanus: ypsêloes (ΥΨΗΛΟΙϹ). Translation: heights

• Fragment Tischendorfianus: ypsêlotatoes (ΥΨΗΛΟΤΑΤΟΙϹ). Translation: high places

• LXX 93: ypsêlotataes (υΨΗλοτΑτΑιϲ). Translation: high places

• Aleppo Codex: bmwt (כמות). Translation: bamahs

• Leningrad Codex: bamot (בָּמֹות). Translation: bamahs

• Targum Jerusalem: bāmôtā (בָּמֹותָא). Translation: bamahs

Bamahs were stone platforms built at the tops of hills, where sacrifices were made to gods in ancient Canaan and Assyria. These bamahs generally included an altar for barbecuing the sacrifices, a stele, a seat for the god (which the priest would sit in), a tree representing Asherah, and a cistern for water. These bamahs were also generally accompanied by a banquet hall, and a 'low stone' used for slaughtering and butchering the animal. Bamahs were the main religious centers used by the Israelites until King Josiah banned and destroyed them circa 625 BC. After that, all Jews were required by law to worship at the temple in Jerusalem.

# 3rd Kingdoms: Chapter 4

King Solomon reigned over Israel. These are the princes which he had: Azariah son of Zadok, the scribes Elihoreph and Ahijah the son of Sheba, and the recorder Jehoshaphat the son of Ahilud. Benaiah the son of Jehoiada was in charge of the army, and Zadok and Abiathar were the priests. Ornia the son of Nathan was in charge of the officers, and Zabud son of Nathan was the king's friend. Ahishar was steward, Eliac the chief steward, and Eliab the son of Saph was over the family, and Adoniram the son of Abda over the tribute.

Solomon had twelve officers over all Israel, to provide for the king and his household, each one's turn came to supply for a month in the year. These were their names:

Been the son of Hur in the mountains of Ephraim.

The son of Dekar, in Makez, Shaalbim, Bethshemesh, and Elon as far as Bethanan.

The son of Hesed in Aruboth in Sochoh, and all the land of Hepher.

All Nephthador belonged to the son of Abinadab, Taphath daughter of Solomon was his wife.

Baanah the son of Ahilud had Taanach and Megiddo, and he was the whole house of San which was by Sesathan below Jezreel, and from Bethsan as far as Abelmeholah, as far as Maeber Lucam.

The son of Geber in Raboth Gilead, to him, fell the lot of Argob in Bashan, sixty great cities with walls, and bronze bars.

Ahinadab son of Iddo, had Mahanaim.

Ahimaaz was in Naphtali, and he took the Basmath daughter of Solomon as a wife.

Baanah the son of Hushai, in Asher and in Aloth.

Jehoshaphat the son of Phuasud was in Issachar.

Shimei son of Elah, in Benjamin.

Gaber son of Adai in the land of Gad, the land of Sihon king of Heshbon, and of Og king of Bashan, and one officer in the land of Judah.

The officers provided for king Solomon, and they executed everyone in his month all the orders for the table of the king, they omitted nothing. They carried the barley and the straw for the horses and the chariots to the place where the king might be, each according to his charge. These were the requisite supplies for Solomon: in one day thirty measures of fine flour, and sixty measures of fine pounded meal, and ten choice calves, and twenty pastured oxen, and a hundred sheep, besides stags, and choice fatted does. He had dominion on this side the river, and he was at peace on all sides. God gave understanding to Solomon, and very much wisdom, and enlargement of heart, as the sand on the seashore. Solomon abounded greatly beyond the wisdom of all the ancients, and beyond all the wise men of Egypt. He was wiser than all other men, and he was wiser than Ethan the Ezrahite, and than Heman, and than Chalcol and Darda the son of Mahol.

Solomon spoke three thousand proverbs and five thousand songs. He spoke of trees, from the cedar in Lebanon even to the hyssop which comes out through the wall. He spoke also of livestock, and of birds, and of reptiles, and of fishes. All the nations came to hear the wisdom of Solomon, and ambassadors from all the kings of the earth, as many as heard of his wisdom. Solomon took to himself the daughter of Pharaoh as a wife and brought her into the city of David until he had finished the Temple of Lord, and his own house, and the wall of Jerusalem. Then went up Pharaoh the king of Egypt, and took Gazer, and burnt it and the Canaanites living in Mergab, and Pharaoh gave them as a dowry to his daughter the wife of Solomon, and Solomon rebuilt Gazer.

# 3rd Kingdoms: Chapter 5

King Hiram of Tyre sent his servants to anoint Solomon in place of David his father because Hiram always loved David. Solomon sent to Hiram, saying, "You knew my father, David, that he could not build a temple in the name of Lord the god because of the wars that raged around him until the Lord put them under the steps of his feet. Now Lord the god has given me peace. There is no one plotting against me, and there is no evil trespass against me. And, look, I intend to build a house to the name of Lord the god, as Lord the god said to my father David, 'Your son whom I will set on your throne in your place, he will build a house to my name.' Now command, and let men cut wood for me in Lebanon, and my servants will be with your servants, and I will give you the wages of your service, whatever you ask because you know that we have no one skilled in cutting timber like the Sidonians."

As soon as Hiram heard the words of Solomon, he rejoiced greatly, and said, "Blessed be God today, who has given to David a wise son over this numerous people."

He sent to Solomon, "I have listened concerning all that you have sent to me for. I will do all your will, as for timber of cedar and fir, my servants will bring them down from Lebanon to the sea. I will form them into rafts, and bring them to the place which you will tell me about. I will land them there, and you will take them up, and you will do my will, in giving bread to my household."

So Hiram gave to Solomon cedars, and fir trees, and all his desire. Solomon gave to Hiram twenty thousand measures of wheat as food for his house, and twenty thousand baths of beaten oil annually. The Lord gave the wisdom to Solomon as he promised, and there was peace between Hiram and Solomon, and they made a covenant between them. The king raised a levy out of all Israel, and the levy was thirty thousand men. He sent them to Lebanon, ten thousand taking a turn each month.

They were a month in Lebanon and two months at home, and Adoniram was in charge of the levy. Solomon had seventy thousand laborers, and eighty thousand stone-masons in the mountains, besides the rulers that were appointed over the works of Solomon, there were three thousand six hundred masters who worked in the works. The king commanded and they brought great stones, precious stones for the foundation of the house, and uncut stones. They prepared the stones and the timber for three years.

# 3rd Kingdoms: Chapter 6

In the four hundred and fortieth year[1] after the departure of the Israelites out of Egypt, in the fourth year and second month of the reign of King Solomon over Israel, the king commanded that they should take great and costly stones for the foundation of the house, and cut stones.

The men of Solomon and the men of Hiram cut the stones and laid them for a foundation. In the fourth year, he laid the foundation of the Temple of the Lord, in the month of Shorm,[2] the second month. In the eleventh year, in the month of Bwl,[3] this is the eighth month, the house was completed according to all its plan, and according to all its arrangement. The temple that the king built for the Lord was forty cubits long, and twenty cubits wide, and its height twenty-five cubits. The porch in front of the temple was twenty cubits long according to the width of the temple in front of the house, and he built the temple and finished it.

He made for the temple hidden windows inclining inward, and against the wall of the temple, he set rooms around it in the temple for the box. The underside was five cubits wide, and the middle part six, and the third was seven cubits wide, for he formed an interval to the temple around outside the temple, that they might not touch the walls of the temple. The temple was built from rough-cut stones, and there were no sounds or hammers or axes, nor any iron tool, in the temple while it was being built. The porch of the underside was below the right-wing of the temple, and there was a winding ascent into the middle room, and from the middle to the third story. So he built the temple and finished it, and he made the ceiling of the temple with cedars.

He made the partitions through all the temple, each five cubits high, and enclosed each partition with cedar boards. He framed the walls of the temple within with cedar boards, from the floor of the temple and on to the inner walls and to the beams, he lined the parts enclosed with boards within and encompassed the inward parts of the temple with planks of fir. He built the twenty cubits from the top of the wall, one side from the floor to the beams, and he made it from the oracle to the holiest place. The temple was forty cubits in extent, in front of the oracle in the middle of the temple within, in order to put there the box of the covenant of the Lord.

The length was twenty cubits, and the width was twenty cubits, and the height of it was twenty cubits. He covered it with perfect gold, and he made an altar in front of the oracle and covered it with gold. He covered the whole temple with gold until he had finished gilding the whole temple. He made in the oracle two sphinxes[4] ten cubits high. The wing of one sphinx was five cubits, and his other wing was five cubits, ten cubits from the tip of one wing to the tip of the other wing. It was the same with the other sphinx, both were identical. The height of the one sphinx was ten cubits, and so was the second sphinx. Both the sphinxes were in the middle of the innermost part of the temple, and they spread out their wings, and one wing touched the wall, and the wing of the other sphinx touched the other wall, and their wings in the middle of the temple touched each other. He covered the sphinxes with gold.

He engraved all the walls of the temple all around it, with carvings of sphinxes and phoenixes[5] inside and outside. He covered the floor of the house within and outside with gold. For the door-way of the oracle he made doors of juniper wood, there were porches in a four-fold way. In both the doors were planks of fir. One door had two beams and their hinges, and the other door had two beams and turned on hinges, being carved with sphinxes and phoenixes around a horseshoe-shaped path, and it was coated with gold guilded onto the engraving. He built the inner court, three rows of cut stones, and a row of worked cedar around it, and he made the curtain of the court of the porch of the house that was in front of the temple.

# 3rd Kingdoms: Chapter 6 Notes

**1** Codex Vaticanus: tessaracostô cae tetracosiostô eti (ΤΕCCΑΡΑΚΟCΤѠ ΚΑΙ ΤΕΤΡΑΚΟCΙΟCΤѠ ΕΤΕΙ). Translation: fortieth and four hundred (440) year

• Fragment Tischendorfianus: ogdoêcostô cae tetracosiostô eti (ΟΓΔΟΗΚΟCΤѠ ΚΑΙ ΤΕΤΡΑΚΟCΙΟCΤѠ ΕΤΕΙ). Translation: eightieth and four hundred (480) year

• Codex Coislinianus: tessaracostô omoeôs cae to ebraecon basemonim echi o esti p′ cae tetracosiostô eti (ΤΕCCΑΡΑΚΟCΤѠ ΟΜΟΙѠCΚΑΙΤΟ ΕΒΡΑΙΚΟΝ ΒΑCΕΜΟΝΕΙΜ ΕΧΕΙ Ο ΕCΤΙ Π′ ΚΑΙ ΤΕΤΡΑΚΟCΙΟCΤѠ ΕΤΕΙ). Translation: fortieth (the same verse in the Hebrew accepted texts has 80) and four hundred (440) year

• LXX 249: tetracosiostô cae tessaracostô eti (τότρ̆Διοσιοστοο μ̆Δι τόσσΔρ̆Διοστοο όΤόι). Translation: four hundred and fortieth (440) year

• LXX 64: tessaracostô cae en tô tetracosiostô eti (τόσσΔρ̆Διοστοο μ̆Δι όʎ τοο τότρ̆Διοσιοστοο όΤόι). Translation: fortieth and in the four hundred (440) year

• Aleppo Codex: bšmwnym šnh wǎrbô mǎwt šnh ( בשמונים שנה וארבע מאות שנה ). Translation: eightieth and four hundred (480) year

• Leningrad Codex: vishmovnim shanah ve'arba me'ovt shanah (בִּשְׁמוֹנִים שָׁנָה וְאַרְבַּע מֵאוֹת שָׁנָה). Translation: eightieth and four hundred (480) year

• Targum Jerusalem: ve'arba me'ah vetamnan shenin ( בְּאַרְבַּע מְאָה וְתַמְנָן שְׁנִין ). Translation: four hundred eightieth (480) year

This verse of the Septuagint does not correlate with either the Masoretic texts or the earlier sections of the Septuagint. This verse dates the exodus from Egypt to 1406 BC, while the Masoretic version places the exodus in 1446 BC. The earlier books of Exodus, Joshua, Judges, and 1st Kingdoms in the Septuagint date the exodus to approximately 1547 BC.

This deviation, along with several others in 2ⁿᵈ and 3ʳᵈ Kingdoms are probably redactions dating to the early Christian era, likely based on Origen of Alexandria's Hexapla, published circa 240 AD, which itself drew on both the Old Greek translation, and the translation made the Jewish scholar Theodotion circa 150 AD. Theodotion retranslated the Septuagint into Greek from the Hebrew texts being used by Jews in the 2ⁿᵈ century. The surviving copies of 2ⁿᵈ and 3ʳᵈ Kingdoms include both text that appears to have been redacted by the Hasmoneans, and text that appears to be pre-Hasmonean, strongly indicating it originated in the Hexapla.

**2** Codex Vaticanus: Nisô (ΝΙϹѠ)

- LXX 12: Nisôn (Νισων)

- LXX 127: Nêsô (Νλσω)

- LXX 56: Nisan (Νισλν)

- LXX 82: Ziou mêni (Ζιου μλνι). Translation: Ziou month

- LXX 119: Diou (Δϭιου)

- Aleppo Codex: Zw (וו)

- Leningrad Codex: Ziw (וֹ)

- Vetus Latina: Xiiu

- Targum Jerusalem: Ziv (זיו)

The Greek name is a transliteration of the name Nisan, the first month of Babylonian (𒌗𒁀), Aramaic (ניסן), and Hebrew (ניסן) calendars. It is unlikely the month of Nisan would have been referred to as the second month by any Aramaic or Hebrew speaking person, suggesting it was part of Origen of Alexandria's Hexapla, published circa 240 AD, which itself drew on both the Old Greek translation, and the translation made the Jewish scholar Theodotion circa 150 AD.

It is sometimes mistaken for the name of the second month on a pre-Babylonian Canaanite calendar, however, the word ziw (זִו) simply means 'this,' and was not the recorded name of any month on any known calendar. Proponents to the month of Ziw generally assume the name is a misspelling of zyw (זיו), meaning 'brightness,' however, there is no known month of Brightness on any recorded calendar form the region. The second month of the Babylonian calendar was <sup>iti</sup>Ayari (𒌚𒄞) which was adopted as the Aramaic åyr (𐡀𐡉𐡓) and Hebrew Iyyar (אִיָּר).

The corresponding month on the Gezer Calendar, a Canaanite tablet dating to the 10<sup>th</sup> century BC, lists this as the month of Šôrm (𐤔𐤒𐤓𐤌), meaning 'grain,' as it was the month when grain was harvested. This Canaanite name appears to have been translated into Neo-Babylonian cuneiform as Še'um (𒊺), which also meant grain, however, was also the way the month <sup>iti</sup>Addari (𒌚𒊺) was spelled, the twelfth month in the Neo-Babylonian calendar, which was later adopted as the Aramaic Ådrå (𐡀𐡃𐡓𐡀), and Hebrew Adar (אֲדָר).

The Cuneiform translation had to have been made prior to the Arameans and Judahites adopting the Babylonian calendar or the name would have been translated as the name of the month <sup>iti</sup>Ayari (𒌚𒄞) instead of the word for grain (𒊺), however, by the time they translated the text into Aramaic the identification of the month of Adar as the second month would have been impossible, and therefore the name was transliterated using the old Sumerian transliteration technique, rendering še (𒊺) as zw (זו), which would have later been transliterated directly into Hebrew as zw (זו). The existence of this word in 3<sup>rd</sup> Kingdoms is fairly conclusive evidence that the Neo-Babylonain cuneiform version of the book was translated from a Canaanite version, likely during the Babylonian captivity, before being translated into Aramaic during the Persian era.

2<sup>nd</sup> Kingdoms also includes the word zê (ζη), which appears to be the Greek transliteration of zw (זו), confirming that the word was once in the Septuagint's Kingdoms. As the Aramaic text the Greeks translated could not have used the name Nisan for the second month, the

Canaanite name Šôrm (𐤔𐤓𐤌) is restored as Shorm. The second month of the Hebrew calendar, Iyar is equivalent to late April and early May on the Gregorian Calendar.

**3** Codex Vaticanus: Baad (ΒΑΑΔ)

- LXX 19: Bald (βαλα)

- LXX 56: Bouad (βουαα)

- LXX 119: Boual (βουαλ)

- LXX 509: Gaad (Γααα)

- Aleppo Codex: Bwl (בול)

- Leningrad Codex: Bul (בּוּל)

- Vetus Latin: Bahal

- Targum Jerusalem: Ziv (זיו)

The month of Bwl (𐤁𐤅𐤋) was also mentioned on the Sarcophagus of Eshmunazar II from Sidon, which is dated to the early 5th century BC, confirming that it was a Canaanite month, and strongly supporting the existence of the Canaanite source text for the Cuneiform translation. The name of the eighth month was not listed on the Gezer Calendar, which listed it as one of two months for gathering. As the Geeks appear to have mistranslated Bwl as variations of Baal, the Canaanite name is restored as Bwl. The eight-month in the modern Hebrew calendar is Cheshvan, equivalent to October and November on the Gregorian Calendar.

**4** Codex Vaticanus: cheroubin (ΧΕΡΟΥΒΕΙΝ)

- Codex Alexandrinus: cherebin xylôn cyparisinôn (ΧΕΡΕΒΕΙΝ ΞΥΛΩΝΚΥΠΑΡΙCΙΝΩΝ). Translation: cherubs of cypress wood

- Codex Coislinianus: cheroubin xylôn cyparissinôn (ΧΕΡΟΥΒΕΙΝ ΞΥΛΩΝΚΥΠΑΡΙCCΙΝΩΝ). Translation: cherubs of cypress wood

- Codex Basiliano-Vaticanus: cheroubi (ⲭⲉⲣⲟⲩⲃⲉⲓ)

- LXX 247: cheroubim en (χόβουμμ ϭν)

- LXX 158: chaeroubêm ec xylôn cyparissinôn (χαιβουαλμ ϭι ξυλοον ᴌυπαβιϭϭιⲛⲟⲟⲛ). Translation: cherubs of cypress wood

- LXX 106: cheroub (χόβουμ)

- Aleppo Codex: krwbym (כרובים). Translation: cherubs (or griffins, sphinxes)

- Leningrad Codex: cheruvim (כְרוּבִים). Translation: cherubs (or griffins, sphinxes)

- Targum Jerusalem: keruvin (כְרוּבִין). Translation: cherubs (or griffins, sphinxes)

The Greek term is a transliteration of the Aramaic krbyn (ᱧᱧᱫᱧᱤ), indicating the Greek translation of 3rd Kingdoms was made from an Aramaic source. The word 'cherub' (ܟܪܘܒ / כרוב / ᱧᱧᱫ / ᱤᱧᱫ) was the West Semitic term for the mythical creature generally called a 'griffin' today. Based in the archaeological record of Canaan, it appears that the concept of the cherub was based on the Egyptian sphinx, as the earliest cherub statues found in Canaan were Egyptian statues of sphinxes. Archaeologists are not sure if the sphinxes of Anatolia were based on the Canaanite cherub, or the Egyptian sphinxes directly, however, all three mythical beings are closely related in the archaeological record.

**5** Codex Vaticanus: phoenices (ⲫⲟⲓⲛⲓⲕⲉⲥ). Translation: phoenixes (or Phoenicians, dates)

- Codex Alexandrinus: phoenices cae periglypha encyptonta (ⲫⲟⲓⲛⲓⲕⲉⲥ ⲕⲁⲓ ⲡⲉⲣⲓⲅⲗⲩⲫⲁ ⲉⲅⲕⲩⲡⲧⲟⲛⲧⲁ). Translation: phoenixes (or Phoenicians, dates) and carved out bowing down

- Codex Coislinianus: phoenicas (ⲫⲟⲓⲛⲓⲕⲁⲥ). Translation: phoenixes (or Phoenicians, palms)

- LXX 247: phoenices cae periglypha (ϕοινιϰὸϲ ϰλι πόϼιγλυϕλ πόϼιγλυϕλ πόϼιγλυϕλ ϭγϫυπτοντλ). Translation: phoenixes (or Phoenicians, dates) and carved out feathers bending down

  - Aleppo Codex: tmrt (תמרת)

  - Leningrad Codex: timorot (תִמֹרֹת)

  - Targum Jerusalem: diklin (דִקְלִין). Translation: palm trees

The Masoretic term is unclear, but generally assumed to be derived from the Hebrew term tamar (תָּמָר), meaning 'date palms,' and therefore, a common English translation is 'palm tree.' The word is not proper Aramaic either, as the Imperial Aramaic word for 'date palms,' was tmrtå (תַּמְרְתָא). The Greek translation of 'Phoenixes' is no more illuminating, as 'Phoenixes' has multiple meanings, one of which was 'dates,' as the Greeks imported dates from Phoenicia. The longer text found in some Greek manuscripts confirms that the translators did view the 'Phoenixes' as winged beings of some kind, however, it is unclear where the longer text came from.

As a result, most translators settle for the translation of 'palm trees,' however, rabbinical and academic interpretations have disagreed for more than a thousand years, as the interpretation of 'date palm' is anachronistic to the era of Solomon. The proto-Semitic root term 'tamar' relates to being awake or standing watch, suggesting that the term referred to engravings of 'guardians,' and not 'palm trees.' If these 'guardians' were anything like the Greek concept of the Phoenix firebird, they were probably the Winged Suns that are found engraved on the important buildings in Canaan from the era.

The Winged Sun iconography seems to have originated in the Egyptian Old Kingdom, were Egyptologts label it as 'Behdety.' At the time, the Behdety represented the sun god Horus in the southern Egyptian city of Edfu. Later it was imported into the Old Assyrian and Old Babylonian Empires, where it represented royal power. It appears to have been used the same way in Samaria and Judah until the Neo-Babylonian Empire conquered Judah and destroyed Jerusalem.

The Greek term phoenix is also paradoxical as the Hebrew 'tamar,' as the Greeks believed the mythical Phoenix fire-bird came from Egypt, yet they named it 'Phoenician,' suggesting that they learned the myth of the Phoenix from Phoenicians. Egyptologists believe the root of the Phoenix fire-bird myth originates in the myth of the Bennu solar-bird, one of the creator gods worshiped in Heliopolis. The Old Kingdom era Pyramid Texts refer to the Bennu solar-bird as an aspect of the creator Atum, similar to the eye of Horus-Ra, of the later New-Kingdom era. During the New Kingdom era, the Bennu was depicted as a heron in Egyptian artwork, meaning that if the Winged Sun was based on the Bennu, it had to have been adopted into Canaan before the fall of the Hyksos Dynasty, circa 1550 BC.

Both the north Egyptian Bennu and south Egyptian Behdety probably have a common origin in pre-Dynastic Egypt, although Egyptologists are not sure what the root of the story would have been. As the term 'Phoenix' is probably not related to palm trees, the Greek translation of phoenixes is imported into this translation.

# 3rd Kingdoms: Chapter 7

King Solomon sent and brought Hiram from Tyre, the son of a widowed woman, and he was of the tribe of Naphtali, and his father was a Tyrian, a worker of brass, and accomplished and skilled and knowledge in every work of brass, and he was brought to King Solomon, and he created all the works.

He cast the two pillars for the porch of the temple. The two pillars were eighteen cubits high, and a circumference was fourteen cubits around it, the thickness of the pillar. The flutings were four fingers wide, and the other pillar formed the same way. He made two molten chapiters to put on the heads of the pillars, the height of one chapiter was five cubits, and the height of the other chapiter was five cubits. He made two ornaments of nettings to cover the chapiters of the pillars, including a net for one chapiter, and a net for the other chapiter, and hanging work, composed of two rows of bronze pomegranates, formed with nettings, hanging row on row, and likewise he framed the ornaments for the second chapiter.

He set up the pillars of the porch of the temple, and he set up the one pillar and called its name Jachum, and he set up the second pillar and called its name Boloz. On the heads of the pillars he made lily-work against the porch, of four cubits, and a room over both the pillars and above the sides an addition equal to the room in width. He made the sea, ten cubits from one rim to the other, the same was completely circular around it. Its height was five cubits and its circumference thirty-three cubits. Underneath its rim around it, the circumference was ten cubits.

There were twelve oxen under the sea, three looking to the north, and three looking to the west, and three looking to the south, and three looking to the east, and all their hind sections were inward, and the sea was above on them. and its rim was as the work of the rim of a cup, a lily-flower, and the thickness of it was a span. He made ten bronze bases: the length of one base was five cubits, and four cubits the width of it, and its height was six cubits. This work of the bases was formed with a border for them, and there was a border between the ledges. On their borders between the projection were lions, and oxen, and sphinxes: and on the projections, even so above, and also below were the places of lions and oxen, hanging work. There were four bronze wheels to one base, and there were bronze bases, and their four sides answering to them, side pieces under the bases. There were axles in the wheels under the base. The height of one wheel was a cubit and a half. The work of the wheels was as the work of chariot wheels: their axles, and their rims, and the rest of their work were all molten.

The four side pieces were at the four corners of each base, its shoulders were formed of the base. On the top of the base half, a cubit was the size of it, there was a circle on the top of the base, and there was the top of its spaces and its borders, and it was open at the top of its spaces. Its borders were sphinxes, and lions, and phoenixes, upright, each was joined in front and within and around it According to the same form he made all the ten bases, even one order and one measure to all. He made ten bronze lavers, each laver containing forty baths, and measuring four cubits, each laver placed on several bases throughout the ten bases. He put five bases on the right side of the house, and five on the left side of the house: and the sea was placed on the right side of the house eastward in the direction of the south. Hiram made the cauldrons, and the pans, and the bowls, and Hiram finished making all the works that he worked for King Solomon in the Temple of Lord: two pillars and the wreathed works of the pillars on the heads of the two pillars, and the two networks to cover both the wreathed works of the flutings that were on the pillars.

The four hundred pomegranates for both the networks, two rows of pomegranates for one network, to cover both the wreathed works of the bases belonging to both pillars. The ten bases, and the ten lavers on the bases. One sea, and the twelve oxen under the sea. The cauldrons, and pans, and bowls, and all the furniture, which Hiram made for king Solomon for the Temple of the Lord: and there were eight and forty pillars of the house of the king and of the Temple of the Lord: all the works of the king which Hiram made were entirely of brass. There was no calculating of the brass of which he made all these works, from its great abundance there was no end of the weight of the brass.

In the country around Jordan, he cast them, in the clay land between Booths and Sira. King Solomon took the furniture which Hiram made for the Temple of Lord, the golden altar, and the golden table of showbread. He put the five candlesticks on the left, and five on the right in front of the oracle, being of pure gold, and the lamp-stands, and the lamps, and the snuffers of gold. There were made the porches, and the nails, and the bowls, and the spoons, and the golden censers, of pure gold. The panels of the doors of the innermost part of the temple, even the holy of holies, and the golden doors of the temple. So the work of the Temple of the Lord which Solomon worked was finished, and Solomon brought in the holy things of David his father, and all the holy things of Solomon, he put the silver, and the gold, and the furniture, into the treasures of the Temple of the Lord.

Solomon spent thirteen years building a palace for himself. He built the palace with the wood of Lebanon, its length was a hundred cubits, and its width was fifty cubits, and its height was thirty cubits, and it was made with three rows of cedar pillars, and the pillars had side-pieces of cedar. He formed the palace with rooms above on the sides of the pillars, and there were 45 pillars in each row, and there were three rooms and space between spaces in three rows.

All the doors and spaces formed like rooms were square, and from door to door was a correspondence in three rows. He made the porch of the pillars, they were fifty cubits long and fifty wide, the porch joining them in front, and the other pillars and the thick beam were in front of the house by the porches. There was the porch of seats where he would judge, the porch of judgment. Their palace where he would live, had one court connecting with these in the construction, and he built the palace for the daughter of Pharaoh whom Solomon had taken, connecting to this porch. All these were of costly stones, sculptured at intervals within even from the foundation even to the top, and outward to the great court, founded with large costly stones, stones of ten cubits and eight cubits long.

Above with costly stones, according to the measure of cut stones, and with cedars. There were three rows of cut stones around the great hall, and a row of sculptured cedar, and Solomon completed all his palace.

# 3rd Kingdoms: Chapter 8

When Solomon had finished building the Temple of the Lord and his own palace, after twenty years, then King Solomon assembled all the elders of Israel in Zion, to bring the box of the covenant of the Lord out of the city of David (this is Zion), in the month of Athanin.[1] The priests picked up the box, and the tabernacle of testimony, and the holy furniture that was in the tabernacle of testimony. The king and all Israel were occupied before the box, sacrificing sheep and oxen, beyond counting. The priests carried the box into its place, into the oracle of the house, to the sacred of sacred, under the wings of the sphinxes. The sphinxes spread out their wings over the place of the box, and the sphinxes covered the box and its holy things above.

The holy staffs projected, and the ends of the holy staffs appeared out of the holy places in front of the oracle and were not seen outside. There was nothing in the box except the two tablets of stone, the tablets of the covenant which Moses put there in Horeb, where the Lord made a covenant with the Israelites when they left the land of Egypt. When the priests left the sacred place, the cloud filled the temple. The priests could not stand to minister because of the cloud, because the glory of the Lord filled the house.

The king turned his face, and the king blessed all Israel, (and the whole assembly of Israel stood,) and he said, "Blessed be Lord the god of Israel today, who spoke by his mouth regarding David my father, and who fulfilled it with his hands, saying, 'From the day that I brought out my people Israel out of Egypt, I have not chosen a city in any tribe of Israel to build a temple, so that my name should be there, but I chose Jerusalem that my name should be there, and I chose David to be over my people Israel.' It was in the heart of my father to build a temple to the name of Lord the god in Israel."

"The Lord said to David my father, 'Inasmuch as it came into your heart to build a temple to my name, you did well that it came in your heart. Nevertheless, you will not build the temple, but your son that has proceeded out of your sides, he will build the house to my name.' Lord has confirmed the word that he spoke, and I am risen up in the place of my father David, and I have sat down on the throne of Israel, as Lord spoke, and I have built the house to the name of Lord the god in Israel. I have set there a place for the box, in which is the covenant of the Lord, which the Lord made with our fathers when he brought them out of the land of Egypt."

Solomon stood up in front of the altar before all the congregation of Israel, and he spread out his hands towards the sky and said, "Lord the god of Israel, there is no god like you in the sky above and on the earth beneath, keeping covenant and mercy with your servant who walks before you with all his heart, which you have kept towards your servant David my father. You have spoken by your mouth and you have fulfilled it with your hands, as on this day. Now, Lord the god of Israel, keep for your servant David my father, the promises when you said to him, 'There will not be taken from you a man sitting before me on the throne of Israel, provided only your children will pay attention to their ways, to walk before me as you have walked before me.'"

"Now, Lord the god of Israel, let, I beg you, your word to David my father be confirmed. But will God indeed live with men on the earth? If the sky, and the sky of Shamyim will not be enough for you, how much less even this temple which I have built to your name? Yet, Lord the god of Israel, you will look on my petition, to hear the prayer which your servant prays to you in your presence this day, that your eyes may be open towards this house day and night, even towards the place which you said, 'My name will be there, to hear the prayer which your servant prays at this place day and night.' You will listen to the prayer of your servant, and of your people Israel, which they will pray towards this place, and you will hear in your living-place in the sky, and you will do and be gracious."

"Whatever trespasses anyone will commit against his neighbor, and if he will take on him an oath so that he should swear, and he will come and make confession before your altar in this house, then will you hear from the sky, and do, and you will judge your people Israel, that the wicked should be condemned, to recompense his way on his head, and to justify the righteous, to give to him according to his righteousness. When your people Israel falls before enemies, because they will sin against you, and they will return and confess to your name, and they will pray and supplicate in this house, then will you hear from the sky, and be gracious to the sins of your people Israel, and you will restore them to the land which you gave to their fathers."

"When the sky is restrained, and there is no rain, because they will sin against you, and the will pray towards this place, and they will make confession to your name and will turn from their sins when you have humiliated them, then you will hear from the sky, and be merciful to the sins of your servant and of your people Israel. You will show them a good way to walk in it, and you will give rain on the earth which you have given to your people for an inheritance."

"If there should be famine, if there should be death, because there should be storm, or locust, or if there be mildew, and if their enemy oppresses them in anyone of their cities, with regard to every calamity, every trouble, every prayer, every supplication whatever will be made by any man, as they will know each the plague of his heart, and will spread wide his hands to this temple, then you will hear from the sky, out of your established home, and will be merciful, and will do, and repay every man according to his ways, as you will know his heart, for you alone know the heart of all the children of men, that they may fear you all the days that they live on the land, which you have given to our fathers. For the stranger who is not of your people, when they will come and pray towards this place, then you will hear them from the sky, out of your established home, and you will do all that the stranger will call on you for, so all the nations may know your name, and fear you, as do your people Israel, and may know that your name has been called on this temple which I have built."

"If it is that your people will go out to war against their enemies in the way by which you will turn them, and pray in the name of the Lord towards the city which you have chosen, and the temple which I have built to your name, then you will hear from the sky their supplication and their prayer, and will execute judgment for them. If it is that they will sin against you, (for there is not a man who will not sin,) and you will bring them and deliver them up before their enemies, and they that take them captive will carry them to a land far or near, and they will turn their hearts in the land to whatever place they have been carried captives, and turn in the land of their captivity, and beg you, saying, 'We have sinned. We have done unjustly. We have transgressed,'" and they will turn to you with all their heart, and with all their mind, in the land of their enemies to whatever place you have carried them captives, and will pray to you towards their land, which you have given to their fathers, and the city which you have chosen, and the temple which I have built to your name, then you will hear from the sky your established home, and you will be merciful to their unrighteousness in which they have trespassed against you, and according to all their transgressions where they have transgressed against you, and you will cause them to be pitied before those who carried them captives, and they have compassion on them, as they are your people and your inheritance, whom you brought out of the land of Egypt; out of an iron smelting furnace."

"Let your eyes and your ears be opened to the supplication of your servant, and to the supplication of your people Israel, to listen to them in all things for which they will call on you. Because you have set them apart for an inheritance to yourself out of all the nations of the earth, as you said by the hand of your servant Moses, when you brought our fathers out of the land of Egypt, my Lord the god."

Then Solomon spoke regarding the temple, when he had finished building it. He said to the sun in the sky, "The Lord said he would live in darkness, 'Build my temple, a beautiful palace for yourself to live in again.' Look, is not this written in the Book of the Song?"

When Solomon had finished praying to the Lord all these prayers and supplication, he rose up from before the altar of the Lord, after having knelt on his knees, and his hands were spread out towards the sky. He stood, and blessed all the congregation of Israel with a loud voice, saying, "Blessed is the Lord this day, who has given rest to his people Israel, according to all that he said, 'There has not failed one word among all his good words which he spoke by the hand of his servant Moses.' May the Lord our god be with us, as he was with our fathers. Let him not desert us nor turn from us, that he may turn our hearts towards him to walk in all his ways, and to keep all his commandments, and his ordinances which he commanded our fathers. Let these words, which

I have prayed before the Lord our god, be near to the Lord our god day and night, to maintain the cause of your servant, and the cause of your people Israel forever, so all the nations of the earth may know that Lord the god, is God, and there is none beside."

"Let our hearts be perfect towards the Lord our god, to walk also holily in his ordinances, and to keep his commandments, as at this day. The king and all the Israelites offered sacrifice before the Lord. King Solomon offered for the sacrifices of peace-offering which he sacrificed to the Lord, 22,000 oxen, and 120,000 sheep, and the king and all the Israelites dedicated the Temple of the Lord."

"In that day the king consecrated the middle of the court in the front of the Temple of the Lord. For there he offered the whole burnt offering, and the sacrifices, and the fat of the peace-offerings because the bronze altar which was before the Lord was too little to carry the whole burnt offering and the sacrifices of peace-offerings. Solomon kept the feast in that day, and all Israel with him, even a great assembly from the entering in of Hamath to the river of Egypt, before the Lord our god in the house which he built, eating and drinking, and rejoicing before the Lord our god seven days. On the eighth day he sent away the people: and they blessed the king, and each departed to his tabernacle rejoicing, and their heart was glad because of the good things which Lord had done to his servant David, and to Israel his people."

# 3rd Kingdoms: Chapter 8 Notes

**1** Codex Vaticanus: Athamin (ΑΘΑΜΕΙΝ)

• Codex Alexandrinus: Athanim en tê eortê autos o mên ebdomêcostos ebdomos (ΑΘΑΝΕΙΜ ΕΝ ΤΗ ΕΟΡΤΗ ΑΥΤΟC Ο ΜΗΝ ΕΒΔΟΜΗΚΟCΤΟC ΕΒΔΟΜΟC). Translation: Athanim in the festival it is, not seventy seven

• Codex Coislinianus: archaeô (ΑΡΧΑΙω)

• Codex Basiliano-Vaticanus: athani (ΑΘΑΝΕΙ)

• LXX 52: Athanin ê goun en mêni athanin (ΑΘΑΝΙΝ ἣ γουν ἐν μὴνι ΑΘΑΝΙΝ). Translation: Athanin that is the month Athanin

• LXX 82: Athemin (ΑΘϬμϬΙΝ)

• LXX 243: Athanen (ΑΘΑΝϬΝ)

• Dead Sea Scroll 6QpapKgs: -y- (-ܝ-). Only one letter survives, however, the text of 6QpapKgs is different enough that it is not enough to confirm the word was in the scroll.

• Dead Sea Scroll 4QKgs: -m (ם-). Only the final letter survives, however, it is enough to indicate the word was in the scroll.

• Aleppo Codex: åtnym (אתנים)

• Leningrad Codex: etanim (אֵתָנִים)

• Targum Jerusalem: kadma'ah (קַדְמָאָה). Translation: former

It is believed that this is a reference to the seventh month in the old Canaanite calendar, equivalent to Tishrei in the modern Hebrew calendar, and September and October in the Gregorian Calendar.

# 3<sup>rd</sup> Kingdoms: Chapter 9

When Solomon had finished building the Temple of the Lord, and the king's palace, and all the works of Solomon, whatever he wished to perform, the Lord appeared to Solomon a second time, as he appeared in Gibeon.

The Lord said to him, "I have heard the voice of your prayer, and your supplication which you made before me. I have done for you according to all your prayer. I have hallowed this house which you have built to put my name there forever, and my eyes and my heart will be there always. If you will walk before me as David your father walked, in holiness of heart and uprightness, and to do according to all that I commanded him, and will keep my ordinances and my commandments, then will I establish the throne of your kingdom in Israel forever, as I said to David your father, 'There will not fail from you a man to rule in Israel. But if you or your children do in any way revolt from me, and do not keep my commandments and my ordinances, which Moses set before you, and you go and serve other gods, and worship them, then will I cut off Israel from the land which I have given them, and this house which I have consecrated to my name I will throw out of my sight. Israel will be a desolation and an example to all nations. This temple, which is high, will become so that everyone who passes by will be amazed, and will hiss, and they will say, 'The Lord has done this to this land, and to this temple!' Men will say, 'Because they forgot the Lord their god, who brought out their fathers from Egypt, out of the house of slavery, and they attached themselves to strange gods, and worshiped them, and served them, and therefore the Lord has brought this evil on them.'"

Then Solomon brought up the daughter of Pharaoh out of the city of David into his palace which he built for himself in those days. During the twenty years in which Solomon was building the two houses, the Temple of the Lord, and the palace of the king, Hiram king of Tyre helped Solomon with cedarwood, and fir wood, and with gold, and all that he wished for, then the king gave Hiram twenty cities in the land of Galilee. So Hiram traveled from Tyre and went into Galilee to see the cities which Solomon gave to him, and they did not please him. He asked, "What are these cities which you have given me, brother?"

He called them Boundary until this day. Hiram brought to Solomon a hundred and twenty talents of gold, with which King Solomon built a ship in Ezion Geber near Elath on the shore of the edge of the sea in the land of Edom. Hiram sent in the ship both servants of Solomon, and servants of his own, mariners to row, men acquainted with the sea. They traveled to Sauvira,[1] and took there a hundred and twenty talents of gold, and brought them to King Solomon.

# 3<sup>rd</sup> Kingdoms: Chapter 9 Notes

**1** Codex Vaticanus: Sôphêra (ⲥⲱϥⲏⲣⲁ)

- Codex Alexandrinus: Sôphara (ⲥⲱϥⲁⲣⲁ)

- LXX 19: Sôphira (ⲥⲱ$ⲋⲓⲣ̇ⲁ)

- LXX 52: Sophêra (ⲥⲟ$ⲗ̇ⲣ̇ⲁ)

- LXX 247: Sophira (ⲥⲟ$ⲋⲓⲣ̇ⲁ)

- LXX 158: Ôphêra (ⲱ$ⲗ̇ⲣ̇ⲁ)

- LXX 93: Ôphira (ⲱ$ⲋⲓⲣ̇ⲁ)

- Aleppo Codex: Åwpyrh (אֹפִירה)

- Leningrad Codex: Ofirah (אֹפִֽירָה)

- Targum Jerusalem: Ofir (אוֹפִיר)

The location of this civilization has been a matter of debate for centuries. Given the list of items imported from Sôphêra/Ofira, it was likely the ancient Pakistani Kingdom of Sauvira on the Indus River. Imported items include gold, silver, sandalwood, pearls, ivory, apes, and peacocks. Sandalwood trees are indigenous to South and Southeast Asia and have traditionally been considered sacred by the Hindus, Jainists, Buddhists, and Zoroastrians, as well as other Asian cultures. Peacocks are indigenous to South and Southeast Asia, as well as the Congo Rain-forest, however, Sandalwood trees are not found in the Congo Rain-forest.

Apes were still living in South and Southeast Asia circa 1000 BC, along with most of Africa. An alternate theory regarding the location of Sôphêra was that is was a trading port in Southern Arabia or Somalia, however, the ships of Solomon were said to take three years to travel between Edom and Sôphêra/Åwpyrh, which makes the location of Sauvira more likely.

The Kingdom of Sauvira is listed in ancient Late Vedic period and early Buddhist literature, as well as the Mahabharata, based around its capital of Rohri in the modern Pakistani state of Sindh. This civilization is recorded as having existed from the Early Vedic period, before 1100 BC, meaning it would have existed in the time of Solomon.

# 3ʳᵈ Kingdoms: Chapter 10

The Queen of Saba[1] heard of the name of Solomon, and the name of Lord and she traveled to test him with riddles. and the name of the Lord and she traveled to test him with riddles. She traveled to Jerusalem with an exceedingly great caravan and brought camels carrying spices, and a great deal of gold, and precious stones. She traveled to Solomon and told him all that was in her heart. Solomon answered all her questions, and there was not a question ignored by the king. The Queen of Saba saw all the wisdom of Solomon, and the house which he built, and the provision of Solomon and the sitting of his attendants, and the standing of his servants, and his clothing, and his cup-bearers, and his whole burnt offering which he offered in the Temple of the Lord, and she was completely amazed.

She said to king Solomon, "It was a true report which I heard in my land of your words and your wisdom. But I did not believe them who told me, until I came and saw with my own eyes, and look, the words that they reported to me are not even half of it. You have exceeded all the report which I heard in my land. Blessed are your wives, blessed are your servants who stand before you continually, who hear all your wisdom. Blessed is Lord the god, who has taken pleasure in you, to set you on the throne of Israel, because Lord loved Israel and established him forever, and he has made you king over them, to execute judgment with justice, and in their causes." She gave to Solomon a hundred and twenty talents of gold, and a great number of spices, and precious stones. There had not come any other spices in such abundance as those which the Queen of Saba gave to king Solomon.

The ship of Hiram which brought the gold from Sauvira also brought a great deal of lumber and precious stones. The king made the lumber into buttresses of the Temple of the Lord and the king's palace, and lyres and harps for singers. Lumber like it had not come on the earth, nor have been seen anywhere until today. King Solomon gave to the Queen of Saba all that she desired, whatever she asked, and she returned, and traveled into her own land, along with her servants.

The weight of gold that came to Solomon in one year was six hundred and sixty-six talents of gold. Besides the tributes of them that were subjects, both merchants and all the kings of the country beyond the river, and of the princes of the land. Solomon made three hundred spears of beaten gold, three hundred shekels of gold per spear. Three hundred shields of beaten gold, three pounds of gold per shield, and the king put them in the palace in the forest of Lebanon.

The king made a great ivory throne and gilded it with pure gold. The throne had six steps, and calves in bold relief to the throne behind it, and side-pieces on either hand of the place of the seat, and two lions standing by the side-pieces, and twelve lions standing there on the six steps on either side. This was not done in any other kingdom. All the vessels made by Solomon were of gold, and the lavers were golden, and all the vessels of the House of the Forest of Lebanon were of pure gold. There was no silver, for it was not counted of in the days of Solomon. Solomon had a ship of Tartessos[2] in the sea with the ships of Hiram: one ship came to the king every three years out of Tartessos, loaded with gold and silver, and worked stones, and cut stones.

This was the arrangement of the provision which king Solomon brought to build the Temple of Lord, and the house of the king, and the wall of Jerusalem, and the citadel, and to fortify the cities of David, Asshur, Magdal, Gazer, Upper Bethhoron and Jethermath, and all the cities of the chariots, and all the cities of the cavalry, and the fortifications of Solomon which he build in

Jerusalem and in all the land, so that none of the people should rule over him that were left of the Cypriots,[3] Amorites, Perizzites, Canaanites, Mitanni,[4] Jebusites, Girgasites, and whoever else was not of the Israelites, their descendants who had been left with him in the land, who the Israelites could not completely exterminate, and Solomon made them tributaries until this day. Of the Israelites, Solomon demanded nothing, as they were the warriors, and his servants and rulers, and captains of the third order, and the captains of his chariots, and his cavalry.

Solomon became greater than all the kings of the Earth in wealth and wisdom. All the kings of the earth wanted to visit the presence of Solomon, to hear the wisdom which the Lord had put into his heart. They brought their gifts, vessels of gold, and clothing, and stacte, and spices, and horses, and mules, every year. Solomon had four thousand mares for his chariots and twelve thousand cavalry, and he put them in the cities of his chariots. As the king in Jerusalem, he ruled over all the kings from the river to the land of the Gentiles, and to the borders of Egypt. The king made gold and silver as common in Jerusalem as stones, and he made cedars as common as sycamores in the plain.

The source of Solomon's cavalry also came from Egypt, and the king's merchants were in Canopus,[5] and they bought them from of Canopus. That which was bought from Egypt cost a hundred shekels of silver per chariot, and fifty shekels of silver per horse for, and the same for all the kings of Cyprus, and the kings of Syria who traded by sea.

# 3ʳᵈ Kingdoms: Chapter 10 Notes

**1** Codex Vaticanus: Saba (ⲥⲁⲃⲁ)

- LXX 245: Sabaa (ⲥⲁⲩⲁⲁ)

- LXX 554: Sabba (ⲥⲁⲩⲩⲁ)

- LXX 93: Sama (ⲥⲁⲙⲁ)

- Aleppo Codex: Šbå (שבא)

- Leningrad Codex: Sheva (שְׁבָא)

- Targum Jerusalem: Sheva (שְׁבָא)

Saba was a country in the territory of modern Yemen between 1200 BC and 275 AD. This nation is also mentioned in the Septuagint's books of Job, Joel, Ezekiel, and Isaiah, as well as the Quran's An-Naml and Saba surahs. This country was ultimately conquered by the neighboring Himyarite Kingdom around 275 AD, which was itself then conquered by the Ethiopian Axumite Empire around 525 AD.

The Himyarite Kingdom was an officially Jewish State after 390 AD and is likely the origin of the early Arabic language version of the Kebra Nagast, which was later translated into Ge'ez, and Ethiopianized, making the 'Queen of Saba' a monarch from the Ethiopian Highlands. The Kebra Nagast has never been used by the Beta Israel community in Ethiopia, who consider it a later Christian work.


**2** Codex Vaticanus: Tharsis (ⲑⲁⲣⲥⲉⲓⲥ)

- LXX 245: Tharsês (ⲑⲁⲣⲟⲏⲥ)

- LXX 509: Thrausis (ⲑⲣⲁⲩⲥⲓⲥ)

- LXX 74: Thrausis (ⲑⲣⲁⲩⲥⲓⲥ)

- Aleppo Codex: Tršyš (תרשיש)

- Leningrad Codex: Tarshish (תַרְשִׁישׁ)

- Targum Jerusalem: Afrika (אַפְרִיקָא). Translation: Africa (the Roman province in modern Tunisia)

This civilization was mentioned in a number of ancient documents, including the inscriptions of Esarhaddon from Assyria and the Nora Stone from Phoenicia. Based on the various descriptions of the land in Phoenician, Hebrew, and Assyrian sources, Tharsis was in the Mediterranean or the Atlantic Ocean, somewhere west of Malta. The Greek historian Herodotus recorded that at his time, circa 450 BC, the city of Tartessos was a major trading center, past the 'Pillars of Herakles' or in modern terms, outside the Mediterranean, on the Atlantic Coast somewhere. This is generally considered to be the same civilization, implying it existed from at least 1000 BC to at least 450 BC.

The dominant theory of the past century is that it was the 'Tartessos' culture of southwest Spain. The name Tartessos was adopted from the Greek geography by modern archaeologists, and it is unclear if they called their civilization something that sounded like Tartessos. A number of ancient ruins and inscriptions have been found in the area, using the Phoenician script, but written in a language dubbed 'Tartessian.' The records of the Hebrews, Phoenicians, and Assyrians all record that Tarshish was a metal-rich land, which exported large amounts of silver, iron, tin, and other metals. The records of the ancient Greeks reported the same about Tartessos. Modern archaeology in the region around Cadiz does support that this was a metal exporting nation, and therefore the evidence is strongly supportive of this being the civilization referred to in 3<sup>rd</sup> Kingdoms.

Several other locations have historically been proposed as the potential location of Tharsis, including Sardinia, Italy, Britain, West Africa, and Southern India. Most of these proposals predated the discovery of the Assyrian and Phoenician records of Tharsis, however, the proposal that Tharsis was in Britain is still supported by some, as the British were also exporting tin to the Phoenicians at the time.

**3** Codex Vaticanus: Chettaeou (ⲭⲉⲧⲧⲁⲓⲟⲨ)

- LXX 55: Chetaeou (χόταιου)

- Aleppo Codex: Ḥtym (חתים). Translation: Cypriots

- Leningrad Codex: Chittim (חִתָּים). Translation: Cypriots

- Targum Jerusalem: Chitta'ei (חִתָּאֵי)

As the term referred to the entire island of Cyprus in Aramaic, the translations of 'Cyprus' and 'Cypriots' are used here.

**4** Codex Vaticanus: Euaiou (ⲉⲨⲁⲓⲟⲨ)

This verse is missing from the Masoretic texts. In other places in the Leningrad Codex they are called the Chivvi (חִוִּי), while in the Aleppo Codex they are called the ḥwy (חוי).

The term is believed to have been derived from the name of the Hurrians, however, is derived separately from the other term Chori (חֹרִי). Chori is accepted as referring to the Hurrians, which the Egyptians called Ḥårw (𓉐 𓏏 𓈙), and the Babylonians called Ḥuurri (𒄷𒌨𒊑). The Hurrians were one of the oldest cultures in the Middle East, however, became largely a slave culture within the Akkadian and Old Babylonian empires. Under the Mitanni empire, they rose to a position of wealth, and formed the noble caste. The Greek transliteration of this term was variations of Chorrhaeous (Χορραιους), which, like the Hebrew term, was used interchangeably in the texts with Eyaeon (Ευαιον) / Chivvi (חִוִּי), although that term generally applied to the rules and priests.

The ultimate origin of the terms Eyaeon (Ευαιον) and Chivvi (חִוִּי), both appear to be the cuneiform word Éan (𒂍𒀭), meaning temple or sacred. In the Amarna Letters, which date to the 1330s BC, the term Éan (𒂍𒀭) was the name of a people, who appear to be the Mitanni, or the Mitanni-Aryan priesthood within the Mitanni. A similar correlation between the terms is found in the Septuagint's 1<sup>st</sup> Paralipomenon and Masoretic Divrei-hay Yamim, where the Greek translation uses

Beithani (Βαιθανι), however, the Hebrew uses the term Mitni (מִתְנִי). This term also refers to a group of people, meaning the underlying Edomite text the Greeks translated would have been 'people of the House of Ån' (𐤉𐤀 𐤕𐤉𐤁), a direct Canaanite translation of É An (𓉐𓇳).

While Mitni was the transliteration used in the Edomite text that formed the basis of the Hebrew translation of Divrei-hayYamim, it was replaced with Chivvi (חִוִּי) in the Judahite texts, which served as the basis of most of the Masoretic texts. This likely originated in a Judahite copy of the text, after the Aramaic translation had been made, where an n (𐤍) was replaced with a w (𐤅). The Aramaic translation would have already been made in the time of King Manasseh, were the term was transliterated as Hyån (𐡇𐡉𐡍), itself a transliteration of the early Canaanite Hyån (𐤇𐤉𐤍).

**5** Codex Vaticanus: Thecoue (ΘΕΚΟΥΕ)

- Codex Alexandrinus: Thecoueem (ΘΕΚΟΥΕΕΜ)

- LXX 509: Scotous (Cκοτουc)

- LXX 158: Thecou ex ec Damascou (Θεκου εξ εκ Δαμασκου). Translation: Thecou its by Damascus

- LXX 19: Thecou cae ec Damascou (Θεκου και εκ Δαμασκου). Translation: Thecou and near Damascus

- LXX 246: Thecou cae ec Aigyptou (Θεκου και εξ Αιγυπτου). Translation: Thecou and in Egypt

- Aleppo Codex: Qwh (קוה)

- Leningrad Codex: Keveh (קְוֵה)

- Targum Jerusalem: Keveh (קְוֵה)

The Hebrew name is believed to be derived from the Ancient Egyptian name of the city the Greeks called Canopus (Κανωπος). At the time of Solomon the city is believed to have been called Gåwty (𓎡𓃭𓇋𓍯),

which is probably where the Hebrew name was derived. Later during the Persian Era when the Aramaic translation would have been made, the city was known as Per-Gwṭ (ᴊʃ∿ᴗ_ᴊᴊ), and later under the Ptolemy's the city's Egyptian name was Peguat (◻◻𓂧𓏛𓈖) in Egyptian. Thecoue doesn't correlate with any of the names of the city, but was the Greek spelling of the name of Teqoa (תוקוע), a town in central Judah at the time of Solomon, and it is possible that the name Thecoue was not the original term the Greeks transliterated, but part of Origen of Alexandria's Hexapla, published circa 240 AD.

As the Hebrew name indicates Canopus, that name is used in this translation. Canopus was Egypt's major trading port on the Mediterranean at the time of Solomon, near the later port-cities of Menouthis, Herakleion, and Alexandria.

# 3rd Kingdoms: Chapter 11

King Solomon was a lover of women. He had seven hundred wives, all princesses, and three hundred concubines. He took strange women, as well as the daughter of Pharaoh, Moabite, Ammanite, Syrian, Edomite, Mitanni, and Amorite women. All of the nations that the Lord forbade the Israelites, saying, "You will not go into them, and they will not go into you, in case they turn away your hearts after their idols." Solomon clung to these in love. It came to pass in the time of the old age of Solomon, that his heart was not perfect with Lord his god, as was the heart of David his father.

The strange women turned away his heart after their gods. Then Solomon built a bamah to Chemosh the idol of Moab, and to King Moloch the idol of the Ammonites,[1] and to Astarte[2] the abomination of the Sidonians. He did this with all his strange wives, who burnt incense and sacrificed to their idols.

Solomon did that which was evil in the sight of the Lord. He did not follow the Lord, as David his father. The Lord was angry with Solomon because he turned away his heart from Lord the god of Israel, who had appeared twice to him, and ordered him concerning this matter, by no means to go after other gods, but to pay attention to do what Lord the god commanded him. His heart was not perfect with the Lord, like the heart of David his father. The Lord said to Solomon, "Because it has been so with you, and you have not kept my commandments and my ordinances which I commanded you, I will certainly rip your kingdom out of your hand, and give it to your servant. Only, I will not do it in your days, for David your father's sake, but I will take it out of the hand of your son. Only I will not take away the whole kingdom, I will give one tribe to your son for David my servant's sake, and for the sake of Jerusalem, the city which I have chosen."

The Lord raised up an enemy against Solomon, Hadad the Edomite, and Rezon son of Eliadah who lived in Raama, and Hadadezer king of Zobah his master. (Men gathered around him, and he was head of the conspiracy, and he seized Damascus.) They were adversaries to Israel all the days of Solomon: and Hadad the Edomite was of the royal seed in Edom. It had happened, that while David was completely destroying Edom, while Joab captain of the army was burying the dead after they killed every male in Edom. (Joab and all Israel lived there six months in Edom until he completely destroyed every male in Edom.) Hadad had ran away, he and all the Edomite servants of his father with him, and they went to Egypt, and Hadad was then a little child. Men rose up out of the city of Midian, and they went to Paran, and took men with them, and went to Pharaoh, king of Egypt, and Hadad went to Pharaoh, and he gave him a house and appointed him a provision.

Hadad found great favor in the sight of Pharaoh, and he gave him his wife's sister in marriage, the elder sister of Thekemina. The sister of Thekemina carried for Hadad, Genubath her son, and Thekemina raised up among the sons of Pharaoh. Hadad heard in Egypt that David slept with his fathers and that Joab the captain of the army was dead, and Hadad said to Pharaoh, "Let me go, and I will return to my country."

Pharaoh replied to Hadad, "What do you lack with me, that you seek to return to your country?"

Hadad answered him, "By all means let me go," and Hadad returned to his country. This is the evil which Hadad did, and he was a bitter enemy of Israel, and he reigned in the land of Edom. Jeroboam the son of Nebat, the Ephrathite of Zereda, the son of a widow, was a servant of Solomon. This was the occasion of his lifting up his hands against king Solomon: now king Solomon built the citadel, he completed the fortification of the city of David his father. The man Jeroboam was very strong, and Solomon saw the young man that he was active, and he set him over the levies of the house of Joseph.

At that time when Jeroboam went out from Jerusalem, and Ahijah the Shilonite, the prophet, found him on the road and made him to turn aside off the road, and Ahijah was wearing a new robe, and the two were alone in the field. Ahijah took hold of the new robe that was on him, and tore it into twelve pieces, and he said to Jeroboam, "Take for yourself ten pieces, for Lord the God of Israel said, 'Look, I rip the kingdom out of the hand of Solomon, and will give you ten tribes. Yet he has two tribes, for my servant David's sake, and for the sake of Jerusalem, the city which I have chosen out of all the tribes of Israel. Because he forgot me and sacrificed to Astarte the abomination of the Sidonians, and to Chemosh, and to the idols of Moab, and to King the abomination of the Ammonites, and he did not follow my ways, to do that which was right before me, as David his father did.'

"How is it I will not take the whole kingdom out of his hand, (for I will certainly resist him all the days of his life,) for David my servant's sake, whom I have chosen. But I will take the kingdom out of the hand of his son, and give you ten tribes. But to his son, I will give the two remaining tribes, that my servant David may have an establishment continually before me in Jerusalem, the city which I have chosen for myself to put my name there. I will take you, and you will reign as your mind desires, and you will be king over Israel.' It will come to pass, if you will keep all the commandments that I will give you, and will follow in my ways, and do that which is right before me, to keep my ordinances and my commandments, as David my servant did, that I will be with you, and will build you a secure house, as I built for David."

Solomon wanted to kill Jeroboam, but he arose and fled into Egypt, to Shoshenq I,[3] King of Egypt, and he was in Egypt until Solomon died. The rest of the history of Solomon, and all that he did, and all his wisdom, look are not these things written in the book of the Life of Solomon? The days during which Solomon reigned in Jerusalem over all Israel were forty years. Solomon slept with his fathers, and they buried him in the city of David his father. When Jeroboam son of Nebat heard of it, even while he was still in Egypt, (as he had fled from the face of Solomon and lived in Egypt), he immediately returned to his own city, in the land of Zereda in the Mountains of Ephraim. King Solomon slept with his fathers, and Rehoboam his son reigned in his place.

# 3ʳᵈ Kingdoms: Chapter 11 Notes

**1** Codex Vaticanus: basili autôn idôlô uiôn Ammon (ΒΑϹΙΛΕΙ ΑΥΤѠΝ ΕΙΔѠΛѠ ΥΙѠΝ ΑΜΜѠΝ). Translation: king the idol of sons of Amman

- Codex Alexandrinus: melcho idôlô uiô Ammon (ΑΥΤѠΝ ΜΕΛΧΟ ΕΙΔѠΛѠ ΥΙѠ ΑΜΜѠΝ). Translation: Melcho the idol of sons of Amman

- LXX 19: Melchôm idôlô huiôn Ammon (Μόλχοομ ϭιΔῶλω υιοον Ἀμμοον). Translation: Melchom idol of sons of Amman

- LXX 55: Melchom basili autôn idôlô huiôn Ammon (Μόλχομ μΔσιλόι Δυτοον ϭιΔῶλω υιοον Ἀμμοον). Translation: Melchim king, the idol of sons of Amman

- LXX 372: Moloch basili autôn idôlô huiôn Ammon (Μολοχ μΔσιλόι Δυτοον ϭιΔῶλω υιοον Ἀμμοον). Translation: Moloch king, the idol of sons of Amman

- LXX 127: Melchom idôlô uiôn Ammon en tô ori o epi prosôpon Ierousalêm (Μόλχομ ϭιΔοολω υιοον Ἀμμοον ϭν τοο ορόι ο ϭπι πϸοσοοπον ιϭϸουσΔλλημ). Translation: Melchom idol of sons of Amman on the mountain the peak in front of Jerusalem

- LXX 82: Melchoma idolôn huiôn Ammon (ΜόλχομΔ ϭιΔολοον υιοον Ἀμμοον). Translation: Melchoma, idol of sons of Amman

- LXX 120: basili Molchom idolôn huiôn Ammon (μΔσιλόι Μολχομ ϭιΔολοον υιοον Ἀμμοον). Translation: King Molchom, idol of sons of Amman

- LXX 107: basili Molchôm idôlô huiôn Ammon (μΔσιλόι Μολχοομ ϭιΔῶλω υιοον Ἀμμοον). Translation: King Molchom, idol of sons of Amman

- LXX 158: Molchôn idôlô huiôn Ammon (Μολχοον ϬιΔϪλοο υιοον Ѧμμοον). Translation: Molchon, idol of sons of Amman

- LXX 243: Molchol idôlou huiôn Ammon (Μολχολ ϬιΔοολου υιοον Ѧμμοον). Translation: Molchol, idol of sons of Amman

- LXX 52: Melchol idôlô huiôn Ammon (Μϭλχολ ϬιΔϪλοο υιοον Ѧμμοον). Translation: Melchol, idol of sons of Amman

- LXX 489: Melchôl idôlô huiôn Ammon (Μϭλχοολ ϬιΔϪλοο υιοον Ѧμμοον). Translation: Melchol, idol of sons of Amman

- LXX 245: Moloch idôlô huiôn Ammon (Μολοχ ϬιΔϪλοο υιοον Ѧμμοον). Translation: Moloch, idol of sons of Amman

- Aleppo Codex: åḥry mlkm šqs Ômnym (אחרי מלכס שקץ עמנים). Translation: after Mlkm, abomination of Ammonites

- Leningrad Codex: acharei Milkom shikkutz Ammonim ( אַחֲרֵי מִלְכֹּם שִׁקֻּץ עַמּֽוֹנִים). Translation: after Milkom, abomination of Ammonites

- Targum Jerusalem: vatar Milkom shikutz Amona'ei ( בָּתַר מִלְכּוֹם שִׁקּוּץ עֲמוֹנָאֵי). Translation: after Milkom, idol of Ammonites

The name of this Ammonite god appears inconsistently in the Masoretic text and Septuagint. He is called Milkom here and Molech (מֹלֶךְ) later in the Masoretic chapter, and variations of Moloch (Μόλοχ) in the Septuagint's translation of Amos, but generally just called King (Βασιλεῖ / מלך) in both texts. As the only difference between the name Molech (מֹלֶךְ) and 'king' (מלך) are the vowel pointers the Masorites added, the name of the Ammonite god does translate as 'King.'

The name Milcom (מִלְכֹּם), used in this verse in the Masoretic text, is not a Canaanite or Aramaic word, but the transliteration of malkum (𒈬𒌑𒁀𒌑), the Neo-Babylonian translation of the Canaanite (Samaritan, Judahite, and Ammonite) mlk (𐤌𐤋𐤊), meaning 'king.' The presence of this word confirms that there was a Neo-Babylonian translation of 3<sup>rd</sup>

Kingdoms, which was itself based on a Canaanite text, and was later translated back into Judahite or Samaritan in the Second Temple Era, separately from the Aramaic translation that Greeks used as a source.

As most Septuagint manuscripts use variations of 'king' and Moloch, the term King Moloch is used here, however, the original text likely just read 'King.'

**2** Codex Vaticanus: Astartê (ᴀᴄᴛᴀ𝆑ᴛн)

- LXX 314: Astratê (ᴀσ𝆑ᴀᴛᴌ)

- Aleppo Codex: Ôštrt (עשתרת)

- Leningrad Codex: Ashtoret (עַשְׁתֹּרֶת)

- Targum Jerusalem: Ashtoret (עַשְׁתּוֹרֶת)

Astarte was the Greek name of the Canaanite goddess Ôštrt (𐤕𐤀𐤕𐤅𐤏 / ⟨𐤋⟩). Local versions of her were worshiped throughout the Middle East and the Mediterranean Sea. In Akkadian she was a god known as ᵃⁿAsdartú (𒀭𒁹𒈹), while in Babylonian she was known as ᵃⁿIštar (𒀭𒈹), and in Etruscan she was known as Uni-al-Astres (𐌔𐌄𐌐𐌕𐌔𐌀𐌋𐌀𐌉𐌍𐌖).

The Greek goddess Aphrodite appears to be derived from an early Cypriot version of her, while the Roman goddess Venus appears to be derived indirectly through Uni-al-Astres. During the New Kingdom era of Egyptian history, circa 1549 to 1077 AD, Astarte was incorporated into the Egyptian pantheon as one of the daughters of Ra, as she appeared in the book entitled the 'Contest between Horus and Set.' According to the Phoenician scholar Sanchuniathon, who supposedly lived circa 1200 BC, Astarte's sister was Asherah. The word Asherah also appears in the Septuagint many times and appears to be widely worshiped by the early Israelites.

**3** Codex Vaticanus: Sousacim (ⲤⲞⲨⲤⲀⲔⲈⲒⲙ)

- LXX 158: Sousacêm (Ϲουσάκημ)

- LXX 242: Oysacim (Ουσάκιμ)

- Aleppo Codex: Šyšq (שׁישׁק)

- Leningrad Codex: Shishak (שִׁישַׁק)

- Targum Jerusalem: Shishak (שִׁישַׁק)

Based on the era when he lived, he is generally accepted as Shoshenq I (𓇓𓇓 𓈎 ) who campaigned in Canaan during the era of King Rehoboam.

# 3rd Kingdoms: Chapter 12

King Rehoboam went to Shechem, and all Israel went to Shechem to make him king. The people said to King Rehoboam, "Your father made our weight heavy, but if you now lighten somewhat the hard service of your father, and of his heavy weight which he put on us, we will serve you."

He replied to them, "Leave for three days, and return to me."

They departed, and the king referred the matter to the elders, who stood before Solomon his father when he was still alive, asking, "How do you advise me to answer these people?"

They answered him, "If you will this day be a servant to these people, and will serve them, and will speak to them good words, then they will be your servants forever."

But he ignored the counsel of the old men and consulted with the young men who were raised with him, who stood in his presence.

He asked them, "What counsel do you give? What will I say to these people who speak to me, asking, 'Lighten somewhat of the weight that your father has put on us?'"

The young men who had been raised with him, who stood before him, answered, "Say to these people who have said to you, 'Your father made our weight heavy, and now lighten it from off us:' 'My little finger will be thicker than my father's loins. And whereas my father did load you with a heavy weight, I also will add to your weight. My father chastised you with whips, but I will chastise you with scorpions."

All Israel returned to King Rehoboam on the third day, as the king asked them, "Return to me on the third day." The king answered the people harshly, and Rehoboam ignored the counsel of the old men. He answered them according to the counsel of the young men, and said, "My father made your yoke heavy, and I will add to your yoke. My father chastised you with whips, but I will chastise you with scorpions."

The king did not listen to the people, because the change was from the Lord, that he might implement his word which he said through Ahijah the Shilonite concerning Jeroboam the son of Nebat. All Israel saw that the king did not listen to them, and the people answered the king, "What portion have we in David? Neither have we any inheritance in the son of Jesse. Leave, Israel, to your tents, now feed your own house, David."

So the Israelites departed to his tents. The king sent Adoniram who was over the tribute, and they stoned him to death. King Rehoboam hurried to rise to flee to Jerusalem. So Israel rebelled against the house of David until this day. When all Israel heard that Jeroboam had returned out of Egypt, they sent and called him to the assembly, and they made him king over Israel, and none followed from the house of David except among the tribe of Judah and Benjamin. Rehoboam went into Jerusalem, and he assembled the congregation of Judah, and the tribe of Benjamin, a hundred and twenty thousand young warriors, to fight against the house of Israel, to reconquer the kingdom for Rehoboam the son of Solomon.

The voice of Lord came to Shemaiah the prophet, "Speak to Rehoboam the son of Solomon, King of Judah, and to all the house of Judah and Benjamin, and to the remnant of the people, saying, 'The Lord says, 'You will not go up, or fight with your brothers the sons of Israel. Return each man to his own home. This thing is from me.'"" They listened to the word of the Lord, and they stopped from going up, according to the word of the Lord.

King Solomon slept with his fathers and was buried with his fathers in the city of David. Rehoboam his son reigned in his place from Jerusalem, being sixteen years old when he began to reign, and he reigned twelve years in Jerusalem. His mother's name was Naanan, daughter of Anah son of Nahash king of the Ammonites. He did that which was evil in the sight of the Lord and did not follow the path of David his forefather.

There was a man from Mount Ephraim, a servant of Solomon, whose name was Jeroboam. His mother's name was Zereda, a prostitute, and Solomon had made him head of the levies of the house of Joseph. He fortified Shechem for Solomon, in mount Ephraim. He had three hundred chariots, and he built the citadel with the levies of the house of Ephraim. He fortified the City of David, and aspired to the kingdom, Solomon wanted to kill him, and he was afraid, and escaped to Shoshenq I, King of Egypt, and was with him until Solomon died.

Jeroboam heard in Egypt that Solomon was dead, and he said to Shoshenq I, King of Egypt, "Let me go, and I will leave into my land."

Shoshenq I said to him, "Ask and request, and I will grant it to you."

Shoshenq I gave to Jeroboam Ano the oldest sister of Thekemina his wife. She was great among the daughters of the king, and she carried for Jeroboam Abiah his son, and Jeroboam said to Shoshenq I, "Let me indeed go, and I will leave."

Jeroboam departed out of Egypt and came into the land of Saria that was in mount Ephraim, and there the whole tribe of Ephraim assembled, and Jeroboam built a fortress there.

His young child was sick with a very severe sickness, and Jeroboam went to inquire concerning the child. He said to Ano his wife, "Rise, go and inquire of God concerning the child, whether he will recover from his sickness." There was a man in Shiloh, his name was Ahijah, and he was sixty years old, and the word of the Lord was with him. Jeroboam said to his wife, "Rise, and take in your hand loaves for the prophet, and cakes for his children, and grapes, and a pot of honey."

The woman rose and took in her hand bread, and two cakes, and grapes, and a pot of honey, for Ahijah. The man was old, and his eyes were dim so that he could not see. She arose, up from Shechem and went to Ahijah the Shilonite, and Ahijah said to his servant, "Go out now to meet Ano the wife of Jeroboam, and say to her, 'Come in, and don't stand still, as the Lord says, 'I send terrible warnings to you.'"

Ano went to the prophet, and Ahijah asked her, "Why have you brought me bread and grapes, and cakes, and a pot of honey? The Lord says, 'Look, you will leave from me, and when you have entered into Shechem, your girls will come out to meet you, and will say to you, 'The child is dead,' for the Lord said, 'Look, I will destroy every male of Jeroboam, and there will be the dead of Jeroboam in the city, and the dogs will eat them, and he will lament for the child,' saying, 'Woe to me, Lord! For there has been found in him some good thing touching the Lord.'

The woman departed when she heard this, and it happened as she entered into Shechem, that the child had died, and wailing came out to meet her. Jeroboam went to Shechem in mount Ephraim and assembled there the tribes of Israel, and Rehoboam the son of Solomon went up there. The word of the Lord came to Samaias son of Enlami, saying, "Take for yourself a new robe which has not been washed and rip it into twelve pieces. You will give some to Jeroboam, and will say to him, 'The Lord says, 'Take for yourself ten pieces to cover yourself.'

Jeroboam took them, and Samaias said, "The Lord said regarding the ten tribes of Israel. 'The people said to Rehoboam the son of Solomon, 'Your father made his weight heavy on us and made the meat of his table heavy, and now you will lighten them on us, and we will serve you.' Rehoboam replied to the people, 'Wait three days, and I will give you an answer,' and Rehoboam said, 'Bring to me the elders, and I will take counsel from them of what I will answer to the people on the third day.'"

"So Rehoboam asked what the people sent to him had said, and the elders of the people answered, 'Do as the people have asked of you.' Rehoboam rejected their counsel, as it did not please him, and he sent and brought in those who had been raised with him, and he asked them, 'Such and such have the people sent to me to ask,' and they that had been raised with him answered, 'Say this to the people, 'My little finger will be thicker than my father's loins. My father scourged you with whips, but I will rule you with scorpions.' The idea pleased Rehoboam, and he answered the people like the young men that were raised with him counseled. All the people spoke as one man, everyone to his neighbor, and they cried out all together, saying, 'We have no part in David or inheritance in the son of Jesse, so return to your tents, Israel, everyone, for this man is not a prince or a ruler over us. All the people were dispersed from Shechem, and they departed every one to his tent."

Rehoboam strengthened himself and departed, and mounted his chariot, and entered into Jerusalem, and the whole tribe of Judah followed, and the whole tribe of Benjamin. At the beginning of the year, Rehoboam gathered all the men of Judah and Benjamin and went up to fight with Jeroboam at Shechem. The word of Lord came to Sameas the prophet, saying, "Speak to Rehoboam king of Judah, and to all the house of Judah and

Benjamin, and to the remnant of the people, saying, 'The Lord says, 'You will not go up, and you will not fight with your brothers the sons of Israel, return every man to his house, for this thing is from me." They listened to the word of the Lord and refused to go up, according to the word of the Lord.

Jeroboam built Shechem in Mount Ephraim and lived in it, and went out from there and built Penuel. Jeroboam said in his heart, "Look, now the kingdom will return to the house of David. If these people will go up to offer sacrifice in the Temple of the Lord at Jerusalem, then the heart of the people will return to the Lord, and to their master, to Rehoboam king of Judah, and they will kill me."

The king took counsel, and went, and made two golden heifers, and said to the people, "Let it be enough for you to have gone until now to Jerusalem. See your gods, Israel, who brought you up out of the land of Egypt."

He put one in the Temple of El[1] and he put the other in Dan. This thing became a sin, and the people went before one as far as Dan and left the Temple of the Lord. He made houses on the bamahs and made priests of any part of the people, who were not of the sons of Levi. Jeroboam appointed a feast in the eighth month, on the fifteenth day of the month, according to the feast in the land of Judah, and went up to the altar which he made in the Temple of El to sacrifice to the heifers which he made, and he placed in the Temple of El the priests from the bamahs which he had appointed. He went up to the altar which he had made, on the fifteenth day in the eighth month, at the feast which he devised out of his own heart, and he made a feast for the Israelites, and went up to the altar to sacrifice.

# 3rd Kingdoms: Chapter 12 Notes

**1** Codex Vaticanus: Baethêl (ʙⲁⲓⲑ̄ⲏ̄ⲗ)

• Codex Codex Basiliano-Vaticanus: Bethêl (ʙⲉⲑ̄ⲏ̄ⲗ)

• Aleppo Codex: byt ål (**בית אל**). Translation: house (or temple) of El (or god)

• Leningrad Codex: veit-El (בֵּית־אֵל). Translation: house (or temple) of El (or god)

• Targum Jerusalem: veit El (בֵית אֵל). Translation: house (or temple) of El (or god)

The term Bethel meant several things in ancient Canaan. The term translates as 'house of god,' which can be translated as either 'Temple of God (or El)' or 'sky/heaven.' Bethel was worshiped as a god by the ancient Canaanites, the brother of El and Dagon according to Sanchuniathon, who referred to him as Baitylos, which is the name used in this translation when the god is denoted. The term can also be translated as 'meteorite' as meteorites were believed to be parts of the god Baitylos that had fallen to the Earth, and shrines were built around them.

# 3rd Kingdoms: Chapter 13

A prophet came out of Judah following the word of the Lord, and traveled to the Temple of El, where Jeroboam stood at the altar to sacrifice. He shouted against the altar by the word of the Lord, "'Altar, altar,' the Lord says, 'See, a son is to be born to the house of David, by the name of Josiah, and he will sacrifice the priests of the bamahs on you! Those who sacrifice on you, he will burn the men's bones on you. On that day one will give a sign, saying, 'This is the word which the Lord spoke, 'Look, the altar is torn, and the fatness on it will be poured out.'"

When King Jeroboam heard the words of the prophet who called on the altar that was in the Temple of El, the king stretched out his hand from the altar, saying, "Take hold of him," and his hand that he stretched out against him, withered, and he could not pull it back to himself. The altar was torn, and the fatness was poured out from the altar, as per the sign which the prophet gave by the word of the Lord. King Jeroboam said to the prophet, "Ask Lord the god, and let my hand be restored to me."

The prophet begged the Lord, and he restored the king's hand to him, and it became as it had been previously. The king said to the prophet, "Enter with me into the temple and eat, and I will give you a gift. The prophet said to the king, "If you should give me half of your palace, I would not go in with you, nor will I eat bread, nor will I drink water in this place. The Lord ordered me, "Eat no bread, and drink no water, and do not return by the road by which you came." So he departed by another road and did not return by the road on which he had traveled to Bethel.

There lived an old prophet in Bethel, and his sons came and told him all the works that the prophet did on that day in the Temple of El, and the words which he spoke to the king, and they turned the face of their father. Their father asked them, "Which way did he go?" and his sons told him the road on which the prophet who came out of Judah left. He ordered his sons, "Saddle my donkey!" and they saddled the donkey for him, and he mounted it and chased after the prophet, and found him sitting under an oak. He asked him, "Are you the prophet that came out of Judah?"

He answered him, "I am."

He replied to him, "Come with me, and eat bread."

He said, "I will not by any means be able to return with you, nor will I eat bread, nor will I drink water in this place. For Lord commanded me, "Do not eat bread there, and do not drink water, and do not return by the road by which you came.""

He replied to him, "I am also a prophet, as you are, and a messenger told me the words of the Lord, saying, "Bring him back to you into your house and let him eat bread and drink water," however, he lied to him. He brought him back, and he ate bread and drank water in his house. While they were sitting at the table, the word of the Lord came to the prophet that brought him back, and he said to the prophet that came out of Judah, "The Lord says, 'Because you have resisted the word of the Lord, and have not kept the commandment which Lord the god commanded you, but have returned, and eaten bread and drank water in the place of which he said to you, 'You will not eat bread, and will not drink water,' therefore your body will not enter into the sepulcher of your fathers."

After he had eaten bread and drank the water, he saddled the donkey, and he turned and departed. A lion found him on the road and killed him, and his body was thrown down on the road, and the donkey stood by it, and the lion also stood by the body.

Men passing by, saw the carcass thrown on the road, and the lion standing near the carcass.

They went and spoke about it in the city where the old prophet lived. The prophet that turned him back on the road heard, and said, "This is the prophet who rebelled against the word of the Lord." He ordered his sons, "Saddle my donkey!" and they saddled it. He went and found the body lying in the road, and the donkey and the lion were standing by the body, and the lion had not devoured the body of the prophet and had not killed the donkey.

The prophet picked up the body of the prophet and laid it on his donkey, and the prophet brought him back to his city, to bury him in his own tomb, and he mourned him, saying, "Alas, brother."

After he had mourned him, he said to his sons, "Whenever I die, bury me in this tomb in which the prophet is buried. Lay me by his bones, so my bones may be preserved with his bones. For it will certainly happen, that which he declared as the word of the Lord against the altar in the Temple of El, and against the bamahs in Samaria."

After this Jeroboam did not turn from his sin, but he turned and made some of the people priests of the bamahs, whoever he liked, he consecrated them, and they became priests for the bamahs. This thing became sin to the house of Jeroboam, even until its destruction and its removal from the face of the Earth.

# 3rd Kingdoms: Chapter 14

Rehoboam the son of Solomon ruled over Judah. Rehoboam was forty-one years old when he began to reign, and he reigned seventeen years from the city of Jerusalem, where the Lord chose to put his name, out of all the tribes of Israel. His mother's name was Naama the Ammanitess. Rehoboam did evil in the sight of the Lord, and he provoked him in all the things which their fathers did in their sins which they sinned. They built for themselves bamahs, and pillars, and planted groves on every high hill, and under every shady tree. There was a conspiracy in the land, and they did according to all the abominations of the nations which Lord removed from before the Israelites.

It happened in the fifth year of the reign of Rehoboam, Shoshenq I king of Egypt attacked Jerusalem, and took all the treasures of the Temple of the Lord, and the treasures of the king's palace, and the golden spears which David took out of the hand of the sons of King Adrazaar of Zobah, and took to Jerusalem, and the golden shields which Solomon had made, and carried them all away into Egypt. King Rehoboam made bronze shields to replace them, and the chiefs of the golden shields which Solomon had made, and the chiefs of the bodyguard, who kept the gate of the house of the king, were placed in charge over them. When the king went into the Temple of the Lord, the bodyguard took them up and fixed them in the room of the bodyguard. The rest of the history of Rehoboam and all that he did, see, are they not written in the book of the Chronicles of the Kings of Judah?

There was a war between Rehoboam and Jeroboam continually. Rehoboam slept with his fathers and was buried with his fathers in the City of David, and Abijam his son reigned in his place.

# 3<sup>rd</sup> Kingdoms: Chapter 15

In the eighteenth year of the reign of Jeroboam son of Nebat, Abijam the son of Rehoboam reigned over Judah. He reigned three years over Jerusalem, and his mother's name was Maachah, daughter of Absalom. He walked in the sins of his father which he worked in his presence, and his heart was not perfect with Lord his god, as was the heart of his father David. It was for David's sake the Lord gave him a remnant, that he might establish his children after him, and might establish Jerusalem, as David did that which was right in the sight of the Lord, and he did not turn from anything that he commanded him all the days of his life. The rest of the history of Abijam and all that he did, see, are not these written in the book of the Chronicles of the Kings of Judah?

There was a war between Abijam and Jeroboam. Abijam slept with his fathers in the twenty-fourth year of Jeroboam, and he was buried with his fathers in the City of David. Asa his son reigned in his place. In the twenty-fourth year of Jeroboam king of Israel, Asa began to reign over Judah. He reigned forty-one years in Jerusalem, and his mother's name was Anah, daughter of Absalom. Asa did that which was right in the sight of Lord, as David his father.

He removed the sacrifices out of the land and abolished all the practices which his fathers had maintained. He removed Anah his mother from being queen, as she gathered a meeting in her grove, and Asa cut down her retreats and burnt them with fire in the brook of Kidron. He did not remove the bamahs, however the heart of Asa was perfect with Lord all his days. He brought in the pillars of his father, he even brought in his gold and silver pillars into the Temple of the Lord, and his vessels. There was a war between Asa and Baasha king of Israel all their days. Baasha king of Israel attacked Judah and built Ramah so that no one should go out or come in for Asa king of Judah. Asa took all the silver and the gold that was found in the treasures of the Temple of the Lord, and in the treasures of the king's palace, and gave them into the hands of his servants, and sent them out to the son of Hadad, the son of Tabrimon son of Hezion king of Syria, who lived in Damascus, saying, "Make a covenant between you and I, and between my father and your father. Look! I have sent out to you gold and silver as gifts. Come, dissolve your alliance with Baasha king of Israel, that he may go up from me."

The son of Hadad listened to King Asa and sent the chiefs of his forces to the cities of Israel, and they struck Ijon, Dan, and Abel of the house of Maacah, and all Chinnereth, as far as the whole land of Naphtali. When Baasha heard it, he stopped building Ramah and returned to Tirzah. King Asa ordered all Judah without exception, and they picked up the stones of Ramah and its timbers with which Baasha was building. King Asa built with them the whole hill of Benjamin and the watch-tower. The rest of the history of Asa, and all his mighty deeds which he worked, and the cities which he built, see, are these not written in the book of the Chronicles of the Kings of Judah? Nevertheless, in the time of his old age, he was diseased in his feet. Asa slept with his fathers and was buried with his fathers in the city of David his father, and Jehoshaphat his son reigned in his place. Nebat son of Jeroboam reigned over Israel in the second year of Asa king of Judah, and he reigned two years in Israel. He did that which was evil in the sight of Lord and walked in the way of his father, and in his sins in which he caused Israel to sin. Baasha son of Ahijah, who was over the house of Belaan son of Ahijah, conspired against him and attacked him in Gibbethon of the Gentiles. Nebat and all Israel besieged Gibbethon. Baasha killed him in the third year of Asa, the son of Asa, king of Judah and reigned in his place. When he reigned, he attacked the whole house of Jeroboam, and left none that breathed of Jeroboam, until he has destroyed him completely, according to the word of Lord which he spoke by his servant Ahijah the Shilonite, for the sins of Jeroboam, who led Israel into sin, even by his provocation where he provoked Lord God in Israel. The rest of the history of Nebat and all that he did, see, are these not written in the book of the Chronicles of the Kings of Israel?

There was a war between Asa and Baasha king of Israel in all their days. In the third year of Asa king of Judah, Baasha the son of Ahijah began to reign over Israel in Tirzah, for twenty-four years. He did that which was evil in the sight of Lord and walked in the way of Jeroboam the son of Nebat, and in his sins, as he caused Israel to sin.

# 3rd Kingdoms: Chapter 16

The word of the Lord came by the hand of Jehu, son of Hanani, to Baasha, saying, "Inasmuch as I lifted you from the earth, and made you ruler over my people Israel, and you have followed in the way of Jeroboam, and have caused my people Israel to sin, to provoke me with their vanities, Look, I raise enemies after Baasha, and after his house, and I will make your house like the house of Jeroboam son of Nebat. He who dies of Baasha, in the city, the dogs will devour, and he that dies of his in the field, the birds of the sky will devour. Now the rest of the history of Baasha, and all that he did, and his mighty acts, look, are not these written in the book of the Chronicles of the Kings of Israel?

Baasha slept with his fathers, and they buried him in Tirzah, and Elah his son reigned in his place. The Lord spoke by Jehu the son of Hanani against Baasha, and against his house, against all the evil which he worked before the Lord to provoke him to anger by the works of his hands, in being like the house of Jeroboam, and because he killed him. Elah son of Baasha reigned over Israel two years in Tirzah. Zimri, captain of half his cavalry, conspired against him, while he was in Tirzah, drinking himself drunk in the house of Osa the steward at Tirzah. Zimri went in and struck him and killed him, and reigned in his place.

When he reigned, when he sat on his throne, he slaughtered all the house of Baasha, according to the word which Lord spoke against the house of Baasha, and to Jehu the prophet, for all the sins of Baasha and Elah his son, as he led Israel astray to sin, to provoke Lord God in Israel with their vanities. The rest of the deeds of Elah which he did, look, are not these written in the book of the Chronicles of the Kings of Israel? Zimri reigned in Tirzah seven days, and the army of Israel was camped against Gibbethon of the Gentiles. The people heard in the army, "Zimri has conspired and killed the king," and the people of Israel made Omri the captain of the army king in that day in the camp over Israel.

Omri went up, and all Israel with him, out of Gibbethon, and they besieged Tirzah. When Zimri saw that his city was taken, he went into the inner room of the house of the king, and burnt the king's palace over him, and he died, because of his sins which he committed, doing that which was evil in the sight of the Lord, to follow in the way of Jeroboam the son of Nebat, and in his sins in which he caused Israel to sin. The rest of the history of Zimri and his conspiracies in which he conspired look are these not written in the book of the Chronicles of the Kings of Israel?

Then the people of Israel divided, half the people went after Tibni the son of Ginath to make him king, and half the people followed Omri. The people who followed Omri overpowered the people who followed Tibni the son of Ginath, and Tibni died and Joram his brother at that time, and Omri reigned after Tibni. In the thirty-first year of King Asa, Omri began to reign over Israel twelve years, he reigned six years in Tirzah. Omri bought Mount Shomron in Samaria, the mountain of Lord, for two talents of silver, and he built on the mountain, and they called the name of the mountain on which he built, after the name of Samaria, the mount of Lord in Shomron. Omri did that which was evil in the sight of the Lord and worked wickedly beyond all that was before him. He followed the  way of Jeroboam the son of Nebat, and in his sins where he caused Israel to sin, to provoke Lord the God of Israel by their vanities. The rest of the acts of Omri, and all that he did, and all his might, see, are not these things written in the book of the Chronicles of the Kings of Israel? Omri slept with his fathers and is buried in Samaria, and Ahab his son reigned in his place.

In the eleventh year of Omri, Jehoshaphat the son of Asa reigned, being thirty-five years old at the beginning of his reign, and he reigned twenty-five years in Jerusalem. His mother's name was Gazuba, daughter of Seli. He followed in the ways of Asa his father, and did not turned from it, from doing right in the eyes of the Lord. Only they did not removed any of the bamahs, and they sacrificed and burnt incense on the bamahs. Now the engagements which Jehoshaphat made with the king of Israel, and all his mighty deeds which he performed, and the enemies whom he fought against, see, are these not written in the book of the Chronicles of the Kings of Judah? The remains of the prostitution which they practiced in the days of Asa his father, he removed out of the land, and there was no king in Syria, but a deputy.

King Jehoshaphat made a ship of Tartessos to go to Sauvira for gold, but it did not, as the ship was broken at Ezion Geber.[1] Then the king of Israel said to Jehoshaphat, I will send out your servants and my servants in the ship, but Jehoshaphat would not. Jehoshaphat slept with his fathers and is buried with his fathers in the City of David, and Joram his son reigned in his place.

In the second year of Jehoshaphat king of Judah, Ahab son of Omri reigned over Israel in Samaria for twenty-two years. Ahab did that which was evil in the sight of the Lord and did more wickedly than all that were before him. It was not enough for him to follow in the sins of Jeroboam the son of Nebat, but he took as a wife, Jezebel the daughter of Ethbaal, king of the Sidonians. He went and served Ba'al,[2] and worshiped him. He set up an altar to Ba'al in the temple of his abominations which he built in Samaria. Ahab made an Asherah,[3] and Ahab did yet more abominably, to provoke Lord the god in Israel, and to sin against his own life so that he should be destroyed. He did evil above all the kings of Israel that were before him.

In his days Hiel the Bethelite rebuilt Jericho. He laid the foundation of it with Abiram his firstborn, and he set up the doors of it with Segub his younger son, according to the word of Lord which he spoke by Joshua the son of Nun.

# 3ʳᵈ Kingdoms: Chapter 16 Notes

**1** Codex Vaticanus: Gasiôngaber (ΓΑϹΙШΝΓΑΒΕΡ)

- LXX 108: Gaesiôngaber (Γαισιωνγαβερ)

- LXX 93: Gaesêôngambre (Γαισεωνγαμβρε)

- LXX 19: Gesiôngaber (Γεσιωνγαβερ)

The Masoretic text does not include this story, however, Etzyovn-gever (עֶצְיֹון־גֶּבֶר) is mentioned in other chapters. Ezion Geber was recorded as being near Elath, on the Gulf of Aqaba. This story implies that King Jehoshaphat attempted to move one of his long-range freighters from the Mediterranean to the Red Sea, which would have needed to be transported overland at the time, however, they could not reassemble the ship in Ezion Geber. Cleopatra VII and Mark Antony attempted something similar in the 1ˢᵗ century BC when they had the Egyptian fleet dragged overland from the Mediterranean Sea to the Gulf of Suez.

As there was no canal linking the Nile to the Red Sea at the time, the alternate interpretation is that a ship was sent from Tartessos to the Gulf of Aqaba by circumnavigating Africa. There is genetic evidence of Canaanites mating with the Khoi people of South Africa circa 1000 BC, supporting the early circumnavigation of Africa. Nevertheless, the earliest known circumnavigation of Africa was 350 years after King Jehoshaphat's time, by a Canaanite expedition sent by the Egyptian King Necho II.


**2** Codex Vaticanus: Baal (ΒΑΑΛ)

- Aleppo Codex: Bôl (בעל). Translation: lord (or owner, master, husband)

- Leningrad Codex: Baal (בַּעַל). Translation: lord (or owner, master, husband)

- Targum Jerusalem: Ba'ala (בַּעֲלָא). Translation: husband

The Greek term Baal is a transliteration of the Canaanite word Ba'al, meaning 'Lord.'

**3** Codex Vaticanus: alsôs (ⲀⲀⲤⲞⲤ). Translation: grove (or woods)

• Aleppo Codex: ăšrh (אשרה). Translation: Asherah

• Leningrad Codex: Asherah (אֲשֵׁרָה). Translation: Asherah

• Targum Jerusalem: Asherata (אֲשֵׁרְתָא)

Asherah was the name of an Israelite goddess before the time of Elijah in the 9th century, described as the mother of Yahweh, as well as the wife of El. It is unclear exactly how Asherah was worshiped, however, is is believed she was worshiped by planting oak trees, similar to her Egyptian counterpart Iusaaset, who was worshiped by planting acacia trees.

# 3rd Kingdoms: Chapter 17

Elijah[1] the prophet, the Tishbite, from Thesbae in Gilead, said to Ahab, "As the god Lord Sabaoth, the god in Israel[2] lives, before whom I stand, there will not be dew or rain these years, except by the word of my mouth."

The words of the Lord came to Elijah, saying, "Leave here and go east, and hide by the brook of Cherith, that is near the Jordan. You will drink the water of the brook, and I will order the ravens to feed you there."

Elijah followed the word of the Lord, and he sat by the brook of Cherith near the Jordan. The ravens brought him loaves in the morning, and meat in the evening and he drank the water of the brook. After some time the brook became dry, as there had been no rain on the earth. The word of the Lord came to Elijah, saying, "Rise and go to Sarepta[3] in the Sidonian lands. Look, I have commanded a widowed-woman there to take care of you."

He rose and went to Sarepta, and came to the gate of the city, and saw a widowed-woman was there gathering sticks. Elijah called to her, and said to her, 'Fetch me, I beg you, a little water in a vessel, that I may drink.'

She went to fetch it, and Elijah called to her, and said, "Bring me, I beg you, a morsel of the bread that is in your hand."

The woman said, "As Lord the god lives, I have no cake, but only a handful of meal in the pitcher, and a little oil in a cruse, and look, I am going to gather two sticks, and I will go in and dress it for myself and my children, and we will eat it or die."

Elijah said to her, "Be of good courage, go in and do according to your word, but make me a little cake, and bring it out to me first, and then make something for yourself and your children afterward. As the Lord says, 'The pitcher of the meal will not fail, and the cruse of oil will not diminish, until the day that the Lord gives rain on the earth.'"

The woman went and did so, and ate, both of them, with her children. The pitcher of meal didn't fail, and the cruse of oil was not diminished, according to the word of the Lord which he spoke by the hand of Elijah. Afterward, the son of the woman, the mistress of the house was sick, and his sickness was very severe until there was no breath left in him. She said to Elijah, "What have I to do with you, prophet? Have you come to me to bring my sins to remembrance, and to kill my son?"

Elijah said to the woman, "Give me your son."

He took him out of her bosom and took him up to the room in which he himself lodged, and laid him on the bed. Elijah cried out loud, "Alas, Lord, in witness of the widow with whom I stay, you have worked evil for her in killing her son."

He breathed on the child three times, and called on Lord, and said, "Lord the god, let, I beg you, the mind of this child return to him," and it was so, and the child cried out, and he brought him down from the upper room into the house and gave him to his mother, and Elijah said, "See, your son lives."

The woman said to Elijah, "Look, I know that you are a prophet, and the word of the Lord in your mouth is true."

# 3rd Kingdoms: Chapter 17 Notes

**1** Codex Vaticanus: Êliou (ΗΛΕΙΟΥ)

- Codex Alexandrinus: Êliou (ΗΛΙΟΥ)

- LXX 19: Êlias (ΗλιΔc)

- LXX 61: Êlion (Ηλιον)

- Aleppo Codex: Aʾlyhw (אליהו)

- Leningrad Codex: Eliyyahu (אֵלִיָּהוּ)

- Targum Jerusalem: Eliyahu (אֱלִיָּהוּ)

The early surviving Greek transliterations of the name of Elijah seem to confirm that the name was the same in Aramaic as it is in Hebrew, composed of the Canaanite word ål (𐤋𐤀), meaning 'god,' and the word Yahw (𐤉𐤄𐤅), which the Greeks generally translated as the name Iaô (Ιαω). The Aramaic name Yhw (𐤉𐤄𐤅) was commonly used by Israelites in the Persian and Greek eras, however, the common Judahite version of the name transitioned to Yhwh (𐤉𐤄𐤅𐤄) at some point after the Babylonian destruction of Jerusalem. In this case, as the name Aʾlyhw was not Aramaic, it was transliterated directly into Greek. The Hebrew name is commonly anglicized as Elijah from Aʾlyh (אליה), the shorter version of the name found in the Masoretic version of Kings, while the Greek name is commonly anglicized as Elias. As Elijah is the more common form, it is used here.

**2** Codex Vaticanus: c̄s o t̄hs tôn dynameôn o t̄hs Israêl (ΚϹΟΘϹΤШΝ ΔΥΝΑΜΕШΝΟΘϹΙϹΡΑΗΛ). Translation: lord the god the forces the god Israel

- Aleppo Codex: Yhwh ålhy Yšrål (יהוה אלהי ישראל). Translation: Yhwh god of Israel

- Leningrad Codex: Yehvah elohei Yisra'el (יְהֹוָה אֱלֹהֵי יִשְׂרָאֵל). Translation: Yehwah god of Israel

- Targum Jerusalem: Yeyah elaha deYisra'el (יְיָ אֱלָהָא דְיִשְׂרָאֵל). Translation: Yahw god of Israel

**3** Codex Vaticanus: Sarepta (ⲤⲀⲣⲉⲡⲧⲀ)

- Codex Alexandrinus: Sephtha (ⲤⲉⲫⲐⲀ)

- Codex Basiliano-Vaticanus: Arephtha (ⲀⲣⲉⲫⲐⲀ)

- LXX 554: Sarephtha (ⲤⲀⲣⲉⲫⲐⲀ)

- LXX 82: Arepta (ⲀⲣⲉⲡⲧⲀ)

- Aleppo Codex: Srpth (צרפתה)

- Leningrad Codex: Tzarefatah (צָרְפַתָה)

- Targum Jerusalem: Tzarefat (צָרְפַת)

The city of Sarepta was a Phoenician port-city between Sidon and Tyre, in modern Lebanon.

# 3rd Kingdoms: Chapter 18

After many days, the word of the Lord came to Elijah in the third year, saying, "Go and appear before Ahab, and I will bring rain on the face of the earth."

Elijah went to appear before Ahab, and the famine was severe in Samaria. Ahab called Obadiah the steward. Now Obadiah was terrified of the Lord. When Jezebel had slaughtered the prophets of the Lord, Obadiah had taken a hundred prophets, and hidden them by fifties in caves, and fed them with bread and water. Ahab said to Obadiah, "Come, and let us go through the land, and to the fountains of water, and to the brooks, if by any means we may find grass, and may save the horses and mules, and so they will not perish from the tents."

They divided the land between them to survey it, Ahab traveled one road, and Obadiah traveled alone by another road. Obadiah was alone on the road, and Elijah came along to meet him. Obadiah rushed, and fell on his face, and said, "My lord Elijah, are you really him?"

Elijah answered him, "I am. Go tell your master, 'Look, Elijah is here.'"

Obadiah asked, "What sin have I committed, that you give your servant into the hand of Ahab to kill me? As Lord the god lives, there is not a nation or kingdom, where my lord has not sent to search for you. If they said, 'He is not here,' then he set fire to the kingdom and its territories because he had not found you. Now you say, 'Go, tell your lord, 'Look, Elijah is here.'" When I have departed from you, if the Spirit of Lord will carry you off to a land which I don't know, and I will go in to tell the matter to Ahab, and he will not find you and will kill me, yet your servant has feared Lord from his youth. Has it not been told to you my lord, what I did when Jezebel killed the prophets of the Lord, that I hid a hundred men of the prophets of the Lord, by fifties in caves, and fed them with bread and water? Now you say to me, 'Go, tell your master, 'Look, Elijah is here,'' and he will kill me.''

Elijah said, "As Lord Sabaoth,[1] before whom I stand lives, today I will appear before him.''

Obadiah went to meet Ahab and told him, and Ahab rushed out and went to meet Elijah. When Ahab saw Elijah, Ahab asked Elijah, "Are you he who perverts Israel?''

Elijah answered, "I do not pervert Israel, but you and your father's house do, in that you forgot Lord the god, and you have gone after Ba'als. Now send, gather to me all Israel to Mount Carmel, and the four hundred and fifty disgraceful prophets, and the four hundred prophets of Asherah that ate at Jezebel's table.''

Ahab sent to all Israel and gathered all the prophets to Mount Carmel. Elijah drew near to them all, and Elijah said to them, "How long will you stand on both feet? If Lord is god, follow him, but if Ba'al, follow him.''

The people did not answered a word. Elijah said to the people, "I am left, the only one prophet of the Lord, and the prophets of Ba'al are four hundred and fifty men, and the prophets of Asherah are four hundred. Let them give us two oxen, and let them choose one for themselves, and cut it in pieces, and lay it on the wood, and put no fire on the wood, and I will dress the other bull, and put on no fire. Do you call loudly on the name of your gods, and I will call on the name of Lord the god, and it will come to pass that the god who will answer by fire, he is God.''

All the people answered and said, "The word which you have spoken is good.''

Elijah said to the prophets of shame, "Choose to yourselves one calf, and dress it first, for you are many, and call on the name of your god, but apply no fire. They took the calf and dressed it, and called on the name of Ba'al from morning until noon, and said, hear us, Ba'al, hear us. There was no voice, neither was there hearing, and they ran up and down on the altar which they had made."

It was noon, and Elijah the Tishbite mocked them, and said, "Call with a loud voice, for he is a god, maybe he is meditating, or else perhaps he is engaged in business, or perhaps he is asleep and is to be awoken."

They cried with a loud voice, and cut themselves according to their custom with knives and daggers until the blood gushed out on them. They prophesied until the evening came, and it came to pass as it was the time of the offering of the sacrifice, that Elijah the Tishbite spoke to the prophets of the abominations, saying, "Stand by for the present, and I will offer my sacrifice."

They stood aside and departed. Elijah said to the people, "Come near to me."

All the people came near to him. Elijah took twelve stones, according to the number of the tribes of Israel, as Lord spoke to him, saying, "Israel will be your name."

He built up the stones in the name of Lord and repaired the altar that had been broken down, and he made a trench that would hold two measures[2] of seed round about the altar. He piled the split wood on the altar which he had made, and divided the whole burnt offering, and laid it on the wood, and laid it in order on the altar, and said, "Fetch me four pitchers of water, and pour it on the whole burnt offering, and on the wood." They did so.

He said, "Do it the second time." They did it the second time.

He said, "Do it the third time." They did it the third time. The water ran around the altar, and they filled the trench with water.

Elijah cried aloud to the sky, and said, "Lord, the God of Abraham, and Isaac, and Israel, answer me, Lord, answer me this day by fire, and let all these people know that you are Lord the God of Israel, and I am your servant, and for your sake I have worked these works. Hear me, Lord, hear me, and let these people know that you are Lord the god, and you have turned back the heart of these people."

Then fire fell from the Lord out of the sky and devoured the whole burnt offerings, and the wood and the water that was in the trench, and the fire licked up the stones and the earth. All the people fell on their faces, and said, "Truly Lord the god, is God."

Elijah said to the people, "Take the prophets of Ba'al, don't let one of them escape."

They took them, and Elijah brought them down to the brook Kisson, and he killed them there. Elijah said to Ahab, "Go up, and eat and drink, for there is a sound of the coming of rain."

Ahab went up to eat and to drink, and Elijah went up to Carmel, and stooped to the ground, and put his face between his knees, and said to his servant, "Go up, and look towards the sea."

The servant looked, and said, "There is nothing."

Elijah said, "Then go again seven times." The servant went again seven times, and it came to pass at the seventh time, that, look, a little cloud like the sole of a man's foot brought water.

He said, "Go up, and say to Ahab, prepare your chariot, and leave, in case the rain overtakes you."

It came to pass in the meanwhile, that the sky grew black with clouds and wind, and there was a great rain. Ahab wept and went to Jezreel. The hand of Lord was on Elijah, and he girded up his loins and ran before Ahab to Jezreel.

# 3rd Kingdoms: Chapter 18 Notes

**1** Codex Vaticanus: c̄s tôn dynameôn (K̄CTⲰNⲆYNⲀMEⲰN). Translation: Lord of the forces

• Aleppo Codex: Yhwh ṣbảwt (**יהוה צבאות**). Translation: Yhwh of forces (or army, war, warfare)

• Leningrad Codex: Yehvah tzeva'ovt (יְהֹוָה צְבָאֹות). Translation: Yehwah of forces (or army, war, warfare)

• Targum Jerusalem: Yeyah tzeva'ovt (יְיָ צְבָאֹות). Translation: Yahw of desires

The Greek translations of the four books of Kingdoms are not consistent at this point, with the term translated in 2nd and 3rd Kingdoms as 'of forces' (των δυνάμεων) being transliterated directly as Sabaoth (Σαβαωθ) in 1st and 4th Kingdoms, as well as in 1st Paralipomenon. As both the Septuagint and Masoretic texts support the name Sabaoth having once been in the Aramaic version of this verse, it is restored in this translation.

**2** Codex Vaticanus: metrêtas (ΜΕΤΡΗΤⲀC). Translation: meters (or measurements, measures)

• Aleppo Codex: såtym (**סאתים**). Translation: messenger se'ahs

• Leningrad Codex: satayim (סָאתַיִם). Translation: se'ahs

• Targum Jerusalem: satan (סָאתָן). Translation: se'ahs

The Masoretic term is the plural form of the Aramaic såtå (סְאתָא), a volume measurement used in ancient Canaan and Syria equaling medium sized 144 chicken eggs. The Hebrew spelling is se'ah (סְאָה), commonly transliterated into English as se'ah, proving that this section of Masoretic Kings was translated from an Aramaic source. The Greeks simplified the term to 'measures,' which is used here as the term in the Masoretic text could not have been the measurement used in the original text of the Chronicles of the Kings of Samaria. The measurement

732

does not appear have been used in Babylon either, indicating that it was originally introduced to the text in the late Persian era Aramaic translation.

# 3rd Kingdoms: Chapter 19

Ahab told Jezebel his wife all that Elijah had done, and how he had slaughtered the prophets with the sword. Jezebel sent to Elijah, and said, "You are Elijah and I am Jezebel. God do so to me, and more also, if I do not make your life like one of their lives by this time tomorrow."

Elijah was afraid, and rose, and ran for his life, and he went to Bathsheba in the land of Judah, and he left his servant there. He himself went a day's journey in the wilderness, and came and sat under a juniper tree, and asked concerning his life that he might die, and said, "Let it be enough now, Lord, take, I beg you, my life from me, for I am no better than my fathers."

He lay down and slept there under a tree, and look, some one touched him, and said to him, "Rise and eat."

Elijah looked, and, saw at his head there was a cake of meal and a cruse of water, and he arose, and ate and drank, and returned and lay down. The messenger of the lord[1] returned again, and touched him, and said to him, "Rise, and eat, for the journey is far from you."

He rose, and ate and drank, and traveled in the strength of that food for forty days and forty nights to Mount Horeb. He entered there into a cave, and rested there, and look, the word of the Lord came to him, and he said, "What do you here, Elijah?"

Elijah said, "I have been very jealous for Lord Sabaoth[2] because the Israelites have forgotten you. They have ripped down your altars, and have slain your prophets with the sword, and I am the only one left, and they seek to take my life."

He said, "You will go out tomorrow, and will stand before the Lord in the mountain, and see the Lord will pass by."

He saw a powerful twisting wind[3] shake the mountains and break the rocks before the Lord, but the Lord was not in the wind. After the wind came a loud noise,[4] but the Lord was not in the loud noise. After the loud noise, came a fire, but the Lord was not in the fire. After the fire, came a voice in a gentle breeze. When Elijah heard, he wrapped his face in his collar, and went out and stood in the cave, and heard the voice come to him and ask, "What do you here, Elijah?"

Elijah answered, "I have been very jealous for Lord Sabaoth, for the Israelites have forgotten your covenant, and they have overthrown your altars, and have slain your prophets with the sword! I am left entirely alone, and they seek my life to take it."

Lord said to him, "Go, return, and you will come into the way of the wilderness of Damascus, and you will go and anoint Hazael to be king over Syria. Jehu the son of Nimshi will you anoint to be king over Israel, and Elisha the son of Shaphat will you anoint to be prophet in your room. It will come to pass, that he that escapes from the sword of Hazael, Jehu will kill, and he that escapes from the sword of Jehu, Elisha will kill. You will leave in Israel seven thousand men, all the knees which had not bowed themselves to Ba'al, and every mouth which had not worshiped him."

He left there, and found Elisha the son of Shaphat, and he was plowing with oxen, there were twelve yoked before him, and he with the twelve. He passed by him, and threw his mantle on him. Elisha left the livestock, and followed after Elijah and said, "I will kiss my father, and follow after you."

Elijah said, "Return, for I have work for you."

He returned from following him, and took a yoke of oxen, and killed them, and boiled them with the instruments of the oxen, and gave to the people, and they ate, and he rose, and went after Elijah, and ministered to him.

# 3ʳᵈ Kingdoms: Chapter 19 Notes

**1** Codex Vaticanus: angelos c̄u (ⲀⲅⲅⲉⲗⲟⲥⲕⲨ). Translation: messenger lord

• LXX 246: angelon Cyriou (Ἀγγϭλον Κυβϑου). Translation: messenger Lord

• Aleppo Codex: mlåk Yhwh (מלאך יהוה). Translation: messenger Yhwh

• Leningrad Codex: malak Yehvah (מַלְאַךְ יְהוָה). Translation: messenger Yehwah

• Targum Jerusalem: mal'acha daYyah (מַלְאָכָא דַיְיָ). Translation: messenger of Yahw

**2** Codex Vaticanus: c̄ō pantocratori (Ⲕ̄ⲰⲠⲀⲚⲦⲞⲔⲢⲀⲦⲞⲢⲓ). Translation: Lord omnipotent

• Codex Alexandrinus: Cyriô pantocratori (ⲔⲨⲢⲓⲱ ⲠⲀⲚⲦⲞⲔⲢⲀⲦⲞⲢⲉⲓ). Translation: Lord omnipotent

• Aleppo Codex: Yhwh ålhy sbåwt (יהוה אלהי צבאות). Translation: messenger Yhwh god of forces

• Leningrad Codex: Yhvah | elohei tzeva'ovt (יְהוָה ׀ אֱלֹהֵי צְבָאוֹת). Translation: Yhwah, god of forces

• Targum Jerusalem: Yeyah elaha tzeva'ovt (יְיָ אֱלָהָא צְבָאוֹת). Translation: Yahw god Sebaot (or desires)

As pantocrator (παντοκράτωρ) is accepted as the translation of Šdy (שדי), the Aramaic text the Greeks worked from could not have mirrored the Hebrew translation. As both the Septuagint and Masoretic texts support the name Sabaoth having once been in the Aramaic version of this verse, it is restored in this translation.

**3** Codex Vaticanus: p̄n̄a mega crataeon (ΠΝΛ ΜΕΓΛ ΚΡΑΤΛΙΟΝ). Translation: spirit (or breath, wind) big (or great, loud, awesome) powerful (or mighty)

• LXX 106: mega pneuma crataeon (μεγλ πνδυμλ ιβΑτλιον). Translation: big (or great, loud, awesome) wind (or breath, spirit) powerful (or mighty)

• Aleppo Codex: rwh gdwlh whzq (רוח גדולה וחזק). Translation: wind (or breath, spirit) twisting (in Aramaic, or 'big' in Hebrew) and strong (or loud)

• Leningrad Codex: ruach gedovlah vechazak (רוּחַ גְּדוֹלָה וְחָזָק). Translation: wind (or breath, spirit) twisting (in Aramaic, or 'big' in Hebrew) and strong (or loud)

• Targum Jerusalem: mal'achei rucha (מַלְאֲכֵי רוּחָא). Translation: messenger wind (or space, breath)

Based on the other Aramaic loanwords in Masoretic Kings, it seems likely that this was a description of a tornado. While the Greek translation does follow the Hebrew interpretation of gdwlh instead of the Aramaic, the way Lord Sabaoth is interpreted in 3<sup>rd</sup> Kingdoms indicates the surviving Greek translation is a later redaction, influenced by Theodotion's Greek translation from circa 150 AD, and therefore the older Aramaic meaning of gədôlâ is imported from the Masoretic text.

**4** Codex Vaticanus: syssismos (ϹΥϹϹΕΙϹΜΟϹ). Translation: with earthquake

• Codex Alexandrinus: sysismos (ϹΥϹΕΙϹΜΟϹ)

• Aleppo Codex: rôš (רעש). Translation: loud noise (or commotion)

• Leningrad Codex: ra'ash (רָעַשׁ). Translation: loud noise (or commotion)

• Targum Jerusalem: zi'a (זִיעָא). Translation: messenger tempest (or commotion)

# 3ʳᵈ Kingdoms: Chapter 19 Notes

The Greek and Hebrew translations do not directly correlate. The Greek could be read as 'with earthquake,' although that reading seems improbable. The Hebrew could be interpreted as the beginning of ra'ash Adamah (רַעַשׁ אֲדָמָה), meaning 'earthquake,' however, that would require the original text of 3ʳᵈ Kingdoms to have been written in Edomite, and the Hasmoneans to have dropped the name Adamah, the Edomite earth-goddess.

While an Edomite origin is plausible, the Greek addition of 'with' (συς) makes no sense in either Greek or Semitic languages, suggesting that the Aramaic translation used the word swssysm (סוסיסיא), meaning 'bird-horses,' or 'pegasuses,' which also appears to have been used in the Aramaic precursor to 4ᵗʰ Kingdoms, where it was mirrored by se'arah (סְעָרָה), meaning 'storm,' or 'whirlwind,' in the Masoretic text. The presence of bird-horses in the Aramaic translations suggests that the text was altered in the Greek era, when the Philip the Phrygian was the high-priest at the Second Temple in Jerusalem, as the Phryrian god Sabazious flew on a flying horse, which was probably the origin of Zeus' winged horse, the Pegasus. As the Hebrew translation of 'loud noise' makes more sense than the Greek 'with earthquake,' or theoretical Aramaic 'pegasuses,' the Hebrew term is used in this translation.

# 3rd Kingdoms: Chapter 20

Nabuthai the Jezraelite had a vineyard, near the threshing floor of King Ahab of Samaria. Ahab said to Nabuthai, "Give me your vineyard, and I'll have it as a garden of plants, as it is near my house, and I will give you another vineyard better than it. Or if it pleases you, I will give you silver, the price of this, your vineyard, and I'll have it for a garden of plants."

Nabuthai said to Ahab, "My God forbids me to give you the inheritance of my fathers."

The spirit of Ahab was troubled, and he lay down on his bed, and covered his face, and ate no bread. Jezebel his wife went to him, and asked him, "Why is your spirit troubled, and why do you eat no bread?"

He answered her, "Because I said to Nabuthai the Jezraelite, 'Give me your vineyard for silver, or if you prefer, I'll give you another vineyard for it,' and he said, 'I will not give you the inheritance of my fathers.'"

Jezebel his wife said to him, "Do you now thus act the king over Israel? Rise, and eat bread, and be your own master, and I will give you the vineyard of Nabuthai the Jezraelite."

She wrote a letter in the name of Ahab, and sealed it with his seal, and sent the letter to the elders, and to the freemen who lived with Nabuthai. And it was written in the letters, saying, "Keep a fast and set Nobah in a chief place among the people.

Set two men, sons of transgressors, before him, and let them testify against him, saying, "He blessed God and the king, and let them lead him forth, and stone him, and let them die." The men of his city, the elders, and the nobles who lived in his city did as Jezebel sent to them, and as it had been written in the letters which she sent to them. They proclaimed a fast and set Nebuthai in a chief place among the people.

Two men, sons of transgressors, came in, and sat opposite him, and witnessed against him, saying, "You have blessed God and King."[1] They led him out of the city and stoned him with stones, and he died. They sent to Jezebel, saying, "Nabuthai is stoned, and is dead."

When Jezebel heard it, she said to Ahab, "Rise, take possession of the vineyard of Nabuthai the Jezraelite, who would not sell it to you." Nebuthai is not alive, for he is dead. When Ahab heard that Nabuthai the Jezraelite was dead, he tore his garments, and put on sackcloth. Afterward, Ahab rose and went down to the vineyard of Nabuthai the Jezraelite, to take possession of it.

The Lord spoke to Elijah the Tishbite, saying, "Rise, and go down to meet Ahab king of Israel, who is in Samaria, in the vineyard of Nabuthai, for he has gone down there to take possession of it."

You will say to him, "The Lord says, 'Inasmuch as you have slain and taken possession, therefore' says the Lord, 'in every place where the swine and the dogs have licked the blood of Nabuthai, there, the dogs will lick your blood, and the prostitutes will wash themselves in your blood."

Ahab asked Elijah, "Have you found me, my enemy?"

He answered, "I have found you, because you have wickedly sold yourself to work evil in the sight of the Lord, to provoke him to anger, look, I bring evil on you, and I will kindle a fire after you, and I will completely destroy every male of Ahab, and him that is locked up and him that is left in Israel. I will make your house like the house of Jeroboam the son of Nebat, and as the house of Baasha son of Ahijah, because of the provocations where you have provoked me, and caused Israel to sin."

The Lord spoke of Jezebel, saying, "The dogs will devour her within the fortification of Jezreel. He who dies of Ahab in the city, the dogs will eat, and he who is dead from him in the field, will the birds of the sky eat."

Ahab did wickedly, in that he sold himself to do that which was evil in the sight of the Lord, as his wife Jezebel led him astray. He did very abominably in following after the abominations, according to all that the Amorites did, who the Lord completely destroyed from before the Israelites. Because of the word, Ahab was pierced with sorrow before the Lord, and he left crying, and tore his clothes, and dressed in sackcloth, and fasted. He put on sackcloth again, like on the day that he struck Nabuthai the Jezraelite, and went his way.

The word of the Lord came by the hand of his servant Elijah concerning Ahab, and the Lord said, "Have you seen how Ahab has been stabbed to the heart before me? I will not bring on the evil in his days, but in his son's days I will bring on the evil."

# 3rd Kingdoms: Chapter 20 Notes

**1** Codex Alexandrinus: autou legontes êylogêcas theon cae basilea (ΑΥΤΟΥ ΛΕΓΟΝΤΕϹ ΗΥΛΟΓΗϹΕΝ ΘΕΟΝ ΚΑΙΒΑϹΙΛΕΑ). Translation: you have said, 'praise god and king.'

• Codex Basiliano-Vaticanus: autou legontes eulogêcas theon cae basilea (ΑΥΤΟΥ ΛΕΓΟΝΤΕϹ ΕΥΛΟΓΗΚΑϹ ΘΕΟΝ ΚΑΙΒΑϹΙΛΕΑ). Translation: you have said, 'bless god and king.'

• LXX 106: autou legontes eulogêsas theon cae basilea (Δυτου λϙγοντόϲ ϭυλογℏσΔϲ θϭον ℏΔι uΔσιλϙΔ). Translation: you have said, 'speak well of god and king.'

• LXX 93: autou legontes eulogêce nabouthae theon cae basilea (Δυτου λϙγοντόϲ ϭυλογℏℏϭ ΝΔμουθΔι θϭον ℏΔι uΔσιλϙΔ). Translation: you have said, 'speak well of Nebuthai's god and king.'

• LXX 82: autou legontes êylogêsen nabouthe theon cae basilea (Δυτου λϙγοντόϲ ℏυλ℥γℏοϭν ΝΔμουθϭ θϭον ℏΔι uΔσιλϙΔ). Translation: you have said, 'praise Nebuthai's god and king.'

• LXX 158: auton legontes eulogêcas theon Basilea (Δυτον λϙγοντόϲ ϭυλογℏℏΔϲ θϭον βΔσιλϙΔ). Translation: you have said, 'bless god King.'

• Aleppo Codex (in chapter 21: lảmr brkt ảlhym wmlk (**לאמר ברכת אלהים ומלך**). Translation: declaring 'praise Elohim and King (or Moloch)'

• Leningrad Codex (in chapter 21: lemor berachta elohim vamelech (לֵאמֹר בֵּרַכְתָּ אֱלֹהִים וָמֶלֶךְ). Translation: declaring 'praise Elohim and King'

• Targum Jerusalem (in chapter 21: lemeimar gadeifta kodam Yeyah umalka (לְמֵימַר גְּדֵיפְתָּא קֳדָם יְיָ וּמַלְכָּא). Translation: declaring 'fortune comes from Yahw and King'

The charge appears to have originally been that he was worshiping both Elohim and Moloch, however, the Masoretes added vowel points that indicating he was charged with 'praising God and king.'

# 3rd Kingdoms: Chapter 21

The son of Hadad gathered all his forces, and went up and besieged Samaria, he and thirty-two kings with him, and all his horses and chariots, and they went up and besieged Samaria, and fought against it. He sent into the city to Ahab king of Israel, and said to him, "The son of Hadad said, 'Your silver and your gold are mine, and your wives and your children are mine.'"

The king of Israel answered and said, "As you have said, 'My lord, my king, I am yours, and all mine also.'"

The messengers came again, and said, "The son of Hadad said, 'I sent to you, saying, 'You will give me your silver and your gold, and your wives and your children. At this time tomorrow, I will send my servants to you, and they will search your house, and the houses of your servants, and it will be that all the desirable objects of their eyes on which they will lay their hands, they will take them.'"

The king of Israel called all the elders of the land, and said, "Take notice now and consider, that this man seeks evil, for he has sent to me concerning my wives, and concerning my sons, and concerning my daughters, yet I have not held back from him my silver and my gold."

The elders and all the people said to him, "don't listen, and don't consent."

He said to the messengers of the son of Hadad, "Say to your master, 'All things that you have sent to your servant about before I will do, but this thing I cannot do.'"

The men departed and carried back the answer to him. The son of Hadad sent to him, saying, "God do so to me, and more also, if the dust of Samaria will be enough for foxes, besides all the people in my infantry."

The king of Israel answered, "It will be sufficient. Don't let the humpbacked boast like he who is upright."

When he returned him this answer, he and all the kings with him were drinking in tents, and he said to his servants, "Dig a trench," and they dug a trench around the city.

A prophet came to King Ahab of Israel, and said, "The Lord says, 'Have you seen this great multitude? Look, I give it into your hands today, and you will know that I am the Lord."

Ahab asked, "How?"

He answered, "The Lord said, 'By the young men of the heads of the districts.'"

Ahab asked, "Who will begin the battle?"

He answered, "You."

Ahab counted the young men the heads of the districts, and they were two hundred and thirty. Afterward, he counted the people, including every man fit for war, totaling seven thousand. He went out at noon, a son of Hadad was drinking and getting drunk in Booths, he and the kings, the thirty-two kings, his allies. The young men, the heads of the districts, went out first, and they sent a report to the king of Syria, saying, "There are men come out of Samaria."

He said to them, "If they come forth peaceably, take them alive, and if they come out to war, take them alive, and don't let the young men the heads of the districts go out of the city."

The force that was behind them struck each one the man next to him, and each one a second time struck the man next to him,

748

and Syria fled, and Israel pursued them. The son of Hadad, the king of Syria, escaped on the horse of a cavalryman. The king of Israel went out, and took all the cavalry and the chariots, and struck the enemy with a great slaughter in Syria. The prophet came to the king of Israel, and said, "Strengthen yourself, and observe, and see what you will do. For at the return of the year the son of Hadad king of Syria comes up against you."

Even the servants of the king of Syria said, "The god of Israel is a god of mountains, and not a god of valleys, which is why he has prevailed against us. If we should fight against them in the plain, we will prevail against them. Do this thing, 'Send away the kings, each one to his home, and set princes in their place.' We will give you another army like the army that was destroyed, and cavalry like the cavalry, and chariots like the chariots, and we will fight against them in the plain, and we will prevail against them."

He listened to their voice and did so. At the return of the year, the son of Hadad reviewed Syria, and went up to Aphek to war against Israel. The Israelites were counted and came to meet them, and Israel camped before them like two little flocks of goats, but Syria filled the land. The prophet came and said to the king of Israel, "The Lord says, 'Because Syria has said, 'Lord the god in Israel is a God of the hills, and he is not a god of the valleys, therefore, I will give this great army into your hand, and you will know that I am the Lord.'"

They camped one against the other before them for seven days. It came to pass on the seventh day that the battle drew on, and Israel struck Syria, even a hundred thousand infantry in one day. The rest fled to Aphek, into the city, and the wall fell on twenty-seven thousand men that were left, and the son of Hadad fled and entered into an inner room, and into a closet. He said to his servants, "I know that the kings of Israel are merciful kings. Let us now put sackcloth on our loins, and ropes on our heads, and let us go out to the king of Israel if by any means he will leave our minds alive."

So they girded sackcloth on their loins, and put ropes on their heads, and said to the King of Israel, "Your servant the son of Hadad says, 'Let our minds live, I beg you.'"

He asked, "Does he yet live?"

He is my brother. The men divined and offered drink-offerings, and they caught the word out of his mouth, and said, "Your brother, the son of Hadad."

He said, "Go in and fetch him."

The son of Hadad went out to him, and they had him go up to him on a chariot. He said to him, "The cities which my father took from your father I will restore to you, and you will make streets for yourself in Damascus, as my father made streets in Samaria, and I will let you go with a covenant." He made a covenant with him, and let him go.

A certain man of the sons of the prophets said to his neighbor by the word of the Lord, "Strike me, I beg," but the man would not strike him.

He said to him, "Because you have not listened to the voice of the Lord, therefore, look, as you leave from me, a lion will kill you," and as he departed from him a lion found him and killed him.

He found another man, and said, "Strike me, I beg you."

The man struck him, and in striking wounded him. The prophet went and stood before the king of Israel by the road, and bound his eyes with a bandage. As the king passed by, he cried out to the king, "Your servant went out to war, and, look, a man brought another man to me, and said to me, 'Keep this man, and if he should by any means escape, then your life will go for his life, or you will pay a talent of silver. However, when your servant looked around this way and that way, the man was gone."

The king of Israel said to him, "Look, you have also destroyed snares set for me."

He rushed and took away the bandage from his eyes, and the king of Israel recognized him, that he was one of the prophets. He said to him, "Lord says, 'Because you have allowed a man appointed to destruction to escape out of your hand, therefore your life will go for his life, and your people for his people."

The king of Israel departed confused and discouraged and returned to Samaria.

# 3rd Kingdoms: Chapter 22

He rested three years, and there was no war between Syria and Israel. In the third year, Jehoshaphat king of Judah went to the king of Israel. The king of Israel said to his servants, "Do you know Remmath in Gilead is ours, even though we are slow to take it out of the hand of the king of Syria?" The king of Israel asked Jehoshaphat, "Will you go up with us to Remmath in Gilead to battle?"

Jehoshaphat answered, "As I am, so are you also. My people are your people. My horses are your horses."

Jehoshaphat the king of Judah said to the King of Israel, "Inquire, I beg you, of Lord today."

The king of Israel gathered all the prophets together, about four hundred men, and the asked them, "Will I go up to Remmath in Gilead to battle, or will I not?"

They answered, "Go up, and the Lord will certainly give it into the hands of the king."

Jehoshaphat said to the King of Israel, "Is there not here a prophet of the Lord, that we may inquire of the Lord through him?"

The king of Israel said to Jehoshaphat, "There is one man here for us to inquire of Lord, but I hate him, for he does not speak good of me, but only evil: Micah the son of Imlah."

Jehoshaphat king of Judah said, "Don't let the king say this!"

The king of Israel called a eunuch and said, "Bring Micah the son of Imlah here quickly."

The King of Israel and Jehoshaphat king of Judah sat, each on his throne, armed in the gates of Samaria, and all the prophets prophesied before them. Zedekiah the Canaanite made for himself iron horns, and said, "The Lord says, 'With these, you will gore Syria until it is consumed.'"

All the prophets prophesied in a similar manner, saying, "Go up to Remmath in Gilead, and it will be profitable, and the Lord will deliver it and the king of Syria into your hands."

The messenger that went to call Micah said to him, "Look, now, all the prophets speak with one mouth good concerning the king. Let your words be like the words of one of them, and speak good things."

Micah replied, "As Lord lives, whatever Lord will say to me, that I will speak."

He went to the king, and the king asked him, "Micah, will I go up to Remmath in Gilead to battle, or will I not?"

He said, "Go up, and Lord will deliver it into the hand of the king."

The king said to him, "How often will I make you sware, that you speak to me truth in the name of the Lord?"

He said, "None. I saw all Israel scattered on the mountains like a flock without a shepherd, and the Lord said, 'Isn't Lord the god of these? Let each one return to his home in peace."

The King of Israel said to Jehoshaphat king of Judah, "Didn't I tell you that this man does not prophesy good for me, for he speaks nothing but evil?"

Micah said, "Not so. It is not me. Listen to the word of Lord. Is it not so? I saw the god in Israel sitting on his throne, and all the army of the sky stood around him on his right hand and on his left. The Lord said, 'Who will deceive Ahab king of Israel, that he may go up and fall in Remmath in Gilead?' And one spoke one way, and another another way. There came out a spirit and stood before the Lord, and said, 'I will deceive him.' The Lord asked him, 'How?' He answered, 'I will go out, and will be a false spirit in the mouth of all his prophets.' He said, 'You will deceive him, yes, and will prevail, go out, and do so.' Now, look, the Lord has put a false spirit in the mouth of all your prophets, and the Lord has spoken evil against you."

Zedekiah, the son of Canaan, approached and slapped Micah on the cheek, and said, "What sort of a spirit of the Lord has spoken in you?"

Micah said, "Look, you will see on that day when you will go into an innermost room to hide there."

The king of Israel said, "Take Micah, and carry him away to Samaria, to the guardians of the city, and tell Joash the king's son to put him in prison, and to feed him with the bread of affliction and water of affliction until I return in peace."

Micah said, "If you return at all in peace, Lord has not spoken by me."

So the king of Israel went up, and Jehoshaphat king of Judah with him to Remmath in Gilead. The king of Israel said to Jehoshaphat king of Judah, I will disguise myself, and enter into the battle, and you put on my clothing."

So the king of Israel disguised himself and went into the battle. The king of Syria had ordered the thirty-two captains of his char- iots, "Don't attack the small or the great, but seek out the king of Israel only."

When the captains of the chariots saw Jehoshaphat king of Judah, they said, "This must be the king of Israel." They surrounded him about to fight against him, and Jehoshaphat called out. When the captains of the chariots saw that this was not the King of Israel, that turned from him.

One drew a bow with a good aim and struck the king of Israel between the lungs and the breast-plate, and he said to his charioteer, "Turn your hands, and take me away out of the battle, as I am wounded."

The war was turned on that day, and the king was standing on the chariot, against Syria from morning until evening, and he bled out of his wound to the bottom of the chariot and died in the evening. The herald of the army stood at sunset, and said, "Let every man go to his own city and his own land, for the king is dead."

They came to Samaria and buried the king in Samaria. They washed the chariot at the fountain of Samaria, and the swine and the dogs licked up the blood, and the prostitutes washed in the blood, according to the words of the Lord. The rest of the acts of Ahab, and all that he did, and the ivory house which he built, and all the cities which he built, look, are these things not written in the book of the Chronicles of the Kings of Israel?

Ahab slept with his fathers, and Ahaziah his son reigned in his place. Jehoshaphat the son of Asa reigned over Judah. In the fourth year of King Ahab of Israel, Jehoshaphat began to reign. Thirty-five years old he was, when he began to reign, and he reigned twenty-five years in Jerusalem. His mother's name was Azuba daughter of Salai. He followed in all the ways of Asa his father, and he did not turn from it, from doing that which was right in the eyes of the Lord. He did not destroy any of the bamahs, and the people still sacrificed and burnt incense on the bamahs. Jehoshaphat was at peace with the king of Israel. The rest of the acts of Jehoshaphat, and his mighty deeds, whatever he did, look, are these things not written in the book of the Chronicles of the Kings of Judah?

Jehoshaphat slept with his fathers and was buried by his fathers in the City of David his forefather, and Joram his son reigned in his place. Ahaziah son of Ahab reigned over Israel in Samaria. In the seventeenth year of King Jehoshaphat of Judah, Ahaziah son of Ahab began to reigned over Israel in Samaria, and continued for two years. He did that which was evil in the sight of the Lord and followed in the ways of Ahab his father, and in the way of Jezebel his mother, and in the sins of the house of Jeroboam the son of Nebat, who caused Israel to sin. He served Ba'als, and worshiped them, and provoked Lord the God of Israel, like to all that had been done before him.

# 4<sup>th</sup> Kingdoms: Chapter 1

The land of Moab rebelled from the rule of Israel after the death of King Ahab.

King Ahaziah fell through the floor of his attic in Samaria and was injured, and he sent messengers, and saying, "Go and inquire of Ba'al Myian,[1] the god[2] of Ekron, whether I will recover of this my sickness," and they went to inquire of him.

The messenger of the lord[3] said to Elijah[4] the Tishbite, "Rise, and go to meet the messengers of Ahaziah king of Samaria, and ask them, 'Is it because there is no god in Israel, that you go to inquire of Ba'al Myian, the god of Ekron? It will not be so.' The Lord[5] says, 'The bed on which you have laid down, you will not rise from, for you will certainly die.'"

Elijah went and spoke to them.

The messengers returned to him, and he asked them, "Why have you returned?"

They answered him, "A man came up to meet us, and said, 'Go, return to the king that sent you, and say to him, the Lord says, 'Is it because there is no god in Israel, that you go to inquire of Ba'al Myian, the god of Ekron? It will not be so! The bed on which you have laid down, you will not rise from, for you will certainly die.'"

When they returned and reported to the king what Elijah had said, he asked them, "What was the manner of the man who went up to meet you, and spoke to you these words?"

They answered him, "He was a hairy man, and girded with a leather girdle about his loins."

He said, "This is Elijah the Tishbite!"

He sent to him a captain and fifty of his soldiers, and he went up to him and found Elijah sitting on the top of a mountain. The captain of the fifty said to him "Prophet, the king has called you, come down."

Elijah answered and said to the captain of the fifty, "If I am a prophet, fire will come down out of the sky, and devour you and your fifty," and fire came down out of the sky, and devoured him and his fifty.

The king sent another captain with fifty more soldiers, and the captain of fifty spoke to him, and said, "Prophet, the king commands, 'Come down quickly.'"

Elijah answered him, "If I am a prophet, fire will come down out of the sky, and devour you and your fifty," and fire came down out of the sky, and devoured him and his fifty.

The king yet again sent a captain with fifty soldiers, and the third captain of fifty came, and knelt on his knees before Elijah, and begged him, and said to him, "Prophet, let my life, and the life of these fifty your servants, be precious in your eyes. Fire came down from the sky and devoured the two first captains and their fifty, and now, I beg, let my life be precious in your eyes."

The messenger of the Lord spoke to Elijah, and said, "Go down with him, do not be afraid of them," so Elijah rose up, and went down with him to the king.

Elijah said to him, "The Lord says, 'Why have you sent messengers to inquire of Ba'al Myian, the god of Ekron? It will not be so! The bed on which you have laid down, you will not rise from, for you will certainly die," and he died according to the word of the Lord which Elijah had spoken. The rest of the acts of Ahaziah which he did, look, are they not written in the book of the Chronicles of the kings of Israel?

Joram son of Ahab reigned over Israel in Samaria twelve years beginning in the eighteenth year of Jehoshaphat king of Judah, and he did that which was evil in the sight of the Lord, only not as much as his brothers, or as his much as his mother, and he removed the steles of Ba'al which his father made, and broke them in pieces. He also enjoyed the sins of the house of Jeroboam, who had led Israel in sin, and did not stop them. The Lord was very angry with the house of Ahab.

# 4ᵗʰ Kingdoms: Chapter 1 Notes

**1** Codex Vaticanus: Baal muian (ɃΑΑΛΜΥΙΑΝ). Translation: Baʻal of flies

- LXX 245: Baal (βΑΑΛ). Translation: Baʻal

- LXX 127: Baal muian cae prosochthisma (βΑΑΛ μυιΑν ↳Αι πϱοσοχθιϭμΑ). Translation: Baʻal of flies and troublesome things

- LXX 19: Baal muian prosochthisma (βΑΑΛ μυιΑν πϱοσοχθιϭμΑ). Translation: Baʻal of flies troublesome things

- Aleppo Codex: bôl zbwb (בַּעַל זְבוּב). Translation: Lord fly

- Leningrad Codex: Vaʼal zevuv (בַּעַל זְבוּב). Translation: Lord fly

- Targum Jerusalem: vaʼal zevuv (בַּעַל זְבוּב). Translation: Lord fly

The god in question is unknown within Canaanite archaeology. It is possible that the translators at the Library of Alexandria were referring to the Greek term Myiagros, 'he who chases off flies.' A number of early Greek cults seemed to have beliefs around chasing away flies, and therefore it is likely the ancient Pelesets in Canaan did as well.

The nature of the fly cults is unclear, however, a number of similar cults are noted lasting as late as the 3ʳᵈ century AD, including Myiagros at Alipheira in Arcadia, Zeus Apomyios in Elis at Olympia, Myiodes among the Akarnanians, and the Alipheiran cult. Based on the records of Pliny the Elder, the origin of the cult may have been an attempt to keep away swarms of disease-causing flies.

**2** Codex Vaticanus: theon (ΘΕΟΝ) Translation: god

- LXX 247: theôn (θϭ∞ν). Translation: god

- LXX 71: theon deute eperôtêsate dia tou baal muian prosôchthisma (θϭον Δϭυτϭ ϭπϭϱ∞τↄσΑτϭ ΔιΑ του ↳ΑΛΛ μυιΑν πϱοσ∞χθιϭμΑ). Translation: god, your inferior consultations through Baal of flies provoke

- Aleppo Codex: ålhy (אלהי). Translation: god

- Leningrad Codex: elohei (אֱלֹהֵי). Translation: god

- Targum Jerusalem: ta'avat (טָעֲוֹת). Translation: error

**3** Codex Vaticanus: angelos c̄u (ⲀⲄⲄⲈⲗⲟⲥⲕⲨ). Translation: messenger lord

- LXX 19: angelos theôn (ἀγγέλος θεῶν). Translation: messenger god

- Aleppo Codex: mlåk Yhwh (מלאך יהוה). Translation: messenger Yhwh

- Leningrad Codex: mal'ach Yehvah (מַלְאַךְ יְהוָֹה). Translation: messenger Yehwah

- Targum Jerusalem: mal'acha daYyah (מַלְאָכָא דַיְיָ). Translation: messenger of Yahw

**4** Codex Vaticanus: Êliou (ⲎⲗⲈⲒⲞⲨ)

- Codex Alexandrinus: Êliou (ⲎⲗⲒⲞⲨ)

- LXX 19: Êlian (ⲎλιⲀⲛ)

- Aleppo Codex: Ålyh (אליה)

- Leningrad Codex: Eliyyah (אֵלִיָּה)

- Targum Jerusalem: Eliyahu (אֵלִיָּהוּ)

The spelling of Elijah's name transitions in the Masoretic text from Ålyhw (אליהו), used in the first half of Kings (3<sup>rd</sup> Kingdoms) to Ålyh (אליה), used in the second half of Kings (4<sup>th</sup> Kingdoms), indicating that the two texts were translated into Hebrew from separate sources. Ålyh (אליה) is generally accepted as the older of the two variants, and it the source of the English transliteration of Elijah. The later name Ålyhw (אליהו) incorporated the Aramaic name Yahw (יהו), indicting that the first half of Masoretic Kings (3<sup>rd</sup> Kingdoms) was translated from an

Aramaic source, while the second half of Masoretic Kings (4<sup>th</sup> Kingdoms) was probably based on a Judahite or Samartian text. As the Greeks transliterated the name consistently in both 3<sup>rd</sup> and 4<sup>th</sup> Kingdoms, it is likely they were using Aramaic versions of both books.

**5** Codex Vaticanus: c̄s ( K̄C̄). Translation: lord (or main, chief, dominant, master)

- Aleppo Codex: Yhwh (יהוה)

- Leningrad Codex: Yehvah (יְהֹוָה)

- Targum Jerusalem: Yeyah (??). Translation: Yahw

Fragments of older Septuagint manuscripts still exist that contain the Aramaic version of the name, Yhw (יהו), transliterated into Greek as Iaô (Ιαω), however, none of the fragments of the books of 4<sup>th</sup> Kingdoms include the name.

# 4<sup>th</sup> Kingdoms: Chapter 2

When the Lord was going to take Elijah up to the sky in the whirlwind,[1] Elijah and Elisha left Gilgal, and Elijah said to Elisha, "Stay here, I beg you, for God has sent me to the sky."[2]

Elisha said, "As the Lord lives and your mind lives, I will not leave you," so they both traveled to the Temple of El.

The sons of the prophets who were in the Temple of El came to Elisha, and asked him, "Do you know, that the Lord is going to take your lord away from you this day?"

He answered, "Yes, I know it. Be silent."

Elijah said to Elisha, "Stay here, please, for the Lord has sent me to Jericho."

He said, "As the Lord lives and your mind lives, I will not leave you," and so they came to Jericho.

The sons of the prophets who were in Jericho approached Elisha, and said to him, "Do you know that the Lord is about to take away your master from you today?"

He answered, "Yes, I know it. Hold your peace."

Elijah said to him, "Stay here, please, for the Lord has sent me to the Jordan."

Elisha replied, "As the Lord lives and your mind lives, I will not leave you, and they both continued traveling."

Fifty men of the sons of the prophets went also, and they stood nearby a ways off, and both stood on the bank of Jordan. Elijah took his mantle, and wrapped it together, and struck the water, and the water was divided on this side and on that side, and they both traveled into the wilderness on dry ground. It came to pass while they were crossing over, that Elijah said to Elisha, "Ask what I will do for you before I am taken up away from you."

Elisha answered, "Let there be, please, a double portion of your spirit on me."

Elijah replied, "You have asked a difficult thing. If you will see me when I am taken up from you, then will it be so to you. If not, it will not be so."

It came to pass as they were going, they continued talking, and, saw a fire-vehicle and fire-horse,[3] and it separated them and Elijah was taken up in a storm[4] to the sky. Elisha saw, and cried out, "Father, father, the vehicle of Israel, and its rider!"[5] Then he saw him no more, and he took hold of his garments and tore them into two pieces.

Elisha picked up the mantle of Elijah, which fell from off of him, and Elisha returned and stood on the bank of the Jordan, and he took the mantle of Elijah and struck the water, and said, "Where is Lord the god of Elijah?"

He struck the waters, and they were divided here and there, and Elisha went over. The sons of the prophets who were in Jericho on the opposite side saw him, and said, "The spirit of Elijah has rested on Elisha."

They came to meet him, and paid respect to him, bowing to the ground, and to him, "Look now, here are with your servants, fifty strong men. Let them go now, and seek your lord. Perhaps the Wind Lord[6] has picked him up, but dropped him into the Jordan, or onto one of the mountains, or onto one of the hills."

Elisha replied, "Do not send them."

They pressed him until he was ashamed, and he said, "Send."

They sent fifty men, and searched three days, and did not find him. They returned to him, where he lived, in Jericho, and Elisha said, "Did I not tell to you, 'don't go?'"

The men of the city said to Elisha, "Look, the situation of the city is good, as our lord sees, but the waters are bad, and the ground barren."

Elisha ordered, "Bring me a new pitcher, and put salt in it."

They took one and brought it to him, and Elisha went out to the spring of the waters, and cast salt into it, and said, "The Lord says, 'I have healed these waters. There will not be any longer death here or barren land."

The waters were healed until this day also by the word that Elisha spoke. He from there to the Temple of El, and as he was going up by the road, some little children came out from the city, who mocked him, and said to him, "Go away, bald-head, go away."

He turned towards them, and saw them, and cursed them in the name of the Lord, and two bears out of the woods and tore the forty-two children apart. He went from there to Mount Carmel and returned from there to Samaria.

# 4th Kingdoms: Chapter 2 Notes

**1** Codex Vaticanus: synsismô (ⲤⲨⲚⲤⲈⲒⲤⲘⲰ)

- Codex Alexandrinus: synsismô (ⲤⲨⲚⲤⲒⲤⲘⲰ)

- LXX 707: theôn (συσσϭισμ∞). Translation: earthquake

- LXX 82: syssismon (συσσϭισμον). Translation: earthquake

- Aleppo Codex: sôrh (סערה). Translation: storm

- Leningrad Codex: se'arah (סְעָרָה). Translation: storm

- Targum Jerusalem: al'ola (עַלְעוֹלָא). Translation: whirlwind

The actual term here seems to not be understood by the translators in Alexandria, it is generally assumed that the Masoretic text maintain the correct term, as a 'with earthquake' taking Elijah to the sky doesn't seem likely. The Greeks had several terms that could have been used as a translation for 'storm,' including laelaps (λαιλαψ) meaning tornado, typhôs (τυφως) meaning cyclone, prêstêr (πρηστηρ) meaning gale, thyella (θυελλα) meaning squall, and aella (αελλα) meaning whirlwind. People were sometimes described as traveling via whirlwind to the sky or the moon in ancient Greco-Roman literature, such as Lucian's True History, and so it is unclear why the translators in Alexandria chose so use a word composed of the words 'with earthquake' unless the original word was not whirlwind, and they were unclear on what it meant.

If the Greek term was a transliteration of an Aramaic term instead of a translation, the Aramaic word would have been swssysm (ךֹׁ^ֹׁ^ֹׁ), meaning 'bird horses,' which does fit the context of the story. The presence of bird-horses in the Aramaic translations suggests that the text was altered in the Greek era, when the Philip the Phrygian was the high-priest at the Second Temple in Jerusalem, as the Phryrian god Sabazious flew on a flying horse, which was probably the origin of Zeus' winged horse, the Pegasus. The same term appears to have been in the Aramaic translation of 3rd Kingdoms, where the Greeks transliterated it as syssismos (συσσεισμός).

In the Masoretic verse of Kings that mirrored it, the Hebrew translation was ra'ash (רַעַשׁ), meaning 'loud noise' or 'commotion' in Hebrew and Aramaic. As the Hebrew translations do not correlate, the Judahite precursor to the Aramaic translation probably used different terms, and as the 'bird-horses' are almost certainly a Phyrgian alteration, the Hebrew term 'whirlwind' is imported.

**2** Codex Vaticanus: Baethêl (ΒΑΙΘΗΛ)

- LXX 707: Bethêl (βεθϊλ)

- LXX 19: Ιορδανου (ιοβΔΔνου). Translation: Jordan

- Aleppo Codex: Byt Âl (בֵּית אֵל). Translation: Temple (or house) of El (god)

- Leningrad Codex: veit-El (בֵּית־אֵל). Translation: Temple (or house) of El (god)

- Targum Jerusalem: veit El (בֵּית אֵל). Translation: Temple (or house) of El

The term Bethel meant several things in ancient Canaan. The term translates as 'house of god,' which can be translated as either 'Temple of God (or El)' or 'sky/heaven.' Bethel was worshiped as a god by the ancient Canaanites, the brother of El and Dagon according to Sanchuniathon, who referred to him as Baitylos, which is the name used in this translation when the god is denoted. The term can also be translated as 'meteorite' as meteorites were believed to be parts of the god Baitylos that had fallen to the Earth, and shrines were built around them. A Temple of El was built in the region by Jacob in Cosmic Genesis.

**3** Codex Vaticanus: arma pyros cae ippos pyros (ΑΡΜΑ ΠΥΡΟC ΚΑΙ ΙΠΠΟC ΠΥΡΟC). Translation: chariot fire (or lightning, wheat, grain) and horse (or cavalry) fire (or lightning, wheat, grain)

• Codex Alexandrinus: arma pyros cae ippoe pyros (ΑΡΜΑ ΠΥΡΟC ΚΑΙ ΙΠΠΟΙ ΠΥΡΟC). Translation: chariot fire (or lightning, wheat, grain) and mare (or cavalry) fire (or lightning, wheat, grain)

• Aleppo Codex: rkb åš wswsy åš (**רכב אש וסוסי אש**). Translation: vehicle-fire and horse fire

• Leningrad Codex: rechev-esh vesusei esh (רֶכֶב־אֵשׁ וְסוּסֵי אֵשׁ). Translation: vehicle-fire and horse (or stallion) fire

• Targum Jerusalem: retichin de'eshta vesusevan de'eshta (רְתִיכִין דְּאֶשְׁתָּא וְסוּסְוָן דְּאֶשְׁתָּא). Translation: in the center of fire and horses of fire

**4** Codex Vaticanus: synsismô ôs is ton o̅n̅ (CΥΝCΕΙCΜΩ ΩC ΕΙC ΤΟΝ O̅N̅). Translation: synsismô as (or since, because, how, where) into the vaulted sky (or universe, Uranus)

• Codex Alexandrinus: synsismô is ton ouranon (CΥΝCΙCΜΩ ΕΙC ΤΟΝ ΟΥΡΑΝΟΝ). Translation: synsismô into the vaulted sky (or universe, Uranus)

• LXX 19: syssismô eôs is ton ouranon (συσσ6ισμω 6ωc 6ιc τον ουβληθν). Translation: with earthquake into the vaulted sky (or universe, Uranus)

• Aleppo Codex: bsôrh hŠmym (**בסערה השמים**). Translation: in (or with) storm the Shamayim (or skies)

• Leningrad Codex: basse'arah haShamayim (בַּסְּעָרָה הַשָּׁמָיִם). Translation: in (or with) storm the Shamayim (or skies)

• Targum Jerusalem: be'il'ola letzeit shemaya (בְּעִלְעוֹלָא לְצֵית שְׁמַיָּא). Translation: in a storm that obeyed the sky

• As the Greek term syssismô (συσσεισμω) appears to be another transliteration of the Aramaic swssysm (לy^לyלy), indicating another Phrygian alteration, the Hebrew term 'storm' is imported.

**5** Codex Vaticanus: arma israêl cae ippeus autou (ΑΡΜΑ ΙϹΡΑΗΛ ΚΑΙ ΙΠΠΕΥϹ ΑΥΤΟΥ). Translation: chariot Israel and its rider (or charioteer)

• LXX 158: harma Israêl hippeus autou (ἁρμα ιϲραλλ ιππευϲ ἀυτου). Translation: chariot Israel its rider (or charioteer)

• Aleppo Codex: rkb yšrål wpršyw (רכב ישראל ופרשיו). Translation: in (or with) storm the Shamayim (or skies)

• Leningrad Codex: rekeb Yisra'el ufarashav (רֶכֶב יִשְׂרָאֵל וּפָרָשָׁיו). Translation: vehicle (or chariot) Israel and cavalier (or horseman) his (or its)

• Targum Jerusalem: lehon leYisra'el bitzluteih meretichin (לְהוֹן לְיִשְׂרָאֵל בִּצְלוֹתֵיה מֵרְתִיכִין). Translation: rising of Israel from sanctuary in it's center


**6** Codex Vaticanus: pneuma cyriou (ΠΝΕΥΜΑ ΚΥΡΙΟΥ). Translation: wind (or spirit) lord

• Aleppo Codex: rwh yhwh (רוח יהוה). Translation: wind (or spirit) Yhwh

• Leningrad Codex: ruach Yehvah (רוּחַ יְהֹוָה). Translation: wind (or spirit) Yehwah

• Targum Jerusalem: ruach min kodam Yeyah (רוּחַ מִן קֳדָם יְיָ). Translation: wind coming from Yahw

# 4ᵗʰ Kingdoms: Chapter 3

Joram the son of Ahab began to reign in Israel in the eighteenth year of Jehoshaphat king of Judah, and he reigned for twelve years. He did that which was evil in the sight of the Lord, only not as much his father, or as his mother, and he removed the steles of Ba'al[1] which his father had made. He continued to the sin of Jeroboam the son of Nebat, who made Israel sin, and he did not stop it. King Mosa of Moab was a shepherd, and he delivered to the king of Israel at the beginning of each year, a hundred thousand lambs, and a hundred thousand rams, with their wool. After the death of Ahab, the king of Moab rebelled against the king of Israel. King Joram went out on that day from Samaria and counted Israel. He sent to Jehoshaphat king of Judah, asking, "The king of Moab has rebelled against me. Will you go to war against Moab with me?"

He answered, "I will go. You are like me, and I am like you. My people are like your people, as my horses are like your horses," and he asked, "What route will I travel?"

He replied, "The road through the wilderness of Edom."

The king of Israel traveled with the king of Judah against the king of Edom, and they prepared gear for a seven days' journey, but there was no water for the army or the livestock that they took with them. The king of Israel said, "Alas! That the Lord should have called the three kings on their way, to give them into the hand of Moab."

Jehoshaphat asked, "Is there no prophet of the Lord here, that we may inquire through him of the Lord?"

One of the servants of the king of Israel answered, "There is Elisha son of Asaph, who washed the hands of Elijah."

Jehoshaphat said, "He has the word of the Lord."

The king of Israel, and Jehoshaphat king of Judah, and the king of Edom, went to him, and Elisha said to the king of Israel, "What have I to do with you? Go to the prophets of your father, and the prophets of your mother."

The king of Israel asked him, "Has the Lord called the three kings to deliver them into the hands of Moab?"

Elisha said, "As Lord Sabaoth[2] before whom I stood lives, only because I respect the presence of Jehoshaphat the king of Judah, I had seen you. Now, fetch me a harpist!"

As the harpist played, the hand of the Lord came on him, and he said, "The Lord says, 'Make this brook full of trenches,' as the Lord says, 'You will not see wind, neither will you see rain, yet this valley will be filled with water, and you, and your slaves, and your livestock will drink. This is a minor thing in the eyes of the Lord. I will also deliver Moab into your hand. You will strike every strong city, and you will cut down every good tree, and you will stop all wells of water, and spoil every good piece of land with stones."

In the morning, when the sacrifice was offered, waters came from the direction of Edom, and the land was filled with water. All of Moab heard that the three kings were coming to fight against them, and they cried out from every side, all who were dressed in a girdle, and they said, "Ho!" and stood on the border.

They rose early in the morning, and the sun rose on the waters, and Moab saw the waters on the opposite side red as blood. They said, "This is the blood of the sword, and the kings have fought, and each man has struck his neighbor. Now then, to the plunder, Moab!"

They entered into the camp of Israel, and Israel rose and struck Moab, and they fled from before them, and they slaughtered Moab as they went. They razed the cities, and threw every man his stone on every good piece of land and filled it. They stopped every well and cut down every good tree until they left only the stones of the wall knocked down, and the slingers surrounded the land and destroyed it. The king of Moab saw that the battle was lost, and he took with him seven hundred men that drew swords to cut through to the king of Edom, but they could not. He took his oldest son who he had intended to reign in his place and offered him up for a whole burnt offering on the walls. There was great indignation against Israel, and they departed from him and returned to their land.

# 4<sup>th</sup> Kingdoms: Chapter 3 Notes

**1** Codex Vaticanus: stêlas sentas stê tou baal (ᴄᴛʜᴀᴀᴄᴄᴇɴᴛᴀᴄᴄᴛʜ ᴛᴏʏʙᴀᴀᴧ). Translation: stele (or column) errected to the Ba'al

• Codex Coislinianus: stêlas tou baal (ᴄᴛʜᴀᴀᴄᴛᴏʏʙᴀᴀᴧ). Translation: stele (or column) of the Ba'al

• Aleppo Codex: mṣbt hbôl (מצבת הבעל). Translation: pillar (or tombstone) of the Ba'al (or lord, master)

• Leningrad Codex: matzevat habba'al (מַצְבַת הַבַּעַל). Translation: pillar (or tombstone) of the Ba'al (or lord, master)

• Targum Jerusalem: a'dei yat kamat be'ala (אַעְדֵי יַת קָמַת בְּעָלָא). Translation: that wooden erected lord

**2** Codex Vaticanus: c̄s tôn dynameôn (ᴋᴄᴛⲱɴᴀʏɴᴀᴍᴇⲱɴ). Translation: Lord of the forces

• Aleppo Codex: Yhwh ṣbâwt (יהוה צבאות). Translation: Yhwh forces (or army, war, warfare, service)

• Leningrad Codex: Yehvah tzeva'ovt (יְהוָה צְבָאוֹת). Translation: Yehwah forces (or army, war, warfare, service)

• Targum Jerusalem: Yeyah tzeva'ovt (יְיָ צְבָאוֹת). Translation: Yahw of desires

The Greek translations of the four books of Kingdoms also do not appear consistent at this point, with the term translated in 2<sup>nd</sup> and 3<sup>rd</sup> Kingdoms as 'of forces' (των δυνάμεων) being transliterated directly as Sabaoth (Σαβαωθ) in 1<sup>st</sup> and 4<sup>th</sup> Kingdoms, as well as in 1<sup>st</sup> Paralipomenon. In 4<sup>th</sup> Kingdoms, the term is translated both ways, indicating the text as redacted at some point. This indicates that the surviving version of 2<sup>nd</sup>, 3<sup>rd</sup>, and 4<sup>th</sup> Kingdoms found in the Septuagint manuscripts was probably based on Origen of Alexandria's Hexapla, published circa 240 AD, which itself drew on both the Old Greek translation, and the translation made the Jewish scholar Theodotion circa 150

AD. Theodotion retranslated the Septuagint into Greek from the Hebrew texts being used by Jews in the 2nd century. The surviving copies of 2nd and 3rd Kingdoms include both text that appears to have been redacted by the Hasmoneans, and text that appears to be pre-Hasmonean, strongly indicating it originated in the Hexapla. As both the Septuagint and Masoretic texts support the name Sabaoth having once been in this verse, it is restored in this translation, however, the evidence from 4th Kingdoms is that the name Iaw (יהוה) was not in Samuel until the Hasmonean redaction, several decades after the Greek translation at the Library of Alexandria, and therefore the translation of 'Lord Sabaoth' is used, as it appears in the Greek translations of 1st and 4th Kingdoms.

# 4<sup>th</sup> Kingdoms: Chapter 4

One of the wives of the sons of the prophets cried to Elisha, "Your servant my husband is dead, and you know that your servant was afraid of the Lord, and a creditor has come to take my two sons to be his slaves."

Elisha asked, "What can I do for you? Tell me what you have in the house."

She answered, "Your servant has nothing in the house except oil, which I anoint myself with."

He said to her, "Go and borrow empty vessels from your neighbors, borrow a lot of them. You will go in and close the door behind you and your sons, and you will pour out into these vessels, and take our those which are filled."

She left him and closed the door behind herself and her sons. They brought the vessels to her, and she poured into them until the vessels were filled. She said to her sons, "Bring more vessels."

They replied to her, "There are no more vessels."

Oil still remained, and she came and told the prophet Elisha, who said, "Go and sell the oil, and pay your debts. You and your sons will live off the remaining oil."

A day came when Elisha passed over to Shunem, and there was a great lady there, and she constrained him to eat bread. Whenever he went into the city, he turned aside to eat there. The woman said to her husband, "See now, I know that this is a holy prophet who comes over continually to us. Now, let's build an upper room for hims, a small place. Let us put there for him a bed, and a table, and a stool, and a candlestick, and it will come to pass that when he comes to us, he will stay there."

One day he went there and turned stayed in the upper room, and laid down. He said to Gehazi his servant, "Call me this Shunammite, and he called her, and she stood before him."

He said to him, "Say to her now, look you have taken all this trouble for us, what should I do for you? Have you any request to make to the king, or the captain of the army?"

She answered, "I live among my people."

He asked Gehazi, "What should we do for her?"

Gehazi his servant answered, "She has no son, and her husband is old."

He called her, and she stood by the door. Elisha said to her, "At this time next year, as the season is, you will be alive, and embrace a son."

She said, "No, my lord, do not lie to your servant."

The woman conceived, and carried a son at the very time, as the season was, being alive, as Elisha told her. The child grew, and when he went out to his father to the reapers, that he said to his father, "My head, my head," and his father told a servant, carry him to his mother. He carried him to his mother, and he lay on her knees till noon, and died. She carried him up and laid him on the bed of the prophet, and she shut the door on him and left.

She called her husband, and said, "Send now for me one of the young men, and one of the donkeys, and I will ride quickly to the prophet, and return."

He said, "Why are you going to him today? It is neither a new moon or a Sabbath."

She answered, "Peace, it is okay," and she saddled the donkey, and said to her servant, "Be quick and go! Don't stop, unless I tell you. Go, and you will travel until you come to the prophet on Mount Carmel."

She rode and came to the prophet on the mountain, and when Elisha saw her coming, he said to Gehazi his servant, "See now, that Shunammite comes. Run to meet her, and ask, 'Are you well? Peace! Is your husband well? Is the child well?'"

She answered, "All is well."

She came to Elisha in the mountain and grabbed his feet, and Gehazi approached and pushed her away."

Elisha said, "Leave her alone, as her mind is grieved, and the Lord has hidden it from me and has not told it to me."

She said, "Did I ask a son of my lord? Didn't I say, 'Don't lie to me?'"

Elisha said to Gehazi, "Prepare yourself, and take my wand[1] in your hand, and go. If you meet any man, you will not bless him, and if a man salutes you, you will not answer him, and you will lay my wand on the child's face."

The mother of the child said, "As the Lord lives and as your mind lives, I will not leave you."

Elisha rose and followed after her. Gehazi went on ahead of her and laid his wand on the child's face, but there was no voice or hearing. So he returned to meet him and told him, "The child will not wake."

Elisha went into the house, and the dead child was laid on his bed. Elisha entered the house, and the two closed the door behind themselves and prayed to the Lord. He went up, and lay on the child, and put his mouth on his mouth, and his eyes on his eyes, and his hands on his hands, and laid himself on him, and the flesh of the child grew warm. He returned and paced around in the house, and he went up and laid himself on the child seven times, and the child opened his eyes. Elisha told Gehazi, "Call the Shunammite!"

So he called her, and she came to him, and Elisha said, "Take your son."

The woman went in, and fell at his feet, and paid respect, bowing to the ground, and she took her son and left. Elisha returned to Gilgal, and famine was in the land. The sons of the prophets sat before him, and Elisha said to his servant, "Set on the great pot, and boil stew for the sons of the prophets."

He went out into the field to gather plants, and found a vine in the field, and gathered from it wild bitter apples until his garment was full, and he threw them into the cauldron of stew, for they did not know them. He poured it out for the men to eat, and when they were eating of the stew, they cried out, "There is death in the pot, prophet," and they could not eat. He said, "Take meal, and throw it into the pot."

Elisha said to his servant Gehazi, "Pour out for the people, and let them eat," and there was no longer anything poisonous in the pot.

A man came from the House of Shershah² and brought to the prophet twenty barley loaves and cakes of figs, of the first-fruits. He said, "Give to the people, and let them eat."

His servant asked, "Why should I set this before a hundred men?"

He said, "Give to the people, and let them eat, as the Lord says, 'They will eat and leave.'

They ate and left, according to the word of the Lord.

# 4<sup>th</sup> Kingdoms: Chapter 4 Notes

**1** Codex Vaticanus: bactêrian (ΒΑΚΤΗΡΙΑΝ). Translation: wand (or cane, baton, staff)

- Aleppo Codex: mšônt (מִשְׁעַנְת). Translation: staff (or wand, crutch)

- Leningrad Codex: mish'anti (מִשְׁעֶנְתָּ). Translation: staff (or wand, crutch)

- Targum Jerusalem: chuterei (חוּטְרֵי). Translation: staff


**2** Codex Vaticanus: Baethsarisa (ΒΑΙΘΣΑΡΙΣΑ)

- Aleppo Codex: bôl šlšh (בַּעַל שָׁלִשָׁה). Translation: Ba'al Shlshh

- Leningrad Codex: ba'al shalishah (בַּעַל שָׁלִשָׁה). Translation: the lord of three (in Aramaic)

- Targum Jerusalem: Roma (רוֹמָא). Translation: Rome

Many texts exist from the Second Temple era that use the terms Beth and Ba'al interchangeably as the beginning of town's names. Both the names Sarisa and Shalishah appear to be derived from the Aramaic word šeršah (ﹲﹲﹲﹲ), meaning 'root,' 'ground,' 'foundation,' or 'beginning.' The Greek is a direct transliteration, while the Hebrew is a transliteration where the R (ﹲ) was mistranslated as an L (ל).

# 4th Kingdoms: Chapter 5

Now Naaman, the captain of the army of Syria, was a great man before his master, and highly respected, because through him the Lord had saved to Syria, and the man was mighty in strength, but a leper. The Syrians went out in small raiding bands, and captured in the land of Israel a young girl: and she waited on Naaman's wife.

She said to her mistress, "If only my lord was before the prophet of God in Samaria, then he would recover him from his leprosy."

She went in and told her lord, and said, "The girl from the land of Israel has said this."

The king of Syria said to Naaman, "Go, go and I will send a letter to the king of Israel."

He went and took in his hand ten talents of silver, and six thousand pieces of gold, and ten changes of robes. He brought the letter to the King of Israel, saying, "Now then, as soon as this letter will reach you, look, I have sent to you my servant Naaman, and you will cure him of his leprosy."

When the king of Israel read the letter, he tore his garments, and said, "Am I God, to kill and to make alive, that this man is sent to me to cure him of his leprosy? Consider, however, please, and see that this man seeks an occasion against me."

When Elisha heard that the king of Israel had torn his garments, he sent word to the king of Israel, "Why have you torn your garments? Let Naaman, please, come to me, and let him know that there is a prophet in Israel."

So Naaman came with horse and chariot and stood at the door of the house of Elisha. Elisha sent a messenger to him, saying, "Go and wash seven times in the Jordan, and your flesh will return to you, and you will be cleansed."

Naaman was angry, and departed, and said, "Look, I said, 'He will come out to me, and stand, and call on the name of his god, and lay his hand on the place, and heal the leprosy. Aren't the Abana and Pharpar, rivers of Damascus, better than all the waters of Israel? May I not go and wash in them, and be clean?" and he turned and went away in a rage.

His servants approached and asked him, "Suppose the prophet had asked a great thing to you, would you not do it? Yet he has only told you, 'Wash, and be cleansed.'"

So Naaman went down, and dipped himself seven times in the Jordan, following the word of Elisha, and his flesh returned to him like the flesh of a little child, and he was cleansed. He and all his company returned to Elisha, and he came and stood in front of him, and said, "Look, I know that there is no god in all the earth, other than in Israel, and now receive a blessing of your servant."

Elisha said, "As the Lord lives, before who I stand, I will not take one."

He insisted he take one, but he would not. Naaman said, "Well then, if not, let there be given to your servant, please, the load of a yoke of mules. and you will give me of the red earth, for from now on your servant will not offer whole burnt offering or sacrifice to other gods, but only to the Lord because of this thing. And let the Lord be propitious to your servant when my master goes into the house of Rimmon to worship there, and he will lean on my hand, and I will bow down in the house of Rimmon when he bows down in the house of Rimmon, even let the Lord, please, be merciful to your servant in this matter."

Elisha replied to Naaman, "Go in peace," and he departed from him a little way.

Gehazi the servant of Elisha said, "Look, my Lord has spared this Syrian Naaman, so as not to take from his hand what he has brought. As the Lord lives, I will certainly run after him, and take something from him."

So Gehazi followed after Naaman, and Naaman saw him running after him, and turned back from his chariot to meet him. Gehazi said, "All is well. My master has sent me, saying, "Look, two young men have just come to me from the sons of the prophets of Mount Ephraim. Please, give them a talent of silver, and two changes of clothing."

Naaman said, "Take two talents of silver."

He took two talents of silver in two bags, and two changes of clothing, and put them on two of his slaves, and they carried them before him. He came to a secret place, and took them from their hands, and hid them in the house, and dismissed the men. He went in and stood before his master, and Elisha asked him, "Where have you come from, Gehazi?"

Gehazi answered, "Your servant has not been here or there."

Elisha said to him, "Didn't my heart go with you when the man returned from his chariot to meet you? Now you have received silver, and now you have received clothing, and olive yards, and vineyards, and sheep, and oxen, and men-slaves, and girl-slaves. The leprosy of Naaman will cling to you, and your seed forever."

He left his presence, leprous as snow.

# 4<sup>th</sup> Kingdoms: Chapter 6

The sons of the prophets said to Elisha, "Look now, the place in which we live with you is too small for us. Let us go, please, to the Jordan, and take from there each man a beam, and build a house there for ourselves."

He answered, "Go."

One of them asked politely, "Come with your servants."

He answered, "I will go," and he went with them, and they came to the Jordan and began to cut down trees.

While one was cutting down a beam, and the ax-head fell into the water, and he cried out, "Alas, Master!" as he could not see it.

The prophet asked, "Where did it fall?" and he showed him the place. He snapped off a stick and threw it in there, and the ax-head floated to the surface. He said, "Pick it up," and he reached out his hand, and took it.

The king of Syria was at war with Israel, and he consulted with his servants, saying, "I will camp in such a place."

Elisha sent to the king of Israel, saying, "Pay attention that you do not pass by that place, for the Syrians are hidden there."

The king of Israel sent scouts to the place which Elisha mentioned to him and saved himself from going there. The mind of the king of Syria was very much disturbed concerning this thing, and he called his servants, and said to them, "Will you not tell me who betrays me to the king of Israel?"

One of his servants said, "No, my lord, my king, for Elisha the prophet is in Israel reports to the king of Israel all the words whatever you may say, even from the closet in your bedroom."

He ordered, "Go, find this man, and I will send some to capture him."

They sent word to him, saying, "Look, he is in Dothan."

He sent horses and chariots there, with a mighty army that came by night and surrounded the city.

The servant of Elisha rose up early and went out, and saw an army surrounding the city, and horses and chariots. The servant asked him, "Master, what will we do?"

Elisha said, "Don't be afraid, for they who are with us, are more than they who are with them."

Elisha prayed, "Lord, please open the eyes of the servant, and let him see."

The Lord opened his eyes, and he saw the mountain was covered with horses, and there were chariots of fire around Elisha. They came down to him, and he prayed to the Lord, and said, "Strike, please, this nation with blindness." He struck them with blindness, according to the word of Elisha.

Elisha said to them, "This is not the city, and this is not the road. Follow me, and I will bring you to the man whom you seek."

He led them away to Samaria. It came to pass when they entered into Samaria, that Elisha said, "Please, Lord, open their eyes and let them see."

The Lord opened their eyes, and they saw they were in the middle of Samaria. When he saw them, the king of Israel asked Elisha, "Will I not completely slaughter them, my father?"

He said, "You will not slaughter them unless you would slaughter those whom you have taken captive with your sword and with your bow. Set bread and water out for them, and let them eat and drink, and return to their master."

He set before them a great feast, and they ate and drank, and he dismissed them and they departed to their master. The raiding bands of Syria stopped coming into the land of Israel. After this, the son of Arad king of Syria gathered all his army, and went out, and besieged Samaria. There was a great famine in Samaria, and, look, they besieged it, until a donkey's head was valued at fifty pieces of silver, and a quarter of a kav[1] of dove's dung at five pieces of silver. The king of Israel was passing by on the wall, and a woman cried to him, saying, "Help, my lord, my king."

He replied to her, "Unless the Lord helps you, from where will I help you? From the grain-floor, or from the wine-press? What is the matter with you?"

The woman answered him, "This woman said to me, 'Give your son, and we will eat him today, and we will eat my son tomorrow.' So we boiled my son and ate him, and I said to her on the second day, 'Give your son and let us eat him,' and she has hidden her son."

When the king of Israel heard the words of the woman, he tore his garments. He passed by on the wall, and the people saw sackcloth covering his body. He said, "God do likewise to me and more also, if the head of Elisha will stay on him this day!"

Elisha was sitting in his house, and the elders were sitting with him, and the king sent a man before him before the messenger came to him, he also said to the elders, "Do you see that this son of a murderer has sent to take away my head? See, as soon as the messenger will come, shut the door, and forcibly detain him at the door, is not the sound of his master's feet behind him?"

While he was yet speaking with them, a messenger came to him, and he said, "Look, this evil is from the Lord. Why should I wait for the Lord any longer?"

# 4ᵗʰ Kingdoms: Chapter 6 Notes

**1** Codex Vaticanus: cabou (ΚΑΒΟΥ)

- Aleppo Codex: qb (קב)

- Leningrad Codex: kav (קָב)

- Targum Jerusalem: kabba (קַבָּא)

The kav was a dry measurement used in ancient Judea and Samaria, equal to approximately 1.5 liters.

# 4<sup>th</sup> Kingdoms: Chapter 7

Elisha said, "Listen to the word of the Lord! The Lord says, 'As at this time, tomorrow a measure of fine flour will be sold for a shekel, and two measures of barley for a shekel, at the gates of Samaria."

The officer on whose hand the king rested, answered Elisha, "Look, even if the Lord will make flood-gates in the sky, how will this thing be?"

Elisha said, "Look, you will see with your eyes, but will not eat it."

There were four leprous men by the gate of the city, and one said to his neighbor, "Why do we sit here until we die? If we say, 'Let us go into the city,' then there is a famine in the city, and we will die there, and if we sit here, then we will die. Now then come, and let us attack the camp of the Syrians. If they should capture us alive, then we will live, and if they should put us to death, then we will only die."

They got up while it was still night, to go into the camp of Syria. They came into part of the camp of Syria, and saw there was no one there. The Lord had made the army of Syria hear the sounds of chariots, and a sound of horses, and the sound of a great army, and the men said, "The king of Israel has hired the kings of the Cypriots[1] against us, and the kings of Egypt have come against us!"

They rose and fled while it was still dark, and left their tents, and their horses, and their donkeys in the camp as they were, as they fled for their lives. The lepers entered a little way into the camp, and went into one tent, and ate and drank, and took the silver and gold and clothing, and they left and returned, and entered into another tent, and took from there and went and hid the spoil. One man said to his neighbor, "We are not doing well like this. This day is a day of good news, and we keep quiet, and are waiting until the morning light, and will find problems. Come, and let us go into the city, and report to the house of the king."

So they went and called at the gate of the city, and reported to them, "We went into the camp of Syria, and, look, there is not there a man, or a voice of man, only tied horses and donkeys, and their tents as they were."

The porters cried out loud and reported to the house of the king within. The king rose up by night, and said to his servants, "I will now tell you what the Syrians have done to us. They knew that we are hungry, and they have gone out from the camp and hidden in the fields, saying, 'They will come out of the city, and we will catch them alive, and go into the city.'"

One of his servants answered, "Let them take five of the horses that are left, which are left here. Look, they are all the number left from all the multitude of Israel, and we will send them there and see.

They sent two horsemen, and the king of Israel sent them to follow the king of Syria, ordering, "Go, and see."

They followed them even as far as the Jordan, and all the road was littered with garments and vessels, which the Syrians had dropped in their panic. The messengers returned and brought word to the king, and the people went out and plundered the camp of Syria, and a measure of fine flour was sold for a shekel, according to the word of the Lord, and two measures of barley for a shekel. The king appointed the officer on whose hand the king leaned to have command at the gate, and the people trampled on him in the gate, and he died, as the prophet had said, who spoke when the messenger went to him.

So it came to pass, as Elisha had told to the king, "Two measures of barley will be sold for a shekel, and a measure of fine flour for a shekel, and it will be at this time tomorrow in the gate of Samaria."

The officer had answered Elisha, and said, "Look, even if the Lord will make flood-gates in the sky, how will this thing be?"

Elisha had said, "Look, you will see it with your eyes, but you will not eat it."

It was so, for the people trampled on him at the gate, and he died.

# 4ᵗʰ Kingdoms: Chapter 7 Notes

1 Codex Vaticanus: Chettaeôn (ϪЄΤΤΑΙШΝ)

• Aleppo Codex: Ḥtym (חתים)

• Leningrad Codex: Chittim (חִתָּים)

• Targum Jerusalem: Chitta'ei (חִתָּאֵי)

As the term referred to the entire island of Cyprus in Aramaic, the translations of 'Cyprus' and 'Cypriots' are used here.

# 4ᵗʰ Kingdoms: Chapter 8

Elisha said to the woman, whose son he had resurrected to life, "Rise, and go with your household, and stay wherever you may stay, for the Lord has called for a famine on the land. It has come on the land for seven years. The woman rose, and did according to the word of Elisha, both she and her household, and they stayed in the land of the Gentiles seven years. After the end of the seven years, the woman returned out of the land of the Gentiles to the city, and went to ask the king for her house and for her lands.

The king spoke to Gehazi the servant of Elisha the prophet, saying, "Tell me, please, all the great things which Elisha has done."

As he was telling the king how he had resurrected to life the dead son, the woman whose son Elisha resurrected to life came to the king asking for her house and for her lands. Gehazi said, "My lord, my king, this is the woman, and this is her son, whom Elisha resurrected to life."

The king asked the woman, and she told him, and the king appointed her a eunuch, saying, "Restore all that was hers and all the fruits of the field from the day that she left the land until now."

Elisha traveled to Damascus, and the king of Syria the son of Arad was ill, and they brought him word, saying, "The prophet has come here."

The king said to Hazael, "Take in your hand a gift, and go to meet the prophet, and inquire of the Lord through him, "Will I live?"

Hazael went to meet him, and he took a gift in his hands, and all the good things of Damascus, forty camel loads, and came and stood before him, and said to Elisha, "Your son, the son of Arad, the king of Syria, has sent me to you to inquire, "Will I recover of my disease?"

Elisha answered, "Go, say, 'You will certainly live, yet the Lord has shown me that you will certainly die."

He stood before him frozen in confusion until he was ashamed, and the prophet wept. Hazael asked, "Why does my lord cry?"

He answered, "Because I know all the evil that you will do to the Israelites. You will completely destroy their strongholds with fire, and you will kill their best men with the sword, and you will dash their infants against the ground, and their women with children you will rip apart."

Hazael asked, "Who is your servant? A dead dog, that he should do this thing?"

Elisha said, "The Lord has shown me you ruling over Syria."

He departed from Elisha and went to his lord, and he asked him, "What did Elisha tell you?"

He answered, "He said to me, 'You will certainly live.'"

The next day he took a thick rug, and dipped it in water, and put it on his face, and he died, and Hazael reigned in his place. In the fifth year of Joram the son of Ahab king of Israel, and while Jehoshaphat was king of Judah, and Joram the son of Jehoshaphat was king of Judah he began to reign. Thirty-two years old he was when he began to reign, and he reigned eight years in Jerusalem. He followed in the ways of the kings of Israel, as the house of Ahab did, as the daughter of Ahab was his wife. He did that which was evil in the sight of the Lord. But the Lord would not destroy Judah for David his servant's sake, as he said he would give a light to him and to his sons continually.

In his days Edom revolted from under the hand of Judah, and they declared a king for themselves. Joram went up to Zair, and all the chariots that were with him, and it came to pass after he had risen, that he slaughtered Edom who surrounded him, and the captains of the chariots and the people fled to their tents. Yet Edom revolted from under the rule of Judah until this day. Then Libnah revolted at that time. The rest of the acts of Joram, and all that he did, look, are these not written in the book of the Chronicles of the Kings of Judah? So Joram slept with his fathers and was buried with his fathers in the city of David, his fore-father, and Ahaziah his son reigned in his place.

In the twelfth year of Joram the son of Ahab king of Israel, Ahaziah son of Joram began to reign. Ahaziah was 22 years old when he began to reign, and he reigned for one year in Jerusalem. The name of his mother was Athaliah, the daughter of Omri king of Israel. He followed in the ways of the house of Ahab and did that which was evil in the sight of the Lord, like the house of Ahab did. He went with Joram the son of Ahab to war against King Hazael of the Syrians at Ramah in Gilead, and the Syrians wounded Joram. King Joram returned to be healed of the wounds in Jezreel, the wounds they had inflicted on him in Ramah when he fought with Hazael king of Syria. Ahaziah son of Joram went down to see Joram the son of Ahab in Jezreel because he was sick.

# 4th Kingdoms: Chapter 9

Elisha the prophet called one of the sons of the prophets, and said to him, "Prepare yourself, and take this jar of oil in your hand, and go to Ramah in Gilead. Enter and will see Jehu the son of Jehoshaphat the son of Nimshi, and will go in and make him rise up from among his brothers, and will bring him into a secret room. You will take the jar of oil, and pour it on his head, and say, "The Lord says, 'I have anointed you king over Israel,' and you will open the door, and run, and don't wait."

The young man, the prophet went to Ramah in Gilead. He went to where the captains of the army were sitting, and he said, "I have a message for you, captain."

Jehu asked, "For which of all us?"

He answered, "For you, captain."

He rose and went into the house, and he poured the oil on his head, and said to him, "The Lord God in Israel says, 'I have anointed you to be king over the people of the Lord, even over Israel. You will completely destroy the house of Ahab your master from before me and will avenge the blood of my servants the prophets, and the blood of all the servants of the Lord, at the hand of Jezebel, and at the hand of the whole house of Ahab, and you will completely cut off from the house of Ahab every male, and him that is shut up and left in Israel. I will make the house of Ahab like the house of Jeroboam the son of Nebat, and as the house of Baasha the son of Ahijah. The dogs will eat Jezebel in the portion of Jezreel, and there will be none to bury her."

He opened the door and fled. Jehu went out to the servants of his lord, and asked him, "Is all well? Why did the mad man come to you?"

He answered them, "You know the man and his message."

They said, "Is it wrong? Tell us now."

Jehu said to them, "He told me this," saying, "and he said, 'The Lord says "I have anointed you to be king over Israel.""'"

When they heard it, they rushed, and took every man his garment, and put it under him on the top of the stairs, and blew with the trumpet, and said, "Jehu is king!"

So Jehu the son of Jehoshaphat the son of Nimshi conspired against Joram, and Joram was defending Ramah in Gilead, he and all Israel, because of Hazael king of Syria. King Joram had returned to be healed in Jezreel of the wounds which the Syrians had given him, in his war with Hazael king of Syria. Jehu said, "If your heart is with me, let there not leave out of the city one fugitive, to go and report to Jezreel."

Jehu rode and advanced, and traveled to Jezreel, for Joram king of Israel was getting healed in Jezreel of the arrow-wounds where the Syrians had wounded him in Ramah in the war with Hazael king of Syria, for he was strong and a mighty man and Ahaziah king of Judah had come down to see Joram. There was a watchman on the tower of Jezreel and saw the dust made by Jehu as he approached, and he shouted, "I see dust."

Joram said, "Take a horseman, and send to meet them, and let him say, Peace."

A horseman went to meet them, and said, "The king says, Peace."

Jehu said, "What have you to do with peace? Follow me."

The watchman reported, "The messenger went to them, and has not returned."

He sent another horseman, and he came to him, and said, "The king says, 'Peace.'"

Jehu said, "What have you to do with peace? Follow me!"

The watchman reported, "He went out to them, and has not returned. The driver drives Jehu the son of Nimshi, and is furious with speed."

Joram said, "Get ready."

The chariot was prepared, and Joram the king of Israel went out, and Ahaziah king of Judah, each in his chariot, and they went to meet Jehu and found him in the portion of Nobah the Jezreelite.

When Joram saw Jehu, he asked, "Is it peace, Jehu?"

Jehu said, "How can it be peace? When there is yet the prostitutes of your mother Jezebel, and her sorcerers are abundant?"

Joram turned and fled, and said to Ahaziah, "Treachery, Ahaziah!"

Jehu bent his bow with his full strength and struck Joram between his arms, and his arrow went out through his heart, and he fell to his knees. Jehu said to Bidkar his chief officer, "Throw him to the ground of Nobah the Jezreelite, for I and you remember, riding as we were on chariots after Ahab his father, that the Lord took up this burden against him, saying, "Certainly, I have seen yesterday the blood of Nobah, and the blood of his sons. The Lord says, 'I will recompense him in this portion.' Now then, please, take him up and cast him into the portion, according to the word of the Lord."

Ahaziah king of Judah saw it and fled by the way of Bethan. Jehu chased after him, and said, "Kill him as well."

One struck him in the chariot at the Ascent of Ai, (which is Ibleam), and he fled to Megiddo and died there. His servants put him on a chariot and brought him to Jerusalem, and they buried him in his sepulcher in the City of David. In the eleventh year of Joram king of Israel, Ahaziah began to reign over Judah. Jehu came to Jezreel, and Jezebel heard of it, and colored her eyes, and adorned her head, and looked through the window. Jehu entered into the city, and she said, "Has Zimri, the murderer of his master, peace?"

He lifted his face towards the window, and saw her, and said, "Who are you? Come down with me."

Two eunuchs looked down towards him. He said, "Throw her down."

They threw her down, and some of her blood was sprinkled on the wall, and on the horses, and they trampled on her. Jehu went in and ate and drank, and said, "Look after this cursed woman, and bury her, for she is a king's daughter."

They went to bury her, but they found nothing of her but the skull, and the feet, and the palms of her hands. They returned and told him. He said, "It is the word of the Lord, which he spoke by the hand of Elijah the Tishbite, when he said, 'In the portion of Jezreel will the dogs eat the flesh of Jezebel. The carcass of Jezebel will be as dung on the face of the field in the portion of Jezreel so that they will not say, This is Jezebel.'

# 4<sup>th</sup> Kingdoms: Chapter 10

Ahab had seventy sons in Samaria. Jehu wrote a letter, and sent it into Samaria to the rulers of Samaria, and to the elders, and to the guardians of the children of Ahab, saying, "Now then, as soon as this letter has reached you, whereas there are with you the sons of your master, and chariots and horses, and fortified cities, and arms, you should search out the best and strongest among your master's sons, and set him on the throne of his father, and fight for the house of your master."

They were greatly afraid, and said, "Look, two kings could not stand before him, and how will we stand?"

So they who were in command of the house, and they who were in command of the city, and the elders and the guardians, sent to Jehu, saying, "We are your servants, and whatever you will say to us we will do. We will not make any man king. We will do that which is right in your eyes."

Jehu wrote them a second letter, saying, "If you are for me, and listen to my voice, take the heads of the men your master's sons, and bring them to me at this time tomorrow in Jezreel."

The king had seventy sons, and these great men of the city brought them up. When the letter came to them, that they took the king's sons, and killed them, even seventy men, and put their heads in baskets, and sent them to him at Jezreel.

A messenger came and told him, saying, "They have brought the heads of the king's sons."

He said, "Lay them in two heaps by the door of the gate until the morning."

The morning came, and he went out, and stood, and said to all the people, "You are righteous. Look, I conspired against my master, and killed him, but who killed all these? See now that there will not fall to the ground anything of the word of the Lord which the Lord spoke against the house of Ahab, for the Lord had performed all that he spoke of by the hand of his servant Elijah."

Jehu killed all that were left of the house of Ahab in Jezreel, and all his great men, and his acquaintance, and his priests, so as not to leave him any remnant. He arose and went to Samaria, and he was in the house of sheep-shearing in the way. Jehu found the brothers of Ahaziah king of Judah, and asked, "Who are you?"

They answered, "We are the brothers of Ahaziah, and we have come down to salute the sons of the king and the sons of the queen."

He ordered, "Capture them alive." They executed them later at the shearing-house, all 42 men. He did not leave a man alive from among them.

He went there and found Jehonadab the son of Rechab coming to meet him, and he saluted him, and Jehu asked him, "Is your heart right with my heart, as my heart is with your heart?"

Jehonadab answered, "It is."

Jehu said, "If it is, then give me your hand." He gave him his hand, and he took him up with him in the chariot.

He said to him, "Come with me, and see me zealous for Lord Sabaoth."[1] He made him sit in his chariot.

He entered into Samaria and slaughtered all that were left of Ahab in Samaria, until he had completely annihilated them, following the orders of the Lord, which he spoke to Elijah. Jehu gathered all the people, and said to them, "Ahab served Ba'al a little, Jehu will serve him a lot! Now then all you the prophets of Ba'al call all his servants and his priests to me. Don't let a man be lacking, for I have a great sacrifice to offer to Ba'al. Everyone who will be missing will die!" however, Jehu was being deceptive, so he might murder the servants of Ba'al.

Jehu said, "Sanctify a solemn festival to Ba'al," and they made a proclamation. Jehu sent throughout all Israel, saying, "Now then let all Ba'al's servants, and all his priests, and all his prophets come, let none be missing. I am going to offer a great sacrifice! Whoever is missing, will not live!"

So all the servants of Ba'al came, and all his priests, and all his prophets. There was no one left who did not come. They entered the temple of Ba'al, and the Temple of Ba'al was filled from one end to the other. He said to the man who was in charge of the house of the wardrobe, "Bring out a robe for all the servants of Ba'al."

The keeper of the robes brought them out. Jehu and Jehonadab the son of Rechab entered into the Temple of Ba'al, and said to the servants of Ba'al, "Look, and see if there is any among you of the servants of the Lord, or only the servants of Ba'al, by themselves."

He went in to offer sacrifices and whole burnt offerings, and Jehu set for himself eighty men outside, and said, "Every man who will escape from the men who I bring into your hands, whoever spares him will lose his own life."

When he had finished offering the whole burnt offering, Jehu said to the infantrymen and to the officers, "Go in and kill them! Don't let a man escape!"

So they slaughtered them with the edge of the sword, and the infantry and the officers threw the bodies out and went to the city of the Temple of Ba'al. They brought out the stele of Ba'al and burnt it. They tore down the steles of Ba'al and made his temple into a latrine until this day. So Jehu abolished Ba'al out of Israel.

Nevertheless, Jehu did not stop from following the sins of Jeroboam the son of Nebat, who led Israel in sin. These were the golden cows in the Temple of El and in Dan. The Lord said to Jehu, "Because of all your deeds in which you have acted well in doing that which was right in my eyes, according to all things which you have done to the house of Ahab as they were in my heart, your sons to the fourth generation will sit on the throne of Israel."

But Jehu did not listen, to follow in the law of Lord the God of Israel with all his heart. He did not stop following the sins of Jeroboam, who made Israel sin. In those days the Lord began to cut Israel short, and Hazael slaughtered them in every frontier of Israel, from the Jordan east through all the land of Gilead belonging to the Gadites, of Gadi and that of Reuben, and of Manasseh, from Aroer, which is on the brink of the brook of Arnon, and Gilead and Bashan. The rest of the acts of Jehu, and all that he did, and all his might, and the wars in which he engaged, are these things not written in the book of the Chronicles of the Kings of Israel? Jehu slept with his fathers, and they buried him in Samaria, and Jehoahaz his son reigned in his place. The days in which Jehu reigned over Israel were twenty-eight years in Samaria.

# 4<sup>th</sup> Kingdoms: Chapter 10 Notes

**1** Codex Vaticanus: tô Curiô Sabaôth (ⲦⲰⲔⲨⲢⲓⲰⳞⲀⲃⲀⲰⲑ). Translation: the Lord Sabaoth

- Aleppo Codex: lYhwh (לִיהוה). Translation: the Yhwh

- Leningrad Codex: laYhvah (לִיהֹוָה). Translation: the Yhwah

- Targum Jerusalem: Yeyah (??). Translation: Yahw

The Greek translations of the four books of Kingdoms also do not appear consistent at this point, with the term translated in 2<sup>nd</sup> and 3<sup>rd</sup> Kingdoms as 'of forces' (των δυναμεων) being transliterated directly as Sabaoth (Σαβαωθ) in 1<sup>st</sup> and 4<sup>th</sup> Kingdoms, as well as in 1<sup>st</sup> Paralipomenon. In 4<sup>th</sup> Kingdoms, the term is translated both ways, indicating the text as redacted at some point. This indicates that the surviving version of 2<sup>nd</sup>, 3<sup>rd</sup>, and 4<sup>th</sup> Kingdoms found in the Septuagint manuscripts was probably based on Origen of Alexandria's Hexapla, published circa 240 AD, which itself drew on both the Old Greek translation, and the translation made the Jewish scholar Theodotion circa 150 AD. Theodotion retranslated the Septuagint into Greek from the Hebrew texts being used by Jews in the 2<sup>nd</sup> century.

The surviving copies of 2<sup>nd</sup> and 3<sup>rd</sup> Kingdoms include both text that appears to have been redacted by the Hasmoneans, and text that appears to be pre-Hasmonean, strongly indicating it originated in the Hexapla. As both the Septuagint and Masoretic texts support the name Sabaoth having once been in this verse, it is restored in this translation, however, the evidence from 4<sup>th</sup> Kingdoms is that the name Iaw (יהוה) was not in Samuel until the Hasmonean redaction, several decades after the Greek translation at the Library of Alexandria, and therefore the translation of 'Lord Sabaoth' is used, as it appears in the Greek translations of 1<sup>st</sup> and 4<sup>th</sup> Kingdoms.

# 4<sup>th</sup> Kingdoms: Chapter 11

Athaliah the mother of Ahaziah saw that her son was dead, and she destroyed all the royal seed. Jehosheba, the daughter of king Joram and sister of Ahaziah, took Joah the son of her brother, and stole him from among the king's sons that were put to death, hiding him and his nurse in the bedroom, and hid him from the face of Athaliah, and he was not killed.

He remained with her hidden in the Temple of the Lord for six years while Athaliah reigned over the land. In the seventh year, Jehoiada sent and took the captains of the hundreds of the conscripts,<sup>1</sup> and the volunteers,<sup>2</sup> and brought them to him in the Temple of the Lord, and made a covenant of the Lord with them, and adjured them, and Jehoiada showed them the king's son, and ordered them, "This is what you will do. Let a third of you go in on the sabbath-day, and keep the watch of the king's palace in the porch, and another third in the gate of the high way, and a third at the gate behind the infantrymen, and guard the temple. There will be two parties among you, even every one that goes out on the Sabbath, and they will keep the guard of the Lord's Temple before the king. Surround the king, every man with his weapon in his hand, and he that goes into the ranges will die. They will be with the king in his going out and in his coming in."

The captains of hundreds did all things that the wise Jehoiada commanded, and they took each his men, both those that went in on the sabbath-day, and those that went out on the sabbath-day, and went to Jehoiada the priest. The priest gave to the captains of hundreds the swords and spears of King David that were in the Temple of the Lord. The infantrymen stood each with his weapon in his hand from the right corner of the temple to the left corner of the house, by the altar and the temple around the king. He brought out the king's son, and put the crown on him and gave him the testimony, and he made him king and anointed him, and they clapped their hands, and said, "Long live the king."

Athaliah heard the sound of the people running, and she went with the people to the Temple of the Lord. She looked and saw the king standing near a pillar, and the singers and the trumpeters were before the king and all the people of the land even rejoicing and sounding with trumpets, and Athaliah tore her clothes, and cried, "A conspiracy, a conspiracy!"

Jehoiada the priest commanded the captains of hundreds who were over the army, and said to them, "Bring her out without the ranks, and he that goes in after her will certainly die by the sword. For the priest said, 'Let her not, however, be slain in the Temple of the Lord.'"

They laid hands on her and went in by the path of the horses' entrance into the Temple of the Lord, and she was killed there. Jehoiada made a covenant between the Lord and the king and the people, that they should be the Lord's people, also between the king and the people. All the people of the land went into the Temple of Ba'al and tore it down, and completely broke in pieces his altars and his columns, and they killed Mattan the priest of Ba'al before the altars. The priest appointed overseers over the Temple of the Lord. He took the captains of the hundreds of the conscripts and the volunteers, and all the people of the land, and brought down the king out of the Temple of the Lord, and they went in by the way of the gate of the infantrymen of the king's palace, and seated him there on the throne of the kings. All the people of the land rejoiced, and the city was at peace. They killed Athaliah with the sword in the house of the king. Joah was seven years old when he began to reign.

# 4ᵗʰ Kingdoms: Chapter 11 Notes

**1** Codex Vaticanus: chorrhi (χοῤῥι)

- Aleppo Codex: kry (כרי)

- Leningrad Codex: kari (כָּרִי)

- Targum Jerusalem: gibbaraya (גִּבָּרַיָּא). Translation: mighty

This term generates some debate, as the Hebrew term means 'pillows,' and the Greek is a transliteration of the same term. The word is similar to the Aramaic word for kryå (𐡍𐡏𐡉) meaning 'short.' It is most likely a reference to the Hurrians (𐤈𐤋𐤋𐤀𐤇𐤊), who had been made perpetual slaves in Israel when Joshua had occupied Samaria. The dispute over the meaning of the word originates in its use in this sentence, where it is listed with the captains of the army, suggesting a division of Hurrians served in the army at the time, however, there are not other references to Hurrians existing this late in history. Given that the accompanying term appears to mean 'volunteers,' this term appears to have referred to conscripts.


**2** Codex Vaticanus: rasim (ρᾱϲιμ)

- Aleppo Codex: rsym (רצים)

- Leningrad Codex: ratzim (רָצִים)

- Targum Jerusalem: rahataya (רְהָטַיָּא). Translation: runners

This term has caused some confusion. The Hebrew word is a plural form of 'satisfy,' however, also appears to be the Aramaic plural form of 'consenter ' transliterated into the Hebrew script, indicating the original meaning would be akin to 'volunteers.'

# 4th Kingdoms: Chapter 12

Joah began to reign in the seventh year of Jehu, and he reigned forty years in Jerusalem. His mother's name was Zibiah from Beersheba. Joah did that which was right in the sight of the Lord all the days that Jehoiada the priest instructed him. Except that none of the bamahs[1] were removed, and the people still sacrificed there and burnt incense in the bamahs.

Joah said to the priests, "As for all the silver of the holy things that is brought into the Temple of the Lord, the silver of valuation, as each man brings the silver of valuation, all the silver which any man may feel disposed to bring into the Temple of the Lord, let the priests take it for themselves, every man from the proceeds of his sale, and they will repair the breaches of the temple in all places wherever a breach will be found."

In the twenty-third year of King Joah, the priests had not repaired the breaches of the temple. King Joah called Jehoiada the priest, and the other priests, and asked them, "Why have you not repaired the breaches of the temple? Now then take no more silver from your sales, instead, you will give it to repair the breaches of the temple."

The priests agreed to take no more silver from the people, while not repairing the breaches of the temple. Jehoiada the priest took a chest, and bored a hole in the lid of it, and set it by the altar in the house of a man belonging to the Temple of the Lord, and the priests who kept the door, put into it all the silver that was found in the Temple of the Lord.

When they saw that there was a great deal of silver in the chest, the king's scribe and the high priest went up, and they counted the silver that was found in the Temple of the Lord. They gave the silver that had been collected to the hands of those who crafted the works, the overseers of the Temple of the Lord, and they gave it out to the carpenters and to the builders that worked in the Temple of the Lord. To the quarry workers and the stonemasons to purchase timber and cut stone to repair the breaches of the Temple of the Lord, and all that was spent on the Temple of the Lord to repair it.

Only there were no silver plates, studs, bowls, or trumpets, any vessel of gold or vessel of silver made for the Temple of the Lord, as the silver that was brought into the Temple of the Lord, was given to the workmen, and they repaired the Temple of the Lord with it. Also, they took no account of the men into whose hands they gave the silver to give to the workmen, for they acted faithfully. silver for a sin-offering, and silver for a trespass-offering, whatever happened to be brought into the Temple of the Lord, went to the priests.

Then King Hazailu[2] of Aram[3] went and attacked Gath[4] and captured it, and Hazailu decided to attack Jerusalem. Joah king of Judah took all the holy things which Jehoshaphat, Joram, and Ahaziah, his fathers, and kings of Judah had consecrated, and what he had himself dedicated, and all the gold that was found in the treasures of the Lord's Temple and the king's palace, and he sent them to King Hazailu of Syria, and he went up from Jerusalem.

The rest of the acts of Joah, and all that he did, look, aren't these things written in the book of the Chronicles of the Kings of Judah? His servants rose up and organized a conspiracy, and killed Joah in the house of Millo that is in Silla. Jozachar the son of Shimeath, and Jehozabad Shomer's son, his servants, struck him, and he died. They buried him with his fathers in the City of David, and Amaziah his son reigned in his place.

# 4th Kingdoms: Chapter 12 Notes

**1** Codex Vaticanus: ypsêlôn (ΥϯΗΛѠΝ). Translation: heights

- Aleppo Codex: bmwt (במות). Translation: bamahs

- Leningrad Codex: bamot (בָּמֹות). Translation: bamahs

- Targum Jerusalem: bamata (בָּמָתָא)

Bamahs were stone platforms built at the tops of hills, where sacrifices were made to gods in ancient Canaan and Assyria. These bamahs generally included an altar for barbecuing the sacrifices, a stele, a seat for the god (which the priest would sit in), a tree representing Asherah (Ashteroth), and a cistern for water. These bamahs were also generally accompanied by a banquet hall, and a 'low stone' used for slaughtering and butchering the animal. Bamahs were the main religious centers used by the Israelites until King Josiah banned and destroyed them circa 625 BC. After that, all Jews were required by law to worship at the temple in Jerusalem.


**2** Codex Vaticanus: Azaêl (ΑΖΑΗΛ)

- Aleppo Codex: ḥzȧl (חזאל)

- Leningrad Codex: chaza'el (חֲזָאֵל)

- Targum Jerusalem: chaza'el (חֲזָאֵל)

Hazailu (𒄩𒍝𒀸𒌑) was the king of the Aramean kingdom of Damascus, who reigned circa 842 to 796 BC. In the aftermath of the great earthquake that devastated the Samaritan Empire, Damascus became an independent kingdom, which under King Hazailu conquered northern Israel and central Syria. Artifacts from his reign have been found as far west as the island of Samos in the Aegean Sea, suggesting that the Arameans were trading with the Greeks at the time.

**3** Codex Vaticanus: Syrias (ϹΥΡΙΛϹ). Translation: Syria

• Aleppo Codex: Årm (אָרֶס). Translation: Aram

• Leningrad Codex: Aram (אֲרָ֖ם). Translation: Aram

• Targum Jerusalem: Aram (אֲרָם). Translation: Aram

Syria was the Greek name of Aram, the ancient Aramean Kingdom, in the region of modern Syria.


**4** Codex Vaticanus: Geth (ΓΕΘ)

• Aleppo Codex: Gat (גַּת)

• Leningrad Codex: Gat (גַּת)

• Targum Jerusalem: Gat (גַּת)

The Egyptians recorded two cities named Gath (Gintu), one in the region of the modern Palestinian Gaza Strip, and another near Mount Carmel (Ginti-kirmil) in northern modern Israel. The northern Gath is likely the city Hazailu attacked.

# 4<sup>th</sup> Kingdoms: Chapter 13

In the twenty-third year of Joah son of Ahaziah king of Judah, Jehoahaz, the son of Jehu, began to reign in Samaria, and he reigned seventeen years. He did that which was evil in the sight of the Lord and followed the sins of Jeroboam the son of Nebat, who led Israel in sin. He did not depart from them. The Lord was very angry with Israel, and delivered them into the hand of Hazailu king of Syria, and into the hand of the son of Arad, son of Hazailu, all their days. Jehoahaz implored the Lord, and the Lord listened to him, for he saw the affliction of Israel, because the king of Syria afflicted them. The Lord gave deliverance to Israel, and they escaped from under the hand of Syria, and the Israelites lived in their tents as before now.

However, they did not stop the sins of the house of Jeroboam, who led Israel in sin, they continued them, and Asherah[1] also remained in Samaria. There was no army remaining for Jehoahaz, except fifty horsemen, and ten chariots, and ten thousand infantry, for the king of Syria had destroyed them, and they trampled them like dirt. The rest of the acts of Jehoahaz, and all that he did, and his mighty acts aren't these things written in the book of the Chronicles of the Kings of Israel? Jehoahaz slept with his fathers, and they buried him in Samaria, and Joah his son reigned in his place.

In the thirty-seventh year of King Joah of Judah, Joah the son of Jehoahaz began to reign over Israel in Samaria sixteen years. He did that which was evil in the sight of the Lord, he did not depart from all the sins of Jeroboam the son of Nebat, who led Israel sin, he followed it. The rest of the acts of Joah, and all that he did, and his mighty acts which he performed together with Amaziah king of Judah, aren't these written in the book of the Chronicles of the Kings of Israel?

Joah slept with his fathers, and Jeroboam sat on his throne, and he was buried in Samaria with the kings of Israel. Now Elisha was sick, and dying, and Joah king of Israel went to him, and cried over his face, and said, "My father, my father, the chariot of Israel, and the horseman!"

Elisha said to him, "Take a bow and arrows."

He took for himself a bow and arrows, and said to the king, "Put your hand on the bow."

Joah put his hand on it, and Elisha put his hands on the king's hands, and he said, "Open the window to the east."

He opened it, and Elisha said, "Shoot."

He shot, and Elisha said, "The arrow of the Lord's deliverance, and the arrow of deliverance from Syria. You will slaughter the Syrians in Aphek until you have consumed them."

Elisha said to him, "Take a bow and arrows."

He took them, and he said to the king of Israel, "Strike the ground."

The king struck three times and stopped, and the prophet was sad for him, and said, "If you had struck five or six times, then you should have slaughtered Syria until they were annihilated, but now you will slaughter Syria only three times."

Elisha died, and they buried him.

The bands of the Moabites came into the land, at the beginning of the year, as they were burying a man, and they saw a band of men, and they threw the man into the grave of Elisha, and as soon as he touched the bones of Elisha, he revived and stood up on his feet. Hazailu greatly slaughtered Israel all the days of Jehoahaz. The Lord had mercy and compassion on them, and had respect to them because of his covenant with Abraham, and Isaac, and Jacob, and the Lord would not destroy them and did not throw them out from his presence.

Hazailu king of Syria died, and the son of Arad his son reigned in his place. Joah the son of Jehoahaz returned, and took the cities out of the hand of the son of Arad the son of Hazailu, which he had taken out of the hand of Jehoahaz his father in the war. Three times Joah attacked him, and he recaptured the cities of Israel.

# 4<sup>th</sup> Kingdoms: Chapter 13 Notes

**1** Codex Vaticanus: alsos (ᴀᴧᴄⲟⲥ). Translation: grove (or woods)

- Aleppo Codex: Åšrh (אשרה). Translation: Asherah

- Leningrad Codex: Asherah (אֲשֵׁרֹה). Translation: Asherah

- Targum Jerusalem: Asheirata (אֲשֵׁירְתָא). Translation: Asherah

Asherah was the name of an Israelite goddess before the time of Elijah in the 9<sup>th</sup> century, described as the mother of Yahweh, as well as the wife of El. It is unclear exactly how Asherah was worshiped, however, is is believed she was worshiped by planting oak trees, similar to her Egyptian counterpart Iusaaset, who was worshiped by planting acacia trees.

In Cosmic Genesis Deborah was buried under the Oak of Mourning, which King Josiah tore down, suggesting that the trees were used as living gravestones. Many of the oaks were named, including the Oak of Visions and the Oak of Sedition, suggesting that the oaks were viewed as spirits or demi-gods.

# 4<sup>th</sup> Kingdoms: Chapter 14

In the second year of Joah the son of Jehoahaz king of Israel, Amaziah who was also the son of Joah the king of Judah began to reign. Twenty-five years old was he when he began to reign, and he reigned 29 years in Jerusalem. His mother's name was Jehoaddan from Jerusalem. He did that which was right in the sight of the Lord, but not as much as David his forefather, as he did according to all things that his father Joah did. Only he did not remove the bamahs, and the people still sacrificed and burnt incense on the bamahs.

When the kingdom was established in his hand, he killed his servants that had slain the king his father. But he did not kill the sons of those that had slain him, following as it is written in the book of the laws of Moses, as the Lord commanded, "The fathers will not be put to death for the children, and the children will not be put to death for the fathers, but everyone will die for his own sins."

He slaughtered ten thousand Edomites in the valley of salt, and captured Petra[1] in the war, and called its name Joktheel until this day. Then Amaziah sent messengers to Joah, son of Jehoahaz, son of King Jehu of Israel, saying, "Come, let's speak face to face."

Joah the king of Israel sent to Amaziah king of Judah, saying, "The thistle that was in Lebanon sent to the cedar that was in Lebanon, saying, 'Give my daughter to your son asa wife, and the wild beasts of the field that were in Lebanon passed by and trod down the thistle. You have struck and wounded Edom, and your heart has lifted you up. Stay at home and praise yourself. Why are you quarrelsome to your hurt? So both you will fall and Judah with you."

Nevertheless, Amaziah did not listen, so Joah king of Israel went up, and he and Amaziah king of Judah looked one another in the face in the Temple of Shemesh² in Judah. Judah was overthrown before Israel, and every man fled to his tent. King Joah of Israel captured Amaziah, the son of Joah, the son of Ahaziah, in the Temple of Shemesh, and he traveled to Jerusalem, and broke down the wall of Jerusalem, beginning at the gate of Ephraim as far as the gate of the corner, four hundred cubits. He took the gold, and the silver, and all the vessels that were found in the Temple of the Lord, and in the treasures of the king's palace, and the hostages, and returned to Samaria. The rest of the acts of Joah, even all that he did in his strength, how he warred with Amaziah king of Judah, are not these things written in the book of the Chronicles of the Kings of Israel? Joah slept with his fathers and was buried in Samaria with the kings of Israel, and Jeroboam his son reigned in his place.

Amaziah the son of Joah king of Judah lived after the death of Joah son of Jehoahaz king of Israel fifteen years. The rest of the acts of Amaziah, and all that he did, are these not written in the book of the Chronicles of the Kings of Judah? They formed a conspiracy against him in Jerusalem, and he fled to Lachish, and they sent after him to Lachish and killed him there. They brought him on horses, and he was buried in Jerusalem with his fathers in the City of David. All the people of Judah took Azariah when he was sixteen years old, and made him king in the place of his father Amaziah.

He rebuilt Aeloth, and restored it to Judah after the king slept with his fathers. In the fifteenth year of Amaziah the son of Joah king of Judah began Jeroboam son of Joah to reign over Israel in Samaria for 41 years. He did that which was evil in the sight of the Lord, and he departed not from all the sins of Jeroboam the son of Nebat, who led Israel sin. He recovered the coast of Israel from the entering in of Hamath to the sea of Arabah, according to the word of Lord the god in Israel, which he spoke by his servant Jonah the son of Amittai, the prophet of Gathhepher.

The Lord saw that the affliction of Israel was very bitter and that they were few in number, straightened and in lack, and destitute, and Israel had no helper. The Lord said that he would not stamp out the seed of Israel from under the sky, so he delivered them by the hand of Jeroboam the son of Joah. The rest of the acts of Jeroboam and all that he did, and his mighty deeds, which he achieved in war, and how he reconquered Damascus and Hamath to Judah and Israel, aren't these things written in the book of the Chronicles of the Kings of Israel? Jeroboam slept with his fathers, even with the kings of Israel, and Zachariah his son reigned in his place.

# 4ᵗʰ Kingdoms: Chapter 14 Notes

**1** Greek: Petran (ΠЄΤΡΔΝ). Translation: Petra

• Aleppo Codex: Slô (סלע). Translation: Petra

• Leningrad Codex: Sela (סֶּלַע). Translation: Petra

• Targum Jerusalem: kerakka (כְּרַכָּא). Translation: walled city (or fortress)

Both the Greek and Hebrew terms are translations of the word 'rock' the name of the ancient Edomite capital.


**2** Codex Vaticanus: Baethsamys (ΒΔΙΘϹΔΜΥϹ)

• Aleppo Codex: byt šmš (בית שמש). Translation: House (or temple) of Shemesh (or sun)

• Leningrad Codex: beit Shemesh (בֵית שֶׁמֶשׁ). Translation: House (or temple) of Shemesh (or sun)

• Targum Jerusalem: beit Shemesh (בֵּית שֶׁמֶשׁ). Translation: House (or temple) of Shemesh (or sun)

Shemesh was the Canaanite sun god, whose worship was later banned by King Josiah circa 625 BC.

# 4<sup>th</sup> Kingdoms: Chapter 15

In the twenty-seventh year of Jeroboam king of Israel Azariah the son of Amaziah king of Judah began to reign. He was sixteen years old when he began to reign, and he reigned fifty-two years in Jerusalem. His mother's name was Jecholiah of Jerusalem. He did that which was right in the eyes of the Lord, like all things that Amaziah his father did. Only he did not remove any of the Bamahs, and the people continued to sacrifice and burnt incense on the Bamahs. The Lord plagued the king, and he was leprous until the day of his death, and he reigned in a separate house. Jotham the king's son was over the household, judging the people of the land. The rest of the acts of Azariah, and all that he did, aren't these written in the book of the Chronicles of the Kings of Judah?

Azariah slept with his fathers, and they buried him with his forefathers in the City of David, and Jotham his son reigned in his place. In the thirty-eighth year of Azariah king of Judah Zachariah the son of Jeroboam began to reign over Israel in Samaria for six months. He did that which was evil in the eyes of the Lord, as his fathers had done. He did not stop the sins of Jeroboam the son of Nebat, who made Israel sin. Shallum the son of Jabesh and others conspired against him, and they murdered him in Keblaam, and he reigned in his place. The rest of the acts of Zachariah, look, they are written in the book of the Chronicles of the Kings of Israel.

This was the word of the Lord which he said to Jehu, "Your sons of the fourth generation will sit on the throne of Israel, and it was so."

Shallum the son of Jabin reigned, and in the thirty-ninth year of King Azariah of Judah, Shallum reigned for a full month in

Samaria. Menahem the son of Gadi left Tharsila, and came to Samaria, and struck Shallum the son of Jabin in Samaria, and killed him. The rest of the acts of Shallum, and the conspiracy that he was engaged in, see, they are written in the book of the Chronicles of the Kings of Israel.

Then Menahem struck both Tirzah and all that was in it, and its borders extending beyond Tirzah, because they opened not to him, and he struck it, and ripped up the pregnant women. In the thirty-ninth year of King Azariah of Judah, Menahem the son of Gadi, began to reign over Israel from Samaria, for ten years. He did that which was evil in the sight of the Lord. He did not stop the sins of Jeroboam the son of Nebat, who led Israel in sin.

In his days King Tiglath-Pileser III[1] of the Assyrians invaded against the land, and Menahem gave to King Tiglath-Pileser III a thousand talents of silver to aid him with his power. Menahem raised the silver by a tax on Israel, on every rich man, to give to the king of the Assyrians, fifty shekels levied on each man, and the king of the Assyrians departed and did not remain in the land. The rest of the acts of Menahem, and all that he did, look, are these not written in the book of the Chronicles of the Kings of Israel?

Menahem slept with his fathers, and Pekahiah his son reigned in his place. In the fiftieth year of King Azariah of Judah, Pekahiah the son of Menahem, began to reign over Israel from Samaria for two years. He did that which was evil in the sight of the Lord, he did not stop the sins of Jeroboam the son of Nebat, who made Israel sin. Pekah the son of Remaliah, his officer, conspired against him, and struck him in Samaria in the front of the king's palace, with Argob and Arieh, and with him there, were fifty men of the four hundred, and he killed him and reigned in his place. The rest of the acts of Pekahiah, and all that he did, look, they are written in the book of the Chronicles of the Kings of Israel.

In the fifty-second year of Azariah king of Judah, Pekah the son of Remaliah began to reign over Israel in Samaria for twenty years. He did that which was evil in the eyes of the Lord, he did not depart from all the sins of Jeroboam the son of Nebat, who led Israel sin. In the days of Pekah king of Israel came King Tiglath-Pileser III[2] of the Assyrians, and conquered Ijon, Abel, Thmaachah, Janoah, and Kedesh, and Hazor, and Gilead, and Galilee, even all the land of Naphtali, and carried them away to the Assyrians.

Hoshea son of Elah led a conspiracy against Pekah the son of Remaliah, and struck him, and killed him, and reigned in his place, in the twentieth year of Jotham the son of Azariah. The rest of the acts of Pekah, and all that he did, look, these are written in the book of the Chronicles of the Kings of Israel. In the second year of Pekah, the son of King Remaliah of Israel, Jotham the son of King Azariah of Judah began to reign.

He was twenty-five years old when he began to reign, and he reigned sixteen years in Jerusalem. His mother's name was Jerusha, the daughter of Zadok. He did that which was right in the sight of the Lord, according to all things that his father Azariah did. Nevertheless, he did not destroy the Bamahs, and the people sacrificed and burnt incense on the Bamahs. He built the upper gate of the Lord's Temple. The rest of the acts of Jotham, and all that he did, are not these written in the book of the Chronicles of the Kings of Judah? In those days the Lord began to send out against Judah Rezin king of Syria, and Pekah son of Remaliah. Jotham slept with his fathers and was buried with his fathers in the City of David his forefather, and Ahaz his son reigned in his place.

# 4<sup>th</sup> Kingdoms: Chapter 15 Notes

**1** Codex Vaticanus: Phoul (ⲪⲞⲨⲀ)

- Aleppo Codex: Pwl (פול)

- Leningrad Codex: Ful (פּוּל)

- Targum Jerusalem: Ful (פּוּל)

Tiglath-Pileser III is the more common throne name of General Pulu, after he usurped the throne of Assyria in 745 BC. This name was also used for Tiglath-Pileser III in the Babylonian King List and Ptolemaic Canon, as well as later Greco-Roman historical works.

**2** Codex Vaticanus: Thaglathphellasar (ⲐⲀⲅⲖⲀⲐⲪⲈⲗⲗⲀⲤⲀⲣ)

- Aleppo Codex: Tglt Plåsr (תגלת פלאסר)

- Leningrad Codex: Tiglat pil'eser (תִּגְלַת פִּלְאֶסֶר)

- Targum Jerusalem: Tiglat Pileser (תִּגְלַת פִּלְאֶסֶר)

Tiglath-Pileser III was the ruler of the Assyrian Empire between 745 and 727 BC, who forged the Neo-Assyrian Empire.

# 4th Kingdoms: Chapter 16

In the seventeenth year of Pekah, the son of Remaliah, Ahaz the son of King Jotham of Judah began to reign. Ahaz was twenty years old when he began to reign, and he reigned for sixteen years in Jerusalem. He did not do that which was right in the eyes of Lord the God, faithfully as David his forefather had done. He followed in the way of the kings of Israel. He even made his son pass through the fire, like the abomination of the tribes that the Lord drove out from before the Israelites. He sacrificed and burnt incense on the Bamahs, and the hills under every shady tree.

King Rezin of Syria and Pekah son of King Remaliah of Israel went to war against Jerusalem, and besieged Ahaz, but could not conquer him. At that time King Rezin of Syria reconquered Elath for Syria, and drove out the Judahites from Elath, and the Edomites came to Elath and lived there until this day. Ahaz sent messengers to King Tiglath-pileser III of the Assyrians, saying, "I am your servant and your son. Come up, deliver me out of the hand of the king of Syria, and out of the hand of the King of Israel, who are rising up against me."

Ahaz took the silver and the gold that was found in the treasures of the Temple of the Lord, and of the king's palace, and sent gifts to the king. The King of the Assyrians listened to him, and the king of the Assyrians went to Damascus and captured it, deported the inhabitants, and executed King Rezin. King Ahaz went to Damascus to meet King Tiglath-pileser III of the Assyrians at Damascus, and he saw an altar at Damascus. King Ahaz sent to Uriah the priest, the design of the altar, and its dimensions, and all its workmanship.

Uriah the priest built the altar, according to all the directions which King Ahaz sent from Damascus. The king saw the altar, and went up to it, and offered his whole burnt offering, and his meat-offering, and his drink-offering, and poured out the blood of his peace-offerings on the bronze altar that was before the Lord. He brought forward the one before the Temple of the Lord from between the altar and the Temple of the Lord, and he set it openly by the side of the altar to the north.

King Ahaz ordered Uriah the priest, "Offer on the great altar the whole burnt offering in the morning and the meat-offering in the evening, and the whole burnt offering of the king, and his meat-offering, and the whole burnt offering of all the people, and their meat-offering, and their drink-offering, and you will pour all the blood of the whole burnt offering, and all the blood of any other sacrifice on it, and the bronze altar will be for me in the morning."

Uriah the priest followed all that King Ahaz commanded him. King Ahaz cut off the borders of the bases, and removed the laver from off them, and took down the sea from the bronze oxen that were under it, and set it on a base of stone. He made a base for the throne in the Temple of the Lord, and he made the king's entrance outside the Temple of the Lord because of the king of the Assyrians. The rest of the acts of Ahaz, all that he did, aren't these written in the book of the Chronicles of the Kings of Judah? Ahaz slept with his forefathers and was buried in the City of David, and Hezekiah his son reigned in his place.

# 4th Kingdoms: Chapter 17

In the twelfth year of King Ahaz of Judah, Hoshea the son of Elah, began to reign in Samaria over Israel, and he reigned nine years. He did evil in the eyes of the Lord, only not as much as the kings of Israel that were before him. King Shalmaneser[1] of the Assyrians attacked them, and Hoshea became his servant and paid tribute to him.

The king of the Assyrians found iniquity in Hoshea, in that he sent messengers to King Osorkon[2] of Egypt, and paid no a tribute to the king of the Assyrians in that year. The king of the Assyrians besieged him, and confined him in the prison-house. The king of the Assyrians invaded the land, and went into Samaria, and besieged it for three years. In the ninth year of Hoshea, the king of the Assyrians took Samaria, and deported Israel away to the Assyrians, and settled them in Halaf,[3] and in Habor on the Khabur River,[4] and to the mountains of the Medes.[5]

The Israelites transgressed against Lord the God, who had brought them up out of the land of Egypt, from under the hand of Pharaoh king of Egypt, and they were afraid of other gods, and followed the statutes of the nations which the Lord drove out before the face of the Israelites. As the kings of Israel had done these things, the Israelites had secretly practiced the customs. Not as they should have, against Lord the God, and they built for themselves bamahs for all their cities, from the tower of the watchmen to the fortified city.

They made for themselves steles and groves on every high hill, and under every shady tree, and burnt incense on all Bamahs, as the nations did whom the Lord removed from before them, and dealt with familiar spirits, and they carved statues to provoke the Lord to anger. They served the idols, of which the Lord said to them, "You will not do this thing against the Lord".

The Lord testified against Israel and Judah by the hand of all his prophets, and of every seer, saying, "Turn from your evil ways and follow my commandments and my ordinances, and all the law which I commanded your fathers and all that I sent to them by the hand of my servants the prophets." But they did not listen and made their neck stiffer than the neck of their fathers.

They did not keep any of his commandments which he ordered them, and they followed vanities and became vain, and after the nations round about them, concerning which the Lord had ordered them not to do. They forgot the commandments of Lord the god and made themselves engraved statues, including the two cows, and they made groves, and worshiped all the forces of the skies,[6] and served the Ba'al.[7] They gave their sons and their daughters to the fire, and used divination and omens, and sold themselves to work wickedness in the sight of the Lord, to provoke him. The Lord was very angry with Israel and removed them out of his sight, and there was only left the tribe of Judah quite alone.

Not even Judah followed the commandments of Lord the god, but they walked according to the customs of Israel which they practiced and rejected the Lord. The Lord was angry with the whole seed of Israel, and troubled them, and gave them into the hand of those who ruined them until he threw them out of his presence. Because Israel revolted from the house of David, and they made Jeroboam the son of Nebat king, and Jeroboam drew off Israel from following the Lord, and led them to sin a great sin. The Israelites followed in all the sin of Jeroboam which he committed, they did not stop it, until the Lord removed Israel from his presence, as the Lord had stated by all his servants, the

prophets, and Israel was removed from off their land to the Assyrians until this day.

The king of Assyria brought Babylonians from Kutha,[8] from
Ivah,[9] from Hama,[10] and the Sipparites,[11] and they were settled in
the cities of Samaria in the place of the Israelites, and they were
awarded Samaria and were settled in its cities. At the beginning of
their establishment there, they were not afraid of the Lord, and
the Lord sent lions among them, and they killed some of them.
They said to the king of the Assyrians, "The people who you
have relocated to the cities of Samaria, replacing the Israelites,
don't know the ways of the god of the land, and he has sent the
lions to attack them, and they are slaying them because they don't
know the way of the god of the land."

The king of the Assyrians commanded, "Take some Israelites
there and let them live there, and they will teach them the ways
of the god of the land."

They brought one of the priests who they had been removed
from Samaria and settled him in the House of El, and he taught
them how they should fear the Lord. But the people made each
their own god and put them in the house of the Bamahs which
the Samaritans had made, each nation in the cities in which they
lived. The Babylonians celebrated the Festival of Akitu,[12] the men
of Kutha celebrated Nergal,[13] and the men of Hama made
Ashima,[14] the Mitanni[15] made Ribhus[16] and Tarkshya,[17] and the
inhabitants of the Sippars did evil when they burnt their sons in
the fire to King Adad[18] and King An,[19] the gods of the Sipparites.[20]
They were afraid of the Lord, yet they established their abominations in the temples of the bamahs which they built in Samaria,
each nation in the city in which they lived. They were afraid of
the Lord, yet they appointed for themselves priests of the bamahs
and sacrificed for themselves in the temples of the bamahs. They

were afraid of the Lord and served their gods according to the customs of the nations from where their lords brought them. Until this day they did according to their customs, they fear the Lord, and they do according to their customs, and according to their manner, and according to the law, and according to the commandment which the Lord commanded the sons of Jacob, whose name he made Israel.

The Lord made a covenant with them, and ordered them, "You will not fear other gods. You will you worship them, nor serve them, nor sacrifice to them. Only to the Lord, who brought you up out of the land of Egypt with great strength and with a strong arm you will fear and worship, and to him will you sacrifice. You will observe continually the ordinances, and the judgments, and the law, and the commandments which he wrote for you, and you will not fear other gods. Neither will you forget the covenant which he made with you, and you will not fear other gods, but you will fear Lord the god, and he will deliver you from all your enemies. Neither will you comply with their practice, which they follow." These nations were afraid of the Lord, and served their engraved statues. Yes, their sons and their son's sons do until this day even as their fathers did.

# 4th Kingdoms: Chapter 17 Notes

**1** Codex Vaticanus: Salamanasar (ϹΑλΑΜΑΝΑϹΑΡ)

- Aleppo Codex: Šlmnåsr (שלמנאסר)

- Leningrad Codex: Shalman'eser (שַׁלְמַנְאֶסֶר)

- Targum Jerusalem: Shalman'eser (שִׁלְמַנְאֶסֶר)

King Shalmaneser V, was the son and heir to King Tiglath-Pileser III, how ruled the Assyrian Empire between 727 and 722 BC. Prior to becoming king, he was the governor of Zimirra in Phoenicia.


**2** Codex Vaticanus: Sêgôr (ϹΗΓϢΡ)

- Codex Alexandrinus: Sôa (ϹϢΑ)

- Aleppo Codex: Swå (סוא)

- Leningrad Codex: So (סוֹא)

- Targum Jerusalem: So (סוֹא)

King Sêgôr/Swå is generally, although not universally, accepted as being King Usermaatre Osorkon IV, the heir to Shoshenq V, and the last king of the 22nd Dynasty, generally dated between 730 to 713 BC. Osorkon IV was de facto ruler of Northern Egypt while Egypt was divided during a dark age called the Third Intermediate Period.


**3** Codex Vaticanus: Alae (ΑλΑΕ)

- Aleppo Codex: Hlh (חלה)

- Leningrad Codex: Chelach (חְלַח)

- Targum Jerusalem: Chelach (חֲלָח)

The city in question is believed to be at Tell Halaf in northern Syria. This site was inhabited by the 6th millennium BC, by a culture now called the Halaf Culture. The city that existed there circa 1000 BC was called Guzana, and the source of the Assyrian name of the Khabur River: Gozan River.

**4** Codex Vaticanus: Abôr potamoes Gôzan (ΑΒѠΡΠΟΤΑΜΟΙϹ ΓѠΖΑΝ). Translation: Habur river Gozan

• Aleppo Codex: Hbwr nhr Gwzn (**חבור נהר גוזן**). Translation: Habur river Gozan

• Leningrad Codex: Chavovr nehar Govzan (חָבוֹר נְהַר גּוֹזָן). Translation: Habur river Gozan

• Targum Jerusalem: Chavovr nehar Govzan (חָבוֹר נְהַר גּוֹזָן). Translation: Habur river Gozan

The exact location is unclear, however, it is assumed to be one of several archaeological sites along the Khabur River, which is the source of the river's name in many languages, including English: Khabur, Arabic: al-khābūr (الخـابور), Syriac: hābur (ܚܒܘܪ), Greek: Abórrhas (Ἀβόρρας), and Latin: Chabura.

**5** Codex Vaticanus: orê Mêdôn (ΟΡΗΜΗΔѠΝ). Translation: Mountains of the Medes

• Aleppo Codex: ôry mdy (**ערי מדי**). Translation: cities of Media

• Leningrad Codex: arei Madai (עָרֵי מָדָי). Translation: cities of Media

• Targum Jerusalem: kirvei Madai (קִירְוֵי מָדִי). Translation: frontiers of Media

At the height of the Assyrian Empire, the western Median lands in the eastern region of modern Turkey and northwestern Iran fell under the control of the Assyrians. The region where the Khabur River originates in eastern Turkey is likely the region implied. The book of Tobit was set in this region a century later when the Medes were rebelling from Assyrian rule.

**6** Codex Vaticanus: dynami tou ouranou (ⲆⲨⲚⲀⲘⲈⲓⲦⲞⲨⲞⲨⲢⲀⲚⲞⲨ). Translation: forces of the skies (or Uranus)

• Aleppo Codex: kl ṣbå hšmym (**כל צבא השמים**). Translation: entire force (or army) of the skies (or Shamayim)

• Leningrad Codex: chol-tzeva haShamayim (כָל־צְבָא הַשָּׁמַיִם). Translation: entire force (or army) of the skies (or Shamayim)

• Targum Jerusalem: chol cheilei shemaya (כָּל חֵילֵי שְׁמַיָּא). Translation: entire force (or army) of the sky

The term 'forces of the sky' appears to be part of the Hasmonean redaction that originated with the authorized Hebrew translation, as the Hebrew translation of Daniel uses the same term tzeva haShamayim (צְבָא הַשָּׁמַיִם) where the Old Greek text of the Chisianus Codex uses the phrase asterôn tou ouranou (αστερων του ουρανου), meaning 'stars of the sky.' Theodotion's Greek translation of the Hebrew and Aramaic version of Daniel from circa 150 AD substituted the term dynameôs tou ouranou (δυναμεως του ουρανου), which was almost universally accepted in later copies of the Septuagint, including the Vaticanus, Sinaiticus, and Alexandrinus codices.

**7** Codex Vaticanus: tô Baal (ⲦⲰⲂⲀⲀⲗ). Translation: the Ba'al

• Aleppo Codex: åt hbôl (**את הבעל**). Translation: to (or you) the Lord

• Leningrad Codex: et-habba'al (אֶת־הַבַּעַל). Translation: to (or you) the Lord

• Targum Jerusalem: yat be'ala (יַת בְּעָלָא). Translation: the husband

Based on the previous reference to the 'forces of the skies' which was likely the 'stars of the skies' before the Hasmonean redaction, the Ba'al in question was almost certainly Ba'al Shamin, the Lord of Dusk and the 'Winged Serpent' of the galactic Great Rift. The Great Rift is the dark band that obscures the center of the galactic plane, which was interpreted as a serpent, dragon, or winged serpent' by many Afro-Eurasian cultures, and the 'Emu in the sky' by ancient Australian cultures.

# 4th KINGDOMS: CHAPTER 17 NOTES

The statue of Ba'al erected by King Solomon, who was named after Lord Shalim, when he built the Temple of Solomon (Shalim), was described as looking like a seraph, or winged serpent, before King Hezekiah destroyed it in the time of Isaiah. Archaeological evidence indicated that King Hezekiah instituted sun worship, replacing the seraph iconography with the winged-sun iconography, matching the Behdety iconography of Egypt, which was used to represent both the kings of Egypt and Assyria at the time.


**8** Codex Vaticanus: Chountha (ΧΟΥΝΘΑ)

- Aleppo Codex: Kwth (כותה)

- Leningrad Codex: Kutah (כּוּתָה)

- Targum Jerusalem: Kutah (כּוּתָה)

The ruins of Kutha are believed to be at Tell Ibrahim (تَلَ إِبْرَاهِيم), historically known as Kutha Rabba (كُوثَى رَبَّا) in Babil Governorate, Iraq.


**9** Codex Vaticanus: Aia (ΑΙΑ)

- Codex Alexandrinus: Auta (ΑΥΤΑ)

- Aleppo Codex: Ôwå (עוא)

- Leningrad Codex: Avva (עַוָּא)

- Targum Jerusalem: Avah (עַוָה)

The city of Ivah was on the Euphrates, between the cities of Sepharvaim and Henah.


**10** Codex Vaticanus: Aimath (ΑΙΜΑΘ)

- Aleppo Codex: Ḥmt (חמת)

- Leningrad Codex: Chamat (חֲמָת)

- Targum Jerusalem: Chamat (חֲמָת)

842

# 4ᵗʰ Kingdoms: Chapter 17 Notes

The city of Hama is located in western Syria and has been inhabited since at least 6000 BC.

**11** Codex Vaticanus: Seppharouaen (ϹΕΠΦΑΡΟΥΑΙΝ)

- Aleppo Codex: Sprwym (ספרוים)

- Leningrad Codex: Sefarvayim (סְפַרְוַיִם)

- Targum Jerusalem: Sefarvayim (סְפַרְוַיִם)

The Greek is a transliteration of the Aramaic and Hebrew term, which was referring to the people from the twin cities of Sippar-Yahrurum and Sippar-Amnanum. Ruins of the two cities are located on the Euphrates approximately 30 km (20 miles) southwest of Baghdad at Tell Abu Habbah and Tell ed-Der, covering a region of approximately 100 hectares (247 acres). As the term refers to people from both the Sippars, the translation of 'Sipparites' is used.

**12** Codex Vaticanus: Socchôthbaenith (ϹΟΚΧѠѲΒΑΙΝΙѲ)

- Aleppo Codex: skwt bnwt (סכות בנות). Translation: booths (or corals, agricultural festival) of daughters (or girls)

- Leningrad Codex: sukkovt benovt (סֻכּוֹת בְּנוֹת). Translation: booths (or corals, agricultural festival) of daughters (or girls)

- Targum Jerusalem: sukkovt benovt (סֻכּוֹת בְּנוֹת). Translation: Saturn (via Assyrian, or twigs) daughter

The goddess mentioned in the Masoretic text is unknown from archaeology, however, based on the Talmud, it was represented with a Hen and her Chicks, and therefore associated with the Pleiades constellation. The more likely explanation was that it was originally a reference to the Festival of Akitu.

In addition to the literal interpretation of sukkôt (סֻכּוֹת) as booths or corrals, the word is also the name of an agricultural festival mandated in Exodus by Moses. The festival was originally called chag hakkatzir (חַג

הַקָצִיר) in Exodus, meaning 'Festival of the Harvest.' The name 'Festival of the Sukkot' (חַג הַסֻּכּוֹת) was introduced in Leviticus chapter 23, during King Josiah's reforms of circa 625 BC, a century later, replacing the 'Festival of the Harvest' that Moses had commanded with a festival that was intended to commemorate the trek from Egypt. By the era the Aramaic translation was made, the Judahite agricultural festival appears to have been established under the name of Sukkot.

As the text of the Kingdoms appears to have been written in Akkadian Cuneiform during the Neo-Babylonian era, the term bintu (𒌍𒊩𒌆) would have meant 'daughter' and not 'daughters.' Bint refers to an individual daughter in most Semitic languages, including the Arabic bint (بِنْت), Maltese bint, and Sabaean bnt (𐩨𐩬𐩩). Canaanite dialects appear to be the exception among Semitic languages, where 'daughter' was bt (𐎁𐎚) and daughters was bnt (𐎁𐎐𐎚) in Ugaritic, which continues into modern Hebrew as bat (בַּת) and banot (בְּנוֹת).

If this was a reference to an agricultural festival of the 'daughter' in Babylon, it would have been the Festival of Akitu, the festival at the beginning of the planting season, generally on the 4<sup>th</sup> through 11<sup>th</sup> days of the month of Nisani (𒊑𒊍), approximately March 17 through 24. During the festival of Akitu, the kings of Sumer, and later Babylon, would legitimize their position as king of the land by acting out a sacred marriage ceremony with the high-priestess of Ishtar (𒀭𒈹), who was the 'daughter of God,' after which he became the Sukkal (𒋫), meaning visor or envoy of Ishtar for the following year. It really isn't clear who she was the daughter of, as different priesthoods claimed she was the daughter of the sky god An (𒀭), the moon god Sin (𒀭𒌍), the 'great lady' (𒀭𒊩𒌆), the lord of spirit Enlil (𒀭𒂗𒇸), or the lord of Earth Enki (𒀭𒂗𒆠), all the primordial gods of Mesopotamia. The original festival was probably based on Inanna's (the Sumerian version of Ishtar's), role as daughter of the Great Lady, as the Great Lady was also an agricultural goddess, similar to the Canaanite Eretz, Edomite Adama, and Greek Ge.

**13** Codex Vaticanus: Nêrigel (ΝΗϜΙΓΕΛ)

- Aleppo Codex: Nrgl (נרגל)

- Leningrad Codex: Neregal (נֵרְגַל)

- Targum Jerusalem: Nirgal (נִרְגַל)

Nergal was a major god in Mesopotamia from the time of the Akkadians, until the Christian era. Nergal was interpreted a variety of ways, including war-god to the Akkadians, underworld god to the Babylonians, and another version of Aplu to the Hittites, who was later known as Apollo to the Greeks and Romans.

**14** Codex Vaticanus: Asimath (ΑϹΙΜΑΘ)

- Aleppo Codex: Åšymå (אשימא)

- Leningrad Codex: Ashima (אֲשִׁימָא)

- Targum Jerusalem: Ashima (אֲשִׁימָא)

Ashima was a Semitic goddess of fate, also known as Manāt in Arabia. Both the names Ashim-Yahw, meaning Ashima wife of Yahweh, and Ashim-Bytål meaning Ashima withof Baitylos, have been found in the ruins of the early Persian Era Israelite Temple in Elephantine, Egypt.

**15** Codex Vaticanus: Eyaeoe (ΕΥΑΙΟΙ)

- Aleppo Codex: Ôwym (עוים)

- Leningrad Codex: Avvim (עַוִּים)

- Targum Jerusalem: Ava'ei (עַוָּאֵי)

The term is believed to have been derived from a name of the Hurrians, however, is derived separately from the other term Hurrians (חֹרִי). As the Avvim are routinely reported to be rulers, the term appears to represent the Mitannian nobility, while the other term used represented the Hurrians themselves. While the Mitanni civilization was destroyed in the 1300s BC, a Mitanni priesthood continued to operate at Mount Hor in Edom, interchangeably referred to as Hurrians in the texts of the era.

In this verse, the Egyptian gods Nephthys and Set appear to be referenced, although the identifications of the gods in question are debated. Nevertheless, it suggests that the Avvim were the descendants of the Hyksos, and supports the theory that the Hyksos and Mitannians were the same people.

**16** Codex Vaticanus: Eblazer (ЄΒΛΑΖЄΡ)

• Codex Alexandrinus: Abaazer cae tên Naebas (ΑΒΑΑΖЄΡ ΚΑΙ ΤΗΝ ΝΑΙΒΑϹ). Translation: Abaazer and the Naebas

• Aleppo Codex: Nbhz (נבחז)

• Leningrad Codex: Nivchaz (נִבְחַז)

• Targum Jerusalem: Nivchaz (נִבְחַז)

Both the Babylonian Talmud (Sanhedrin 63b), and Jerusalem Talmud (Avoda Zara 3:2 claim the original spelling the name was Nbhn (נבחן), not Nbhz (נבחז). The Semitic words nabāḫu (𒈾𒁀𒄷), nbhn (נבחן), nbhå (ܢܒܚ), and nabahnā (نَبَحْنَا) translate as approximately 'to bark,' and the god in question is described as dog-like. Rabbis have debated whether the Talmuds' spelling or the Masoretic text's is correct for centuries, however, the Septuagint supports the name having a Z (ז) in the Aramaic version the Greek and Hebrew translations were made from, which is not easy to mistake for an Aramaic N (ן).

As the Eyaeoe / Avvim were clearly not a Semitic people, there is no reasoned their gods should have Semitic names, and if they were the Indo-Aryan Mitanni priesthood who worshiped the Rigvedic deities, then this was originally probably about the Ribhus (ऋभु), a group of Vedic gods associated with winds and stars, and specifically a dog-star, which some interpret as a reference to the star Sirius.

**17** Codex Vaticanus: Tharthac (ΘΑΡΘΑΚ)

- Aleppo Codex: Trtq (תרתק)

- Leningrad Codex: Tartak (תַּרְתָּק)

- Targum Jerusalem: Tartak (תַּרְתָּק)

The Talmud claims this was donkey-like god, and the 'prince of dark-ness,' which appears to be based on the Egyptian god Set (Sutekh), who was depicted with a donkey's head from the time of Late Period onward, and considered evil from the New Kingdom onward.

Assuming that the Eyaeoe / Avvim were the Indo-Aryan Mitanni priesthood, who worshiped the Rigvedic deities, then the god this was originally about was probably Tarkshya, the bird (Rigveda 5.51) horse (Rigveda 1.89.6 god 'with intact wheel-rims' (Rigveda 10.178.1, similar to the earlier reference to the bird-horse of Elijah's vision in chapter 2.

**18** Codex Vaticanus: Adramelech (ΑΔΡΑΜΕΛΕΧ)

- Aleppo Codex: Ådrmlk (אדרמלך)

- Leningrad Codex: Adrammelech (אַדְרַמֶּלֶךְ)

- Targum Jerusalem: Anamelech (אַדְרְמֶלֶךְ)

The name is composed of the name Adra (אדר) and the word king (מלך). The name Adra is unknown among Semitic gods, and has been theorized as a misspelling of Adad via a substitution of an R (𐤓) for a D (𐤃), meaning that the text must have previously been written in Cunei-form. Ba'al Hadad was the king of the Canaanite gods after the Ba'al Cyle, however, he was known as <sup>an</sup>Adad (✳𒐖𒄭𒂁) in Cuneiform. As the following god was likewise a Mesopotamian god, King An, the translation of King Hadad is used.

**19** Codex Vaticanus: Anêmelech (ⲀⲚⲎⲘⲈⲖⲈⲬ)

• Aleppo Codex: Ônmlk (עֲנמלךְ)

• Leningrad Codex: Anammelech (עֲנַמֶּלֶךְ)

• Targum Jerusalem: Anamelech (אַדְרַמֶּלֶךְ)

This name is composed of the name An (עַנ) and the word king (מלךְ). The reference to An, the Septuagint's god of Moses, as Moloch (מלךְ), the god who the Judahites were sacrificing their children to a few decades later, confirms that the Judahites viewed Moloch as Moses' god at the time, explaining why King Josiah needed to issue a new Torah with the Levitical amendments to Moses laws in Exodus.


**20** Codex Vaticanus: theois Seppharouain (ⲐⲈⲞⲒⲤⲤⲈⲦⲦⲪⲀⲢⲞⲨⲀⲒⲚ). Translation: gods of Siparites

• Aleppo Codex: ålh sprym [ålhy sprwym] (אלה ספרים [אלהי ספרויס]). Translation: god (in Aramaic, or goddess in Hebrew) of Sipars [my gods (in Aramaic, or my goddesses in Hebrew) of Siparites]

• Leningrad Codex: Eloah [q] elohei [k] sefarim [q] sefarvayim [k] (אֱלֹהַּ [כ] אֱלֹהֵי [ק] סְפָרִים [כ] סְפַרְוָיִם [ק]). Translation: goddess (Hebrew) [k] god (Aramaic) [q] of Sipars [k] of Siparites [q]

Targum Jerusalem: ta'avat sefarvayim (טַעֲוַת סְפַרְוָיִם). Translation: error of Siparites

# 4<sup>th</sup> Kingdoms: Chapter 18

In the third year of King Hoshea the son of Elah in Israel, Hezekiah the son of King Ahaz of Judah began to reign. He was twenty-five years old when he began to reign, and he reigned twenty-nine years in Jerusalem. His mother's name was Abi, the daughter of Zachariah. He did that which was right in the sight of the Lord, like all that his father David did. He removed the bamahs and broke in pieces the steles, and completely destroyed Asherah, and the bronze serpent that Moses had made, because until those days the Israelites had burnt incense to it, which he had called Neesthan.[1]

He trusted in Lord the god in Israel, and since him, there were none like him among the kings of Judah, nor were like him among those before. He served the Lord and did not stop obeying him. He kept his commandments, all that he commanded Moses. The Lord was with him, and he was wise in all that he undertook, and he revolted from the King of the Assyrians and stopped serving him. He slaughtered the foreigners all the way to the border of Gaza, from the tower of the watchmen all the way to the fortified city.

In the fourth year of King Hezekiah, (this was the seventh year of Hoshea son of Elah, king of Israel,) King Shalmaneser V of the Assyrians invaded Samaria, and besieged it. He captured it at the end of three years, in the sixth year of Hezekiah, (this is the ninth year of Hoshea king of Israel when Samaria was captured.) The king of the Assyrians deported the Samaritans to Assyria, and put them in Halah and Habor, by the Khabur River, and in the mountains of the Medes, because they did not listen to the voice of Lord the god and transgressed his covenant, in all things that Moses the servant of the Lord commanded, and did not listen to them or do them.

In the fourteenth year of King Hezekiah, King Sennacherib[2] of the Assyrians attacked the fortified cities of Judah and captured them. King Hezekiah of Judah sent messengers to the king of the Assyrians in Lachish, saying, "I have offended, leave from me. Whatever you will lay on me, I will accept."

The king of Assyria laid on King Hezekiah of Judah a tribute of three hundred talents of silver and thirty talents of gold. Hezekiah gave all the silver that was found in the Temple of the Lord, and the treasury of the king's palace. At that time Hezekiah cut down the gold from the doors of the temple, and from the steles which Hezekiah king of Judah had overlaid with gold, and gave it to the king of the Assyrians. The king of the Assyrians sent Tartans and Resafa and Rabshakeh from Lachish to King Hezekiah with a strong force against Jerusalem. They went up and came to Jerusalem, and stood by the aqueduct of the upper pool, which is by the road of the fuller's field.

They called to Hezekiah, and to him came Eliakim the son of Hilkiah the steward, and Shebna the scribe, and Joah the son of Asaph the recorder. Rabshakeh said to them, "Say now to Hezekiah, 'The great king of the Assyrians says, 'What is this confidence in which you trust?' You have said, (but they are mere words,) 'I have counsel and strength for war.' Now then in whom do you trust, that you have revolted from me? See now, are you trusting for yourself on this broken wand of reed, even on Egypt? Whoever will lean himself on it, it will even go into his hand and pierce it, this is what Pharaoh king of Egypt is to all who trust in him. However, you have said to me, 'We trust in Lord the god. Is not this he whose Bamahs and altars Hezekiah has removed and has said to Judah and Jerusalem, 'You will worship before this altar in Jerusalem?' Now, please, make an agreement with my lord the king of the Assyrians, and I will give you two thousand horses if you are able on your part to set riders on them. 'How then will you turn away the face of one petty governor, from among the least of my lord's servants? Yet you trust for yourself in Egypt for chariots and cavalry. Now have we come up without the Lord against this place to destroy it?' the Lord said to me, 'Go up against this land, and destroy it.'"

Eliakim the son of Hilkiah, and Shebna, and Joah, said to Rabshakeh, "Speak now to your servants in Aramaic,[3] for we understand it, and don't speak with us in Judahite.[4] Why do you speak in the ears of the people that are on the wall?"

Rabshakeh said to them, "Has my master sent me to your master, and to you, to speak these words? Has he not sent me to the men who sit on the wall, that they may eat their own dung, and drink their own water together with you."

Rabshakeh stood, and cried with a loud voice in Judahite, and said, "Hear the words of the great king of the Assyrians. The king says, 'Don't let Hezekiah encourage you with words, for he will not be able to deliver you out of his hand. Don't let Hezekiah cause you to trust in the Lord, saying, 'the Lord will certainly deliver us, this city will not be delivered into the hand of the king of the Assyrians, don't listen to Hezekiah, for the king of the Assyrians says, 'Gain my favor, and come out to me, and every man will drink of the wine from his own vine, and every man will eat of his own fig tree, and will drink water out of his own cistern, until I come and relocate you to a land like your own land, a land of grain and wine, and bread and vineyards, a land of olive oil, and honey. You will live and not die, so do not listen to Hezekiah, for he lies to you, saying, 'The Lord will save you.' Have the gods of the nations at all delivered each their own land out of the hand of the king of the Assyrians? Where is the god of Hama, and of Arpad? Where is the god of the Sippars, Hena, and Ivah? For have they delivered Samaria out of my hand? Who is there among all the gods of the countries, who have delivered their countries out of my hand, that the Lord should deliver Jerusalem out of my hand?"

The men were silent, and did not answer him, for there was a commandment of the king, saying, "You will not answer him."

Eliakim the son of Hilkiah, the steward, and Shebna the scribe, and Joah the son of Asaph the recorder came to Hezekiah, having torn their garments, and they reported to him the words of Rabshakeh.

# 4ᵗʰ Kingdoms: Chapter 18 Notes

**1** Codex Vaticanus: Neesthan (ΝΕΕϹΘΑΝ)

• Aleppo Codex: nhš hnhšt (נחש הנחשת). Translation: serpent this copper

• Leningrad Codex: nechash hannechoshet (נְחַשׁ הַנְּחֹשֶׁת). Translation: serpent this copper

• Targum Jerusalem: Yh nechushetann (יה נְחוּשְׁתָן). Translation: Yah of copper


**2** Codex Vaticanus: Sennachêrim (ϹΕΝΝΑΧΗΡΙΜ)

• Aleppo Codex: Snhryb (סנחריב)

• Leningrad Codex: Sancheriv (סַנְחֵרִיב)

• Targum Jerusalem: Sancheriv (סַנְחֵרִיב)

King Sennacherib was the king of the Assyrian Empire between 705 and 681 BC.


**3** Codex Vaticanus: Syristi (ϹΥΡΙϹΤΙ). Translation: Syrian (or Aramaic)

• Aleppo Codex: Årmyt (ארמית). Translation: Aramaic

• Leningrad Codex: Aramit (אֲרָמִית). Translation: Aramaic

• Targum Jerusalem: Aramit (אֲרָמִית). Translation: Aramaic

'Syristi' was the Greek translation of the word 'Aramaic,' and therefore the original term is restored.


**4** Codex Vaticanus: Ioudaesti (ΙΟΥΔΑΙϹΤΙ). Translation: Judahite

• Aleppo Codex: Yhwdyt (יהודית). Translation: Judahite

• Leningrad Codex: Yehudit (יְהוּדִית). Translation: Judahite

# 4<sup>th</sup> KINGDOMS: CHAPTER 18 NOTES

- Targum Jerusalem: Yehudit (יְהוּדִית). Translation: Judahite

# 4th Kingdoms: Chapter 19

When King Hezekiah heard it, he tore his clothes, and put on sackcloth, and went into the Temple of the Lord. He sent Eliakim the steward, and Shebna the scribe, and the elders of the priests clothed with sackcloth, to Isaiah, the prophet the son of Amos. They said to him, "Hezekiah says, "This day is a day of tribulation, and rebuke, and provocation. The children have come to be born, but the mother has no strength. The Lord God may hear all the words of Rabshakeh, who the king of Assyria his master has sent to reproach the living God and to insult him with the words which Lord the god has heard, therefore you will offer your prayer for the remnant that is found."

So the servants of King Hezekiah came to Isaiah, and Isaiah said to them, "You will say this to your master, 'the Lord says, 'do not be afraid of the words which you have heard, where the servants of the king of the Assyrians have blasphemed. Look, I send a spirit on him, and he will hear a report and will return to his own land, and I will overthrow him with the sword in his own land.'"

So Rabshakeh returned and found the king of Assyria warring against Libnah, and he heard that he had departed from Lachish. He heard concerning King Taharqa[1] of Kush,[2] 'Look, he is come out to fight with you,' and he left.

He sent messengers to Hezekiah, saying, "Don't let your god in who you trust encourage you, saying, 'Jerusalem will not be delivered into the hands of the king of the Assyrians.' Look, you have heard all that the kings of the Assyrians have done in all the lands, to destroy them completely, and you will be saved? Have the gods of the nations who my fathers destroyed saved them? Both Gozan, and Harran, and Resafa,[3] and the sons of Eden[4] who were at the hill of Assur?[5] Where is the king of Hama, and the king of Arpad? Where is the king of the Sippar cities of Anah[6] and Ivah?"

Hezekiah took the letter from the hand of the messengers, and read it, and he went up to the Temple of the Lord, and Hezekiah spread it before the Lord, and said, "Lord the god in Israel who lives above the sphinxes, you are the only god in all the kingdoms of the earth! You have made the sky and earth. Incline your ear, the Lord, and hear! Open, the Lord, your eyes, and see! Hear the words of Sennacherib, which he has sent to insult the living god. Truly, Lord, the kings of Assyria have wasted the nations, and have thrown their gods into the fire, because they are no gods, but the works of men's hands, wood and stone, and they have destroyed them. Now, Lord the god, save us out of his hand, and all the kingdoms of the earth will know that you alone are Lord the god."

Isaiah the son of Amos sent to Hezekiah, saying, "The god Lord Sabaoth, the god in Israel says, 'I have heard your prayer to me concerning Sennacherib king of the Assyrians.' This is the word which the Lord has spoken against him. 'The virgin daughter of Zion has made light of you, and mocked you, the daughter of Jerusalem has shaken her head at you. Who have you reproached, and whom have you criticized? Against who have you lifted your voice, and raised your eyes? It is against the holiness[7] of Israel! By your messengers you have reproached the Lord, and have said, 'I will go up with the multitude of my chariots, to the height of the mountains, to the sides of Lebanon, and I have cut down the height of his cedar, and his choice cypresses, and I have come into the middle of the forest and of Carmel. I have refreshed myself, and have drunk strange waters, and I have dried up with the sole of my foot all the rivers of fortified places. I have brought about the matter, I have brought it to a conclusion, and it is come to the destruction of the bands of warlike prisoners, even of fortified cities. They that lived in them were weak in hand, they shake and were confounded, they became like the grass of the field, or as the green plant, the grass growing on houses, and that which is trodden down by him that stands on it.' But I know your laying down, and your going out, and your rage against me."

"Because you were angry with me, and your fierceness is come up into my ears, therefore will I put my hooks in your nostrils, and my bridle in your lips, and I will turn you back by the way by which you came. This will be a sign for you: Eat this year the things that grow of themselves, and next year the things which spring up, and in the third year let there be sowing, and reaping, and planting of vineyards, and eat the fruit of them. He will increase who has escaped from the house of Judah, and the remnant will strike root beneath, and it will produce fruit above. For from Jerusalem will go out a remnant, and he who escapes from the mountain of Zion, the zeal of Lord Sabaoth will do this. Is it not so?'"

"The Lord says this concerning the king of the Assyrians, 'He will not enter into this city, and he will not shoot an arrow there, neither will a shield come against it, neither will he heap a mound against it. By the road by which he comes, on it will he return, and he will not enter into this city," says the Lord. "I will defend this city as with a shield, for my own sake, and for my servant David's sake." At night that messenger of the lord went out, and slaughtered the camp of the Assyrians a hundred and eighty-five thousand. They woke early in the morning, and saw these were all dead corpses. King Sennacherib of the Assyrians departed, and returned and lived in Nineveh. It happened, while he was worshiping Gugalanna[8] in the temple of his god, that Prince Adra[9] and Shar-usur[10] his sons killed him with the sword, and they escaped into the land of Urartu,[11] and Esarhaddon[12] his son reigned in his place.

# 4<sup>th</sup> Kingdoms: Chapter 19 Notes

**1** Codex Vaticanus: Tharaca (ⲐⲀⲢⲀⲔⲀ)

- Aleppo Codex: Trhqh (תרהקה)

- Leningrad Codex: Tirhakah (תִּרְהָקָה)

- Targum Jerusalem: Tirhakah (תִּרְהָקָה)

King Taharqa was a Nubian King whose reign is generally dated to between 690 and 664 BC. At the time the Nubian Empire ruled Egypt. He fought a series of wars against the Assyrians. There is some debate as to whether King Tharaka/Tirhaqah was Taharqa or one of his predecessors: Shabaka or Shebitku, due to the conflicting records of the Egyptians, however, the majority of modern scholars accept that this is a reference to Taharqa.

**2** Codex Vaticanus: Aithiopôn (ⲀⲒⲐⲒⲞⲡⲱⲚ). Translation: Aethiopia

- Aleppo Codex: Kwš (כוש)

- Leningrad Codex: Kush (כּוּשׁ)

- Targum Jerusalem: Chush (כוּשׁ)

The term Aethiopians was applied to all dark-skinned nations that the Greeks encountered, both in Sub-Saharan Africa and Southern India, however, the empire that King Taharqa ruled at the time was the Empire of Kush, based in modern Sudan, which had at that time conquered Egypt.

**3** Codex Vaticanus: Raphes (ⲢⲀⲫⲉⲤ)

- Aleppo Codex: Rsp (רצף)

- Leningrad Codex: Retzef (רֶצֶף)

- Targum Jerusalem: Retzef (רֶצֶף)

Resafa was a city on the Euphrates until the Byzantine era, also known in later times as Sergiopolis and Anastasiopolis. The ruins are called Al-Resafa, in modern Syria.

**4** Codex Vaticanus: Edem (ⲈⲆⲈⳘ)

• Aleppo Codex: Ôdn (עֶדֶן)

• Leningrad Codex: Eden (עֶדֶן)

• Targum Jerusalem: Eden (עֶדֶן)

The term Edem/Eden is generally treated as a reference to the plains of southern Iraq in ancient Israelite, Judahite, and Aramean texts, based on the ancient Akkadian Cuneiform name edinu (𒂔 𒌍 𒄖) meaning 'plain,' itself based on the earlier Sumerian word eden (𒂔) also meaning 'plain.'

**5** Codex Vaticanus: Thaesthen (ⲐⲀⲈⲤⲐⲈⲚ)

• Aleppo Codex: Tlăšr (תלאשר)

• Leningrad Codex: Telasar (תְּלַאשָׂר). Translation: Hill of Assur

• Targum Jerusalem: Telasar (תְּלַסָר)

This reference is debated, however, it is likely referring to the ancestral capital of Assyria: Assur. During the reign of King Ashur Nasir Pal II between 883 and 859 BC the capital had been moved to Nimrud, farther north. The capital of the empire was moved by King Sargon II to a new city he built and named after himself Dur-Sharrukin (Fortress of Sargon), which was abandoned by King Sennacherib, who moved the capital to Nineveh. According to Assyrian history, Assur existed before the Assyrian tribes settled there, and therefore the reference to the 'sons of Eden who were at the hill of Assur,' was likely a reference to the Sumerians that lived there before it was conquered by the Assyrians.

**6** Codex Vaticanus: Ana (ᗅNᗅ)

- Aleppo Codex: Hnô (הֹנֵע)

- Leningrad Codex: Hena (הֵנַע)

- Targum Jerusalem: Taltilunun (טַלְטִילוּנוּן)

Anah is a town on the Euphrates in Al-Anbar province, Iraq. The town was more significant in ancient times. Its earliest recorded name was Hanat, during the Old Babylonian era, which was derived from the name of the war-goddess Anat. By the time of the Assyrian era, the town was called Anat in the records of King Ashur Nasir Pal II.

**7** Codex Vaticanus: agion (ᗅΓΙΟΝ). Translation: saint

- Aleppo Codex: qdwš (קדוש). Translation: sacred (or Qetesh)

- Leningrad Codex: kadosh (קָדוֹשׁ). Translation: sacred (or Qetesh)

- Targum Jerusalem: kadisha (קָדִישָׁא). Translation: sacred (or ring)

Kadesh was a Canaanite goddess whose name is believed to have begun as a title for the goddess Asherah. Her main center of worship was in the city of Qadesh, in Syria. Her worship was carried into Egypt by the large number of Canaanites that settled there during the Second Intermediate Period, where she was known as Qetesh. As this is the same time period that the Israelites were described as living in Egypt, it is likely they were worshiping her at the time, although, based on the number of references to Asherah in the Hebrew texts, it is likely that they generally knew her as Asherah.

**8** Codex Vaticanus: Neserach (ΝΕϹΕΡᗅΧ)

- Aleppo Codex: Nsrk (נסרך)

- Leningrad Codex: Nisroch (נִסְרֹךְ)

- Targum Jerusalem: Nisroch (נִסְרוֹךְ)

There is no known Assyrian deity with this name. It is theorized by some researchers to be a scribal error, and the original text would have read Ninurta. This hypothetical error would result from the Hebrew letter m (מ) being replacing with s (ס) and the letter d (ד) being replaced with a ch (ך). There was a major temple of Ninurta in Nimrud, near Nineveh. If this theory is correct then the error would have been in the source text the Aramaic and Phoenician texts were made from, in order to be in both the Greek and Hebrew translations.

It seems unlikely that ᵃⁿNinurta (⸗⊢⊨⊟⊔) could have been mistransliterated into nsrk (ץץ℘), and if this word began as a cuneiform word, which was translated following Sumerian norms like other words transliterated into Aramaic, then it would have ⁿⁱⁿSarik (⊦⊟⊢⩗), which would have been the Akkadian translation of Bôl Šr (٩ᵂ ∠O9), the Canaanite name of the 'Great Bull in the Sky' Gugalanna (⊏▷⊟⊢⸗), now known as the constellation Taurus.

Conversely the Talmud claims that the original Hebrew word was neser, not nisroch, which translates as a plank of wood. As the text is unlikely to be referencing a plank of wood, the translation of Gugalanna is used, although the translation of 'Taurus' may be equally applicable.

**9** Codex Vaticanus: Adramelech (ΑΔΡΑΜΕΛΕΧ)

- Aleppo Codex: Ȧdrmlk (אדרמלך)

- Leningrad Codex: Adrammelech (אַדְרַמֶּלֶךְ)

- Targum Jerusalem: Adramelech (אֲדְרַמֶלֶךְ)

Arda-Mulissu was one of Sennacherib's sons, called Adrammelech in Hebrew texts. He assassinated his father King Sennacherib in 681 BC in an attempt to usurp the throne. His brother Nabu Shar-usur assisted him, however, his other brother Esarhaddon had support of the military, and drove Arda-Mulissu from the throne. Arda-Mulissu and Nabu Shar-usur fled to Uratu, in the Armenian highlands.

The difference between his name and in both the Greek and Hebrew translations, and his name in the Assyrian records indicates the original term in the Akkadian cuneiform text of Kingdoms used the term Adra 'malku' (), meaning 'Prince' Adra. As the name Adra was a transcription error of Arda, the term Prince Arda is used in this translation.

**10** Codex Vaticanus: Sarasar (ϹΑΡΑϹΑΡ)

- Aleppo Codex: Šråṣr (שראצר)
- Leningrad Codex: Shar'etzer (שַׂרְאֶצֶר)
- Targum Jerusalem: Shar'etzer (שַׂרְאֶצֶר)

Nabu Shar-usur was one of Sennacherib's sons. He helped Arda-Mulissu assassinate his father King Sennacherib in 681 BC in an attempt to usurp the throne. Their other brother Esarhaddon had the support of the military, and drove Arda-Mulissu from the throne. Arda-Mulissu and Nabu Shar-usur fled to Uratu, in the Armenian highlands, and it is not known what happened to them.

**11** Codex Vaticanus: gên Ararat (ΓΗΝΑΡΑΡΑΤ). Translation: land of Ararat

- Aleppo Codex: årṣ Årrt (ארץ אררט). Translation: land of Ararat (or of Urartu)
- Leningrad Codex: eretz Ararat (אֶרֶץ אֲרָרָט). Translation: land of Ararat
- Targum Jerusalem: ar'a Kardu (אַרְעָא קַרְדוּ). Translation: land of Kurdistan

The Mountains of Ararat are in the Armenian Highlands of eastern Turkey. At the time, the highlands were home to the Kingdom of kurU-rartu (), which translates as 'land of Urartu,' and almost certainly the original term used in the Cuneiform books of the Kingdoms. As this was the land that Prince Arda and Shar-usur fled to, the name Urartu is used in this translation. The Targum Jerusalem uses the name 'Cordune,' which was a common reinterpretation of Urartu during the Classical Era, however, was to the south of the ancient kingdom of Urartu.

**12** Codex Vaticanus: Asordan (ασορδαν)

- Aleppo Codex: Åsr Ḥdn (אסר חדן)

- Leningrad Codex: Esar-chaddon (אֱסַר־חַדֹּן)

- Targum Jerusalem: Esarchadon (אֱסָרְחַדוֹן)

Esarhaddon is the more common name of King Aššur-Aḫa-Iddina, Sennacherib's youngest son and heir. The name Esarhaddon is derived from the Latin Hazor Haddan, which was in turn derived from the Greek Asarchaddon (Ασαρχαδδων), which was used in direct translations from Assyrian texts. The name Asordan (Ασορδαν) used in the Septuagint is a direct transliteration of the Aramaic spelling of Aššur: Åšor (אשור), followed by the rest of the Assyrian name -adin (𒀸𒋙), confirming that the Greek translation was made from an Aramaic translation was was in turn made from a Cuneiform version of the book.

# 4th Kingdoms: Chapter 20

In those days was Hezekiah sick, and close to death. The prophet Isaiah the son of Amos came to him, and said, "The Lord says, 'Give orders to your household, for you will die.'"

Hezekiah turned to the wall, and prayed to the Lord, "The Lord, remember, please, how I have walked before you in truth and with a perfect heart, and have done that which is good in your eyes," and Hezekiah wept greatly.

Isaiah was in the middle court, when the word of the Lord came to him, saying, "Go back and say to Hezekiah the ruler of my people, 'Lord the god of your father David says, 'I have heard your prayer, and I have seen your tears. I will heal you. In three days you will go up to the Temple of the Lord, and I will add to your days fifteen years. I will deliver you and this city out of the hand of the king of the Assyrians, and I will defend this city for my own sake, and for my servant's David sake.'"

He said, "Let them take a cake of figs, and lay it on the ulcer, and he will be well."

Hezekiah said to Isaiah, "What is the sign that the Lord will heal me, and I will go up to the Temple of the Lord on the third day?"

Isaiah said, "This is the sign from the Lord, that the Lord will perform the word which he has spoken, the shadow of the dial will advance ten degrees, or if it should go back ten degrees this would also be the sign."

Hezekiah said, "It is a light thing for the shadow to go down ten degrees. No, but let the shadow return ten degrees backward on the dial." Isaiah the prophet cried to the Lord, and the shadow moved back ten degrees on the dial.

At that time King Marduk Apla-Iddina,[1] son of Baladan[2] of Babylon, sent letters and a present to Hezekiah because he had heard that Hezekiah was sick. Hezekiah rejoiced at them and them showed all the house of his spices, the silver and the gold, the spices, and the fine oil, and the armory, and all that was found in his treasures. There was nothing that Hezekiah did not show them in his house, and in all his dominion.

Isaiah the prophet went to King Hezekiah, and asked him, "What did these men say? Where did they come to you from?"

Hezekiah answered, "They came to me from a distant land, from Babylon."

He said, "What did they see in your house?"

He said, "They saw all the things that are in my house. There was nothing in my house which I did not show them. Yes, all that was in my treasury also."

Isaiah said to Hezekiah, "Hear the word of the Lord, 'Look, the days come, that all things that are in your house will be taken to Babylon, and all that your fathers have treasured up until this day. There will not fail a word,' which the Lord has spoken. As for your sons which you will father, the enemy will take them, and they will be eunuchs in the house of the king of Babylon."

Hezekiah said to Isaiah, "Good is the word of the Lord which he has spoken. Only let there be peace in my days." The rest of the acts of Hezekiah, and all his might, and all that he made, the fountain and the aqueduct, and how he brought water into the city, aren't these things written in the book of the Chronicles of the Kings of Judah? Hezekiah slept with his fathers and Manasseh his son reigned in his place.

# 4<sup>th</sup> Kingdoms: Chapter 20 Notes

**1** Codex Vaticanus: Marodachbaladan (ΜΑΡѠΔΑΧΒΑΛΑΔΑΝ)

- Aleppo Codex: Brådk Blådn (בראדך בלאדן)

- Leningrad Codex: Berodach bal'adan (בְּרֹאדַךְ בַּלְאֲדָן)

- Targum Jerusalem: Berodach bal'adan (בְּרֹאדַךְ בַּלְאֲדָן)

The more common name of this king today is Marduk Apla-Iddina II, who wrestled control of Babylon from the hands of the Assyrians in 722 BC, and ruled until 710 BC when the Assyrian King Shalmaneser V managed to recapture the city. Marduk Apla-Iddina II escaped to Elam (southern Iran) when Babylon fell, and later returned in 703 BC, and managed to seize control of Babylon for 9 months, afterwhich the Assyrian King Sennacherib recaptured the city. He died in exile in Elam. As the Greek and Hebrew versions of the verse differ slightly, his actual name is imported from ancient Babylonian and Assyrian historical records.

**2** Codex Vaticanus: Baladan (ΒΑΛΑΔΑΝ)

- Aleppo Codex: Blådn (בלאדן)

- Leningrad Codex: Bal'adan (בַּלְאֲדָן)

- Targum Jerusalem: Bal'adan (בַּלְאֲדָן)

# 4<sup>th</sup> Kingdoms: Chapter 21

Manasseh was twelve years old when he began to reign, and he reigned fifty-five years in Jerusalem. His mother's name was Hephzibah. He did that which was evil in the eyes of the Lord, according to the abominations of the nations which the Lord drove out from before the Israelites. He rebuilt the bamahs, which Hezekiah his father had demolished, and set up an altar to Ba'al, and rebuilt Asherah as Ahab king of Israel made them, and worshiped all the army of Shamayim, and served them. He built an altar in the Temple of the Lord, where he had said, "In Jerusalem, I will place my name."

He built an altar to all the army of Shamayim in the two courts of the Temple of the Lord. He caused his sons to pass through the fire, and used divination and omens, and made groves, and multiplied wizards, to do that which was evil in the sight of the Lord, to provoke him to anger. He set up the engraved statues of Asherah[1] in the temple which the Lord said to David, and to Solomon his son, "In this house, and in Jerusalem which I have chosen out of all the tribes of Israel, I will place my name forever. I will not again remove the foot of Israel from the land which I gave to their fathers, of all those who will keep all that I commanded, according to all the commandments which my servant Moses commanded them."

They did not listen and Manasseh led them astray to do evil in the sight of the Lord, beyond the nations whom the Lord completely destroyed from before the Israelites. The Lord said through his servants the prophets, "Manasseh the king of Judah has worked all these evil abominations, beyond even which the Amorites did, who lived before him, and who has led Judah also into sin through their idols. This must not be."

Lord the god in Israel says, "Look, I bring calamities on Jerusalem and Judah so that both the ears of everyone that hears will tingle. I will stretch out over Jerusalem the measure of Samaria, and the plummet of the house of Ahab, and I will wipe Jerusalem as a jar is wiped, and turned upside down in the wiping. I will reject the remnant of my inheritance and will deliver them into the hands of their enemies, and they will be as plunder and as a spoil to all their enemies. As they have done wickedly in my sight, and have provoked me from the day that I brought their fathers out of Egypt, even until this day. Moreover, Manasseh shed a great deal of innocent blood, until he filled Jerusalem with it from one end to the other, beside his sins with which he caused Judah to sin, in doing evil in the eyes of the Lord."

The rest of the acts of Manasseh, and all that he did, and his sin which he sinned, are these things not written in the book of the Chronicles of the Kings of Judah? Manasseh slept with his fathers and was buried in the garden of his palace, in the garden of Uzza,[2] and Amon his son reigned in his place.

Amon was twenty-two years old when he began to reign, and he reigned for two years in Jerusalem. His mother's name was Meshullemeth, daughter of Haruz of Jotbah. He did that which was evil in the sight of the Lord, as Manasseh his father did. He followed in all the ways in which his father walked, and served the idols which his father served, and worshiped them. He forgot Lord the god of his fathers and did not follow the ways of the Lord.

The servants of Amon conspired against him and killed the king in his palace. The people of the land killed all that had conspired against king Amon, and the people of the land made Josiah king in his room. The rest of the acts of Amon, all that he did, look, are these not written in the book of the Chronicles of the Kings of Judah? They buried him in his tomb in the garden of Uzza, and Josiah his son reigned in his place.

# 4<sup>th</sup> Kingdoms: Chapter 21 Notes

**1** Codex Vaticanus: alsous (ⲀⲗⲥⲟⲨⲥ). Translation: grove (or park with trees)

• Aleppo Codex: Åšrh (אשרה). Translation: visa (or permit, Asherah, Astarte)

• Leningrad Codex: Asherah (אֲשֵׁרָה). Translation: visa (or permit, Asherah, Astarte)

• Targum Jerusalem: Asheirata (אֲשֵׁירְתָא)

The Greek word 'grove' makes no sense in the context of this verse, and therefore the Masoretic name Asherah is imported.


**2** Codex Vaticanus: Oza (ⲟⲍⲀ)

• Aleppo Codex: Ôzå (עזא). Translation: goat (in Aramaic, or 'Uzzā in Arabic)

• Leningrad Codex: Uzza (עֻזָּא). Translation: goat (in Aramaic, or 'Uzzā in Arabic)

• Targum Jerusalem: Uza (עֻזָא)

The nature of the Garden of Uzza has been debated since the Classical era. It is unlikely that the name was derived from the Aramaic word for goat, as Aramaic would not have been widely spoken in Judah at the time. The alternate interpretation is that this was either a garden named after the Arabian goddess al-'Uzzā (العزى), one of the three major goddesses of Arabia in the pre-Islamic era. Al-'Uzzā was the goddess of the planet Venus, and the Arabian equivalent of the Greek Aphrodite.

As the text appears to have been written in Akkadian Cuneiform, and no other references to the Garden of Uzza have been found that date to the era, it is possible this was a Canaanite name that was translated into Akkadian, in which case the word was probably uzuzzu (𒍪𒄿𒍪) meaning 'the presence,' and suggesting a mortuary grove, like it groves that King Josiah later destroyed. As the meaning of the name is unclear, the name is transliterated directly from the Hebrew in this translation.

# 4ᵗʰ Kingdoms: Chapter 22

Josiah was eight years old when he began to reign, and he reigned thirty-one years in Jerusalem. His mother's name was Jedidah, the daughter of Adaiah of Boscath. He did that which was right in the sight of the Lord and walked in all the ways of David his forefather, he did not turn aside to the right hand or the left. In the eighteenth year of King Josiah, in the eighth month, the king sent Shaphan the son of Azaliah the son of Meshullam, the scribe of the Temple of the Lord, saying, "Go to Hilkiah the high priest, and account of the silver that is brought into the Temple of the Lord, which the doormen have collected from the people. Let them give it into the hands of the workmen that are appointed in the Temple of the Lord."

He gave it to the workmen in the Temple of the Lord, to repair the damage to the temple, to the carpenters, and builders, and masons, and also to purchase timber and cut stones, to repair the damage to the temple. They did not call them to account for the silver that was given to them, because they dealt faithfully. Hilkiah the high priest told Shaphan the scribe, "I have found the book of the law in the Temple of the Lord."

Hilkiah gave the book to Shaphan, and he read it. He traveled from the Temple of the Lord to the king, and reported to the king, "Your servants have collected the silver that was found in the Temple of the Lord, and have given it into the hands of the workmen that are appointed in the Temple of the Lord."

Shaphan the scribe told the king, "Hilkiah the priest has given me a book."

Shaphan read it to the king, and when the king heard the words of the book of the law, he tore his garments. The king commanded Hilkiah the priest, and Ahikam the son of Shaphan, and Achbor the son of Micah, and Shaphan the scribe, and Asahiah the king's servant, "Go, inquire of the Lord for me, and for all the people, and for all Judah, and concerning the words of this book that has been found. The anger of the Lord that has been started against us is great because our fathers did not listen to the words of this book, to do according to all the things written concerning us."

So Hilkiah the priest went, and Ahikam, and Achbor, and Shaphan, and Asahiah, to Huldah the prophetess, the mother of Shallum the son of Tikvah son of Harhas, keeper of the robes, (she lived in Jerusalem in Mishneh) and they spoke to her. She answered them, "Lord the god in Israel says, "Say to the man that sent you to me, 'the Lord says, "Look, I bring evil on this place, and on those who live in it, even all the words of the book which the king of Judah has read, because they have forgotten me, and burnt incense to other gods, that they might provoke me with the works of their hands. My anger will burn forth against this place, and will not be quenched."'

To the king of Judah that sent you to inquire of the Lord, tell him this, 'Lord the god in Israel says, 'As for the words which you have heard, because your heart was softened, and you were humiliated before me when you heard all that I spoke against this place, and against the inhabitants of it, that it should be completely destroyed and cursed, and you ripped your clothes, and cried before me, I have also heard,' says the Lord. 'Therefore it will not happen. Look, I will add you to your fathers, and you will be gathered to your tomb in peace, and your eyes will not see any among all the evils which I bring on this place.'"

# 4<sup>th</sup> Kingdoms: Chapter 23

They reported the word to the king, and the king gathered all the elders of Judah and Jerusalem to himself. The king went up to the Temple of the Lord, and every man of Judah and all who lived in Jerusalem with him, and the priests, and the prophets, and all the people small and great, and he read in their ears all the words of the book of the covenant that was found in the Temple of the Lord. The king stood by a pillar, and made a covenant before the Lord, to follow the Lord, to keep his commandments and his testimonies and his ordinances with all the heart and with all the mind, to confirm the words of this covenant, even the things written in this book. All the people agreed to the covenant.

The king commanded Hilkiah the high priest, and the priests of the second order, and those who kept the door, to bring out of the temple of the Lord all the vessels that were made for Ba'al, and for Asherah, and all the army of Shamayim, and he burnt them outside of Jerusalem in the fields of Kidron, and took the ashes of them to the Temple of El. He burnt the sacred male prostitutes, who the kings of Judah had appointed, and those who burnt incense in the Bamahs and in the cities of Judah, and the places around Jerusalem, and those that burnt incense to Ba'al, Shemesh,[1] Yarikh,[2] the Zodiac,[3] and the power of the armies of Shamayim.

He carried out the Asherah from the Temple of the Lord to the brook Kidron, and burnt it at the brook Kidron, and ground it to powder, and threw its powder on the sepulchers of the sons of the people. He pulled down the Palace of Kadosh that were by the Temple of the Lord, where the women wove tents for the Asherah. He brought up all the priests from the cities of Judah and defiled the bamahs where the priests burnt incense, from Geba even to Beersheba.

He pulled down the house of the gates that were by the door of the gate of Joshua the ruler of the city, on a man's left hand at the gate of the city. The priests of the bamahs did not go up to the altar of the Lord in Jerusalem, and they only ate leavened bread among their brothers. He defiled sacrificial shine[4] in the valley of the son of Hinns,[5] for a man to pass his son or for a man to pass his daughter to Moloch in fire.[6] He burnt the horses which the king of Judah had given to Shemesh in the entrance of the Temple of the Lord, by the treasury of Nathan the king's eunuch, in the suburbs, and he burnt the Chariot of Shemesh with fire.

The altars that were on the roof of the upper room of Ahaz, which the kings of Judah had made, and the altars which Manasseh had made in the two courts of the Temple of the Lord, the king pulled down and forcibly removed from there and threw their dust into the Brook of Kidron. The king defiled the temple that was near Jerusalem, to the right of the mountain of rubbish[7] that Solomon, king of Israel, built to Astarte[8] the abomination of the Sidonians, and to Chemosh the abomination of Moab, and to Moloch the abomination of the Ammonites. He broke in pieces the steles, and completely destroyed Asherah, and filled their places with the bones of men. Also the high altar in the Temple of El, which had been built by Jeroboam the son of Nebat, who made Israel sin, even that high altar he tore down, and broke in pieces the stones of it, and reduced it to powder, and burnt Asherah.

Josiah turned aside, and saw the tombs that were there in the city, and sent, and took the bones out of the tombs, and burnt them on the altar, and defiled it, following the word of the Lord which the prophet spoke, when Jeroboam stood by the altar at the feast, and he turned and raised his eyes to the tomb of the prophet that spoke these words. He said, "What is that mound which I see?"

The men of the city said to him, "It is the grave of the prophet that came out of Judah, and uttered these imprecations which he imprecated on the altar of the Temple of El."

He said, "Leave him alone. Let no one disturb his bones," and so his bones were spared, together with the bones of the prophet that came out of Samaria. Moreover, Josiah removed all the temples of the bamahs that were in the cities of Samaria, which the kings of Israel made to provoke the Lord, and did to them all that he did in the Temple of El. He sacrificed all the priests of the bamahs that were there. on the altars and burnt the bones of the men on them, and returned to Jerusalem.

The king commanded all the people, "Keep the Passover to Lord the god, as it is written in the Book of the Covenant," as a Passover had not been kept since the days of the judges who judged Israel, until the days of the kings of Israel and Judah. In the eighteenth year of king Josiah, was the Passover kept to the Lord in Jerusalem. Moreover, Josiah removed the sorcerers, and the wizards, and the icons,[9] and the idols, and all the abominations that had been set up in the land of Judah and in Jerusalem, that he might keep the words of the law that were written in the book, which Hilkiah the priest found in the Temple of the Lord.

There was no king like him before him, who turned to the Lord with all his heart, and with all his mind, and with all his strength, according to all the law of Moses, and after him, there did not rise another one like him. Nevertheless, the Lord did not turn from the fierceness of his great anger against Judah, because of the provocations, where Manasseh provoked him. The Lord said, "I will also remove Judah from my presence, as I removed

Israel, and will reject this city which I have chosen even Jerusalem, and the house of which I said, 'My name will be there.'"

The rest of the acts of Josiah and all that he did are these things not written in the book of the Chronicles of the Kings of Judah?

In his days Pharaoh Necho,[10] king of Egypt went up with the king of the Assyrians to the river Euphrates. Josiah went out to meet him, and Necho II killed him in Megiddo when he saw him. His servants carried him dead from Megiddo, and brought him to Jerusalem, and buried him in his sepulcher, and the people of the land took Jehoahaz the son of Josiah, and anointed him, and made him king in the room of his father. Jehoahaz was 23 years old when he began to reign, and he reigned three months in Jerusalem. His mother's name was Hamutal, the daughter of Jeremiah of Libnah.

He did that which was evil in the sight of the Lord, like all that his forefathers did. Pharaoh Necho removed him to Riblah in the land of Hamath, so that he should not reign in Jerusalem, and imposed a tribute on the land of one hundred talents of silver, and one hundred talents of gold. Pharaoh Necho made Eliakim, the son of King Josiah of Judah, king, to rule over them in the place of his father Josiah, and he changed his name to Jehoiakim, and he took Jehoahaz to Egypt, and he died there.

Jehoiakim gave the silver and the gold to Pharaoh, but he assessed the land to give the silver at the command of Pharaoh. They gave the silver and the gold to each man according to his assessment together with the people of the land to give to Pharaoh Necho. Twenty-five years old was Jehoiakim when he began to reign, and he reigned eleven years in Jerusalem. and his mother's name was Jidlaph, daughter of Pedaiah of Rumah. He did that which was evil in the eyes of the Lord, like all that his forefathers had done.

# 4th Kingdoms: Chapter 23 Notes

**1** Codex Vaticanus: Êliô (ΗλιϹϡ). Translation: Helios (or sun)

- Aleppo Codex: Šmš (שמש). Translation: Shemesh (or sun)

- Leningrad Codex: Shemesh (שֶׁמֶשׁ). Translation: Shemesh (or sun)

- Targum Jerusalem: shimsha (שִׁמְשָׁא). Translation: sun

Shemesh (𐤔𐤌𐤔) was the Canaanite god of the sun, the equivalent of the Akkadian Shamshu (𒀭), Greek Helios (Ἡλίω), and Egyptian Ra (☉𓏃𓎼). By the era of King Josiah, the sun gods were dominant throughout the region, with the Babylonians worshiping ᵃⁿMarduk (𒀭𒀫𒌓) the 'sun-calf god' as the supreme God, and the Egyptians worshiping Amen (𓇋𓏶𓈖𓏏) as the sun god, father god in the Theban trinity, and supreme God of Egypt. Based on 1st Ezra, after the king of Egypt killed King Josiah, he restored the worship of the 'Lord,' which had to have been been Shemesh, as Egyptian records report he was a worshiper Ra, Amen, and Atum, the Egyptian sun gods.


**2** Codex Vaticanus: Selênê (ϹελΗΝΗ). Translation: Selene (or moon)

- Aleppo Codex: Yrḥ (ירח). Translation: Yarikh (or moon)

- Leningrad Codex: Yareach (יָרֵחַ). Translation: Yarikh (or moon)

- Targum Jerusalem: Sihara (סִיהֲרָא). Translation: moon

Yrḥ (𐤉𐤓𐤇) / Yrḥ (𐤁𐤒𐤆) was the Canaanite god of the moon, the equivalent of the Sabaen Wrḥ (𐩥𐩧𐩭), Aramaic Yrḥå (𐡉𐡓𐡇𐡀), Sumerian ᵃⁿNanna (𒀭𒋀𒆠), Akkadian Sin (𒀭𒌍), South Egyptian Khonsu (𓃹𓈖𓇳𓏤), North Egyptian Iahw (𓇋𓂝𓎛𓅱𓇳), and Greek Selene (Σελήνη). The moon god may have been dominant in Southern Canaan and Hejaz Mountains, which the Neo-Babylonian king Nabonidus believed, however, that would have been long before the era of Josiah. The city of Jericho appears to have been named after the Canaanite moon god Yrḥ, and was one of the major fortified cities in the region for thousands of years before it was destroyed around 1500 BC. Nabonidus attempted to restore the worship of the moon god briefly, however, lost his empire to the Persians.

**3** Codex Vaticanus: mazourôth (ΜΑΖΟΥΡѠΘ)

- Aleppo Codex: mzlwt (מִזְלוֹת)
- Leningrad Codex: mazzalot (מַזָּלוֹת)
- Targum Jerusalem: mazlata (מַזְלָתָא)

The Greek word is almost certainly based on the Aramaic mzrwt (מזרות), itself derived from the Neo-Babylonian mazraåtu (𒂍𒐊𒐽𒀀𒈨), meaning 'mansions' or 'manors.' The Hebrew translators appear to have made a transliteration error, replacing an R (ר) with an L (ל). The Jewish interpretation of the Hebrew word has traditionally been a reference to the zodiac, which does appear to be what the Babylonian word would mean in this context.

**4** Codex Vaticanus: Tapheth (ΤΑΦΕΘ)

- Aleppo Codex: tpt (תפת)
- Leningrad Codex: tofet (תֹּפֶת)
- Targum Jerusalem: tofet (תּוֹפֶת)

Both the Greek and Hebrew words appear to be transliterations ultimately from the Neo-Babylonian tiptu (𒀴𒁹𒈨), meaning 'sacrificial shine.' If tiptu was transliterated directly into Aramaic it would be rendered as tpt (תפת), which is the direct transliteration of the term in the Masoretic text. As both the Greek and Hebrew terms are transliterations of the word, the Akkadian term is restored.

**5** Codex Vaticanus: pharangi huiou Ennom (ϷΑΡΑΓΓΙΥΙΟΥ ЄΝΝΟΜ). Translation: gorge (or canyon) sons Ennom

- Aleppo Codex: bny [bn] hnm (בְּנִי [בֶּן] הִנֹּם). Translation: sons [son] of Hinns

- Leningrad Codex: venei K [ven-hinnom Q] (בְנֵי־ כ [בֶן־הִנֹּם ק]). Translation: sons K [son the sleep Q]

- Targum Jerusalem: bar Hinom (בַּר הִנוֹם). Translation: sons of the sleep

The exact location of the (gorge of) the sons of sleep is disputed. In modern terminology, the 'Valley of Hinnom' is the valley south and west of Jerusalem's Old City and Mount Zion, however, this is not necessarily the ancient context. An alternate location is Wadi ar-Rababi, which runs east from Mount Zion. The Septuagint includes a different name in Joshua chapter 18, refering to the place as the 'Forest of Shonnam' (ναπης Σονναμ), where the Masoretic text reads Valley of the Sons of Hinnom (גֵּי בֶן־הִנֹּם). The name change of Hinnom to Shonnam is easy to explain as a translation error when the Aramaic version was created, as the Canaanite H (𐤄) and the Ś (𐤔) looked quite similar. A virtually identical error is found in the Judahite Apocalypse of Ezra, which rendered the Sea of Edom as the Sea of Sodom.

The origin of the word 'hinnom' is likely a plural of hinn (حِنّ), a reference to an ancient extinct type of being that once lived on the Earth in Semitic folklore. The hinns continue to be part of the Islamic and Druze religions, although their roles in the religions vary. It is agreed that they are extinct, however, it isn't clear what they were. Many sources describe the hinn and binn as powerful, gigantic primordial creatures, suggesting they were influenced by finding the bones of extinct animals. Conversely, the Revelations of 'Abdullah Al-Sayid Muhammad Habib claims the hinn were air creatures, and the binn were water creatures, while the medieval Islamic historian al-Tabari claimed they were created from poisonous fire (سموم). In most versions of the stories, they fought in part of a series of wars for control of the earth before the creation of humanity, and most of the ancient species became extinct, including the hinn.

The substitution of 'forest' or 'grove' for the 'valley of the sons...' is clearly not a translation error. The combination of 'valley/abyss/gorge' and 'forest/grove' suggests it is a reference to a gravesite, and not a physical valley. At the time, Canaanites marked gravesites by planting trees, usually oak, which was known as the 'Asherah' tree, because it could self-pollinate, and was therefore seen as a 'virgin' tree. In the context of a gravesite, it is likely that the term 'sons of hinns' did not refer to some known people, but an ancient gravesite of a by then unknown people. Oak trees are known to live over 1000 years, and reproduce, so the gravesite in question could have already been thousands of years old.

**6** Codex Vaticanus: tô Moloch en pyri (ΤШΜΟΛΟΧΕΝΠΥΡΙ). Translation: to Moloch in fire

- Aleppo Codex: båš--lmlk (בּאשׁ--לַמְלְךְ). Translation: in fires of king

- Leningrad Codex: ba'esh lamMolech (בָּאֵשׁ לַמֹּלֶךְ). Translation: in fire to Molek

- Targum Jerusalem: benura laMolech (בְּנוּרָא לַמוֹלֶךְ). Translation: gave in fear to Molek

The Greeks translated the word Moloch as a name instead of translating it as 'king' indicating that the word was spelled as mlk (𐤌𐤋𐤊) in the Aramaic texts they translated. The Aramaic spelling of 'king' was mlkā (𐤌𐤋𐤊𐤀), indicating the term was transliterated as a name in the Aramaic text. As the Neo-Babylonian spelling of 'king' was malkum (𒈗) this 'name' had to have been transliterated into the cuneiform text from the older Phoenician (Judahite/Samaritan) mlk (𐤊𐤋𐤌), meaning 'king.'

According to Roman and Greek records, the Carthaginians in Tunisia had a similar practice of sacrificing their children to Baal Hammon, which the Greeks considered to be the Phoenician version of Kronos, and the Roman considered to be Saturn. The remains of children's bones mixed with animal bones in Tunisia discover in the 1920s, are been considered conclusive proof of the child sacrifice the Greeks and Romans described.

Similar human and animal remains discovered in a temple in Amman, Jordan in the 1960s, indicate that human sacrifice was happening there since 1400 BC. As Moses' laws required the sacrifice of the first born, and Baruch later claimed that God turned against the Judahites because they were doing something no one should ever do, they were following the laws of Moses and consuming their children, it is clear that this 'King' was considered Moses' god by those sacrificing their children. Josiah's reforms in Leviticus specifically amended Moses' laws, prohibiting the sacrifice of the first born, meaning it was still being practiced until his time.


**7** Codex Vaticanus: arous tou Mosoath (ⲞⲢⲞⲨⳭⲦⲞⲨⲘⲞⳭⲞⲀⲐ). Translation: mountain of Mosoath

• Aleppo Codex: hr hmshcht (**הר המשחית**). Translation: mountain of waste

• Leningrad Codex: har-hammashchit (הַר־הַמַּשְׁחִית). Translation: mountain of waste

• Targum Jerusalem: tur zeitaya (טוּר זֵיתָיָא). Translation: mount of olives

The Greek name appears to be a translation of the term found in the Hebrew translation, which translates as approximately 'waste' or 'rubbish,' appears to be an attempt to describe his contempt for what Solomon built on the mountain, not the name of the mountain itself, so the Hebrew meaning is imported in this translation. The author of the Targum Jerusalem, generally accepted as Jonathan ben Uzziel, identified the mountain in question as the Mount of Olives.

**8** Codex Vaticanus: Astartê (ΑϹΤΑΡΤΗ)

- Aleppo Codex: Ôštrt (עשתרת)

- Leningrad Codex: Ashtarot (עַשְׁתָּרֹת)

- Targum Jerusalem: Ashtoret (עַשְׁתּוֹרֶת)

Astarte was the Greek name of the Canaanite goddess Ôštrt (𐤕𐤓𐤕𐤏 / ⟨⟩). Local versions of her were worshiped throughout the Middle East and the Mediterranean Sea. In Akkadian she was a god known as ᵃⁿAsdartú (𒀭𒅗𒁯𒌅), while in Babylonian she was known as ᵃⁿIštar (𒀭𒈹), and in Etruscan she was known as Uni-al-Astres (SEPᛏSALᴚINV).

The Greek goddess Aphrodite appears to be derived from an early Cypriot version of her, while the Roman goddess Venus appears to be derived indirectly through Uni-al-Astres. During the New Kingdom era of Egyptian history, circa 1549 to 1077 AD, Astarte was incorporated into the Egyptian pantheon as one of the daughters of Ra, as she appeared in the book entitled the 'Contest between Horus and Set.' According to the Phoenician scholar Sanchuniathon, who supposedly lived circa 1200 BC, Astarte's sister was Asherah. The word Asherah also appears in the Septuagint many times and appears to be widely worshiped by the early Israelites.


**9** Codex Vaticanus: theraphin (ΘΕΡΑΦΙΝ)

- Aleppo Codex: trpym (תרפים)

- Leningrad Codex: terafim (תְּרָפִים)

- Targum Jerusalem: ta'avata (טַעֲוָתָא). Translation: idols

The Greek term is a transliteration from the Hebrew, although the exact meaning is unclear. Scholarly consensus is that these were fetishes or icons representing household gods.

**10** Codex Vaticanus: pharaô Nechaô (ⲫⲁⲣⲁⲱⲛⲉⲭⲁⲱ). Translation: pharaoh Nechao

- Aleppo Codex: prôh Nkh (פרעה נכח). Translation: Pharaoh Nkh

- Leningrad Codex: par'oh Nechoh (פַּרְעֹה נְכֹה). Translation: pharaoh Nekoh

- Targum Jerusalem: par'oh Chagira (פַּרְעֹה חֲגִירָא). Translation: pharaoh Hagirah

This king is known by his more common Egyptian name Necho II. He was a Nubian king of the 26<sup>th</sup> Dynasty, who ruled between 610 and 585 BC. Necho II launched a number of campaigns into Canaan and attempted to restore the Assyrian dynasty to their homeland after they were driven out by a combination of the resurgent Babylonian Empire, and the raids of the Cimmerians from Eastern Europe and Scythians from Central Asia. The 1<sup>st</sup> century Jewish historian Josephus recorded an alternate view of Necho's invasions of Asia as an attempt to conquer the Canaan and Syria for the Egyptian empire, not restore the Assyrian Empire. Necho II also initiated a number of building projects in Egypt and launched what is considered the first recorded circumnavigation of the African continent.

# 4ᵗʰ Kingdoms: Chapter 24

In his days King Nebuchadnezzar of Babylon invaded, and
Jehoiakim became his servant for three years, and then he turned
and revolted from him. The Lord sent against him bands of the
Chaldeans, Syrians, Moabites, and Ammonites, and sent them into
the land of Judah to conquer it, according to the word of the Lord,
which he had foretold by his servants the prophets. Moreover, it
was the purpose of the Lord concerning Judah, to remove them
from his presence, because of the sins of Manasseh, according to all
that he did. Moreover, he shed innocent blood and filled
Jerusalem with innocent blood, and the Lord would not pardon it.
The rest of the acts of Jehoiakim, and all that he did, look, are not
these not written in the book of the Chronicles of the Kings of
Judah? Jehoiakim slept with his fathers, and Jehoiakim his son
reigned in his place.

The king of Egypt did not venture out of Egypt again, for the
king of Babylon conquered all that belonged to the king of Egypt
from the river of Egypt as far as the river Euphrates. Eighteen
years old was Jehoiakim when he began to reign, and he reigned
three months in Jerusalem. His mother's name was Nehushta,
daughter of Elnathan from Jerusalem. He did that which was evil
in the sight of the Lord, like all that his forefathers did.

At that time King Nebuchadnezzar of Babylon besieged
Jerusalem. King Nebuchadnezzar of Babylon came against the
city, and his servants besieged it. Jehoiakim king of Judah came
out to the king of Babylon, he and his servants, and his mother,
and his princes, and his eunuchs, and the king of Babylon took
him in the eighth year of his reign. He took out from there all the
treasures of the Temple of the Lord and the treasures of the king's
palace and he cut up all the golden vessels which Solomon the
king of Israel had made in the Temple of the Lord, following the

word of the Lord. He deported the inhabitants of Jerusalem and all the captains, and the mighty men, taking captive ten thousand prisoners, and every craftsman and smith, and only the poor of the land were left.

He deported Jehoiakim to Babylon, and the king's mother, and the king's wives, and his eunuchs, and he took the mighty men of the land into captivity from Jerusalem to Babylon. All the men of might, all seven thousand, and one thousand craftsmen and smiths, and all were mighty men who were fit for war. The king of Babylon took them captive to Babylon. The king of Babylon made Mattaniah his son king in his place and called his name Zedekiah. Twenty-one years old was Zedekiah when he began to reign, and he reigned eleven years in Jerusalem. His mother's name was Hamutal daughter of Jeremiah. He did that which was evil in the sight of the Lord, according to all that Jehoiakim did. For it was according to the Lord's anger against Jerusalem and on Judah, until he threw them out of his presence, that Zedekiah revolted against the king of Babylon.

# 4<sup>th</sup> Kingdoms: Chapter 25

In the ninth year of his reign, in the tenth month, Nebuchadnezzar the king of Babylon came with his army and besieged Jerusalem. He camped near it and built a mound around it. The city was besieged until the eleventh year of king Zedekiah on the ninth day of the month. The famine prevailed in the city, for there was no bread for the people of the land. The city was broken up, and all the men of war went out by night, by the way of the gate between the walls, this is the gate of the king's garden, and the Chaldeans were set against the city around it. The king fled by the road on the plain, and the force of the Chaldeans pursued the king and caught up to him in the plains of Jericho, and all his army was dispersed from about him.

They captured the king and brought him to the king of Babylon to Riblah, and he gave judgment on him. He killed the sons of Zedekiah before his eyes, and cut out the eyes of Zedekiah, and bound him in shackles, and brought him to Babylon. In the fifth month, on the seventh day of the month (this is the nineteenth year of King Nebuchadnezzar of Babylon), came Nebuzaradan, captain of the guard, who stood before the king of Babylon, in Jerusalem. He burnt the Temple of the Lord, and the king's palace and all the houses of Jerusalem. The captain of the guard burned burned down every house. The force of the Chaldeans pulled down the walls around Jerusalem. Nebuzaradan the captain of the guard removed the rest of the people that were left in the city, and the men who had deserted to the king of Babylon, and the rest of the multitude. But the captain of the guard left of the poor the land to be vine-tenders and husbandmen.

The Chaldeans broke to pieces the bronze steles that were in the Temple of the Lord, and the bases, and the bronze sea that was in the Temple of the Lord, and carried their brass to Babylon. The cauldrons, and the shovels, and the bowls, and the censers, and all the bronze vessels with which they ministered, he took. The captain of the guard took the fire-pans, and the gold and silver bowls. Two steles, and one sea, and the bases which Solomon made for the Temple of the Lord, there was no weight of the brass of all the vessels. The height of one pillar was eighteen cubits, and the chapiter on it was of brass, and the height of the chapiter was three cubits: the border and the pomegranates on the chapiter round about were all of brass: and so it was with the second pillar with its border.

The captain of the guard took Seraiah the high-priest, and Zephaniah the second in order, and the three doorkeepers. They took out of the city one eunuch who was commander of the men of war, and five men that saw the face of the king, that were found in the city, and the secretary of the commander-in-chief, who took account of the people of the land, and sixty men of the people of the land that were found in the city. Nebuzaradan the captain of the guard took them and brought them to the king of Babylon to Riblah. The king of Babylon struck them and killed them at Riblah in the land of Hamath. So Judah was carried away from his land.

As for the people that were left in the land of Judah, who King Nebuchadnezzar of Babylon had left, he placed Gedaliah the son of Ahikam the son of Shaphan over them. All the captains of the army, they and their men, heard that the king of Babylon had appointed Gedaliah, and they came to Gedaliah to Mizpah, both Ishmael the son of Nethaniah, and Johanan son of Careah, and Seraiah, son of Tanhumeth the Netophathite, and Jaazaniah son of a Maachathite, they with their men. Gedaliah swore to them and their men, and said to them, "Don't be afraid of the incursion of the Chaldeans. Live in the land, and serve the king of Babylon, and it will go well for you."

In the seventh month Ishmael, the son of Nethaniah, the son of Elishama, of the royal seed, came, and ten men with him, and he murdered Gedaliah, and the Judeans and the Chaldeans that were with him in Mizpah. All the people, great and small rose up, they and the captains of the forces went into Egypt, because they were afraid of the Chaldeans. It came to pass in the thirty-seventh year of the deportation of Jehoiakim king of Judah, in the twelfth month, on the twenty-seventh day of the month, that King Amel-Marduk[1] of Babylon in the first year of his reign lifted the head of Jehoiakim king of Judah, and brought him out of his prison-house. He spoke kindly to him and set his throne above the thrones of the kings that were with him in Babylon, changed his prison garments, and he ate bread with him for days. His portion, a continual portion, was given him out of the house of the king, a daily rate for every day all the days of his life.

# 4th Kingdoms: Chapter 25 Notes

1 Codex Vaticanus: Euilmarôdach (ⲉⲩⲓⲗⲙⲁⲣⲱⲇⲁⲭ)

• Aleppo Codex: Åwyl Mrdk (אויל מרדך)

• Leningrad Codex: Evil Merodach (אֱוִיל מְרֹדַךְ)

• Targum Jerusalem: Evil Merodach (אֱוִיל מְרוֹדָךְ)

King Amel-Marduk was the king of the Neo-Babylonian Empire between 562 and 560 BC. His predecessor was Nebuchadnezzar II, and his successor Neriglissar.

# Septuagint Manuscripts

The following is a list of the Septuagint manuscripts referenced in the notes for this book.

LXX א (Codex Sinaiticus) is dated to the 4$^{th}$ century. Sections are currently located at British Library (Add. 43725) in London, Leipzig University (Gr. 1 in Leipzig, National Library of Russia (Gr. 2, Gr. 259, Gr. 843, and Fonds. d. Ges. f. alte Lit. Oct 156) in St, Petersburg, and Saint Catherine's Monastery (МΓ 1 on Mount Sinai.

LXX A (Codex Alexandrinus) is dated to the 5$^{th}$ century. It is currently located at the British Library (Royal 1 D. VIII) in London.

LXX B (Codex Vaticanus) is dated to the 4$^{th}$ century. It is currently located at the Vatican Library (Gr. 1209) in Vatican City.

LXX M (Codex Coislinianus) is dated to the 7$^{th}$ century. It is currently located at National Library of France (Coisl. Gr. 1 in Paris.

LXX N (Codex Basiliano-Vaticanus) is dated to the 8$^{th}$ century. It is currently located at Vatican Library (Vat. gr. 2106) in Vatican City.

LXX V (Codex Venetus) is dated to the 8$^{th}$ century. It is currently located at the Marciana Library (Gr. 1 in Venice.

LXX Z (Fragment Tischendorfianus) is dated to sometime in the 4$^{th}$ through 8$^{th}$ century. Sections are currently located at the Vatican Library (Vat. Syr. 162) in Rome, and at the British Library (Add 14665; Z$^{I}$; Z$^{II}$; Z$^{III}$; Z$^{IV}$; Z$^{V}$; Z$^{VI}$) in London.

LXX 19 is dated to the 12$^{th}$ century. It is currently located at the Chigi Palace (R. VI. 38) in Rome.

LXX 29 is dated to the 14$^{th}$ century. It is currently located at the Marciana Library (Gr. 2 in Venice.

LXX 44 is dated to the 15$^{th}$ century. It is currently located at the Stadtbibliothek (A 1 in Zittau.

LXX 46 is dated to the 15$^{th}$ century. It is currently located at the National Library of France (Coisl. Gr. 4 in Paris.

LXX 52 is dated to the 14th century. It is currently located at the Laurentian Library (Acquisti 44) in Florence.

LXX 55 is dated to the 10th century. It is currently located at the Vatican Library (Regin. Gr. 1 in Vatican City.

LXX 56 is dated to 1093. It is currently located at the National Library of France (Gr. 3 in Paris.

LXX 58 is dated to the 11th century. It is currently located at the Vatican Library (Regin. Gr. 10 in Vatican City.

LXX 62 is dated to the 11th century. It is currently located at the New College (44) in Oxford.

LXX 64 is dated to the 10th century. It is currently located at the National Library of France (Gr. 2 in Paris.

LXX 71 is dated to the 13th century. It is currently located at the National Library of France (Coisl. Gr. 1 in Paris.

LXX 74 is dated to the 13th century. It is currently located at the Laurentian Library (S. Marco 700) in Florence.

LXX 76 is dated to the 13th century. It is currently located at National Library of France (Coisl. Gr. 4 in Paris.

LXX 82 is dated to the 12th century. It is currently located at the National Library of France (Coisl. Gr. 3 in Paris.

LXX 92 is dated to the 11th century. It is currently located at the National Library of France (Coisl. Gr. 3 in Paris.

LXX 93 is dated to the 13th century. It is currently located at the British Library (Royal 1 D. II) in London.

LXX 98 is dated to the 13th century. It is currently located at the Royal Library (Σ-II-19 in El Escorial.

LXX 106 is dated to the 14th century. It is currently located at the Biblioteca Comunale Ariostea (187 I-III) in Ferrara.

LXX 107 is dated to 1334. It is currently located at the Biblioteca Comunale Ariostea (188 I) in Ferrara.

LXX 108 is dated to the 13th century. It is currently located at the Vatican Library (Gr. 330) in Vatican City.

LXX 119 is dated to the 10th century. It is currently located at the National Library of France (Gr. 7 in Paris.

LXX 120 is dated to the 11th century. It is currently located at the Biblioteca Marciana (Gr. 4 in Venice.

LXX 121 is dated to the 10th century. It is currently located at the Biblioteca Marciana (Gr. 3 in Venice.

LXX 122 is dated to the 15th century. It is currently located at the Biblioteca Marciana (Gr. 6 in Venice.

LXX 125 is dated to the 14th century. It is currently located at the State Historical Museum (Gr. 30) in Moscow.

LXX 126 is dated to the 1475. It is currently located at the State Historical Museum (Gr. 19 in Moscow.

LXX 127 is dated to the 10th century. It is currently located at the State Historical Museum (Gr. 31) in Moscow.

LXX 130 is dated to the 12th or 13th centuries. It is currently located at the Austrian National Library (Theol. Gr. 23) in Vienna.

LXX 131 is dated to the 10th century. It is currently located at the Austrian National Library (Theol. Gr. 57) in Vienna.

LXX 134 is dated to the 11th centuries. It is currently located at the Biblioteca Marciana (Plut. 5.1 in Venice.

LXX 158 is dated to the 13th centuries. It is currently located at the Universitätsbibliothek Basel (B. VI. 22) in Basel.

LXX 236 is dated to the 11th century. It is currently located at the Vatican Library (Vat. Gr. 331) in Vatican City.

LXX 241 is dated to the 17<sup>th</sup> century. It is currently located at the British Museum (Harley MS 7522 A) in London.

LXX 242 is dated to the 14<sup>th</sup> century. It is currently located at the Austrian National Library (Theol. gr. 135) in Vienna.

LXX 243 is dated to the 10<sup>th</sup> century. It is currently located at the National Library of France (Coisl. 8 in Paris.

LXX 244 is dated to the 11<sup>th</sup> century. It is currently located at the Vatican Library (Gr. 333) in Vatican City.

LXX 245 is dated to the 12<sup>th</sup> century. It is currently located at the Vatican Library (Vat. gr. 334) in Vatican City.

LXX 246 is dated to 1195. It is currently located at the Vatican Library (Gr. 1238) in Vatican City.

LXX 247 is dated to the 12<sup>th</sup> century. It is currently located at the Vatican Library (Urbin. Gr. 1 in Vatican City

LXX 248 is dated to the 13<sup>th</sup> century. It is currently located at the Vatican Library (Vat. Gr. 346) in Vatican City.

LXX 249 is dated to the 13<sup>th</sup> century. It is currently located at the Vatican Library (Pii. II Gr. 1 in Vatican City.

LXX 311 is dated to the 12<sup>th</sup> century. It is currently located at the State Historical Museum of Russia (Syn. gr. 354) in Moscow.

LXX 314 is dated to the 13<sup>th</sup> century. It is currently located at the National Library of Greece (44) in Athens.

LXX 318 is dated to the 10<sup>th</sup> or 11<sup>th</sup> centuries. It is currently located at the Vatopedi (598) on Mount Athos.

LXX 319 is dated to 1021. It is currently located at the Vatopedi (600) on Mount Athos.

LXX 340 is dated to the 11<sup>th</sup> century. It is currently located at the Vatopedi (39) on Mount Athos.

LXX 370 is dated to the 11$^{th}$ through 14$^{th}$ centuries. It is currently located at the Vatican Library (Chis. R VIII 61) in Vatican City.

LXX 376 is dated to the 15$^{th}$ century. It is currently located at the Royal Library (Y (Griech.)-II-5 in El Escorial.

LXX 381 is dated to the 11$^{th}$ century. It is currently located at the Royal Library (Ω-1-13 in El Escorial.

LXX 392 is dated to the 10$^{th}$ century. It is currently located at the Abbey of Saint Mary of Grottaferrata (A. γ. I) in Grottaferrata.

LXX 402 is dated to the 14$^{th}$ century. It is currently located at the Patriarchal Library (Σάβα 105) in Jerusalem.

LXX 489 is dated to the 10$^{th}$ century. It is currently located at the Bavarian State Library (Gr. 454) in Munich.

LXX 534 is dated to the 11$^{th}$ century. It is currently located at the National Library of France (Coisl. Gr. 18 in Paris.

LXX 538 is dated to the 12$^{th}$ century. It is currently located at the National Library of France (Coisl. Gr. 191) in Paris.

LXX 542 is dated to the 9$^{th}$ century. It is currently located at the National Library of France (Gr. 10 in Paris.

LXX 554 is dated to the 14$^{th}$ century. It is currently located at the National Library of France (Gr. 133) in Paris.

LXX 583 is dated to the 14$^{th}$ century. It is currently located at the National Library of France (Gr. 1087) in Paris.

LXX 670 is dated to the 14$^{th}$ century. It is currently located at the Vatican Library (Vat. Gr. 335) in Vatican City.

LXX 671 is dated to the 15$^{th}$ century. It is currently located at the Vatican Library (Vat. Gr. 348) in Vatican City.

LXX 707 is dated to the 10$^{th}$ or 11$^{th}$ centuries. Sections are currently located at Saint Catherine's Monastery (Codex Gr. 1 in the Sinai, and the National Library of Russia (Gr. 260) in St. Petersburg.

# SEPTUAGINT MANUSCRIPTS

LXX 728 is dated to the 14$^{th}$ or 15$^{th}$ centuries. It is currently located at the Biblioteca Marciana (Append I 13 in Venice.

LXX 771 is dated to the 10$^{th}$ century. Sections are currently located at Vatopedi Monastery (290 + 1213 Bl. 13-51) on the Mount Athos, and the National Library of Russia (Gr. 260) in St. Petersburg.

LXX 996 (Oxyrhynchus Papyri LXV 4443) is dated to 1$^{st}$ century. It is currently located in the Ashmolean Museum (LXV 4443), in Oxford.

# Alternative Translations

The following is a list of alternative translations that were used for comparative analysis.

The Aleppo Codex is dated to circa 920 AD. For centuries it was housed at the Central Synagogue of Aleppo, from which its name is derived. It was the oldest known complete copy of the Hebrew scriptures used within Judaism until 1947, when it was seized and divided among Jewish families during anti-Jewish riots in Aleppo. The sections that have resurfaced are currently at the Israel Museum in Jerusalem. Approximately 40% is still missing.

The Leningrad Codex is dated to 1008 (or 1009) AD. It is currently located at the National Library of Russia (Firkovich B 19 A) in St. Petersburg. The Leningrad Codex is the oldest complete copy of the Hebrew scriptures used within Judaism.

Targum Jerusalem has historically been misidentified as the Targum Jonathan, and is commonly called the Targum Pseudo-Jonathan in academic literature. Its oldest name is the Targum Jerusalem, which is used here. It is written in Palestinian-Aramaic, and generally dated to sometime between the 4th and 11th centuries. Some scholars believe it originated in the 4th century, and was modified after the Islamic conquest of Palestine, as it includes some Arabic names generally found in Islamic sources. It existed before the crusades, as it was documented at the time.

The Targum of Ruth was published in the 1516 edition of the Mikraot Gedolot, a Hebrew language translation and commentary on the Hebrew Bible, that included Aramaic targums on the various books. The origin of the Targum on Ruth is unknown,however, it is accepted as being composed earlier than 600 AD.

The Peshitta is the Syriac translation of the Christian bible. The Old Testament was translated from older Aramaic and Hebrew sources during the late 2nd century AD.

# ALTERNATIVE TRANSLATIONS

The Sahidic manuscripts are translations of the Septuagint into Sahidic (also known as Thebaic), one of the six dialects of Coptic, the classical era form of the Egyptian language. Sahidic was the dominant form of Coptic used before the 11th century, and is believed to have originated in the region around Hermopolis, at the boundary between Upper and Lower Egypt. Translations of the Septuagint into Sahidic are known to have existed by the 4th century, however, early non-dialect specific translations are generally accepted as having been made as early as the 1st century AD, with some scholars suggesting the 1st century BC. The early non-dialect specific forms of Coptic are generally grouped with Sahidic, as Sahidic did not have a standardized spelling until the 6th century.

The Armenian bible was translated from the Septuagint in the 5th century, replacing the older Armenian bible that had been translated from Aramaic texts, however, includes some of the older names.

The Ge'ez manuscripts are Classical Ethiopic translations of various ancient Israel books that comprise the Christian bible, Jewish Tanakh, and Beta Israeli Orit. They were sources from texts in multiple languages, including Coptic, Greek, Aramaic, and Arabic.

The Vetus Latina are the old Latin translations of the Septuagint and other Israelite texts that predate Jerome's Latin Orthodox Bible in the 5th century. Some of the texts appear to have been translated directly from Aramaic or Hebrew source texts, however, most appear to have been translations from the Greek translations. The version of Tobit found in the Vetus Latina manuscripts is far closer to the Codex Sinaiticus' version of Esther than the more common versions found in Septuagint manuscripts, suggesting it was translated from an Aramaic source.

# Dead Sea Scrolls

The following is a list of the Dead Sea Scrolls mentioned in the notes for this book. Most are held by the Israel Museum in Jerusalem.

DSS 4Q47 (4QJosh$^a$) is dated to the Herodian Dynasty in Judea (37 BC to 6 AD).

DSS 4Q48 (4QJosh$^b$) is dated to the Herodian Dynasty in Judea (37 BC to 6 AD).

DSS 4Q49 (4QJudg$^a$) is dated to the Hasmonean Dynasty in Judea (140 to 37 BC).

DSS 4Q50 (4QJudg$^b$) is dated to the Hasmonean Dynasty in Judea (140 to 37 BC).

DSS 4Q104 (4QRuth$^a$) is dated to the Hasmonean Dynasty in Judea (140 to 37 BC).

DSS 4Q51 (4QSam$^a$) is dated to the Herodian dynasty in Judea (37 BC to 6 AD).

DSS 4Q52 (4QSam$^b$) is dated to the Maccabean Revolt (165 to 140 BC).

DSS 4Q54 (4QKgs) is dated to the Herodian Dynasty (37 BC to 6 AD).

DSS 6Q4 (6QpapKgs) is dated to the Hasmonean Dynasty (140 to 37 BC).

# Also Available

# ALSO AVAILABLE

- Octateuch: The Original Orit

ENOCH AND METATRON SERIES:
- Books of Enoch Collection

- Books of Enoch and Metatron Collection

- Books of Metatron Collection

- Secrets of Enoch

OTHER TRANSLATIONS:
- Apocalypses of Ezra

- Arabic Maccabees

- Hebrew Maccabees

- Life of Adam and Eve

- Memories of the New Kingdom

- Septuagint's Esther and the Vetus Latina Esther

- Septuagint's Ezekiel and the Ba'al Cycle

- Septuagint's Proverbs and the Wisdom of Amenemope

- The Amarna Letters

- Testaments of the Patriarchs Collection

- Tobit and Ahikar

- Ugaritic Texts: Ba'al Cycle

- Wisdom of Ahikar